The Enduring Vision

# The Enduring Vision

## A HISTORY OF THE AMERICAN PEOPLE
### Concise Third Edition

## VOLUME 1: TO 1877

### Paul S. Boyer
*University of Wisconsin, Madison*

### Clifford E. Clark, Jr.
*Carleton College*

### Sandra McNair Hawley
*San Jacinto College*

### Joseph F. Kett
*University of Virginia*

### Neal Salisbury
*Smith College*

### Harvard Sitkoff
*University of New Hampshire*

### Nancy Woloch
*Barnard College*

Houghton Mifflin Company   Boston  New York

Sponsoring editor: Pat Coryell
Associate editor: Jeffrey Greene
Senior project editor: Rosemary Winfield
Production/design coordinator: Jennifer Meyer
Senior designer: Henry Rachlin
Manufacturing coordinator: Sally Culler
Marketing manager: Charles Cavaliere

Cover: design by Len Massiglia; cover image: View of Fort Snelling by E. K. Thomas, oil
painting. The Minneapolis Institute of Arts.

Printed in the U.S.A.

Library of Congress Catalog Card Number: 97-72446

ISBN: 0-395-85827-5

456789-VH-01 00 99

# Preface

In this new concise edition of *The Enduring Vision* we have tried to maintain the strengths of the previous edition—a strong narrative that interweaves political, diplomatic, and economic history with social, cultural, and environmental analysis in a brief but thorough text that reflects both traditional concerns and the cutting edge of contemporary historical research. We have tried to use a readable style throughout, eliminating the social science jargon that both instructors and students (quite correctly) dislike.

This concise edition of *The Enduring Vision* interweaves traditional and more recent approaches to the study of history. In addition to political, diplomatic, and economic history, for example, the book examines and integrates social history, cultural history, the histories of the diverse peoples who make up our pluralistic society, and environmental history. We have maintained a balance that reflects the best of both traditional and the new emphases in historical scholarship, a blend that will serve the modern student well.

Like its predecessor, this is not a "lite" version of American history. We have retained all the major topics and issues from the original text to make this a book suitable for any introductory United States history course at the freshman or sophomore level, whether in four-year colleges and universities or two-year community and junior colleges. With nearly 40 percent fewer pages than the longer book, this concise edition affords the instructor the opportunity to assign more outside readings for greater depth.

Throughout this third edition the reader will encounter substantial changes, changes meant to deepen, broaden, and clarify our discussion of major issues. For example, Chapters 2 and 3 have been extensively reordered to bring together diverse aspects of early colonization and to strengthen the discussion of slavery and its transfer across the Atlantic. Other significant changes include greater discussion of the Taos pueblo and the Pueblo Revolt; British perspectives of the coming of the American Revolution; the rise of the Republican party; the Civil War in the Trans-Mississippi West; shifting attitudes toward the environment; fuller analysis of both Keynesianism and the roots of isolationist ideology; the Kennedy presidency; recent social and cultural trends such as mass marketing, mass entertainment, and the growing political clout of evangelical Christians; and the complexities and paradoxes of the first Clinton administration, the "Republican Revolution," the new worlds of the post–Cold War era and the postindustrial economy, and the 1996 presidential election. Chronologies and suggested readings have been brought up to date as well.

This concise edition features a generous array of maps. Reproduced in two colors, they vividly establish the physical and spatial setting of American history, enabling the student to grasp both the immensity of the United States and of the North American continent and the complexities of Native American and European settlement of that continent. We chose photographs not only for their freshness and visual impact but also for their complementarity with the text. Clear, easily understood charts and other graphics round out the illustrations. Each chapter has an extensive chronology at the end to help the student to set events in historical context, and an extensive annotated bibliography of the works for further reading or research.

A wide range of ancillaries to aid both instructor and student is available with *The Enduring Vision*, Concise Third Edition. They include the *Instructor's Resource Manual with Test Items*, the *Study Guide with Map Exercises*, and a computerized test bank for

Macintosh and IBM-compatible computers. The instructor may also opt to use some of the following additional supplements for the course and should contact a Houghton Mifflin sales representative for more information:

- *Getting the Most out of Your U.S. History Course: The History Student's Vade Mecum* by Neil R. Stout—a handy, concise student guide to getting the most out of the U.S. history survey course

- *Reading and Writing American History* by Peter Charles Hoffer and William W. Stueck, Volumes 1 and 2—a skills-based sourcebook for U.S. history students

- Map transparencies

- *Enduring Voices Document Sets* by James J. Lorence, Volumes 1 and 2

- *Surveying the Land: Skills and Exercises in U.S. Historical Geography* by Robert B. Grant, Volumes 1 and 2

- *Atlas of American History*

- *The Houghton Mifflin Guide to the Internet for History*

Writing and publishing a book of this complexity is never easy, and I would like to thank those individuals whose support and help has made this revised edition possible with minimum stress: my daughter, Lee Anne Hawley; my friends, especially James D. Heil; my colleagues, especially James A. Hall; and the editorial and production staff at Houghton Mifflin. We changed publishers in the midst of preparations for this third edition, and the hard work and intelligence of the Houghton Mifflin people made what could have been a logistical nightmare into a smooth transition. My special thanks to Pat Coryell, senior sponsoring editor; Jeff Greene, senior associate editor; and Rosemary Winfield, senior project editor.

Finally, reviewers at all stages of the revision process have made this a stronger and better book through their suggestions and their general enthusiasm. However, we must note that errors are ours alone.

Robert H. Tomlinson, Southwest Virginia Community College

Ronald C. McArthur, Atlantic Community College

James W. McKee, Jr., East Tennessee State University

George C. Rable, Anderson University

Karin A. Wulf, American University

Martin B. Cohen, George Mason University

Geoffrey Plank, University of Cincinnati

Michael J. Morgan, Rose State College

We are most grateful to them all.

We welcome all our readers' suggestions, queries, and criticisms. Please send them to Houghton Mifflin at this e-mail address: history@hmco.com.

S. M. H.

# Contents

# *America Begins*

1

# *Transatlantic Encounters and Colonial Beginnings, 1492–1630*

15

# Expansion and Diversity:
# The Rise of Colonial America

39

# The Forge of Nationhood,
# 1776–1788

**7**

# Launching the New Republic, 1789–1800

144

**8**

# Jeffersonianism and the Era of Good Feelings

168

# The Transformation of American Society, 1815–1840

190

# Immigration, Expansion, and Sectional Conflict, 1840–1848

271

16

# *The Crises of Reconstruction, 1865–1877*

341

# Maps

## Charts, Graphs, and Tables

The Enduring Vision

Volume 1: To 1877

## America Begins

The history of the Americas began thousands of years before Christopher Columbus's first voyage. Over that time, an indigenous American history unfolded, separate from that of the Old World of Africa, Asia, and Europe.

Some Native Americans eked out their existences in precarious environments, whereas others enjoyed prosperity; some lived in small bands, but others dwelled in large cities; some believed that the first humans came from the sky, and others thought that they originated underground. Wherever and however they lived, and whatever they believed, native peoples together made North America a human habitat and gave it a history.

(Right) Adena stone effigy pipe, c. 400–100 B.C.

**The First Americans**

❧

**The Indians' Continent**

❧

**New World Peoples on the Eve of European Contact**

# The First Americans

The origins of the human species extend far back in time. More than 5 million years ago, direct human ancestors evolved in the temperate grasslands of Africa. Between 300,000 and 100,000 years ago, humans began peopling the Old World. Between 40,000 and 15,000 years ago, northern Asian hunting bands pursued large game animals across a broad land bridge then connecting Siberia and Alaska. In doing so, they became the first Americans.

Most Native Americans are descended from these earliest migrants, but a few trace their ancestry to later arrivals who crossed the land bridge about 9,000 years ago, and spread over much of northern and western Canada and southern and central Alaska. Some later migrated southward to become the Apaches and the Navajos of the Southwest. Eskimos and Aleuts began crossing the Bering Sea—which had submerged the land bridge—from Siberia about 5,000 years ago, and the Hawaiian Islands remained uninhabited until after A.D. 300.

## The Peopling of North America: The Paleo-Indians

About 10,000 B.C., the Ice Age neared its end. Melting glaciers opened an ice-free corridor from Alaska to the northern Plains, and bands of hunters moved along this route. Others probably traveled south along the Pacific coast in boats. As they emerged from the glacier-covered north, they discovered a hunter's paradise. Giant mammoths, mastodons, bison, caribou, and moose roamed the continent, innocent of the ways of human predators. In this bountiful world, the Paleo-Indians, as archaeologists call these hunters, fanned out and multiplied with astonishing speed. Within 1,000 years, descendants of the first Americans had spread throughout the Western Hemisphere.

Most Paleo-Indians lived in small bands of fifteen to fifty people. The men hunted; the women prepared the food and cared for the children. The band lived together for the summer but split into smaller groups of one or two families for fall and

**The First Americans**
*The arrow shows the "ice corridor" through which most ancestors of Native Americans passed before dispersing throughout the Western Hemisphere.*
SOURCE: Dean R. Snow, *The Archaeology of North America.* Copyright © 1989 by Chelsea House Publishers, a division of Main Line Book Co. Used by permission.

winter. Although they moved constantly, they remained within informal boundaries except when they traveled to favored quarries to obtain jasper or flint for making tools. Here they encountered other bands, with whom they traded and joined in religious ceremonies.

Even before leaving Alaska, the Paleo-Indians developed distinctly "American" ways. Their most characteristic innovation was the fluted point, which the Indians fitted to spears. Fluted points have been found throughout the Western Hemisphere, but none in Siberia. By 9000 B.C. many big-game species, including mammoths and mastodons, had vanished. Paleo-Indian hunters contributed to this extinction, as did a warming climate and ecological changes that altered or destroyed the large animals' food chains.

## Archaic Societies

Climatic warming continued until about 4000 B.C. with dramatic effects for North America. Sea levels rose, flooding the shallow continental shelf, and glacial runoff filled the Great Lakes, the Mississippi River basin, and other waters. As the glaciers receded northward, so did the cold, icy arctic or subarctic environments that had previously extended into what are now the "lower forty-eight" states of the United States. Treeless plains and evergreen forests yielded to deciduous forests in the East, grassland prairies on the Plains, and desert in much of the West. An immense range of plants and animals covered the landscape.

Descendants of the Paleo-Indians prospered amid this abundance and diversity. These Archaic peoples, as archaeologists term native North Americans from 8000 B.C. to 1500 B.C., lived off wide varieties of smaller mammals, fish, and wild plants rather than big game. Greater efficiency in hunting and gathering permitted larger populations to inhabit smaller areas. In rich areas such as the East and Midwest, large populations lived in villages for virtually the entire year. For example, a year-round village that flourished near present-day Kampsville, Illinois, from 3900 to 2800 B.C. supported 100 to 150 people. Its residents procured fish and mussels from local lakes to supplement the deer, birds, nuts, and seeds available in the surrounding area.

Archaic peoples' cultures were diverse in other ways. Besides using many varieties of stone, they utilized bone, shell, copper, ivory, clay, leather, asphalt, and horn to make tools, weapons, utensils, and ornaments. Often Native Americans obtained these materials through trade with neighbors and through long-distance networks. Obsidian from the Yellowstone region, copper from the Great Lakes, and marine shells from ocean coasts appear at sites thousands of miles from their points of origin.

Archaic peoples, like their Indian descendants, believed that such minerals contained supernatural power. A few large sites, among them Indian Knoll in western Kentucky, which dates to 2500–2000 B.C., served as major trade centers for such minerals.

Ideas as well as materials traveled along the trade networks. Techniques that developed in one place for making tools, procuring food, or using medicinal plants eventually spread over wide areas, far beyond the boundaries of community, language, and ethnicity. This diffusion created regional cultural patterns. Trade also served to spread religious beliefs, including ideas and practices relating to death. Archaic burials grew increasingly elaborate as Native Americans interred their dead with personal possessions and with objects fashioned from valued substances such as obsidian and copper. They often sprinkled the corpses with bright red hematite (an iron-bearing ore) so that they resembled a newborn. Ideas of death as a kind of rebirth were widespread in North America by the time Europeans arrived.

Archaic Americans developed neither ranks nor classes, nor did they centralize political power. However, the growing complexity of their diets and technologies led them to sharpen many distinctions between women's and men's roles. Men took responsibility for fishing and hunting; women harvested and prepared wild plants, including grinding and milling seeds. Men and women each made the tools needed for their tasks. In general, men's activities entailed travel, and women's work kept them close to the village, where they bore and raised children. At Indian Knoll and elsewhere, men were buried with tools related to hunting and fishing, and women with implements related to nut cracking and seed grinding. Objects used by shamans, or religious healers, were distributed equally between male and female graves, a practice implying that these key roles were not divided by gender.

# The Indians' Continent

By 1500 B.C. in much of North America, Indians were developing new cultures that transcended those of the Archaic peoples. Some practiced specialized methods of food production and actively shaped their environment to their needs. In the Southwest, the Southeast, and the Eastern Woodlands, the advent of agriculture and of large centers of trade and population constituted a radical departure from Archaic patterns and hunting-gathering bands. Most Indians, however, still dwelled in small bands and retained their traditional reliance on hunting, fishing, and gathering.

Despite the differences emerging among native societies, ties among them remained strong. Expanded trade networks permitted goods and ideas to be carried over ever-widening areas. Ceramic pottery and the bow and arrow came into extensive use. Virtually everywhere, Indians continued to prefer seasonal food procurement and communities based on kinship, abandoning or resisting more centralized systems when they proved to be unworkable or oppressive.

## The Northern and Western Perimeters

In western Alaska the post-Archaic period marked the beginning of a new arctic way of life. Eskimos and Aleuts had brought sophisticated tools and weapons from their Siberian homeland, including harpoons and spears for hunting sea mammals and caribou. By 1500 B.C., through their continued contacts with Siberia, the Eskimos were making and using the Americas' first bows and arrows, ceramic pottery, and pit houses, structures set partially below ground level. As they perfected ways of living in regions of vast tundras (treeless plains with a permanently frozen subsoil), Eskimos spread across upper Canada to the shores of Labrador, western Newfoundland, and Greenland.

Long before Columbus, the Eskimos made contact with Europeans and used certain of their material goods. From about A.D. 1 some iron tools reached Alaska by way of Russia and Siberia, but not enough to affect Eskimo culture substantially. Direct contacts with Europeans began in Greenland, Newfoundland, and Labrador, where Norse people from

Scandinavia planted colonies in the late tenth century. At first the Norse traded metal goods for ivory near their Newfoundland settlement, but growing hostility ended peaceful commerce. By the eleventh century, the Norse had withdrawn from Vinland, as they called Newfoundland. The Norse colonies had no long-term impact on the indigenous peoples of North America. The colonies were short-lived, colonists were few, and, most important, the Norse did not carry the epidemic diseases that would be brought, with disastrous results for the Native Americans, by later colonists.

Along the Pacific coast, from Alaska to southern California, improvements in the production and storage of food enabled Indians to develop more settled ways of life. From the Alaskan panhandle to northern California, natives spent brief periods each year catching salmon and other fish. The Northwest Coast Indians dried and stored enough fish to last the year, and their seasonal movements gradually gave way to settled life in permanent villages of cedar-plank houses. In the Columbia Plateau, Indians built villages of pit houses and ate salmon through the summer. They left these communities in spring and fall for hunting and gathering.

By A.D. 1 many Northwest Coast villages numbered several hundred people. Trade and warfare strengthened the power of chiefs and other leaders, whose families had greater wealth and prestige than commoners. Leading families proclaimed their status in elaborate totem poles depicting supernatural beings linked to their ancestors and in potlatches, ceremonies in which the Indians gave away or destroyed much of their material wealth. The artistic and architectural achievements of Northwest Coast Indians awed Europeans. "What must astonish most [observers]," a French explorer wrote in 1791, "is to see painting everywhere, everywhere sculpture, among a nation of hunters."

At about the same time, Indians farther south, along the coast and in the interior valleys of what is now California, began to live in villages of one hundred or more people. Acorns dominated their diet. After the fall harvest, Indians ground the

UNINHABITED LANDS

Eskimos

Aleuts
Ingaliks
Tanainas
Kutchins
Dogribs
Eskimos
Kaskas
Slaveys
Chippewyans
Eskimos
Naskapis
Tlingits
Tsimshians
Beavers
Crees
Beothuks
Haidas
Sarsis
Crees
Montagnais
Micmacs
Kwakiutls
Nootkas
Shuswaps
Thompsons
Sanpoils
Blackfeet
Salish
Gros Ventres Assiniboins
Abenakis
Chinooks
Yakimas
Nez Percés
Ojibwas
Sioux
Ottawas
Hurons
Iroquois
Mohawks
Oneidas
Onondagas
Cayugas
Senecas
Massachusette
Flatheads
Crows
Mandans
Menominis
Winnebagos
Sacs
Foxes
Wampanoags
Narragansetts
Pequots
Yuroks
Cheyennes
Arikaras
Potawatomis
Susquehannocks
Delawares
Pomos
Shoshones
Pawnees
Miamis
Shawnees
Eries
Illinois
Yokuts
Washos
Arapahos
Powhatans
Chumash
Paiutes
Utes
Osages
Wichitas
Tuscaroras
Walapais
Mohaves
Hopis
Navajos
Zunis
Kiowas
Cherokees
Catawbas
Luiseños
Yumas
Papagos
Pimas
Rio Grande
Pueblos
Apaches
Chickasaws
Choctaws
Creeks
Guales
(Yamasees)
Caddos
Natchez
Mobiles
Coahuiltecs
Calusas

PACIFIC OCEAN

ATLANTIC OCEAN

GULF OF MEXICO

0        500 Miles
0        500 Kilometers

**Cultural Areas**

Arctic
Subarctic
Northwest Coast
Plateau
Great Basin
California
Southwest
Plains
Eastern Woodlands – Northeast
Eastern Woodlands – Southeast

**Culture Areas of Native Americans and Locations of Selected Tribes, A.D. 1500**

*"Culture area" is a convention enabling archaeologists and anthropologists to generalize about regional patterns among pre-Colombian Native American cultures.*

acorns into meal, leached them of bitter tannic acid, and then roasted, boiled, or baked the nuts before eating or storing them. Intense competition for acorns forced California bands to define territorial boundaries rigidly and to combine several villages under a single chief. Chiefs conducted trade, diplo-

macy, and religious ceremonies with neighboring groups and, when necessary, led their people in battle. Supplementing game, fish, and plants, acorns enabled California's Indians to prosper.

The end of the Archaic period produced little change in the forbidding aridity of the Great Basin, encompassing present-day Nevada, western Utah, southern Idaho, and eastern Oregon. The area continued to support small hunting and gathering bands. Change came only in the fourteenth or fifteenth century A.D., when Paiute, Ute, and Shoshone Indians absorbed or displaced earlier inhabitants across the Great Basin. The newcomers' more efficient seed processing enabled them to support increased populations, which in turn occupied ever-larger territories.

The Hawaiian Islands were part of the south and central Pacific lands of Oceania. By 1600 B.C. the Austronesian peoples of Australia and New Guinea had developed agriculture and were making pottery, tools, and giant outrigger canoes. They began settling formerly uninhabited South Pacific islands but did not reach Hawaii until the fourth century A.D.

These first Hawaiians lived in self-sufficient communities. They cultivated sweet potatoes, yams, and taro (which they made into a fermented paste) and exploited a variety of fish and shellfish. Each community distinguished sharply between commoners and chiefs. Hawaiian chiefs collected food and goods from subordinate communities and allies and occasionally waged war for territorial conquest and subjugation of other peoples.

When Europeans arrived in Hawaii in the late eighteenth century, the islands contained about 400,000 people in communities averaging 200 people each. Thereafter, European diseases devastated the native population, which plummeted to 40,000 by 1890.

## The Southwest

Although peoples of the Pacific coast cultivated tobacco, they never farmed food-bearing plants. Abundant food resources left them little incentive to take the risks that agriculture entailed, especially in California, with its dry summers. In other areas of North America, however, agriculture became central to Indian life. In the arid Southwest, natives concentrated community energies on irrigation for agriculture, but in the humid Eastern Woodlands, plant cultivation came more easily. In both regions

the advent of agriculture was a long, slow process that never entirely replaced other food-procuring activities.

New World farming began about 5000 B.C.—the same era in which agriculture was being introduced in Europe from southwestern Asia—when Indians in central Mexico planted seeds of certain wild crops that they had customarily harvested, including squash, corn, and beans. Plant domestication slowly spread, first reaching western New Mexico about 3500 B.C. Agriculture remained relatively unimportant for several thousand years, until a more drought-resistant strain of corn from Mexico enabled the inhabitants to move to dry lowlands. Populations then rose rapidly, and two influential new cultures arose, the Hohokam and the Anasazi.

Hohokam culture emerged in the third century B.C. when ancestors of Pima and Papago Indians began farming in the Gila River and Salt River valleys of southern Arizona. The Hohokam people built elaborate canal systems for irrigation that enabled them to harvest two crops each year, an amazing feat in such an arid environment. The construction and maintenance of the canals demanded large, coordinated work forces. The Hohokams therefore built permanent villages of several hundred residents, and many such communities were joined in confederations linked by canals. The central village in each confederation coordinated labor, trade, and religious and political life for all.

The Hohokam way of life drew on materials and ideas from outside the Southwest. From about the sixth century A.D., the larger Hohokam villages had ball courts and platform mounds such as those in Mexico, and ball games became major public events. Mexican art influenced Hohokam artists, who used clay, stone, turquoise, and shell. Seashells from California appeared in Hohokam pottery as backing for turquoise mosaics and as material for intricate etchings. Archaeologists have found Mexican items such as rubber balls, macaw feathers, and copper bells at Hohokam sites.

Among the last southwesterners to make farming the focus of their subsistence were a people known as the Anasazis, a Navajo term meaning "ancient ones." Their culture originated in the Four

bank, Indians, and capitalism/making money, go together with the attitudes of Americans at the time.

4.    What is the significance of the frontier in American history? What was the powerful myth that Americans developed regarding the frontier? How did Hollywood and television affect that myth? You might wish to concentrate on the role of the Western Hero, the gun, or women.

5.    What were some of the factors that led to the Industrial Revolution in America? You might wish to consider natural resources, banks and capital investments, agriculture, transportation, or mass production. Or you might wish to trace why the Industrial Revolution was so revolutionary, and how it affected the American National character.

did some Americans become so anti-Catholic when Catholics began coming in
mbers to this country? Stress the political, moral, and economic factors. How
an attitudes towards Catholics changed, and what is the place of Catholics
ay? You may concentrate on Irish Catholics if you wish, and you
o some outside research/reading if you answer this question.

oals of the Ante Bellum Reform movement? How many of the
may wish to discuss the Temperance movement,
nd abolitionism.

Corners area where Arizona, New Mexico, Colorado, and Utah meet. Although they adopted village life and agriculture late, the Anasazis expanded rapidly in the sixth century A.D. and dominated a wide area. They traded with Indians in Mexico, California, and elsewhere but took few artistic or cultural ideas from them. Instead, their neighbors borrowed from the Anasazis.

The Anasazis had a distinctive architecture. They constructed their early dwellings, round pit houses, in the shape of *kivas*, the partly underground, circular structures where Anasazi men conducted religious ceremonies. Because the Anasazis believed that the first humans reached the earth from underground, their homes also featured small holes in the floor known as *sipapus*. As their population grew, the Anasazis built aboveground, rectangular apartment houses containing small *kivas*. Anasazi-style apartments and *kivas* are characteristic of the architecture of the modern-day Pueblo Indians, who are descendants of the Anasazis.

From the tenth through the mid-twelfth century, an unusually wet period, the Anasazis expanded over much of what today is New Mexico and Arizona. Village populations grew to 1,000 or more. In Chaco Canyon in northwestern New Mexico, a cluster of twelve villages forged a powerful confederation numbering 15,000 people. Perfectly straight roads radiated from the canyon to satellite pueblos up to sixty-five miles away. The builders carved out stairs or footholds in the sides of steep cliffs. The largest village, Pueblo Bonito, had 1,200 inhabitants and two Great Kivas, each fifty feet in diameter. People traveled from outlying areas to Chaco Canyon for religious ceremonies. Chaco Canyon was the center of the turquoise industry that manufactured beads for trade with Mexico, and its pueblos supplied the outlying people with food in times of drought. An elaborate system of controlling rainwater runoff through small dams, terraces, and other devices permitted this agricultural surplus.

Devastating droughts in the late twelfth and thirteenth centuries destroyed classic Anasazi culture. Suddenly, the amount of farmland was drastically reduced for a population that had grown rapidly during the preceding centuries. The Indians abandoned the great Anasazi centers and scattered. Some formed new pueblos along the upper Rio Grande, and others moved south and west to establish the Zuñi and Hopi pueblos. Descendants of the Anasazis still inhabit many of these pueblos. Other large agricultural communities, such as those of the Hohokams, also dispersed when droughts came. With farming peoples consequently clustered in the few areas with sufficient water, the drier southwestern lands attracted the foraging Apaches and Navajos, whose arrival at the end of the thirteenth century ended their long migration from northwestern Canada.

## The Eastern Woodlands

Indians of the Eastern Woodlands, the vast forests from the Mississippi Valley to the Atlantic coast, also experimented with village life and political centralization, but without farming. After doing so, however, they developed an extraordinarily productive agriculture.

By 1200 B.C. about 5,000 people had concentrated in a single village at Poverty Point on the Mississippi River in Louisiana. Two large mounds flanked the village, and six concentric embankments—the largest over half a mile in diameter surrounded it. During the spring and autumn equinoxes, a person standing on the larger mound could watch the sun rise directly over the village center. Solar observations formed the basis for these Indians' religious beliefs as well as for their calendar.

Poverty Point lay at the center of a large political and economic unit. It imported quartz, copper, obsidian, crystal, and other sacred materials from eastern North America and distributed them to nearby communities. These communities almost certainly supplied the labor for the earthworks. The Olmec peoples of Mexico clearly influenced the design and organization of Poverty Point. The settlement flourished for only three centuries and then declined, for reasons that are unclear. Nevertheless, it foreshadowed later Mississippi Valley developments.

A different mound-building culture, the Adena, emerged in the Ohio Valley in the fifth century B.C. Adena villages rarely exceeded 400 inhabitants, but

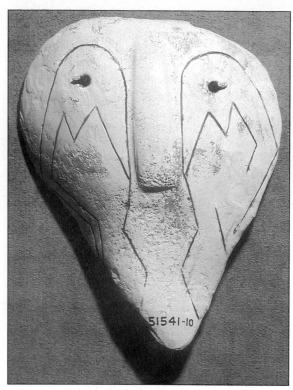

**Mississippian Engraved Shell**
*Engraved conch shells, often with highly abstract designs, were among the goods traded by Mississippian peoples in the Southeast.*

the Adena people spread over a wide area and built hundreds of mounds, most of them containing graves. The largest, Grave Creek Mound in West Virginia, was 240 feet in diameter and 70 feet high. In Adena culture, a person's social and political status apparently determined his or her treatment in death: some corpses were cremated (burned), others were placed in round clay basins, and still others were given elaborate tombs.

The Adena mounds constituted the heart of a religious movement whose adherents scattered over much of the Northeast. Although Adena burial practices—the inclusion of grave goods, the painting of red hematite on some corpses—were familiar

in the Northeast, the burial rituals themselves and many of the manufactured objects were new. As the Adena culture flourished, trade networks distributed these objects far across the Northeast.

During the first century B.C., Adena culture evolved into a more developed and widespread culture known as Hopewell. Hopewell ceremonial centers, larger and more elaborate than those of the Adena, mushroomed along the Ohio and Illinois river valleys. Some centers contained two or three dozen mounds within enclosures of several square miles. The graves of elites contained elaborate burial goods: freshwater pearls, copper ornaments, mica, quartz, or other sacred substances. Hopewell artisans used raw materials from throughout America east of the Rockies. Through trade networks Hopewell influence spread to communities as distant as places in modern-day Wisconsin, Florida, and New York. The great Hopewell centers of the Ohio and Illinois Valleys were abandoned in the fifth century A.D. for reasons that remain unknown, but they exerted enormous influence.

Amazingly, the people who created the sophisticated Hopewell culture were primarily hunter-gatherers, not farmers. Although they did grow some crops, agriculture became a dietary mainstay for Woodlands people only between the seventh and twelfth centuries A.D.

The first full-time farmers in the East were the Mississippians, who lived on the flood plains of the Mississippi River and its major tributaries. Their culture incorporated elements from the Hopewell culture and new ideas from Mexico into their own traditions. The volume of Mississippian craft production and of long-distance trade dwarfed those of the Hopewell and Adena cultures. Mississippian towns, containing hundreds or even thousands of people, were built around open plazas like those of central Mexico. Religious temples and elite residences stood atop large mounds next to the plazas. Religious ceremonies focused on worship of the sun as the source of agricultural fertility. Chiefs claimed to be related to the sun, and when they died, wives and servants were killed to accompany them to the afterlife. Artisans produced sophisticated work in clay, stone, shell, copper, and wood, largely for religious and funeral rituals.

Many Mississippian centers were built not by local natives but by outsiders seeking to combine farming and riverborne trade. By the tenth century most Mississippian centers were part of larger confederacies based on trade and shared religious beliefs. Powerful "supercenters" and their chiefs dominated these confederacies. The most powerful confederacy revolved around the magnificent city of Cahokia, near modern St. Louis; its influence extended from the Appalachians to the edge of the Plains and from the Great Lakes to the Gulf of Mexico.

A city of about 20,000 people, Cahokia covered more than 6 square miles and contained more than 120 earthworks. At its center a four-terraced structure called Monk's Mound covered fifteen acres (more than the Great Pyramid of Egypt) and rose 100 feet at its highest point. Surrounding the city, a 125-square-mile metropolitan area encompassed ten large towns and more than fifty farming villages. In addition, Cahokia dominated a giant network of commercial and political alliances extending over much of the American heartland. Like other Mississippian societies, Cahokia, influenced by ideas and crops from Mexico, erected ever-more-complex political, economic, and religious institutions. Many scholars believe that by the twelfth century, Cahokia was the capital of a potential nation-state.

Cahokia reigned supreme for two and a half centuries, but by the thirteenth century, it and allied centers were beginning to suffer food shortages. Neighboring peoples, moreover, challenged them militarily, and the inhabitants fled. By the fifteenth century, Indians in the central Mississippi Valley were living in small villages linked by mutual interdependence, not coercion. Similar temple-mound centers in the Southeast also declined, and although new centers rose, European diseases destroyed them after 1500.

The demise of the Mississippian culture, like that of the Hopewell, ended a trend toward political centralization among Indians in eastern North America. Nonetheless, the Mississippians profoundly affected native culture in the East. They

**Cahokia, c. A.D. 1200**   *This depiction of Cahokia by a twentieth-century artist shows the Indian city's central area as defined by a defensive stockade. The four-terraced Monk's Mound and other public structures are within the stockade walls.*

## CHRONOLOGY

| | |
|---|---|
| c. 5,000,000 B.C. | Earliest human ancestors appear in Africa. |
| c. 2,000,000 B.C. | Ice Age begins. |
| c. 300,000–100,000 B.C. | Humans spread throughout Eastern Hemisphere. |
| c. 40,000–15,000 B.C. | Ancestors of Native Americans cross Alaska-Siberia land bridge. |
| c. 10,000 B.C. | Ice Age ends. |
| c. 10,000–9000 B.C. | Paleo-Indians spread throughout Western Hemisphere. |
| c. 9000 B.C. | Extinction of big-game mammals. |
| c. 8000 B.C. | Archaic era begins. |
| c. 7000 B.C. | Athapaskan-speaking peoples arrive in North America. |
| c. 5000 B.C. | First domesticated plants grown in Western Hemisphere. |
| c. 3500 B.C. | First domesticated plants grown in North America. |
| c. 3000–2000 B.C. | Eskimo and Aleut peoples arrive in North America. |
| c. 1500 B.C. | Archaic era ends. Bow and arrow and ceramic pottery introduced in North America. |
| c. 1200 B.C. | Poverty Point flourishes in Louisiana. |
| c. 400–100 B.C. | Adena culture flourishes in Ohio Valley. |
| c. 250 B.C. | Hohokam culture begins in Southwest. |
| c. 100 B.C. | Anasazi culture begins in Southwest. |
| c. 100 B.C.–A.D. 600 | Hopewell culture thrives in Midwest. |
| c. A.D. 300 | First people arrive at Hawaiian Islands. |
| c. A.D. 700 | Mississippian culture begins. |
| c. A.D. 900 | Stockade and first mounds built at Cahokia. |
| c. A.D. 1000–1100 | Norse settlement of Vinland flourishes on Newfoundland. |
| c. A.D. 1150 | Anasazi peoples disperse to form pueblos. |
| c. A.D. 1200–1300 | Cahokia declines. |
| c. A.D. 1400 | League of the Iroquois formed. |

## FOR FURTHER READING

John Bierhorst, *The Mythology of North America* (1985). An excellent introduction to Native American mythology, organized regionally.

Brian Fagan, *Ancient North America: The Archaeology of a Continent* (1991). An informative, comprehensive introduction to the continent's history before Europeans' arrival.

Åke Hultkrantz, *The Religions of the American Indians* (1979). A stimulating discussion by the leading scholar on the subject.

Gwyn Jones, *The Norse Atlantic Saga,* rev. ed. (1986). A single volume combining recent scholarship on Norse, Eskimos, and Indians with translations of the most important sagas.

Alvin M. Josephy, Jr., *America in 1492: The World of the Indian Peoples Before the Arrival of Columbus* (1992). Outstanding essays on life in the Western Hemisphere on the eve of European contact.

William C. Sturtevant, gen. ed., *Handbook of North American Indians* (20 vols. projected, 1978–   ). A partially completed reference work providing basic information on the history and culture of virtually every known native society.

The concepts of New World and Old World had not existed prior to Christopher Columbus's voyages from 1492 to 1504. To Europeans before Columbus, there was only one world—theirs, the world that stretched from Europe to Africa and Asia. Pre-Columbian Native Americans were equally sure that they inhabited the only world. In many ways the Columbian voyages triggered not just a meeting of two worlds previously unknown to each other but a collision between them.

Each group's fascination with the strangeness of the "other" world would all too quickly sour. The Indians, whom Europeans first saw as gullible, as potential servants or slaves, would become lazy and deceitful "savages" in whites' eyes. Native Americans would lose their wonder at European "magic"—guns and gunpowder, metal tools, and glass beads—and would realize that this magic, and the diseases that the Europeans brought, could be destructive.

*(Right)* ***Englishman Bartholomew Gosnold Trading with Indians at Martha's Vineyard, Massachusetts,*** *by Theodore de Bry, 1634*

# Transatlantic Encounters and Colonial Beginnings, 1492–1630

**Old World Peoples**

❧

**European Expansion**

❧

**Footholds in North America**

In much of what is now Latin America, the arrival of the Europeans led to conquest. In the future United States and Canada, however, European mastery came more slowly; more than one hundred years would pass before self-sustaining colonies were established. Nevertheless, from the moment of Columbus's landing on October 12, 1492, the American continents became the stage for the encounter of the Old and New worlds.

# Old World Peoples

The Eastern Hemisphere gave birth to the human race. Early humans evolved for several million years on Africa's warm savannas (grasslands) before spreading slowly across the rest of Africa, Asia, and Europe. These continents hosted a vast array of societies ranging from hunter-gatherers to powerful states with armed forces, bureaucracies, religious institutions, proud aristocracies, and toiling commoners. All would play a role in the collision of the Old and New worlds.

## West Africa and Its Peoples

For almost 5,000 years the barren Sahara Desert across northern Africa cut most of the continent off from the rest of the Old World. West Africa was further isolated from the land to its north by the prevailing Atlantic winds, which carried old-fashioned sailing ships south but hampered their northward return. And the yellow fever rampant in the West African rain-forest coastline generally killed adult newcomers, who lacked immunity to the disease. But a broad, hospitable savanna covered much of the rest of Africa. In the first millennium B.C., the region's peoples radiated outward, eventually leaving their imprint on virtually all of sub-Saharan Africa. By the sixteenth century, sub-Saharan Africa, twice the landmass of the United States, had a population of perhaps 20 million.

Camel caravans crossing the Sahara ended West Africa's isolation and stimulated trade in gold and salt with Mediterranean North Africa. Powerful West African empires—Ghana, Mali, and Songhai—arose and flourished for a millennium, from 600 to 1600 A.D. Nominally Islamic, these wealthy empires were famed throughout North Africa. By 1492 the last of the great empires, Songhai, stood at the height of its power, its bureaucracy and army dominating much of the African interior. Songhai's major city, Timbuktu, boasted flourishing markets and a renowned university.

Compared to the savanna empires, coastal West Africa was relatively insignificant. During the first millennium A.D., small Islamic states arose in Senegambia, at Africa's westernmost bulge, and in Guinea's coastal forests. The best-known state was Benin, where artisans fashioned magnificent ironwork for centuries.

Then in the fifteenth century foreign demand for the gold that Africans panned from streams and dug from the earth triggered a population rise in Guinea. Savanna warriors and merchants poured into Guinea and Senegambia, seeking opportunity and occasionally founding or expanding Islamic states. By the mid-fifteenth century, the Portuguese, using new maritime technology, were sailing along West Africa's coast in search of gold and slaves.

West African leaders wielded sharply different amounts and kinds of political power. Grassland emperors claimed semigodlike status, which they only thinly disguised after adopting Islam. Rulers of smaller kingdoms depended on their ability to persuade, to conform to custom, and sometimes to redistribute wealth justly among their people.

In sub-Saharan Africa, kinship groups knitted societies together. Parents, aunts, uncles, distant cousins, and those who shared clan ties formed networks of mutual obligation. In centuries to come, the tradition of strong extended families would help enslaved Africans to endure the breakup of nuclear families by sale. In addition, polygyny (the custom whereby a man had several wives) and bridewealth (a prospective husband's payment to his bride's kin before marriage) were widespread in West Africa. Europeans often saw both practices as evidence of African barbarism. Wives generally maintained lifelong links with their own kin group, and children

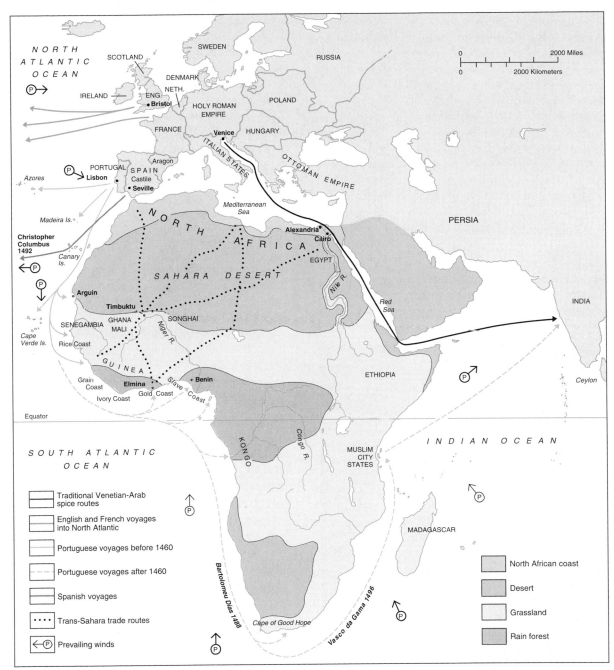

**Europe, Africa, and the Near East in 1492**

*In 1492 Europeans had little knowledge of the outside world apart from the Mediterranean basin and Africa's west coast. Since the Azores, the Canary Islands, and the Cape Verde Islands had been discovered recently in the eastern Atlantic, many Europeans were not surprised when Columbus found new islands farther west in 1492.*

traced descent through the mother's bloodline. These traditions buttressed women's standing in society.

Sub-Saharan Africans believed that kin groups enjoyed inalienable rights to land that their ancestors had cultivated and that they had a duty to honor ancestors and earth spirits by proper cultivation. Like North Americans, Africans did not treat land as a commodity to be bought and sold.

Cultivation was difficult in Africa and required the labor of both genders. As in all tropical regions, scorching sunlight and frequent downpours lowered soil fertility. Like Indians in eastern North America, many Africans practiced slash-and-burn agriculture

**Mali Horseman, c. 13th–14th century**
*This terra-cotta figure originated in Mali, one of several powerful empires in West Africa before the arrival of Europeans.*

to maintain soil fertility. In coastal rain forests, root crops, primarily yams, dominated. On the Senegambia savanna, rice was the staff of life. In the seventeenth and eighteenth centuries, both rice and its Senegambian cultivators would be transplanted (the latter, as slaves) to North America.

Religion permeated African life. West African, like Native American, religion recognized spiritual presences throughout nature. The power of earth spirits and of agricultural ancestors reinforced the esteem that Africans accorded to cultivators. An enslaved eighteenth-century West African who eventually managed to purchase his freedom from slavery, Olaudah Equiano, gave Europeans a glimpse of African religion:

> *The natives believe that there is one Creator of all things, and that he lives in the sun, [and] . . . that he governs events. . . . Some . . . believe in the transmigration of souls [reincarnation] to some degree. Those spirits, who are not transmigrated, such as their dear friends or relations, they believe always attend them, and guard them from the bad spirits of their foes.*

Magic and the placating of spiritual powers, moreover, were important in African life. In both African and Native American societies, shamans maintained contact with the spiritual world, and belief in witchcraft was widespread. Unlike Indian religion, however, African religion focused on ancestor worship.

Religious motifs saturated African art. West Africans used their ivory, cast-iron, and wood sculptures in ceremonies reenacting creation myths and honoring spirits. A strong moralistic streak ran through African folktales. Oral reciters transmitted these stories in dramatic public presentations with ritual masks, dance, and music of a complex rhythmic structure. West African art and music powerfully influenced twentieth-century art and jazz.

Much in traditional African culture clashed with the great monotheistic religions, Islam and Christianity. Among Africans, Islam appealed primarily to merchants trading with Muslim North Africa and to grassland rulers eager to consolidate their power. By the sixteenth century, Islam had only just begun to affect the daily lives of grassland cultivators and artisans. Christianity, which accompanied the Portuguese to Africa in the fifteenth and sixteenth centuries, had little impact on Africans until the nineteenth century.

## European Culture and Society

When Columbus reached the New World in 1492, Europe was approaching the height of the Renaissance, the rebirth of classical Greek and Roman culture. Splendid architecture decorated European cities, and wealthy patrons commissioned artists to create works of idealized human beauty. Scholars strove to reconcile Christian faith and ancient philosophy, to explore the mysteries of nature, to map the world, and to explain the motions of the heavens.

But European society was quivering with tension. The era's artistic and intellectual creativity stemmed partly from intense social and spiritual stress as Europeans groped for stability by glorifying order, hierarchy, and beauty. A concern for power and rank, or "degree," dominated European life in the fifteenth and sixteenth centuries. Gender, wealth, inherited position, and political power affected every European's status, and few lived beyond the reach of some political authority's claim to tax and rule. But this order was shaky. Conflicts between ranks, between religions, and between rich and poor threatened the balance, making Europeans cling all the more eagerly to order and hierarchy.

Democracy had no place in this world. To Europeans of the era, democracy meant mob rule and the destruction of social distinctions. Hierarchy and its strict rules seemed safer. Kings dominated the European hierarchy, but they were concerned less with their people's welfare than with consolidating and enlarging their own power. To that end, they waged costly wars using mercenary armies and spreading disease and misery everywhere.

Europeans believed that kings, not queens, were meant to rule. In addition, they knew that a queen's marriage would ultimately transfer the crown to a foreign dynasty or to a new domestic one. Either situation would threaten stability and hierarchy. In England, where Queens Mary I and Elizabeth I reigned for half a century, people felt this fear most keenly.

Although Mary (ruled 1553–1558) blundered repeatedly as queen and saved the day only by dying early, Elizabeth (ruled 1558–1603) took England's interests to heart. Remaining the unmarried "virgin queen," she artfully managed Parliament, which represented upper-class landowners and merchants. By choosing prudent advisers and shrewdly manipulating royal favors, Elizabeth retained control of the kingdom's intricate political system for a half century.

Elizabeth's reign demonstrated the degree to which royal power depended on the upper classes' cooperation. The men who dominated Parliament saw officeholding as a form of property and as a legitimate way to improve their fortunes. No monarch could ride roughshod over such men, and in defending their own liberties, they preserved the principle of limited government against encroaching despotism. But England's upper classes had problems of their own as well. A tradition of free spending to maintain status and a stagnant economy pinched not only members of the aristocracy, or noblemen with titles, but also many of the gentry, the "respectable" untitled landowners who traditionally lived without doing manual labor and who played prominent political roles in local government and Parliament.

At the bottom of the social heap toiled the ordinary people. Europe remained rural in these times, and four-fifths of its population were peasants. Taxes, rents, and other dues to landlords and church officials were heavy. Poor harvests or war drove even well-to-do peasants to starvation.

Sharp population increases worsened conditions. The plague known as the Black Death had killed one-third of Europe's people in the late fourteenth century, but by 1660 dramatic growth was driving up the population to 100 million. Food supplies, however, did not rise as rapidly. Peasant families survived on pitifully low yields of wheat, barley, and oats. Plowing, sowing, and harvesting together, they also grazed livestock on jointly owned "commons" composed of pastureland and forest. But with new land at a premium, landlords, especially the English gentry, began to "enclose" the commons, thus making them private property. Peasants with no *written* title to their lands were particularly vulnerable. Those with strong titles, however, could either keep their land or profit by joining the landlord in enclosing.

Though numerous, European towns usually contained only a few thousand inhabitants. London, a great metropolis of 200,000 people by 1600, was an exception. Large or small, towns were dirty and disease-ridden, and townspeople lived close-packed with their neighbors.

People of the times saw towns as centers of opportunity for the ambitious. Immigration from the countryside therefore swelled urban populations. But peasants transplanted to towns remained at the bottom of the social order, unable to earn enough money to marry and to live independently. Manufacturing took place in household workshops, where artisan masters ruled their subordinates. Successful artisans and merchants formed guilds to control employment, prices, and the sale of goods. Dominated by the richest citizens, urban governments enforced social conformity by "sumptuary laws" that forbade dressing inappropriately for one's social rank.

The consequences of rapid population growth were acute in England, where the population doubled from 2.5 million in 1500 to 5 million by 1620. In parts of the countryside, the gentry grew rich selling wool, but because of technological stagnation, per capita output and household income among textile workers fell. In effect, more workers competed for fewer jobs as European markets for English cloth diminished and as food prices rose. Land enclosure aggravated unemployment and forced large numbers of people to wander the countryside in search of work. These "vagabonds" seemed to threaten law and order. Parliament passed "Poor Laws" ordering vagrants whipped and sent home, where hard-pressed taxpayers maintained them on relief.

Thus the hopes and ambitions that drew people to towns usually yielded to frustration. Some English people blamed the wealthy for raising prices, goading the poor to revolt, and giving too little to charity. Others, such as writer Thomas Nashe, spread the blame more widely:

> From the rich to the poor . . . there is ambition, or swelling above their states [proper place in society]; the rich citizen swells against the pride of the prodigal courtier; the prodigal courtier swells against the wealth of the citizen. One company swells against another. . . . The ancients [elderly], they oppose themselves against the younger, and suppress them and keep them down all that they may. The young men, they call [the elderly] dotards, and swell and rage.

Nashe and other conservative moralists stoutly upheld the value of social reciprocity. As in the New World and Africa, traditional society in Europe rested on long-term, reciprocal relationships. Because it sought smooth social relationships between individuals of unequal status, reciprocity required the upper classes to act with self-restraint and dignity and the lower classes to show deference to their "betters." It demanded strict economic regulation, too, to ensure that sellers charged a "just" price—one that covered costs and allowed the seller to profit but barred him from taking advantage of buyers' and borrowers' misfortunes, or of shortages, to make "excessive" profits.

Yet the ideals of traditional economic behavior had been withering for centuries. By the sixteenth century, nothing could stop the practices of charging interest on borrowed money and of increasing prices in response to demand. New forms of business organization such as the joint-stock company, the ancestor of the modern corporation, steadily spread. Demand for capital investment grew, and so did the supply of accumulated wealth. Gradually, a new economic outlook arose that justified the unimpeded acquisition of wealth and unregulated economic competition. Its adherents insisted that individuals owed one another only the money necessary to settle each market transaction. This "market economy" capitalism stood counter to traditional demands for the strict regulation of economic activity to ensure social reciprocity and to maintain "just prices."

Sixteenth- and seventeenth-century Europeans therefore were ambivalent about economic enterprise and social change. A restless desire for fresh opportunity kept life simmering with competitive tension. However, even those who prospered still sought the security and prestige of traditional social distinctions, and the poor longed for the age-old values that they hoped would restrain irresponsible greed. Intellectuals and clergy defended traditional standards, but ideal and reality grew steadily further apart.

Fundamental change in European society could also be seen in the rising importance of the nuclear family. In such a family, the power of the senior male challenged traditional kinship networks. The nuclear family represented a "little commonwealth" within which the father's rule mirrored God's rule over Creation and kings' lordship over their subjects. The ideal, according to a German writer, was that "wives should obey their husbands and not seek to dominate them; they must manage the home efficiently. Husbands . . . should treat their wives with consideration and occasionally close an eye to their faults." In practice, however, the father's domination often had to make room for the wife's management of family affairs and her assistance in running the farm or the workshop.

## Europeans and Their God

Sixteenth-century Europeans believed in the biblical explanation of the origins of the world and its peoples. Christianity taught that Jesus Christ, God's Son, redeemed sinners through his crucifixion and resurrection. As real as God to European Christians was the devil, Satan, who lured people to damnation by tempting them to do evil. Jewish and Muslim European minorities shared Christians' worship of a single supreme being, based on the God of the Old Testament.

But many sixteenth-century Europeans also believed in witchcraft, magic, and astrology. They saw nature as a "chain of being" infused by God with life and tingling with spiritual forces. Deeply embedded in folklore, such supernaturalism also marked the "high culture" of educated Europeans. Indeed, the sixteenth-century European "mentality" had more in common with Indian and African mindsets than with modern views.

The medieval Christian church taught that Christ had founded the church to save sinners from hell. Every time a priest said Mass, Christ's sacrifice was repeated, and divine grace flowed to sinners through sacraments that priests alone could administer—especially baptism, confession, and the Eucharist (communion). In most of Europe the "church" was a huge network of clergymen set apart from laypeople by ordination into the priesthood and by the fact that they did not marry. The pope, the "vicar (representative) of Christ," topped this hierarchy. His authority reached throughout Europe, except in Russia, Greece, and the Balkan peninsula.

The papacy wielded awesome spiritual power. Fifteenth- and sixteenth-century popes claimed the authority to dispense extra blessings, or "indulgences," to repentant sinners in return for "good works," such as donating money to the church. Indulgences also promised time off from future punishment in purgatory. Given peoples' anxieties over sin, indulgences were enormously popular. A German seller of indulgences even advertised that

> As soon as the coin in the cash box rings,
> The soul from purgatory's fire springs.

But the sale of indulgences provoked charges of materialism and corruption. In 1517 Martin Luther, a German friar, attacked the practice. When the papacy tried to silence him, Luther broadened his criticism to include the Mass, priests, and the pope. His revolt sparked the Protestant Reformation, which changed Christianity forever.

To Luther, the selling of indulgences was evil not only because it bilked people but also because the church did harm by falsely assuring people that they could "earn" salvation by doing good works.

Luther believed instead that God alone chose whom to save and that believers should trust only God's love, not the word of priests and the pope. Luther's own spiritual struggle and experience of being "born again" constituted a classic conversion experience—the heart of Protestant religion as it would be preached and practiced for centuries in England and North America.

Luther's assault on church abuses won a fervent following among the German public, but Protestant reformers themselves could not agree on what God's word really meant. Thus Luther and French reformer John Calvin (1509–1564) interpreted salvation differently. Calvin, unlike Luther, insisted on the doctrine of predestination, in which an omnipotent God "predestined" most sinful humans to hell, saving only a few to exemplify his grace. Calvinists and Lutherans, as the followers of the two Reformation leaders came to be called, alike were horrified by radical Protestants such as the Anabaptists, who criticized the rich and powerful and restricted baptism to adults who had undergone a conversion. Viewing the Anabaptists as a threat to the social order, governments and mainstream churches persecuted them.

The Catholic church's remarkable resilience also dismayed Protestants. Indeed, the papacy vigorously attacked church corruption and combated Protestant viewpoints. The popes also sponsored a new religious order committed to the papacy, the Jesuits, whose members would distinguish themselves for centuries as teachers, missionaries, and royal advisers. This Catholic revival, known as the Counter-Reformation, created the modern Roman Catholic church.

Those in all religious camps who hoped that eventual Christian harmony would overcome religious quarrels were disillusioned. Religious warfare consumed much of western and central Europe from the mid-sixteenth to the mid-seventeenth century. Well-established international rivalries, such as those between Protestant England and Catholic Spain, assumed religious dimensions. In England the crown itself was entangled in religious controversy. Henry VIII (ruled 1509–1547) wanted a male heir to ensure political stability. But when his queen, Catherine of Aragon, failed to bear a son, Henry in 1527 requested a papal annulment of their marriage. When the pope denied his request, in 1533–1534 Henry had Parliament dissolve his marriage and proclaim him "supreme head" of the Church of England (Anglican church). He then seized and sold vast tracts of land owned by Catholic monasteries as a means of raising revenue.

## The Rise of Puritanism in England

Religious strife troubled England for over a century after Henry's break with Rome. Henry's sale of monastic lands had created a vested interest against returning to the old order, but Henry never quite decided that he was Protestant. Under his son Edward VI (ruled 1547–1553), however, the English church veered sharply toward Protestantism. Then Henry's daughter Mary assumed the throne in 1553 and tried to restore Catholicism, in part by burning several hundred Protestants at the stake.

The reign of Mary's successor, Elizabeth I, who became queen in 1558, marked a crucial watershed. Most English people were now Protestant; *how* Protestant was the question. A militant Calvinist minority, the Puritans, demanded wholesale "purification" of the Church of England from "popish abuses." As Calvinists, they affirmed salvation by predestination, denied Christ's presence in the Eucharist, and believed that a learned sermon was the heart of true worship. They wished to free each congregation from outside interference and encouraged lay members to participate in parish affairs.

Puritans argued that leading an outwardly moral life was not enough to earn salvation. They believed that Christians also must forge a commitment to serve God through an act of spiritual rebirth, the conversion experience. At this moment of being "reborn," a soul confronted its own unworthiness and felt the power of God's grace. Through "sanctification," the convert was cemented to God as a "saint"—a member of the "elect," or the chosen. Only saints could join Puritan congregations.

In preparing for spiritual rebirth, Puritans struggled to master their own wills, to internalize an idealistic code of ethics, and to forge the inner strength to survive in a world of economic and moral chaos. By the time of his or her redemption, the Puritan had undergone a radical transformation that replaced doubt with certainty, producing a strong sense of purpose, a willingness to sacrifice, and an ironclad discipline.

Puritanism appealed mainly to the growing middle sectors of English society—the gentry, university-educated clergymen and intellectuals, merchants, shopkeepers, artisans, and well-to-do peasants. Self-discipline had become central to both the worldly and the spiritual dimensions of these people's lives, and from their ranks would come the settlers of New England (see Chapter 3). Puritanism attracted few of the titled nobility, who enjoyed their wealth and privilege, and few of the desperately poor, who were struggling for mere survival.

Queen Elizabeth distrusted Puritan militancy and favored the traditional, dignified worship of the Anglican church. Until the pope declared her a heretic in 1570 and urged Catholics to overthrow her, she even avoided breaking with the Catholic church. Thereafter she saw all English Catholics as potential traitors and became more openly Protestant. Although Puritan sentiment steadily gained ground, Elizabeth never embraced it. By courting influential Puritans and embracing militant anti-Catholicism, Elizabeth maintained most Puritans' loyalty. But after her death, religious tensions came to a boil.

The Stuart monarchs, James I (ruled 1603–1625) and Charles I (ruled 1625–1649), bitterly opposed Puritan efforts to eliminate the office of bishop; not only did bishops, appointed by the king, compose one-quarter of Parliament's upper house, but they also could, and did, silence clerical critics of the monarchs. "No bishop, no king," snapped James I, more prophetically than he realized.

Abandoning the earlier hope of transforming the Church of England into independent congregations of "saints," Puritan *Separatists* decided to leave the corrupt state church. Some Separatists went first to Calvinist Holland and from there to Plymouth

Plantation in New England. *Nonseparatists* continued to strive to reform the Church of England from within. Some of their rank would later lead the colonization of Massachusetts Bay and Connecticut (see Chapter 3).

Under Charles I, Anglican authorities campaigned to eliminate Puritan influence within the church. Bishops insisted that services be conducted according to the Book of Common Prayer, which prescribed rituals similar to Catholic practice, and they dismissed Puritan ministers who refused to perform these "High Church" rites. Church courts harassed Puritans with fines and even excommunication.

Hard economic times compounded the Puritans' plight. Wages fell by 50 percent between 1550 and 1650, a growing population spawned massive unemployment, and war on the European continent threw the weaving industry of England's heavily Puritan southeastern counties into a recession as Germany was prevented from importing large amounts of English cloth after 1618. Puritans believed that these problems were contributing to a spiritual and moral crisis in England. Indeed, one Puritan minister wrote that the dwindling economic opportunities were tempting everyone "to pluck his means, as it were, out of his neighbor's throat."

Seeking escape from religious, political, and economic misery, a group of Puritan merchants bought the charter of the failed Virginia Company of Plymouth in 1628 and obtained a royal charter for land north of the Plymouth colony between the Charles and Merrimack rivers in 1629.

## Legacies of the Reformation

The Reformation left four major legacies. First, it created almost all the major Christian traditions that took root on American soil: Protestantism, modern Roman Catholicism, and the radical Protestantism that would later flower into dozens of denominations and groups seeking human perfection. Second, Protestants valued literacy. Luther's conversion sprang from his long study of the Bible, and Protestants demanded that believers carefully read

God's Word translated from Latin into contemporary spoken languages. Newly invented printing presses spread the new faith; wherever Protestantism flourished, so did general education and religious teaching. Third, Protestants denied that God endowed priests with special powers. Instead, Luther claimed, the church was a "priesthood of all believers." People were responsible for their own spiritual and moral condition. Finally, the Reformation and Counter-Reformation created a new crusading spirit in Europe that coincided with overseas expansion. From Christopher Columbus onward, this spirit justified Europeans' assumption of superiority over the non-Christian peoples of Africa and the Americas and the seizing of their land, resources, and labor.

The Reformation also created in many people a longing for the simplicity and purity of the ancient Christian church. Protestantism condemned the replacement of traditional reciprocity by marketplace values and questioned the pursuit of excessive wealth. In a world of troubling change, it forged individuals of strong moral determination and gave them the fortitude to survive and prosper. Protestantism's greatest appeal was to those who brooded over their chances for salvation and valued the steady performance of duty.

# European Expansion

Europe's outward thrust began centuries before Columbus's first voyage in 1492. Norse adventurers had reached North America in the tenth century, but their colonies had collapsed. European attention had turned eastward after 1096 as a series of crusading armies tried to wrest Palestine from Muslim control. A brisk trade with the Middle East begun in these years had brought silks and spices to Europe. Marco Polo and other thirteenth-century merchants had even traveled overland to East Asia, to buy directly from the Chinese. Fourteenth- and fifteenth-century Italian merchants grew rich from the spice and silk trade and used their fortunes to finance the early Renaissance and overseas expansion by European monarchs.

## Seaborne Expansion

In the mid-fifteenth century Europe experienced renewed prosperity and population growth. Competing for commercial advantage, the newly centralized European states projected their power overseas.

Improved maritime technology permitted this European expansion. In the early fifteenth century shipbuilders added the triangular Arab sail to their heavy cargo ships, creating a highly maneuverable ship, the caravel, to sail the stormy Atlantic. Further, the growing use of the compass and astrolabe permitted mariners to calculate their bearings on the open sea. Hand in hand with the technological advances of this "maritime revolution," Renaissance scholars corrected ancient geographical data and drew increasingly accurate maps. The new geography and sophisticated use of Arabic mathematics sharpened Europeans' knowledge of the world.

The Portuguese first felt the itch to explore new worlds. Their zeal for continuing the struggle against the Muslims, recently driven from Portugal, combined with an anxious search for new markets. Prince Henry "the Navigator" of Portugal (1394–1460) embodied both impulses. He encouraged Portuguese seamen to pilot their caravels farther down the African coast searching for weak spots in Muslim defenses and for trade opportunities. By the time of Henry's death, the Portuguese had built a profitable slaving station at Arguin; shortly after, they had penetrated south of the equator. In 1488 Bartolomeu Días reached Africa's southern tip, the Cape of Good Hope, opening the possibility of direct trade with India, and in 1498 Vasco da Gama led a Portuguese fleet around the cape and on to India. For more than a century the Portuguese remained an imperial presence in the Indian Ocean and the East Indies (modern Indonesia). But far more significantly, they brought Europeans face to face with black Africans.

**The "New Slavery"**

*In this early depiction, African slaves work and look for gold in the New World, under the supervision of a watchful European master.*

## The "New Slavery" and Racism

Slavery was well established in fifteenth-century West Africa, as elsewhere. The grassland emperors as well as individual families depended on slave labor. But most slaves or their children were absorbed into African families over time. First Arabs, and then Europeans, however, turned African slavery into an intercontinental business. A fifteenth-century Italian reported that the Arabs

> have many Berber horses, which they trade, and take to the Land of the Blacks, exchanging them with the rulers for slaves. . . . These slaves are brought to the market town of Hoden. . . . [Some] are taken . . . and sold to the Portuguese leaseholders of Arguin. . . . Every year the Portuguese carry away from [Arguin] a thousand slaves.

The Portuguese kept most competitors from the lucrative African slave trade until about 1600. They exploited existing African commercial and social patterns, often trading slaves and local products to other Africans for gold. The local African kingdoms were too strong for the Portuguese to attack, and black rulers traded—or chose not to trade—according to their own self-interest.

The coming of the Portuguese slavers changed West African societies. Small kingdoms in Guinea and Senegambia expanded to "service" the trade, and some of their rulers became rich. Farther south, in modern Angola, the kings of Kongo used the slave trade to consolidate their power and adopted Christianity. Kongo flourished until attackers from the interior severely weakened it at the end of the sixteenth century. African kings and their communities used the slave trade to dispose of "undesirables," including troublesome slaves whom they already owned, lawbreakers, and persons accused of witchcraft. But most slaves were simply victims of raids or wars. Muslim and European slave trading greatly stimulated conflicts among communities in Africa.

Europeans had used slaves since ancient Greece and Rome, but ominous changes took place in European slavery once the Portuguese began making voyages to Africa. First, the new slave trade was a high-volume business that expanded at a steady rate as Europeans colonized the Western Hemisphere and established plantation societies there. Between 1500 and 1600, perhaps 250,000 African slaves would reach the New World, and 50,000 would perish en route. Between 1601 and 1621, 200,000 more would arrive. Before the Atlantic slave trade ended in the nineteenth century, nearly 12 million Africans would be shipped across the sea. Slavery on this scale had been unknown since the Roman Empire. Second, African slaves received exceptionally harsh treatment. In medieval Europe slaves had primarily performed domestic service, but by 1450 the Portuguese and Spanish had created large slave-labor plantations on their Atlantic and Mediterranean islands. Using African slaves who toiled until death, these plantations produced sugar for European markets. In short, the African slaves owned

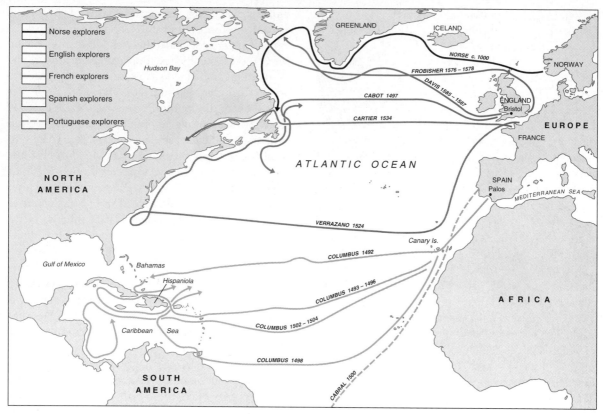

**Major Transatlantic Explorations, 1000–1587**

*Following Columbus's 1492 voyage, Spain's rivals soon began laying claim to parts of the New World based on the voyages of Cabot for England, Cabral for Portugal, and Verrazano for France. Later English and French exploration focused on finding a passsage to Asia around or through Canada.*

by Europeans performed exhausting, mindless labor. By 1600 the "new slavery" had become a brutal link in an expanding commerce that ultimately would encompass all major Western nations.

Finally, race became the explicit basis of the "new slavery." Africans' blackness and alien religion dehumanized them in European eyes. As racial prejudice hardened, Europeans found it easy to justify black slavery. European Christianity, moreover, made few attempts to soften slavery's rigors. Because the victims of the "new slavery" were physically distinctive and culturally alien, slavery became a lifelong, hereditary, and despised status.

## Europeans Reach America

The fascinating, contradictory figure of Christopher Columbus (1451–1506) embodied Europeans' varied motives for expansion. The son of an Italian weaver, Columbus became obsessed by the idea that Europeans could reach Asia by sailing westward across the Atlantic. Combining an overestimation of Asia's eastward thrust with an underestimation of the earth's circumference, he concluded that the world was much smaller than it actually is and that the open-sea distance from Europe to Asia was roughly 3,000 miles, not the actual 12,000 miles.

Religious fervor led Columbus to dream of carrying Christianity around the globe, but he also hungered for wealth and glory.

Europeans had ventured far into the Atlantic before Columbus: besides the early Norse, fifteenth-century English fishers may have reached North America's coast. What distinguished Columbus was his persistence in hawking his "enterprise of the Indies" around Europe's royal courts. In 1492 the rulers of newly united Spain, Isabella of Castile and Ferdinand of Aragon, accepted Columbus's offer, hoping to break a threatened Portuguese monopoly on Asian trade. Picking up the westerly trade winds, Columbus's three small ships made landfall within a month off the North American coast at a small island that he named San Salvador.

Word of Columbus's discovery fired Europeans' imaginations. It also induced the Spanish and Portuguese to sign the Treaty of Tordesillas in 1494, dividing all future discoveries between themselves. Columbus made three further voyages, in the course of which he established Spanish colonies, but never fulfilled his promise of reaching Asia. Meanwhile, England's Henry VII (ruled 1485–1509) ignored the Treaty of Tordesillas and sent an Italian navigator known as John Cabot westward across the northern Atlantic in 1497. Cabot claimed Nova Scotia, Newfoundland, and the rich Grand Banks fisheries for England, but he vanished at sea on a second voyage. Like Columbus, Cabot believed that he had reached Asia.

The more Columbus and others explored, the more apparent it became that a vast landmass blocked the western route to Asia. In 1500 the Portuguese claimed Brazil, and other voyages outlined a continuous coastline from the Caribbean to Brazil. In 1507 a publisher brought out a collection of voyagers' tales, including one from the Italian Amerigo Vespucci. A shrewd marketer, the publisher devised a catchy name for the new continent: America.

Getting past America to Asia remained the early explorers' goal. In 1513 the Spaniard Vasco Núñez de Balboa crossed the narrow isthmus of Panama and chanced upon the Pacific Ocean. In 1519 the Portuguese mariner Ferdinand Magellan, sailing under the Castilian flag, began a voyage around the world through the stormy straits at South America's southern tip, now named the Straits of Magellan. He crossed the Pacific to the Philippines, only to die fighting with natives. One of his five ships and fifteen emaciated sailors returned to Spain in 1522, the first people to have sailed around the world. But Europeans desired an easier way to Asia's fabled wealth. The French dispatched Giovanni da Verrazano and Jacques Cartier to search for a "northwest passage" to Asia. Their voyages probed the North American coast from Newfoundland to the Carolinas but found neither gold nor a northwest passage.

## The Conquerors

Columbus was America's first slave trader and the first Spanish *conquistador*, or conqueror. On Hispaniola he exported Indian slaves and created *encomiendas*, grants for both land and the labor of the Indians who lived on it.

From the beginning, *encomienderos*, those given the *encomiendas*, harshly exploited the native people. As disease, overwork, and malnutrition killed thousands of Indians, Portuguese slave traders supplied shiploads of Africans to replace them. Although shocked Spanish friars sent to convert the Native Americans reported the Indians' exploitation, and King Ferdinand attempted to forbid the practice, no one worried about African slaves' fate. Spanish settlers were soon fanning out across the Caribbean in pursuit of slaves and gold. In 1519 the young nobleman Hernán Cortés (1485–1547) led a small band of Spaniards to the Mexican coast. Destroying his boats and enlisting Indian allies, he marched inland to conquer Mexico.

Since reaching America, Spaniards had dreamed of a prize as rich as Mexico. The Aztec civilization, the product of 3,000 years of cultural evolution, was both powerful and wealthy. A centralized bureaucracy ruled from the capital, Tenochtitlán, whose 300,000 inhabitants made it one of the largest cities in the world. The Aztecs used fresh water carried by elaborately engineered aqueducts, and their artisans produced fine pottery as well as implements and statues of stone, copper, silver, and gold. "We were amazed . . . and some of our soldiers even asked whether the things that we saw were not a dream," recalled one *conquistador* of his first glimpse of Tenochtitlán's pyramids, lakes, and causeways. But the golden gifts that the Aztecs offered in vain hopes of buying off the invaders were no dream. Recalled an Indian, "Their bodies swelled with greed. . . . They hungered like pigs for that gold."

Cortés attacked and swiftly prevailed, owing partly to firearms and horses, which terrified the Aztecs, and partly to initial Aztec suppositions that the Spanish were the white, bearded gods foretold in legends. Cortés cunningly exploited the Aztec emperor Moctezuma's fears, the Indians' decimation by epidemics, and a revolt by the Aztecs' subject peoples. By 1521 Cortés had defeated the Aztecs and had begun to build Mexico City on the ruins of Tenochtitlán. Within twenty years, Central America lay at the Spaniards' feet. Thus was New Spain born.

During the rest of the sixteenth century, other *conquistadores* consolidated a great Hispanic empire stretching from New Spain (Mexico) to Chile. Spaniards stilled any doubts about the legitimacy of conquest by demanding that the Indians convert to Christianity—and by attacking them if they refused. From the beginning, however, the Spanish church and government had worried that the *conquistadores* were too powerful and abusive. The monarchy consequently sent hundreds of bureaucrats across the ocean to govern in the hierarchical European manner and to defend Indian rights. Further, an army of Spanish friars established missions among the Indians and tried to lessen their suffering, often clashing with civilian authorities. The result was a cumbersome system that seldom worked well.

The conquest came at enormous human cost. When Cortés landed in 1519, the Aztec empire contained 25 million people. By 1600 it had shrunk to between 1 and 2 million. Peru experienced similar devastation. Disease, not war or slavery, was the greatest killer. Native Americans lacked resistance to European and African infections, especially the

**Indian View of Spanish Colonizers** *This pictograph—a painting or drawing on rock—was sketched in the early colonial period in Cañón del Muerto, Arizona.*

deadly, highly communicable smallpox. From the first years of contact with Europeans, terrible epidemics decimated Indian communities. In the West Indies the native population vanished within a half century, and disease opened the mainland for conquest as well. "The people began to die very fast, and many in a short space," an Englishman later remarked. From the early sixteenth century on, smallpox and other epidemics ravaged the defenseless Indians. Up to 90 percent of the native population was lost in some areas. In return, a virulent form of syphilis spread from the New World to the Old shortly after Columbus's first voyage.

The "Columbian exchange"—the biological encounter of the Old and New Worlds—went beyond deadly germs. Europeans brought horses, cattle, sheep, swine, chickens, wheat, coffee, sugar cane, and numerous fruits and vegetables with them, as well as an astonishing variety of weeds. African slaves carried rice and yams across the Atlantic. The list of New World gifts to the Old was equally impressive: it included corn, white and sweet potatoes, many varieties of beans, tomatoes, squash, pumpkins, peanuts, vanilla, chocolate, avocados, pineapples, chilis, tobacco, turkeys, canoes, kayaks, hammocks, snowshoes, and moccasins. European weeds and domesticated animals often, especially in North America, overwhelmed indigenous plant life and drove away native animals dependent on those plants. Settlers' crops, intensively cultivated on land never allowed to lie fallow, frequently exhausted American soils. Nonetheless, the worldwide exchange of food products enriched human diets and made possible enormous population growth. Today, nearly 60 percent of all food crops worldwide trace their roots to the Native American garden.

Another dimension of the meeting of the two worlds was the mixing of peoples. Within Spain's empire, a great human intermingling occurred. From 1500 to 1600 between 100,000 and 300,000 Spaniards immigrated to the New World, 90 percent of them male. A racially mixed population developed, particularly in towns. Spaniards fathered numerous children with African or Indian mothers, most of them slaves. Such racial mixing would

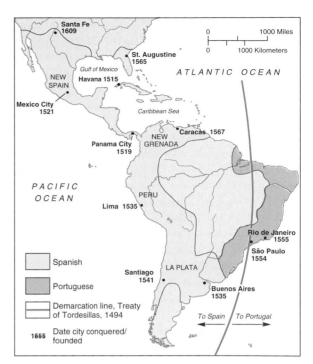

**The Spanish and Portuguese Empires, 1610**
*By 1610 Spain dominated Latin America, including Portugal's possessions. Having devoted its energies to exploiting Mexico and the Caribbean, Spain had not yet expanded into what is now the United States, aside from establishing outposts in Florida and New Mexico.*

occur, although far less commonly, in French and English colonies as well.

The New World supplied seemingly endless wealth for Spain. West Indian sugar plantations and Mexican sheep and cattle ranches enriched many. Much of Spain's wealth, however, was dug from the silver mines of Mexico and Peru. After 1540 enormous amounts of silver flowed across the Atlantic, far more than the small Spanish economy could absorb, setting off an inflation that eventually engulfed Europe. But, bent on dominating Europe, Spanish kings needed even more American silver to pay for their ships and armies. Several times they went bankrupt, and in the 1560s their efforts to squeeze more taxes from their subjects provoked revolt in Spain's Netherlands provinces (modern

Belgium, Holland, and Luxembourg). In the end, gaining access to American wealth cost the Spanish dearly.

The bloody history of Spain's American conquests and efforts to dominate Europe created the "Black Legend"—Protestant Europeans' vision of tyrannical, fanatically Catholic Spain intent on conquering everything in sight. Ironically, much of this grimly lurid picture came from the writings of a devout Spanish friar, Bartolomé de Las Casas (1474–1566), who had repented his own participation in the subjugation of Hispaniola and argued for a more humane Indian policy. By the end of the sixteenth century, Las Casas's hopes of justice for the Indians lay shattered. The Spanish church had grown increasingly bureaucratic and intolerant, fueling the Black Legend. As Spain's struggle to regain the Netherlands and to subdue France spilled near England, the Protestant English shuddered. They looked for opportunities across the Atlantic to strike back at Spain—and to enrich themselves.

# Footholds in North America

Spain's New World wealth attracted other Europeans. Throughout the sixteenth century they sailed the North American coast, exploring, fishing, trading for furs, and smuggling. But except for a Spanish fort at St. Augustine, Florida, all sixteenth-century attempts at colonizing North America failed. Unrealistic dreams of easy wealth and pliant Indians brought French, English, and Spanish attempts to grief. Only the continued ravaging of the Indians by disease, declining Spanish power, and rising French, Dutch, and English power finally made colonization possible.

In 1607–1608 the English and French finally established permanent colonies. By 1614 the Dutch had followed. Within a generation North America's modern history took shape as each colony developed an economic orientation, pattern of Indian relations, and direction of geographic expansion.

## New Spain's Northern Frontier

The Spanish built their New World empire on the wealth of the Aztec and other Indian states. But in the frontier lands north of Mexico, the absence of visible wealth and organized states discouraged conquest. Nonetheless, a succession of hopeful *conquistadores* marched across much of what would become the United States. Earliest came Juan Ponce de León, the conqueror of Puerto Rico, who trudged through Florida in search of gold and slaves twice, in 1512–1513 and in 1521, and then died in an Indian skirmish. The most astonishing early expedition began when 300 explorers left Florida in 1527 to explore the Gulf of Mexico. Indian attacks whittled their numbers until only a handful survived. Stranded in Texas, the survivors, led by Cabeza de Vaca, were passed from Indian tribe to tribe, often as slaves. They finally escaped and made their way to New Mexico and then south to Mexico in 1536.

Cabeza de Vaca inspired two would-be conquerors, Hernando de Soto and Francisco Vásquez de Coronado. In 1539–1543 de Soto and his party blundered from Tampa Bay to the Appalachians and back to southern Texas, scouring the land for gold and harrying the Indians. Although de Soto died without finding gold or conquering any Indians, his and other expeditions touched off epidemics that destroyed most of the remaining Mississippian societies. By the time Europeans returned to the southeastern interior late in the seventeenth century, only the Natchez people on the lower Mississippi River still inhabited their temple-mound center. Depopulated, the Cherokee and Creek Indians had adopted the less centralized village life of other eastern tribes.

As de Soto roamed the Southeast, the Southwest drew others with dreams of conquest, lured by rumors that the fabled Seven Golden Cities of Cíbola lay north of Mexico. In 1538 an expedition sighted the Zuñi pueblos and assumed them to be the golden cities. In 1540–1542 Francisco Vásquez de Coronado led a massive expedition bent on conquest. Coronado plundered several pueblos and roamed from the Grand Canyon to Kansas before returning to Mexico, thinking himself a failure. A third expedition under Juan Rodríguez Cabrillo sailed north along the California coast but found nothing worth seizing.

For decades after these failures, Spain's principal interest in the lands north of Mexico lay in establishing a few strategic bases in Florida to keep out intruders. In 1565 Spain planted the first successful European settlement on mainland North America, the fortress of St. Augustine. Then in the 1580s the Spanish returned to the southwestern pueblo country, preaching Christianity and scouting for wealth. In 1598 Juan de Oñate led 500 Spaniards into the upper Rio Grande valley, where he proclaimed the royal colony of New Mexico, distributed *encomiendas,* and demanded tribute from the Indians.

The new colony barely survived. In 1606 the Spanish replaced Oñate because of his excessive brutality. Finding no gold, many settlers left. In 1609 those who remained established Santa Fe; still others migrated to isolated ranches and fought off Navajo and Apache raiders. By 1630 Franciscan missionaries had established more than thirty missions stretching from the Rio Grande valley to Hopi villages in Arizona, 250 miles to the west. They had converted about 20,000 Indians to Christianity. Eventually, the missions' demands for labor and their attempts to uproot native religions would provoke an Indian backlash (see Chapter 3). Spanish New Mexico would not be secure for a century.

## France: Initial Failures and Canadian Success

In 1534 Jacques Cartier of France, searching for the northwest passage, explored the St. Lawrence River, the center of French colonization after 1600. But a half century of failure preceded France's ultimate success.

France made its first attempt at colonizing North America in 1541, when ten ships sailed into the St. Lawrence Valley. Having alienated many of the Indians along the St. Lawrence in two previous expeditions, Cartier built a fortified settlement on Indian land and thus ended all possibility of peaceful Indian-French relations. Steady Indian attacks and scurvy (for which the Indians could have shown them a cure) drove the French off within two years.

This fiasco underlined one Spaniard's view that "this whole coast as far [south] as Florida is utterly unproductive." In 1562 French Huguenots (Calvinists) made the next French attempt at colonization, establishing a base in modern South Carolina. Two years later they founded a settlement in Florida, which the Spanish quickly destroyed. These failures as well as a civil war between French Catholics and Huguenots ended France's first attempts at colonization.

## The Enterprising Dutch

Having secured independence from Spain by 1588, the Dutch Republic became one of the seventeenth century's great powers. The Dutch empire, based on sea power, would stretch from Brazil to West Africa to the East Indies, modern Indonesia. North American colonies were a small part of this vast empire, but the Dutch nonetheless played a key role in European colonization of the continent.

In 1609 Henry Hudson sailed up the broad, deep river that today bears his name, and in the next year Dutch ships sailed up the Hudson to trade with Indians. In 1614 the Dutch established Fort Nassau at the site of modern Albany, New York, and in 1625 planted another fort on an island at the mouth of the Hudson. Within two years Peter Minuit, director-general of the colony, bought the island from local Indians, named it Manhattan, and began a settlement christened New Amsterdam.

Furs, particularly beaver pelts, became the New Netherlanders' chief economic staple. The Mohawks as well as the other nations of the Iroquois Confederacy became the Dutch colonists' chief sup-

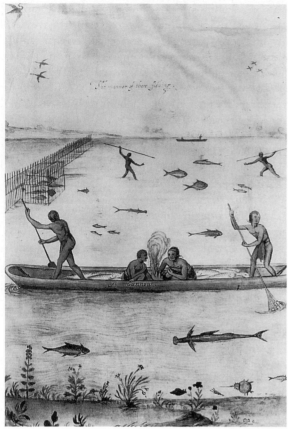

**Carolina Indians Fishing,** *by John White, 1585*
*Using weirs (traplike enclosures), nets, and spears, these Carolina coastal Indians depended on fishing as an important source of their food. The artist, John White, accompanied Sir Walter Raleigh in setting up the Roanoke colony.*

pliers of furs and soon found themselves embroiled in competition with the French-supported Hurons.

## Elizabethan England and the Wider World

When Elizabeth I became queen in 1558, England, a minor power, stood on the sidelines as Spain and France grappled for European supremacy. England's claims to North America had receded, and religious division and domestic instability preoccupied the English.

This very instability, however, helped to propel Elizabethan expansion. Shipping the unemployed poor overseas would relieve England's economic woes, and these "surplus" people could provide markets for English cloth and produce raw materials. And the gentry of England's West Country—including the adventurers and seafarers Sir Francis Drake, Sir John Hawkins, Sir Humphrey Gilbert, and Sir Walter Raleigh—were lusting for action and ready to lead overseas ventures.

But Spain blocked the way. Good relations between Elizabethan England and imperial Spain had broken down as England worried about Spanish attempts to crush rebellion in the Netherlands and about Spain's intervention in France's religious wars. By 1570 Elizabeth was secretly aiding the French Huguenots and Dutch rebels as well as encouraging English "sea dogs" such as Sir Francis Drake and Sir John Hawkins, from whose voyages she took a share of the plunder.

Meanwhile, England's position in Ireland had deteriorated. By 1565 English troops were fighting to impose Elizabeth's rule throughout the island, where a Protestant English government was battling Irish Catholic rebels aided by Spain. In a war that ground on through the 1580s, English troops drove the Irish clans from their strongholds and established "plantations," or settlements, of Scottish and English Protestants. The English resorted to starvation and mass slaughter to break the Irish spirit. Elizabeth's generals justified these atrocities by calling the Irish savages. The Irish experience gave England strategies that it later used against North American Indians, whose customs, religion, and method of fighting seemed to absolve the English from guilt in waging exceptionally cruel warfare.

England had two objectives in the Western Hemisphere in the 1570s. The first was to find the northwest passage to Asia, preferably one lined with gold. The second, as Drake said, was to "singe the king of Spain's beard" by raiding Spanish fleets and cities. The search for a northwest passage proved fruitless, but the English did stage spectacularly successful and profitable privateering raids against the

Spanish. The most breathtaking enterprise of the era was Drake's voyage around the world in 1577–1580 in quest of sites for colonies.

In 1587 Sir Walter Raleigh, dreaming of founding an American colony where English, Indians, and even blacks liberated from Spanish slavery could live together productively, sponsored a colony on Roanoke Island, off the modern North Carolina coast. An earlier settlement (1585) had failed, in part because the colonists refused to grow their own food, expecting the Indians to feed them, and had worn out their welcome. One hundred ten colonists, many of them members of families, reached Roanoke in late summer 1587. Almost immediately the colony's leader, John White, returned to England for more supplies, leaving behind the settlers.

Spain's attempt to crush England with the Great Armada in 1588 prevented White from returning to Roanoke until 1590. When he did, he found only rusty armor, moldy books, and the word CROATOAN carved into a post. To this day, no one knows what happened to the "Lost Colony." The miserable failure at Roanoke would postpone the establishment of English colonies for seventeen more years.

Roanoke's fate illustrated several stubborn realities. First, even a large-scale, well-financed colony could fail, given settlers' unpreparedness for the American environment. Second, Europeans falsely assumed that the Indians would feed them and thus neglected to carry enough food supplies to carry them through the first winter. Third, colonizing attempts would have to be self-financing: a fiscally

### European Settlements in Eastern North America, 1565–1625

*Except for St. Augustine, Florida, and Sante Fe, New Mexico, all European settlements founded before 1607 were abandoned by 1625. Despite the migration of 10,000 Europeans to North America's Atlantic coast by 1625, the total number of Spanish, English, French, and Dutch on the continent was then about 1,800, of whom two-thirds lived in Virginia. For French and Spanish settlement in the late colonial period, see map on p. 80.*

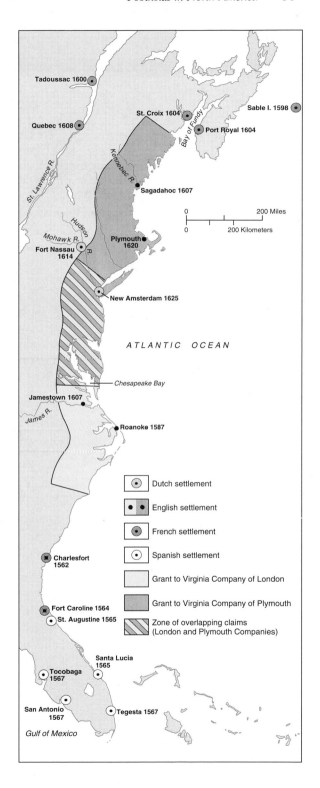

Tadoussac 1600
Sable I. 1598
St. Croix 1604
Quebec 1608
Port Royal 1604
Bay of Fundy
Kennebec R.
St. Lawrence R.
Sagadahoc 1607
0        200 Miles
0    200 Kilometers
Mohawk R.
Fort Nassau 1614
Hudson R.
Plymouth 1620
New Amsterdam 1625
ATLANTIC OCEAN
Chesapeake Bay
Jamestown 1607
James R.
Roanoke 1587

⊙ Dutch settlement
●■ English settlement
◉ French settlement
⊙ Spanish settlement
☐ Grant to Virginia Company of London
▓ Grant to Virginia Company of Plymouth
▨ Zone of overlapping claims (London and Plymouth Companies)

Charlesfort 1562
Fort Caroline 1564
St. Augustine 1565
Santa Lucia 1565
Tocobaga 1567
San Antonio 1567
Tegesta 1567
Gulf of Mexico

strapped monarch such as Elizabeth would not throw good money after bad. Finally, conflict with Spain hung menacingly over every other European attempt to gain a foothold in North America.

England's victory over the Spanish Armada in 1588 preserved English independence, kept the island Protestant, and demonstrated that England could repel invaders. But the war with Spain churned on. In 1595 Drake and Hawkins died fighting in the Caribbean, while Raleigh squandered his fortune and his health on unsuccessful ventures.

To sustain public interest in the New World, Richard Hakluyt published collections of explorers' accounts, *The Principal Navigations, Voyages, and Discoveries of the English Nation* (1589, 1601). Meanwhile, a new means of financing colonies appeared, the joint-stock company. A kind of business corporation, the joint-stock company raised capital through the sale of stock to the public. Each investor faced only a limited risk, but large sums could be amassed. The English government henceforth would leave colonization to the private initiative of individuals or groups.

## The Beginnings of English Colonization: Virginia

The hopes of would-be English colonial investors rose after 1600. Peace between England and Spain, concluded in 1604 by Elizabeth's successor, James I (ruled 1603–1625), opened the way for new colonization attempts in the New World. The Spanish not only agreed to peace but also renounced their claims to Virginia, leaving England a free hand.

On April 10, 1606, James I granted charters to two separate joint-stock companies, one based in London and the other in Plymouth. The Virginia Company of Plymouth received a grant extending from modern Maine to the Potomac River; the Virginia Company of London, a grant from Cape Fear north to the Hudson River. The grants overlapped, with the land in question to go to the first successful colonizer. The colonists would be business employees, not citizens of a separate political jurisdiction, and the stockholders of each company would regu-

late the colonists' behavior. Both companies dispatched colonists in 1607.

The Virginia Company of Plymouth sent 120 men to Sagadahoc at the mouth of the Kennebec River in Maine. The following year the colony disintegrated, the victim of Indian hostility (generally provoked) and hard Maine winters. The company subsequently became dormant. The Virginia Company of London dispatched 105 settlers to a site on the James River near Chesapeake Bay that they named Jamestown. But the first colonists, who included many gentry, hunted for gold and failed to plant crops. When relief ships arrived in January 1608, they found only 38 survivors.

Near anarchy reigned at Jamestown until September 1608, when desperate councilors, representatives of the Virginia Company of London, turned to a brash soldier of fortune, Captain John Smith. Only twenty-eight, Smith found that his experiences fighting the Spanish and the Turks had prepared him well to assume control in Virginia. By instituting harsh discipline, organizing the settlers, and requiring them to build houses and plant food, he ensured Jamestown's survival. During the winter of 1608–1609, Smith lost just 12 men out of 200.

Smith also became the colony's best diplomat. After local Indians captured him late in 1607, Smith displayed such impressive courage that Powhatan, the leader of the nearby Powhatan Confederacy, arranged an elaborate ceremony in which Pocahontas, his daughter, "saved" Smith's life during a mock execution. Smith maintained satisfactory relations with the Powhatan Confederacy partly through his personality and partly through calculated demonstrations of English military strength.

When serious injuries forced Smith to return to England in 1609, discipline again crumbled. Expecting the Indians to furnish corn, the settlers had not laid away enough food for winter. One colonist reported that Jamestown residents ate dogs, cats, rats, and snakes in order to survive. He gruesomely added that "many besides fed on the corpses of dead men." Of the 500 residents at Jamestown in September 1609, only 100 lived to May 1610. An influx of new recruits and the imposition of military rule, however, enabled Virginia to win the First Anglo-

Powhatan War (1610–1614) and, by 1611, to expand west to modern Richmond. The English population remained small—only 380 by 1616—and produced nothing of value for the stockholders.

Tobacco saved Virginia. John Rolfe, an Englishman who married Pocahontas, perfected a salable variety of tobacco for planting there, and by 1619 Virginia was exporting large, profitable amounts of the crop. Thereafter the Virginia Company poured supplies and settlers into the colony.

To attract labor and capital, the company awarded fifty-acre land grants ("headrights") to anyone paying his or her own passage or that of a laborer. By financing the passage of indentured servants, planters could accumulate large tracts of land. Thousands of single young men and a few hundred women became indentured servants, choosing the uncertainty of Virginia over poverty in England. In return for their passage, they worked a fixed term, usually four to seven years.

In 1619 the Virginia Company ended military rule and provided for an elected assembly, the House of Burgesses. Although the company could veto the assembly's actions, 1619 marked the beginning of representative government in North America. However, Virginia still faced three serious problems. First, local officials systematically defrauded shareholders, in the process sinking the company deeply into debt. Second, the colony's death rate soared. Malnutrition, typhus, dysentery, and salt poisoning (from drinking polluted river water) killed thousands of immigrants. Third, Indian relations worsened. After Powhatan's death in 1618, the new leader, Opechancanough, worried about the relentless expansion of the English colony. In 1622 the Indians killed 347 of the 1,200 settlers in a surprise attack. With their livestock destroyed, spring planting impossible, and disease spreading through crowded stockades, hundreds more colonists died in the ensuing months.

The Virginia Company sent more men, and Governor Francis Wyatt took the offensive. Using tactics developed during the Irish war, Wyatt destroyed the Indians' food supplies, conducted winter campaigns to drive them from their homes when they would suffer most, and fought (according to

John Smith) as if he had "just cause to destroy them by all means possible." By 1625 the English had won the war, and the Indians had lost their best chance of forcing out the intruders.

But the struggle bankrupted the Virginia Company. After receiving complaints about its management, James revoked its charter and made Virginia a royal colony in 1624. Only 500 Old World settlers lived there, including a handful of Africans of uncertain status. The roots from which Virginia's Anglo-American and African-American peoples grew were fragile indeed.

## The Origins of New England: Plymouth Plantation

Another rival entered the competition for the North American fur trade: the English who settled New England. In 1620 the Virginia Company of London granted a patent for a settlement to some English merchants headed by Thomas Weston. Weston dispatched eighteen families (102 people) in a small, leaky ship, the *Mayflower*. The colonists promised to send back lumber, furs, and fish for seven years, after which they would own the tract.

The expedition's leaders, and half its members, belonged to a small religious community from the northern English town of Scrooby. Separatist Puritans, they had earlier fled to the Netherlands to practice their religion freely. Fearing that their children were adopting Dutch ways, they decided to immigrate to America under Weston's sponsorship.

In November 1620 the *Mayflower* landed at Plymouth, outside the bounds of Virginia. Because they had no legal right to be there, the leaders forced the adult males in the group to sign the Mayflower Compact before they landed. By this document they constituted themselves a "civil body politic"—a civil government—under James I's sovereignty and established the colony of Plymouth Plantation.

Weakened by their journey and unprepared for winter, half the self-styled Pilgrims died within four months. Two Indians helped the others to survive: Squanto, a local Patuxet, and Samoset, an Abenaki from Maine who had traded with the English. To stop the Pilgrims from stealing their food, the Indians taught the newcomers how to grow corn. Squanto and Samoset also arranged an alliance between the Pilgrims and the local Wampanoag Indians, who were headed by Chief Massasoit. With firearms, the Pilgrims became the dominant partner, and the Wampanoags were forced to acknowledge English sovereignty.

Plymouth's relations with the Indians gradually worsened. Learning of the Virginia massacre of 1622, the Pilgrims militarized their colony and threatened their Indian "allies" with their monopoly of firepower. Although Massasoit remained loyal, this conduct offended many Wampanoags.

Meanwhile, systematically cheated by English patrons, the Pilgrims had sunk deeply into debt after seven years and faced fifteen years' additional labor to free themselves. Fishing was unprofitable, but the Pilgrims traded their surplus corn with nonagricultural Indians for furs, and in 1627 they agreed to divide the New England fur and wampum trade with the Dutch. By the time Plymouth fulfilled its financial obligations, the settlement had grown to several hundred people on Cape Cod and in the southeastern corner of modern Massachusetts.

The Pilgrims' importance was twofold. First, they helped to inspire the ideal of Americans as sturdy, self-reliant, God-fearing folk who endured hardship to govern themselves freely. Second, they foreshadowed the coercive methods that later generations of white Americans would use to gain mastery over the Indians. In both respects, the Pilgrims represented the vanguard of a massive Puritan migration in the 1630s.

## CONCLUSION

The founding of North American colonies was part of Europe's halting modernization, which saw commercial capitalism, nation-states, and postmedieval Christianity emerge during the sixteenth century. In fact, expansion and colonization strengthened the forces of modernity by providing new fields for investment and profit as well as new foundations for national power.

The displacement of Indians and the enslavement of Africans tarnished the early history of European settlement in the New World. Despite devastation by disease, however, Native Americans yielded only slowly to foreign incursions. As for Africans, even the horrors of the Atlantic slave trade did not strip them of their heritage, which became the basis of a distinctive African-American culture.

During the first third of the seventeenth century, the general outlines of European claims in North America emerged, as did the basic elements of the various colonies' economic life. Establishing ranches in New Mexico and fortresses in Florida, Spain advanced as far north as seemed worthwhile. Virginia's victory over the Indians strengthened the English position in the Chesapeake, where tobacco became the principal crop. Here, as in the fragile Plymouth colony, English settlers depended mainly on farming. Dutch, Swedish, and French colonists traded in fish and furs, with New France positioned to penetrate deep into the continent. All these enterprises needed stable relations with Native Americans for success and security.

By the 1630s the tiny European outposts in North America had an air of permanence. Discontented Europeans began to dream of creating new societies across the Atlantic free of the Old World's inherited problems. Most of these dreamers seldom crossed the ocean, and those who did generally lost their illusions—and often their lives—to the rigors of a strange environment. The transplantation of Europeans into North America was hardly a story of inevitable triumph.

## CHRONOLOGY

| | |
|---|---|
| **c. 600–1600** | Rise of the great West African empires. |
| **1271–1295** | Marco Polo travels to East Asia. |
| **c. 1400–1600** | Renaissance era—first in Italy, then elsewhere in Europe. |
| **1440** | Portuguese slave trade in West Africa begins. |
| **1488** | Bartolomeu Días reaches the Cape of Good Hope. |
| **1492** | Christopher Columbus lands at San Salvador. |
| **1497** | John Cabot reaches Nova Scotia and Newfoundland. |
| **1512–1521** | Juan Ponce de León explores Florida. |
| **1517** | Protestant Reformation begins in Germany. |
| **1519** | Ferdinand Magellan embarks on round-the-world voyage. Hernán Cortés begins conquest of Aztec empire. |
| **1534** | Church of England breaks from Roman Catholic Church. |
| **1534–1542** | Jacques Cartier explores eastern Canada for France. |
| **1539–1543** | Hernando de Soto explores the southeastern United States. |
| **1540–1542** | Francisco Vásquez de Coronado explores the southwestern United States. |
| **1558** | Elizabeth I becomes queen of England. |
| **1565** | St. Augustine founded by Spanish. |
| **1565–1580s** | English attempt to subdue Ireland. |
| **1577** | Francis Drake circumnavigates the globe. |
| **1578** | Humphrey Gilbert secures a patent to establish an English colony in Newfoundland. |
| **1584–1587** | Roanoke colony explored and founded. |
| **1588** | English defeat the Spanish Armada. |
| **1598** | New Mexico colony founded. |
| **1603** | James I becomes king of England. |
| **1607** | English found colonies at Jamestown and Sagadahoc. |
| **1608** | Samuel de Champlain founds Quebec. |
| **1609** | Henry Hudson explores the Hudson River for the Dutch Republic. |
| **1610–1614** | First Anglo-Powhatan War. |
| **1614** | New Netherland colony founded. |
| **1619** | Large exports of tobacco from Virginia begin. House of Burgesses, first elected assembly, established in Virginia First Africans arrive in Virginia. |
| **1620** | Mayflower Compact signed; Plymouth Plantation founded. |
| **1622–1632** | Second Anglo-Powhatan War. |
| **1624** | James I revokes Virginia Company's charter. |

## FOR FURTHER READING

J. F. A. Aiayi and Michael Crowder, eds., *History of West Africa*, vol. I (1972). A comprehensive collection of essays covering the period prior to 1800.

Robert J. Berkhofer, Jr., *The White Man's Burden: Images of the American Indian from Columbus to the Present* (1978). A penetrating analysis of the shaping of European and American attitudes, ideologies, and policies toward Native Americans.

Carl Bridenbaugh, *Vexed and Troubled Englishmen, 1590–1642* (1968). A highly readable account of England at the start of the colonial era.

Alfred W. Crosby, Jr., *Ecological Imperialism: The Biological Expansion of Europe, 900–1900* (1986). An outstanding discussion of the environmental and medical history of European overseas expansion.

D. W. Menig, *The Shaping of America, vol. I: Atlantic America, 1492–1800* (1986). A geographer's engrossing study of Europeans' encounter with North America and the rise of colonial society.

J. H. Parry, *The Age of Reconnaissance* (1963). A comprehensive analysis of European exploration and the rise of European overseas empires from the fifteenth to the seventeenth century.

David B. Quinn, *North America from Earliest Discoveries to First Settlements: the Norse Voyages to 1612* (1977). A thorough, learned account of European exploration, based on a wide range of scholarship.

Kirkpatrick Sale, *The Conquest of Paradise: Christopher Columbus and the Columbian Legacy* (1990). A polemical but informed critique of Columbus and his role in opening the Americas to European exploitation.

Eric Wolf, *Europe and the People without History* (1982). An anthropologist's sweeping view of the causes and consequences of Europe's worldwide expansion.

The seventeenth century witnessed a flood of English migration across the Atlantic. In 1600 no English person had lived along the North American seacoast. By 1700, however, nearly 250,000 people of English birth or ancestry were dwelling in the New World, 200,000 of them in what became the United States. Large numbers of Dutch, French, Spanish, Irish, Scottish, and German settlers joined them. A second wave carried 300,000 West Africans to the New World. Whereas English immigrants to America hoped to realize economic opportunity or religious freedom, Africans and their descendants were owned by others. The majority of Africans taken to the Caribbean and North America went to West Indies sugar plantations; a minority, to the mainland plantation colonies; and a few, to New England. A third demographic upheaval, the depopulation and uprooting of Native Americans, made these two other migrations possible. Epidemic disease did much of the work of destroying the Indians, but warfare played an important role as well. About 1 million Indians had died as a result of contact with Europeans by 1700.

*(Right) African slave making sugar (detail)*

# Expansion and Diversity: The Rise of Colonial America

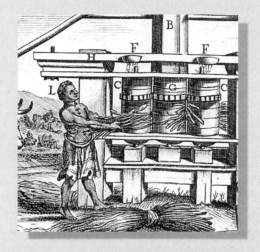

**The New England Way**

❧

**Chesapeake Society**

❧

**Spread of Slavery: The Caribbean and Carolina**

❧

**The Middle Colonies**

❧

**Rivals for North America**

Invading Englishmen and their African slaves settled not in wilderness but on lands that Indian peoples had long inhabited. The wealth and vitality of the English colonies by 1700 resulted from this unequal encounter of peoples from three continents.

# The New England Way

As England's religious and political environment grew worse in the 1620s, many Puritans became interested in colonizing New England. Large-scale Puritan migration would begin in 1630, as the intensely religious Puritans built a community based on religious ideals, the first utopian society in America.

### A City upon a Hill

In 1628 several Puritan merchants obtained a charter to settle north of the Separatist colony at Plymouth. Organized as the Massachusetts Bay Company, they moved the seat of their colony's government to New England, paving the way for Massachusetts to be self-governing.

In 1630 the company dispatched a "great fleet," eleven ships and 700 passengers, to New England. As the ships crossed the Atlantic, Governor John Winthrop delivered a lay sermon, "A Model of Christian Charity," in which he explained how and why the new colony would differ from England itself.

Winthrop boldly announced that "we shall be as a city upon a hill, the eyes of all people are upon us." The settlers would build a godly community whose compelling example would shame England. The English government would then truly reform the church, and a revival of piety would create a nation of saints. Denouncing economic jealousy, Winthrop explained that God intended "in all times some must be rich and some poor." The rich would practice charity and mercy, and the poor show their faith in God's will by practicing patience and fortitude. In a godly state, the government would prevent the greedy among the rich from exploiting the poor and the lazy among the poor from

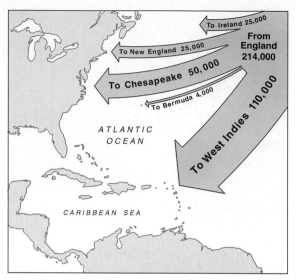

**The Great English Migration, 1630–1660**
*During the great transatlantic English migration, the present-day United States received just one-third of English immigrants. The West Indies attracted twice as many colonists as went to the Chesapeake and over four times as many as settled in New England.*

burdening their fellow citizens.

Winthrop's sermon expressed both traditional European ideas of social reciprocity (see Chapter 2) and the Puritans' dismay at the economic forces battering—and changing—English society.

The old England of self-sufficient farm families living for generations in tight-knit communities had vanished. Instead, a handful of gentry families owned half of England's village land, while "yeoman" farmers, 20 percent of the remaining population, owned the other half.

For much of England's village population, life was brutal and desperate. Community ties frayed and family life deteriorated as people scattered to find work and as children were hired out as servants or apprentices. Lacking land, England's people competed fiercely for jobs and became individualistic, acquisitive, and materialistic. Winthrop blamed this competitive spirit for fostering apathy toward human suffering. Charity should moderate the drive for profit, he believed, so that goods would be ex-

**John Winthrop (1588–1649)**
*During the passage to America, Winthrop urged his ship-mates to build a society about which "men shall say of succeeding plantations: 'The Lord make it like that of New England.'"*

great thing," wrote an early New Englander, "to be a foundation stone in such a spiritual building."

## Development of a Puritan Orthodoxy

The great fleet of Puritans reached Boston Harbor in June 1630; by fall six towns had sprung up. During the unusually severe first winter, one-third of the Puritans died; however, spring brought 1,300 new settlers, and thousands more followed. The disciplined and highly motivated Puritans put Massachusetts Bay Colony on a firm footing in its first year. Though Nonseparatists, they created a system of self-governing congregations (congregationalism) unique to America. Unlike the Separatists of Plymouth and (later) Rhode Island, the Puritans of Massachusetts and Connecticut proclaimed themselves spiritual members of the Church of England, but at the same time they completely ignored the authority of Anglican bishops.

The chief architect of the Nonseparatists' congregationalism was the Reverend John Cotton. His plan placed the control of each congregation in the hands of the male saints, in contrast to the system in England, where a few wealthy members of the gentry controlled each congregation. In New England the male saints chose their minister, elected "elders" to handle finances, and otherwise controlled their church. The New England system thus was more democratic than Anglicanism.

Congregationalism fused elements of separating and nonseparating Puritanism. It followed the Separatist tradition by allowing only saints to take communion and to baptize their children, but adopted the Nonseparatist practice of requiring all adults (except for a few scandalously wicked individuals) to attend services and to pay for the support of the churches. New England thus had a state-sponsored, "established" church; the meetinghouse, used for both religious services and town business, symbolized the relationship of church to government.

This "New England Way" set high standards for identifying saints. Massachusetts Puritans insisted that candidates for church membership provide a soul-baring "relation," or account of their conversion, before the congregation. This public revela-

changed, wages set, and interest calculated in a way that would allow a decent life for all. The rich would serve God with their money, giving generously in time of need, and the less fortunate would sacrifice their time to serve in church, government, or the military.

Winthrop and his fellow Puritans saw Massachusetts Bay not, like other colonies, as an extension of England and its harshly competitive ways, but as a reaction to it. Moral self-restraint would prevent merchants from squeezing out excessive profits; if necessary, the government could step in. Above all, the Puritans wanted to turn religious idealism into a renewed sense of community. "It is a tion of intimate spiritual matters could be embarrassing and painful for candidate and congregation, and it often intimidated those seeking church membership. The conversion relation ultimately became the New England Way's most vulnerable point and a major cause of its demise.

Literacy was essential to conversion. Children were drilled in catechism, young people read the Bible to feel the quickening of God's grace, and saints recorded their lapses and spiritual insights in diaries. In 1647 the Massachusetts Bay Colony passed the Old Deluder Act because "one chief project of that old deluder, Satan [is] to keep men from knowledge of the Scriptures." Every town of fifty or more households was to appoint one teacher from whom all children could receive instruction, and every town of one hundred households or more was to maintain a grammar school with a teacher capable of preparing students for university-level learning. This law, echoed by other Puritan colonies, was New England's first step toward public education, although attendance remained optional and boys were more likely to be taught reading and writing than girls. In any case, the family remained the chief guardian of education.

Clergymen bore responsibility for leading people to repentance and for stimulating piety. The minister was to stir his congregation's faith with direct, logical, and moving sermons understandable to average listeners. An educated clergy was essential, and so in 1636 Massachusetts founded Harvard College to produce learned ministers. In its first thirty-five years, the college turned out 201 graduates, 111 of them ministers. These alumni made New England the only American colony with a college-educated elite during the seventeenth century and ensured that the New England Way would not falter for lack of properly trained clergymen.

## Dissenting Puritans

Some Puritans dissented from their leaders' vision of social order and religious conformity. The first to challenge the New England Way was Roger Williams, who arrived in America in 1631. Radiating the joy of serving God, he quickly became one of the most respected and popular figures in Massachusetts Bay. But when he questioned the legal basis of congregationalism, insisting that church and state be separate, the Massachusetts Bay government silenced him.

Although agreeing that the church must be free of state control, Puritans believed that a holy commonwealth required cooperation between church and state. Williams argued that civil government had to remain absolutely uninvolved with religious matters. He derived his ideas from the Anabaptist tradition (see Chapter 2), which held that saints had to limit their association with sinners to prevent contamination. Williams opposed compulsory church service and interference with private religious beliefs because he feared that the state would eventually corrupt the church and its saints.

Believing that the purpose of the colony was to protect true religion and to prevent heresy, political authorities declared Williams's opinions subversive and banished him in 1635. Williams went south to the edge of Narragansett Bay to a place that he later named Providence, which he purchased from the Indians. A steady stream of dissenters drifted to the group of settlements near Providence, forming Rhode Island in 1647. The only New England colony to practice religious toleration, Rhode Island grew to 800 settlers by 1650.

Anne Hutchinson, "a woman of haughty and fierce carriage, of a nimble wit and active spirit" according to her enemy John Winthrop, presented a second challenge to the New England Way. Ironically, Hutchinson's ideas derived from the much-respected minister John Cotton. Cotton insisted that true congregationalism required the saints to be free of religious or political control by anyone who had not undergone a conversion experience. His refusal to give authority or power over religion to anyone not "reborn" applied even to those who led blameless lives—at least until they had been reborn spiritually.

Hutchinson extended Cotton's ideas to a broad attack on clerical authority. She began to imply that her own minister was not a saint and then asserted that saints in the congregation could ignore his views if they believed that he lacked saving grace. Ultimately, she declared that only two ministers in the colony, John Cotton and her brother-in-law John Wheelright, had been reborn and thus were fit to exercise authority over the saints.

Hutchinson's ideas directly attacked the clergy's authority to interpret and teach Scripture; critics charged that her beliefs would delude individuals into imagining that they were accountable only to themselves. Her followers were labeled Antinomians, meaning those opposed to the rule of law. Anne Hutchinson bore the additional liability of being a woman challenging traditional male roles in church and state. Her gender made her seem an especially dangerous foe.

Massachusetts Bay split into pro- and anti-Hutchinson forces. Her opponents prevailed, bringing Hutchinson to trial for sedition before the Massachusetts Bay legislature (the General Court) and then for heresy before a panel of ministers. Hutchinson's knowledge of Scripture was so superior to that of her inquisitors that she might well have been acquitted had she not claimed to communicate directly with the Holy Spirit. Because Puritans believed that God had ceased to make known matters of faith by personal revelation since New Testament times, Hutchinson was condemned by her own words. Banished from the colony along with other Antinomians, Hutchinson settled in Rhode Island and then moved to New Netherland, where she was killed in that colony's war with Indians in 1643. Her banishment effectively ended the last challenge capable of splitting congregationalism and ensured the survival of the New England Way for two more generations.

New restrictions on women's independence and on equality within Puritan congregations followed antinomianism's defeat. Increasingly, women were prohibited from assuming the kind of public religious role claimed by Hutchinson and were even required to relate their conversion experiences in private to their ministers rather than publicly before their congregations.

Economics as well as ideas posed serious threats to Winthrop's "city upon a hill." While most Puritans shared Winthrop's view of community, self-discipline, and mutual obligation, a large minority had come to America for prosperity and social mobility. The most visibly ambitious colonists were merchants, whose activities fueled New England's economy but whose way of life challenged its ideals.

Merchants fit uneasily into a religious society that equated financial shrewdness with greed. They clashed repeatedly with government leaders, who were trying to regulate prices so that consumers would not suffer from the chronic shortage of manufactured goods that afflicted New England. In 1635 the General Court forbade the sale of any item at above 5 percent of its cost. Led by Robert Keayne, merchants protested that they needed to sell some goods at higher rates to offset losses incurred by shipwreck and inflation. In 1639 authorities heavily fined Keayne for selling nails at 25 percent above cost and forced him to apologize in front of his congregation.

Though he was a pious Puritan whose annual profits averaged just 5 percent, Keayne symbolized the danger that a headlong rush for prosperity would lead New Englanders to forget that they were their brothers' keepers. Controversies such as that involving Keayne were part of a struggle for the New England soul. At stake was the Puritans' ability to insulate their city upon a hill from a market economy that threatened to strangle the spirit of community within a harsh world of frantic competition.

## Puritan Government and Community Life

To preserve the New England Way, the Puritans created political and religious institutions with far more popular participation than those in England. Its headquarters established in America, the Massachusetts Bay Company allowed all male saints to elect the governor and his council. By 1634 each town had gained the right to send two delegates to the General Court; ten years later court and council separated to create a bicameral (two-chamber) leg-islature. Although in England stringent property re-quirements allowed less than 30 percent of adult males to vote, 55 percent of Massachusetts's adult males could vote.

In England the basic unit of local government was the county court. Its magistrates, appointed by the king, not only decided legal cases but also per-formed administrative duties. By contrast, in New England the county court was primarily a court of law; the town meeting oversaw matters of local administration.

Towns were formed when a legislature granted land to several dozen heads of families. These indi-viduals had almost unlimited freedom to lay out the settlement, design its church, distribute land among themselves, and make local laws. Generally, all adult male taxpayers, even nonsaints, participated in town meetings. In turn, the meetings ran the town and granted land rights to new settlers.

Most New England towns were uniform farm communities resembling traditional English vil-lages; seaports, with their transient populations, were the chief exception. Each family generally re-ceived a one-acre house lot (just enough room for a vegetable garden) within a half mile of the meeting-house. Each household also received strips of land or small fields farther away for crops and livestock. In-dividuals often owned several scattered parcels of land and had the right to graze a few extra animals on the town "commons."

Most towns attempted to maintain communi-ties of tightly clustered settlers by distributing only as much land as was necessary for each family to support itself. The remaining land would be dis-tributed to future generations as needed. Forcing residents to live close together was an attempt to foster social reciprocity. New England's generally compact system of settlement made people interact with each other and established an atmosphere of mutual watchfulness that promoted godly order. Town meetings open to all property-owning males and Sunday church services attended by everyone reinforced this strong sense of community.

## Puritan Families

"The little commonwealth"—the nuclear family—was the foundation of Puritan society. "*Well-ordered families,*" declared minister Cotton Mather in 1699, "naturally produce a *Good Order* in other *Societies.*" A well-ordered family was one in which wife, chil-dren, and servants dutifully obeyed the husband and in which the "true wife" thought of herself "in sub-jection to her husband's authority."

New Englanders defined matrimony as a con-tract, not a sacrament. Puritans were thus married by justices of the peace rather than ministers. As a civil institution, marriage could be dissolved by the courts in cases of desertion, bigamy, adultery, or physical cruelty. However, New England courts saw divorce as a remedy only for extremely wronged spouses, such as the Plymouth woman who discov-ered that her husband also had wives in Boston, Barbados, and England. Massachusetts courts granted just twenty-seven divorces from 1639 to 1692.

Because Puritans believed that healthy families were crucial to the community's welfare, they inter-vened whenever they discovered serious problems in a household. Courts disciplined unruly young-sters, disobedient servants, disrespectful wives, and irresponsible husbands. Churches also censured, and even expelled, spouses who did not maintain do-mestic tranquillity.

New England wives enjoyed significant legal protections against spousal violence and nonsupport and had more freedom than their English counter-parts to escape a failed marriage. But they suf-fered the legal disabilities borne by all women under English law. A wife had no property rights indepen-dent of her husband except by premarital agree-ment. Only if there were no other heirs or if a will so specified would a widow receive control of house-hold property, although law entitled her to lifetime use of one-third of the estate.

New England's families enjoyed greater stability and lived longer lives than their English counter-parts. The region's cold climate limited the impact of disease, especially in winter, when limited travel between towns slowed the spread of infection. Easy access to land contributed to a healthy diet, which strengthened resistance to disease and lowered death rates associated with childbirth. Life expectancy for Puritan men reached sixty-five, and women lived nearly that long. These life spans were ten years or more longer than those of England. More than 80 percent of all infants survived long enough to marry. Because so many of the 20,000 immigrants who arrived in New England between 1630 and 1642 came as members of families, an even sex ratio and a rapid natural increase of population followed.

Families were economically interdependent. Male heads of family managed the household's crops and livestock, conducted its business transactions, and represented it at town meetings. Wives bore and nurtured children; performed or oversaw work in the house, garden, and barn; and participated in community networks that assisted at childbirths and aided the poor and vulnerable. Sons depended on parents to provide them with acreage for a farm, and parents encouraged sons to stay at home and work in return for a bequest of land later on. Young males often tended their fathers' fields until their late twenties before receiving their own land. The average family, raising four sons to adulthood, could count on thirty to forty years of work if their sons delayed marriage until age twenty-six. Families with many sons and daughters enjoyed a labor surplus and sometimes hired out their children to work for others. Although inefficient, this system of family labor was all that New Englanders could afford.

There were other benefits. Prolonged dependence for sons ensured that the family line and property would continue in the hands of capable, experienced men. Although daughters performed vital labor, they would marry into another family. Young women with many childbearing years ahead of them were the most valuable potential wives, and first-generation women tended to marry by the age of twenty-one.

Saddled with the triple burdens of a short grow- ing season, rocky soil salted with gravel, and an inefficient system of land distribution that forced farmers to cultivate widely scattered strips, the colonists nevertheless managed to feed their families and to keep ahead of their debts. Few grew wealthy from farming. For wealth, New Englanders turned lumbering, shipbuilding, fishing, and rum distilling into major industries that employed perhaps one-fifth of all adults full-time. As its economy diversified, New England prospered. Increasingly concerned more with profit than prophecy, the Puritans discovered, to their dismay, that fewer of their children were emerging as saints.

## The Demise of the Puritan Errand

As New England struggled for stability and conformity, old England fell into chaos and civil war. Alienated by years of religious harassment, Puritans gained control of the revolt, beheaded Charles I in 1649, and governed without a king for more than a decade. In 1660 a provisional English government recalled the Stuarts and restored Charles II to the throne.

The Stuart Restoration doomed Puritanism in England as High Church Anglicans took their revenge; "God has spit in our face," lamented one Puritan. The Restoration also left American Puritans without a mission. Having conquered a wilderness and built their city upon a hill, they found that the eyes of the world were no longer fixed on them.

An internal crisis also gripped New England. First-generation Puritans had believed that they held a covenant, a holy contract, with God to establish a scripturally ordained church and to charge their descendants with its preservation. However, understandably reluctant to submit to a public review of their spirituality, relatively few second-generation Puritans were willing to join the elect by making the required conversion relation before the congregation. Through its passivity, the second generation expressed a preference for a more inclusive religious community, organized on traditional English practices. This generation also rejected the ritual of public conversion relation as an unnecessary source of division and bitterness that undermined Christian fellowship.

Because Puritan churches baptized only babies born to saints, first-generation Puritans faced the prospect that their own grandchildren would remain unbaptized unless the standards for church membership were lowered. They solved their dilemma in 1662 through a compromise known as the Half-Way Covenant, which permitted the children of all baptized members, including nonsaints, to be baptized. Church membership would pass down from generation to generation, but nonsaints would be "halfway" members, unable to take communion or to vote in church affairs. When forced to choose between a church system founded on a pure membership of the elect and one that embraced the entire community, New Englanders opted to sacrifice purity for community.

The Half-Way Covenant marked the end of the New England Way. The elect had been unable to raise a new generation of saints whose religious fervor equaled their own. Most adults chose to remain in "halfway" status for life, and the saints became a shrinking minority in the third and fourth generations. By the 1700s there were more female than male saints in most congregations. But because women could not vote in church affairs, religious authority stayed in male hands. Nevertheless, ministers publicly recognized women's role in upholding piety and the church itself.

## Expansion and Native Americans

In contrast to the settlement of Virginia, the Puritan colonization of New England initially met little resistance from Native Americans, whose numbers had been drastically reduced by disease. Between 1616 and 1618 an epidemic killed 90 percent of New England's coastal Indians, and a second epidemic in 1643–1644 inflicted comparable casualties on Indians throughout the Northeast. The Massachusett Indians dwindled from 20,000 in 1600 to a few dozen in 1635 and sold most of their land. By 1675, New England's Native American population had shrunk from 125,000 in 1600 to about 10,000. During the 1640s Massachusetts Bay passed laws prohibiting Indians from practicing their own religion and encouraging missionaries to convert them to Christianity. Beginning in 1651 the Indians surrendered much of their independence and moved into "praying towns" such as Natick, a reservation established by the colony.

The expansion of English settlement farther inland, however, aroused Indian resistance. As settlers moved into the Connecticut River valley, beginning in 1633, friction developed with the Pequots, who controlled the trade in furs and wampum with New Netherland. After tensions escalated into violence, the English waged a ruthless campaign against the Pequots, using tactics similar to those devised to break Irish resistance (see Chapter 2). In a predawn attack, troops led by Captain John Mason surrounded and set fire to a Pequot village at Mystic, Connecticut, and then cut down all who tried to escape. Several hundred Pequots, mostly women and children, were killed. The Puritans found the grisly massacre a cause for celebration. Wrote Plymouth's governor William Bradford, "It was a fearful sight to see them [the Pequots] thus frying in the fire and the streams of blood quenching the same . . . but the victory seemed a sweet sacrifice, and they [the English] gave the praise to God, who had wrought so wonderfully for them." By late 1637 Pequot resistance was crushed, and English settlement of the new colonies of Connecticut and New Haven could proceed unimpeded.

Indians felt the English presence in many ways. The fur trade, initially beneficial to Native Americans of the interior, became a burden. Once Indians began hunting for trade instead of for their subsistence needs alone, they quickly depleted the supply of beavers and other fur-bearing animals. Because English traders advanced trade goods on credit before the hunting season began, many Indians fell into debt. Traders increasingly took Indian land as collateral and sold it to settlers.

English townspeople, eager to expand their agricultural output and provide for their sons, voted themselves much larger amounts of land after 1660.

For example, Dedham, Massachusetts, had distributed only 3,000 acres from 1636 to 1656; by 1668 it had allocated another 15,000 acres. Many farmers built their homes on their outlying tracts, crowding closer to the Indians' settlements and their hunting, fishing, and gathering areas.

Expansion put pressure on the natives and the land alike. By clearing trees for fields and for use as fuel and building material, the colonists were altering the entire ecosystem by the mid-1600s. Deer no longer grazed freely, and the wild plants on which the Indians depended for food and medicine could not grow. Deforestation not only dried the soil but also brought frequent flooding. Encroaching white settlers allowed their livestock to run wild, according to English custom. Pigs damaged Indian cornfields and shellfish-gathering sites. Cattle and horses devoured native grasses, which the settlers replaced with English varieties.

Powerless to reverse the alarming decline of population, land, and food supplies, many Indians became demoralized. Some turned to alcohol, which became increasingly available during the 1660s despite colonial attempts to suppress its sale to Native Americans. Interpreting the crisis as one of belief, other Indians converted to Christianity. By 1675 Puritan missionaries had established about thirty "praying towns." Supervised by missionaries, each praying town had its own Native American magistrate, and many congregations had Indian preachers. Although missionaries struggled to convert the Indians to "civilization"—English culture and ways of life—most Indians integrated the new faith with their native cultural identities, reinforcing the hostility of settlers who believed that all Indians were irrevocably "savage" and heathen.

Anglo-Indian conflict became acute in the 1670s because of pressure on the Indians to sell their land and to accept missionaries and the legal authority of white courts. Tension was especially high in the Plymouth colony, where Puritans had engulfed the Wampanoag tribe and forced a series of humiliating concessions from their leader Metacom, "King Philip," the son of the Pilgrims' onetime ally Massasoit.

In 1675 Plymouth hanged three Wampanoags for killing a Christian Indian; several other Wampanoags were shot while burglarizing a farmhouse. In response to the escalation of violence, Metacom organized two-thirds of the Native Americans, including many praying Indians, into a military alliance. "But little remains of my ancestors' domain. I am resolved not to see the day when I have no country," Metacom declared as he and his men touched off the conflict known as King Philip's War.

The war raged across New England. Metacom's forces, as well armed as the Puritans, devastated the countryside, wiping out twelve of New England's ninety towns and killing 600 colonists. The following year, 1676, saw the tide turn as Puritan militia destroyed their enemies' food supplies and sold hundreds of captives into slavery, including Metacom's wife and child. Perhaps 3,000 Indians died in battle or starved, including Metacom himself.

King Philip's War reduced southern New England's Indian population by almost 40 percent and eliminated open Indian resistance to white expansion. It also deepened whites' hostility toward all Native Americans, even the Christian Indians who had fought against King Philip. In 1677 ten praying towns were disbanded and all Indians were restricted to the remaining four. Missionary work ceased. "There is a cloud, a dark cloud upon the work of the Gospel among the poor Indians," mourned Puritan missionary John Eliot. In the face of poverty and discrimination, the remaining Indians struggled to maintain their communities and cultural identity. To compensate for the loss of traditional sources of sustenance, many became seamen or indentured servants, served in English wars against French Canada, or made and sold baskets and other wares.

## Economics, Gender, and Satan in Salem

In the three decades after adoption of the Half-Way Covenant, the Puritan clergy unleashed a stream of jeremiads (angry lamentations, named after the Old Testament prophet Jeremiah) at their congregations, berating them for failing to preserve the idealism of the first generation. "New-England is originally a plantation of Religion, not a plantation of trade," one minister proclaimed, but in fact New Englanders were becoming more worldly, more individualistic, and far less patient with restrictions on their economic behavior. Indeed, by 1690 the Puritans, having built a society from the ground up, no longer felt an overriding need to place collective, community interests first. As New Englanders pursued economic gain more openly and as populations dispersed away from town centers, the fabric of community frayed. Friction easily arose between the townspeople still dwelling near the meetinghouse (who usually dominated politics) and the "outlivers," those living on outlying tracts of land, who were less influential because of their distance from town.

The rough equality of early New England, when most people had been small landowners with few luxuries, also began to vanish. By the late seventeenth century, the distribution of wealth was growing more uneven, especially in large, prosperous port cities. New England's rising involvement in international trade, moreover, encouraged competitiveness and impersonality. John Winthrop's vision of a religious community sustained by reciprocity and charity faded before the reality of a world increasingly materialistic and acquisitive—like the one that the early Puritans had fled.

Nowhere in New England did these trends have more disturbing effects than in Salem, Massachusetts, made up of the port of Salem Town and the farm community of Salem Village. Trade and rapid growth had made Salem Town the region's second-largest port. By 1690 prosperous merchants controlled much of the wealth and political power of Salem as a whole, and the community was vulnerable to conflict between its prosperous merchants and its struggling farmers.

Salem Village (now Danvers) lay six miles west of Salem Town's meetinghouse, and its citizens resented Salem Town's political dominance. Salem Village was divided between the supporters of two families, the Porters and the Putnams. Well connected with the merchant elite, the Porters enjoyed

political prestige in Salem Town and lived in the village's eastern section, whose residents farmed richer soils and benefited more from Salem Town's prosperity. In contrast, most Putnams lived in Salem Village's less fertile western half, shared little in Salem Town's commercial expansion, and had lost their political influence. Rivalry between Porters and Putnams mirrored the tensions between Salem's urban and rural dwellers.

In late 1691 several Salem Village girls encouraged an African slave woman, Tituba, to tell fortunes and talk about sorcery. When the girls began behaving strangely, villagers assumed that they were victims of witchcraft. Pressed to identify their tormenters, they named two local white women and Tituba.

So far the incident was not unusual. Belief in witchcraft existed at all levels of American and European society. But by April 1692 the girls had denounced two prosperous farm wives long considered saints in the local church and had identified the village's former minister as a wizard (male witch). Fear of witchcraft soon overrode considerable doubts about the girls' credibility and led local judges to sweep aside normal procedural safeguards. Specifically, the judges ignored legal bans on "spectral evidence," testimony that a spirit resembling the accused had been seen tormenting a victim. Thereafter charges multiplied until the jails overflowed with accused witches.

The pattern of hysteria and accusations reflected Salem Village's internal divisions. Most charges came from the western side of the village—one-third from the Putnams alone—and were lodged against people who lived outside the western half and who were connected by economics or marriage to the Porters. Two-thirds of all accusers were girls aged eleven to twenty, and more than one-half had lost one or more parents in conflicts between Indians and settlers in Maine. They and other survivors had fled to Massachusetts, where most worked as servants in other families' households. They most frequently named as witches middle-aged wives and widows—women who had escaped the poverty and uncertainty that they themselves faced. At the same time, the "possessed" accusers

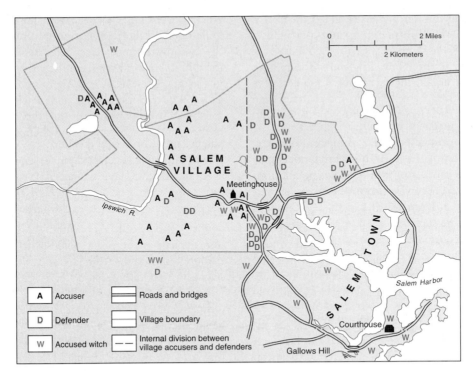

### The Geography of Witchcraft: Salem Village, 1692

*Geographic patterns of witchcraft testimony mirrored tensions within Salem Village. Accused witches and their defenders lived mostly in the village's eastern division or in Salem Town, whereas their accusers overwhelmingly resided in the village's western sector.*

SOURCE: Adapted from *Salem Possessed: The Social Origins of Witchcraft* by Paul Boyer and Stephen Nissenbaum. Copyright © 1974 by the President and Fellows of Harvard College. Reprinted by permission of Harvard University Press.

gained momentary power and prominence by voicing the anxieties and hostilities of many others in their community and by virtually dictating the course of events in and around Salem for months.

Those found guilty of witchcraft tried to stave off death by implicating others. As the pandemonium spread, fear dissolved ties of friendship and family. A minister was condemned by his granddaughter, a mother by her seven-year-old daughter, and a husband and father by his wife and daughter. Fifty saved themselves by confessing, but twenty were condemned and executed.

By late 1692 doubts about the charges were surfacing. Clergymen objected to the emphasis on spectral evidence, crucial to most convictions. By accepting such evidence in court, minister Increase Mather warned, the Puritans had fallen victim to a deadly game of "blind man's buffet" set up by Satan and were "hotly and madly mauling one another in the dark." In October Governor William Phips forbade any further imprisonments for witchcraft. One hundred were still in jail, and 200 more stood accused. In early 1693 Phips ended the terror by pardoning all those who were convicted or suspected of practicing witchcraft.

The witchcraft hysteria reflected profound anxieties over social change. The underlying causes of this tension became clear as Salem Village's communally oriented farmers directed their wrath toward Salem Town's competitive and individualistic merchants. This clash of values revealed the extent to which John Winthrop's city upon a hill had lost its relevance to new generations forced into economic enterprise by New England's stingy soil, harsh climate, and meager natural resources. The tensions pervading New England society had been heightened by the crown's revoking the Massachusetts charter in 1684 and subsuming several colonies in the Dominion of New England in 1686 (see Chapter 4).

By 1700 New Englanders had begun a transition from Puritans to "Yankees." True to their Puritan roots, they retained strong religious convictions and an extraordinary capacity for perseverance. Increasingly grafted to these roots were ingenuity, sharpness, and an eye for opportunity, traits that would enable New Englanders to build a thriving international commerce and later an industrial revolution.

As New England moved away from its roots, the Chesapeake region to the south also underwent radical transformation. But the differences between the two areas of English settlement remained as great as ever.

## Chesapeake Society

Virtually ignored by King James I (who took over the colony in 1624 from the bankrupt Virginia Company) and his successors, Virginia developed on its own. The English monarch's indifference worked to the colonial elite's advantage, leaving them room to experiment with local administration and to force reluctant royal governors to cooperate with their legislature. Tobacco and the environment shaped the colonists' destiny not only in Virginia but also in Maryland and in what became North Carolina.

### State and Church in Virginia

James I planned to rule Virginia through appointed officials, but Virginians petitioned repeatedly for the restoration of their elected assembly, the first in the New World. James I's successor, Charles I, grudgingly relented in 1628, but only in order to induce the assembly to tax tobacco exports so as to transfer the cost of government from the crown to Virginia's taxpayers. After 1630, seeking more taxes, Virginia's royal governors called regular assemblies. During the 1650s the assembly split into two chambers, the elected House of Burgesses and the appointed Governor's Council. Later royal colonies also adopted this bicameral pattern.

Local government officials were appointed, rather than elected, during Virginia's first quarter-century. In 1634 Virginia adopted England's county-court system. Appointed by the royal governor, justices of the peace acted as judges, set local tax rates, paid county officials, and oversaw the construction and maintenance of roads, bridges, and public buildings. Thus south of New England, unelected county courts became the basic unit of local government.

In contrast to Puritan New England, Virginia had the Church of England as its established church. Anglican vestries governed each parish; elected vestrymen handled church finances, determined poor relief, and investigated complaints against the minister. Taxpayers were legally obliged to pay fixed rates to the Anglican church. Because of the large distances between settlements and churches as well as a chronic shortage of clergymen, few Virginians regularly attended services. In 1662 Virginia had just ten ministers to serve its forty-five parishes. Compared to New Englanders, Chesapeake dwellers felt religion's influence lightly.

### Virginia's First Families

Three generations passed before Virginia evolved a social elite willing and able to provide disinterested public service. The gentry sent out by the Virginia Company were ill suited for a frontier society; by 1630 most had either died or returned to England. Then from 1630 to 1660 a generation of leaders emerged who had acquired great wealth through tobacco or through fraud. They dominated the Royal Council and used their power to increase their

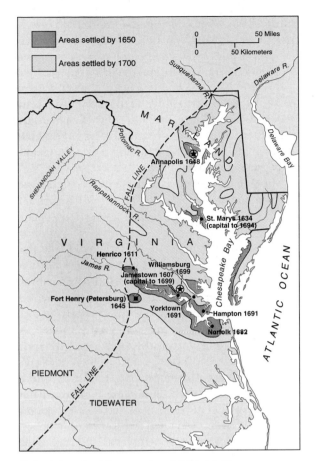

**Colonizing the Chesapeake, 1607–1660**

*The Chesapeake frontier expanded slowly until after Indian defeat in the Second Powhatan War of 1644–1646. By 1700, when the European and African population had reached 110,000, newcomers had spread virtually throughout the tidewater.*

wealth, but few had children to assume their place, and their influence died with them.

From 1660 to 1675 a third cycle of immigrants reached for power in Virginia. Generally the members of English merchant families who traded with Virginia, they brought wealth, education, and ambition with them. Becoming planters, they soon controlled the Royal Council; many profited from "public" service by obtaining huge land grants. They

bequeathed both wealth and power to future generations, later known as the First Families of Virginia. Among them, Burwell, Byrd, Carter, Harrison, Lee, Ludwell, Randolph, and Taylor were prominent names. The First Families would dominate Virginia politics for two centuries, and four of the first five American presidents would be descended from them.

## Maryland

Beginning in the 1630s, grants by the crown to reward English politicians replaced joint-stock companies as the primary mechanism of colonization. The first such grant, or proprietorship, went in 1632 to Lord Baltimore (Cecilius Calvert); he named the large tract east of Chesapeake Bay Maryland in honor of England's Queen Henrietta Maria. Lord Baltimore enjoyed broad power, lessened only by the stipulations that an elected assembly had to approve all laws and that the crown would control both war and trade.

With Charles I's consent, Baltimore intended to make Maryland a refuge for England's Catholics, who could neither worship in public nor hold political office and who had to pay tithes to the Anglican church. To make Maryland a haven, Baltimore tried to install the old English manor system. In theory, a manor lord would employ a Catholic priest as chaplain and allow others to hear Mass and to receive the sacraments on the manor. In practice, this arrangement never worked, for relatively few Catholics settled in Maryland, which was overwhelmingly Protestant from the beginning. Cheap land lured settlers who did not need to become tenants on the manors, and Baltimore's scheme fell apart. By 1675 all sixty of Maryland's nonproprietary manors had become plantations.

Religious tension gradually developed in Maryland society. The Protestant majority dominated the elected lower house of government, but many Catholics had become large landowners, held high public office, and dominated the appointive upper house. Until 1642 Catholics and Protestants shared the chapel at St. Mary's, the capital, but they began to argue over its use. As antagonisms intensified, Baltimore drafted, and the assembly passed, the Act for Religious Toleration (1649), America's first law affirming liberty of worship.

Unfortunately, the toleration act did not secure religious peace. In 1654 the Protestant majority barred Catholics from voting; ousted Governor William Stone, a Protestant; and repealed the toleration act. Stone raised an army, both Protestant and Catholic, to regain the government but met defeat at the Battle of the Severn River in 1655. The victors imprisoned Stone and hanged three Catholic leaders. Maryland remained in Protestant hands until 1658. Although Lord Baltimore was restored to control that year (ironically, at the command of English Puritans), Protestant resistance to Catholic political influence continued to cause problems in Maryland.

## Tobacco Shapes a Way of Life

Chesapeake settlers were scattered across the landscape. A typical community included only 24 families in a twenty-five-square-mile area, a mere six people per square mile. (In contrast, New England often had 500 people squeezed onto one square mile.) Most Chesapeake inhabitants lived in a world of few friendships and considerable isolation; typical was Robert Boone, a Maryland farmer, who died at age seventy-nine "on the same Plantation where he was born in 1680, from which he never went 30 miles in his Life."

Isolated Chesapeake settlers shared a life governed by one overriding factor: the price of tobacco. After an initial boom, tobacco prices plunged 97 percent in 1629 before stabilizing at 10 percent of their original high. Tobacco was still profitable as long as it was grown on fertile soil near navigable water. As a result, 80 percent of Chesapeake homes were located along a riverbank, both for the fertile soil and for the cheap transportation thus afforded; ships literally could come to the plantation's front door. Wealthy planters shipped their tobacco and small farmers' crops from their own wharves and distributed imported goods. Neither towns nor a merchant class was needed, and urbanization was slow

in the Chesapeake. Maryland's capital, St. Mary's, was a hamlet of thirty houses as late as 1678.

Wealth lay in the cultivation of large amounts of tobacco, and that in turn required a large work force. From 1630 to 1700, 110,000 English, most of them indentured servants, migrated to the Chesapeake. A headright system further stimulated migration by offering land for each person transported. Because most of these immigrants were destined for field work, men dominated; four out of every five servants were males aged about twenty.

## Mortality, Gender, and Kinship

So few women immigrated to the Chesapeake that before 1650, only one-third of male servants could find brides and then only after completing their indentures. Female scarcity gave women an advantage in negotiating favorable marriages. Many female indentured servants married prosperous planters who paid off their remaining time of service.

Death ravaged Chesapeake society and left domestic life exceptionally fragile. In 1650 malaria joined the killer diseases typhoid, dysentery, and salt poisoning as the marshy lowlands of the tidewater Chesapeake became fertile breeding grounds for the mosquitoes that spread malaria. Life expectancy in the 1600s was twenty years lower in the Chesapeake than in New England. Servants died at appalling rates; 40 percent were dead within a decade of arrival and 70 percent before reaching age fifty.

Chesapeake widows often enjoyed substantial property rights. The region's men wrote wills giving their wives perpetual and complete control of their estates so that their own children could inherit them. A widow in such circumstances had a degree of economic independence but faced enormous pressure to remarry, particularly a man who could produce income by farming her fields.

The lopsided sex ratio and high death rates contributed to slow population growth in the Chesapeake. Although perhaps 110,000 English immigrated to the Chesapeake between 1630 and 1700, the white population was just 69,000 in 1700. Change come gradually as children acquired childhood immunities, life spans lengthened, and the sex

**Virginia Indian, c. 1645**
*At the time that this contemporary sketch was made, Virginia's white settlers and Indians were embroiled in the Third Anglo-Powhatan War.*

ratio evened out. By 1720 most Chesapeake residents were native born.

## Tobacco's Troubles

Chesapeake society became increasingly unequal. A few planters used the headright system to build up large landholdings and to profit from their servants' labor. Wretchedly exploited, and poorly fed, clothed, and housed, servants faced a bleak future even when their indentures ended. Although some were able to claim fifty acres of land in Maryland, the majority who went to Virginia had no such prospects. Indeed, in Virginia after 1650 most riverfront land was held by speculators, and upward mobility became virtually impossible.

In 1660 Chesapeake tobacco prices plunged by 50 percent, setting off a depression that lasted fifty years. Despite losses, large planters earned some income from rents, interest on loans, and shopkeeping, while small landowners scrambled to sell corn and cattle in the West Indies. A typical family in this depression era lived in a small wooden shack, slept on rags, and ate mush or stew cooked in the single pot. Having fled poverty in England or the West Indies, people often found utter destitution in the Chesapeake. Ex-servants in particular became a frustrated and embittered underclass that seemed destined to remain landless and poor.

## Bacon's Rebellion

By the 1670s these bleak conditions had locked most Virginia landowners into a losing battle against poverty and had left the colony's freedmen in despair. Both groups were capable of striking out in blind rage if an opportunity to stave off economic disaster presented itself. In 1676 this human powder keg exploded in violence.

Virginians had been free of serious conflict with the Indians since the end of the Third Anglo-Powhatan War in 1646. By 1653 tribes encircled by English settlements had begun agreeing to remain within boundaries set by the government—in effect, on reservations. White settlement continued to expand northward to the Potomac River, and by 1675 whites outnumbered Indians by a ten-to-one ratio.

In June 1675 a dispute between some Doeg Indians and a Virginia farmer escalated. A force of Virginia and Maryland militia pursuing the Doegs murdered fourteen friendly Susquehannocks and later executed five of their chiefs. The violence was now unstoppable. While Governor William Berkeley proposed defending the frontier by a costly system of forts, small farmers preferred the cheaper solution: a war of extermination against the Indians. Some 300 settlers elected Nathaniel Bacon, a distant relative of Berkeley and member of the Royal Council, to lead them against nearby Indians in April 1676. The expedition found only peaceful Indians but slaughtered them anyhow.

Returning to Jamestown, Virginia's capital, in June 1676, Bacon asked for authority to wage war "against all Indians in general." The legislature voted for a program designed to appeal to both hard-pressed taxpayers and landless ex-servants. All Indians who had left their villages without permission (even if fleeing Bacon) were declared enemies, and their lands were forfeited. Bacon's troops could seize any "enemy" property and enslave Indian prisoners.

But Governor Berkeley soon had second thoughts about the slaughter and recalled Bacon and his 1,300 men. Forbidden to attack Indians, Bacon's forces turned against the government and burned Jamestown. The rebels offered freedom to any servants or slaves owned by Berkeley's allies who would join them and then looted enemy plantations. What had begun as Indian warfare was now a social rebellion. Before the uprising could proceed further, however, Bacon died of dysentery in late 1676, and his followers dispersed.

Bacon's Rebellion revealed a society under deep internal stress. Begun as an effort to displace escalating tensions among whites onto the Indians, it became an excuse to plunder other whites. Economic opportunism as well as racism had spurred the small farmers and landless ex-servants to rise up. This rebellion was an outburst of pent-up frustrations by marginal taxpayers and ex-servants driven to desperation by the tobacco depression.

### Slavery

The tensions and social instability underlying Bacon's Rebellion grew in large part from the plight of indentured servants trying to become free agents in an economy that offered them little. Even before the rebellion, however, potential for class conflict was diminishing as planters gradually substituted black slaves for white servants.

Racial slavery developed in three stages in the Chesapeake. Africans first appeared in 1619, but their early status was generally indistinguishable from the standing of white servants. By 1640 blacks and some Indians were being treated as slaves, and their children inherited their status. Thus their situation had become inferior to that of indentured white servants. In the final phase, after 1660, laws defined slavery as a lifelong, inheritable status based on color. By 1705 strict legal codes defined the place of slaves in society and set standards of racial etiquette.

Slavery was a system for blacks and Indians only. Whites never enslaved their white enemies; rather, they reserved the complete denial of human rights for nonwhites. The English embarked on slavery as a response to nonwhite peoples, whom they considered inferior to whites.

Not until the 1680s were there significant numbers of black slaves in the Chesapeake, but by 1700 nearly 20,000 slaves resided in the region. Economics as well as race underlay the replacement of indentured servitude by slavery. In England a population decline between 1650 and 1700 reduced the potential pool for overseas labor and drove up wages. In addition, with the end of the Royal African Company's monopoly on the shipping and sale of slaves in the 1690s, an expanded supply of slaves arrived in the Chesapeake.

The emergence of slavery served to relax the economic tensions that had triggered Bacon's Rebellion. After 1690 even poor whites who owned no slaves believed that they shared a common interest with upper-class planters in maintaining social control over an alien and dangerous race.

Slavery's establishment as the principal form of labor in the Chesapeake was part of a larger trend among England's plantation colonies, one that had begun in the Caribbean and would spread to the new mainland colony of Carolina.

## Spread of Slavery: The Caribbean and Carolina

As Puritans settled New England, a second immigrant wave carried twice their number, some 40,000 English people, to the West Indian islands in the Caribbean. The English West Indies strongly influenced English North America. First, the islands were a major market for New England's surplus foodstuffs, dried fish, and lumber. Second, they

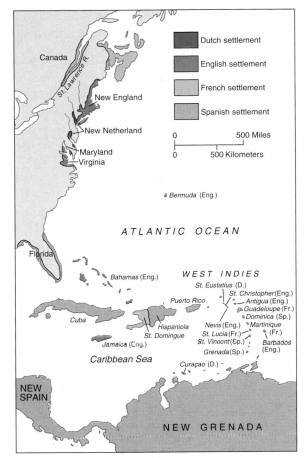

**The Caribbean Colonies, 1660**
*Aside from Jamaica, England's sugar colonies were clustered in the eastern Caribbean's Leeward Islands. Lying within easy reach of seaborne attack, every English island but Barbados was the scene of major fighting.*

adapted their economy to large-scale slave labor and devised a code of social conduct for nonwhites. In these latter ways, the West Indies pioneered techniques of racial control that were later adopted in the mainland colonies' plantation societies.

After 1660 large numbers of English islanders migrated to the Chesapeake and to Carolina, carrying with them the habits and prejudices of plantation slaveholding. By 1710 the population of

Carolina, like that of the Caribbean colonies, was predominantly black and enslaved.

## The Chaotic Caribbean

In the sixteenth century Spain claimed the entire Caribbean but concentrated on holding the four largest islands: Santo Domingo (Hispaniola), Puerto Rico, Cuba, and Jamaica. The English, French, and Dutch all scrambled to settle the uninhabited Caribbean islands. English freebooters became especially bold after Spain and Holland went to war in 1621. By 1640 England had established twenty communities from the Bahamas to the Nicaraguan coast. St. Kitts, Barbados, Montserrat, Nevis, and Antigua survived a Spanish counterattack, and Jamaica fell to England in 1655.

Born of war, England's West Indian colonies matured in turmoil. Between 1640 and 1713 they suffered the constant threat and frequent reality of both invasion and piracy. Seven slave revolts rocked the English islands before 1713 and left a bitter legacy of racial hatred.

Caribbean life went on amid constant violence inflicted on slaves by masters, on Catholics by Protestants, and on humans by nature. Bubonic plague killed one-third of the islanders from 1647 to 1649. Five thousand militiamen (every sixth Englishman in the Caribbean) died in the battle to capture Jamaica from Spain in the 1650s. Hurricanes regularly killed hundreds, and malaria and yellow fever felled thousands. In 1692 an earthquake killed 7,000 on Jamaica, one-sixth of the population. Few lived more than twenty years from their arrival in the islands.

## Sugar and Slaves

Initially, the English West Indies developed along lines similar to Virginia, with tobacco the dominant crop. Because a single worker could tend only three acres of tobacco, tobacco farming demanded a large population. By 1640 more colonists lived on England's five West Indian islands than in all of Virginia.

**Tobacco Label**
*The slave's central role in growing tobacco and serving his white master (here enjoying a smoke) is depicted.*

Tobacco, requiring little equipment beyond a curing shed, was cheap to raise, and tobacco cultivation gave individuals with little money a chance at upward mobility. Through the 1630s the West Indies remained a society with a large percentage of independent landowners, an overwhelmingly white population, and no extreme inequality of wealth.

Sugar cane soon changed that, revolutionizing the islands' economy and society. Encouraged by Dutch merchants, wealthy English planters began to raise this enormously lucrative crop. Sugar sold at high prices, which escalated steadily over the next century, and could make a planter fabulously wealthy, but it required large amounts of capital and labor and elaborate machinery. With tobacco prices remaining low, most farmers could not afford to raise sugar. On Barbados a few sugar planters closed off all opportunity to small farmers by aggressively bidding up the price of land by more than 1,000 percent; by 1680 a mere 7 percent of landowners held over half the acreage. A typical sugar planter's estate was 200 acres, whereas most Barbadians scratched a meager living from 10 acres or less.

Because the profit from sugar vastly exceeded that from any other crop, West Indian planters turned every available acre into cane fields. Deforesting the islands (except Jamaica's mountains), they also virtually eliminated land for growing grain or raising livestock. Suddenly dependent on outside sources even for food, the Indies became a flourishing market for New England farmers, fishers, and loggers.

Moreover, the demand for labor soared because sugar required triple the labor force of tobacco. African slaves soon replaced indentured white servants in the fields. Most planters preferred black slaves to white servants because they could be driven harder and maintained more cheaply. Also, African slaves could better withstand the tropical diseases of the Caribbean, they had no rights under contract, and they toiled until they died. Although slaves initially cost two to four times more than indentured servants, they were an economical long-term investment. Some English immigrants to the Caribbean copied the example already set by the Spanish and enslaved both Indians and Africans.

By 1670 the sugar revolution had transformed the British West Indies into a predominantly black and slave society. In 1713 slaves outnumbered whites by four to one; the slave population had leaped from 40,000 in 1670 to 130,000 in 1713, with the white population remaining stable at 33,000. Meanwhile, driven from the Indies by high land prices, thousands of English settlers went north to the mainland. Settling in Carolina, they resumed tobacco cultivation.

## West Indian Society

At the bottom of Caribbean society were the slaves, who lived under a ruthless system of racial control expressed in laws known as slave codes. The Barbados slave code of 1661 served as a model for both the Caribbean and the mainland colonies. The code required but never defined adequate shelter and diet for slaves, in effect allowing masters to let their slaves run almost naked, to house them in rickety shacks, and to work them to exhaustion. Slaves were stripped of all legal rights and protections: they could not be tried by juries and had no guarantee of a fair legal hearing.

In this way West Indian governments granted masters almost total control over their human property. As there were no limits on punishment, slaves suffered vicious beatings and whippings. A master who killed a slave could be punished only if a jury determined that the act was intentional—and then the punishment was limited to fines. Slave codes effectively legalized assault, battery, and manslaughter. The codes left slaves at the mercy of all whites, not just their owners; any white who caught a slave at large without a pass could give the slave a "moderate whipping," up to fifty lashes. Cruel and extreme punishments were prescribed to guarantee obedience. Judges could order ears sliced off, slaves torn limb from limb, and accused rebels burned alive.

Mortality among slaves was frightfully high. Sugar production required arduous labor, but it was so profitable that planters had little incentive to keep slaves healthy; they could easily replace those killed by overwork. Exhaustion and abuse killed most slaves within a decade of their arrival. Although planters imported 264,000 slaves between 1640 and 1699, the slave population stood at just 100,000 in 1700.

Despite these appalling conditions, slaves tried to maintain a semblance of normal existence. Many married and formed families. But the staggering rate of mortality cut most slave marriages short, and more than one-half of slave children died before reaching age five. Slaves preserved much of their African heritage in work songs, ceremonial dances and chants, and lamentations. Few slaves became Christian; most kept their faith in ancestral spirits, and some committed suicide in the belief that their ghosts would return home to Africa. The islands'

black culture retained far more of an African imprint than the African-American life that would emerge on the mainland.

Among island whites, family cohesion was weak. Men outnumbered women four to one, and most white islanders lived wild bachelor lives. Organized religion withered in the absence of family and community support. A Caribbean joke maintained that on founding a settlement, the Spanish built a church, the Dutch built a fort, and the English built a barroom. "Old Kill-Devil," the local rum, was consumed in great quantities.

Wealthy island planters generally hired overseers to run their estates and retired in luxury to England. Poor whites left in droves for other colonies. The English Caribbean was a society of fortune seekers trying to get rich quickly before death overtook them and of slaves being worked to death.

The West Indies were the first English colonies to become plantation societies. They contained the most extreme examples of labor exploitation, racial subordination, and social inequality, but similar patterns would also characterize the Chesapeake Bay settlements and the coastal region known as Carolina.

## Carolina: The First Restoration Colony

In 1663 Charles II bestowed the swampy coast between Virginia and Spanish Florida on several English supporters, making it the first of several Restoration colonies. The proprietors named their colony Carolina in honor of Charles (*Carolus* in Latin).

Settlers from New England and the West Indies had established outposts along the northern Carolina coast in the 1650s; the proprietors organized them into a separate district with a bicameral legislature. In 1669 one of the proprietors, Anthony Ashley Cooper, accelerated settlement by offering immigrants fifty-acre headright grants for every family member, indentured servant, or slave they brought in. The next year 200 Barbadian and English people began the settlement of southern Carolina near modern Charleston, "in the very chops of the Spanish." In the settlement they called Charles Town, they formed the colony's nucleus, with a bicameral legislature distinct from that of the northern district.

Cooper and his secretary, John Locke, devised an intricate plan for Carolina's settlement and government. Their Fundamental Constitutions of Carolina attempted to ensure the colony's stability by decreeing that political power and social rank should accurately reflect settlers' landed wealth. Thus they invented a three-tiered nobility that would hold two-fifths of all land, make laws through a council of nobles, and dispense justice through manorial courts. Ordinary Carolinians were expected to defer to the nobility and pay them rent, although they would enjoy religious toleration and the benefits of English common law. But new arrivals, hungry for land, saw no reason to accept the system and all but ignored it.

In the early years Carolina's population mainly consisted of small landowners. Southern Carolinians raised livestock, and colonists in northern Carolina exported tobacco, lumber, and pitch. In neither north nor south did the people realize enough profit to maintain slaves, and so self-sufficient white families predominated. But southern Carolinians eagerly sought a cash crop. In the early 1690s they found it—rice. Probably introduced to America by enslaved West Africans, rice cultivation enriched the few settlers with capital enough to acquire the dikes, dams, and slaves necessary to grow it. By earning annual profits of 25 percent, successful rice planters within a generation became the only colonial mainland elite whose wealth rivaled that of the Caribbean sugar planters.

Rice planters reaped their riches at the expense of African slaves. Knowledgeable about rice cultivation, slaves became tutors to their owners. The typical rice planter, with 130 acres in cultivation, needed sixty-five slaves. Demand drove the proportion of slaves in southern Carolina's population from 17 percent in 1680 to 67 percent in 1720, when the region officially became South Carolina. By 1776 the colony, with at least 100,000 slaves, would have more bondsmen than any other mainland colony in the eighteenth century. It would be

Britain's only eighteenth-century mainland colony with a black majority.

Rice thrived in a narrow coastal strip extending from Cape Fear (now in North Carolina) to Georgia. Malaria, carried in from Africa but to which many Africans had partial immunity, ravaged this hot, humid lowland. In the worst months planters' families escaped to the relatively healthful climate of Charles Town, while overseers supervised the harvest.

As the black majority increased, whites relied on force and fear to control their slaves. In 1696 Carolina adopted the galling restrictions and gruesome punishments of the Barbados slave code. Bondage in the mainland colony grew as cruel and harsh as in the West Indies.

White Carolinians' attitudes toward Native Americans likewise hardened. The most vicious result was the trade in Indian slaves. White Carolinians armed allied Indians, encouraged them to raid and capture unarmed Indians to the south and west, and sold the captives to the West Indies during the 1670s and 1680s. A recent study estimates that the Carolina traders enslaved tens of thousands of Indians. Once shipped to the West Indies, most Native Americans died because they lacked immunities to European and tropical diseases.

Not surprisingly, Indian wars racked Carolina in the early eighteenth century. In 1711 some Tuscaroras, provoked by whites' encroachments and enslavement of Indians, destroyed the frontier settlement of New Bern. North Carolinians enlisted the aid of southern Carolina and its Indian allies. By 1713, after 1,000 Tuscaroras (about one-fifth of their population) had been killed or enslaved, the Native Americans surrendered.

Having helped to defeat the Tuscaroras, Carolina's Indian allies grew increasingly resentful of English traders' cheating, violence, and encroachment on their land. In 1715 the Yamasees attacked English trading houses and settlements. Only by arming some 400 slaves and enlisting the aid of the powerful Cherokees did the Carolinians crush the uprising. The surviving Yamasees fled to Florida or to the Creek nation.

In two generations Carolinians, with little help

from distant proprietors, had developed a thriving economy and had ended resistance from hostile Native Americans. Exasperated South Carolinians asked the British monarchy to take control, and in 1720 a temporary royal governor was appointed. Proprietary rule came to an end in 1729 when both North Carolina and South Carolina became royal colonies.

## The Middle Colonies

Between the Chesapeake and New England, the third mainland colonial regions, the middle colonies, gradually emerged. In 1664 England seized New Netherland from the Dutch, and in 1681 Charles II authorized a colony where New Sweden had stood. Thus were laid the foundations for the Restoration colonies of New York, New Jersey, and Pennsylvania. By the end of the seventeenth century, the middle colonies composed North America's fastest-growing region.

### *Precursors: New Netherland and New Sweden*

New Netherland became North America's first multiethnic society. Barely half the settlers were Dutch; most of the rest comprised Germans, French, Scandinavians, and Africans, both free and slave. In 1643 the population included Protestants, Catholics, Jews, and Muslims, speaking eighteen European and African languages. The trading company that had established the settlement struggled to control the settlers, whose get-rich-quick attitude sapped company profits as private individuals traded illegally in furs. Eventually, the company legalized the private trade.

Privatization rapidly increased the number of guns in the hands of New Netherland's Iroquois allies, giving them a distinct advantage over other tribes. As overhunting depleted local fur supplies and smallpox epidemics raged, the Iroquois encroached on Huron territory for pelts and captives (who were adopted into Iroquois families to replace

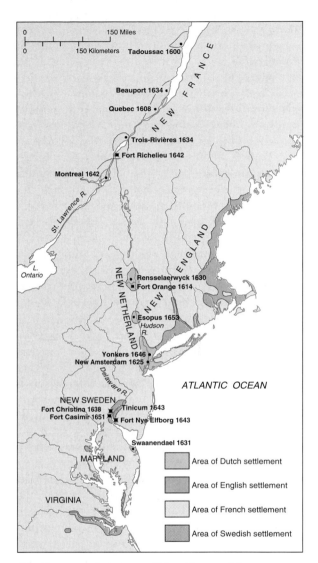

**The Riverine Colonies of New France, New Netherland, and New Sweden, c. 1650**
*England's imperial rivals located their colonies along major river routes to the interior so that they could easily buy furs trapped by Indians farther inland. The French settled along the St. Lawrence, the Dutch along the Hudson, and the Swedes along the Delaware.*

the dead). After 1648 the Dutch-armed Iroquois destroyed the Hurons and attacked French settlements along the St. Lawrence. "They come like foxes, they attack like lions, they disappear like birds," wrote a French Jesuit.

Although the Dutch had allied with the Iroquois, relations with the nearer Indian neighbors were terrible. With greedy settlers and military weakness, New Netherland largely had itself to blame. In 1643 an all-out war erupted when Governor Willem Kiefft massacred previously friendly Algonquian-speaking Indians. By 1645 the Dutch had temporarily prevailed, but only by enlisting English help and by inflicting atrocities. But the fighting cut New Netherland's Indian population from 1,600 to 700.

Another European challenger, Sweden, distracted the Dutch in their war with the Algonquians. In 1638 Sweden had planted a small fur-trading colony in the lower Delaware Valley that was diverting furs from New Netherland. In 1655 the Dutch colony's stern soldier-governor Peter Stuyvesant marched against New Sweden, whose 400 residents peacefully accepted Dutch annexation. But New Netherland paid dearly for its victory. With the militia absent, the Algonquians destroyed scattered Dutch settlements and forced Stuyvesant to ransom white captives.

Although tiny, the French, Dutch, and Swedish colonies were significant. New France became the nucleus of modern French Canada. New Netherland fell to the English in 1664, but the Dutch presence in what became New York has lent a distinctive flavor to American life. Even short-lived New Sweden left a mark, the log cabin, introduced to the continent by Finnish settlers in the Swedish colony. Above all, the Dutch and Swedish colonies bequeathed a religious and ethnic diversity that would continue in England's "middle colonies."

## English Conquests: New York and the Jerseys

Like the Carolinas, New York and the Jerseys originated with Restoration-era proprietors hoping to grow rich from rents collected from settlers within a hierarchical society. New York marginally achieved this dream, but the Jerseys did not.

In 1664, at war with the Dutch Republic, Charles II attacked the Dutch colony of New Netherland. Four hundred poorly armed Dutch civilians under Governor Peter Stuyvesant surrendered peacefully. Charles II made his brother James, duke of York, proprietor of the new English colony and renamed it New York. With James's ascension to the throne in 1685, he converted New York into a royal colony. By 1700 immigration had swelled the population to 20,000, of whom just 44 percent were descended from the original Dutch settlers.

New York's governors rewarded their influential political supporters with large land grants. By 1703 five families held 1.75 million acres, which they carved into manors and rented to tenants. By 1750 the enormous income they earned from rents had made the New York *patroons* a landed elite second in wealth only to the Carolina rice planters.

Ambitious plans collided with American realities in the Jerseys, also carved out of New Netherland. In 1664 the duke of York awarded a group of supporters the Jerseys, at the time inhabited by a few hundred Dutch and Swedes and several thousand Delaware Indians. Within a decade thousands of troublesome New England Puritans settled in the Jerseys, and the proprietors sold the region to Quakers, who split the territory into East and West Jersey.

East Jersey's new Scottish Quaker proprietors worked no more successfully with the local Puritans than had their predecessors, and in West Jersey the English Quakers squabbled constantly among themselves. The Jerseys' Quakers, Anglicans, Puritans, Scottish Presbyterians, and Dutch Calvinists quarreled with each other and got along even worse with the proprietors. The governments collapsed between 1698 and 1701, and in 1702 the disillusioned proprietors surrendered their political powers to the Crown, which made New Jersey a royal colony.

## Quaker Pennsylvania

In 1681 Charles II paid off a huge debt by appointing a supporter's son, William Penn, as proprietor

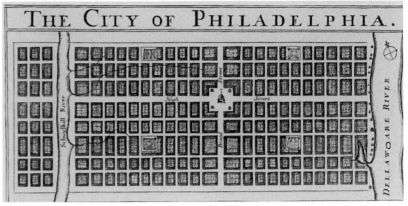

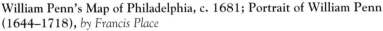

**William Penn's Map of Philadelphia, c. 1681; Portrait of William Penn (1644–1718),** *by Francis Place*
*Central to Penn's master plan for Philadelphia was the idea that each residence should stand in the middle of its plot, encircled by gardens and orchards. This portrait is thought to be the most accurate likeness of Penn extant.*

of the last unallocated tract of American territory at the king's disposal. Penn, a Quaker, thus founded the colony as a "holy experiment" based on the teachings of the English preacher George Fox. Penn also hoped for financial gain.

Quakers in late-seventeenth-century England stood well beyond the fringe of respectability. Challenging conventional foundations of social order, they appealed to those at the bottom of the economic ladder. But they also attracted some well-educated, well-to-do individuals disillusioned by the quarreling of rival religious faiths, including significant numbers of merchants. The members of this radical religious sect, which had been born in war-torn England during the 1640s and 1650s, called themselves the Society of Friends, but most others dubbed them Quakers.

At the heart of their founder George Fox's theology was the belief that the Holy Spirit, or "Inner Light," could inspire every soul. Mainstream Christians found this claim highly suspicious. Although trusting such direct inspiration, Quakers took pains to ensure that individual opinions would not be mistaken for God's will. Indeed, they felt confident that they understood the Inner Light only after hav-

ing reached near-unanimous agreement through intensive discussion. In their religious services ("meetings"), Quakers sat silently until the Inner Light prompted one of them to speak. Quakers believed that the Inner Light could "speak in the female as well as the male," and they thus accorded women unprecedented equality.

Quaker behavior often seemed disrespectful to government and to the social elite and thus aroused hostility. For example, Quakers refused to tip their hats to their social betters, insisting that spiritual state, not wealth or status, deserved recognition. Their refusal to bear arms, moreover, appeared unpatriotic and cowardly.

Quakers in England faced intense pressure to conform to the established church, but they throve on persecution. Quakers absent from Anglican services were fined, and constables seized their farm tools, equipment, and livestock. Under Charles II, 15,000 Quakers were jailed. But Quakers maintained their reputation for industriousness even in prison. Jailed in 1669, Penn found his fellow Quaker inmates weaving, spinning, and absorbed in prayer during work breaks.

Care and planning made the Quaker migration

to Pennsylvania one of the most successful initial transplantations of Europeans in any North American colony. After sending an advance party, Penn arrived in 1682. He named his new capital Philadelphia, the "City of Brotherly Love." Within five years, 8,000 English Quakers had joined him. Quakers migrated in family groups, and the resulting high birthrate generated rapid population growth. (Pennsylvania's religious toleration attracted not only Quakers but also many other religious groups: Presbyterians, Baptists, Anglicans, and Catholics from England and Lutherans and radical sectarians from Germany.)

A victim of persecution, Penn hated intolerance and arbitrary governance. He offered Quakers the opportunity to make laws according to their ideals. His Frame of Government (constitution) featured a strong executive branch (a governor and governor's council) and a lower chamber (the assembly) with limited power. Friends, a majority in the colony, dominated the assembly, and Penn generally named Quakers to other positions. Hardly a democrat, Penn feared "the ambitions of the populace which shakes the Constitution" and intended to check the "rabble" as much as possible. To prevent wrangling and to achieve an orderly disposition of property, Penn personally oversaw land sales. He also designed a grid plan for Philadelphia, reserving park areas to keep it a "greene country towne." Penn sought peace with Native Americans by reassuring the Indians that the Quakers wished "to live together as Neighbours and Friends" and by buying land from them fairly.

Pennsylvania seemed an ideal colony—intelligently organized, well financed, tolerant, open to all industrious settlers, and at peace with the Indians. Rich lands and a lengthy growing season produced bumper crops. West Indian demand for grain generated widespread prosperity. By 1700 Philadelphia had become a major port. In 1704 counties along the lower Delaware River, where Swedes and Dutch had settled long before Penn, gained the right to elect their own legislature and became the colony of Delaware.

However, by this time Penn's "peaceable king-

dom" had bogged down in human bickering. In 1684 Penn had returned to England, and during his fifteen-year absence the settlers had quarreled incessantly. An opposition party had attacked his efforts to monopolize foreign trade and to collect a small annual fee from each landowner. Struggles between pro- and anti-Penn forces had deadlocked the government. Penn's return from 1699 to 1701 had restored some order, but before leaving again, he made the legislature unicameral (one chamber) and allowed it to initiate measures.

Religious controversy meanwhile had erupted in the 1690s when prominent Quaker preacher George Keith urged the Quakers to adopt a formal religious creed. Doing so would have changed the democratically functioning Quakers into a conventional clergy-dominated church. In 1692 a majority of Quakers had rejected Keith's views, and he had joined the Church of England. But Keith's departure had begun a major decline in the Quaker share of Pennsylvania's population. In 1748 Penn's sons, who inherited the proprietorship, would become Anglican, and Anglicans thereafter would hold the highest political offices, although Friends would still dominate the colony's assembly.

Sadness darkened Penn's last years. His fortune spent in Pennsylvania, he served time in a debtor's prison and died in debt in 1718. He had long despaired at battling the legislature's politicians, bent as they were on economic and political advantage. As early as 1685 he had begged them, "For the love of God, me, and the poor country, be not so governmentish; so noisy and open in your disaffection."

Penn's anguish summed up the dilemmas of the English who had established the Restoration colonies. Little had gone as planned. Yet the Restoration colonies had succeeded. Before they were a quarter century old, the middle colonies had demonstrated that English America could benefit by encouraging pluralism. New York and New Jersey successfully integrated Dutch and Swedish populations; Pennsylvania, New Jersey, and Delaware refused to require residents to support any official church. But the virtual completion of English claim staking along the Atlantic coast had set England on a collision course with France and Spain, which also were vying for American territory.

# Rivals for North America

Unlike England, with its compact seacoast colonial settlements in North America, France and Spain had cast enormous nets of widely separated trading posts and missions across the interior. The two Catholic nations had converted many Indians to Christianity and made them trading partners and allies. By 1720 scattered missionaries, fur traders, and merchants had spread French and Spanish influence across two-thirds of today's United States. The French government invested heavily in its American enterprise, but Spain, its empire decaying, made little effort to influence North American affairs. Local officials and settlers assumed the burden of extending imperial control for both powers.

## France Claims a Continent

Under King Louis XIV (reigned 1661–1715), France sought to subordinate its American colony to French interests, following the doctrine of *mercantilism*. According to this doctrine, colonies should serve as sources of raw materials and as markets for manufactured goods so that the colonial power did not have to depend on rival nations for trade. The French wanted New France in order to increase fur trade, provide agricultural surplus to ship to France's West Indies colonies, and export timber for those colonies, and for the French Navy. To achieve this, the French government transformed New France into a royal colony, confronted and sought to stifle the Iroquois, and encouraged French immigration to Canada.

The Iroquois had long limited French colonial profits by intercepting convoys of fur pelts. In the 1660s Louis XIV had dispatched French troops to New France. The French Army had burned Mohawk villages. Sobered by the destruction, the Iroquois Confederacy had made a peace that had permitted New France's rapid expansion of fur ex-

ports. The French obtained furs in exchange for European goods, including guns.

In the 1660s France dispatched about 600 settlers a year to Canada, half of them indentured servants. But many immigrants gave up farming for the fur trade. By 1670 one-fifth had become *coureurs de bois*, independent traders free of government authority. Living and intermarrying with the Indians, the *coureurs* built a French empire resting on trade and goodwill among native peoples throughout central North America. Alarmed by the rapid expansion of England's colonies, France sought to contain them, and to prevent Spain from linking Florida with New Mexico, by dominating the North American heartland.

## The Spanish Borderlands

English and French expansion, particularly René-Robert La Salle's building a fort in Spanish Texas in the 1680s, alarmed the Spanish. Yet the first permanent Spanish settlements in Texas did not appear until 1716. Instead, Spain concentrated on New Mexico. By 1680, 2,300 Europeans and 17,000 Pueblo Indians lived in New Mexico's Rio Grande valley.

However, many of the Indians chafed under Spanish control. Taos, a large pueblo in northern New Mexico, had long been a magnet for Native Americans resentful of Spanish rule, and in 1680 it would become the center of a major rebellion against the Spanish. Several factors triggered the uprising: prolonged drought, epidemics of European diseases, and Spanish attempts to suppress traditional religious ceremonies and symbols. The leader of the Taos revolt was Popé, a religious leader from a nearby pueblo who had fled to Taos to avoid persecution. In August 1680 Popé and others—many disillusioned Christian converts—led a massive uprising against the Spanish. The rebels slew more than 400 colonists and missionaries; hundreds more fled south into Mexico, leaving behind their horse herds and other livestock. Twelve years would pass before the Spanish recaptured Taos and the rebel Indians submitted to Spanish rule once again. The

**Taos Pueblo, North House Block, 1880**
*The Taos pueblo of northern New Mexico became the site of a major anti-Spanish rebellion by Native Americans in 1680. As a result of this rebellion and the Spanish flight, Plains tribes gained access to horses for the first time.*

Pueblo Revolt of 1680 would remain the largest Native American rebellion against Spain, although resentment continued to simmer. Perhaps the most important legacy of the Pueblo Revolt was the acquisition of the horse by Plains Indians quick to recognize the enormous advantages of mobility and speed; within a generation mounted warriors peopled the Great Plains from Canada to Texas, a formidable force arrayed first against Spanish and then against Anglo-American settlers.

In Florida the Spanish fared little better. Forced labor and missionization led to periodic Indian rebellions before 1680, and after that slave raiders from Carolina wreaked havoc among Indians under Spanish rule, as did disease. After 1715 Creek neutrality permitted the Spanish to enter the deerskin trade and even to stage counterraids into the British colony of Carolina. The Spanish also offered freedom to English-owned slaves who made their way to Florida. When a new round of warfare erupted in Europe at the end of the decade, Spain was ill prepared to defend its beleaguered North American colonies.

## CONCLUSION

In less than a century, from 1630 to 1715, Europeans had laid claim to most of the area composing the United States from the Atlantic Ocean to the Rocky Mountains. Although France and Spain claimed vast domains, the population of England's colonies stood at 250,000, compared with 15,000 for France and 4,500 for Spain.

With the English colonies, several distinct regions emerged. Southern colonies, like those of the West Indies, focused on plantation production of cash crops, relying more and more on slave labor. New England's Puritans became far more worldly as a commercial economy boomed, and religious fervor slackened. The middle colonies, ethnically and religiously pluralistic, also embraced the market economy. During the first half of the eighteenth century, all three regions would be integrated into the first empire in history rooted in commercial capitalism.

## CHRONOLOGY

**1627**   English establish Barbados.

**1630**   John Winthrop, "A Model of Christian Charity." Massachusetts Bay colony founded.

**1630–ퟏ660**   The great English migration to North America.

**1633**   First English settlements in Connecticut.

**1634**   Cecilius Calvert (Lord Baltimore) founds proprietary colony of Maryland.

**1635**   Roger Williams banished from Massachusetts Bay; founds Providence, Rhode Island, in 1636.

**1636**   Harvard College established.

**1637**   Anne Hutchinson tried by Massachusetts Bay Colony and banished to Rhode Island.
Pequot War.

**1638**   New Sweden established.

**1640s**   Large-scale slave-labor system takes hold in the West Indies.

**1642**   English Civil War begins.

**1644**   Williams obtains permission to establish a legal government in Rhode Island.

**1644–ퟏ646**   Third Anglo-Powhatan War in Virginia.

**1649**   Maryland's Act for Religious Toleration.
King Charles I beheaded.

**1651**   First New England "praying town" established at Natick, Massachusetts.

**1653**   First Indian reservation established in Virginia.

**1655**   New Netherland annexes New Sweden.

**1660**   Charles II becomes king of England.

**1661**   Barbados government creates first comprehensive slave code.
Maryland defines slavery as a lifelong, inheritable racial status.

**1662**   Half-Way Covenant drafted.

**1663**   Carolina founded as English colony.
New France made a royal colony.

**1664**   English conquer the Dutch colony of New Netherland, which becomes the English colony of New York.
New Jersey established.

**1670**   Settlement of southern Carolina begins.
Virginia defines slavery as a lifelong, inheritable racial status.

**1672**   Louis Jolliet and Jacques Marquette explore the Mississippi River.

**1675–ퟏ676**   King Philip's War in New England.

**1676**   Bacon's Rebellion in Virginia.
Quakers organize the colony of West Jersey.

**1680–ퟏ692**   Pueblo revolt in New Mexico.

**1681**   William Penn founds the Pennsylvania colony.

| | |
|---|---|
| 1682 | Quakers organize the colony of East Jersey. The Sieur de La Salle descends the Mississippi River to the Gulf of Mexico and claims the Mississippi basin for France. |
| 1690s | Collapse of the Royal African Company's monopoly on selling slaves to the English colonies; large shipments of Africans begin reaching the Chesapeake. |
| 1692–1693 | Salem witchcraft trials. |
| 1698 | French begin settlements near the mouth of the Mississippi River. |
| 1711–1713 | Tuscarora War in Carolina. |
| 1715–1716 | Yamasee War in Carolina. |

## FOR FURTHER READING

Paul Boyer and Stephen Nissenbaum, *Salem Possessed: The Social Origins of Witchcraft* (1974). A study of the witchcraft episode as the expression of social conflict in one New England community.

William Cronon, *Changes in the Land: Indians, Colonists, and the Ecology of New England* (1983). A pioneering study of the interactions of Native Americans and European settlers with the New England environment.

W. J. Eccles, *France in America*, rev. ed. (1991). An interpretive overview of French colonization in North America and the Caribbean by a distinguished scholar.

Jack P. Greene, *Pursuits of Happiness: The Social Development of Early Modern British Colonies and the Formation of American Culture* (1988). A brilliant synthesis of the colonial history of English America.

Winthrop D. Jordan, *The White Man's Burden: Historical Origins of Racism in the United States* (1974). A brief, yet definitive analysis of racism's origins.

Carol F. Karlsen, *The Devil in the Shape of a Woman: Witchcraft in Colonial New England* (1987). An examination of the relationship between witchcraft episodes and gender in New England society.

Edmund S. Morgan, *American Slavery, American Freedom: The Ordeal of Colonial Virginia* (1975). The most penetrating analysis yet written on the origins of southern slavery.

Alan Simpson, *Puritanism in Old and New England* (1955). A good brief introduction to Puritanism.

David J. Weber, *The Spanish Frontier in North America* (1992). A masterful synthesis of Spanish colonial history north of the Caribbean and Mexico.

# Colonial Society Comes of Age, 1660–1750

With the English Civil War's end in 1646, the flow of English settlers to America became a torrent. New colonies soon dotted the Atlantic seaboard from French-held Canada to Spanish-controlled Florida. Although English immigrants peopled most of these colonies, significant numbers of Germans, Irish, Scottish, Dutch, and French arrived and contributed to the emerging American culture. So, too, did the increasing African-American population, which slowly became English-speaking and Christian.

A generation of imperial crisis and war against the French from 1685 until 1713 forged among Anglo-America's whites a strong sense of shared allegiance to the English crown and of deeply felt Protestant heritage. During the peace that prevailed from 1713 to 1744, two vital but conflicting currents of European culture challenged British-American provincialism. The first was the Enlightenment, a movement among the educated public

*(Right) Rhode Island colonists relaxing at teatime (detail)*

**Restoration and Rebellion**

∝

**A Maturing Colonial Economy and Society**

∝

**Competing for a Continent**

∝

**Enlightenment and Awakening**

characterized by a faith in reason and an appreciation of natural science. Joining and opposing this movement was a second current, a religious revival that pulsed across Protestant Europe in the 1730s and 1740s, a movement known as the Great Awakening in the American colonies.

The peace and prosperity of mid-eighteenth-century British North America would have astonished the seventeenth-century colonists who had clung to their uncertain footholds on the edge of the wilderness. But even though life had become reasonably stable and secure by the 1740s, especially for upper-class Anglo-Americans, the Great Awakening unleashed spiritual and social tremors that jolted colonial self-confidence.

## Restoration and Rebellion

Although English colonies dated to Virginia in 1607, there was no serious attempt to weld the diverse colonies into an empire until Charles II (ruled 1660–1685) ascended the throne. The "restoration" of the Stuart dynasty ended two decades of civil war and republican experiment. England began to expand its overseas trade and tried to subordinate to its own interests the commercial and political interests of the colonies.

### Stuart Policies

To benefit England's commercial interests, Parliament began "tidying up" the North American colonies by passing a series of laws collectively known as the Navigation Acts beginning in 1651. The 1660 and 1663 acts, expanding on the 1651 act, forced colonial merchants to export valuable commodities such as sugar and tobacco only to England and banned the importation of goods in non-English ships. Meanwhile, a new wave of colony building gave England control of the North American coast from Maine to South Carolina.

Charles II intended the Navigation Acts and the new colonies to reward his supporters in England. The proprietors who oversaw the colonies' government expected to create prosperous settle-

**The Restoration Colonies**
*England's Restoration colonies were carved out of the claims or earlier colonial territory of rival European powers. Spain claimed the territory chartered as Carolina in 1663. Out of England's takeover of Dutch New Netherland in 1664 came the colonies of New York, East Jersey, West Jersey, Pennsylvania, and Delaware.*

ments and a stable social hierarchy. But such plans collided with the colonists' determination to better themselves, and by 1689 English attempts to impose a uniform system of rule had provoked a series of colonial rebellions.

### Royal Centralization

The sons of a king executed by Parliament, the last Stuart monarchs, Charles II and James II, disliked representative government. They tried to rule England as much as possible without Parliament and eyed American colonial assemblies suspiciously.

As Duke of York during his brother Charles's rule, James showed his disdain for colonial assemblies almost as soon as he became the proprietor of New York. Calling elected assemblies "of dangerous consequence," he forbade legislatures to meet from 1664 to 1682. Charles himself often appointed high-ranking army officers as colonial governors. Technically civilians, these officers commanded the militia and used it to crush civilian dissent. In his twenty-five-year reign, more than 90 percent of the governors whom Charles II appointed were army officers, a serious violation of the English tradition of holding the military accountable to civilian authority. When James became king, he continued the policy.

Ever resentful of outside meddling, New Englanders resisted such centralization of power. In 1661 the Massachusetts assembly declared its citizens exempt from all English laws and royal decrees except declarations of war. Ignoring the Navigation Acts, New Englanders welcomed Dutch traders. "The New England men . . . trade to any place that their interest lead them," lamented Virginia's governor William Berkeley.

Provoked, Charles targeted Massachusetts for punishment. In 1679 he carved a new royal territory, New Hampshire, from Massachusetts. In 1684 he declared Massachusetts a royal colony and revoked its charter, the very foundation of the Puritan city upon a hill. Puritan minister Increase Mather called on the colonists to resist, even to the point of martyrdom.

James II's accession to the throne intensified royal centralization in America. In 1686 the new king merged five separate colonies—Massachusetts, New Hampshire, Connecticut, Rhode Island, and Plymouth—into the Dominion of New England, later adding New York and the Jerseys. Under the new system, these colonies' legislatures ceased to exist. Sir Edmund Andros, a former army officer, became the Dominion's governor.

Andros's arbitrary actions ignited burning hatred. He limited towns to one annual meeting and jailed prominent citizens in order to crush protests. He forced a Boston Puritan congregation to share its meetinghouse with an Anglican minister. And Andros enforced the Navigation Acts. "You have no more privileges left you," Andros reportedly told a group of colonists, "than not to be sold for slaves."

Tensions also ran high in New York, where Catholics held high political and military posts under the Duke of York's rule. Anxious colonists feared that these Catholic officials would betray the colony to France. When Andros's local deputy allowed harbor forts to deteriorate, New Yorkers suspected the worst.

## The Glorious Revolution in England and America

Puritans in England also worriedly monitored Stuart displays of pro-Catholic sympathies. The Duke of York himself became a Catholic in 1676, and Charles II converted on his deathbed. Both rulers violated English law by allowing Catholics to hold high office and to worship openly. James II had Anglican bishops who denounced these practices tried as state enemies.

The English tolerated James II's Catholicism only because his heirs, daughters Mary and Anne, remained Anglican. But in 1688 his second wife bore a son, who would be raised—and perhaps would rule—as a Catholic. Aghast at the idea, English political leaders asked Mary and her husband, William of Orange (the Dutch Republic's leader), to intervene. When William and Mary led a small army to England in November 1688, royal troops defected to them, and James II fled to France.

This bloodless coup, the "Glorious Revolution," created a "limited monarchy" as defined by England's Bill of Rights of 1689. The monarchs promised to summon Parliament annually, to sign its bills, and to respect civil liberties. Neither the English nor Anglo-Americans would ever forget this vindication of limited representative government. Anglo-Americans struck their own blows for political liberty as well when Massachusetts, New York, and Maryland rose up against their Stuart-appointed rulers.

News of the Glorious Revolution electrified Massachusetts Puritans, who arrested Andros and his councilors. (He tried to flee in women's clothing but was caught when a guard spotted this "lady" in army boots.) Acting in the name of William and Mary, the Massachusetts elite resumed its own government. In fact, the new monarchs would have preferred continuing the Dominion but prudently consented to its dismantling. They allowed Connecticut and Rhode Island to resume election of their own governors and permitted Massachusetts to absorb the Plymouth colony. But Massachusetts enjoyed only a partial victory. The colony's new royal charter of 1691 reserved to the crown the appointment of the governor. Moreover, property ownership, not church membership, became the criterion for voting. Worst of all, the Puritan colony had to tolerate Anglicans, who were proliferating in the port towns.

New York's counterpart of the anti-Stuart uprising was Leisler's Rebellion. In May 1689 the city militia, under Captain Jacob Leisler, had seized the harbor's main fort, begun to repair its defenses, and called elections for an assembly. Andros's deputy, his authority strangled, had sailed for England. In 1691 Leisler, still riding high, denied newly arrived English troops entry to key forts for fear that they were loyal to James II. But after a brief skirmish, Leisler was arrested and charged with treason for firing on royal troops. New Yorkers who considered themselves ill treated by Leisler packed the jury, and both he and his son-in-law were convicted and hanged.

Arbitrary government and fears of Catholic plots had also brought turmoil to Maryland by 1689, where the Protestant-dominated lower house and the Catholic upper chamber were feuding. When the Glorious Revolution had toppled James II, Lord Baltimore, away in England, had dispatched a courier to Maryland, commanding obedience to William and Mary. But the courier died en route. Maryland's Protestants widely suspected that their proprietor was a traitor who supported James II.

Protestant rebel John Coode organized the Protestant Association to secure Maryland for William and Mary. In July 1689 Coode and his co-conspirators seized the capital, removed Catholics from office, and requested that the crown take over the colony. Maryland became a royal province in 1691 and made the Church of England an established religion in 1692. Catholics, composing less than one-fourth of the population, lost the right to vote and to worship in public. In 1715 the fourth Lord Baltimore joined the Church of England and regained the proprietorship of Maryland. Maryland remained a proprietary colony until 1776.

The revolutionary events of 1688–1689 reestablished the colonies' legislative government and ensured Protestant religious freedom. William and Mary allowed colonial elites to reassert local control and encouraged Americans to identify their interests with England, laying the foundation for an empire based on voluntary allegiance, not raw force.

## A Generation of War

The Glorious Revolution ushered in a quarter century of war that convulsed both England and the colonies. In 1689 England joined a European coalition against France's Louis XIV and plunged into the War of the League of Augsburg (which Anglo-Americans called King William's War).

In 1690, at the outbreak of King William's War, New Yorkers and Yankees launched an invasion of England's enemy, New France. The invasion deteriorated into cruel but inconclusive border raids by both sides. The Iroquois, allied to the English and Dutch, bore the brunt of the war. French forces, enlisting the aid of virtually every other tribe from Maine to the Great Lakes, played havoc with Iroquois land and peoples. By 1700 one-fourth of the Iroquois warriors had been killed or taken prisoner, or had fled to Canada. In twelve years the Iroquois population fell from 8,600 to 7,000. By comparison, English and Dutch casualties were fewer than 900, while the French probably lost no more than 400. In 1701 the Iroquois agreed to let Canada's governor settle their disputes with other Indians and to remain neutral in future wars. Thereafter, playing French and English off against each other, the Iroquois maintained control of their lands, rebuilt their population, and held the balance of power along the Great Lakes.

In 1702 a new European war pitted England against France and Spain. During what the colonists called Queen Anne's War, Anglo-Americans became painfully aware of their own military weakness. French and Indian raiders from Canada destroyed New England towns, while the Spanish invaded southern Carolina and nearly took Charles Town in 1706. Colonial vessels fell to French and Spanish warships. English forces, however, gained control of the Hudson Bay region, Newfoundland, and Acadia (henceforth called Nova Scotia). The peace signed in 1713 allowed Britain to keep these lands but left the French and Indians in control of their interior.

These wars had a profound political consequence. Anglo-Americans, newly aware of their military weakness, realized how much they needed the protection of the Royal Navy, and consequently they became more loyal than ever to the English crown. War thus reinforced the Anglo-American sense of British identity.

# A Maturing Colonial Economy and Society

Britons visiting mid-eighteenth-century America found a sophisticated society and widespread prosperity. "The nobleness of the town surprised me more than the fertile appearance of the country," wrote an English naval officer of New York in 1756. "I had no idea of finding a place in America, consisting of near 2,000 houses, elegantly built of brick . . . and the streets paved and spacious, . . . but such is this city that very few in England can rival it in its show."

Such prosperity and social development were relatively new. By 1750 the colonies' brisk economic growth had been under way for fifty to seventy-five years, depending on the region. During that time colonial exports had grown steadily, allowing Anglo-Americans to enjoy a relatively high living standard despite parliamentary controls.

## British Economic Policy Toward America

Between 1651 and 1733 Parliament enacted laws to govern commerce between Britain and its overseas colonies. Historians label the rules of trade set forth in these laws the navigation system, and they use the word *mercantilism* to describe the underlying legal assumptions. The navigation system and mercantilism deeply affected North America's relationship with Great Britain.

Mercantilism was not an elaborate economic theory. Instead, the word refers in general to European policies aimed at guaranteeing prosperity by making their own country as self-sufficient as possible—by eliminating its dependence on foreign suppliers, damaging its foreign competitors' commerce, and increasing the national stock of gold and silver by selling more goods abroad than it bought. Mercantilism was the direct opposite of a competitive free-market system, which would receive its first great theoretical description in Scottish economist Adam Smith's *The Wealth of Nations* (1776). Until then, mercantilism would dominate British policy.

In 1651 the English Parliament passed the first Navigation Act to undercut the Dutch Republic. It excluded the Dutch from English trade in order to force England to build its own merchant fleet. The Stuart restoration in 1660 brought more laws to protect English manufacturers from foreign competition. By 1750 a long series of Navigation Acts was affecting the colonial economy in four major ways.

First, the laws limited imperial trade to British-owned ships whose crews were three-quarters British (which was broadly defined to include all colonists, even blacks). At first the American colonists and some in the English business community objected because the Dutch offered better prices, credit, and merchandise. After 1700, however, the rising quality of the British merchant marine removed this cause for complaint.

This new shipping restriction helped Britain to become Europe's foremost shipping nation and laid the foundations for an American merchant marine. By the 1750s Americans owned one-third of all imperial vessels. The swift growth of this merchant marine diversified the colonial economy and made it more self-sufficient. The expansion of colonial shipping in turn demanded centralized docks, warehouses, and repair shops, and thus hastened urbanization. Philadelphia and New York both grew rapidly. Shipbuilding became a major industry, and by 1770 one-third of the British merchant marine was American built.

Second, the Navigation Acts barred the colonies' export of "enumerated goods" unless they first passed through England or Scotland. Among these were tobacco, rice, furs, indigo, and naval stores (masts, hemp, tar, and turpentine). (Before the mid-eighteenth century, at least, Parliament did not restrict grain, livestock, fish, lumber, or rum, which constituted 60 percent of colonial exports.) Furthermore, American tobacco exporters received a monopoly on the British tobacco market. Parliament also refunded taxes on tobacco and rice later shipped from Britain to other countries—amounting eventually to about 85 percent of American tobacco and rice.

Third, the navigation system encouraged economic diversification. Parliament paid modest bounties to Americans producing silk, iron, dyes, hemp, lumber, and other products that Britain would otherwise have had to import from foreign countries. Parliament also erected protective tariffs against foreign goods.

Fourth, the trade laws forbade Americans from competing with British manufacturers of clothing and steel—an apparently negative consequence for the colonies. In practice this regulation meant little because it referred to *large-scale* manufacturing and thus did not interfere with the tailors, hatters, and housewives who produced most American clothing in their households or in small shops. Americans would establish a profitable clothing industry only after 1820 and did not develop a successful steel industry until the 1840s. The colonists were free to produce iron, however, and by 1770, 250 colonial ironworks were employing 30,000 men. That year the colonies produced more iron than England and Wales; and only Sweden and Russia exceeded American output.

Before the mid-eighteenth century, the Navigation Acts did not overburden the colonists. The trade regulations, which fell primarily on rice and tobacco producers, lowered their income by only 3 percent. The cost of non-British merchandise rose, but not enough to encourage smuggling (except for tea from India and molasses from the French Caribbean). The great volume of colonial trade proceeded lawfully. In addition, Anglo-American commerce provided mutual advantages. Although Parliament intended the laws only to benefit Britain, British North America's economy grew at a per capita rate of 0.6 percent annually from 1650 to 1770 under the navigation system—twice as fast as Britain's.

## A Burgeoning, Diversifying Population

European cities were too poor and crowded for marriage and families, Benjamin Franklin noted in 1751, but British America, with its open spaces and small cities, seemed destined to grow and flourish. Estimating the colonies' population at 1 million, Franklin predicted that it would double every 25 years. Not only were his estimates amazingly precise, but modern research has also confirmed his analysis of factors affecting population growth.

After 1700, when life expectancy and family size in the South rose to levels typical of those of the North, Anglo-America's growth far outpaced Britain's. Colonial women had an average of eight children and forty-two grandchildren, compared to five children and fifteen grandchildren for their British counterparts. In 1700 England's population outnumbered the colonies' by twenty to one; by 1775 the ratio would be only three to one.

In the eighteenth century continuing immigration contributed significantly to colonial population growth. In the forty years after Queen Anne's War, 350,000 newcomers had reached the colonies. The percentage of English-born immigrants among whites decreased sharply. Rising employment and higher wages in England made emigration less attractive than before, but economic hardship elsewhere in the British Isles and in northern Europe guaranteed an ethnically more diverse North America.

Ironically, enslaved Africans, some 140,000 in number, constituted the largest group of newcomers. Most were from Africa's west coast, and all had survived a sea crossing of sickening brutality. Ship captains closely calculated how many slaves they could jam into their vessels. Kept below deck in near-darkness, surrounded by filth and stench, numbed by depression, the Africans frequently fell victim to disease.

More than 100,000 newcomers in this era were from Ireland. Two-thirds of these were "Scots-Irish," the descendants of sixteenth-century Scottish Presbyterian settlers of northern Ireland. The Scots-Irish generally immigrated as complete families. In contrast, 90 percent of Irish Catholic immigrants consisted of unmarried males who, once in

America, typically abandoned their faith to marry Protestant women.

Germany contributed some 65,000 settlers, the majority seeking escape from desperate poverty. One-third were "redemptioners" who had sold themselves or their children as indentured servants. Lutherans and Calvinists predominated, but a significant minority belonged to small, pacifist sects that desired above all to be left alone.

Immigrants shunned areas where land was scarce and expensive because most of them were poor. Philadelphia became the immigrants' primary port of entry. By 1775 the English accounted for only one-third of Pennsylvania's population.

Indentured servants had to work one to four years for a master who might exploit them cruelly.

**Architect's Plan of a Slave Ship**
*This plan graphically depicts the crowded, unsanitary conditions under which slaves were transported across the Atlantic.*

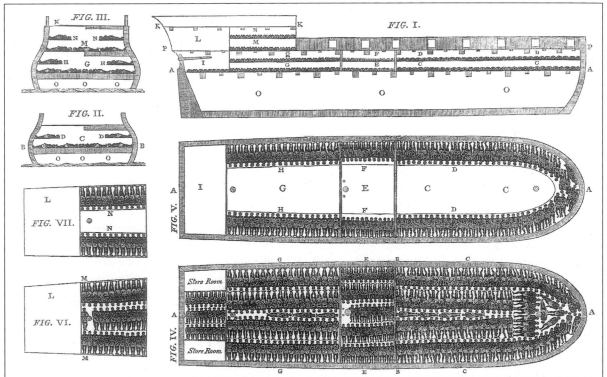

Servants could be sold or rented out, beaten, kept from marrying, and sexually harassed; attempted escape usually meant an extension of service. At the end of their term, most collected "freedom dues," which helped them to marry and to acquire land.

The piedmont, a broad, rolling upland stretching along the eastern slope of the Appalachians, drew many immigrants. Upper New York, Pennsylvania, and Maryland attracted large numbers of Germans and Scots-Irish. Charles Town became a popular gateway for immigrants who later moved westward to the Carolina piedmont to become small farmers. In 1713 few Anglo-Americans lived more than fifty miles from the Atlantic, but by 1750 one-third of the colonists resided in the piedmont.

English-descended colonists did not relish the arrival of so many foreigners. Benjamin Franklin wrote:

> *Why should the Palatine boors [Germans] be suffered to swarm into our settlements, and, by herding together, establish their language and manners, to the exclusion of ours? Why should Pennsylvania, founded by the English, become a colony of aliens, who will shortly be so numerous as to Germanize us instead of us Anglicizing them, and will never adopt our language or customs any more than they can acquire our complexion?*

Franklin also objected to slave trade because, he argued, it would increase America's black population at the expense of industrious whites.

## Eighteenth-Century Living Standards

A tenfold increase in exports drove colonial living standards up dramatically after 1700, especially in the Chesapeake. As tobacco exports tripled from 1713 to 1774, and as exports of corn and wheat also soared, prosperity replaced poverty in the region, although slaves and a small underclass of struggling white farmers remained poor. A landholding small-planter class arose, and a wealthy elite of large landowners and slavemasters flourished atop Chesapeake society after 1700. Perhaps 30 percent of white families owned slaves.

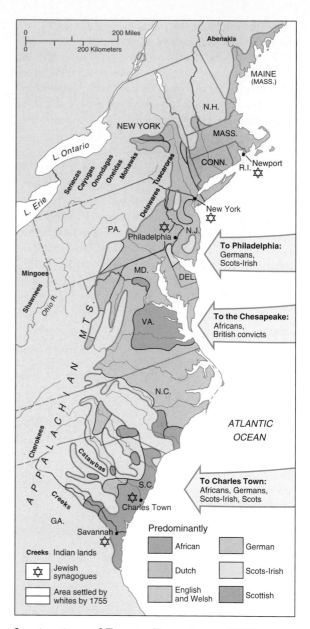

**Immigration and Frontier Expansion, to 1755**
*A sharp rise in the importance of African slaves made much of the southern tidewater a predominantly African-American region. Immigrants from Germany, Ireland, and Scotland tended to settle in the piedmont. A significant Jewish population emerges in the seaports.*

The mid-Atlantic, stretching from New York to Delaware, had the highest living standards. In 1770 per capital wealth here stood 40 percent above the colonial average. Prosperity rested on the region's rich soil, on a long-term climatic warming that lengthened the growing season, and on a brisk demand for livestock, wheat, and corn in the West Indies and southern Europe.

New Englanders prospered least. Their wealth, on average, was only half that of other colonists. Mediocre soil and a short growing season forced New Englanders to import grain. A long-term decline in the price of lumber also hurt the New England economy. By 1750 New England towns teemed with more young men than the land could support. Migration to the frontier eased this population pressure. The sea also provided a means of survival for many New Englanders. By 1700 the Yankee merchant marine and fishing industry were the largest in the colonies, providing employment for every seventh man. But prosperity carried a heavy price: the sea took one sailor in five to a watery grave.

By 1750 the American colonies enjoyed a standard of living roughly equal to that of England and far higher than those of Scotland and Ireland. Steady overseas demand for colonial products spawned a prosperity that enabled Americans to consume a huge volume of British products. In 1700 the colonies took just 5 percent of Britain's exports; by 1760 they absorbed almost 40 percent.

## Rural Men and Women

Because the vast majority of colonial landowners had just enough acreage for a working farm, most could not provide land for their children when they married. Moreover, with longevity increasing, children often did not receive their inheritances until middle age or later; and, because families were large, a farmer's wealth was typically divided into small portions. Under these circumstances, a young man typically worked from about age sixteen to twenty-three as a field hand to save money just to buy farm equipment, and a young husband generally had to rent land until he reached his mid-thirties.

Landownership came fastest to those farmers who took part-time work to increase their savings. Carpentry, fur trapping, and wintertime jobs such as draining meadows and fencing land supplemented farm incomes.

The payment of mortgages was slow. A farmer could expect to earn 6 percent cash income per year, which barely equaled mortgage interest. After making a down payment of one-third, a husband and wife generally paid the next third through their inheritances. The final third would be paid when the children reached their teens and helped to double the regular farm income. Most colonial parents found themselves free of debt only as they reached their late fifties.

Rural families depended somewhat on barter and much more on what wives and daughters manufactured: soap, preserved food, knitted goods, yarn,

**Women's Work**
*Rural women were responsible for most household and garden tasks. This print, dating to 1780, shows young women tending onions in Wethersfield, Connecticut.*

and the products of dairy, orchard, and garden. In this way women made significant contributions to the family's cash income and well-being. Legal constraints, however, bound colonial women. A woman's most independent decision was her choice of a husband. Once married, she lost control of her dowry. Nevertheless, widows controlled substantial property—an estimated 8 to 10 percent of all property in eighteenth-century Anglo-America—and some ran large estates or plantations.

## Colonial Farmers and the Environment

As English settlement expanded, the environment east of the Appalachians changed rapidly. Eighteenth-century settlers cleared forest land in order to plant crops in its fertile soil. New England farmers also cleared from their land innumerable large rocks, debris from the last Ice Age. The felled trees provided timber to construct houses, barns, and fences and to burn as fuel for cooking and heating. Urban dwellers bought their firewood and construction timber from farmers and planters. Six years after Georgia's founding, a colonist noted that there was "no more firewood in Savannah; . . . it must be brought from the plantations [and is] already right expensive."

Removal of trees (deforestation) deprived large forest creatures such as bears, panthers, and wild turkeys of their habitat, while the planted land provided free lunch for rabbits, mice, and possums. Deforestation removed protection from winds and sun, producing warmer summers and harsher winters and, ironically, reinforcing the demand for firewood. By hastening the runoff of spring waters, deforestation led to heavier flooding and, where water could not escape, to more extensive swamps. Volatile temperatures and water levels rapidly reduced the number of fish in colonial streams and lakes. By 1766 naturalist John Bartram noted that fish "abounded formerly when the Indians lived much on them" but that "now there is not the 100[th] or perhaps the 1000th [portion] to be found."

Deforestation also dried and hardened the soil; colonial crops had even more drastic effects. Native Americans had rotated their crops to protect against soil depletion, but many colonial farmers lacked enough land to do so—and many more were unwilling to sacrifice short-term profits for long-term benefits. As early as 1637 a dismayed New England farmer found that his soil "after five or six years [of planting corn] grows barren beyond belief and puts on the face of winter in the time of summer." Tobacco yields in the Chesapeake region declined in fields planted only three or four consecutive years. As the Chesapeake tobacco growers abandoned tidewater fields and moved to the piedmont, they contributed to increased soil erosion. By 1750, in order to remain productive, many shifted from tobacco to wheat.

Well-to-do Europeans had already turned to conservation and "scientific farming." North American colonists ignored such techniques. Some could not afford to implement them, and virtually all believed that America's vast lands, including those still held by Indians, would sustain them and future generations indefinitely.

## The Urban Paradox

Cities were colonial America's economic paradox. Although they shipped the livestock, grain, and lumber that enriched the countryside, at the same time they were caught in a downward spiral of declining opportunity.

After 1740 the 4 percent of colonists in cities found economic success elusive. Philadelphia, New York, and Boston faced escalating poverty. Debilitating ocean voyages left many immigrants too weak to work, and every ship from Europe carried widows and orphans. The cities' poor rolls, moreover, always bulged with the survivors of mariners lost at sea; unskilled, landless men; and women (often widows) and children from the countryside. And a high population density and poor sanitation left colonial cities vulnerable to the rapid spread of contagious diseases. As a result, half of all city children died before twenty-one, and urban adults averaged ten fewer years of life than rural residents.

Even the able-bodied found cities economically treacherous. Traditionally, artisans trained apprentices and employed them as journeymen until they could open their own shops. After 1750, however, more employers released their workers when business slowed. And from 1720 onward recessions hit frequently, creating longer spells of unemployment. As urban populations ballooned, wages shrank, while the cost of rent, food, and firewood shot up. Economic frustration bred violence. Between 1710 and 1750, for example, Boston experienced five major riots.

In the South most cities were little more than large towns, although Charles Town was North America's fourth-largest city. South Carolina's capital offered gracious living to wealthy planters during the months of heat and insect infestations on their plantations. But shanties on the city's outskirts sheltered a growing crowd of destitute whites. Like their counterparts in northern port cities, Charles Town's poor whites competed for work with urban slaves whose masters rented out their labor. Racial tensions simmered.

Middle-class urban women faced less manual drudgery than their rural counterparts. Nonetheless, they managed complex households, often including servants and other nonfamily members. Although they raised poulty and vegetables, sewed, and knitted, urban women generally purchased their cloth and most of their food. Household servants, usually young single women or widows, helped with cooking, cleaning, and laundering. Wives also worked in family businesses, usually located in the owner's home.

Widows and less affluent wives took in boarders and often spun and wove cloth for local merchants. Grim conditions in Boston forced many widows with children to look to the community for relief. Although their Puritan ancestors had seen providing care for poor dependents a matter of Christian charity, affluent Bostonians turned an increasingly wary eye toward the needy.

## Slavery's Wages

From 1713 to 1754 five times as many slaves poured into mainland Anglo-America as in all the preceding years. The proportion of African-Americans in the colonies doubled, reaching 20 percent by midcentury. Fifteen percent of American slaves lived north of Maryland, mostly in New York and New Jersey.

Because West Indian and Brazilian slave buyers outbid North Americans, only 5 percent of transported Africans reached the mainland Anglo-American colonies. Mainland slaveowners, unable to buy enough male field hands, bought female workers and protected their investment by maintaining their slaves' health. These factors promoted family formation and increased life expectancy far beyond the levels in the Caribbean. By 1750 population growth among African-Americans equaled that of whites.

Masters could usually afford to keep slaves healthy, but they rarely made their human chattels comfortable. Slave upkeep generally cost 60 percent less than the maintenance of indentured servants. White servants ate 200 pounds of beef or pork a year; slaves, 50 pounds. A master would spend as much providing beer and hard cider for a servant as food and clothing for a slave. Adult slaves received eight quarts of corn and one pound of pork weekly and were expected to grow vegetables and to raise poultry.

Slaves worked for a longer portion of their lives than whites. Slave children worked part-time from the age of seven and full-time as early as eleven. African-American women performed hard work alongside men and tended tobacco and rice crops even when pregnant. Most slaves toiled until they died, although those in their sixties rarely did hard labor. The rigors of bondage, however, did not crush the slaves' spirits. Slaves proved resourceful at maximizing opportunities. Some even accumulated small amounts of property by staking out exclusive rights to their gardens and poultry. And in the Carolina and Georgia rice country, the task system gave slaves some control of their work. Under tasking, each slave spent a half day caring for a quarter acre, after which his or her duties ended. Ambitious slaves used the rest of the day to keep hogs or to grow vegetables for sale in Charles Town.

By midcentury slaves constituted 20 percent of New York City's population and formed a majority

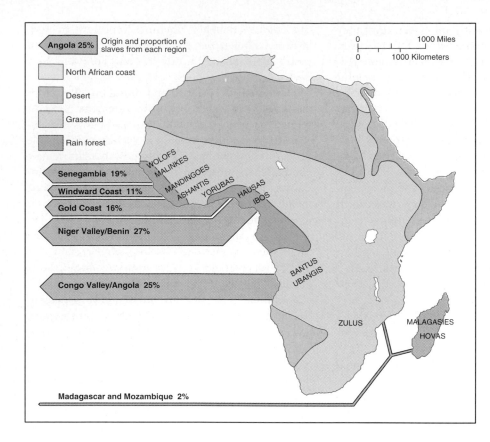

Angola 25%  Origin and proportion of slaves from each region

North African coast

Desert

Grassland

Rain forest

WOLOFS
MALINKES
MANDINGOES
ASHANTIS
YORUBAS
HAUSAS
IBOS
BANTUS
UBANGIS
ZULUS
MALAGASIES
HOVAS

Senegambia 19%
Windward Coast 11%
Gold Coast 16%
Niger Valley/Benin 27%
Congo Valley/Angola 25%
Madagascar and Mozambique 2%

0          1000 Miles
0     1000 Kilometers

**African Origins of North American Slaves, 1690–1807** *Virtually all slaves brought to English North America came from West Africa, between Senegambia and Angola. Most were captured or bought inland and marched to the coast, where they were sold to African merchants who in turn sold them to European slave traders.*

in Charles Town and Savannah. Skilled urban slaves hired themselves out and kept part of their wages. By 1770 one-tenth of Savannah's slaves were living in rented rooms away from their owners. Despite substantial personal freedom, they remained slaves. Although city life afforded them some freedom of association, it did not extend to them the opportunities of their owners.

The independence of South Carolina's slaves, and the fact that they constituted a majority in the colony, aroused planters' fears. To retain control, the white minority passed a number of laws restricting slaves' behavior. A 1735 law imposed a dress code limiting slaves to fabrics worth less than ten shillings a yard and prohibited their wearing their owners' cast-off clothes. Concern about the dangers of gatherings of large numbers of blacks uncon-

trolled by whites led in 1721 to a 9:00 P.M. curfew on blacks in Charles Town; the colony of South Carolina placed local slave patrols under the colonial militia. Slaves responded to such vigilance, and to harsher punishments, with increased incidents of arson, theft, flight, and violence.

Tensions erupted in 1739 when a slave uprising known as the Stono Rebellion jolted South Carolina. Stealing guns and ammunition from a store at the Stono River Bridge, one hundred slaves headed for Floridia crying "Liberty!" Along the way they burned seven plantations and killed twenty whites. Within a day, however, mounted militiamen surrounded the runaways, cut them down, and spiked a rebel head on every milepost back to Charles Town. Whites expressed their fears in a new slave code stipulating constant surveillance for slaves. The code threatened masters with fines for not disciplining slaves and required legislative approval for manumission (the freeing of individual slaves). The Stono Rebellion thus accelerated South Carolina's emergence as a racist and fear-ridden society. The rebels' failure showed slaves that armed uprisings were suicidal. After the uprising slaves' resistance took the form of feigning stupidity, running away, committing arson or sabotage, or poisoning masters. Not until 1831 would significant slave violence of a comparable scale erupt on the mainland.

The Carolinas' phenomenal economic and political success cost innumerable lives and untold suffering for enslaved blacks and displaced Native Americans. Whites meanwhile lived in an atmosphere of anxiety. Grim reality had triumphed over hazy English dreams of a stable society.

## The Rise of the Colonial Elites

For white colonial Americans, wealth defined status. "A man who has money here, no matter how he came by it, is everything," wrote a Rhode Islander in 1748. Once wealthy, a man was expected to be responsible, dignified, and generous and to act as a community leader—to act like a gentleman. His wife was expected to be a skillful household manager and a refined, yet deferential hostess—a lady.

Before 1700 class structure in the colonies was relatively invisible; the rural elite spent its resources on land, servants, and slaves instead of conspicuous luxuries. A traveler visiting one of Virginia's richest planters noted that his host owned only "good beds but no curtains and instead of cane chairs . . . stools made of wood." After 1720, however, the display of wealth became more ostentatious. The greater gentry—the richest 2 percent of the population—built splendid estate homes such as New Jersey's Low House and Virginia's Shirley Mansion. The lesser gentry, or second-wealthiest 2 to 10 percent, lived in more modest fieldstone or wood-frame houses, and middle-class farmers typically inhabited one-story wooden buildings with four small rooms.

The gentry also exhibited their wealth after 1720 by living in the European "grand style." They wore costly English fashions, drove carriages, and bought expensive china, books, and furniture. They pursued a gracious life by studying foreign languages, learning formal dances, and cultivating polite manners. Horse racing replaced cockfighting as a preferred spectator sport. A few young colonial males received English educations.

Chesapeake planters, even the frugal, accumulated debt. Tobacco planters, perpetually short of cash, were in hock to British merchants who bought their crops and sold them expensive goods on credit. Planters had two options. They could strive for self-sufficiency, or they could diversify by growing wheat or cutting timber. Both self-sufficiency and economic diversification became more widespread as the eighteenth century progressed.

In eighteenth-century colonial cities wealth remained concentrated. New York's wealthiest 10 percent owned 45 percent of the property. Similar patterns characterized Philadelphia and Boston. Juxtaposed against the growth of a poor urban underclass, these statistics underscored the polarization of status and wealth in urban America on the eve of the Revolution. No American cities, however, experienced the vast gulf between wealth and poverty typical of European cities.

## Elites and Colonial Politics

The colonial elite dominated politics as well as society. Governors appointed members of the greater gentry to serve on councils and as judges in the highest courts. The upper gentry, along with militia majors and colonels, also dominated among the representatives elected to the legislatures' lower houses (the assemblies). Members of the lesser gentry sat less often in the legislatures, but they commonly served as justices of the peace in the county courts.

Outside New England property restrictions barred 80 percent of white men from running for the assembly. In any case few ordinary citizens could have afforded the high costs of elective office. Assemblymen received meager living expenses, which did not cover the cost of staying at the capital,

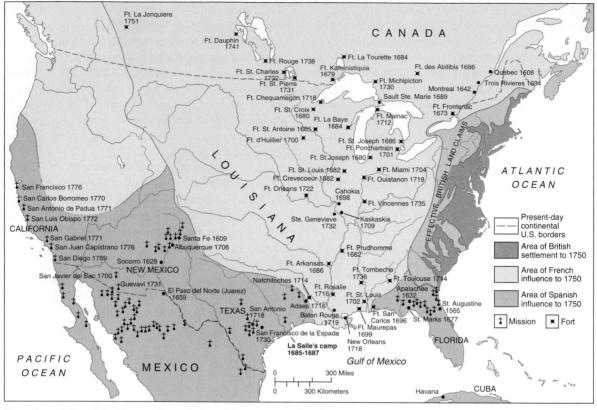

**French and Spanish Occupation of North America, to 1776**
*French fur traders became entrenched along the Great Lakes and upper Mississippi River between 1666 and 1700, after which they built many settlements in territory claimed by Spain along the Gulf of Mexico. Spanish colonization was concentrated in Florida, central Texas, the Rio Grande Valley, and (after 1769) southern California.*

much less make up for six to ten weeks of missed work. Even members of the gentry grumbled about legislative duty, many of them viewing it as "a sort of tax . . . to serve the public at their own Expense besides the neglect of their business." Consequently, political leadership fell to a small number of wealthy families with a tradition of public service.

The colonies generally set liberal qualifications for male voters, but all excluded women, blacks, and Indians from voting. In seven colonies voters had to own land (usually forty to fifty acres), and in the others they had to have enough property to furnish

a house and to work a farm. Most of the 40 percent who could not meet these requirements were indentured servants, single sons living with parents, or young men just beginning family life. Most white males in Anglo-America could vote by age forty, whereas across the Atlantic, two-thirds of all Englishmen and 90 percent of Irishmen could never vote.

Rural voting participation was low, averaging 45 percent. Governors called elections randomly so that after years without an election one could be called on short notice. Voters in isolated areas often did not know of an upcoming election. Voting took place at the county seat, and many voters did not risk traveling long distances over poor roads to reach the voting place. In many colonies voters stated their preference publicly, often face to face with the candidates, a practice that discouraged dissenters. There were no political parties to stimulate popular interest or to mobilize voters. Candidates nominated themselves and ran on their reputations, not on issues.

In view of these factors, political indifference was widespread. For example, to avoid paying legislators' expenses, many Massachusetts towns refused to elect assemblymen. From 1731 to 1760 one-third of South Carolina's elected assemblymen neglected to take their seats. Apathy might have been even greater had not candidates plied voters with alcohol. George Washington dispensed almost two quarts of liquor for each voter when first elected to Virginia's assembly in 1758.

Only in the major seaports did political life flourish. Here greater population density, better communications, and the use of secret ballots (except in New York) accounted for a relatively high voter turnout. Furthermore, the cities' acute economic difficulties stimulated political participation among voters, ever hopeful that government might ease their problems.

The most important political development after 1700 was the rise of the assembly as the dominant force in colonial government. Except in Connecticut and Rhode Island, the crown or proprietors chose colonial governors, who in turn named a council, or upper legislative house. Only in the lower house, or assembly, could members of the gentry defend their interests. Until 1689 governors and councils drafted laws, and the assemblies generally followed passively. Thereafter assemblies assumed a more central role in politics as colonial leaders argued that their legislatures should exercise the same rights as Parliament. Indeed, they viewed their assemblies as miniature Houses of Commons and believed that colonial governors should be as restricted as monarchs. Parliament's victory in the Glorious Revolution convinced Americans that their governors had limited powers and should defer to the assemblies.

The lower houses refused to permit meddling in their procedures, took control over taxes and budgets, and kept a tight rein on executive salaries. Governors remained vulnerable to such financial pressure: they received no salary from Britain and relied on the assemblies for income. This "power of the purse" often forced governors to sign laws opposed by the crown.

Moreover, Britain's lack of interest in colonial politics allowed the assemblies to seize considerable power. The Board of Trade, established by Parliament in 1696 to monitor American affairs, had neither the staff, the energy, nor the vision to maintain royal authority by supporting embattled governors. This vacuum in royal power allowed the colonies to become self-governing in most respects except for regulating trade, printing money, and declaring war. This autonomy, reinforced by self-assertive assemblies, would haunt British authorities when they attempted to exercise more direct rule after 1763 (see Chapter 5).

From 1700 to 1750, then, class distinctions sharpened as many colonists flourished and some grew wealthy. The upper classes' hold on wealth ensured their domination of public life.

# Competing for a Continent

Europeans transformed North America in the first half of the eighteenth century as they expanded their territorial claims, opened new areas for settlement, and engaged in more intensive trade and warfare with Native Americans. In turn, Native Americans welcomed some of these developments and resisted others.

## France and Native Americans

With the end of the War of the Spanish Succession in 1713, France aggressively expanded and strengthened its North American empire, especially Louisiana. The French began to settle the mouth of the Mississippi and its environs, founding New Orleans in 1718. French traders moved onto the southern plains, exchanging goods, including guns, with Comanches and other Plains tribes that raided Spanish Texas.

Louisiana quickly acquired a foul reputation, and few French immigrated there willingly. To boost its population, the government sent paupers and criminals, recruited German refugees, and encouraged slave importation. By 1732 two-thirds of lower Louisiana's 5,800 people were slaves. Life was dismal for everyone. Corruption riddled local government, famine threatened constantly, and the missionary priests quarreled among themselves.

Louisiana's sluggish export economy forced settlers and slaves to find other means of support. Like the Indians, they hunted, fished, gathered wild plants, and cultivated gardens. And red, white, and black Louisianans traded with one another. Indians provided corn, tallow, and above all deerskins to merchants in return for blankets, kettles, axes, chickens, hogs, guns, and alcohol. Indians from west of the Mississippi brought horses and cattle, usually stolen from Spanish ranches in Texas. West African slaves, familiar with cattle from their homelands, managed many of Louisiana's herds; some became rustlers and illicit traders of beef.

French attention also turned to the Ohio Valley, which, thanks to Iroquois neutrality, had become a refuge for dislocated Native American tribes such as the Kickapoos, Shawnees, and Delawares. In order to counter growing English influence and to secure commercial and diplomatic ties with the Indians, the French expanded their trade. Several French posts, including Detroit, ballooned into sizable villages of Indian, French, and mixed-ancestry residents. Nonetheless, increased English trade in the area led most Indians to prefer an independent course.

Although the French were generally more successful than the English among the Indians, the French never won over the Chickasaws, who were supported by Carolina and whose frequent attacks made life miserable for the French and their Indian allies. Another southeastern tribe, the Creeks, played French, Spanish, and British off against one

another, while the Fox Indians kept French traders from direct contact with Sioux tribes. In 1729–1730 the French brutally suppressed the Natchez Indians, the last of the Mississippian peoples, in order to open up land in Louisiana for tobacco and sugar cultivation.

By 1744 French traders had explored as far west as North Dakota and Colorado, buying beaver pelts and Indian slaves on the Great Plains. These traders and their competitors spread trade goods, including guns, to Native Americans throughout central Canada and the Plains. Meanwhile, Indians in the southern Plains and Great Basin had acquired horses from the thousands left behind by fleeing Spaniards after the Pueblo Revolt of 1680. Horses and guns enabled tribes such as the Lakota Sioux and Comanche to move onto the Plains and build a new, highly mobile way of life based on the pursuit of the buffalo. Widely scattered settlements along the Mississippi in modern-day Illinois and Missouri completed France's domain, an immense territory precariously dependent on often shaky relations with Native Americans.

## Native Americans and British Expansion

The depopulation and dislocation of Native Americans made possible the colonies' rapid expansion. Epidemic diseases, environmental changes, war, and political pressure opened new land for Europeans. Pennsylvania coerced the Delawares into selling more than 50,000 acres between 1729 and 1734. In 1735 the colony's leaders produced a patently fraudulent treaty, dated to 1686, in which the Delawares promised to sell their land as far west as a man could walk in a day and a half. The colony hired three men to walk west as fast as they could. They covered nearly 60 miles, forcing the Delawares to cede 1,200 square miles of land in what became known as the Walking Purchase. The Delawares were forced to move, and the proprietors made a huge profit from land sales.

By helping remove the Delawares from Pennsylvania, the Iroquois tried to accommodate the English and consolidate their own power. Late in the seventeenth century the Iroquois had entered into a series of agreements, known as the Covenant Chain, to relocate Indians whose lands the colonists desired. These tribes were moved to areas of New York and Pennsylvania, on the periphery of the Iroquois' homeland, to serve as buffers against English expansion. By agreeing to the covenant, and by incorporating the Tuscaroras into their confederacy, the Iroquois created a center of Native American power distinct from, but cooperative with, the British.

Indians elsewhere along the westward-moving frontier faced pressure from settlers on one side and the Iroquois on the other. For example, having earlier abandoned some villages being encroached on by white settlers, the Catawbas of the Carolina piedmont, facing a dramatic decrease in wild game, moved westward and ran into the Iroquois. To counter the Iroquois, whose alliances with most of the northern colonies left them well armed, the Catawbas turned for aid to South Carolina. By ceding land and helping to defend that colony against other Indians, the Catawbas received guns, food, and clothing. Temporarily, their relationship with the English afforded the Catawbas security. But the growing gap in numbers between them and the settlers, and their competition with settlers for resources, made the Indians vulnerable and dependent.

## British Settlement in the South: Georgia

In 1732 Parliament chartered a new colony, Georgia. It was to be a refuge for debtors, whose settlement would buffer South Carolina against attacks from Spanish Florida. Further, the new English colony would export expensive commodities such as wine and silk. To fulfill these plans, Parliament even spent money on the colony, the only North American colony except Nova Scotia in which the British government invested.

James Oglethorpe, who dominated the provincial board of trustees, shaped Georgia's early years. He established the port of entry, Savannah, in 1733. By 1740 nearly 3,000 colonists resided in Georgia. Almost half were non-English, immigrants from Germany, Switzerland, and Scotland, and most had their overseas passage paid by the government. A small number of Jews were among the early settlers. Thus Georgia began as the least English colony.

Idealism and concerns about security led Oglethorpe to ban slavery from Georgia. "If we allow slaves," he wrote to the trustees, "we act against the very principles by which we associated together, which was to relieve the distressed." Oglethorpe thought that slavery degraded blacks, made whites lazy, and presented a terrible risk. Aware of the Stono Rebellion, he worried that reliance on slave labor courted a slave revolt. Parliament thus made Georgia the only colony where slavery was forbidden. Oglethorpe also tried to bar the importation of rum. An abstainer from hard liquor, he feared the effects of encouraging local Indians to drink.

Oglethorpe's well-intentioned plans failed completely. Few debtors arrived because of Parliament's restrictions on their release from prison. Limitations that Oglethorpe had secured on settlers' rights to enlarge or sell their holdings discouraged immigrants, as did the ban on slavery. Georgia exported neither wine nor silk; only rice proved profitable. After a decade of struggle against economic reality, Oglethorpe yielded. In 1750 slavery became legal, and restrictions on landholdings vanished. As a result, Georgia boomed. Its 4,000 residents of 1750 mushroomed to 23,000 by 1770, almost half of them African-American.

Georgia's founding completed British settlement of the Atlantic seaboard. After 1750 westward expansion virtually halted—Anglo-Americans would not cross the Appalachians until the 1770s—but the population continued to grow at the rapid rates that Franklin had predicted.

## Spain's Struggles

While trying to maintain an empire in the face of Native American, French, and British adversaries, Spain spread its language and culture over much of North America, especially the Southwest. To repopulate New Mexico with settlers after the Pueblo Revolt (see Chapter 3), Spain handed out huge land grants and constructed fortifications, primarily for defense against the Apaches. Settlers typically built houses on small lots around the church plaza, farmed separate fields nearby, grazed livestock, and shared community woodlands and pasture. Livestock-raising *ranchos* (ranches) monopolized vast amounts of land along the Rio Grande and blocked the establishment of further towns. On these *ranchos* mounted herders of cattle and sheep (*vaqueros*) created the way of life later adopted by the American cowboy, featuring lariat and roping skills, cattle drives, and roundups.

By 1750 New Mexico contained just 5,200 Spanish and 13,500 Pueblos. Intergrated into New Mexico society, most Pueblos practiced both Catholicism and their traditional religion. Along the frontier, Navajos and Apaches made peace with New Mexico to gain support against raids by Utes from the north and Comanches from the east.

To counter growing French influence among the Comanches and other Native Americans on the southern plains, Spain colonized Texas. In 1716 the Spanish established four missions. The most successful of the missions was San Antonio de Valero, where friars constructed a fortified building known as the Alamo. The Spanish presence in Texas remained light, however; by midcentury only 1,200 Spaniards and 1,300 mission Indians lived there under constant threat of Indian raids.

By 1750 the French and Spanish empires had reached their limits in North America. Spain controlled much of the Southeast and Southwest, and France claimed the Mississippi, Ohio, and Missouri River valleys. Both empires, spread thin, depended heavily on Indian goodwill. In contrast, British North America, compact and aggressively expansionist, was generally antagonistic toward Native Americans.

# Enlightenment and Awakening

Eighteenth-century Anglo-America was probably the world's most literate society. Ninety percent of New England's adult white males and 40 percent of its women could write well enough to sign documents. In other colonies the literacy rate varied from 35 to 50 percent. In contrast, in England it stood at just over 30 percent. Nevertheless, ordinary Americans' reading encompassed only a few books: an almanac, a psalter, and the Bible. They inhabited a world of oral culture, in which ideas and information were passed through the spoken word—in conversations, debates, and sermons.

However, members of the gentry, well-off merchants, and educated ministers lived in a world of print culture. Though costly, books and writing paper opened eighteenth-century European civilization to men and women of these classes who could read. And a rich, exciting world it was. Great advances in natural science seemed to explain the laws of nature, human intelligence appeared poised to triumph over ignorance and prejudice, and life itself would surely become more pleasant. For those with time to read and think, an age of optimism and progress had dawned: the Enlightenment.

## The Enlightenment in America

American intellectuals drew inspiration from Enlightenment ideals, which combined confidence in reason with skepticism toward beliefs not based on science or logic. Enlightenment thought drew on the work of the English physicist Sir Isaac Newton (1642–1727), who explained how gravitation ruled the universe. Newton's work demonstrated the harmony of natural laws and stimulated others to search for rational principles in medicine, law, psychology, and government.

No American more embodied the Enlightenment spirit than Benjamin Franklin (1706–1790). Born in Boston, Franklin migrated to Philadelphia at age seventeen, bringing considerable assets: skill as a printer, ambition, and insatiable curiosity. Within a few years he had gathered a small group of other young men with a zest for learning into a club called the Junto. Its members pledged to debate highbrow questions and to collect useful information for their "mutual improvement." In 1732 Franklin began publishing *Poor Richard's Almanack*, a collection of proverbs that made him famous. By age forty-two he had saved enough money to retire from printing and to devote himself to science and community service.

To Franklin, science and community service were intertwined; true science would make everyone's life more comfortable. For example, his experiments in flying a kite during a thunderstorm proved that lightning was electricity and led to the invention of the lightning rod. In 1743 Franklin organized the American Philosophical Society to encourage "all philosophical experiments that let light into the nature of things, tend to increase the power of man over matter, and multiply the conveniences and pleasures of life." By 1769 the society had blossomed into an intercolonial network of amateur scientists.

Although some plantation owners, among them Thomas Jefferson, championed the Enlightenment, it flourished in the seaboard cities, where the latest ideas from Europe circulated and gentlemen and artisans met in small societies to investigate nature. To these individuals, the Royal Society in London, the foremost learned society in the English-speaking world, represented the ideal. The Enlightenment thus initially strengthened ties between British and colonial elites. Its adherents envisioned progress as gradual and proceeding from the top down. They trusted reason far more than they trusted the common people, whose judgment seemed too easily deranged.

Just as Newton inspired the scientific bent of Enlightenment intellectuals, the English philosopher John Locke's *Essay Concerning Human Understanding* (1690) led many to embrace "reasonable" or "rational" religion. Locke contended that ideas are not inborn but are acquired by investigation of, and reflection on, experience. Enlightenment intellectuals believed that the study of the harmony and order of nature provided the best argument for God, a rational Creator. A handful insisted that where the Bible conflicted with reason, one should follow reason. Those—including Franklin and Jefferson—who took the argument furthest were called Deists. They concluded that God, having created a perfect universe, did not miraculously intervene in its workings but instead left it alone to operate according to natural law.

Most Americans influenced by the Enlightenment described themselves as Christians and attended church. But they feared Christianity's excesses, especially the influence of fanatics who persecuted others in religion's name and of "enthusiasts" who claimed miraculous visions and direct mandates from God. Before 1740 colonial intellectuals associated fanaticism and bigotry with the early Puritans and looked on their own time as an era of progressive reasonableness. But a series of religious revivals known as the Great Awakening would shatter their complacency.

## The Great Awakening

Rationalists viewed the world as orderly and predictable. Many Americans, however, had neither worldly goods nor orderly and predictable lives. A diphtheria epidemic in 1737–1738 that killed every tenth child under sixteen from New Hampshire to Pennsylvania starkly reminded the colonists how fragile life was and turned their thoughts to religion.

A quickening of religious fervor in scattered places in the 1730s became passionate revivalism throughout Anglo-America in the 1740s. This "Great Awakening" cut across lines of class, status, and education as even elites realized the inadequacy of reason alone to move their hearts. Above all, the Great Awakening represented an unleashing of anxiety and longing among ordinary people living in a world of oral culture—anxiety about sin, longing for salvation. And it was the spoken word that brought the answers that they craved. But for all—colonial elites comfortable in the print world and commoners accustomed to the oral world—religion was primarily a matter of emotional commitment.

In contrast to rationalists, who stressed the human potential for betterment, the ministers of the Great Awakening emphasized the corruption of human nature, the fury of divine wrath, and the need for immediate repentance. Although well aware of contemporary philosophy and science,

**Jonathan Edwards (1703–1758)**
*Edwards is best known for his sermon "Sinners in the Hands of an Angry God," which warned the wicked of the terrible punishments awaiting them in the afterlife.*

Congregationalist minister Jonathan Edwards drove home this message with breathtaking clarity. In 1735 during a revival in Northampton, Massachusetts, Edwards preached his great sermon "Sinners in the Hands of an Angry God." "The God that holds you over the pit of Hell, much as one holds a spider or other loathsome insect over the fire, abhors you," Edwards intoned. "His wrath toward you burns like fire; He looks upon you as worthy of nothing else but to be cast into the fire."

Other colonial ministers—Presbyterian William Tennent and Dutch Reformed Theodore Frelinghuysen—had anticipated Edwards's fire-and-brimstone style. Pulling the diverse threads of revival together was the arrival in 1739 of the charismatic English cleric George Whitefield. A man of overpowering presence and a booming voice, Whitefield attracted some crowds exceeding 20,000. On a tour through the colonies Whitefield inspired thousands, mainly young adults, to seek salvation. Within four years of Whitefield's arrival, 20 percent of those under age forty-five had been "born again."

Whitefield's powerful allure awed even his critics. But divisions over the revivals developed in Whitefield's wake and were widened by the tactics of his most extreme followers. For example, after leaving Boston in October 1740, Whitefield invited Gilbert Tennent (William's son) to follow "in order to blow up the divine flame lately kindled there." Denouncing Boston's established clergy as "dead Drones" and lashing out at elites, Tennent built a following among the poor and downtrodden.

Exposing colonial society's divisions, Tennent and other radicals corroded support for revivals among established ministers and officials. Increasingly, lines hardened between the revivalists, the "New Lights," and the rationalist clergymen, or "Old Lights," who dominated the Anglican, Presbyterian, and Congregational churches. In 1740 Gilbert Tennent hinted that most Presbyterian ministers lacked saving grace and were bound for hell, and he urged parishioners to abandon them for the New Lights. By sowing doubts about ministers, Tennent undermined one of the foundations of the social order, for if people could not trust their ministers, whom *could* they trust? Old Light rationalists fired back. In 1742 Charles Chauncy, a Boston Congregationalist, condemned revivals as an epidemic of the "enthusiasm" that Enlightened intellectuals so hated. Chauncy especially blasted enthusiasts who mistook the ravings of their overheated imaginations for direct communications from God.

The Great Awakening thus split American Protestantism. In 1741 Old and New Light Presbyterians formed rival branches that reunited in 1758 when the revivalists emerged victorious. The Anglican church lost many members to New Light Presbyterians and Baptists. Congregationalists also splintered badly; by 1760 New Lights had seceded from one-third of all churches and formed separate parishes.

In Massachusetts and Connecticut, where the Congregational church was established by law, the secession of New Light parishes provoked bitter conflict. Old Lights denied new parishes legal status and tried to force New Lights into paying tithes to their former churches. Many New Lights were expelled from the legislature. In Windham County, Connecticut, an extra story was added to the jail to hold the New Lights arrested for failure to pay tithes.

The Great Awakening peaked in 1742 but made steady gains into the 1770s, and its long-term effects far exceeded its immediate impact. First, the revival started a decline in the influence of older sects such as the Quakers, Anglicans, and Congregationalists. In turn, the number of Presbyterians and Baptists increased after 1740, and that of Methodists rose steadily after 1770. These churches have since dominated American Protestantism. Second, the Great Awakening stimulated the founding of new colleges unscarred by religious wars. The College of New Jersey (Princeton, 1746), King's College (Columbia, 1754), the College of Rhode Island (Brown, 1764), Queen's College (Rutgers, 1766), and Dartmouth (1769) trace their roots to this era. Third, the revival drew many African Americans and Native Americans to Protestantism for the first time. Its oral and communal nature and emphasis on piety, rather than learning, blended aspects of both groups' traditional cultures. The Great Awakening marked the real emergence of black Protestantism as New Lights reached out to slaves, some of whom joined white churches and even preached at revival meetings. Meanwhile, a few New Light preachers became missionaries to Indians still residing in the colonies. Some Christian Indians, such as the Mohegan Samson Occom, became preachers themselves.

The Great Awakening, moreover, gave women added prominence in colonial religion. For several decades ministers had praised women—the majority of church members—as the embodiment of Christian piety. Now some New Light sects, mainly Baptist and Congregationalist, granted women the right to speak and vote in church meetings. Some women, like Anne Hutchinson a century earlier, presided over prayer meetings that included women, men, and sometimes even slaves. Unlike Anne Hutchinson, none was prosecuted. The Great Awakening also fostered religious tolerance by blurring theological differences among New Lights. Indeed, revivalism's emphasis on inner experience, rather than doctrinal fine points, helped to prepare Americans to accept the denominational pluralism that emerged after the Revolution.

Historians disagree about whether the Great Awakening had political effects. Although New Lights flayed the wealthy, they neither advocated a social revolution nor developed a political ideology. Yet by empowering ordinary people to criticize those in authority, the revivals laid the groundwork for political revolutionaries a generation later who would preach that royal government had grown corrupt and unworthy of obedience.

## CONCLUSION

By the 1750s the mainland British colonies had matured. For fifty years their wealth and popululion had risen impressively. The mainland colonies were more populous than Scotland and almost one-third the size of England. White colonists' living standard equaled that of England. Literacy was widespread in the northern mainland colonies, and Anglo-America had more institutions of higher learning than England, Scotland, and Ireland combined. Britain and its colonies were a far more formidable presence in North America than their French and Spanish rivals. But after France's defeat, and Spain's weakening, in the Seven Years' War (1756–1763), latent tensions in colonial relations with Britain quickly became irreconcilable differences.

## CHRONOLOGY

| | |
|---|---|
| 1651–1733 | Parliament creates the navigation system to regulate British imperial commerce. |
| 1660 | Restoration of the Stuart dynasty to the English throne. |
| 1685 | Duke of York becomes King James II of England. |
| 1686–1689 | Dominion of New England. |
| 1688 | Glorious Revolution in England; James II deposed. |
| 1689 | William and Mary ascend to English throne. Protestant Association seizes power in Maryland. Leisler's Rebellion in New York. |
| 1689–1697 | King William's War (in Europe, War of the League of Augsburg). |
| 1690 | John Locke, *Essay Concerning Human Understanding*. |
| 1698 | French begin settlements near the mouth of the Mississippi River. |
| 1701 | Iroquois adopt neutrality policy toward European powers. |
| 1702–1713 | Queen Anne's War (in Europe, War of the Spanish Succession). |
| 1716 | San Antonio founded. |
| 1718 | New Orleans founded. |
| 1732 | Georgia colony chartered. Benjamin Franklin begins publishing *Poor Richard's Almanack*. |
| 1734 | "Walking Purchase" of Delaware Indians in Pennsylvania. |
| 1735 | Jonathan Edwards leads revival in Northhampton, Massachusetts. |
| 1739 | Great Awakening begins. Stono Rebellion in South Carolina. |
| 1739–1744 | Anglo-Spanish War. |
| 1750 | Slavery legalized in Georgia. |

# FOR FURTHER READING

Bernard Bailyn, *The Peopling of British North America: An Introduction* (1986). A brief interpretive overview of the causes and effects of European immigration to British North America.

Bernard Bailyn and Philip D. Morgan, eds., *Strangers Within the Realm: Cultural Margins of the First British Empire* (1991). Essays by leading historians examine the interplay of ethnicity and empire occurring in North America, the Caribbean, Scotland, and Ireland.

Richard L. Bushman, *From Puritan to Yankee: Character and the Social Order in Connecticut, 1690–1765* (1967). The best examination of social and cultural transformation in any eighteenth-century colony.

Rhys Isaac, *The Transformation of Virginia, 1740–1790* (1982). Pulitzer Prize–winning study of class relationships, race relations, and folkways during the Great Awakening and American Revolution.

John J. McCusker and Russell R. Menard, *The Economy of British America, 1607–1789*, rev. ed. (1991). A comprehensive discussion of the colonial economy in light of current scholarship.

James H. Merrell, *The Indians' New World: Catawbas and Their Neighbors from European Contact Through the Era of Removal* (1989). A pathbreaking examination, with broad implications for understanding the Native American past, of the interaction between South Carolina colonists and Catawba Indians.

Gary B. Nash, *The Urban Crucible: The Northern Seaports and the Origins of the American Revolution*, abridged ed. (1986). A study of social, economic, and political change in Boston, New York, and Philadelphia during the eighteenth century.

Timothy Silver, *A New Face on the Countryside: Indians, Colonists, and Slaves in South Atlantic Forests, 1500–1800* (1990). A highly readable discussion of the interactions of humans and their environment in one region.

Peter H. Wood, *Black Majority: Negroes in Colonial South Carolina from 1670 Through the Stono Rebellion* (1974). An engrossing study of slavery, racism, and African-American life in the lower South.

# CHAPTER 5

By 1763 Britain had defeated France, its chief competitor for preeminence in North America, and stood at the height of eighteenth-century imperial power. British rule ran undisputed from the Atlantic seacoast to the Mississippi River and from northernmost Canada to the Florida straits. Ironically, this greatest of British triumphs would turn into one of the greatest of British defeats.

The imperial reorganization that war and conquest made necessary after 1763 radically altered Britain's relationship with its American colonies. Conflict arose between Britain and the colonies when Parliament, searching for ways to pay off the enormous debt accumulated during the war, attempted to tighten control over colonial affairs. The colonists, accustomed to legislating for themselves, widely resisted this effort to centralize decision making in London. American leaders interpreted Britain's clampdown as calculated antagonism, intended to deprive them of both prosperity and relative independence.

# The Road to Revolution, 1744–1776

*(Right)* **Captain and Mrs. John Purves** *(detail),* by *Henry Benbridge, 1775*

**Imperial Warfare**

❧

**Imperial Reorganization**

❧

**Era of Anglo-American Crisis**

❧

**Toward Independence**

Other groups, nonelites, had their own perspectives, shaped as much by social-economic tensions as by constitutional crisis. In port cities crowds of poor and working people clashed with British authority in sometimes violent demonstrations, in concert with or in defiance of elite radicals. In remote "backcountry" areas settlers used the language and ideas of urban radicals to resist domination by large landowners and seaboard elites. Throughout the colonies women brought their own perspective to the unfolding crisis.

Colonial resistance to British policies also reflected democratic stirrings in America and throughout the North Atlantic world. Among the products of this democratic urge were both the American Revolution, which erupted in 1776, and the French Revolution, which soon followed in 1789.

Despite apprehension among colonial politicians, they expressed their opposition peacefully from 1763 to 1775, through legislative resolutions and commercial boycotts. Even after fighting erupted, the colonists agonized for more than a year about whether to sever their political relationship with England—which even native-born Americans sometimes referred to affectionately as "home." Of all the world's colonial peoples, none became rebels more reluctantly than Anglo-Americans did in 1776.

## Imperial Warfare

Imperial rivalries between England, on the one hand, and France and Spain, on the other, triggered two major wars that spilled into North America. The War of the Austrian Succession (1740–1748), known as King George's War to the colonists, saw England and its allies emerge victorious. Within a few years the conflict resumed as the Seven Years' War (1756–1763). England and France fought these wars not on the continent of Europe but on the high seas; in India, where they were competing for influence among local rulers; and in North America. Despite the European roots of these conflicts, few

colonists doubted that their continued prosperity depended on British victories.

The wars produced mixed results. They strengthened the bonds between the British and the Anglo-Americans as they fought side by side. But the conclusion of each war planted the seeds first of misunderstanding, then of suspicion, and finally of hostility between the former compatriots.

### King George's War

King George's War followed the pattern of earlier conflicts in the colonies. Battles generally involved fewer than 600 men, and skirmishes consisted of raids along the New French–British frontier. In attacks on New England frontier towns, the French and Indians killed or captured many civilians. Some captives, particularly women and children, chose to remain with their captors after the conflict ended.

King George's War produced a single major engagement. In 1745 almost 4,000 New Englanders assaulted the French bastion of Louisbourg in northern Nova Scotia, which guarded the entrance to the St. Lawrence River. The raw American recruits battered away at the fortress's 250 cannons and thirty-foot-high stone walls for almost seven weeks. Victory cost the Americans only 167 men and brought them control of the fortress and 1,500 prisoners.

But the triumph proved short-lived. In the treaty signed with the French in 1748, Britain traded Louisbourg back to France in exchange for a British outpost in India. The memory of how the stunning achievement at Louisbourg went for naught would embitter the colonists for a decade.

### A Fragile Peace

Neither Britain nor France emerged from King George's War as the dominant power in North America, and each prepared for another war. Although French forts remained on British soil in New York and Nova Scotia, the Ohio Valley became the tinderbox for conflict.

For more than half a century Indians—Delawares, Shawnees, and others—had sought refuge in the Ohio Valley. Initially welcomed as trade partners and bulwarks against English expansion, these Indians irritated the French by their independence, especially their willingness to trade with Anglo-Americans and to fight against France in King George's War. The French derided these Native Americans as "republicans" for their defiance of all outside authority, whether of the French or English or the Iroquois, some of whom had also moved to the area.

By the mid-eighteenth century these "republican" Indians were seeking to balance the French and British off against each other, while the two powers grew increasingly impatient with the Indians' neutrality. After King George's War Virginia pressured some Iroquois into ceding western lands occupied by the Delawares and agreeing to the construction of a fortified trading post at the junction of the Allegheny and Monongahela rivers—the site of modern Pittsburgh, headwaters of the Ohio River, and key to the Ohio Valley. The "republican" Indians consequently began to fear that the English represented the greater threat.

By 1752 Virginia, Pennsylvania, France, the Iroquois, and the "republican" Indians had all claimed the Ohio Valley. In 1753 France started building a chain of forts in order to regain control of the Virginia and Pennsylvania Indian trade. Virginia retaliated by sending a twenty-one-year-old surveyor, George Washington, to demand that the French abandon their forts. When the French refused, Washington recommended that Virginia occupy the point where the Monongahela and Allegheny rivers joined. In 1754 he led 300 colonial volunteers and 100 British regulars west, only to find the French already constructing Fort Duquesne at the juncture of the rivers. Washington withdrew sixty miles southeast to build a crude defensive post christened Fort Necessity, near which his men killed several French soldiers in an ambush that brought swift retaliation. On July 4, 1754, with one-fourth of his men dead, Washington surrendered Fort Necessity.

In mid-1754 seven northern colonies sent delegates to Albany, New York, to plan their mutual defense in the face of certain French retaliation. By showering the wavering Iroquois with wagonloads of presents, the colonists bought Iroquois neutrality. The delegates endorsed a plan for a colonial confederation, the Albany Plan of Union, drawn up by Pennsylvania's Benjamin Franklin and Massachusetts's Thomas Hutchinson. However, the Albany Plan collapsed because no colonial legislature would surrender control over its powers of taxation, not even to fellow Americans and in the face of grave danger. But the Albany Plan would provide a precedent for future American unity.

## The Seven Years' War in America

Although France and Britain remained at peace in Europe until 1756, Washington's action at Fort Necessity had created a virtual state of war in North America. In response, nearly 8,000 colonists enlisted in 1755 to attack the French strongholds in New York and Nova Scotia. The British government sent General Edward Braddock and 1,000 regulars to take Fort Duquesne that same year.

Scornful of colonial soldiers, Braddock expected his disciplined regulars to make short work of the French. He only dimly perceived the strength and resourcefulness of the forces gathering against him. Washington's failure at Fort Necessity and Braddock's arrogance wiped out hope of any Indian support. On July 9, 1755, about 850 French and Indians ambushed Braddock's 2,200 Britons and Virginians near Fort Duquesne. After three hours of steady fire, the British regulars broke and retreated, leaving Washington's Virginians to cover the withdrawal. Nine hundred regular soldiers and colonists died, including Braddock.

After Braddock's defeat Indian raids convulsed Pennsylvania, Maryland, Virginia, and New Jersey. Two thousand New Englanders managed to seize two French forts that were threatening Nova Scotia. In the aftermath thousands of French-Canadians, or Acadians, were driven from Nova Scotia, and their villages were burned. French Louisiana became the new home for many of these people, who became known there as Cajuns.

**The Seven Years'
War in America**

*After experiencing major defeats early in the war, Anglo-American forces turned the tide
against the French by taking Fort Duquesne and Louisbourg in 1758. After Canada fell in
1760, the fighting shifted to Spain's Caribbean colonies.*

In 1756–1757 New France's daring commanding general Louis Joseph Montcalm maintained the
offensive. Anglo-Americans outnumbered Canadi-
ans twenty to one, but Montcalm benefited from

large numbers of French regulars, Indian support
(including that of the neutral but usually British-
leaning Iroquois), and full-scale mobilization of
the Canadian population. The Anglo-American

cans continued smuggling. In 1766 Britain lowered the duty to 1 pence, less than the usual bribe.

Colonial opponents hesitated to denounce the Sugar Act, which seemingly only amended the Molasses Act. Although nine provincial legislatures protested that the Sugar Act represented an abuse of Parliament's authority to regulate trade, opposition to the law remained fragmented and ineffective. A far more controversial measure would soon overshadow the Sugar Act.

## The Stamp Act

Revenues raised by the Sugar Act did little to ease Britain's financial crisis. Britons groaned under the second-highest tax rates in Europe and looked resentfully at the lightly taxed colonists, who paid an average of 1 shilling per person compared to their 26 shillings per person. Most agreed with Prime Minister George Grenville that fairness demanded a larger colonial contribution.

In March 1765, to force colonists to pay their share of imperial expenses, Parliament passed the Stamp Act. The law obliged Americans to purchase and use specially marked or stamped paper for newspapers, customs documents, wills, contracts, and other public legal documents. Violators faced prosecution in vice-admiralty courts, without juries. Grenville projected yearly revenues of £60,000 to £100,000, which would defray up to 20 percent of North American military expenses. Unlike the Sugar Act, an *external* tax levied on imports, the Stamp Act was an *internal* tax levied directly on property, goods, and services in the colonies. External taxes regulated trade and fell primarily on merchants and ship captains, but internal taxes were designed to raise revenue and had far wider effects. The Stamp Act would tax anyone who made a will, bought or sold property, purchased newspapers, or borrowed money.

William Pitt and others objected to such an internal tax, arguing that the colonies taxed themselves through their elected assemblies. But to Grenville and his supporters, the tax seemed a small price for the benefits of empire, especially since Britons had paid a similar tax since 1695. Grenville

**Stamp Act Protest**
*A Boston crowd burns bundles of the special watermarked paper intended for use as stamps.*

agreed with Stamp Act opponents that Parliament could not tax British subjects unless they enjoyed representation in that body. He contended, however, that the colonists, like many other British adult males who did not vote for members of Parliament, were *virtually* represented. Theoretically, with virtual representation, every member of Parliament considered the welfare of *all* subjects, not just his constituents, in deciding issues. No Briton was represented by any particular member of the House of Commons; but all imperial subjects, including Americans, could depend on each member of Parliament to protect their well-being.

Grenville and his supporters also held that the colonial assemblies had no powers other than those Parliament allowed them. This view clashed directly with the stance of the many colonists who had argued for decades that their assemblies exercised legislative power equivalent to that of Britain's House of Commons.

## The Colonial Perspective

The Stamp Act made many colonists believe that they had to confront parliamentary taxation head-on or surrender any claim to meaningful self-government. However much they admired Parliament, few Americans thought that it represented them. While virtual representation might apply to England and Scotland, they argued, it certainly did not extend across the Atlantic. In the American view, unless a lawmaker shared his constituents' interests, he would have no personal stake in opposing bills contrary to their welfare. Thus the colonists favored *actual*, rather than virtual, representation.

To the colonists, the Stamp Act demonstrated both Parliament's indifference to their interests and the shallowness of virtual representation. Colonial agents in London had lobbied against the law, and colonial assemblies had sent petitions warning against its passage, but to no avail. Parliament "must have thought us Americans all a parcel of Apes and very tame Apes too," concluded Christopher Gadsden of South Carolina, "or they would never have ventured on such a hateful, baneful experiment." The colonists did still concede, however, that Parliament possessed *limited* powers of legislation, and they accepted the parliamentary regulation of imperial trade.

Anglo-Americans considered the essential obligation of British allegiance to be loyalty to the Crown and their one unequivocal duty to be defending the empire in wartime. The colonists insisted that they enjoyed a substantial measure of self-government similar to that of the Protestants in Ireland, whose Parliament alone could tax its people but could not interfere with laws, such as the Navigation Acts, passed by the British Parliament. In a speech opposing the Sugar Act, James Otis had expressed Americans' basic argument: "that by [the British] Constitution, every man in the dominions is a free man; that no parts of His Majesty's dominions can be taxed without consent; that every part has a right to be represented in the supreme or some subordinate legislature." In essence, the colonists saw the empire as a loose federation (union) in which their legislatures possessed considerable autonomy.

## Resisting the Stamp Act

In 1765 a political storm generated by the Stamp Act rumbled through all the colonies. The tempest caught up nearly every member of colonial society, but before it ended, elite leaders had assumed direction of the resistance movement.

In late May Patrick Henry, a twenty-nine-year-old Virginia lawyer with a gift for fiery oratory, expressed the rising spirit of resistance. He persuaded Virginia's House of Burgesses to adopt strong resolutions denying Parliament's power to tax the colonies. Garbled accounts of his resolutions and speeches—he probably never said, "Give me liberty or give me death"—electrified other colonists. By year's end, eight other colonial legislatures had rejected parliamentary taxation.

Meanwhile, active resistance took shape. In Boston by late summer, middle-class artisans and businessmen had created the Loyal Nine to fight the Stamp Act. They recognized that the stamp distributors, who alone could sell the specially watermarked paper, represented the law's weak link. If public pressure could force them to resign before the tax went into effect on November 1, the Stamp Act would not work. The Loyal Nine would propel Boston to the forefront of resistance.

Boston's preeminence in opposing Parliament was no accident. Bostonians lived primarily by trade and distilling, and in 1765 they were not living well, thanks to the Sugar Act. The heavy tax on molasses burdened rum producers, and the act's trade restrictions dried up the wine-import business and interfered with the direct export of New England products to profitable overseas markets. To add to the general distress, the city was still recovering from a disastrous fire in 1760 that had left every tenth family homeless.

This widespread economic distress produced an explosive situation. There was good reason to blame British policy for hard times. Furthermore, Bostonians seemed to enjoy mayhem for its own sake. The high point of each year was Guy Fawkes Day, November 5, when thousands commemorated the failure of a supposed Catholic plot in 1605 to blow up Parliament and to kill King James I. Crowds from the North End and the South End of Boston burned gigantic effigies of the pope as well as of local political leaders and generally poked fun at the "better sorts." High spirits usually overflowed into violent confrontations as crowds battled each other with fists, stones, and barrel staves. In 1764 after Guy Fawkes Day brawlers accidentally killed a small child, a truce united the rival mobs under a South End shoemaker named Ebenezer MacIntosh, the leader of 2,000 young toughs. The Loyal Nine enlisted MacIntosh's frustrated street fighters against Boston's stamp distributor, Andrew Oliver.

The morning of August 14, 1765, found a likeness of Oliver swinging from a tree. Oliver did not take the hint to resign, so at dusk MacIntosh and several hundred followers demolished a new building of his at the dock. The mob then surged toward Oliver's house and vandalized it. Oliver announced his resignation the following morning.

Groups similar to the Loyal Nine, calling themselves the Sons of Liberty, formed throughout the colonies. Several more houses were wrecked, and by November 1 the colonies had only two stamp distributors, who soon resigned. Within three months a movement without central leadership killed Grenville's tax.

The violence was spontaneous and directed against property, not persons. But some of the rampages and assaults raised warning flags, and leaders of the Sons of Liberty recognized that violence could alienate elite opponents of the tax. Thus they began to direct public demonstrations with firm discipline, maneuvering hundreds of protesters like a small army and forbidding their followers to carry weapons. Recognizing the value of martyrs, they resolved that the only lives lost over the issue of British taxation would come from their own ranks.

In October 1765 representatives from nine colonies met in New York City in the Stamp Act Congress. There the colonies agreed on, and boldly articulated, the principle that Parliament had no authority to levy taxes outside Britain or to deny any person a jury trial. The united front of the Stamp Act Congress was a far cry from the only other intercolonial meeting, the Albany Congress of 1754. But while emboldening and unifying the colonies, declarations of principle such as the Stamp Act Congress resolutions seemed futile to many colonists, in view of Parliament's earlier refusal to consider their objections to the stamp duties.

By late 1765 most stamp distributors had resigned or fled, and, without the watermarked paper required by law, most customs officials and court officers refused to perform their duties. In response, legislators compelled them to resume operations by threatening to withhold their pay. At the same time, merchants obtained sailing clearances by insisting that they would sue if their cargoes spoiled while delayed in port. By late December the colonial courts and harbors were again functioning.

In these ways the colonial upper class assumed control of the public outcry against the Stamp Act. Respectable gentlemen kept an explosive situation under control by taking over leadership of local Sons of Liberty, by coordinating protest through the Stamp Act Congress, and by having colonial legislatures resume normal business. But the Stamp Act remained in effect. To force its repeal, New York's merchants agreed on October 31, 1765, to boycott all British goods. Others followed. Because the colonies purchased 40 percent of England's manufactures, this nonimportation strategy triggered panic within England's business community. Its members descended on Parliament to warn that continuing the Stamp Act would result in bankruptcies, massive unemployment, and political unrest.

Meanwhile, the Marquis of Rockingham had succeeded George Grenville as prime minister. Rockingham hesitated to advocate repeal, but parliamentary support for repeal gradually grew—the result of practicality, not principle. In March 1766 Parliament revoked the Stamp Act. Simultaneously, however, Parliament passed the Declaratory Act, affirming parliamentary power to legislate for the colonies "in all cases whatsoever."

Because Americans interpreted the Declaratory Act as merely a face-saving measure on Parliament's part, they ignored it. In truth, however, the House of Commons intended that the colonists take the Declaratory Act literally to mean that they were not exempt from *any* parliamentary statute, including a tax law. The Stamp Act crisis thus ended in a fundamental disagreement between Britain and America over the colonists' political rights.

Although philosophical differences between Britain and America remained unresolved, most colonists put the events of 1765 behind them. Still loyal to "Old England," Anglo-Americans concluded that their resistance to the law had slapped Britain's leaders back to their senses. Yet the crisis led many to ponder British policies and actions more deeply than ever.

## Ideology, Religion, and Resistance

The Stamp Act crisis had caused some Anglo-Americans to discern for the first time a sinister quality in the imperial relationship with Britain. To understand these perceptions, some educated colonists turned to philosophers, historians, and political writers. Many more looked to religion.

The colonists were familiar with John Locke and other Enlightenment political thinkers. Locke argued that in a state of nature, people enjoyed the "natural rights" of life, liberty, and property. To form governments to protect these rights, people entered into a "social contract." A government that encroached on natural rights broke its contract with the people. In such cases the people could resist their government. To many colonial leaders, Locke's concept of natural rights justified opposition to Parliament's arbitrary legislation.

The political writers read most widely in the colonies included a group known as oppositionists. According to John Trenchard and Thomas Gordon, among others, Parliament—the freely elected representatives of the people—formed the foundation of England's unique political liberties and protected them against the inherent corruption and tyranny of executive power. But since 1720, the opposition-

ists argued, prime ministers had exploited the treasury to provide pensions, contracts, and profitable offices to politicians and had bought elections by bribing voters. Most members of Parliament, they held, no longer represented the true interest of their constituents; instead, they had sold their souls for financial gain and joined a "conspiracy against liberty." Referring to themselves as the "country party," these oppositionists feared that a power-hungry "court party" of nonelected officials close to the king was using a corrupt Parliament to gain absolute power.

During the 1760s and 1770s English radicals, notably Joseph Priestly and James Burgh, drew from both Enlightenment and oppositionist authors to fashion a critique of English government and a new way of thinking about politics. At the heart of all political relationships, they argued, raged a struggle between the aggressive extension of artificial *power*, represented by corrupt governments, and the natural *liberty* of the people. To protect their liberty, free people had to avoid corruption in their own lives and resist the encroachment of tyranny. Above all, they had to remain alert for "conspiracies" against liberty.

Influenced by such ideas, a number of colonists detected a conspiracy behind British policy during the Stamp Act crisis. Joseph Warren of Massachusetts wrote that the act "induced some to imagine that [Prime Minister Grenville intended] by this to force the colonies into a rebellion, and from thence to take occasion to treat them with severity, and, by military power, to reduce them to servitude." Over the next decade a thundershower of pamphlets denounced British efforts to "enslave" the colonies through taxation and the imposition of officials, judges, and a standing army directed from London.

Many colonists also followed the lead of Massachusetts assemblyman Samuel Adams, who expressed hope that America would become a "Christian Sparta." By linking religion and ancient history, Adams combined two potent rhetorical appeals. Virtually every colonial American was steeped in Protestantism, and those whose education had gone beyond the basics had imbibed Greek and Latin learning as well as seventeenth-century English literature. These traditions, Americans believed, confirmed the legitimacy of their cause.

Thomas Jefferson of Virginia was typical of educated men of the day in revering the classical Greeks and Romans for their virtuous devotion to liberty. The pamphlets and speeches of gentlemen such as Jefferson, John Dickinson, and Patrick Henry resounded with quotations from the ancients that served as constant reminders of the righteous dignity of their cause. But appeals to ordinary Americans drew on deeper wellsprings of belief, notably the religious fervor that the Great Awakening had stirred.

Beginning with the Stamp Act crisis, New England's clergymen summoned their flocks to stand up for God and liberty. Exhorted one minister, "We are bound in conscience to stand fast in the liberty with which Christ has made us free." (Only Anglican ministers, whose church the king headed, tried to stay neutral or opposed the protest.) Clergymen who exalted the cause of liberty exerted an enormous influence on popular opinion. Far more Americans heard or read sermons than had access to newspapers or pamphlets. A popular theme was how God sent the people woes only to strengthen and sustain them until victory. Even Virginia gentlemen not known for their piety felt moved by such messages and ordered their families to comply with the days of "fasting and public humiliation" proclaimed by the clerical leaders. Moreover, protest leaders' calls to boycott British luxuries meshed neatly with ministers' traditional warnings against frivolity and wastefulness. Few Americans could ignore the unceasing public reminders that solidarity against British tyranny and "corruption" meant rejecting sin and obeying God.

The ebbing of the Stamp Act crisis removed the urgency from such extreme views. But the alarm raised by British actions was not easily quieted. After a gap of two years it would become clear that British and American views of the colonies' place in the empire remained far apart.

# Era of Anglo-American Crisis

From 1767 to 1773 Parliament pursued a confrontational policy that eroded Americans' trust of Britain. The resulting climate of fear and alienation left most colonists convinced that the Stamp Act had been not an isolated mistake but part of a deliberate design to undermine colonial self-government. Growing numbers in Britain likewise questioned economically costly policies and actions that seemed to threaten Britons as well as colonists.

## *The Quartering Act*

In August 1766 George III dismissed the Rockingham government and summoned William Pitt to form a cabinet. An opponent of taxing the colonies, Pitt had the potential to repair the Stamp Act's damage; the colonists respected him highly. However, Pitt's health collapsed in March 1767, and Charles Townshend, the chancellor of the exchequer (treasurer), became the effective leader.

Just as Townshend took office, a conflict arose with the New York legislature over the Quartering Act of 1765, which ordered colonial legislatures to pay for certain goods used by British soldiers stationed within their borders—candles, windowpanes, mattress straw, and a small liquor ration. The act applied only to troops in settled areas, not on the frontier. It did not force citizens to accept soldiers in private homes or require legislatures to erect barracks. The law aroused resentment, however, because it constituted an *indirect* tax. That is, although it did not empower royal officials to collect money directly from the colonists, it obligated assemblies to raise revenue by whatever means they considered appropriate. The act fell lightly on the colonies except New York, where more soldiers were stationed than in any other province. New York refused to grant the supplies.

New York's resistance unleashed a torrent of anti-American feeling in Parliament, still bitter after revoking the Stamp Act. Townshend responded by drafting the New York Suspending Act, which threatened to nullify all laws passed by the colony after October 1, 1767, if it refused to vote the supplies. By the time George III signed the measure, New York had already appropriated the funds. Nonetheless, the conflict over the Quartering Act revealed the depth of anticolonial sentiment in the House of Commons. It demonstrated that British leaders would not hesitate to defend Parliament's sovereignty through the most drastic of all steps: interfering with colonial self-government.

## The Townshend Duties

This new wave of British resentment toward the colonies coincided with an outpouring of frustration over the government's failure to cut taxes from wartime levels. Discontent seethed among the landed gentry, whose members took advantage of their domination of the House of Commons to slash their own taxes in 1767. This move cost the government £500,000 and prompted Townshend to tax imports entering America and to propose laws to increase colonial customs revenues.

Townshend sought to tax the colonists by exploiting a loophole in their arguments against the Stamp Tax. Americans had emphasized their opposition to *internal* taxes but had said nothing about *external* taxes—Parliament's right to tax imports as they entered the colonies. Townshend interpreted this silence as evidence that the colonists accepted Britain's right to impose external taxes. But a now much wiser George Grenville predicted, "They will laugh at you for your distinctions about regulations of trade." Brushing aside such warnings, Parliament passed Townshend's Revenue Act of 1767 (popularly called the Townshend duties) in the summer. The new law taxed glass, paint, lead, paper, and tea imported into the colonies.

On the surface Townshend's case for external taxation was convincing, as the colonists had long accepted parliamentary regulation of trade and had in principle acknowledged taxation as a form of regulation. Americans had protested the Sugar Act not because it imposed taxes but because it set impractical regulations for conducting trade and violated traditional guarantees of a fair trial. But the Townshend duties differed significantly from what Americans considered a legitimate way of regulating trade through taxation. To the colonists, charging a duty was a lawful way for British authorities to control trade only if it excluded foreign goods by making them prohibitively expensive. The Revenue Act of 1767, however, set moderate rates that did not price goods out of the colonial market; clearly, its purpose was to collect money for the treasury. Thus from the colonial standpoint, Townshend's duties were taxes just like the Stamp Act duties.

Townshend had an ulterior motive for establishing an American source of revenue. Traditionally, colonial legislatures set colonial royal governors' salaries and often refused to pay them until the governors signed bills that they opposed. Townshend hoped that the Revenue Act would establish a fund to pay governors' and other royal officials' salaries, freeing them from the assemblies' control. In effect, he would strip the assemblies of their most potent weapon, the power of the purse, and tip the balance of power away from elected representatives and toward appointed royal officials.

The Revenue Act never yielded the income that Townshend had anticipated. Of all the items taxed, only tea produced any significant revenue—£20,000 of the £37,000 expected. And because the measure would serve its purpose only if the colonists could afford British tea, Townshend eliminated £60,000 in import fees paid on East Indian tea entering Britain before transshipment to America. On balance, the Revenue Act *worsened* the British treasury's deficit by £23,000. By 1767 Britain's financial difficulties were more an excuse for political demands to tax the colonies than a driving force. From Parliament's standpoint, the conflict with America was becoming a test of national will over the *principle* of taxation.

## The Colonists' Reaction

Americans learned of the Revenue Act shortly before it went into operation, and they hesitated over their response. The strong-arm tactics that had sent stamp distributors into flight would not work against the Townshend duties, which the Royal Navy could easily collect offshore.

Resistance to the act remained weak until December 1767, when John Dickinson, a Delaware planter and Philadelphia lawyer, published *Letters from a Farmer in Pennsylvania*. These twelve essays, which appeared in nearly every colonial newspaper, emphasized that Parliament had no right to tax trade for the simple purpose of raising revenue. No tax designed to produce revenue could be considered constitutional unless a people's elected representatives voted for it. Dickinson's writings convinced Americans that their arguments against the Stamp Act also applied to the Revenue Act.

In early 1768 the Massachusetts assembly asked Samuel Adams to draft a "circular letter" to other legislatures. Possessing a flair for the push and shove of local politics, the Harvard-educated Adams had helped organize the Sons of Liberty in Boston. Adams's circular letter denounced taxation without representation and the threat to self-governance posed by Parliament's making governors and royal officials independent of the legislatures. Nevertheless, the document acknowledged Parliament as the "supreme legislative Power over the whole Empire" and advocated no illegal activities.

Virginia's assembly warmly approved Adams's eloquent measure and sent out a more strongly worded letter of its own, urging all the colonies to oppose imperial policies that would "have an immediate tendency to enslave them." But most colonial legislatures reacted indifferently to these letters. In fact, resistance might have disintegrated had not the British government overreacted to the circular letters.

Indeed, parliamentary leaders saw even the mild Massachusetts letter as "little better than an incentive to Rebellion." Disorganized because of Townshend's sudden death in 1767, the king's Privy Council (advisers) directed Lord Hillsborough, the first appointee to the new post of secretary of state for the colonies, to express the government's displeasure. Hillsborough ordered the Massachusetts

**Samuel Adams (1722–1803)**
*A central player in the drive for American liberty, Adams wrote in 1774 that "I wish for a permanent union with the mother country, but only in terms of liberty and truth. No advantage that can accrue to America from such a union, can compensate for the loss of liberty."*

assembly to disown its letter, forbade all overseas assemblies to endorse it, and commanded royal governors to dissolve any legislature that violated his instructions.

The tactic backfired. Protesting Hillsborough's bullying, many legislatures previously indifferent to the Massachusetts letter adopted it enthusiastically. The Massachusetts House of Representatives voted 92–17 not to recall its letter. Royal governors responded by dismissing legislatures in Massachusetts and elsewhere, playing into the hands of Samuel

Adams and others who wished to ignite widespread opposition to the Townshend duties.

Increasingly outraged, the colonists still needed an effective means of pressuring Parliament for repeal. Nonimportation seemed especially promising because it offered an alternative to violence and would distress Britain's economy. Thus in August 1768 Boston's merchants adopted a nonimportation agreement, and the tactic spread southward. "Save your money, and you save your country!" trumpeted the Sons of Liberty, which reorganized after two years of inactivity. However, not all colonists supported nonimportation. Many merchants whose livelihood depended on imported goods waited until early 1769 to join the boycott. Far from complete, it probably kept out no more than 40 percent of British imports.

## Wilkes and Liberty

British merchants and artisans, hit hard by the exclusion of 40 percent of imports, demanded repeal of the Townshend duties. Their protests became part of a larger movement in the 1760s against the policies of George III and a Parliament dominated by wealthy landowners. John Wilkes, a fiery London editor whose newspaper regularly and irreverently denounced the king, became both leader and focal point of the protest. A member of Parliament, Wilkes was tried for seditious libel and acquitted, to great popular acclaim. George III's government then shut down his newspaper and persuaded members of the House of Commons to deny Wilkes his seat. After publishing another slashing attack on the king, Wilkes fled to Paris.

In 1768 Wilkes returned to England, defying an arrest warrant, and again ran for Parliament. By then government policies, including the Townshend Acts, had unleashed a flood of protests against the "obnoxious" government ministers, a flood that swept along manufacturers and merchants as well as weavers and other workers. They all rallied around the cry "Wilkes and Liberty."

When the newly elected Wilkes was once again arrested 20,000 to 40,000 angry "Wilkesites" massed on St. George's Fields, outside the prison where he was being held. Soldiers and police responded to rock-throwing demonstrators by opening fire on them, killing eleven protesters. The "massacre of St. George's Fields" furnished martyrs to the protesters, and Wilkes received enormous outpourings of public support from the North American colonies as well as from Britain. Twice more elected from his prison cell, and twice more denied his seat, Wilkes maintained a regular correspondence with Boston's Sons of Liberty. Bostonians celebrated his release from prison in April 1770 with a massive celebration honoring this "illustrious martyr to liberty."

The Wilkes furor sharpened the political ideas of government opponents on both sides of the Atlantic. English voters sent petitions to Parliament proclaiming that its refusal to seat Wilkes was an affront to the electorate's will and calling "virtual representation" a sham. To guard against further arbitrary government actions, some formed the Society of the Supporters of the Bill of Rights "to defend and maintain the legal, constitutional liberty of the subject[s of the King]." Emboldened by the Wilkes and Liberty movement, William Pitt, Edmund Burke, and others forcefully denounced the government's colonial policies. The colonists themselves concluded that Parliament and the government represented a small but powerful minority whose authority they could legitimately question.

## Women and Colonial Resistance

Nonimportation convinced the British—and the colonists—that all Americans were determined to sustain resistance, and it demonstrated that the American cause rested on foundations of impeccable morality and sensible moderation. It also provided a unique opportunity for women to join the protest.

Calling themselves Daughters of Liberty, upper-class female patriots assumed a highly visible role during the Townshend crisis. Convinced that colonial women could exert a persuasive moral influence on public opinion, American leaders encouraged them to protest the Revenue Act's tax on tea. Accordingly, in early 1770 more than 300 "mistresses of families" in Boston denounced the consumption of the beverage. In some ways nonconsumption was more effective than nonimportation, for the colonists' refusal to consume imports would chill merchants' economic incentive to import British goods.

Nonconsumption agreements therefore became popular and were extended to include other goods, mainly clothes. Again, women played a vital role because the boycott would fail unless the colonists replaced British imports with apparel of their own making. Responding to leaders' pleas for an expansion of domestic cloth production, women of all social ranks organized spinning bees. These attracted intense publicity as evidence of American determination to fight parliamentary taxation. The colonial cause, noted a New York woman, had enlisted "a fighting army of amazons . . . armed with spinning wheels." Spinning bees not only helped to undermine the masculine prejudice that women had no place in public life but also endowed spinning and weaving, previously considered routine tasks, with political virtue.

Colonial leaders were waging a battle to convince British public opinion that their society would stand firm in opposing unconstitutional taxes. Only if the Britons believed that Americans—male and female alike—were truly united would they accept repeal of the Townshend duties. Female participation in symbolic protests forced the British public to appreciate the depth of colonial commitment.

## Customs Racketeering

Townshend also sought to increase revenues by extending British surveillance of colonial trade. In 1767 he induced Parliament to create the American Board of Customs Commissioners to strictly enforce the Navigation Acts. At the same time, Parliament increased the number of port officials, funded a colonial coast guard to catch smugglers, and provided money for secret informers. Townshend's hope was that the new system would end widespread

bribery of customs officials by colonial shippers and merchants by bringing honesty, efficiency, and greater revenue to overseas customs operations. Instead the law quickly drew protests because of the ways it was enforced and because it reversed traditional legal process by assuming the accused to be guilty until proved otherwise.

The rapid expansion of the customs service in 1767 coincided with new provisions that awarded an informer one-third of the value of all goods and ships appropriated through a conviction of smuggling. The fact that fines could be tripled under certain circumstances provided an even greater incentive to seize illegal cargoes. Smuggling cases were heard in vice-admiralty courts, where the probability of conviction was extremely high. The prospect of accumulating a small fortune proved too tempting to most commissioners.

Revenue agents commonly perverted the law by filing charges for technical violations of the Sugar Act even when no evidence existed of intent to conduct illegal trade. They most often exploited the provision that declared any cargo illegal unless it had been loaded or unloaded with a customs officer's written authorization. Many vessels transporting lumber or tobacco found it impossible to comply because they typically picked up items piecemeal at a succession of small wharves far from a customhouse. Customs officials created other opportunities for seizures by bending the rules for a time and then suddenly enforcing the law.

Customs commissioners also fanned anger by invading sailors' traditional rights. Long-standing maritime custom allowed crews to supplement their incomes by making small sales between ports. Anything stored in a sailor's chest was considered private property, exempt from the Navigation Acts. But after 1767 revenue agents treated such belongings as cargo, thus establishing an excuse to seize the entire ship. Under this policy, crewmen saw arrogant inspectors break open their trunks and then lost trading stock worth several months' wages. Sailors waited for chances to get even. Not surprisingly, after 1767 inspectors increasingly fell victim to riots dominated by vengeful sailors.

In these ways the commissioners embarked on a program of "customs racketeering" that constituted legalized piracy. This program fed an upsurge in popular violence. Above all, customs commissioners' use of informers provoked retaliation. The *Pennsylvania Journal* in 1769 scorned these agents as "dogs of prey, thirsting after the fortunes of worthy and wealthy men." Informers aroused hatred in those whom they betrayed. Nearly all instances of tarring and feathering in these years represented private revenge against informers, not political reprisals.

Nowhere were customs agents and informers more detested than in Boston, where citizens retaliated in June 1768. When customs agents seized colonial merchant John Hancock's sloop *Liberty* on a technicality, a crowd tried to prevent the towing of Hancock's ship and then began assaulting customs officials. Swelling to several hundred, the mob drove all revenue inspectors from the city.

The wealthy Hancock, a leading opponent of British taxation, had become a chief target of the customs commissioners. Despite a lack of evidence that he was a smuggler, customs commissioners in 1768 used a perjured statement from a customs inspector to seize the *Liberty* for allegedly avoiding £700 in duties on wine worth £3,000. By then requesting the payment of triple charges, they made Hancock liable for a total fine of £9,000, thirteen times greater than the taxes supposedly evaded. During the prosecution that followed, British agents perjured themselves and the judge denied Hancock his right to a fair trial.

Hancock's case made Americans rethink their acceptance of the principle that Parliament had limited authority to pass laws for them. By 1770 it was clear that measures such as the Sugar Act and the act creating the American Board of Customs Commissioners endangered property rights and civil liberties as much as taxes. Realizing this fact, many Americans began to reject any legislation without representation. By 1774 a consensus had emerged that Parliament had no lawmaking authority over the colonies except the right to regulate imperial commerce.

By 1770 the British government, aware of its customs officers' excesses, had begun reforming the service. Smuggling charges against Hancock were dropped. Although the abuses ended, the damage had been done. Townshend's American Board of Customs Commissioners reinforced the colonists' growing suspicion of British motives and their alienation from England.

## Repeal of the Townshend Duties

Meanwhile, in January 1770 Lord North had become prime minister. An able administrator, North favored eliminating most of the Townshend duties to end the commercial boycott, but he insisted on retaining the tax on tea to underscore British authority. In April 1770 Parliament again yielded to colonial pressure and repealed most of the Townshend duties.

This partial repeal presented a dilemma to American politicians. They considered it intolerable that taxes remained on tea, the most profitable item for the royal treasury. In July 1770 the general nonimportation movement collapsed, but the Sons of Liberty resisted external taxation by voluntary agreements not to drink British tea. Revenue from the tea tax consequently fell to only one-sixth the anticipated amount, far too low to pay royal governors' salaries.

Yet American leaders remained dissatisfied. The tea duty was a galling reminder that Parliament still claimed broad authority. The tea tax became a festering sore that slowly poisoned relations between Britain and the colonies. The Townshend crisis had begun the gradual dissolution of American loyalty to Britain.

## The Boston Massacre

Nowhere was the fraying of loyalties more obvious than in Boston. In response to Bostonians' violence, 1,700 British troops landed in Boston in October 1768. In 1770 this military occupation provoked a fresh round of violence as armed sentries and resentful civilians traded insults. The mainly Protestant townspeople resented the authority of the soldiers, especially blacks and Irish Catholics, and bristled at job competition from enlisted men, most of whom could seek work after morning muster.

It was a situation tailor-made for Samuel Adams, a genius in shaping public opinion. By imposing nearly 2,000 redcoats on a crowded, economically distressed, and violence-prone city of 20,000 bullheaded Yankees, the British government had given Adams grist for his propaganda mill. In October 1768 he began publishing the *Journal of the Times*, a magazine claiming to offer factual accounts of abuses committed by the army and customs services. Adams's purpose was to kindle outrage, and thus resistance, toward British authority. The *Journal* seldom lacked stories of citizens assaulted, insulted, or simply annoyed, and Adams exaggerated every incident. With each issue, Boston's hatred of the redcoats grew.

Bostonians endured their first winter as a garrison town without undue trouble and saw half the British troops sail home in mid-1769. But relations between civilians and the remaining soldiers deteriorated. Resentment of British authority boiled over on February 22, 1770, when a customs informer fired bird shot at several children throwing rocks at his house and killed an eleven-year-old boy. Adams organized a burial procession to maximize the horror at a child's death, relying on grief to unite the community in opposition to British policies. "My Eyes never beheld such a funeral," wrote his cousin John Adams. "A vast Number of Boys walked before the Coffin, a vast Number of Women and Men after it. . . . This Shows there are many more Lives to spend if wanted in the Service of their country."

Although the army had played no part in the shooting, it became a target for Bostonians' rage. A week after the funeral, tension erupted at the guardpost protecting the customs office. When an officer tried to disperse a crowd led by Crispus Attucks, a seaman of African and Native American ancestry,

**The Boston Massacre, 1770,**
*Engraving by Paul Revere Shortly after this incident, one Bostonian observed that "unless there is some great alteration in the state of things, the era of the independence of the colonies is much nearer than I once thought it, or now wish it."*

the mob responded with a barrage of flying objects. One soldier, knocked down by a block of ice, fired, and the others opened fire. Their volley killed five people, including Attucks.

Samuel Adams orchestrated a martyrs' funeral for the victims of this so-called Boston Massacre, named to recall the "St. George's Field Massacre" of Wilkes's supporters in London, and used the occasion to solidify American opposition to British authority. To defuse the explosive situation, the product of burning hatreds that sprang from an intolerable situation, royal authorities isolated the British troops on a fortified harbor island and promised a trial for the soldiers who had fired. Patriot leader John Adams defended the men to demonstrate American commitment to impartial justice. But the light punishments given these soldiers, who had shot unarmed civilians, forced the colonists to confront the stark possibility that Britain intended to coerce and suppress them through naked force.

## The Committees of Correspondence

The colonies enjoyed a brief truce in their relations with Britain, but it ended in June 1772 when the customs schooner *Gaspee* ran aground near Providence, Rhode Island. A revenue cutter that engaged in customs racketeering by plundering cargoes for technical violations of the Sugar Act, the *Gaspee* also had an odious reputation among Rhode Islanders for its high-handed captain and crew of petty thieves. Stuck in the mud, the *Gaspee* presented an irresistible target for local inhabitants. That night more than 100 men took revenge by burning it to the waterline.

The British government dispatched a commission with instructions to send all suspects to England for trial. Although the investigators failed to identify any raiders, colonists took alarm at the government's willingness to dispense with another essential civil liberty, an accused citizen's right to be tried by a local jury.

Meanwhile, in fall 1772 Lord North prepared to implement Townshend's goal of paying royal

governors from customs revenue, freeing them from the control of the colonial assemblies. With representative government deeply threatened, Samuel Adams persuaded Boston's town meeting to request that every Massachusetts community appoint people to exchange information and to coordinate measures to defend colonial rights. Within a year most Massachusetts communities had established "committees of correspondence," and the idea spread throughout New England.

The committees of correspondence, the colonists' first attempt to maintain close political cooperation over a wide area, allowed Samuel Adams to conduct a campaign of political education for all New England. He sent messages for each local committee to read at its town meeting, which debated the issues and adopted formal resolutions. The system made tens of thousands of citizens consider evidence that their rights were endangered and committed them to take a stand. Adams's most successful venture in whipping up public alarm came in June 1773 when he published letters from Massachusetts governor Thomas Hutchinson, obtained by Benjamin Franklin, advocating "an abridgement of what are called English liberties" and "a great restraint of natural liberty." The Hutchinson correspondence confirmed Americans' suspicions that a plot was afoot to destroy their basic freedoms.

Patrick Henry, Thomas Jefferson, and Richard Henry Lee had proposed in March 1773 that Virginia establish committees of correspondence, and within a year every province but Pennsylvania had such committees. By early 1774 a communications web linked colonial leaders.

In contrast to the brief, intense Stamp Act crisis, the dissatisfaction spawned by the Townshend duties persisted and gradually poisoned relations between Britain and America. In 1765 strong ties of loyalty and affection had disguised the depth of the division over taxation. By 1773, however, colonial allegiance was becoming conditional.

## Frontier Tensions

On the Appalachian frontier tensions among natives, recent settlers, and colonial authorities underlined a continuing sense of emergency. Rapid population growth had spurred the migration of people and capital to the frontier, where colonists sought access to Indian lands. Land pressures and the lack of adequate revenue from the colonies left the British government helpless to enforce the Proclamation of 1763. The government could neither maintain garrisons at many of its forts, enforce laws and treaties, nor provide gifts to its native allies. Rising violence by colonists against Indians often went unpunished.

Under such pressures, Britain and the Iroquois, in the Treaty of Fort Stanwix (1768), turned land along the Ohio River that was occupied by the Shawnees, Delawares, and Cherokees over to the Virginia and Pennsylvania governments. The Shawnees assumed leadership of the "republican" Indians, who, with the Cherokees, were convinced that appeasement would not stop colonial expansion.

The treaty resolved Virginia's and Pennsylvania's overlapping land claims in Ohio at the Indians' expense. Other frontier disputes led to conflict among the colonists themselves. Settlers in western Massachusetts in the early 1760s, for example, found their titles challenged by New Yorkers. In 1766, threatened with eviction, the New Englanders staged an armed uprising. And in 1769 New Hampshire settlers calling themselves the Green Mountain Boys began guerrilla warfare against New York landlords. The independent government that they formed ultimately became that of Vermont.

Expansion also provoked conflict between frontier settlers and their own colonial governments. In North Carolina westerners, underrepresented in the assembly, found themselves exploited by dishonest officeholders appointed by eastern politicians. Twenty-five hundred armed westerners, known as Regulators, clashed with 1,300 North Carolina militia on May 16, 1771, at the battle of Alamance Creek. Although the Regulator uprising disintegrated, it crippled the colony's subsequent ability to resist British authority. A Regulator movement also arose in South Carolina, in this case to counter the government's unwillingness to prosecute bandits who terrorized the settlers. Fearful that the colony's slave population might revolt if the militia was dis-

patched, South Carolina's government yielded to the Regulators by establishing new courts and allowing jury trials in recently settled areas.

## Toward Independence

By early 1773 British-colonial relations were again tranquil, but deceptively so. Wishful thinking was leading Americans to ignore the tax on tea. Indeed, they expected Lord North to have it repealed. But Parliament's passage of the Tea Act in May 1773 shattered this hope and set off a chain reaction of events from the Boston Tea Party in late 1773 to the colonies' declaration of their independence from England in July 1776.

### The Tea Act

Smuggling and nonconsumption had taken a heavy toll on Britain's East India Company, the holder of the legal monopoly on importing tea into the British Empire. By 1773, as tons of tea rotted in warehouses, the East India Company was teetering on the brink of bankruptcy. But Lord North could not let the company fail because by maintaining British authority in India at its own expense, the East India Company had become a vital component in the British imperial structure.

If the company could control the colonial market, North reasoned, it could increase its profits and its survival would be guaranteed. Americans consumed vast amounts of tea but by 1773 were purchasing just one-quarter of it from the company. In May 1773, to save the beleaguered East India Company, Parliament passed the Tea Act, which eliminated all import duties on tea entering England and thus lowered the selling price to consumers. To reduce the price further, the Tea Act also permitted the company to sell tea directly to consumers rather than through wholesalers. These provisions reduced the cost of East India Company tea in the colonies to well below the price of smuggled tea. Parliament expected economic self-interest to overcome American scruples about buying taxed tea.

But the Tea Act alarmed many Americans,

who recognized that the revenues raised by the law would place royal governors' purses beyond the reach of the colonial assemblies. The law also threatened to seduce Americans into accepting parliamentary taxation in return for a frivolous luxury. The committees of correspondence decided to resist the importation of tea by pressuring the East India Company's agents to refuse acceptance or by preventing the landing of East India Company cargoes.

In Boston on November 28, 1773, the first ship came under jurisdiction of the customhouse, to which duties would have to be paid within twenty days or the cargo would be seized from the captain and the tea would be claimed by the company's agents and placed on sale. When Samuel Adams, John Hancock, and others asked customs officers to issue a special clearance for the ship's departure (to avoid the seizure and sale), Governor Hutchinson refused.

On the evening of December 16, 1773, Samuel Adams convened a meeting in Old South Church, at which he told 5,000 citizens about Hutchinson's insistence on landing the tea, warned them that the grace period would expire in a few hours, and proclaimed that "this meeting can do no more to save the country." About fifty young men disguised as Indians then loosed a few war whoops and headed for the wharf, followed by the crowd. Thousands lined the waterfront to watch them heave forty-five tons of tea overboard; for an hour the only sounds echoing through the crisp, moonlit night were the steady chop of hatchets breaking open wooden chests and the soft splash of tea on the water. Their work finished, the participants left quietly. They had assaulted no one and damaged nothing but the tea.

## The Coercive Acts

Boston's "Tea Party" enraged the British. Only "New England fanatics" could imagine that cheap tea oppressed them, fumed Lord North. A Welsh member of Parliament declared that "the town of Boston ought to be knocked about by the ears, and destroy'd." The great orator Edmund Burke pled in vain for the one action that could end the crisis:

"Leave America . . . to tax herself." But the British government swiftly asserted its authority through the passage of four Coercive Acts, which, along with the Quebec Act, became known to many colonists as the Intolerable Acts.

The first Coercive Act, the Boston Port Bill, was passed on April 1, 1774. It ordered the navy to close Boston harbor unless the town arranged to pay for the ruined tea by June 1. The impossibly short deadline was meant to ensure the harbor's closing, which would plunge Boston into economic distress. The second Coercive Act, the Massachusetts Government Act, revoked the Massachusetts charter and made the colony's government less democratic. The upper house would be appointed for life by the Crown, not elected annually by the assembly. The royal governor gained absolute control over the appointment of judges and sheriffs. Finally, the new charter limited town meetings to one a year. Although these changes brought Massachusetts government into line with other colonies, the colonists interpreted them as hostile toward representative government.

The final two Coercive Acts—the Administration of Justice Act and a new Quartering Act—rubbed salt into the wounds. The first of these permitted any person charged with murder while enforcing royal authority in Massachusetts to be tried in England or in another colony. The second went beyond the Quartering Act of 1765 by allowing the governor to requisition *empty* private buildings for quartering, or housing, troops. These measures, coupled with the appointment of General Thomas Gage, Britain's military commander in North America, as governor of Massachusetts, struck New Englanders as proof of a plan to place them under a military despotism.

Americans learned of the unrelated Quebec Act at the same time as the Coercive Acts. Intended to cement loyalty to Britain among conquered French-Canadian Catholics, the law established Roman Catholicism as Quebec's official religion. Protestant Anglo-Americans, who associated Catholicism with arbitrary government, took alarm. Furthermore, the Quebec Act gave Canada's governor sweeping powers but established no legislature. It also allowed property disputes to be decided by French law, which used no juries. The law extended Quebec's territorial claims south to the Ohio River and west to the Mississippi, a vast area populated by Indians and some French and claimed by several colonies.

The Intolerable Acts convinced New Englanders that the crown planned to corrode traditional English liberties throughout North America. Once the Coercive Acts destroyed these liberties in Massachusetts, many believed, the Quebec Act would serve as a blueprint for extinguishing representative government in other colonies. Parliament would replace all colonial governments with ones like Quebec's. Elected assemblies, freedom of religion for Protestants, and jury trials would vanish.

Intended only to punish Massachusetts, the Coercive Acts thus pushed most colonies to the brink of revolution. Repeal of these laws became the colonists' nonnegotiable demand. The Declaration of Independence would refer to these laws six times in listing colonial grievances justifying the break with Britain.

Virginia's response to the Coercive Acts was crucial, for it could provide more military manpower than any other colony in the event of war. After sentiment for active resistance solidified in the Virginia assembly, leading planters began a program of political education for the colony's apathetic citizens, emphasizing the need to support Massachusetts and persuading voters to commit themselves to resistance by signing petitions against the Coercive Acts. Within two years the gentry mobilized Virginia's free population against Parliament. It was clear that if war erupted, Britain would face united resistance not only in New England but also in Virginia.

## The First Continental Congress

In response to the Intolerable Acts, the committees of correspondence of every colony but Georgia sent delegates to a Continental Congress in Philadelphia. The fifty-six delegates who assembled on September 5, 1774, included the colonies' most prominent politicians: Samuel and John Adams of Massachusetts; John Jay of New York; Joseph Galloway and John Dickinson of Pennsylvania; and Patrick Henry, Richard Henry Lee, and George Washington of Virginia. They were determined to find a way to defend American rights without war.

The Continental Congress endorsed the Suffolk Resolves, extreme statements of principle that proclaimed that the colonies owed no obedience to the Coercive Acts, advocated a provisional government until restoration of the Massachusetts charter, and vowed that defensive measures should follow any attack by royal troops. The Continental Congress also voted to boycott British goods after December 1, 1774, and to stop exporting goods to Britain and its West Indies possessions after September 1775. This agreement, called the Continental Association, would be enforced by locally elected committees of "observation" or "safety." But not all the delegates embraced such bold defiance. Jay, Dickinson, Galloway, and other moderates who dominated the middle-colony contingent feared that a confrontation with Britain would spawn internal colonial turmoil. They vainly opposed nonimportation and unsuccessfully sought support of a plan for an American legislature that would share with Parliament the authority to tax and to govern the colonies.

Finally, the delegates summarized their principles and demands in a petition to George III. They conceded to Parliament the power to regulate colonial commerce but argued that parliamentary efforts to impose taxes, enforce laws through admiralty courts, suspend assemblies, and revoke charters were unconstitutional. By addressing the king rather than Parliament, Congress was imploring George III to end the crisis by dismissing the ministers responsible for passing the Coercive Acts.

## The Fighting Begins

Most Americans hoped that resistance would jolt Parliament into renouncing its claims of authority over the colonies. Only a minority of the colonial elite charged that Congress had made the "breach with the parent state a thousand times more irreparable than it was before," as one colonist observed. In England George III saw rebellion in Congress's actions. His instincts, like those of American loyalists—people loyal to England—were correct: a revolution was indeed brewing.

To solidify defiance, American resistance leaders used coercion against waverers and loyalists ("Tories"). Committees elected to enforce the Continental Association became vigilantes, compelling merchants to burn British imports, browbeating clergymen who preached pro-British sermons, and pressuring Americans to free themselves of dependence on British imports by adopting simpler diets and homespun clothing. In colony after colony, moreover, the committees assumed governmental functions by organizing volunteer military companies and extralegal legislatures. By spring 1775 colonial patriots had established provincial "congresses" that rivaled existing royal governments.

In April 1775 events in Massachusetts shattered the uneasy calm. Citizens had collected arms and organized militia units ("minutemen") to respond instantly in an emergency. The British government ordered Massachusetts governor Gage to quell the "rude rabble" and to arrest the patriot leaders. Aware that most of these had fled Boston, Gage, on April 19, 1775, sent 700 British soldiers to seize colonial military supplies stored at Concord. Two couriers, William Dawes and Paul Revere, alerted nearby towns of the British troop movements. At Lexington on the road to Concord, about 70 minutemen faced the British on the town green. After a confused skirmish in which eight minutemen died and a single redcoat was wounded, the British marched to Concord. They found few munitions but encountered a swarm of armed Yankees. When some minutemen mistakenly concluded that the town was being burned, they exchanged fire with British regulars and touched off a running battle that continued most of the sixteen miles back to Boston. By day's end the redcoats had lost 273 men.

These engagements awakened the countryside. Within a day some 20,000 New Englanders were besieging the British garrison in Boston. In the New England interior the Green Mountain Boys under Ethan Allen overran Fort Ticonderoga on Lake Champlain on May 10, partly with the intent of using its captured cannon in the siege of Boston. That same day the Continental Congress reconvened in Philadelphia. Most delegates still opposed independence and agreed to send a "loyal message" to George III. The resulting Olive Branch Petition presented three demands: a cease-fire in Boston, repeal of the Coercive Acts, and negotiations to establish guarantees of American rights. But the Olive Branch Petition reached London along with news of the battles of Breed's Hill and Bunker Hill just outside Boston. Although the British dislodged the Americans in the clashes, they suffered 2,200 casualties, compared to colonial losses of only 311. After Bunker Hill the British public wanted retaliation, not reconciliation. On August 23 the king proclaimed New England in a state of rebellion, and in December Parliament declared all the colonies rebellious.

## The Failure of Reconciliation

Most Americans still clung to hopes of reconciliation. Even John Adams, who believed separation inevitable, said that he was "fond of reconciliation, if we could reasonably entertain Hopes of it on a constitutional basis." Yet the same Americans who pleaded for peace passed measures that the British could only see as rebellious. Delegates to the Continental Congress voted to establish an "American continental army" and appointed George Washington as commander.

The majority of Americans who resisted independence blamed evil ministers, rather than the king, for unconstitutional measures and expected saner heads to rise to power in Britain. On both counts they were wrong. Americans exaggerated the influence of Pitt, Burke, Wilkes (who finally took his seat in 1774), and their other friends in Britain. In March 1775 when Burke proposed that Parliament acknowledge the colonists' right to raise and dispose of taxes, a thumping majority of Parliament voted him down. Lord North's sole counterproposal was to allow the colonists to tax themselves on condition that they collect whatever sum Parliament ordered, in effect practicing involuntary self-taxation.

Americans' sentimental attachment to the king, the last emotional barrier to independence, crumbled in January 1776 with the publication of Thomas Paine's *Common Sense*. Paine had immigrated to the colonies from England in 1774 with a penchant for radical politics and a gift for plain and pungent prose. Paine told Americans what they had been unable to bring themselves to say: that at the root of the conspiracy against American liberty lay not corrupt politicians but the very institutions of monarchy and empire. Further, America did not need its British connection. "The commerce by which she [America] hath enriched herself are the necessaries of life, and will always have a market while eating is the custom in Europe," Paine argued. And, he pointed out, the events of the preceding six months had made independence a reality. Finally, Paine linked America's awakening nationalism with a sense of religious mission: "We have it in our power to begin the world over again. A situation, similar to the present, hath not happened since the days of Noah until now." America, Paine wrote, would be a new *kind* of nation, a model society free of oppressive English beliefs and institutions.

*Common Sense*, "a landflood that sweeps all before it," sold more than 100,000 copies in three months, one copy for every fourth or fifth adult male in the colonies. By spring 1776 Paine's pamphlet had dissolved lingering allegiance to George III and removed the last psychological barrier to independence.

## Independence at Last

John Adams described the movement toward independence as a coach drawn by thirteen horses, which could not reach its destination any faster than the slowest were willing to run. New England was already in rebellion, and Rhode Island declared itself independent in May 1776. The middle colonies hesitated to support revolution because they feared, correctly, that the war would largely be fought over control of Philadelphia and New York. The South began to press for separation. In April North Carolina authorized its congressional delegates to vote for independence, and in June Virginia followed suit. On July 2 the Continental Congress formally adopted the Virginia resolution and created the United States of America.

The drafting of a statement to justify the colonies' separation from England fell to Virginia's Thomas Jefferson. Congress approved his manuscript on July 4, 1776. Even though parliamentary authority had been the focal point of dispute since 1765, the Declaration of Independence never mentioned Parliament by name because Congress was unwilling to imply that Parliament held any authority over America. Jefferson instead focused on George III, citing "repeated injuries and usurpations" against the colonies. He added that the king's "direct object [was] the establishment of an absolute tyranny over these states."

Like Paine, Jefferson elevated colonial grievances to a struggle of universal dimensions. In the tradition of Enlightenment thought, Jefferson argued that Britain had violated its contract with the colonists, giving them the right to replace it with a government of their own. His emphasis on the equality of all individuals and their natural entitlement to justice, liberty, and self-fulfillment expressed the Enlightenment's deep longing for government that rested on neither legal privilege nor the exploitation of the majority by the few—and deliberately ignored the existence of slavery.

Jefferson addressed the Declaration of Independence as much to Americans uncertain about the wisdom of independence as to world opinion. He wanted to convince his fellow citizens that social and political progress could no longer be accomplished within the British Empire. The declaration never claimed that perfect justice and equal opportunity existed in the now former American colonies, which had become the United States; instead, it challenged the Revolutionary generation and all who followed to bring this ideal closer to reality.

## CONCLUSION

Throughout the long imperial crisis, Americans pursued the goal of reestablishing the empire as it had functioned before 1763, when colonial trade was protected and encouraged and when colonial assemblies exercised exclusive power over taxation and internal legislation. These reluctant revolutionaries now had to face Europe's greatest imperial power and win independence on the battlefield. They also had to decide to what degree they would implement the ideals evoked in Jefferson's declaration. Neither task would prove easy.

## CHRONOLOGY

1733  Molasses Act.

1754– French and Indian War (in Europe, the Seven
1760  Years' War, 1756–1763).

1760  George III becomes king of Great Britain.
Massachusetts controversy over writs of assistance.

1763  Indian uprising in Ohio Valley and Great Lakes.
Proclamation of 1763.

1764  Sugar Act.

1765  Stamp Act.
Quartering Act.
Loyal Nine formed in Boston to oppose the Stamp Act.
Sons of Liberty band together throughout the colonies.
Stamp Act Congress.
Colonists begin boycott of British goods.

1766  Stamp Act repealed.
Declaratory Act.

1767  New York Suspending Act.
Revenue Act (Townshend duties).
John Dickinson, *Letters from a Farmer in Pennsylvania*.
American Board of Customs Commissioners created.

1768  Massachusetts "circular letter."
Boston merchants adopt the colonies' first nonimportation agreement.
John Hancock's ship *Liberty* seized.
British troops arrive in Boston.
John Wilkes elected to Parliament; arrested.
St. George's Fields Massacre in London.

1770  Townshend duties, except tea tax, repealed.
Boston Massacre.

1771  Battle of Alamance Creek in North Carolina.

1772  *Gaspee* incident in Rhode Island.
Committees of correspondence begin in Massachusetts and rapidly spread.

1773  Tea Act.
Boston Tea Party.

1774  Coercive Acts.
Quebec Act.
First Continental Congress meets in Philadelphia and adopts Suffolk Resolves.
Continental Association.

1775  Battles of Lexington and Concord.
Second Continental Congress meets.
Olive Branch Petition.
Battles at Breed's Hill and Bunker Hill.

1776  Thomas Paine, *Common Sense*.
Declaration of Independence.

## FOR FURTHER READING

Bernard Bailyn, *The Ideological Origins of the American Revolution* (1967). Pulitzer Prize–winning examination of the political heritage that shaped colonial resistance to British authority.

Edward Countryman, *The American Revolution* (1985). An outstanding introduction to the Revolution.

Robert A. Gross, *The Minutemen and Their World* (1976). An eloquent and evocative examination of Concord, Massachusetts, in the revolutionary era.

Pauline Maier, *From Resistance to Revolution: Colonial Radicals and the Development of American Opposition to Britain, 1765–1776* (1972). An insightful, definitive examination of how colonial leaders strove to force the repeal of unconstitutional laws with a minimum use of violence.

Robert Middlekauff, *The Glorious Cause: The American Revolution, 1763–1789* (1982). A learned and highly readable narrative of the events leading to independence.

Edmund S. Morgan and Helen M. Morgan, *The Stamp Act Crisis: Prologue to Revolution*, rev. ed. (1963). A classic analysis of colonial constitutional principles regarding limits on Parliament's taxing power.

Robert R. Palmer, *The Age of the Democratic Revolution:* Vol. I, *The Challenge* (1959). Bancroft Prize–winning examination of the American Revolution in comparison to events in England, Ireland, and France.

Gordon S. Wood, *The Radicalism of the American Revolution* (1992). A sweeping account of the Revolution's long-range impact on American society.

# The Forge of Nationhood, 1776–1788

The Revolution would teach Americans a hard lesson: that *proclaiming* a new nation, as they had done so proudly in 1776, was much easier than *making* a new nation, which they struggled to do from 1776 to 1788.

Before 1775 the outlooks of inhabitants of the various colonies had been narrowly confined within the borders of their individual provinces. With little opportunity and less necessity to work together, each colonist had regarded his own colony as superior to all others. But eight years of war transformed the colonists from citizens of thirteen disparate provinces into American citizens. Only through the collective hardships of the War for Independence did the colonists learn to see each other not just as military allies but as fellow citizens.

Independence and peace in 1783, however, gave Americans a false security. Major problems remained unsolved. The national government's authority withered as states failed to provide financial support for its operations. During the 1780s

America's First Civil War
ฐ
Revolutionary Society
ฐ
Forging New Governments

---

(*Right*) **A Daughter of Liberty**, *woodcut, 1779*

farsighted leaders saw two great challenges. Could they preserve the national spirit born during the war? If so, could they provide the central government with adequate authority, yet not interfere with the rights of individual states or endanger civil liberties? Not until 1789 would they begin to overcome these challenges.

# America's First Civil War

The Revolution was simultaneously a collective struggle of the American people against Britain and a civil war among North Americans, the latter conducted without restraint, mutual respect, or compassion. Militarily, the war's outcome depended on the ability of the supporters of independence, called Whigs, to wear down the British army, and on the Whigs' success in suppressing their fellow North Americans' opposition to independence. The magnitude of these twin tasks often disheartened the Whigs, but it united them as well. The common disappointments and sacrifices endured from 1775 to 1783 forged among Americans the commitment to nationhood that ultimately prevented their new country from splintering into small republics.

## Loyalists and Other British Sympathizers

When independence came in July 1776, many colonists remained unconvinced of its necessity. About 20 percent of all whites actively opposed the rebellion or supported it only when threatened with fines and imprisonment. These opponents of the Revolution called themselves loyalists, but Whigs labeled them Tories.

Loyalists, like Whigs, typically opposed parliamentary taxation of the colonies. Many loyalists thus found themselves fighting for a cause with which they did not entirely agree, and as a result many switched sides during the war. Maryland loyalist Reverend Jonathan Boucher expressed a widespread apprehension: "For my part, I equally dread a Victory by either side." But loyalists believed that separation was illegal and was not necessary to preserve the colonists' constitutional rights. Above all, they revered the crown and equated any failure to defend their king with a sacrifice of personal honor.

Loyalist strength in an area depended on how well prominent local Whigs had convinced voters that the king and Parliament were endangering representative government. From 1772 to 1776 elites in New England, Virginia, and South Carolina mobilized citizens by organizing public meetings and repeatedly explaining the issues. The majority opted for resistance; by 1776 loyalists constituted barely 5 percent of whites in these areas. In contrast, elites in New York and New Jersey remained reluctant to declare allegiance to either side, and their indecision resulted in divided communities. These two states provided half of the 21,000 Americans who would fight in loyalist units.

A second major factor in loyalist strength was the geographic distribution of recent British immigrants, who identified closely with their homeland. These newcomers included thousands of British veterans of the French and Indian War who had remained in the colonies, usually in New York. Further, the 125,000 British immigrants who arrived between 1763 and 1775 formed major centers of loyalist sympathy. In New York, Georgia, and the Carolina piedmont, where these newcomers clustered, loyalists probably constituted 25 to 40 percent of the white population in 1776.

Third, loyalism thrived on the presence of ethnic and religious minorities outside the main currents of colonial society. For example, a few German, Dutch, and French religious congregations that had resisted use of the English language felt indebted to Britain for their religious freedom and doubted that their rights would remain safe in an independent Anglo-American nation. However, German colonists in Virginia, Pennsylvania, and Maryland had embraced emergent American republicanism by 1776, and they would overwhelmingly support the Revolution.

Canada's French Catholics became the most significant white loyalist minority. The Quebec Act of 1774 had guaranteed their religious freedom and their continued use of French civil law. Remembering the bitter denunciations of this measure by their southern neighbors, French Catholics feared that Protestant Anglo-Americans would be far less tolerant. Canadian anxieties intensified in mid-1775 when the Continental Congress ordered Continental forces to "free" Canada from British tyranny and to block a British invasion from the north. In 1775 Continental armies attacked Quebec but were defeated. French Catholics emerged more loyal to the British crown than ever.

Black slaves and Native Americans also widely supported the British. In the earlier 1770s the British, not the Americans, had most often offered liberty to American slaves. In 1775 nearly 800 African-Americans had joined Lord Dunmore, Virginia's governor, who had promised them freedom if they supported the British cause. Hundreds of South Carolina slaves sought refuge on British ships in Charles Town's harbor. During the war itself at least 20,000 slaves would run away to sign on as laborers or soldiers in the Royal Army. Deeply alienated from white society, slaves realized that the Revolution would not benefit them. Finally, most Indians, recognizing the threat that expansion-minded colonists posed, likewise supported the British. Of the handful of tribes that sided with the colonists, the most prominent were two Iroquois tribes, the Oneidas and the Tuscaroras.

Whigs hated loyalists, and loyalists responded to Whigs with equal venom. Each side saw its cause as sacred and viewed opposition to it by a fellow American as a betrayal. Consequently, the worst atrocities of the war were inflicted by Americans on each other.

## The Opposing Sides

Britain entered the war with what should have been two major advantages. First, Britain's 11 million people greatly outnumbered the 2.5 million colonists, one-third of whom were either slaves or loyalists. Second, Britain possessed the world's largest navy and one of its best armies. During the war the army's size more than doubled, from 48,000 to 111,000 men, and Britain hired 30,000 Hessian mercenaries and enlisted 21,000 loyalists to supplement its own fighting force.

Despite a smaller population, the new nation mobilized its people more effectively than Britain. By the war's end the rebels had enlisted or drafted half of all free males aged sixteen to forty-five—about 220,000 troops—compared to the 162,000 Britons, loyalists, and Hessians who served in the British army. Further, peacetime budget cuts after 1763 had weakened British seapower and thus Britain's ability to crush the rebellion. Midway through the war, half of Britain's ships languished in dry dock, awaiting repairs. Of 110,000 new sailors, the navy lost 42,000 to desertion and 20,000 to disease or wounds. In addition, American privateers cost Britain's merchant marine dearly. During the war U.S. Navy ships and privateers would capture more than 2,000 British merchant vessels and 16,000 crewmen.

Britain could ill afford such losses, for supplying its troops in North America was a Herculean task. Although at various times the British army controlled all the major American cities, British soldiers seldom ventured into the agricultural hinterland and thus could not easily round up supplies. Virtually all the food consumed by the army, one-third of a ton per soldier per year, was imported from Britain. Seriously overextended, the navy barely kept the army supplied and never effectively blockaded American ports.

Maintaining public support presented another serious problem for Britain. The war more than doubled the British national debt, adding to the problems of a people already paying record taxes. Burdened by record taxes, the politically influential landed gentry would not vote against their pocketbooks forever.

The new United States faced different but equally severe problems. First, one-fifth of its population was openly pro-British. Second, state militias lacked the training to fight pitched battles. Their hit-and-run guerrilla tactics could not bring victory, nor could avoiding major battles and allowing the British to occupy population centers. Moreover, the

U.S. dependence on guerrilla warfare would convince potential European allies that the Americans could not drive out the British and would doom American efforts to gain foreign loans and diplomatic recognition.

The Continental Army would thus have to fight in European fashion, relying on precision movements of mass formations of troops. Victory would depend on rapid maneuvers to crush an enemy's undefended flank or rear. Attackers would need exceptional skill in close-order drill to fall on an enemy before it could re-form and return fire. After advancing within musket range, opposing troops would stand upright and fire at each other until one line weakened. Discipline, training, and nerve would be essential if soldiers were to hold their line as comrades fell around them. The stronger side would attack at a quick walk, with bayonets drawn, and drive off its opponents.

In contrast to Britain, which had a well-trained army with a tradition of bravery under fire, the Continental Army had neither an inspirational heritage nor experienced officers in 1775. In the war's early years, it suffered heartbreaking defeats. However, to win, the Continentals did not have to destroy the British army but only to prolong the rebellion until Britain's taxpayers lost patience. Until then, American victory depended on the ability of one man to keep his army fighting despite defeat—George Washington.

## George Washington

Few generals looked and acted the role as much as Washington. He spoke with authority and comported himself with dignity. At six feet two inches, he stood a half foot taller than an average contemporary. Powerfully built, athletic, and hardened by a rugged outdoor life, he could inspire troops to heroism.

Washington's military experience had begun at age twenty-two, when he had commanded a Virginia regiment raised to resist French claims in the Ohio Valley (see Chapter 5). Vastly outnumbered, he had lost his first battle. A year later at Braddock's defeat, Washington had assumed the point of great-

est danger, had had two horses shot out from under him, and had had his hat shot off and his coat ripped by bullets. But Washington's mistakes and lost battles had taught him lessons that easy victories might not have. He had discovered the dangers of overconfidence and the need for determination. He had also learned that Americans fought best when led by example and treated with respect.

In 1758, with Virginia's borders secured, Washington had resigned his commission and become a tobacco planter. He had sat in the House of Burgesses, where others respected him and sought his opinion. An early opponent of parliamentary taxation, he had also served in the Continental Congress. In the eyes of the many who valued his advice and his military experience, Washington was the logical choice to head the Continental Army.

## War in Earnest

In March 1776 the British evacuated Boston and moved south to New York, which they wished to use as a base for conquering New England. Under two brothers, General William Howe and Admiral Richard, Lord Howe, 130 warships carried 32,000 troops to New York City in summer 1776. Defending the city were 18,000 poorly trained soldiers under Washington. On August 27, 15,000 British troops nearly annihilated 10,500 American troops on Long Island, just across a river from New York City. But Washington executed a masterly night evacuation, saving 9,500 troops and most of his artillery from capture.

In mid-September 1776 the Continental Army counted 16,000 men. Over the next three months the British killed or took prisoner one-quarter of these troops and drove the survivors across New Jersey. By early December, when Washington retreated from New Jersey into Pennsylvania, he commanded fewer than 7,000 men fit for duty. Thomas Paine called these demoralizing days "the times that try men's souls."

Washington took the offensive before military and national morale collapsed. On Christmas night 1776 he attacked a Hessian garrison at Trenton, New Jersey, and captured nearly 1,000 Germans

**George Washington (1732–1799),**
*by John Trumbull, 1780*
*Washington's brilliant victories at Trenton and Princeton made patriot morale soar and forced the British to reconsider their military strategy.*

with the loss of only 4 men. On January 3, 1777, Washington attacked Princeton, New Jersey, killing or capturing one-third of his 1,200 British opponents and losing only 40. The American victories at Trenton and Princeton had important consequences. First, they boosted civilian and military morale. Second, they undermined the Howes' plans to rally loyalists and skeptics to Britain's cause and forced the British evacuation of New Jersey in early 1777. Washington established winter quarters only twenty-five miles from New York City.

The rebel militia meanwhile drove thousands of New Jersey loyalists, who had been plundering Whig property, into British-held New York, where many joined the Royal Army. The New Jersey militia became a police force dedicated to rooting out political dissent. It disarmed known loyalists, jailed their leaders, and constantly watched suspected Tories. Ironically, the failure by British commanders to prevent widespread looting by their troops undermined New Jersey loyalists' support for the Crown. Facing constant danger of arrest, most loyalists who remained in New Jersey bowed to the inevitable and swore allegiance to the Continental Congress.

British invasions of New York in 1777, Georgia in 1778, and the Carolinas in 1779 produced similar results. As Whigs regained the upper hand, they pursued loyalists and coerced most into renouncing the Crown. But not all loyalists shifted sides; some became political refugees and fled the country. Indeed, the war drove one out of six loyalists into exile.

## The Turning Point

Shortly after the battles of Trenton and Princeton, the marquis de Lafayette, a young French aristocrat, joined Washington's staff. Lafayette was twenty years old, idealistic, brave, infectiously optimistic— and closely connected to the French court. His arrival indicated that France might recognize American independence and declare war on Britain. However, the French first wanted proof that the Americans could win a major battle.

That victory came quickly. In summer 1777 the British planned a two-pronged attack to crush New York State and to isolate New England. Two British columns, one from Montreal and the other from Quebec, were to link up near Albany. Complicating an already intricate scheme, General William Howe launched another major campaign that summer aimed at the American capital, Philadelphia. Because of Howe's fateful decision, no British troops would be able to come to the aid of the Canadian columns.

The first British column, moving south from Montreal under Lieutenant Colonel Barry St. Leger, encountered a Continental force holding a chokepoint at Fort Stanwix. Unable to defeat the rebels after a three-week siege, the British retreated north. Meanwhile, the second British column, led by Gen-

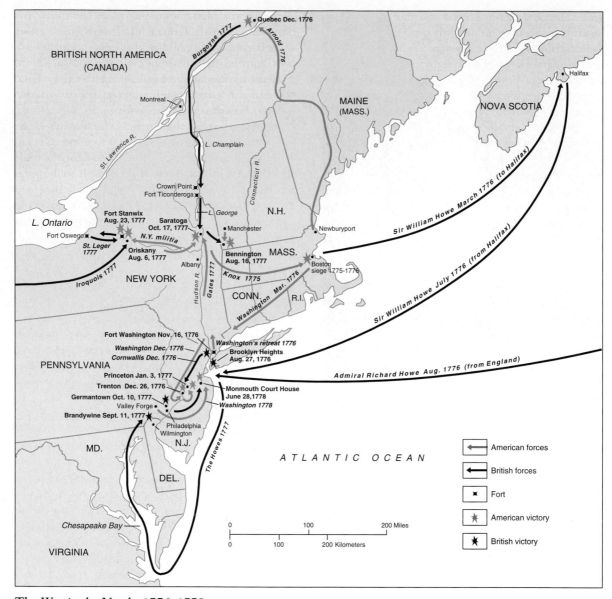

## The War in the North, 1776–1779

*Following the British evacuation of Boston, the war shifted to New York City, which the British held from 1776 to 1783. In 1777 Britain's success in taking the U.S. capital, Philadelphia, was offset by defeat in upstate New York. The hard-fought battle of Monmouth Court House, New Jersey, ended the northern campaigns in 1778.*

eral John Burgoyne, became stranded in western New York, his supply lines overextended and his 8,300 troops depleted by combat and hunger. General Horatio Gates of the Continental Army gathered a force of 17,000 rebels and attacked Burgoyne near Saratoga. Burgoyne's troops, surrounded and outnumbered, surrendered on October 17, 1777.

Saratoga was as important diplomatically as militarily. Benjamin Franklin had arrived in France only a few weeks before news of Saratoga. Renowned for his learning and sophistication, Franklin shrewdly captured French imaginations by wearing a fur cap and playing the part of an innocent backwoods philosopher. Already pro-American, the French court received news of the victory at Saratoga as proof that the Americans could win the war and thus deserved diplomatic recognition. In February 1778 France formally recognized the United States. Four months later France went to war with Britain. Spain and Holland ultimately joined the war as French allies. Facing a coalition of enemies, Britain had no allies.

The colonies' allies made their presence felt. Between 1779 and 1781 Spanish troops prevented the British from taking the Mississippi Valley, and beginning in 1781 French troops contributed to rebel victories. Moreover, Britain sent thousands of soldiers to Ireland and the West Indies to guard against a French invasion, further stretching already depleted manpower reserves. The French and Spanish navies, which together approximately equaled the British fleet, won several large battles, denied Britain control of the sea, and punctured the Royal Navy's blockade.

### The Continentals Mature

In late August 1777 British general Howe landed 18,000 troops near Philadelphia. With Washington at their head and Lafayette at his side, 16,000 Continentals paraded through the imperiled city. "They marched twelve deep," John Adams reported, "and yet took above two hours in passing by." Adams noted that the troops, although uniformed and well armed, had not yet acquired "quite the air of soldiers." They would pay a fearful price for their lack of professionalism when they met Howe's army.

The armies collided on September 11, 1777, at Brandywine Creek, Pennsylvania. After the Continentals crumbled in the face of superior British discipline, Congress fled Philadelphia, allowing Howe to occupy it. In early October Howe defeated the Americans a second time, at Germantown. In four bloody weeks 20 percent of the Continentals were killed, wounded, or captured.

In early December 1777 the 11,000 Continental survivors left Whitemarsh, Pennsylvania. Short on rations and chilled to the bone from marching into a wall of sleet, they took a week to reach their winter headquarters only eleven miles away. One-fourth of them had worn out at least one shoe. On days when the roads froze, they suffered horribly. Washington later recalled, "You might have tracked the army from White Marsh to Valley Forge by the blood of their feet." As the British rested comfortably in Philadelphia, eighteen miles away, the Continentals stumbled around the bleak hills of Valley Forge and huddled, exhausted and hungry, in crude huts.

The army slowly regained its strength but still lacked training. The Saratoga victory had resulted from the Americans' overwhelming numbers, not their superior skill. Meeting Howe on an even basis, the Continentals had lost badly—twice. The key skills of marching and maneuvering were nonexistent. Then in February 1778 the Continental Army's fortunes rose when a German soldier of fortune and drillmaster, Friedrich von Steuben, reached Valley Forge. An administrative genius and immensely popular, he turned the army into a formidable fighting force.

Just how formidable became clear in June 1778. The British, now under General Henry Clinton, evacuated Philadelphia and marched toward New York. The Continentals caught up on June 28 at Monmouth Court House, New Jersey. The battle blazed for six hours, with the Continentals throwing back Clinton's best units. The British finally broke off contact and slipped away under cover of darkness. Never again would they win easy victories against the Continental Army.

The Battle of Monmouth ended the contest for the North. Clinton occupied New York, which the Royal Navy made safe from attack. Washington kept his army on watch nearby, while Whig militia hunted down the last few Tory guerrillas.

## Frontier Campaigns

West of the Appalachians and along New York and Pennsylvania's western borders, a different kind of war unfolded. The numbers engaged along the frontier were small, but the stakes were enormous. In 1776 few Anglo-Americans had any clear idea of the country's western boundaries. By 1783 when the

### The War in the West, 1776–1779

*George Rogers Clark's victory at Vincennes in 1779 gave the United States effective control of the Ohio Valley. Carolina militiamen drove attacking Cherokees far back into the Appalachians in 1776. In retaliation for raids on New York and Pennsylvania, John Sullivan inflicted widespread starvation on the Iroquois by burning their villages and winter food supplies in 1779.*

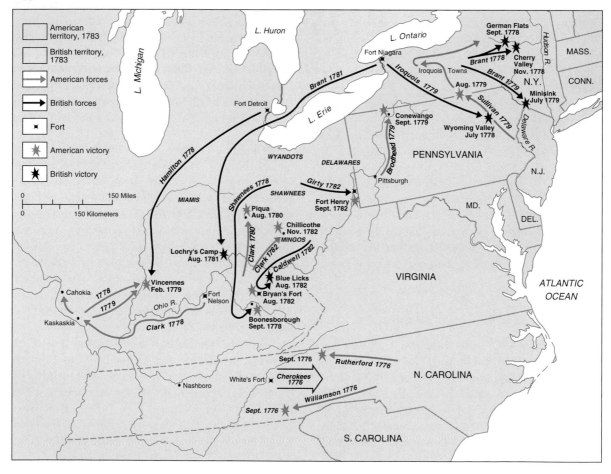

Peace of Paris concluded the war, the new nation would claim the Mississippi River as its western border. So although the frontier campaigns would not determine the war's outcome, they would significantly shape the future of the United States.

Frontier fighting first erupted in the South when Cherokees had begun attacking frontier settlements from Virginia to Georgia in 1776. Within a year retaliatory expeditions had burned most Cherokee towns and forced the Cherokees to cede most of their lands in South Carolina and large tracts in North Carolina and Tennessee. Elsewhere in the region the intense warfare lasted longer. Kentucky saw fierce fighting as rebels under Colonel George Rogers Clark established control of the Ohio River valley from Pittsburgh to the Mississippi after defeating both the British and Native Americans.

In the East pro-British Iroquois under the gifted Mohawk leader Joseph Brant devastated the New York and Pennsylvania frontiers in 1778. General John Sullivan led a Continental force, with Tuscarora and Oneida allies, against the Iroquois. Victorious at what is now Elmira, New York, in 1779, Sullivan and his forces burned two dozen Iroquois villages and destroyed a million bushels of corn. The Iroquois fled north to Canada, and hundreds starved to death. Sullivan had destroyed the heartland of the Iroquois; their population declined by one-third during the Revolutionary War. Although Brant's warriors laid waste to Pennsylvania and New York in one final spasm of fury in 1780, the Iroquois never recovered.

## Victory in the South

After 1778 the British focus shifted to the South. France and Spain's entry had embroiled Britain in an international struggle that raged from India to Gibraltar and from the West Indies to the North American mainland. If the British could secure the South, they could easily shuffle forces between the West Indies and the mainland. And the South looked like an easy target: in 1778, 3,500 British troops had taken Savannah, Georgia, without difficulty, and Clinton expected a southern invasion to tap a huge reservoir of loyalist support. British strategy called for seizing key southern ports and, aided by loyal militiamen, moving back north, pacifying one region after another.

At first the plan unfolded smoothly. Sailing from New York with 4,000 men, Clinton captured Charles Town, South Carolina, in May 1780. He then returned to New York, leaving the mop-up operation to Lord Charles Cornwallis. Clinton's miscalculation of loyalist strength rapidly became apparent. Southern Tories used the British occupation to take revenge for their harsh treatment under rebel rule, and patriots struck back. The war engulfed the lower South and became intensely personal, with individuals choosing sides not for political reasons but for simple revenge.

Meanwhile, battles between British troops and Continental regulars led to a string of Continental defeats. America's worst loss of the entire war came at Camden, South Carolina, in August 1780. General Horatio Gates's combined force of professionals and militiamen faced Cornwallis's army. The militiamen fled after the first volley, and the badly outnumbered Continentals were overrun. Washington sent General Nathanael Greene to confront Cornwallis. Under Greene, the rebels lost three major battles in 1781 but won the campaign anyhow. Greene gave the patriot militiamen the protection that they needed to hunt down loyalists, stretched British supply lines until they snapped, and inflicted heavy casualties. Greene's dogged resistance forced Cornwallis to abandon the Carolina backcountry and to lead his battered troops into Virginia.

Still secure in New York, Clinton wanted Cornwallis to return to Charles Town, but Cornwallis had other plans. He established a base at Yorktown, Virginia, where the York and James rivers empty into Chesapeake Bay. He hoped to fan out into Virginia and Pennsylvania but never got the chance. On August 30, 1781, a French fleet dropped anchor off the Virginia coast and landed troops near Yorktown. Lafayette joined them, and Washington led his Continental Army south to

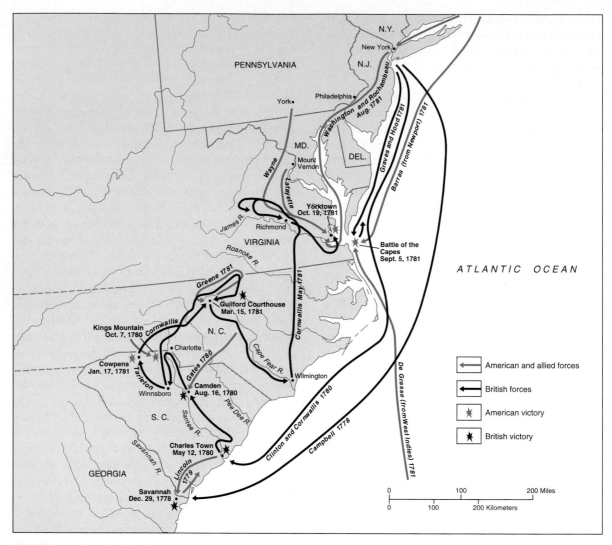

**The War in the South, 1778–1781**

*By 1780 Britain held the South's major cities, Charles Town and Savannah, but could not establish control over the backcountry because of resistance from Nathanael Greene's Continentals. By invading Virginia, Lord Cornwallis placed himself within striking distance of Washington's U.S. and French forces, a decision that rapidly led to the British surrender at Yorktown in October 1781.*

tighten the noose. Trapped and besieged at Yorktown, Cornwallis's 6,000 troops lasted three weeks against 8,800 Americans and 7,800 French. On October 19, 1781, they surrendered.

## The Peace of Paris

"Oh God!" Lord North exclaimed on hearing of Yorktown. "It's all over." Indeed, Cornwallis's surrender had extinguished the overtaxed people's will to fight and forced the government to begin peace negotiations. Talks opened in Paris in June 1782, with John Adams, Benjamin Franklin, and John Jay as America's principal diplomats.

Military realities largely dictated the terms of the peace treaty. Britain recognized American independence and promised the evacuation of all royal troops from U.S. soil. Moreover, the British had little choice but to award the new nation the vast territory east of the Mississippi, for by 1783 20,000 Anglo-American settlers lived west of the Appalachians and George Rogers Clark's victories had given Americans control of the Northwest.

The settlement favored the United States but left some problems unresolved. In a separate treaty Britain transferred East and West Florida back to Spain, but the designated boundaries were ambiguous. Further, the Peace of Paris contained seeds of future British-American controversy: although the United States promised to urge state legislatures to compensate loyalists for property losses, several states would later refuse to comply. And notably missing from the treaty was any reference to the Native Americans, most of whom had supported the British. The treaty left them to deal with the new American republic on their own. Not surprisingly, many Indians did not acknowledge the new nation's claims to sovereignty over their territory.

Independence carried a heavy price. At least 5 percent of free white males aged sixteen to forty-five had died in the war. If the present-day United States were to suffer comparable casualties, 2.5 million would die. And the peace left two important issues unsettled: what kind of society the United States would become and what sort of government it would possess.

# Revolutionary Society

Two forces shaped the Revolution's social effects: the principles articulated in the Declaration of Independence and the dislocations caused by the war. These factors combined to change relationships between members of different classes, races, and genders momentously.

## Egalitarianism

Between 1700 and 1760 social relations between elites and common people had grown more formal, distant, and restrained. Members of the colonial gentry lived sumptuously to emphasize their position. By the late 1760s, however, many in the upper class were wearing homespun clothing in support of boycotts of British goods. When the First Families of Virginia organized militia companies in 1775, they dressed in plain hunting shirts so that even the poorest farmer would not find his humble appearance too embarrassing to enlist. By 1776 visible distinctions of wealth had noticeably lessened.

The war accelerated the erosion of class differences by forcing gentry-officers to respect ordinary men serving as privates. Indeed, the soldiers demanded to be treated with consideration, especially in light of the ringing statement of the Declaration of Independence that "all men are created equal." Soldiers followed commands, but not if they were addressed and treated as inferiors. The best officers realized this fact immediately. For example, General Israel Putnam of Connecticut, inspecting fortifications being dug near Boston in 1776, ordered a noncommissioned officer to throw a large stone onto the outer wall. "Sir, I am a corporal," the man protested. "Oh," Putnam responded, "I ask your pardon, sir," and he hurled the rock himself.

The war exposed most men of military age to such treatment. Soldiers who expected officers to recognize their worth as individuals carried their new self-esteem and insistence on respect back into civilian life. Personal pride gradually translated into political behavior and beliefs, and candidates took care not to scorn the common people. The war thus fundamentally democratized Americans' political assumptions. The gentry's sense of social rank also diminished as they met men who rose through ability and observed middle-class farmers and artisans handling duties previously thought above their station. This egalitarianism did not extend to propertyless males, women, and nonwhites, but it did undermine the tendency to believe that wealth or family background conferred a special claim to public office.

In short, Revolutionary-generation Americans insisted that virtue and sacrifice, not wealth, defined worth. They came to see the "natural aristocracy"—those who demonstrated fitness for government service by their personal accomplishments—as ideal candidates for political office. This natural aristocracy included self-made men such as Benjamin Franklin as well as those, like Thomas Jefferson and John Hancock, born into wealth.

## A Revolution for African-Americans

The wartime condition of African-Americans contradicted the ideals of equality and justice for which Americans fought. About 500,000 black persons, composing one-fifth of the total population, inhabited the United States in 1776. All but 25,000 were slaves. Free blacks could not vote, lived under curfews, and lacked the guarantees of equal justice afforded to even the poorest white criminal. Grudging toleration was all that free blacks could expect, and few slaves ever became free.

The war nevertheless presented new opportunities to African-Americans. Some slaves took advantage of the confusion of war to run off and pose as freemen. A 1775 ban on black soldiers was collapsing by 1777. All states but Georgia and South Carolina eventually recruited blacks. Approximately 5,000 African-Americans, mainly from the North, served in the Continental Army. Most were slaves serving with their masters' consent, usually in racially integrated units.

Manpower demands, not a white commitment to equal justice, largely opened these opportunities. In fact, until the mid-eighteenth century most in the Western world saw slavery as part of the natural order. By the 1760s, however, some American opposition to slavery had blossomed. The Quakers led the way; by 1779 most Quaker slaveowners had freed their slaves. The Declaration of Independence's broad assertion of natural rights and human equality spurred a larger attack on slavery. By 1804 all the states from Pennsylvania north, except New Hampshire, had abolished slavery.

The antislavery movement reflected the Enlightenment's emphasis on gradual change. By priming public opinion to favor a weakening of the institution over time, leaders sought to bring about its demise. Most state abolition laws provided for gradual emancipation, typically declaring free all children born of a slave woman after a certain date, often July 4. (These individuals still had to work, without pay, for their mother's master for up to twenty-eight years.) Furthermore, Revolutionary leaders did not press for decisive action against slavery in the South, where the institution was embedded in the economy. They feared that widespread southern emancipation would either bankrupt or disrupt the Union. They argued that the United States, deeply in debt, could not finance immediate abolition in the South and that any attempt to do so without compensation would drive the region to secession.

Although slavery gnawed at Whig consciences even in the South, no state south of Pennsylvania abolished slavery. Most, however, passed laws making it easier to free slaves. Between 1775 and 1790 the number of free blacks in Virginia and Maryland rose from 4,000 to 21,000, or about 5 percent of all African-Americans residing there.

These "free persons of color" faced a future of destitution and second-class citizenship. Most had used up their cash savings to purchase their freedom and were past their physical prime. They found few whites willing to hire them or to pay equal wages. Most free blacks remained poor laborers or tenant farmers. But a few became landowners or skilled artisans. Benjamin Banneker of Maryland, a self-taught mathematician and astronomer, served on the commission that designed Washington, D.C., and published a series of almanacs.

Free blacks relied on one another for help, generally through religious channels. Because many white congregations spurned them, and because racially separate churches provided mutual support, self-pride, and a sense of accomplishment, free blacks began founding their own Baptist and Methodist congregations after the Revolution. In 1787 Philadelphia blacks established the Methodist congregation that by 1816 would become the African Methodist Episcopal church. Black churches, a great source of inner strength and community cohesion for most African-Americans ever since, had their roots in the revolutionary period.

Most states granted important civil rights to free blacks during and after the Revolution. For example, male free blacks who met property qualifications gained the right to vote everywhere by the 1780s. Most northern states repealed or stopped enforcing curfews and other restrictive laws; most also guaranteed free blacks equal treatment in court.

The Revolution neither ended slavery nor brought equality to free blacks, but it did begin a process by which slavery could be extinguished. In half the nation, public opinion no longer condoned human bondage, and southerners increasingly saw slavery as a necessary evil, implicitly admitting its immorality. The shift proved short-lived, as the trend toward egalitarianism faded in the 1790s.

## Women in the New Republic

"To be adept in the art of Government is a prerogative to which your sex lay almost exclusive claim," wrote Abigail Adams to her husband, John, in 1776. One of the era's tartest political commentators and her husband's confidante and best friend, Adams had no public role. Indeed, most Americans in the 1780s believed that a woman's duty lay in maintaining her household and rearing her children.

Apart from some states' easing of women's difficulties in obtaining divorces, the Revolution had little effect on women's legal position. Women gained no new political rights, although New Jersey's constitution of 1776 did not exclude white female property holders from voting, which they did in significant numbers until barred (along with free blacks) in 1807. The assumption of women's natural dependence—on parents and then husbands—dominated discussions of the female role. Nevertheless, the Revolution's ideological currents emphasizing

liberty and equality were significant for white American women.

Women greatly broadened their involvement in the cause, creating a wide range of support activities during the war. Female "camp followers," many of them soldiers' wives, cooked, laundered, and nursed the wounded for both sides. A few women disguised themselves as men and joined the fighting. Women who remained at home managed families, households, farms, and businesses on their own. Despite—and because of—enormous struggles, women gained confidence in their ability to think and act on matters traditionally reserved for men.

The revolutionary era witnessed a challenge to traditional attitudes toward women. American republicans increasingly recognized a woman's right to choose her husband rather than wait for an arranged marriage. Especially in the Northeast, daughters often, deliberately or otherwise, forced fathers' consent by becoming pregnant by prospective husbands. This secured young women economic support in a region depleted of suitors by the exodus of young, unmarried men.

Overall, white women had fewer children than their mothers and grandmothers had had. Before 1770, 40 percent of Quaker women had borne nine or more children; after then, only 14 percent would have that many children. Declining farm size and urbanization were incentives for smaller families, but just as clearly, women were finding some relief from the endless cycle of pregnancy and nursing that had consumed their forebears.

As women's roles expanded, so did republican ideas of male-female relations. A female author calling herself Matrimonial Republican denounced the word *obey* in the marriage service. "The obedience between man and wife," she wrote, "is, or ought to be, mutual." Lack of mutuality contributed to a rising number of divorce petitions submitted by women. A few women even dared challenge the prevailing sexual double standard that portrayed extramarital affairs by men as proof of virility and the same affairs by women as proof of bad character. In 1784 a woman writer calling herself Daphne appealed to her "sister Americans" to "stand by and support the dignity of our own sex" by publicly condemning the seducers, not their victims.

Gradually, the subordination of women became the subject of debate. In the essay "On the Equality of the Sexes," written in 1779, Massachusetts poet and essayist Judith Sargent Murray wrote that the genders had equal intellectual ability and deserved equal education. She hoped that "sensible and informed" women would improve their minds rather than rush into marriage and would instill republican ideals in their children. Like many of her contemporaries, Murray advocated "republican motherhood," which emphasized the importance of educating women in the values of liberty and independence in order to strengthen virtue in the new nation. Women were to infuse their sons as well as their daughters with these values. Even conservative John Adams reminded his daughter that she would be "responsible for a great share of the duty and opportunity of educating a rising family, from whom much will be expected."

After 1780 the urban elite founded numerous private schools, or academies, for girls, providing American women their first widespread opportunity for advanced education. Massachusetts also established an important precedent in 1789 by forbidding any town to exclude girls from its elementary schools. And although the great struggle for female political equality would not begin until the nineteenth century, Revolutionary-era assertions of women's intellectual and moral equality provoked scattered cries for women to be treated as men's political peers. However, republican egalitarianism faced a serious limitation: even an educated woman would be confined to being a virtuous wife and mother.

## Native Americans and the Revolution

Revolutionary ideology held out at least abstract hope for African-Americans and women, but it made no provisions for the many Indians who sought to maintain political and cultural independence. Moreover, in an overwhelmingly agrarian society, the Revolution's promise of equal economic opportunity for all set the stage for territorial expansion beyond settled areas, thereby threatening Indian lands. Even where Indians retained land, the influx of settlers posed dangers in the form of deadly diseases, farming practices hostile to Indian subsistence, and alcohol. Indians were all the more vulnerable because during the wars between 1754 and 1783, their population east of the Mississippi had fallen by about one-half and many villages had been uprooted.

In the face of these uncertainties, Native Americans continued to incorporate aspects of European culture into their lives. From the early colonial period, they had adopted European-made goods of cloth, metal, and glass while retaining some of their traditional clothing, tools, and weapons. Indians also participated in the American economy by occasionally working for wages or selling food, craft items, and other products. Such interweaving of old and new characterized Indian communities throughout the newly independent states.

Thus Native Americans did not hold stubbornly to traditional ways, but they did insist on retaining control of their communities and ways of life. In 1745 some Iroquois had told an Anglo-American missionary, "We are Indians and do not wish to be transformed into white men. The English are our Brethren, but we never promised to become what they are." In the Revolution's aftermath, it remained unclear whether the new nation would accommodate Native Americans on these terms.

## The Revolution and Social Change

The American Revolution left the distribution of wealth in the nation unchanged. Because fleeing Tories represented a cross-section of the population, and because wealthy Whigs snapped up confiscated Tory estates, the upper class owned about the same proportion of national wealth in 1783 as it had in 1776.

In short, the Revolution neither erased nor challenged social distinctions. Class distinctions, racial injustice, and the subordination of women persisted. Slavery remained intact in the South. Yet the Revolutionary era set in motion substantial changes. The gentry increasingly had to treat the common people with courtesy and to earn their respect. The Revolution dealt slavery a decisive blow in the North, enlarged the free-black population, and granted it important political rights. The Revolution also placed issues about relations between the genders on the agenda of national debate. Inevitably, these social changes shaped the new nation's political debates.

# Forging New Governments

Before the Declaration of Independence, few Americans had thought about the colonies' forming governments of their own. The Continental Congress lacked the sovereign powers associated with governments, including the authority to impose taxes.

During the war rebels recognized the need to establish government institutions to sustain the war and to buttress the American claim to independence. But the task of forging a national government proved arduous. Moreover, the state governments formed in wartime reflected two often conflicting impulses: on the one hand, traditional Anglo-American ideas and practices; on the other, new, republican ideals. Americans would find that it was far easier to win a revolution than to transform revolutionary ideals into everyday institutions.

## Tradition and Change

In establishing the Revolutionary state governments, the patriots relied heavily on the colonial experience. For example, most took the value of bicameral legislatures for granted. Colonial legislatures in the royal provinces had consisted of two houses: an appointed upper chamber (council) and an elected lower chamber (assembly). These two-part legislatures resembled Parliament's division into the House of Lords and the House of Commons and symbolized the assumption that a government should represent aristocrats and commoners separately. Despite the Revolution's democratic tendencies, few questioned the long-standing practice of setting property requirements for voters and elected officials. Property ownership, they argued, enabled voters and officeholders to think and act independently.

Americans generally agreed, too, that their elected representatives should exercise independent judgment rather than simply carry out the popular will. The idea of political parties as instruments for identifying and mobilizing public opinion was alien to the Revolutionary era, which equated parties with "factions"—selfish groups that advanced their interests at the expense of the public good. Candidates campaigned on the basis of their reputation and qualifications, not issues. In general, they did not present voters with a clear choice between policies calculated to benefit rival interest groups. Thus voters did not know how candidates stood on specific issues and found it hard to influence government actions.

As in the colonial era, legislatures were divided equally among all counties or towns in the 1780s, regardless of population distribution. A minority of voters normally elected a majority of assemblymen. Offices such as sheriff and county court justice remained appointive.

In sum, the colonial experience provided no precedent for democratization. Yet the imperial crisis of the 1760s and 1770s had pulled political elites in a democratic direction. The assemblies, the most democratic parts of colonial government, had led the fight against British policy. Colonists had embarked on the Revolution dreading executive officeholders and convinced that they could not trust even elected governors. Their recent experience seemed to confirm the "country party" view (see Chapter 5) that those in power tended to become corrupt or dictatorial. Thus revolutionary statesmen proclaimed the need to strengthen legislatures at the governors' expense.

But Revolutionary leaders described themselves as republicans, not democrats. These words had strongly charged meanings in the eighteenth century. At worst, democracy suggested mob rule; at best, it meant the concentration of power in an uneducated people. In contrast, republicanism presumed that government would be entrusted to capable leaders, elected for their talent and wisdom. For republicans, the ideal government would balance the interests of different classes to prevent any group's gaining absolute power. Most Whigs believed that a republic could not include a hereditary aristocracy or even a monarchy. Yet by rejecting these institutions, Whigs created a problem: how to maintain balance in government amid a pervasive distrust of executive power.

## Reconstituting the States

The state governments organized during the Revolution reflected a struggle between democratic elements and elites. Eleven of the thirteen states set up bicameral legislatures. In most states the majority of officeholders continued to be appointed. The most radical constitution, Pennsylvania's, tried to establish election districts roughly equal in population so that a minority of voters could not elect a majority of legislators. Nine states reduced property requirements for voting, but none abolished them.

The persistence of these features should not obscure the pathbreaking nature of the state constitutions. First, their adoption required ratification by the people. Second, they could be changed only by popular vote. Above all, counter to the British view of a constitution as a body of customary practices, the state constitutions were *written* compacts that defined and limited rulers' powers. As a final check on government power, the Revolutionary constitutions contained bills of rights outlining fundamental freedoms beyond government control. Governments would no longer serve as the final judge of the constitutionality of their activities.

The state constitutions strictly limited executive power. In most states the governor became an elected official, and elections were held far more frequently than before—usually every year. In the majority of states legislatures, not governors, appointed judges and other officials. Stripped of the veto and most appointive powers, governors became figureheads.

Having weakened the executive branch and vested more power in the legislatures, the state constitutions also made the legislatures more responsive to the will of the people. Nowhere could the governor appoint the upper chamber. Eight states allowed voters to select *both* houses of the legislature. Pennsylvania and Georgia abolished the upper house and substituted a unicameral (one-chamber) legislature. The Whigs' assault on executive power reflected bitter memories of arbitrary royal governors and underscored the influence of country-party ideologues who had warned against executives' usurpation of authority.

During the 1780s, however, elites gradually reasserted their desires for centralized authority and the political prerogatives of wealth. The Massachusetts constitution of 1780, which established stiff property qualifications for voting and holding office, created state senate districts apportioned according to property values, and increased the governor's powers of veto and appointment, signaled a general trend. Georgia and Pennsylvania had reverted to bicameral legislatures by 1790. Other states raised property qualifications for the upper chamber to make room for men of "Wisdom, remarkable integrity, or that Weight which arises from property."

Troubled far less by differences among social classes and restrictions on the expression of popular will than by the prospect of tyranny, elites nevertheless feared that deep-seated and permanent social divisions could jeopardize republican liberty. Although more committed to liberty than equality, some republicans did use state government legislation to implement major social changes. In Virginia between 1776 and 1780, Thomas Jefferson drafted a series of bills to promote equality. He also attacked two legal bastions of the British aristocracy, primogeniture and entail. Primogeniture required that the eldest son inherit all property if there was no will; entail dictated that an heir and his descendants keep an estate intact—that is, neither sell nor divide it. Jefferson hoped that this legislation would

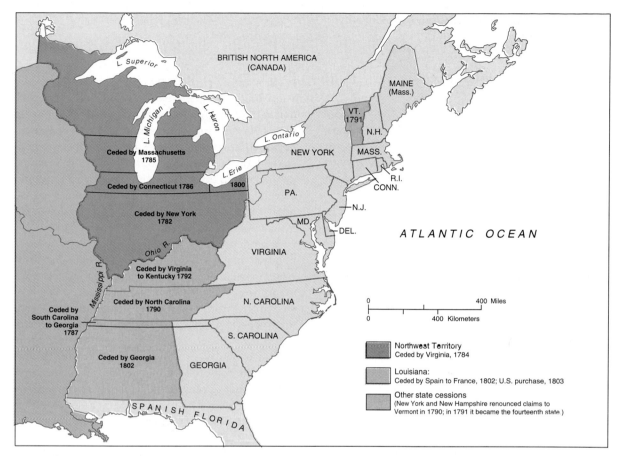

**State Claims to Western Lands and State Cessions to the Federal Government, 1782–1802**

*Eastern states' surrender of land claims paved the way for new state governments in the West. Georgia was the last state to cede its western lands, in 1802.*

ensure a continuous division of wealth and prevent wealthy families from amassing huge landholdings and becoming an aristocracy. By 1791 no state provided for primogeniture, and only two allowed entails.

These years also witnessed the end of most state-established churches. Religiously conservative New Hampshire, Connecticut, and Massachusetts resisted this reform until 1817, 1818, and 1833, respectively, but in every state where the Anglican church was established, such status was abolished by 1786. Jefferson's Statute for Religious Freedom (1786) resoundingly defended religious freedom. "Truth is great," he proclaimed, "and will prevail if left to itself."

In 1782 Thomas Paine wrote that the American Revolution was intended to ring in "a new era and give a new turn to human affairs." In this ambitious declaration, Paine expressed the heart of the republican ideal: that *all* political institutions would be judged by whether they served the public good, not the interests of a powerful few. More than anything else, this way of thinking made American politics revolutionary.

## The Articles of Confederation

Americans' first national government reflected their fears of centralized authority. In 1776 John Dickinson drafted a proposal for a national government, and in 1777 Congress sent a weakened version of this document, the Articles of Confederation, to the states for ratification.

The Articles reserved to each state "its sovereignty, freedom and independence" and made Americans citizens of their states first and of the United States second. John Adams later explained that the Whigs never thought of "consolidating this vast Continent under one national Government" but created instead "a Confederacy of States, each of which must have a separate government."

Under the Articles, the national government consisted of a unicameral congress, elected by the state legislatures, in which each state had one vote. Congress could request funds from the states but could not tax without every state's approval, nor could it regulate interstate or overseas commerce. The Articles provided for no executive branch. Rather, congressional committees oversaw financial, diplomatic, and military affairs. Nor was there a judicial system by which the national government could compel allegiance to its laws.

All thirteen states had to approve the Articles. Maryland refused to sign them until states claiming lands north of the Ohio River turned them over to the national government. Maryland lawmakers wanted to keep Virginia and New York from dominating the new nation. As individual states gradually abandoned their northwestern claims, Maryland relented, and the Articles became law in March 1781.

The new government represented an important step in the process of defining the role of national sovereignty in relation to the sovereignty of individual states and in creating a formal government. Nonetheless, the Whigs' misgivings left the new government severely limited.

## Finance and Trade Under the Confederation

Perhaps the greatest challenge facing the Confederation was putting the nation on a sound financial footing. Winning the war cost $160 million, far more than taxation could raise. The government borrowed from abroad and printed paper money, called Continentals. But from 1776 to 1791 lack of public faith in the government destroyed 98 percent of the Continentals' value—an inflationary disaster. Congress turned to Robert Morris, a wealthy Philadelphia merchant who became the nation's superintendent of finance in 1781. Morris proposed a national import duty of 5 percent to finance the congressional budget and to guarantee interest payments on the war debt, but the duty failed to pass.

In 1783, hoping to panic the country into creating a regular source of national revenue, Morris and New York congressman Alexander Hamilton engineered a dangerous gamble, later known as the Newburgh Conspiracy. They secretly persuaded some army officers, encamped at Newburgh, New York, to threaten a coup d'état unless the treasury obtained the taxation authority necessary to raise their pay, which was months late. George Washington forestalled the conspiracy by appealing to his officers' honor. Morris never intended a mutiny to take place, but his risk taking demonstrated the new nation's perilous financial straits and its political institutions' vulnerability.

When peace came in 1783, Morris found it impossible to fund the government adequately. After New York blocked another congressional tax measure sent to the states, state contributions to Congress fell steadily. By the late 1780s the states lagged 80 percent behind in providing the funds that Congress requested.

Nor could the Confederation pry trade concessions from Britain. Before independence, New England had depended heavily on exports to the West Indies. After independence, Britain had slapped strict limitations on U.S. commerce, allowing British shippers to increase their share of the Atlantic trade at American expense. This loss of

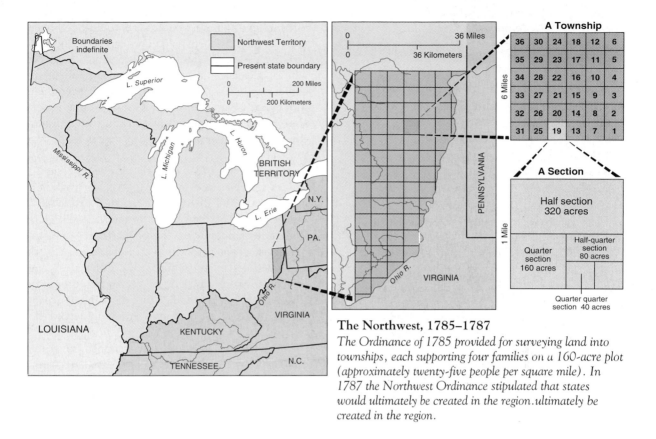

### The Northwest, 1785–1787

*The Ordinance of 1785 provided for surveying land into townships, each supporting four families on a 160-acre plot (approximately twenty-five people per square mile). In 1787 the Northwest Ordinance stipulated that states would ultimately be created in the region.ultimately be created in the region.*

trade contributed to an economic depression that gripped the nation beginning in 1784.

## The Confederation and the West

The postwar settlement and administration of western lands posed another formidable challenge to the new government. Settlers and speculators were determined to possess these lands, and Native Americans were equally determined to keep them out. At the same time, Britain and Spain sought to contain the new nation's territorial expansion.

After the states surrendered claims to more than 160 million acres north of the Ohio River, Congress, in the Ordinance of 1785, established uniform procedures for surveying the region. The law made the basic unit of settlement a township six miles square, subdivided into thirty-six sections of 640 acres each, with one section reserved as a source of income for public schools. A subsequent law, the Northwest Ordinance of 1787, defined the land north of the Ohio River as the Northwest Territory, provided for its later division into states, and forbade slavery in the territory. The Northwest Ordinance outlined three steps for admitting states to the Union. First, Congress would appoint a territorial governor and judges. Second, as soon as 5,000 adult males lived in a territory, the people would write a temporary constitution and elect a legislature. Third, when the population reached 60,000, the settlers would write a state constitution, which Congress would approve before granting statehood.

The Ordinance of 1785 and the Northwest Ordinance became the Confederation's major contributions to American life. They set the principles for surveying the frontier, allowed territorial self-

**Phillis Wheatley, African-American Poet**
*Though a slave, Wheatley was the best-known poet in America at the time of the Revolution. Some of her poems linked the liberty sought by the colonists with a plea for the liberty of slaves. Despite her fame, Wheatley died in poverty in 1784.*

government at an early stage of settlement, and provided reasonable standards for statehood. They became models for organizing territories west of the Mississippi River and established precedents for banning slavery from certain territories. However, because Indians, determined to bar white settlement, controlled virtually the entire Northwest, Congress's ordinances had no immediate effect.

The Northwest Territory offered enough rich land to guarantee future citizens landownership, thus satisfying the republican belief that opening the West would prevent the rise, east of the Appalachians, of a large class of tenant farmers and poor laborers lacking the property needed to vote.

Such a development would poison politics through class conflict and would undermine republican equality. In the anticipated westward push by whites, Jefferson and other republicans hoped to avoid conflict with Indians by assimilating them into white society. However, because Native Americans had no desire to abandon their own cultures, the opening of western lands to whites made war inevitable.

At postwar treaty negotiations U.S. commissioners told Native Americans, "You are a subdued people. . . . We claim the country by conquest." Under threat of continued warfare, some Indian leaders initially yielded. Through treaties the Iroquois lost about one-half their land in New York and Pennsylvania, while the Delawares and Shawnees were obliged to recognize American sovereignty over their lands. But most Indians repudiated the treaties, denying that their negotiators had the authority to give up their nations' lands.

The Indians' resistance also stemmed from their confidence that the British would provide the arms necessary to defy the Americans. Britain had refused to abandon seven forts along the nation's northwestern frontier, ostensibly because Tories remained uncompensated for property losses. In April 1784 the British colonial office secretly ordered Canada's governor to hold onto the forts, hoping to reestablish Britain's claim to the Northwest Territory.

The Mohawk Joseph Brant led Indian resistance to white settlement. Courageous, skilled in diplomacy, and well educated, he organized the northwestern Indians into a military alliance in 1786 to keep out white settlers. But Brant and his followers, who had relocated beyond American reach in Canada, could not win support from other Iroquois such as the Senecas of Jenuchshadago, who remained in New York and feared a military invasion.

The Confederation faced similar problems in the Southeast, where Spain and its Indian allies worked to block American encroachment on their land. The Spanish found an ally in the shrewd Creek diplomat Alexander McGillivray, who was determined to regain surrendered Creek territory. McGillivray negotiated a secret treaty with Spain that promised the Creeks weapons to protect themselves "from the Bears and other fierce Animals." In 1786 he launched an attack on occupants of disputed lands. He offered a cease-fire after winning his objective.

The Spanish also attempted to prevent American infiltration by denying western settlers permission to ship crops down the Mississippi River to New Orleans. After the Spanish closed New Orleans to Anglo-American commerce in 1784, John Jay went to Spain to negotiate trading privileges at New Orleans. Although he failed to win concessions, he returned with a treaty that opened Spanish markets to eastern merchants at the price of relinquishing American export rights through New Orleans. In 1786 Congress rejected this Jay-Gardoqui Treaty, but westerners and southerners, whose interests seemed to have been sacrificed to benefit northern commerce, felt betrayed.

## Shays's Rebellion

Had not violence erupted in Massachusetts, the Confederation might have lasted indefinitely. Massachusetts had suffered two major blows: in the depression that had set in in 1784, it had lost its best market, the British West Indies, and early in 1786 the state legislature had imposed high taxes to pay off its Revolutionary debt rapidly. British creditors and Massachusetts bankers and tax collectors demanded payment in specie (gold and silver coin). Thousands of small farmers, accustomed to paying local creditors with goods and services, often over a period of years, found the idea of paying all debts in hard currency not only alien but also impossible. Farmers in western Massachusetts were hard hit. As they had more than a decade earlier, farmers held rallies to discuss "the Supressing of tyrannical government." This time, however, tyranny stemmed from the state house in Boston, not Parliament in London. Late in 1786 Daniel Shays, a Revolutionary War officer and hard-pressed farmer, led 2,000 angry men in an attempt to shut down the courts

and to prevent foreclosures and tax auctions. Although routed by the state militia, Shays's followers won control of the Massachusetts legislature in 1787, cut taxes, and secured a pardon for Shays.

Although Shays's Rebellion caused little bloodshed and never raised a serious threat of anarchy, critics of the Confederation painted it and similar, less radical movements elsewhere as a taste of the disorder to come under the weak national government. By threatening to seize weapons from a federal arsenal at Springfield, Massachusetts, the Shaysites had unintentionally reminded nationalists how vulnerable to "mobocracy" the United States had become. Meanwhile, rumors that Spain had offered westerners export rights at New Orleans if they would secede from the Union sowed fears that the United States was on the verge of coming apart.

The mid-Atlantic and southern states, emerging from the depression that still gripped New England, generally did not share this alarm about the Confederation's fragility. However, a growing minority was dissatisfied. Urban artisans wanted a strong government that could impose high tariffs to protect their products. Merchants and shippers desired a government powerful enough to secure trading privileges for them, and land speculators and westerners wanted a strong government that would pursue aggressive anti-Indian policies.

Shortly before Shays's Rebellion, delegates from five states, meeting at Annapolis, Maryland, had called for a convention to propose amendments to the Articles of Confederation. Accepting their suggestions, Congress asked the states to send delegates to meet in Philadelphia.

## The Philadelphia Convention

In May 1787 fifty-five delegates, from every state but Rhode Island, began gathering at the Pennsylvania State House (later called Independence Hall) in Philadelphia. Among them were men of established reputation—George Washington, Benjamin Franklin, Robert Morris—as well as talented newcomers such as Alexander Hamilton and James Madison. Most were wealthy, were in their thirties

**James Madison (1751–1836)**
*Although one of the Philadelphia Convention's youngest delegates, Madison of Virginia was among its most politically astute. He played a central role in the Constitution's adoption.*

or forties, and had legal training. Nineteen owned slaves. Most important, they shared a "continental" or "nationalist" perspective. Thirty-nine had served in Congress and knew firsthand the weaknesses of the Articles. They were convinced that without a strong national government, the country would fall victim to foreign aggression or simply disintegrate.

Two basic issues confronted the convention. First, should the delegates merely tinker with the Articles, or should they draw up a new frame of government? Second, how could any government balance the conflicting interests of large and small states? Thirty-six-year-old James Madison of Virginia proposed answers to both questions.

Madison's Virginia Plan, introduced by fellow Virginian Edmund Randolph in late May, boldly called for a national government, not a confederation of states. It gave Congress virtually unrestricted rights of legislation and taxation, power to veto

state laws, and authority to use military force against states. As delegate Charles Pinckney of South Carolina immediately saw, the Virginia Plan was designed "to abolish the State Govern[men]ts altogether." The Virginia Plan specified a bicameral legislation and made representation in both houses of Congress proportional to each state's population. The voters would elect the lower house, which would then choose delegates to the upper house from nominations submitted by the state legislatures. The houses would jointly name the country's president and judges. But opposition to Madison's plan surfaced immediately, particularly his call for proportional representation, which favored Virginia, the largest state.

On June 15 William Paterson of New Jersey offered a counterproposal that, like Madison's plan, strengthened the national government at the states' expense. The New Jersey Plan featured a unicameral legislature in which each state had one vote, just as under the Articles. It went even further than the Virginia Plan by defining congressional laws and treaties as the "supreme law of the land."

The New Jersey Plan exposed the convention's greatest problem: the question of representation. The Virginia Plan gave the four largest states—Virginia, Massachusetts, New York, and Pennsylvania—a majority in both houses. The New Jersey Plan allowed the seven smallest states, with only 25 percent of the U.S. population, to control Congress. By early July the convention was stalemated. To end the impasse, the delegates appointed a "grand committee" dedicated to compromise. This panel adopted a proposal by the Connecticut delegation: an equal vote for each state in the upper house and proportional representation in the lower house. The convention accepted the compromise on July 17 and in two months overcame the remaining hurdles.

As finally approved on September 17, 1787, the Constitution of the United States was an extraordinary document. In addition to reconciling the interests of large and small states, it balanced the delegates' desire for a strong national government against their fear of tyranny. It increased national authority in several ways. It vested in Congress the authority to levy and collect taxes, to regulate interstate commerce, and to conduct diplomacy. Under the Constitution, all acts and treaties of the United States would become "the supreme law of the land." State officials would have to uphold the Constitution, even against acts of their own states. The national government could use military force against any state.

In effect, the Constitution abandoned the principle on which the Articles of Confederation had rested: that the United States was a federation of independent republics known as states. However, the Constitution's framers restrained the new national government in two key ways. First, they established three distinct branches within the new government—the legislative, the executive, and the judicial. Second, they designed a system of checks and balances to prevent one branch from dominating the others. States' equal representation in the Senate offset proportional representation by population in the House, and each chamber could block hasty measures demanded by the other. Further, the president could veto acts of Congress, but to prevent capricious use of the presidential veto, a two-thirds majority in each house could override a veto. The president would conduct diplomacy, but only the Senate could ratify treaties. The president appointed his cabinet, but only with Senate approval. Congress could, by joint vote, remove the president and his appointees from office, but only for "high crimes," not for political disagreements.

To further guarantee the independence of each branch, the Constitution provided that the members of one branch would not choose those of another, except judges, whose independence was protected by lifetime appointments. For example, an electoral college, composed of members chosen by the various state legislatures, would select the president. State legislatures would also elect senators, whereas popular vote would determine delegates to the House of Representatives.

In addition to checks and balances, the Constitution embodied a novel form of federalism—a system of shared power and dual lawmaking by the state and national governments—to limit central authority. Not only did the state legislatures have a key role in electing the president and senators, but

the Constitution could be amended by the votes of three-fourths of the state legislatures. This system differed greatly from Madison's original plan to establish a national government entirely independent of and superior to the states. Federalism assumed that the national government would limit its activities to foreign affairs, national defense, regulation of commerce, and coining of money. Most other political matters were left to the states. The states could otherwise act autonomously on purely internal matters, including slavery.

The Philadelphia convention faced a dilemma: were slaves property or persons? In general, southern states regarded slaves as property; however, since slaves constituted substantial portions of the southern population, southern delegates wanted to count them as persons in determining representation in the lower house. Many northern delegates from the states that were abolishing slavery hesitated to give southern states a political edge by counting as persons slaves who had neither civil nor political rights. At the same time, northern delegates, themselves property owners, balked at questioning southern notions of property rights. Thus they agreed to allow three-fifths of all slaves to be counted for congressional representation and forbade any state's people to prevent the return of runaway slaves to another state. The Constitution did limit slavery by not repudiating the Northwest Ordinance's restrictions on slavery and by permitting Congress to ban the importation of slaves after 1808.

Although leaving much authority to the states, the Constitution established a national government clearly superior to the states in several spheres and utterly abandoned the notion of a confederation of virtually independent states. Having thus strengthened national authority, the convention faced the issue of ratification. Two factors argued against submitting the Constitution to the state legislatures for ratification. First, the state legislatures would probably reject the Constitution, which shrank their power relative to the national government. Second, most of the framers believed that the government had to rest on the consent of the American people themselves. The Constitution's opening words— "We the People of the United States"—embodied this view. In the end the Philadelphia Convention provided for the Constitution's ratification by special state conventions composed of delegates elected by the people. Approval by nine such conventions would enable the new government to operate.

Under the Constitution, the framers expected the nation's "natural aristocracy" to continue exercising political leadership; but did they also intend to rein in the democratic currents that the Revolution had set in motion? In one respect they did—by curtailing the power of popularly elected state legislatures. However, the Constitution made no attempt to control faction and disorder by suppressing liberty—a "remedy," wrote Madison, that would have been "worse than the disease." The House of Representatives did provide one crucial democratic element in the new government. Equally important, the Constitution recognized the American people as the ultimate source of political legitimacy. By making the Constitution flexible and amendable and by dividing political power among competing branches of government, the framers made it possible for the national government to be slowly democratized.

## The Constitution's Ratification

At first the Constitution had little national support. Many Americans hesitated to accept the idea of a radically restructured government. To quiet fears of centralized national authority, the Constitution's supporters shrewdly dubbed themselves Federalists, a term implying that the Constitution successfully balanced the relationship between state and national governments.

The Constitution's opponents became known as Antifederalists, a negative-sounding name that conveyed little of their fears that the Constitution *did not* balance the power of the state and national governments. In fact, many Antifederalists doubted that such a balance was even possible. By augmenting national authority, they believed, the Constitution would ultimately doom the states.

Antifederalist arguments reflected the deep-seated Anglo-American suspicion of any concentration of power, a suspicion that had driven events from the Stamp Act Congress through the War of Independence and the early years of the new republic. Unquestionably, the Constitution gave the national government unprecedented authority in an age when most writers on politics agreed that the sole means of preventing despotism was restraining the power of government officials. Distant from the people, especially in an era when news traveled slowly, the national government would be far less responsive to the popular will than state governments would be. "The vast Continent of America cannot be long subjected to a Democracy if consolidated into one Government. You might as well attempt to rule Hell by Prayer," wrote a New England Antifederalist. Furthermore, no one could be sure that the untried scheme of checks and balances would work. And the Constitution contained no guarantees that the new government would protect the liberties of individuals or the states. The absence of a bill of rights prompted Madison's nationalist ally and fellow Virginian George Mason, the author of the first state bill of rights in 1776, to oppose the Constitution.

The Antifederalists confronted several major disadvantages. For one thing, the Federalists included most of the country's wealthiest and most honored men, including Washington and Franklin. In addition, the majority of newspapers were Federalist and did not hesitate to bias their reporting. Finally, the Antifederalists, largely drawn from state and local leaders, lacked their opponents' contacts and experience at the national level. Ultimately, however, Federalist superiority in funds and political organizing proved decisive. The Antifederalists failed to create a sense of urgency among their supporters, assuming that most would automatically rally to them. However, only one-quarter of the voters turned out to elect delegates to the state ratifying conventions, and most had been mobilized by Federalists.

Federalist delegates prevailed in eight state

**Federalist and Antifederalist Strongholds, 1787–1790**

*Federalists drew their primary backing from densely populated areas along major transportation routes, where trade, mobility, and frequent contact with people in other states encouraged a nationalistic identity. Antifederalist support came from interior regions where geographic isolation bred a localistic perspective. However, some frontier regions, among them Georgia and western Virginia, voted for a strong central government that would push back the Indians or the Spanish.*

conventions between December 1787 and May 1788, in all cases but one by margins of two-thirds or more. Such lopsided voting in favor of the Constitution reflected Federalist aggressiveness more than popular support. In a Pennsylvania Antifederalist's words, the Federalists rammed through approval in some states "before it can be digested or deliberately considered." Only Rhode Island and North Carolina rejected the Constitution.

But unless the large states of Virginia and New York ratified, the new government would be unworkable. Antifederalism ran high in both, especially among small farmers, who believed that the Constitution favored city dwellers and monied interests. Prominent Antifederalists included New York's governor George Clinton and Virginia's Richard Henry Lee, George Mason, Patrick Henry, and future president James Monroe.

On June 21, 1788, the Constitution became the law of the land when the ninth state, New Hampshire, ratified. Debate continued in Virginia, where the Federalists won wide support from settlers in the western part of the state who wanted a strong national government capable of ending Indian raids along the Ohio River. Western Virginians' votes, combined with Madison's logic and tidewater planters' support, ruled the day. On June 25 the Virginia delegates ratified by a narrow 53 percent majority.

The struggle was even hotter in New York. Antifederalists controlled the state convention and probably would have voted down the Constitution had not news arrived of New Hampshire's and Virginia's ratification. Federalists, led by Alexander Hamilton and John Jay, hinted strongly that if the convention rejected the Constitution, New York City would secede and join the Union alone, leaving upstate New York a landlocked enclave. Alarmed, a number of Antifederalists switched sides and New York ratified on July 26 by a 30–27 vote.

Despite the defeat, the Antifederalists left an important legacy. At Antifederalist insistence, the Virginia, New York, and Massachusetts conventions ratified the Constitution with requests that the new charter be amended to include a bill of rights protecting Americans' basic freedoms. Widespread support for a bill of rights made it a major item on the new government's agenda, even as states were choosing members of Congress and presidential electors were unanimously designating George Washington president of the United States.

Antifederalists in New York also stimulated one of the greatest works of political analysis ever written: *The Federalist*, a series of eighty-five newspaper articles by Alexander Hamilton, James Madison, and John Jay. Although *The Federalist* papers did little to influence the New York vote, they provided a glimpse of the framers' intentions in designing the Constitution and thus powerfully shaped the American philosophy of government. The Constitution, insisted *The Federalist*'s authors, had two main purposes: to defend minority rights against majority tyranny and to prevent a stubborn minority from blocking measures necessary for the national interest. There was no reason to fear that the Constitution would allow a single economic or regional interest to dominate. In the most profound essay in the series, *Federalist* No. 10, Madison argued that the nation's size and diversity would neutralize the attempts of factions to steer unwise laws through Congress.

Madison's analysis was far too optimistic, however. The Constitution did indeed afford enormous scope for special interests to influence government. The great challenge for Madison's generation would be maintaining a government that provided equal benefits to all but special privileges to none.

## CONCLUSION

By May 1790 North Carolina and Rhode Island had entered the Union, marking the final triumph of the nationalism born of the War for Independence. The eight-year conflict had swept up one-half of all men of military age and made casualties of one-fifth of them. Never before had such a large part of the population sacrificed in a common cause of this magnitude.

The experience of sacrificing and fighting together made many of the former colonists self-consciously American. Many shared the view of General Nathanael Greene of Rhode Island, who condemned the "prejudices" of those with "local attachments." "I feel the cause and not the place," he said; "I would as soon go to Virginia [to fight] as stay here [New England]." The distractions of peace almost allowed this sentiment to evaporate, but the Constitution offered clear proof that large numbers of Americans viewed themselves as a common people rather than as the citizens of allied states.

## CHRONOLOGY

**1775** Virginia governor Lord Dunmore promises freedom to any slave assisting in the restoration of royal authority.
Mercy Otis Warren, *The Group*.

**1776** British troops evacuate Boston.
British defeat American forces under George Washington in fighting around New York City.
American victory in Battle of Trenton.

**1777** American victory in Battle of Princeton.
British surrender at Saratoga.
Battle of Brandywine Creek; British occupy Philadelphia.
American defeat at Battle of Germantown.
Congress approves Articles of Confederation.

**1778** France formally recognizes the United States.
France declares war on Britain.
Philadelphia evacuated by British; Battle of Monmouth Court House (New Jersey).
British occupy Savannah.
Joseph Brant leads Iroquois attacks in western Pennsylvania and New York.

**1779** Spain declares war on Britain.
George Rogers Clark's recapture of Vincennes.
John Sullivan leads U.S. raids on Iroquois.
Judith Murray, "On the Equality of the Sexes" (published in 1790).

**1780** British seize Charles Town.
Dutch Republic declares war on Britain.

**1781** Articles of Confederation become law.
Battle of Yorktown; British general Charles Cornwallis surrenders.

**1782** Paris peace negotiations begin.

**1783** Peace of Paris.
Newburgh Conspiracy.

**1784** Spain closes New Orleans to American trade.
Economic depression begins.

**1785** Ordinance of 1785.

**1786** Congress rejects Jay-Gardoqui Treaty.
Joseph Brant organizes Indian resistance to U.S. expansion.
Virginia adopts Thomas Jefferson's Statute for Religious Freedom.

**1786–** Shays's Rebellion in Massachusetts.
**1787**

**1787** Northwest Ordinance.
Philadelphia Convention; federal Constitution signed.

**1788** Alexander Hamilton, James Madison, and John Jay, *The Federalist*.
Federal Constitution becomes law.

## FOR FURTHER READING

Edward Countryman, *The American Revolution* (1985). An excellent introduction to developments from the Revolution through ratification of the Constitution.

Jack P. Greene, ed., *The American Revolution: Its Character and Limits* (1987). Leading scholars' analysis of how Americans dealt with the problem of applying their political ideals to an imperfect society without endangering the nation's survival.

Robert Middlekauff, *The Glorious Cause: The American Revolution, 1763–1789* (1982). A comprehensive account of military and political developments through the Philadelphia Convention.

Mary Beth Norton, *Liberty's Daughters: The Revolutionary Experience of American Women, 1750–1800* (1980). A wide-ranging study of changes in the lives and roles of women during the revolutionary era.

Benjamin Quarles, *The Negro in the American Revolution* (1961). An authoritative study of blacks' role in the Revolution and its consequences for them.

Charles Royster, *A Revolutionary People at War: The Continental Army and American Character* (1980). An illuminating analysis of how revolutionary Americans created and fought in an army.

Gordon Wood, *The Creation of the American Republic, 1776–1787* (1969). Comprehensive treatment of the evolution of American political thought from the first state governments to the Philadelphia Convention.

The problems facing George Washington in 1789 underlined the fragility of the United States. North Carolina and Rhode Island still remained outside the Union, westerners were flirting with Spanish agents, and the splintering of the nation into several smaller countries seemed a real threat. In addition, Indians and frontier whites were fighting ceaselessly, foreign restrictions were strangling American exports, the treasury was bankrupt, and government credit was a shambles. Finally, France, Spain, and Britain all menaced American prosperity and independence.

By the end of his second administration in 1797, Washington had helped to overcome some of the most serious obstacles, but at the price of unleashing fiercely emotional party divisions. By 1798 a sense of crisis again gripped the nation. The party in power resorted to political oppression. Afraid of despotism and an unfair election, the opposition party desperately maintained that state legislatures could veto federal laws.

*(Right)* **Liberty and Washington,** *anonymous artist, early nineteenth century*

# Launching the New Republic, 1789–1800

**The Fragile New Nation**

❧

**Constitutional Government Takes Shape**

❧

**National Economic Policy and Its Consequences**

❧

**The United States in a Hostile World**

❧

**Battling for the Nation's Soul**

❧

**Deferring Equality**

In the election of 1800, each side damned the other in irresponsible rhetoric. Only after the election, with Thomas Jefferson in office, was it clear that the United States had avoided dissolution and preserved civil liberties.

# The Fragile New Nation

The postwar years brought problems, not prosperity, to many Americans. Restrictions on export markets endangered the livelihoods of farmers, sailors, and merchants. Foreign efforts to prevent American settlement of the frontier frustrated land speculators as well as pioneers. The Confederation's default on the national debt had injured thousands of Revolutionary creditors by delaying their compensation, and there was no guarantee that the new government would honor their claims. These conditions had convinced Americans of the need for a new constitution, but because of the scope of the problems, the new system could still fail.

Conflicting regional interests would prevent the new government from providing equal nationwide benefits for two decades. And other fissures were deepening within American society: among blacks, Indians, and whites; between emerging capitalists and wage earners; and above all, among citizens with different interpretations of republicanism. These regional and ideological conflicts would not only split the new Congress into hostile parties but also bring into focus a rising demand for a *democratic* republic.

## The West and the South

Most U.S. territory from the Appalachians to the Mississippi River belonged to Native Americans. Divided into more than eighty tribes numbering perhaps 150,000 people in 1789, Indians struggled to preserve their way of life. During the Revolutionary War patriot forces had dealt the Iroquois and Cherokees punishing blows, but most Indians, though bloodied, had continued to hold their land. In 1786 Ohio River tribes formed a defensive confederacy (see Chapter 6). Powerful southeastern na-

tions refused to acknowledge American rule. Great Britain backed Indian resistance in the Northwest, as did Spain in the Southeast.

Confronting the inland Indians were about 200,000 frontier settlers, many of them isolated and vulnerable. By 1786 Indian war parties had spread death, destruction, and panic from Pennsylvania to Georgia. Fifteen hundred of Kentucky's 74,000 settlers were captured or killed in Indian raids from 1784 to 1790, a casualty rate twice that of the Revolutionary War. Frontier people retaliated ruthlessly. "The people of Kentucky," wrote an army officer, "will carry on private expeditions against the Indians and kill them whenever they meet them, and I do not believe there is a jury in all Kentucky will punish a man for it."

Massive military force—enough to raze Indian villages, destroy food supplies, and threaten starvation—represented the key to whites' conquering the Indians. Frontier militias, poorly equipped and trained, lacked sufficient force. In 1786 a lack of supplies forced 1,200 Kentuckians under George Rogers Clark to abandon a campaign against Great Lakes Indians. Defeat of the Indians clearly called for federal forces. But in 1789 the U.S. Army's total strength stood at 672 soldiers, less than one-half the number of warriors in the northwestern Indian confederation. Despairing frontier settlers concluded that the United States had forfeited their loyalty. Clark spoke for many Kentuckians in 1786 when he declared that "no property or person is safe under a government so weak as that of the United States."

Nevertheless, militia raids gradually forced Miamis, Shawnees, and Delawares to evacuate southern Indiana and Ohio. In spring 1788 fifty New Englanders sailed down the Ohio in a bullet-proof barge christened the *Mayflower* to found the town of Marietta. Later that year Pennsylvanians and New Jerseyites established Cincinnati. The contest for the Ohio Valley was nearing its decisive stage.

Westerners felt a special bitterness toward the British, whose continued occupation of seven northwestern forts seemed the mainspring of the endless border fighting. British complaints about American failure to compensate the loyalists were a fig leaf for slowing U.S. expansion until Britain could establish an Indian buffer state south of the Great Lakes and annex the region to Canada.

Spain, unable to prevent American settlers' occupation of land it claimed in the Southeast, sought their allegiance by offering citizenship—and bribes. Most westerners who accepted the gold doled out by Spanish officials meant only to pocket badly needed cash in return for vague promises of goodwill. Nevertheless, many talked openly of secession. "I am decidedly of the opinion," wrote Kentucky's attorney general in 1787, "that this western country will in a few years Revolt from the Union and endeavor to erect an Independent Government."

Meanwhile, southerners watched with concern as Anglo-American fortunes in the West deteriorated. Many southern citizens had acquired a stake in trans-Appalachian affairs when Virginia and North Carolina had awarded revolutionary soldiers with western land. Whether they intended to move west or to sell their rights, the veterans wanted the western territories to prosper. Many planters (including George Washington) hoped to make a quick fortune in land speculation. They had borrowed heavily to buy frontier land, but uncertainty about the West's future endangered their investments. By 1789 a potent combination of small farmers and landed gentry in the South were enraged at foreign barriers to expansion. They eagerly supported politicians, including Thomas Jefferson and James Madison, who urged strong measures against the British and Spanish.

## Regional Economies

The failure of tobacco and rice to regain their prewar export levels intensified the frustrations of southern planter-speculators. In 1770 the South had produced two-thirds of the mainland colonies' exports; by 1790 this portion had shrunk to less than half. Southerners' attempts to diversify their crops had had little effect. Their failure to recover their export base, along with the persistence of barriers to western expansion, raised doubts about the South's future.

In the mid-Atlantic region New York and Pennsylvania benefited from a steady demand for foodstuffs and quickly recovered from the Revolution's ravages. As famine stalked Europe, American farmers in the Delaware and Hudson valleys prospered from climbing export prices.

New England enjoyed less fortune. A short growing season and poor soil kept farm yields low. Farmers barely produced enough grain for local consumption. New Englanders also faced both high taxes to repay Revolutionary debts and tightened credit that spawned countless lawsuits against debtors. And economic depression only aggravated the region's chronic overpopulation. Moreover, British restrictions on West Indian trade (see Chapter 6) hit New England hard. Some resourceful captains carried cargoes to the French West Indies or even to China, and others smuggled foodstuffs to the British West Indies under the nose of the British navy. But with British policy as it was, the number of seamen in the Massachusetts cod and whale fisheries had fallen 42 percent between the 1770s and 1791. Because New Englanders could not force Britain to grant trade concessions, they preferred peaceful accommodation rather than the direct confrontation with Britain that southerners supported.

## Entrepreneurs, Artisans, and Wage Earners

After 1783, however, ambitious, aggressive businessmen reduced northern dependence on farming by investing their profits in factories, ships, government bonds, and banks. Convinced that American strength required a balancing of agriculture with banking, manufacturing, and commerce, they sought to limit U.S. dependence on British manufactures. They also insisted that the nation needed a healthy merchant marine to augment its naval forces in wartime.

These entrepreneurs' innovative business ventures pointed toward the future. In the 1780s the country's first private banks appeared in Philadelphia, Boston, and New York. In 1787 Philadelphia merchants created the Pennsylvania Society for the

Encouragement of Manufactures and the Useful Arts. Among the English artisans whom the society encouraged to bring their knowledge of industrial technology across the Atlantic was Samuel Slater, who helped to establish an early cotton-spinning mill in Rhode Island in 1793 (see Chapter 9). In 1791 New York and Philadelphia investors founded the Society for the Encouragement of Useful Manufactures, and New York merchants and insurance underwriters organized America's first association for trading government bonds, which evolved into the New York Stock Exchange.

Yet in 1789 northeastern cities lacked large factories. Half the work force consisted of "mechanics," or master artisans and journeymen, who produced handmade goods. Journeymen changed jobs frequently; master artisan Samuel Ashton's Philadelphia cabinet shop, for example, kept journeymen an average of just six months. Master artisans and other employers drew on the increasing ranks of low-paid day workers—orphans, widows, drifters, and free blacks.

Mechanics tended to follow their fathers' occupations. They lived in close-knit neighborhoods and drank, marched, and "mobbed" together. Facing stiff competition from British manufacturers using labor-saving machinery and cheap unskilled labor, they supported a national tariff to raise the price of imported goods and wanted a strong, assertive national government. Although a few artisans employed new technologies, most were reluctant to abandon their traditional ways or could not raise the capital to modernize. With opportunities shrinking, many formed societies to set wages and hours.

In 1789 virtually all politically conscious Americans—entrepreneurs and merchants, urban mechanics and frontier settlers, nationalists and Antifederalists, northerners and southerners—expressed their hopes for the nation's future in terms of republican ideals. These lofty goals of selfless service to the general good had helped leaders to rally public resistance to British encroachment since the 1760s. Republican ideology had shaped the state constitutions and the new Constitution and Antifederalist doctrines as well. By the 1790s most

Americans thought that they knew what republican virtue meant, and most condemned rival views as the road to corruption.

# Constitutional Government Takes Shape

The men entrusted with the federal experiment began assembling in the new national capital, New York, in March 1789. The new leaders had to reach decisions on critical questions that the Constitution's framers had left unresolved. For example, the Constitution neither gave the president formal responsibility for preparing a legislative agenda nor specified whether cabinet officers were accountable to Congress or to the president. The Constitution did not say how the federal courts should be organized, and there was no bill of rights. Under these circumstances, the First Congress could have weakened presidential authority, limited access to federal courts, or even called a convention to rewrite the Constitution. In 1789 the nation's future remained unsettled in these and many other regards.

### Defining the Presidency

No office in the new government aroused more suspicion than the presidency. Many feared that the president's powers could make him a king. But George Washington's reputation for honesty checked public apprehension, and Washington himself tried to calm fears of unlimited executive power.

The Constitution mentioned the executive departments of the federal government only in passing, required Senate approval of presidential nominees to head these bureaus, and made all executive personnel liable to being impeached or to being charged with wrongdoing in office. Otherwise, Congress was free to establish the organization and accountability of what became known as the cabinet. The first cabinet consisted of four departments, headed by the secretaries of state, treasury, and war and by the attorney general. A proposal to forbid the president's dismissal of cabinet officers without Senate approval was defeated. This outcome reinforced presidential authority to make and carry out policy; it also separated executive and legislative powers beyond what the Constitution required and made the president a more equal partner of Congress.

President Washington suggested few laws to Congress, seldom criticized opponents of government policy, and generally limited his public statements to matters of foreign relations and military affairs. He deferred to congressional decisions on domestic policy whenever possible and vetoed only two measures in his eight-year tenure. To reassure the public that he was above favoritism and conflicts of interest, Washington balanced his cabinet with southerners and northeasterners. When Secretary of State Thomas Jefferson opposed policies of Secretary of the Treasury Alexander Hamilton, Washington implored Jefferson not to resign, even though the president supported Hamilton.

"He is polite with dignity, affable without familiarity, distant without haughtiness, grave without austerity, modest, wise, and good." So Abigail Adams, the wife of Vice President John Adams, described Washington. The nation's first president genuinely sought to understand the hopes of the two groups that dominated American society— southern planters and northeastern merchants and entrepreneurs. Like most republican leaders, he believed that the proper role for ordinary citizens was not to set policy through elections but to choose well-educated men to make laws in the people's best interest, independently of direct popular influence.

Only reluctantly did Washington accept reelection in 1792. He dreaded dying while in office and setting the precedent for a lifetime presidency. He realized that "the preservation of the sacred fire of liberty and the destiny of the republican model of government are . . . *deeply,* perhaps *finally,* staked on the experiment entrusted to the hands of the American people." Should he contribute to that experiment's failure, Washington feared, his name would live only as an "awful monument."

## National Justice and the Bill of Rights

The Constitution authorized Congress to establish federal courts below the level of the Supreme Court but provided no plan for their structure. The absence of a comprehensive bill of rights, moreover, had led several delegates at Philadelphia to refuse to sign the Constitution and had been a major Antifederalist point of attack. The task of dealing with these gaps fell to Congress.

In 1789 many citizens feared that the new federal courts would ride roughshod over local customs. Every state had a blend of judicial procedures suited to its needs, and any attempt to force the states to abandon their legal heritage would have produced counterdemands for narrowly restricting federal justice. In the face of such sentiments, Congress might have drastically curtailed the scope and power of the federal judiciary or limited the federal judiciary system to the Supreme Court. Congress might also have forbidden federal judges to accept cases from the states on a range of subjects (as permitted by Article III, Section 2). Such actions by Congress would have tipped the balance of power to the states.

However, when it created the federal court system through the Judiciary Act of 1789, Congress did not seek to hobble the national judiciary. The act quieted popular apprehensions by establishing in each state a federal district court that operated according to local procedures. As the Constitution stipulated, the Supreme Court exercised final jurisdiction. Congress's compromise respected state traditions while offering wide access to federal justice.

Behind the movement for a bill of rights lay Americans' long-standing fear that a strong central government would lead to tyranny. Many Antifederalists believed that the best safeguard against tyranny would be to strengthen the powers of the state governments at the expense of the federal government, but many others wanted simply to guarantee basic personal liberties. From the House of Representatives, James Madison battled to preserve a powerful national government. He played the leading role in drafting the ten amendments that became known as the Bill of Rights when ratified in December 1791.

Madison insisted that the first eight amendments guarantee personal liberties, not strip the national government of authority. The First Amendment safeguarded the most fundamental freedoms of expression—religion, speech, press, and political activity. The Second Amendment ensured that each state could form its own militia. Like the Third Amendment, it sought to protect citizens from what Americans saw as the most sinister embodiment of tyranny: standing armies. The Fourth through the Eighth Amendments limited the police powers of the states by guaranteeing fair treatment in legal and judicial proceedings. The Ninth and Tenth Amendments reserved to the people or to the states powers not allocated to the federal government, but Madison headed off proposals to limit federal power more explicitly.

With the Bill of Rights in place, the federal judiciary established its authority. In the case of *Chisholm* v. *Georgia* (1793), the Supreme Court ruled that a nonresident could sue a state in federal court. In 1796 the Court declared its right to determine the constitutionality of federal statutes in *Hylton* v. *United States* and to strike down state laws in *Ware* v. *Hylton*. But in 1794 Congress decided that the *Chisholm* case had encroached too far on states' authority and overturned the decision through a constitutional amendment. Ratified in 1798, the Eleventh Amendment revised Article III, Section 2, so that private citizens could not undermine states' financial autonomy by using federal courts to sue another state's government in civil cases and claim money from that state's treasury.

By endorsing the Eleventh Amendment, Congress expressed its recognition that federal power could threaten vital local interests. The same awareness had ruptured the nationalist coalition that had written the Constitution, secured its ratification, and dominated the First Congress. James Madison's shift from nationalist to critic of excessive federal power in 1790–1791 dramatically illustrated the

split. Up to this time, of the nationalists, only Alexander Hamilton had thought much about how federal power should be used. His bold program alienated many nationalists by demonstrating that federal policies could be shaped to reward special interests.

# National Economic Policy and Its Consequences

Aware that war would jeopardize national survival, Washington concentrated on diplomacy and military affairs. His reluctance to become involved with legislation enabled Secretary of the Treasury Alexander Hamilton to set domestic priorities. Hamilton emerged as the country's most imaginative and dynamic statesman by formulating a sweeping program for national economic development. However, his agenda proved deeply divisive.

### *Alexander Hamilton and His Objectives*

Born in the West Indies in 1755, Hamilton had arrived in New York in 1772 to enroll at King's College (now Columbia University), where he had passionately defended American rights. Having entered the Continental Army in 1775, Hamilton had distinguished himself in battle, and during four years on Washington's staff had developed a close relationship with the commander in chief. For Hamilton, Washington filled the emotional void created by his own father's desertion. For the childless Washington, Hamilton became almost a son. Hamilton thus enjoyed extraordinary influence over Washington.

Hamilton's financial policies had two goals: to strengthen the nation against foreign enemies and to lessen the threat of disunion. The possibility of war with Britain, Spain, or both presented the most immediate danger. To finance a war, the Republic would have to borrow, but because Congress under the Articles had failed to redeem or pay interest on the Revolutionary debt, the nation had little credit. Thus the country's economy seemed unequal to fighting a major European power. War with Britain would mean a blockade, strangling commerce and halting the importation of necessary manufactured goods. The French navy, so helpful during the Revolution, had declined greatly since 1783, while Britain's Royal Navy had vastly improved. In addition, political instability in France made the Revolutionary ally an uncertain friend. Without self-sufficiency in vital industrial products and a strong merchant marine ready for combat, America stood little chance of surviving another war with Britain.

His own service in the Continental Army had imbued him with burning nationalistic faith and had weakened his identification with his adopted state, New York, or any other American locale. To him, the Constitution represented a close victory of national over state authority. Now he worried that the states might reassert power over the new government. If they succeeded, he doubted whether the nation could prevent ruinous trade discrimination between states, deter foreign aggression, and avoid civil war.

Hamilton also feared that the Union might disintegrate because he believed that Americans tended to think first of local loyalties and interests.

His view of human nature as well as his wartime experiences shaped Hamilton's political beliefs. He shared the conviction of many nationalists that the vast majority of the Republic's population, like the rest of humanity, would never display the degree of self-sacrifice and virtue that he had shown. Hamilton concluded that the federal government's survival depended on building support among politically influential citizens through a direct appeal to their financial interests. Private ambitions would then serve the national welfare.

Charming and brilliant, vain and handsome, a notorious womanizer, thirsty for fame and power, Hamilton exemplified the worldly citizens whose fortunes he hoped to link to the Republic's future. To his opponents, however, Hamilton embodied

**Alexander Hamilton (1755–1804),** *by John Trumbull As President George Washington's secretary of the treasury, the boldly self-confident Hamilton designed national economic programs that aimed to expand the power and influence of wealthy Americans within society.*

the dark forces luring the Republic to doom—a man who, Jefferson wrote, believed in "the necessity of either force or corruption to govern men."

## Report on the Public Credit

In 1789 Congress directed the Treasury Department to evaluate the Revolutionary debt. Hamilton seized the opportunity to devise policies to strengthen the nation's credit, enable it to defer paying its debt, and entice the upper class to place its prestige and capital at the nation's service. In January 1790 Congress received his Report on the Public Credit. It listed $54 million in U.S. debt: $42 million owed to Americans and the rest to foreigners. Hamilton estimated that on top of the national debt, the states had debts of $25 million that the United States had promised to reimburse.

Hamilton recommended that the federal government "fund" the national debt by raising $54 million in new securities to honor the Revolutionary debt. Purchasers of these securities could choose from several combinations of federal "stock" and western lands. Those who wished could retain their original bonds and earn 4 percent interest. All these options would reduce interest payments on the debt. Creditors would approve this reduction because their investments would become more valuable and secure. The report proposed that the federal government use the same means to pay off state debts remaining from the Revolution.

A deeper motive lay behind Hamilton's argument that the failure of some states to honor their obligations would undermine American credit overseas. Hamilton saw the federal assumption of state debts as a chance for the national government to win the gratitude and loyalty of state creditors. Because state legislatures, awash in debt, were anxious to avoid piling more taxes on voters, they would accept any relief, regardless of the reason.

Hamilton exhorted the government to use the money earned by selling federal lands in the West to pay off the $12 million owed to Europeans as soon as possible, but he suggested that the remaining $42 million owed to Americans be made a permanent debt. If the government paid only the interest on its bonds, investors would hold them for long terms. The sole burden on taxpayers would be the small annual interest. Thus the United States could uphold its credit at minimal expense without ever having to pay off the debt itself.

Above all, Hamilton believed, a permanent debt would tie the economic fortunes of the nation's creditors to the government. In an age of notoriously risky investments, the federal government would protect the savings of wealthy bond holders through conservative policies but still pay an interest rate competitive with that of the Bank of England. The guarantee of future interest payments would link the interests of the moneyed class to those of the nation.

Hamilton's proposals provoked controversy. Many members of Congress objected that those least deserving reward would gain the most. The original owners of more than 60 percent of the debt certificates issued by the Continental Congress had long since sold at a loss, often out of dire necessity. Wealthy speculators, anticipating Hamilton's intentions, had snapped up large holdings at the expense of the unsuspecting original owners and would reap huge gains.

To Hamilton's surprise, Madison became a chief opponent of reimbursing current holders at face value. Sensing disapproval of the plan in Virginia, Madison tried but failed to obtain compensation for original owners who had sold their certificates. Hamilton's policy generated widespread resentment by rewarding rich profiteers while ignoring wartime sacrifice by ordinary citizens.

Opposition to assuming the state debts also ran high, especially in the South. But Hamilton saved his proposal by exploiting Virginians' desire to relocate the national capital in their region. They hoped that moving the capital would keep Virginia the nation's largest, most influential state. Essentially, Hamilton traded the votes necessary to locate the capital along the Potomac for enough votes to win his battle for assumption.

Enactment of the Report on the Public Credit reversed the nation's fiscal standing. By 1792 the United States' soaring fiscal reputation allowed some U.S. bonds to sell at 10 percent above face value.

## Reports on the Bank and Manufactures

In December 1790 Hamilton presented Congress with his Report on a National Bank. Having restored full faith in greatly undervalued certificates, Hamilton had in effect expanded the capital available for investment. Now he intended to direct that money toward projects to diversify the national economy through a federally chartered bank.

The proposed bank would raise $10 million through a public stock offering. Fully four-fifths of the control of the bank would fall to private hands. Private investors could purchase shares by paying for three-quarters of their value in government bonds. In this way the bank would capture a substantial portion of the recently funded debt and make it available for loans; it would also receive steady interest payments from the Treasury. Shareholders would profit handsomely.

Hamilton argued that the Bank of the United States would cost taxpayers nothing and greatly benefit the nation. It would provide a safe place for federal deposits, make inexpensive loans to the government when taxes fell short, and relieve the scarcity of hard cash by issuing paper notes. Further, the bank would regulate the business of state banks and, above all, provide much-needed credit for economic expansion.

Hamilton also called for American economic self-sufficiency. An admirer of the way that factory expansion had stimulated British wealth, he wanted to encourage industrialization in the United States. His Report on Manufactures of December 1791 advocated protective tariffs on imports to foster domestic manufacturing, which would in turn attract immigrants and create national wealth. He also called for assisting the merchant marine against British trade restrictions by reducing duties on goods brought into the country on U.S. ships and by offering subsidies for fishermen and whalers.

## Hamilton's Challenge to Limited Government

To many, Hamilton's plan to establish a permanent national debt violated the principle of equality among citizens by favoring the interests of public creditors. Some detractors also denounced the national bank as a dangerous scheme that gave a small elite special power to influence the government.

The bank controversy drew Thomas Jefferson into the ranks of Hamilton's opponents. Like Madison, Jefferson believed that the Bank of England had undermined the integrity of the government in Britain. Shareholders of the Bank of the United States could just as easily become tools of unscrupulous politicians. Members of Congress who owned bank stock would likely vote in support of the bank even at the cost of the national good. To Jefferson, the bank represented "a machine for the corruption of the legislature [Congress]."

Constitutional issues presented the bank's opponents with their strongest argument. The Constitution did not authorize Congress to issue charters of incorporation; in fact, the constitutional convention had rejected such a proposal. Unless Congress adhered to a "strict interpretation" of the Constitution, critics argued, the central government might oppress the states and trample individual liberties. Strict limits on government powers seemed the surest way to prevent the United States from degenerating into a corrupt despotism, as Britain had.

Congress approved the bank by only a thin margin. Dubious about its constitutionality, Washington asked Jefferson and Hamilton for advice. Jefferson distrusted banking and did not want to extend government power beyond the letter of the Constitution. But Hamilton urged Washington to sign the bill. Because Article I, Section 8, of the Constitution specified that Congress could enact all measures "necessary and proper," Hamilton contended that the only unconstitutional activities were those *forbidden* to the national government. Washington accepted Hamilton's argument, and in February 1791 the Bank of the United States obtained a twenty-year charter. Washington's acceptance of a "loose interpretation" of the Constitution marked the first victory for advocates of an active, assertive national government.

Madison and Jefferson also strongly opposed Hamilton's proposal to use protective tariffs to encourage industry. Such protection, they thought, constituted an unfair subsidy promoting uncompetitive industries that would founder without government support. They argued, moreover, that tariffs doubly injured most citizens, first by imposing heavy import taxes passed on to the consumer and then by reducing the incentive for American manufacturers to produce low-cost goods. The only beneficiaries would be individuals shielded from overseas competition and the institutions, such as the bank, that lent them money. Fearful that American cities would spawn a dangerous class of politically volatile poor, Jefferson and Madison viewed industrialization as a potential menace.

Congress ultimately refused to approve a high protective tariff. Hamilton nevertheless succeeded in setting higher duties on goods brought in by non-American than by American ships, and consequently the tonnage of such goods imported on American ships tripled from 1789 to 1793.

## Hamilton's Legacy

Hamilton built a political base by appealing to people's economic self-interest. His "rescue" of the national credit provided enormous gains for speculators, merchants, and other urban "moneyed men" who by 1790 possessed most of the Revolutionary debt. As holders of bank stock, these same groups had reason to use their prestige on behalf of national authority. Moreover, federal assumption of state debts liberated taxpayers from crushing burdens in New England, New Jersey, and South Carolina, while Hamilton's promotion of industry, commerce, and shipping won favor with the Northeast's budding entrepreneurs and hard-pressed artisans.

Supporters of Hamilton's policies called themselves Federalists in order to associate themselves with the Constitution. But they actually favored a centralized ("consolidated") national government, not a truly federal system that left substantial power to the states. They dominated public opinion in the states that were most benefited by assumption and enjoyed considerable support in Pennsylvania and New York.

However, Hamilton's economic program sowed dissension in areas where it provided little advantage. Resentment ran high among those who felt that the government was rewarding special interests. Southerners especially detested Hamilton's program. Southern states had generally paid off their Revolutionary debts, and few southerners still held Revolutionary certificates. Moreover, the Bank of the United States had few southern stockholders and allocated little capital for southern loans.

Hamilton's plan for commercial expansion and industrial development appeared similarly irrelevant to the West, where agriculture promised exceptional profit once the right of export through New Orleans was guaranteed. Even in New York and Pennsylvania, Hamilton's policies generated some dissatisfaction. Resentment of a supposedly national program that benefited eastern "moneyed men" and Yankees who refused to pay their debts gradually united westerners, southerners, and many people in the mid-Atlantic into a political coalition. Challenging the Federalists for control of the government, these opponents called for a return to true republicanism.

## The Whiskey Rebellion

Hamilton's program helped to ignite a civil insurrection called the Whiskey Rebellion. Severely testing federal authority, this uprising posed the young Republic's first serious crisis.

To augment national revenue, Hamilton had proposed an excise tax on domestically produced whiskey. He maintained that such a tax would not only distribute the expense of financing the national debt evenly but also improve the country's morals by lowering liquor consumption. Although Congress passed Hamilton's program in March 1791, many doubted that Americans, who drank an average of six gallons of hard liquor per adult per year, would submit tamely to sobriety.

Western Pennsylvanians found the new tax especially burdensome. Unable to ship their crops to world markets through New Orleans, most local farmers habitually were distilling their rye or corn into alcohol, which could be carried across the Appalachians at a fraction of the price charged for bulky grain. Hamilton's excise tax, equal to 25 percent of whiskey's retail value, would wipe out frontier farmers' profit.

Because the law specified, in addition, that federal courts would try all cases of alleged tax evasion, any western Pennsylvanian indicted for noncompliance would have to travel 300 or so miles to Philadelphia. Not only would the accused face a jury of unsympathetic easterners, but he would also have to shoulder the cost of a long journey and lost earnings as well as fines and penalties if convicted. Moreover, because Treasury Department officials rarely enforced the law outside western Pennsylvania, the efforts of an especially diligent excise inspector who lived near Pittsburgh to collect the tax enraged local residents.

Initially, most western Pennsylvanians preferred peaceful protest. But a minority turned violent, assaulting federal revenue officers and sometimes their own neighbors, until, in a scene reminiscent of colonial protests against Britain, large-scale resistance erupted in July 1794. One hundred men attacked a U.S. marshal serving delinquent taxpayers with summonses to appear in court in Philadelphia. A crowd of 500 burned the chief revenue officer's house following a shootout with federal soldiers. Roving bands torched buildings, assaulted tax collectors, and raised a flag symbolizing an independent country that they hoped to create from six western counties.

The frontier turmoil played into the Washington administration's hands. Echoing British denunciation of colonial protests, Hamilton blasted the rebellion as simple lawlessness. Washington concluded that a federal failure to respond strongly would encourage outbreaks in other frontier areas where lax enforcement had allowed distillers to escape paying taxes. The president accordingly summoned 12,900 militiamen to march west under his command, but opposition evaporated once the troops reached the Appalachians. Of 150 suspects later seized, 20 were sent in irons to Philadelphia.

The Whiskey Rebellion was a milestone in determining the limits of public opposition to federal policies. In the early 1790s many Americans assumed that it was still legitimate to protest unpopular laws by using the methods that they had employed against British policies. By firmly suppressing the first major challenge to national authority, President Washington served notice that

citizens could change the law only through constitutional procedures—by making their dissatisfaction known to their elected representatives and, if necessary, by electing new representatives.

# The United States in a Hostile World

By 1793 disagreements over foreign affairs had become the primary source of friction in American public life. The division created by controversy over Hamilton's economic program hardened into ideologically oriented factions that disagreed vehemently over whether American foreign policy should become pro-French or pro-British.

The United States faced a particularly hostile international environment in the 1790s. European powers restricted American trade, supported Indian trouble along the frontier, strengthened and expanded their North American empires, and maintained garrisons on U.S. soil. Because the new nation's economic well-being depended on exports, foreign policy issues loomed large in national politics. Disputes over foreign relations roiled public life from 1793 to 1815.

## Foreign Powers and Native Americans in the West

At the same time, Spain attempted to counter potential rivals for North American territory—Russia and Britain on the Pacific coast and the United States and Britain in the Mississippi Valley. In the 1740s traders from Siberia had begun trading with Alaskan natives for sea-otter pelts, spreading deadly diseases in the process. Britain continued its search for a "northwest passage" to link the Canadian interior to the Pacific. To counter these twin threats, Spain flung colonists and missionaries northward along the California coast from San Diego to Sonoma (north of San Francisco). In "New California," the missions fared better than the handful of settlers. However, epidemic and venereal diseases carried by the Spanish raged among the native coastal tribes; between 1769 and 1830 the Indian population plummeted from about 72,000 to about 18,000. Priests sought to "civilize" the survivors by placing them in missions, imposing rigid discipline, and putting them to work in vineyards and other enterprises. Meanwhile, Spain strengthened its position in the southwest by making peace with the Comanches, the Navajos, and most of the Apache nations that threatened its settlements.

Revitalized by these western successes, Spain joined Britain and Native Americans as a formidable barrier to U.S. aims in the Mississippi Valley. In the 1790s the Spanish bribed many well-known political figures in Tennessee and Kentucky, including James Wilkinson, one of Washington's former generals, whose intrigues continued into the next century. Thomas Scott, a congressman from western Pennsylvania, meanwhile schemed with the British. The admission of Vermont, Kentucky, and Tennessee as states between 1791 and 1796 was meant in part to strengthen their sometimes shaky loyalty to the Union.

President Washington tried to keep tight control of foreign policy. Recognizing that the complex western problems would not easily yield, he pursued patient diplomacy to "preserve the country in peace if I can, and to be prepared for war if I cannot." The prospect of peace improved in 1789 when Spain unexpectedly opened New Orleans to American commerce. Secessionist sentiment subsided.

Washington then moved to weaken Spanish influence in the West by neutralizing Spain's most important ally, the Creek Indians. The Creeks numbered more than 20,000, including perhaps 5,000 warriors, and were fiercely hostile toward Georgian settlers, whom they called "the greedy people who want our lands." Under terms of the 1790 Treaty of New York, American settlers could occupy the Georgia piedmont but not other Creek territory. Washington insisted that Georgia restore to the Chickasaws and Choctaws, Creek allies, a vast area along the Mississippi River that Georgia had already begun selling off to land speculators.

Hoping to conclude a similar agreement with Britain's Indian allies, the United States sent an

**Stimafachki of the Koasati Creeks,**
*by John Trumbull, 1790*
*This portrait was sketched during the U.S.-Creek conference that resulted in the Treaty of New York.*

envoy to the Great Lakes tribes. The Miamis responded by burning a captured American to death. Two military campaigns, in 1790 and 1791, failed to force peace and cost the United States 1,100 men.

The Washington administration tried to pacify the Indians through a benevolent policy. Alarmed by the chaos on the frontier, where trespassers invaded Indian lands and the native peoples rejected U.S. claims to sovereignty, the government formally recognized Indian title as secure and inalienable except by the "free consent" of the Indians themselves. To reinforce this policy, Congress passed laws to prohibit trespassing on Indian lands, to punish crimes committed there by non-Indians, to outlaw alcohol, and to regulate trade. The administration also encouraged Indians to become "civilized." By adopting private property and a strictly agricultural livelihood, officials believed, Indians would find a place in American society—and make land available for non-Indians.

Indians, however, were unwilling to give up their traditional ways entirely and to assimilate into an alien culture. And most whites did not want to integrate Native Americans into their society. Consequently, the United States continued to pressure Indians to sell their lands and to move farther west. Washington's frontier policy became a wreck. Not only had two military expeditions suffered defeat in the Northwest, but in 1792 the Spanish had persuaded the Creeks to renounce their treaty with the federal government and to resume hostilities. Ultimately, the damage to U.S. prestige from these setbacks convinced many Americans that only an alliance with France could counterbalance the combined strength of Britain, Spain, and the Indians.

## France and Factional Politics

One of the most momentous events in history, the French Revolution, began in 1789. Americans watched sympathetically as the French abolished nobles' privileges, wrote a constitution, and repelled invading armies. In 1793, after becoming a republic, France proclaimed a war of all peoples against all kings and assumed that the United States would eagerly enlist.

Enthusiasm for a pro-French foreign policy burned brightest in the South and along the frontier. France's war against Britain and Spain, begun in 1793, raised hopes among southern land speculators and western settlers that a French victory would leave those nations too exhausted to continue meddling in the West. The United States could then insist on free navigation of the Mississippi, evacuation of British garrisons, and termination of both nations' support of Indian resistance.

In addition, a slave uprising in France's Caribbean colony of Saint Domingue (later renamed Haiti), in which Britain became involved, aroused passionate anti-British sentiment in the South. White southerners grew alarmed for slavery's future

and their own lives as terrified French planters fled to the United States from Saint Domingue with vivid accounts of how British invaders in 1793 had supported the rebellious slaves. The blacks had inflicted heavy casualties on the French. Southern whites concluded that Britain had intentionally provoked a bloodbath, and they worried that a British-inspired race war would engulf the South as well.

After 1790 economics led to sharp differences between northern and southern reactions to the French Revolution. Growing antagonism toward France among northern merchants reflected their basic conservatism and their awareness that their prosperity depended on good relations with Britain. Virtually all the nation's merchant marine operated from northern ports, and the largest share of U.S. foreign trade was with Britain. Fearful that an alliance with France would provoke British retaliation against this valuable commerce, northerners argued that the United States could win valuable concessions by demonstrating friendly intentions toward Britain.

Southerners had no such reasons to favor Britain. They perceived American reliance on British commerce as a menace to national self-determination and wished to divert most U.S. trade to France. Southern spokesmen such as Jefferson and Madison demanded discriminatory duties on British cargoes. These recommendations threatened ties with Britain, which sold more manufactured goods to the United States than to any other country. Federalist opponents of a discriminatory tariff warned that the English would not stand by while a weak French ally pushed them into depression. If Congress adopted trade retaliation, Hamilton predicted, "an open war between the United States and Great Britain" would result.

After declaring war with Spain and Britain in 1793, France sought to enlist the United States in the war and to strengthen the treaty of alliance between the two nations. France dispatched Edmond Genet as minister to the United States with orders to recruit American mercenaries to conquer Spanish territories and to attack British shipping. Much to France's disgust, President Washington issued a proclamation of neutrality on April 22, 1793.

Meanwhile, Citizen Genet (as he was known in French Revolutionary style) had arrived on April 8. He found numerous southern volunteers for his American Foreign Legion despite official U.S. neutrality. Making generals of George Rogers Clark of Kentucky and Elisha Clarke, Genet ordered them to seize New Orleans and St. Augustine. Clark openly defied the neutrality proclamation by advertising for recruits, and Clarke drilled 300 soldiers along the Florida border. However, the French failed to provide adequate funds for either campaign, and in 1794 both expeditions disintegrated.

However, Genet did not need funds to outfit privateers, whose crews were paid from captured plunder. By summer 1793 nearly 1,000 Americans were at sea in a dozen ships flying the French flag. These privateers seized over eighty British ships and towed them to American ports, where French consuls sold the ships and cargoes at auction.

## The British Crisis

Although Washington swiftly closed the nation's harbors to Genet's buccaneers, the episode provoked an Anglo-American crisis. Britain decided that only a massive show of force would deter American aggression. Thus on November 6, 1793, Britain's Privy Council issued orders confiscating foreign ships trading with the French islands in the Caribbean. The orders were kept secret until most American ships carrying winter provisions to the Caribbean left port so that their captains would not know that they were sailing into a war zone. The Royal Navy seized more than twenty-five American ships, a high price for Genet's mischief making.

Meanwhile, the U.S. merchant marine suffered another galling indignity—the drafting of its crewmen into the Royal Navy. Thousands of British sailors had fled to American ships looking for an easier life than the tough, poorly paying British system. In late 1793 British naval officers began inspecting American crews for British subjects, whom they then impressed (forcibly enlisted) as the king's sailors. Overzealous commanders sometimes exceeded orders by taking U.S. citizens—and in any case Britain did not recognize its former subjects' right to adopt American citizenship. Impressment struck a raw nerve in most Americans.

Next the British challenged the United States for control of the West. In February 1794 at an Indian council, Canada's governor denied U.S. claims north of the Ohio River and urged his listeners to destroy every white settlement in the Northwest. Britain soon erected Fort Miami near Toledo, Ohio. That same year Spain encroached further on U.S. territory by building Fort San Fernando at what is now Memphis, Tennessee.

Hoping to halt the drift toward war, Washington launched a desperate diplomatic initiative, sending Chief Justice John Jay to Great Britain and Thomas Pinckney to Spain. The president also authorized General Anthony Wayne to negotiate a treaty with the Indians of the Ohio Valley.

The Indians scoffed at Washington's peace offer until "Mad Anthony" Wayne led 3,000 regulars and militiamen deep into their homeland, ravaging every village in reach. On August 20, 1794, Wayne's troops routed 2,000 Indians at the Battle of Fallen Timbers, two miles from Britain's Fort Miami. Wayne's army staged a provocative victory march past the British garrison and then built Fort Defiance to challenge British authority in the Northwest. Indian morale plummeted. In August 1795 Wayne compelled twelve northeastern tribes to sign the Treaty of Greenville, which opened most of Ohio to white settlement and temporarily ended Indian hostilities.

Wayne's success allowed John Jay a major diplomatic victory in London: a British promise to withdraw troops from American soil. Jay also gained American access to West Indian markets, but only by bargaining away U.S. rights to load cargoes of sugar, molasses, and coffee from the Caribbean. On other points the British remained unyielding. Few Americans could interpret Jay's Treaty as preserving peace with honor.

Jay's Treaty left Britain free not only to violate American neutrality but also to restrict U.S. trade with French ports during wartime. Moreover, Jay did not succeed in ending impressment. He also failed to gain compensation for slaves taken by the British during the Revolution, an outcome especially galling to southerners. In 1795 the Federalist-dominated Senate ratified the treaty by just one vote.

Jay's Treaty probably represented the most that a weak, politically divided United States could extract from Britain. A major achievement for the Washington administration, it defused an explosive crisis with Britain, ended British occupation of U.S. territory, and provided for arbitration to settle both American and British claims for compensation. Jay's Treaty also stimulated American trade as British governors in the West Indies used the treaty's ratification as an excuse to open their harbors to U.S. ships. Other British officials permitted Americans to develop a thriving commerce with India. Within a few years of 1795, American exports to the British Empire had shot up 300 percent.

On the heels of Jay's Treaty came an unqualified diplomatic triumph engineered by Thomas Pinckney. Ratified in 1796, the Treaty of San Lorenzo (also called Pinckney's Treaty) with Spain gave westerners unrestricted, duty-free access to world markets via the Mississippi River. Spain also promised to recognize the thirty-first parallel as the United States' southern boundary, to dismantle all fortifications on American soil, and to discourage Indian attacks against western settlers.

By 1796 the Washington administration had defended the nation's territorial integrity, restored peace to the frontier, opened the Mississippi for western exports, reopened British markets to U.S. shipping, and kept the nation out of a European war. However, as the outcry over Jay's Treaty showed, foreign policy had left Americans far more divided in 1796 than in 1789.

# Battling for the Nation's Soul

Besides distrusting centralized executive authority, colonial and Revolutionary Americans feared orga-

nized political parties, which they assumed were formed by corrupt conspirators operating against the liberties of the people. Despite these views, politically conscious Americans had split into two hostile political parties, Federalists and Republicans, by the end of Washington's second term.

The struggle transcended the economic and social differences evident in earlier disputes about Hamiltonian finance and the possibility of war with Britain. After 1796 the battle was fought over the very future of representative government. The election of 1800 would determine whether the political elite could accommodate demands from ordinary citizens for more influence in determining policy. No issue was more important or more hotly argued than that of officeholders' accountability to their constituents.

## Ideological Confrontation

The French Revolution led many Americans to reassess their political values. The Revolution's radical turn in 1793–1794, which sent thousands to the guillotine, polarized public opinion, generally along regional lines.

Northern Federalists damned revolutionary France as an abomination—"an open Hell," thundered Massachusetts Federalist Fisher Ames, "still ringing with agonies and blasphemies, still smoking with sufferings and crimes." Conservative and religiously oriented, New Englanders detested the French government's disregard for civil rights and its adoration of reason over the worship of God. Middle Atlantic businessmen, perhaps less religious but no less conservative, condemned French leaders as evil radicals who incited the poor against the rich. But a minority of well-off northern merchants and professionals, loyal to deeply held republican principles, supported the Revolution.

Federalists trembled at the thought of "mob rule" in the nation's future. They took alarm when artisans in New York and Philadelphia bandied the French revolutionary slogan "Liberty, Equality, Fraternity" and exalted pro-French political leaders such as Jefferson. Citizen Genet's recruitment of hundreds of Americans to fight for France reinforced their fears.

By the mid-1790s Federalist leaders had concluded that it was dangerous to involve the public deeply in politics. The people were undependable, too easy a prey for rabble-rousers like Genet. As Senator George Cabot of Massachusetts said, "The many do not think at all." But properly led, they believed, the people presented a powerful (albeit passive) bulwark against anarchy. Federalists in fact trusted ordinary property owners to judge a candidate's personal fitness for high office, but only that personal fitness. They consequently argued that citizens need not be presented with policy choices during elections. Thus Federalists favored a representative government in which elected officials would rule in the people's name, independently of direct popular influence.

Preserving order, Federalists maintained, required forging a close relationship between the government and the upper class. Doing so would reassure citizens that their future was in competent hands and would set high standards that few radicals could meet. As early as 1789 Vice President John Adams had tried (unsuccessfully) to give the president and other officials titles such as "His High Mightiness." In the 1790s government officials dramatized their social distance from average citizens. Congress and the cabinet dressed in high fashion and flaunted their wealth at endless balls and formal dinners. While insisting that they ruled *of* and *for* the people, Federalists took pains to symbolize that their government was not *by* the people.

The Federalists aimed to limit public office to wise and virtuous men who would protect liberty. This objective was consistent with eighteenth-century fears that corruption and unchecked passion would undermine society. In republican theory a "virtuous" government need not be directly responsible to public opinion. If (as many assumed) democracy meant mob rule, then political virtue and direct democracy were incompatible. Conservative colonial political traditions, republican ideology, and social reciprocity (see Chapter 2) shaped Federalists' suspicion of the ordinary people.

Federalist measures alienated many Americans, including Jefferson and Madison, who had a vastly different understanding of republican ideology. Antifederalist sentiment ran high in the South, where republican ideology stressed the corruption inherent in a powerful government dominated by a few highly visible men. Southern Republicans insisted that only the distribution of power among virtuous, independent citizens would protect liberty. Further, many southern planters had absorbed the Enlightenment's faith that the free flow of ideas would ensure progress. Exhilarated by events in France, many white southerners saw the French as fellow republicans, carrying on a revolution that would replace hereditary privilege with liberty, equality, and brotherhood. With their own labor force consisting of enslaved blacks, not free wage workers, southern elites did not fear popular participation in politics. Unlike northern Federalists, then, southern planters faced the future with optimism and viewed attempts to inhibit widespread political participation as unworthy of educated gentlemen.

Self-interest also drove Jefferson, Madison, and likeminded Americans to rouse ordinary citizens' concerns about civic affairs. In the early 1790s widespread political apathy favored the Federalists, making it unlikely that they would be criticized for passing unwise laws. However, if the public held Federalists accountable, they would think twice before enacting measures opposed by the majority; or if they persisted in advocating such policies, they would be removed from office.

In October 1791 organized efforts to turn public opinion against the Federalists began with the publication of the *National Gazette*. Then in 1793–1794 popular dissatisfaction with government policies led to the formation of several dozen Democratic (or Republican) societies. Their membership ranged from planters and merchants to artisans and sailors. Conspicuously absent were clergymen, the poor, and nonwhites. Sharply critical of Federalists, the societies spread dissatisfaction with the Washington administration's policies.

Federalists interpreted the societies' emotional appeals to ordinary people as demagoguery and denounced their followers as "democrats, mobocrats, & all other kinds of rats." They feared that the societies would become revolutionary organizations. Washington privately warned that "if [the clubs] were not counteracted . . . they would shake the government to its foundation." By criticizing them, Washington abandoned his nonpartisanship and aligned himself with the Federalists, a move that would cost him dearly.

## The Republican Party

Neither Jefferson nor Madison belonged to a Democratic society. However, the clubs' criticism of the administration galvanized into political activity many who would later support Jefferson and Madison's Republican party.

In the early 1790s Americans believed that organizing a political faction or party was corrupt and subversive. Republican ideology assumed that parties would fill Congress with politicians of little ability and less integrity, pursuing selfish goals at national expense. Good citizens would shun such partisan scheming. However, these ideals wavered as controversy mounted over Hamilton's program and the Washington administration's foreign policy. Washington tried to set an example of impartial leadership by seeking advice from both camps, but Jefferson resigned from the cabinet in 1793, and thereafter not even the president could halt the widening political split. Each side saw itself as the guardian of republican virtue and attacked the other as an illegitimate faction.

In 1794 party development reached a decisive stage. Shortly after Washington aligned himself with Federalist policies, supporters of Jefferson who had begun to call themselves Republicans won a slight majority in the House of Representatives. The election signaled their transformation from a faction to a broad-based party, the Republican party, capable of coordinating national political campaigns.

Federalists and Republicans alike used the press to mold public opinion. American journalism came of age in the 1790s as the number of newspapers

multiplied from 92 to 242. By 1800 newspapers had perhaps 140,000 paid subscribers (about one-fifth of the eligible voters), and their secondhand readership probably exceeded 300,000. Newspapers of both camps, libelous and irresponsible, cheapened public discussion through constant fear mongering and character assassination. Republicans stood accused of plotting a reign of terror and scheming to turn the nation over to France. Federalists faced charges of favoring hereditary aristocracy and planning to establish an American dynasty by marrying off John Adams's daughter to George III. But despite the mutual distrust thus created, newspaper warfare stimulated citizens to become politically active.

Underlying the inflammatory rhetoric was the Republican charge that the Federalists were bent on enriching the wealthy at taxpayers' expense. Although most Republican leaders were themselves well born, Republicans asserted that the Federalists planned to create a privileged order of men and to re-create the atmosphere of a European court through highly publicized formal dinners and balls. Although wrong in claiming that opponents wanted to introduce aristocracy and monarchy, the Republicans correctly identified the Federalists' fundamental assumption: that citizens' worth could be measured in terms of their money.

Accusations that he secretly supported a plot to establish a monarchy enraged Washington. "By God," Jefferson reported him swearing, "he [the president] would rather be in his grave than in his present situation. . . . He had rather be on his farm than to be made *emperor of the world*." Alarmed by the furor over Jay's Treaty, Washington dreaded the nation's polarization into hostile factions. And Republican abuse stung him. Lonely and surrounded by mediocre men after Hamilton returned to private life, Washington decided in spring 1796 to retire after two terms and called on Hamilton to give a sharp political twist to a farewell address.

In the farewell message Washington vigorously condemned political parties. Partisan alignments, he insisted, endangered the republic's survival, especially if they became entangled in foreign policy disputes. Aside from fulfilling existing treaty obligations and maintaining foreign commerce, the United States had to avoid "political connection" with Europe and its wars. If the United States gathered its strength under "an efficient government," it could defy any foreign challenge; but if it was drawn into Europe's quarrels and corruption, the republican experiment would be doomed. Washington and Hamilton thus turned the central argument of republicanism against their Republican critics. They also evoked a vision of a United States virtuously isolated from foreign intrigue and power politics, an ideal that would remain a potent inspiration until the twentieth century.

Washington left the presidency in 1797 amid a barrage of criticism. The nation's political division into Republicans and Federalists meanwhile hardened. Each party consolidated its hold over particular states and groups of voters, leaving the electorate almost equally divided.

## The Election of 1796

As the election of 1796 approached, the Republicans cultivated a large, loyal body of voters, the first time since the Revolution that the political elite effectively mobilized ordinary Americans. The Republican constituency included the Democratic societies, workingmen's clubs, and immigrant-aid associations.

Immigrants became a prime target for Republican recruiters. During the 1790s the United States absorbed 20,000 French refugees from Saint Domingue and 60,000 Irish. Although few immigrants could vote, the Irish exerted critical influence in Pennsylvania and New York, where public opinion was so closely divided that a few hundred voters could tip the balance. In short, Irish immigrants could provide Republicans a winning margin in both states, and the Republicans' pro-French, anti-British rhetoric ensured enthusiastic Irish support.

In 1796 the presidential candidates were Vice President John Adams, whom the Federalists supported, and the Republicans' Jefferson. Republican strength in the South offset Federalist strength in New England, leaving Pennsylvania and New York as crucial "swing" states where the Irish vote might tip the scales. In the end Jefferson carried Pennsylvania but not New York and lost the presidency by three electoral votes. The Federalists kept control of Congress. But by a political fluke, Jefferson became vice president under the constitutional provision (quickly changed by the Twelfth Amendment) that the candidate receiving the highest number of electoral votes would become president and the candidate amassing the next-highest number would become vice president.

President Adams exemplified the paradoxes of the intellectual. His brilliance, insight, and idealism have seldom been equaled among American presidents. He was more comfortable, however, with ideas than with people, more theoretical than practical, and rather inflexible. He inspired trust and admiration but could not command loyalty or stir the electorate. As Benjamin Franklin observed, Adams was "always an honest man, often a wise one, but sometimes, and in some things, absolutely out of his senses." He was utterly unsuited to unify the country.

## The French Crisis

To Adams's initial good fortune, French provocations produced a sharp anti-Republican backlash. France interpreted Jay's Treaty as an American attempt to assist the British in their war against France. Learning of Jefferson's defeat, the French ordered the seizure of American ships; within a year they had plundered more than 300 U.S. vessels. The French also ordered that every American captured on a British naval ship, even those involuntarily impressed, be hanged.

Seeking to avoid war, Adams dispatched a peace commission to France. The French foreign minister, Charles de Talleyrand, refused to meet with the Americans, instead promising through three unnamed agents ("X, Y, and Z") that talks could begin after he received $250,000 and France obtained a $12 million loan. This barefaced demand for a bribe became known as the XYZ Affair. Outraged Americans adopted the battle cry "Millions for defense, not one cent for tribute."

The XYZ Affair discredited Republican foreign policy views. The party's leaders compounded the damage by refusing to condemn French aggression and opposing Adam's call for defensive measures. While Republicans tried to excuse French behavior, the Federalists rode a wave of patriotism to an enormous victory in the 1798 congressional elections.

Congress responded to the XYZ Affair by arming fifty-four ships to protect U.S. commerce. The new warships joined what became known as the Quasi-War—an undeclared Franco-American naval conflict in the Caribbean from 1798 to 1800, during which U.S. forces seized ninety-three French privateers at the loss of just one ship. The British navy meanwhile extended the protection of its convoys to the U. S. merchant marine. By early 1799 the French no longer posed a serious threat at sea.

Despite Adam's misgivings, the Federalists Congress tripled the regular army to 10,000 men in 1798, with an automatic expansion of land forces to 50,000 in case of war. But the risk of a land war with France was minimal. What Federalist actually wanted was a strong military force ready in case of a civil war, for the crisis had produced near-hysterical fears that French and Irish malcontents were hatching treasonous conspiracies.

## The Alien and Sedition Acts

The Federalists insisted that the possibility of war with France demanded stringent legislation to protect national security. In 1798 the Federalist Congress accordingly passed four measures known collectively as the Alien and Sedition Acts. Although President Adams neither requested nor wanted the laws, he deferred to Congress and signed them.

The least controversial of the four laws, the Alien Enemies Act, was designed to prevent wartime espionage or sabotage. It outlined procedures for determining whether a hostile country's citizens, when staying in America, posed a threat to the United States; if so, they would be deported or jailed. It also established principles to respect the rights of enemy citizens. This law would not be used until the War of 1812.

The second of the laws, the Alien Friends Act, enforceable in peacetime until June 25, 1800, authorized the president to expel foreign residents whose activities he considered dangerous. It required no proof of guilt. Republicans maintained that the law's real purpose was to deport immigrants critical of Federalist policies. Republicans also denounced the third law, the Naturalization Act. This measure increased the residency requirement for U.S. citizenship from five to fourteen years (the last five continuously in one state) to reduce Irish voting.

Finally came the Sedition Act, the only one of these measures enforceable against U.S. citizens. Although its alleged purpose was to distinguish between free speech and attempts to encourage the violation of federal laws or to seed a revolution, the act defined criminal activity so broadly that it blurred distinctions between sedition and legitimate political discussion. Thus it forbade an individual or a group "to oppose any measure or measures of the United States"—wording that could be interpreted to ban any criticism of the party in power. Another clause made it illegal to speak, write, or print any statement that would bring the president "into contempt or disrepute." A newspaper editor could therefore face imprisonment for criticizing Adams or his cabinet. Juries heard sedition cases and could decide whether a defendant had intended to stir up rebellion or merely to express political dissent. However one regarded it, the Sedition Act interfered with free speech. The Federalists wrote the law to expire in 1801 so that it could not be used against them if they lost the next election.

The real target of all this Federalist repression was the opposition press. Four of the five largest Republican newspapers were charged with sedition just as the election of 1800 was getting under way. The attorney general used the Alien Friends Act to drive the Irish journalist John Daly Burk underground. After failing to deport Scottish editor Thomas Callender, an all-Federalist jury sent him to prison for criticizing the president. Federalist leaders intended that a small number of highly visible prosecutions would intimidate journalists and candidates into silence during the election. The attorney general charged seventeen persons with sedition and won ten convictions. Among the victims was Republican congressman Matthew Lyon of Vermont, who spent four months in prison for publishing an article blasting Adams.

Vocal criticism of Federalist repression erupted only in Virginia and Kentucky. In summer 1798 militia commanders in these states mustered their regiments to hear speeches demanding that the federal government respect the Bill of Rights. Entire units signed petitions denouncing the Alien and Sedition Acts. Young men stepped forward to sign the documents on drumheads, a pen in one hand and a gun in the other. Older officers who had fought in the Continental Army looked on approvingly. It was not hard to imagine rifles replacing quill pens as the men who had led one revolution took up arms again.

Ten years earlier opponents of the Constitution had warned that giving the national government extensive powers would endanger freedom. By 1798 these predictions had come true. Shocked Republicans realized that with the Federalists in control of all three branches of government, neither the Bill of Rights nor the system of checks and balances protected individual liberties. In this context the doctrine of states' rights was advanced as a way to prevent the national government from violating freedoms.

James Madison and Thomas Jefferson anonymously wrote two manifestos on states' rights that the assemblies of Virginia and Kentucky endorsed in 1798. Madison's Virginia Resolutions and Jefferson's Kentucky Resolutions proclaimed that state legislatures retained both their right to judge the constitutionality of federal actions and an authority called interposition, which enabled them

to protect the liberties of their citizens. A set of Kentucky Resolutions adopted in November 1799 added that states could "nullify" objectionable federal laws. The authors intended interposition and nullification to protect residents from being tried for breaking an unconstitutional law. Although most states disapproved the resolutions, their passage demonstrated the potential for rebellion in the late 1790s.

## The Election of 1800

In 1800 the Republicans rallied around Thomas Jefferson for president and New York politician Aaron Burr for vice president. The Federalists became mired in wrangling between Adams and the "High Federalists" who looked to Hamilton for guidance. That the nation survived the election of 1800 without a civil war or the disregard of voters' wishes owed much to the good sense of moderates in both parties. Jefferson and Madison discouraged radicalism that might provoke intervention by the national army. Even more credit belonged to Adams for rejecting High Federalist demands that he ensure victory by sparking an insurrection or asking Congress to declare war on France.

"Nothing but an open war can save us," declared one High Federalist. But when the president discovered the French willing to seek peace in 1799, he proposed a special diplomatic mission. "Surprise, indignation, grief & disgust followed each other in quick succession," reported a Federalist senator. Adams obtained Senate approval for his envoys only by threatening to resign and so make Jefferson president. Outraged High Federalists tried, unsuccessfully, to dump Adams. Hamilton denounced him as a fool, but this ill-considered tactic backfired when most New Englanders rallied around the president.

Adams's negotiations with France did not achieve a settlement until 1801, but the expectation of normal relations prevented Federalists from exploiting charges of Republican sympathy for the enemy. With the immediate threat of war removed, voters grew resentful that in just two years taxes had soared 33 percent to support an army that had done virtually nothing. As the danger of war receded, voters gave Federalists less credit for standing up to France and more blame for ballooning the national debt by $10 million.

Two years after triumphing in the 1798 elections, Federalists found their support badly eroded. High Federalists spitefully withheld the backing that Adams needed to win the presidency. Republicans successfully mobilized voters in Philadelphia and New York who were ready to forsake the Federalists. Voter turnouts more than doubled those of 1788, rising from 15 percent to 40 percent, and in hotly contested New York and Pennsylvania more than one-half the eligible voters participated.

Adams lost the presidency by just eight electoral votes, but Jefferson's election was not assured. Because all seventy-three Republican electors voted for both their party's nominees, the electoral college deadlocked in a Jefferson-Burr tie. The election went to the House of Representatives, where, after thirty-five ballots, Jefferson won the presidency by history's narrowest margin.

# Deferring Equality

The election of 1800 did not make the United States more democratic, but it did prevent antidemocratic prejudices from blocking future political liberalization. The Republican victory also repudiated the Federalist campaign to create a base of support through special-interest legislation. After 1800 government policies would be judged by Jefferson's standard of "equal rights for all, special privileges for none."

But not all Americans won equal rights. Women and African-Americans took almost no part in politics, and few people felt that they should. In the case of the Indians, U.S. diplomatic gains came largely at their expense; and national issues rarely were concerned with African-Americans. Meanwhile, white Americans lost much of their Revolutionary idealism and began to assume that

racial minorities would always be second-class citizens at best.

## Indians in the New Republic

By 1795 most eastern Indian tribes had suffered severe reductions in population and territory, owing to battle, famine, and disease. From 1775 to 1795 the Cherokees declined from 16,000 to 10,000 and the Iroquois from 9,000 to 4,000. Between 1775 and 1800 Indians forfeited more land than the area inhabited by whites in 1775. Settlers crowded Indians onto reservations (often illegally), liquor dealers and criminals trespassed on Indian lands, and government agents and missionaries pressured Indians to abandon their lands and cultures.

Demoralized and unable to strike back, Indians often consumed enormous amounts of whiskey and became violent. The Iroquois were typical. "The Indians of the Six Nations," wrote a federal official in 1796, "have become given to indolence, drunkenness, and thefts, and have taken to killing each other." A social and moral crisis gripped tribes threatened by whites' expansion.

Beginning in 1799 a Seneca prophet, Handsome Lake, led his people in a creative effort to resolve the crisis. He tried to end alcoholism among Indians by appealing to their religious traditions. He welcomed Quaker missionaries and federal aid earmarked for teaching Euro-American agricultural methods to Iroquois men in search of new livelihoods after the collapse of the fur trade and the loss of most of their lands. Many Iroquois men welcomed the change. Iroquois women, however, resisted because they stood to forfeit their collective ownership of farmland, their control of the food supply, and their place in tribal councils. Women who rejected Handsome Lake's advice to exchange farming for housewifery were accused of witchcraft, and some were killed.

## Redefining the Color Line

The Republic's first years marked the high tide of African-Americans' Revolutionary-era success in

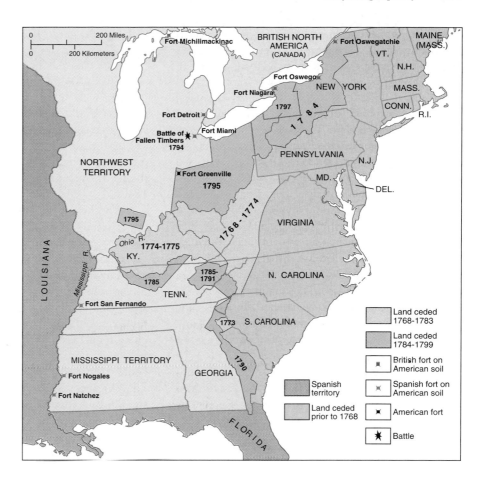

**Indian Land Cessions, 1768–1799**

*Between 1768 and 1775 western Indians sold off vast territories, mostly hunting grounds in mountainous regions. The upheavals of the Revolutionary War, followed by conflicts with U.S. military forces from 1784 to 1799, led to large cessions of inhabited Indian lands.*

bettering their lot. Although racism persisted, Jefferson's eloquent words "all men are created equal" awakened many white consciences. In 1790, 8 percent of African-Americans enjoyed freedom. By 1800, 11 percent were free. State reforms meanwhile attempted to improve slaves' conditions. In 1791 the North Carolina legislature declared that the "distinction of criminality between the murder of a white person and one who is equally an human creature, but merely of a different complexion, is disgraceful to humanity" and authorized the execution of whites who murdered slaves. By 1794 most states had outlawed the Atlantic slave trade.

Hesitant measures to ensure free blacks' legal equality appeared in the 1780s and early 1790s. Most states dropped restrictions on their freedom of movement, protected their property, and allowed them to enroll in the militia. All but three states either permitted free blacks to vote or made no specific attempts to exclude them. But before the 1790s ended, the trend toward lessening the social and legal distances between the races ended. Abolitionist sentiment ebbed, slavery became more entrenched, and whites demonstrated reluctance to accept free blacks as fellow citizens.

Federal law led the way in restricting the rights of African Americans. In 1790 congressional procedures for naturalizing aliens limited eligibility to foreign whites. The federal militia law of 1792 allowed states to exclude free blacks. The navy and marine corps forbade nonwhite enlistments in 1798. By 1807 Delaware, Maryland, Kentucky, and New Jersey had stripped free blacks of the vote. Although free blacks enjoyed rights in some areas, the number of places treating them as the political equals of whites dropped sharply in the early 1800s.

An especially revealing symptom of changing attitudes occurred in 1793 when Congress passed the Fugitive Slave Law. The law required judges to award possession of a runaway slave on a formal request by a master or his representative. Accused runaways were denied jury trials and sometimes were refused permission to present evidence. Slaves' legal status as property disqualified them from claiming these constitutional privileges, but the Fugitive Slave Law denied even *free* blacks the legal protections guaranteed to them under the Bill of Rights. The law marked a striking departure from the atmosphere of the 1780s, when state governments had given whites and free blacks the same legal privileges. By 1793 white Americans clearly found it easy to forget that the Constitution had not limited citizenship to their race.

The bloody slave revolt on Saint Domingue undermined the trend toward abolition and reinforced the kind of fears that spawned racism. Reports of the slaughter of French slaveholders made white Americans more reluctant to criticize slavery and helped to transform the image of blacks from that of victims of injustice to one of potential menaces. In August 1800 a planned insurrection of more than 1,000 slaves in Richmond, Virginia, kindled smoldering white fears. The militia put down the conspiracy and executed 35 slaves, including the leader, Gabriel Prosser. "I have ventured my life in endeavoring to obtain the liberty of my countrymen, and I am a willing sacrifice to their cause," said one rebel before his execution.

Isolated uprisings occurred in the United States for years after "Gabriel's Rebellion," and rumors persisted that a massive revolt was brewing. Antislavery sentiment diminished rapidly. The antislavery movement would not recover from the damage inflicted by the Saint Domingue revolt until the early 1830s.

Another development would strengthen slavery. In the 1790s demand in the British textile industry stimulated the cultivation of cotton in coastal South Carolina and Georgia. Here the soil and climate were ideal for growing long-staple cotton, whose fibers could be separated easily from its seed. In the South's upland and interior regions, however, only short-staple cotton thrived. Its seed clung tenaciously to the fibers and defied cleaning. It was as if southerners had discovered gold but could not mine it. In 1793 a Connecticut Yankee, Eli Whitney, rescued the South by inventing a cotton gin that efficiently cleaned short-staple cotton. Improved by others, Whitney's machine removed a major obstacle to cotton cultivation, gave plantation slavery a new lease on life, and undermined the doubts of those who considered slavery economically outmoded. Thus by the time Thomas Jefferson became president in 1801, free blacks had suffered a subtle erosion of their political gains, and slaves stood no closer to freedom.

## CONCLUSION

The United States had survived its perilous birth. George Washington had steered the country through its initial uncertain years even as political strife led to the formation of political parties and threatened the unity of the fragile nation. In 1800 a peaceful transition of power occurred when the Federalists allowed Thomas Jefferson to become president. By 1801 the dangers of civil war and national disintegration had abated. Yet ideological hatreds remained strong and the West's allegiance to the Union shaky. Racial tensions were growing, not diminishing. It remained to be seen whether Jefferson's liberal version of republicanism could serve as a better philosophy of government than the Federalists' conservative republicanism.

## CHRONOLOGY

**1789**  First Congress convenes in New York.
George Washington sworn in as first president.
Judiciary Act of 1789.
French Revolution begins.

**1790**  Alexander Hamilton submits his Report on the Public Credit and Report on a National Bank to Congress.
Treaty of New York.

**1791**  Bank of the United States is granted a twenty-year charter.
Bill of Rights ratified.
Slave uprising begins in French colony of Saint Domingue.
Hamilton submits his Report on Manufactures to Congress.

**1792**  Washington reelected president.

**1793**  Fugitive Slave Law.
*Chisholm* v. *Georgia*.
Large-scale exodus of French planters from Saint Domingue to the United States.
France declares war on Britain and Spain.
Washington's Neutrality Proclamation.
Citizen Genet arrives in United States.
Democratic societies established.

**1794**  Whiskey Rebellion.
General Anthony Wayne's forces rout Indians in the Battle of Fallen Timbers.

**1795**  Treaty of Greenville.
Jay's Treaty with Britain ratified.

**1796**  *Hylton* v. *United States*.
*Ware* v. *Hylton*.
Treaty of San Lorenzo (Pinckney's Treaty) ratified.
Washington's Farewell Address.
John Adams elected president.

**1798**  XYZ Affair.
Alien and Sedition Acts.
Eleventh Amendment to the Constitution ratified.

**1798–ᅠ1799**  Virginia and Kentucky Resolutions.

**1798–ᅠ1800**  United States fights Quasi-War with France.

**1800**  Gabriel's Rebellion in Virginia.
Thomas Jefferson elected president.

## FOR FURTHER READING

Joyce Appleby, *Capitalism and a New Social Order: The Republican Vision of the 1790s* (1984). A brief, penetrating analysis of Jeffersonian ideology.

Stanley Elkins and Eric McKitrick, *The Age of Federalism: The Early American Republic, 1788–1800* (1993). A magisterial account of politics and diplomacy through the decisive election of 1800.

Richard Hofstadter, *The Idea of a Party System: The Rise of Legitimate Opposition in the United States, 1780–1840* (1969). A classic account of how and why America's founders, originally fearing political parties, came to embrace them.

Drew R. McCoy, *The Elusive Republic: Political Economy in Jeffersonian America* (1980). An insightful portrayal of the influence of economic considerations on early national political thought.

James M. Smith, *Freedom's Fetters: The Alien and Sedition Laws and American Civil Liberties,* rev. ed. (1966). The most comprehensive study of the country's first great crisis in civil rights.

Laurel Thatcher Ulrich, *A Midwife's Tale: The Life of Martha Ballard, Based on Her Diary, 1785–1812* (1990). A Pulitzer Prize–winning study of a woman's life in rural America.

Anthony F.C. Wallace, *The Death and Rebirth of the Seneca* (1969). An anthropologist's masterful account of the Senecas' devastation during the Revolution and their remarkable cultural recovery afterward.

Jefferson's election, a turning point in the history of the young Republic, marked the peaceful transfer of power from one political party to another, a process never before attempted. Given the absence of precedent—the very newness of it all—relatively minor questions such as the replacement of Federalist office-holders spawned major philosophical debates. Perhaps the most important task facing Jefferson was to create and to gain support for ground rules to guide the operations of republican government.

This objective accomplished, the United States experienced extraordinary events in the two decades after Jefferson's election. In swift succession it doubled its land area; stopped all trade with Europe in an attempt to avoid war; went to war anyhow, nearly lost, and proclaimed a moral victory; almost disintegrated in a conflict over slavery and statehood; and staked its claim to preeminence in the New World. An age that began with ferocious political controversy culminated in the "Era of Good Feelings."

*(Right)* **Dolley Madison,** *by Gilbert Stuart, 1804*

# Jeffersonianism and the Era of Good Feelings

**The Age of Jefferson**

❧

**The Gathering Storm**

❧

**The War of 1812**

❧

**The Awakening of American Nationalism**

# The Age of Jefferson

Unemotional himself, Thomas Jefferson aroused deep emotions in others. To admirers, he was an aristocrat who trusted the people and defended popular liberty; to detractors, he was an infidel and a radical. Jefferson had so many facets that misunderstanding him was easy. Trained in law, he had spent much of his life in public service—as governor of Virginia, Washington's secretary of state, Adams's vice president. He designed his own neoclassical mansion, Monticello; studied the violin and numerous languages (including several Native American tongues); and served twenty years as president of the American Philosophical Society, America's oldest and most important scientific organization. Although he saw himself as a humanitarian, he owned more than 200 slaves.

History taught Jefferson that republics fell from within; governments that undermined popular liberty, not hostile neighbors, were the real threat to freedom. Taxes, standing armies, and corrupt officials made governments masters, rather than servants, of the people. In Europe the collapse of the French Revolution and the rise of Napoleonic dictatorship had both dismayed Jefferson and convinced him that he had read history correctly.

To prevent the United States from sinking into tyranny, Jefferson advocated that state governments retain great authority because they were immediately responsive to popular will. Popular liberty required popular virtue, he believed, virtue being the disposition to place public good above private interest and to exercise vigilance in keeping government under control. To Jefferson, the most vigilant and virtuous people were educated farmers, accustomed to acting and thinking with sturdy independence. Least vigilant were the inhabitants of cities, which he saw as breeding grounds for mobs and as menaces to liberty. When Americans "get piled upon one another in large cities, as in Europe," he warned, "they will become corrupt as in Europe."

Although opponents labeled him a dreamy philosopher incapable of governing, Jefferson was in fact intensely practical. He studied science not for its abstract theories but because scientific advances would augment human happiness. Jefferson's practical cast of mind revealed itself in his inventions—including an improved plow and a gadget for duplicating letters—and in his presidential agenda.

## Jefferson's "Revolution"

Jefferson described his election as a revolution, but the revolution he sought was to restore the liberty and tranquillity that (he thought) the United States had enjoyed in its earliest years and to reverse what he saw as a drift into despotism. The $10 million growth in the national debt under the Federalists alarmed Jefferson and his secretary of the treasury, Albert Gallatin. They rejected Alexander Hamilton's argument that debt strengthened the government by giving creditors a stake in its health. Just paying interest on the debt would require taxes, which would suck money from industrious farmers, the backbone of the Republic. The money would then fall into the hands of creditors, parasites who lived off interest payments. Increased tax revenues might also tempt the government to create a standing army, always a threat to liberty.

Jefferson and Gallatin asked Congress to repeal most internal taxes, and they slashed expenditures by closing some embassies and reducing the army. The navy was a different matter because of the Barbary pirates. For centuries rulers in North Africa (the "Barbary Coast") had tried to solve their own budget problems by engaging in piracy and demanding ransom for captured seamen. Jefferson refused to meet their demands for tribute: he calculated that war would be cheaper than giving in to such bribery. In 1801 he dispatched a naval squadron to the Barbary Coast. After the navy had bombarded several ports and the marines had landed at Tripoli, in 1805 the United States concluded a peace treaty with the Barbary rulers. The military solution had cost less than half the annual bribe!

To Jefferson and Gallatin, federal economy outweighed the importance of military preparedness; Gallatin calculated that by holding the line on expenditures, the government could pay off the

the foundation of the region's prosperity. A Massachusetts poet wrote:

> *Our ships all in motion once whitened the ocean,*
> *They sailed and returned with a cargo;*
> *Now doomed to decay they have fallen a prey*
> *To Jefferson, worms, and embargo.*

## The Election of 1808

With Jefferson's blessing, the Republicans nominated James Madison and George Clinton for the presidency and vice presidency in 1808. The Federalists renominated Charles C. Pinckney and Rufus King, the same ticket that had failed in 1804. In 1808 the Federalists staged a modest comeback, but Madison handily won the presidency, and the Republicans continued to control Congress.

The Federalists' revival, modest as it was, rested on two factors. First, the Embargo Act gave them the national issue that they had long lacked. Second, younger Federalists had abandoned their elders' "gentlemanly" disdain for campaigning and deliberately imitated vote-winning techniques such as barbecues and mass meetings that had worked for the Republicans.

## The Failure of Peaceable Coercion

To some contemporaries, "Little Jemmy" Madison, five feet four inches tall, seemed a weak, shadowy figure compared to Jefferson. In fact, Madison's intelligence and capacity for systematic thought equaled Jefferson's. Like Jefferson, Madison believed that American liberty rested on the virtue of the people and that virtue was critically tied to the growth and prosperity of agriculture. Madison also recognized that agricultural prosperity depended on trade—farmers needed markets. The British West Indies, dependent on the United States for much lumber and grain, struck Madison as both a natural trading partner and a tempting target. Britain alone could not fully supply the West Indies. By embargoing its own trade with the Indies, Madison reasoned, the United States could force Britain to its knees before Americans would suffer severe losses.

| The Election of 1808 | | |
| --- | --- | --- |
| Candidates | Parties | Electoral Vote |
| JAMES MADISON | Democratic-Republican | 122 |
| Charles C. Pinckney | Federalist | 47 |
| George Clinton | Democratic-Republican | 6 |

The American embargo, however, was coercing no one. Increased trade between Canada and the West Indies made a shambles of Madison's plan to pressure Britain. On March 1, 1809, Congress replaced the Embargo Act with the weaker, face-saving Non-Intercourse Act, which opened U.S. trade to all nations except Britain and France and authorized the president to restore trade with either of those nations if it stopped violating neutral rights. But neither nation complied. Meanwhile, American shippers kept up their profitable trade with the British and French, despite the restrictions. In May 1810 Congress substituted a new measure, Macon's Bill No. 2, for the Non-Intercourse Act. This legislation reopened trade with both belligerents, France and Britain, and then offered a clumsy bribe to each: if either nation repealed its restrictions on neutral shipping, the United States would halt all trade with the other. Napoleon seized the opportunity to confound both English-speaking nations by promising to repeal his edicts against American trade, hoping to provoke hostility between Britain and the United States. But the French continued to seize American ships. Peaceable coercion had become a fiasco.

## The Push into War

Madison now faced not only a hostile Britain and France but also militant Republicans demanding more aggressive policies. Primarily southerners and westerners, the militants were infuriated by insults to the American flag. In addition, economic recession between 1808 and 1810 had convinced the firebrands that British policies were wrecking their regions' economies. The election of 1810 brought several young militants, christened "war hawks," to Congress. Led by Henry Clay of Kentucky, who preferred war to the "putrescent pool of ignominious peace," the war hawks included John C. Calhoun of South Carolina, Richard M. Johnson of Kentucky, and William R. King of North Carolina—all future vice presidents. Clay was elected Speaker of the House.

### Tecumseh and the Prophet

More emotional and pugnaciously nationalistic than Jefferson or Madison, the war hawks called for expelling Britain from Canada and Spain from the Floridas. Their demands merged with westerners' fears that the British in Canada were recruiting Indians to halt the march of United States settlement. These fears, groundless but plausible, intensified when the Shawnee Indian chief Tecumseh and his half-brother, the Prophet, tried to unite several Ohio and Indiana tribes against westward-moving settlers. Demoralized by the continuing loss of the Indians' land and by alcoholism's ravages on Native American society, Tecumseh and the Prophet (a recovered alcoholic) tried to unite their people and to revive traditional values. Both believed that the Indians had to purge themselves of liquor and other corruptions of white civilization.

The Shawnee leaders were on a collision course with the governor of the Indiana Territory, William Henry Harrison. In the Treaty of Fort Wayne (1809), Harrison had purchased much of central and western Indiana from the Miami and the Delaware tribes for a paltry $10,000. After Tecumseh's Shawnees refused to sign the treaty, Harrison saw the charismatic leader as an enemy and even as a British cat's-paw. Accordingly, in September 1811 Harrison led an army against a Shawnee encampment at the junction of the Wabash and Tippecanoe Rivers. Two months later when the Prophet prematurely attacked Harrison (Tecumseh was away

recruiting Creek Indians), Harrison won a decisive victory. Ironically, the Battle of Tippecanoe, which made Harrison a national hero, accomplished what it had been designed to prevent: it prompted Tecumseh to join with the British.

### Congress Votes for War

By spring 1812 President Madison had concluded that war was inevitable, and he sent a war message

**Tenskwatawa (1768?–1834?), the Prophet**
*In periods of crisis Native American cultures often gave rise to prophets—religious revivalists of sorts—such as Tecumseh's brother Tenskwatawa. Known to non-Indians as the Prophet, Tenskwatawa tried to revive traditional Indian values and customs such as the common ownership of land and the wearing of animal skins and furs. His religious program blended with Tecumseh's political program to unite the western tribes.*

# CHAPTER 9

## The Transformation of American Society, 1815–1840

The years 1815 to 1840 saw rapid, often disorienting changes that affected both those who followed the frontier westward and those who stayed in the East. A revolution in transportation stimulated interregional trade and migration and encouraged an unprecedented development of towns and cities. The new urban dwellers provided a market not only for agricultural produce but also for the manufactures of the industries springing up in New England and major northeastern cities.

Viewed superficially, these changes might seem to have had little effect on the way Americans lived. Whether in 1815 or in 1840, most Americans dwelled outside the cities, practiced agriculture for a living, and traveled on foot or by horse. Yet this impression of continuity misleads us, for by 1840 many farmers had moved west. In addition, the nature of farming had changed as farmers increasingly raised crops for sale in distant markets rather than for their own use. By 1840, moreover, alternatives to farming as a liveli-

*(Right) Rocky Mountain trappers, or "mountain men," were hunters, explorers, and adventurers who lived "a wild Robin Hood kind of life" with "little fear of God and none at all of the Devil."*

**Westward Expansion and the Growth of the Market Economy**

❧

**The Rise of Manufacturing**

❧

**Equality and Inequality**

❧

**The Revolution in Social Relationships**

hood abounded. And the rise of such alternatives impinged on some of the most basic social relationships: between parents and children and between wives and husbands.

# Westward Expansion and the Growth of the Market Economy

The spark igniting these changes was the spread of Americans across the Appalachian Mountains. In 1790 most Americans lived east of the mountains, within a few hundred miles of the Atlantic; by 1840 one-third dwelled between the Appalachians and the Mississippi River. Unforeseen social and economic forces buffeted the settlers of this new West.

## The Sweep West

This westward movement occurred in several thrusts. Americans leapfrogged the Appalachians after 1791 to bring four new states into the Union by 1803: Vermont, Kentucky, Tennessee, and Ohio. From 1816 to 1821 momentum carried settlers farther west, even across the Mississippi River, and six more states entered: Indiana, Mississippi, Illinois, Alabama, Maine, and Missouri. Ohio's population soared from 45,000 in 1800 to more than 1.5 million by 1840 and Michigan's from 5,000 in 1810 to 212,000 in 1840.

Exploration carried some Americans even farther west. Zebulon Pike explored the Spanish Southwest in 1806, sighting the Colorado peak later named after him. By 1811, in the wake of Lewis and Clark, the New York merchant John Jacob Astor had founded a fur-trading post at the mouth of the Columbia River in the Oregon Country. At first whites relied on the Native Americans for furs, but in the 1820s such "mountain men" as Kit Carson and Jedediah Smith penetrated deep beyond the Rockies.

Smith typified these men and their exploits. Originally from western New York, he had moved west as far as Illinois by 1822. That year he signed on with an expedition bound for the upper Missouri River. In the course of this and later explorations, Smith nearly fell victim to a grizzly bear in South Dakota's Black Hills, crossed the Mojave Desert into California and explored the San Joaquin Valley, and hiked back across the Sierras and the Great Basin to the Great Salt Lake, a forbidding trip. His thirst for adventure led to his early death at the hands of Comanche Indians in 1831.

The mountain men, though celebrated, were not themselves typical westward migrants. For most pioneers, the West meant the area between the Appalachians and the Mississippi River, and their goal was stability, not adventure. Pioneers' letters home stressed the bounty and peacefulness of the West rather than its dangers. According to a Missourian in 1816, "There neither is, nor, in the nature of things, can there ever be, any thing like poverty [in this area]. All is ease, tranquility, and comfort."

## Western Society and Customs

Pioneers usually migrated in family groups. To reach markets with their produce, most settled along navigable rivers, particularly the great Ohio-Mississippi system. Not until the coming of canals and then railroads did westerners venture far from rivers. Settlers often clustered with people from the same eastern region; when New Englanders found southerners well entrenched in Indiana, they pushed on to Michigan.

These new westerners craved sociability. Even before towns sprang up, farm families joined their neighbors for sports and festivities. Men met for games that tested strength and agility: wrestling, lifting weights, pole jumping (for distance, not height), and hammer throwing. The games could be brutal. In gander pulling, riders competed to pull the head off a gander whose neck had been stripped of feathers and greased. Women usually combined work and play in quilting and sewing bees, carpet tackings, and even goose and chicken pluckings. At "hoedowns" and "frolics," the settlers danced to a fiddler's tune.

**Merrymaking at a Wayside Inn,** *by Pavel Svinin*

*Country inns served as social centers for rural neighborhoods as well as stopping places for travelers. Although this painting evokes rustic charm, guests at inns complained of the stale odor of rum, pie crusts that tasted like leather, cheese that defied digestion, and a lack of privacy that made them look forward to another day on the road.*

Western farm households usually practiced a clear gender division of labor. Men performed the heavy work such as cutting down trees and plowing fields. Women cooked, spun and wove, sewed, milked, and tended their large families. They also often helped with the butchering—slitting the hog's throat while it was still alive, bleeding it, scooping out the innards, washing the heart and liver, and hanging the organs to dry. Daintiness had been left behind, east of the mountains.

Compared to the East, the West was rough: cowpaths substituted for sidewalks and hand-hewn cabins for comfortable homes. The relative lack of refinement made westerners targets for eastern taunts. Jibed at as half-savage yokels, westerners responded that they at least were honest democrats, not soft would-be aristocrats. Pretension got short shrift. A sojourner at a tavern who hung a blanket to cover his bed from public gaze might find it ripped down, a woman who sought privacy in a crowded room might be dismissed as "uppity," and a politician who came to a rally in a buggy, rather than on horseback, might lose votes.

## The Federal Government and the West

The federal government's growing strength spurred westward expansion. Under the Articles of Confederation, several states had ceded western lands to the national government, creating a bountiful public domain. The Land Ordinance of 1785 had provided for the survey and sale of these lands, and the Northwest Ordinance of 1787 had established a mechanism for transforming them into states. The Louisiana Purchase had brought the entire Mississippi River under American control, and the Adams-Onís Treaty had wiped out the remnants of Spanish control east of the Mississippi. Six million acres of public land had been promised to volunteers during the War of 1812. The National Road, a highway begun in 1811, stretched farther westward, reaching Wheeling, Virginia, in 1818 and Vandalia,

Illinois, by 1838. People crowded along it. One traveler wrote, "We are seldom out of sight, as we travel on this grand track toward the Ohio, of family groups before and behind us."

The same governmental strength that aided whites brought misery to the Indians. Virtually all the foreign policy successes of the Republicans worked to the Native Americans' disadvantage. The Louisiana Purchase and Adams-Onís Treaty had stripped them of Spanish protection, and the War of 1812 had deprived them of British protection. Lewis and Clark bluntly told the Indians that they should "shut their ears up to the counsels of bad birds" and listen only to the Great White Father in Washington.

## The Removal of the Indians

Westward-moving white settlers found in their path sizable numbers of Native Americans, especially in the South, home to the "Five Civilized Tribes"—the Cherokees, Creeks, Choctaws, Chickasaws, and Seminoles. Years of commercial dealings and intermarriage with Europeans had created in these tribes influential minorities of mixed-bloods who had embraced Christianity and agriculture. The Cherokees had adopted Anglo-American culture to a greater extent than any other tribe. Among them were farmers, millers, and even slave owners; they also had a written form of their language, written laws, and their own bilingual newspaper, the *Cherokee Phoenix*.

While welcoming such signs of "civilization" among the Indians, whites did not hesitate to push the tribes out of their way. Although some mixed-bloods sold tribal lands and moved west, others resisted because their prosperity depended on trade with close-by whites. And full-blooded members of the Five Civilized Tribes, contemptuous of whites and mixed-bloods alike, wanted to retain their ancestral lands. When the Creek chief William McIntosh, a mixed-blood, sold most Creek lands in Georgia and Alabama, other Creeks executed him.

Whites' demands for Native American lands reached the boiling point in the 1820s. Andrew

Jackson of Tennessee embodied the new militancy of those who rejected piecemeal and tribe-by-tribe treaties. Jackson believed that the balance between Indians and whites had shifted drastically in recent decades and that the Indians were far weaker than commonly believed. There was no justification for "the farce of treating with the Indian tribes," Jackson proclaimed; the Indians were not independent nations but subject to the laws of their state of residence.

When Jackson became president in 1829, he instituted a coercive removal policy that reflected his disdain for the Indians and his conviction that

**Andrew Jackson as the Indians' Great Father**
*This political cartoon of c.1830 depicts the Native Americans as children or dolls, subject to a fatherly Jackson's dictates.*

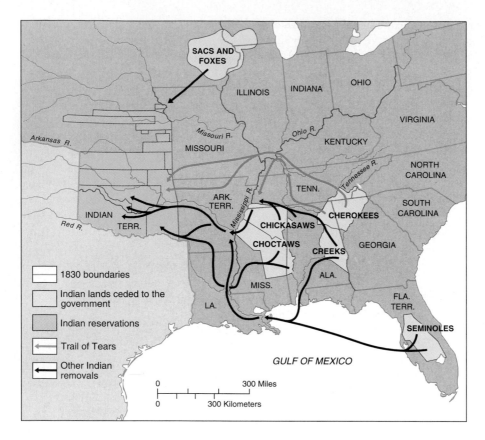

**The Removal of the Native Americans to the West, 1820–1840**
*The so-called Trail of Tears, followed by the Cherokees, was one of several routes along which various tribes migrated on their forced removal to reservations west of the Mississippi.*

"real" Indians, who retained their original ways, were being exploited by whites and mixed-bloods. In 1830 Jackson secured from a divided Congress the Indian Removal Act, granting the president authority to remove the Indians by force if necessary. By then, southern states had intensified pressure on the remaining tribes: a Georgia law had extended state jurisdiction over Cherokee country, begun the confiscation of tribal land, and made it illegal for Indians to testify against whites. The Creeks of Georgia and Alabama had started moving west in the late 1820s. In 1836 the Georgia militia attacked those still in the state, and when starving Creeks raided white settlements for food, federal troops finished the job begun by the militia. In 1836, 15,000 Creeks, most of the Creek nation, were removed—

many in chains—and resettled west of the Mississippi River.

The other southern "civilized" tribes suffered a similar fate. Chickasaws and Choctaws were removed by the early 1830s. French visitor Alexis de Tocqueville witnessed the arrival of the Choctaws along the Mississippi. "I saw them embark to cross the great river, and the sight will never fade from my memory. Neither sob nor complaint rose from that silent assembly. Their afflictions were of long standing, and they felt them to be irremediable." Of the Seminoles, more than half were removed from Florida in 1842 after seven years of bitter warfare.

The Cherokees, however, pursued peaceful resistance by seeking an injunction from the Supreme Court against Georgia's attempts to extend its laws over them and to confiscate their lands. In *Worcester* v. *Georgia* (1832), Chief Justice John Marshall ruled that the Cherokees, who had their own constitution and government, were a "domestic dependent nation" and hence were entitled to federal protection of their lands against Georgia's claims. Marshall concluded that Georgia laws were not valid in Cherokee territory.

President Andrew Jackson reportedly sneered, "John Marshall has made his decision; now let him enforce it," and ignored the ruling. Then in 1835 the U.S. government negotiated the fraudulent Treaty of New Echota with a handful of unauthorized individuals. It ceded most remaining Cherokee lands to the United States for $5.6 million and the Indians' transportation west. The principal signers were killed by other Cherokees in 1839, but by then the tribe's fate was sealed. Sixteen thousand Cherokees straggled west to the Indian Territory between 1835 and 1838 along the so-called Trail of Tears. A total of perhaps 4,000 died along the trail itself and within a year of the initial roundup and hard journey.

Indians in the Northwest Territory fared no better after they signed land-cession treaties. Two uprisings marked their westward removal. The first was quickly crushed, but the second, led by a Sac and Fox chief, Black Hawk, raged along the frontier in Illinois until federal troops and state militiamen virtually annihilated the Indians in 1832. After Black Hawk's defeat, the other northwestern tribes agreed to removal. Between 1832 and 1837 the United States consequently acquired nearly 190 million acres of Indian land in the Northwest for $70 million.

## The Agricultural Boom

In clearing the Indians from their territory, the federal government was responding to whites' pressures for land. Depleted soil and overcrowding had long driven farmers west, but after the War of 1812 soaring agricultural commodity prices and rising demand for western foodstuffs sharpened the land hunger. England and France, exhausted by war,

were importing substantial amounts of American wheat and corn; New England needed food for its burgeoning industrial population. With produce prices skyrocketing, western farmers took advantage of the Ohio-Mississippi river system to ship their grain to foreign markets through New Orleans. In short, federal Indian policy, although devastating to Native Americans, made farming possible in the West, and high prices and high demand made it attractive.

Cotton, and Eli Whitney's cotton gin, provided the impetus for settlement of the Old Southwest, especially Alabama and Mississippi. Indeed, the explosive westward thrust of southern farmers and planters after the War of 1812 resembled a gold rush. By 1817 land prices had shot up from $30 to $50 an acre. By 1820 Alabama and Mississippi produced half the nation's cotton. With a seemingly unlimited British market for raw cotton, production tripled between 1816 and 1831. Between 1831 and 1836 the value of cotton exports rose 300 percent, and cotton accounted for two-thirds of U.S. exports.

## The Market Economy and Federal Land Policy

American farmers, accustomed to growing enough food for their families (subsistence farming) and some grain or cotton for sale (commercial farming for the "market economy"), pursued national and foreign markets with zeal after the War of 1812. But the new commercial farmers encountered serious problems, including wildly fluctuating markets. They also routinely had to borrow money to cover the often long interval between harvest and sale. Thus commercial agriculture forced farmers to accept short-term debt in hope of reaping long-term profits. This debt was frequently worse than expected, particularly because many western farmers had also borrowed money to buy their land.

Federal efforts in this period to put the public domain into the hands of small farmers floundered. In the face of partisan and sectional pressures, the federal government passed various land laws in quick succession, each intended to undo the damage caused by its predecessors.

The Ordinance of 1785 had aimed to ensure the orderly settlement of the public domain by creating townships of thirty-six square miles, divided into 640-acre sections. Because ordinary farmers could not afford such large purchases, the assumption was that they would pool their money to buy sections. It was also assumed that a population of compatible settlers living on adjoining lots would be easier to govern than one of isolated settlers on scattered homesteads.

However, the Federalist administrations of the 1790s undermined this orderly process by encouraging the sale of huge tracts of land to wealthy speculators, who held the land until prices rose and then sold it to farmers. When the Republicans came to power in 1801, they tried to reverse this trend by dropping the minimum land sale to 320 acres; by 1832 the minimum acreage had fallen to 40 acres.

But land speculators remained one step ahead of federal policy, selling more affordable, easier-to-clear 40-acre lots (which farmers preferred) long before 1832. Soaring agricultural prices and easier credit after the War of 1812 also favored speculators; between 1812 and 1817 the value of bank notes in circulation increased from $45 million to $100 million. Many new banks were funded primarily to lend money to their directors for personal investment in land speculation. By 1819 sales of public lands were 1,000 percent greater than average sales from 1800 to 1814.

## The Speculator and the Squatter

Nonetheless, most of the public domain found its way into the hands of small farmers. The desire to recoup investments led speculators to sell quickly, as did the proliferation of squatters.

Squatters had long helped themselves to western land. Proud and independent, they hated land speculators and pressured Congress to allow "preemption" rights—that is, the right to purchase at the minimum price the land that they already lived on and had improved. After passing a series of lim-

ited preemption laws, Congress acknowledged a general right of preemption in 1841.

But these laws were of little use to farmers who had to purchase land from speculators. For them, interest rates ranged as high as 40 percent. Many western farmers, drowning in debt, had to skimp on food and plant cash crops in the hope of paying off creditors. Having moved west to fulfill dreams of self-sufficiency, they found themselves caught in the cash-crop economy, which quickly exhausted their land and forced them to move farther westward in search of new land. Abraham Lincoln's parents, who migrated from the East through several farms in Kentucky and then to Indiana, typified this "moving frontier."

## The Panic of 1819

In 1819 the land boom collapsed like a house of cards, the victim of a financial panic. State banks' loose practices played a major role in causing the panic. These state banks issued their own bank notes, little more than a promise to pay the bearer a certain amount of specie (gold and silver coin) on demand. Such notes were plentiful and had helped fuel the land boom after 1815. Farmers also borrowed to buy more land and plant more crops, certain that sales to Europe would enable them to repay loans. But even as American farmers were becoming more dependent on agricultural exports to repay their debts, bumper crops in Europe combined with an economic slump in England to trim foreign demand for U.S. crops.

The result was a cascade of economic catastrophes. In summer 1819 the Bank of the United States, holder of large amounts of state bank paper, began to insist that the state banks redeem this paper in specie. To pay these debts, state banks demanded that farmers and land speculators repay their loans—in specie. Credit contracted sharply throughout the nation, particularly in the West.

Land speculators suffered as credit dried up and land prices tumbled. Land prices plummeted from $69 an acre to $2 an acre as the credit squeeze drove down commodity prices. Hard-pressed farmers could not pay their debts, speculators could not collect their money, and land values collapsed.

The panic had three major consequences for Americans. First, they came to despise banks, especially the Bank of the United States. Second, they recognized how vulnerable American factories were to foreign competition and began to favor higher tariffs. Third, farmers recognized how deeply they depended on distant markets and began to look for better and cheaper ways to transport their products to these markets.

## The Transportation Revolution: Steamboats, Canals, and Railroads

The transportation systems available in 1820 had serious weaknesses. The great rivers west of the Appalachians ran primarily north to south and hence could not by themselves connect western farmers to eastern markets. Roads were expensive to maintain, and horse-drawn wagons were slow and limited in range. Consequently, after 1820 attention and investment shifted to the development of waterways.

In 1807 Robert R. Livingston and Robert Fulton introduced the steamboat *Clermont* on the Hudson River. They soon gained a monopoly from the New York legislature to run a New York–New Jersey ferry service. Spectacular profits lured competitors, who secured a license from Congress and then filed suit to break the Livingston-Fulton monopoly. In 1824 Chief Justice John Marshall handed down his decision in what was known as the *Gibbons* v. *Ogden* case. Marshall ruled that Article I, Section 8, of the Constitution, which empowered Congress to regulate interstate commerce, applied to navigation as well. In this case, he wrote, the power of Congress to regulate interstate commerce had to prevail over the power of New York; thus the Livingston-Fulton monopoly was void. Marshall's decision not only opened the way for rapid expansion of steamboat traffic but also forcefully reasserted the supremacy of national power over that of the states. In the aftermath of this decision, other state-granted monopolies collapsed and steamboat traffic increased

rapidly. The number of steamboats operating on western rivers jumped from 17 in 1817 to 727 by 1855.

Steamboats assumed a vital role along the Mississippi-Ohio river system. They were far more useful than rafts, which journeyed only one way, or keelboats, which took up to four months to travel upstream from New Orleans to Louisville; in 1817 a steamboat made the identical trip in just twenty-five days. The development of long, shallow hulls permitted navigation of the Mississippi-Ohio system even when hot, dry summers lowered the river level. Steamboats became more ornate as well as more practical. To compete for passengers, they offered luxurious cabins and lounges, called saloons. The saloon of one steamboat, the *Eclipse,* was the length of a football field and featured skylights, chandeliers, and velvet-covered mahogany furniture.

While steamboats proved their value, canals replaced roads and turnpikes as the focus of popular enthusiasm and financial speculation. Although the cost of canal construction was mind-boggling—Jefferson dismissed the idea of canals as "little short of madness"—canals offered the possibility of connecting the Mississippi-Ohio system with the Great Lakes and even the East Coast.

The first major canal project was the Erie Canal, completed in 1825. Ten times longer than any existing canal in North America, it stretched 363 miles from Buffalo to Albany, linking Lake Erie to the Hudson River, New York City, and the Atlantic Ocean. Other canals followed in rapid succession. One of the most spectacular was the Main Line (or Pennsylvania) Canal, which crossed the Alleghenies to connect Philadelphia with Pittsburgh. Canal boats used on the Main Line were built in collapsible sections; taken apart on reaching the mountains, they were carried over the crest on cable cars.

The canal boom slashed shipping costs. Before the Erie Canal, transporting wheat from Buffalo to New York City cost three times its market value; corn, six times its market value; and oats, twelve times. The Erie dramatically cut freight charges, which in the period 1817–1830 dropped from nineteen cents to two cents a ton per mile between the two cities. Similar reductions prevailed nationwide.

Railroads soon were competing with canals and gradually overtook them. In 1825 the first railroad for general transportation began operation in England. The new technology quickly reached the United States, and by 1840 there were 3,000 miles of railroad track, equal to the total canal mileage. Faster, cheaper to build, and able to reach more places, railroads enjoyed obvious advantages over canals, but Americans realized their potential only slowly.

Early railroads connected eastern cities rather than crossing the mountains and carried more passengers than freight. Not until 1849 did freight revenue exceed passenger revenue, and not until 1850 did railroads link the East Coast to Lake Erie. There were two main reasons for this slow pace of development. First, unlike canals, most railroads were built by private companies that tended to skimp on costs, as a result producing lines requiring constant repair. In contrast, canals needed little maintenance. Second, shipping bulky commodities such as iron, coal, and grain was cheaper by canal than by rail.

### The Growth of Cities

The transportation revolution accelerated the growth of towns and cities. Indeed, the forty years before the Civil War, 1820 to 1860, saw the most rapid urbanization in U.S. history. In that time the percentage of people living in places of 2,500 or more inhabitants rose from 6.1 percent to nearly 20 percent. The Erie Canal transformed Rochester, New York, from a village of several hundred in 1817 to a town of 9,000 by 1830. By 1860 New York City's population had rocketed from 124,000 to 800,000, and the number of towns with more than 2,500 inhabitants climbed from 56 to 350 between 1820 and 1850.

Urban growth was particularly fast in the West. The War of 1812 stimulated manufacturing and transformed villages into towns, as did the agricultural boom and the introduction of steamboats after 1815. Virtually all the major western cities were river ports. Of these, Pittsburgh, Cincinnati,

Louisville, and New Orleans were the largest and most prominent. Pittsburgh was a manufacturing center, but the others were basically commercial hubs flooded by people eager to make money.

What the transportation revolution gave, it could also take away. The completion of the Erie Canal gradually shifted the center of western economic activity away from the river cities and toward the Great Lakes; Buffalo, Cleveland, Detroit, Chicago, and Milwaukee were the ultimate beneficiaries of the canal. In 1830 nearly 75 percent of western city dwellers lived in the river ports of New Orleans, Louisville, Cincinnati, and Pittsburgh, but by 1840 the proportion had dropped to 20 percent. The advent of modern manufacturing would multiply the effect of the transportation revolution on the growth of cities.

## The Rise of Manufacturing

Although we associate the word *manufacturing* with factories and machines, it literally means "making by hand." In the colonial era most products were in fact handmade, either in the home or in the workshops of skilled artisans. The years 1815–1860 mark the transition from colonial to modern manufacturing, although factories remained small. Indeed, as late as 1860 the average manufacturing establishment contained only eight workers.

Americans continued to think of themselves as a nation of farmers in this era, but industrialization was taking hold. By 1850, 20 percent of the labor force worked in manufacturing and produced 30 percent of the national output.

Industrialization occurred gradually, in distinct stages. In early manufacturing the production of goods was divided so that each worker made parts rather than entire products. As manufacturing advanced, workers were gathered into factories with rooms devoted to specialized operations performed by hand or simple machines. Finally, power-driven machinery replaced hand manufacturing. Because industrialization grew gradually and unevenly, people did not always realize that traditional manufacturing by skilled artisans was becoming obsolete and that machines would soon tumble artisans from their pedestals.

## Causes of Industrialization

Multiple domestic and foreign factors stimulated industrialization. The Era of Good Feelings saw general agreement that the United States needed tariffs; once protected from foreign competition, American cloth production rose by an average of 15 percent *every year* from 1815 to 1833. At the same time, the transportation revolution enlarged markets and demand. Americans began to prefer factory-made products to homemade ones. Especially in the West, farmers concentrated on their farming and bought shoes and cloth.

Immigration was also vital. Five million people emigrated from Europe to the United States between 1790 and 1860, most of them to pursue economic opportunity. The majority was German or Irish, but the smaller number of British immigrants was most important to industrialization. That process in Britain was a generation ahead of the United States, and British immigrants understood the workings of machines. For example, immigrant Samuel Slater had learned the "mystery" of textile production as an apprentice in England. Although British law forbade emigration by skilled "mechanics" such as Slater, he disguised himself and brought his knowledge of machines and factories to eager Americans.

Americans also freely experimented with various machines and developed their own technologies. In the 1790s wagon maker Oliver Evans built an automated flour mill that a single person could supervise: grain was poured in one side, and flour poured out on the other. With labor scarce in the early Republic, manufacturers sought to cut costs by replacing expensive workers with machines. Eli Whitney borrowed the European idea of interchangeable parts and employed unskilled (and thus cheap) workers to make 10,000 muskets for the U.S. Army. The use of interchangeable parts become so common in the United States that Europeans and Americans alike called it the American system of manufacturing.

**Mill Girls**
*New England's humming textile mills were a magnet for untold numbers of independence-seeking young women in antebellum America.*

## New England Industrializes

New England became America's first industrial region. The trade wars leading up to the War of 1812 had devastated the Northeast's traditional economy and stimulated capital investment in manufacturing. New England's many swift-flowing rivers were ideal sources of waterpower for mills. The westward migration of New England's young men, unable to wrest a living from rocky soil, left a surplus of young women, who supplied cheap industrial labor.

Cotton textiles led the way. Samuel Slater arrived in Pawtucket, Rhode Island, in 1790 and helped to design and build a mill that used Richard Arkwright's spinning frame to spin cotton yarn. His work force quickly grew from nine to one hundred, and his mills multiplied. Slater's mills performed only two operations: carding the cotton (separating cotton bolls into fine strands) and spinning the fiber into yarn. In what was still essentially "cottage" manufacturing, Slater contracted out the weaving to women working in their homes.

The establishment of the Boston Manufacturing Company in 1813 opened a new chapter in U.S. manufacturing. Backed by ample capital, the Boston Company built textile mills in the Massachusetts towns of Lowell and Waltham; by 1836 the company employed more than 6,000 workers.

Unlike Slater's mills, the Waltham and Lowell factories turned out finished products, thus elbowing aside Slater's cottage industry. Slater had tried to preserve tradition by hiring entire families to work at his mills—the men to raise crops, the women and children to toil in the mills. In contrast, 80 percent of the workers in the Lowell and Waltham mills were unmarried women fifteen to thirty years old. Hired managers and company regulations, rather than families, provided discipline. The workers ("operatives") boarded in factory-owned houses or licensed homes, observed a curfew, attended church, and accepted the "moral police of the corporations."

The corporations enforced high moral standards, at least in part to attract New England farm girls to the mills, where working conditions were less than attractive. To prevent threads from snapping, the factories had to be kept humid; windows were nailed shut, and water was sprayed in the air. Flying dust and deafening noise were constant companions. In the 1830s conditions worsened as competition and recession led mill owners to reduce wages and speed up work schedules. The system's impersonality intensified the harshness of the work environment. Owners rarely visited factories; their agents, all men, gave orders to the workers, mainly women. In 1834 and again in 1836 women at the Lowell mills quit work to protest low wages.

## Manufacturing in New York City and Philadelphia

In the 1830s and 1840s New York, Philadelphia, and other cities witnessed a different kind of industrialization. It involved few machines or women workers and encompassed a wide range of products, including shoes, saddles, tools, ropes, hats, and gloves.

Despite these differences, factories in New York City and Philadelphia exposed workers to the same forces encountered by their New England counterparts. The transportation revolution had expanded markets and turned urban artisans and merchants into aggressive merchandiser who scoured the country for orders. By 1835 New York's ready-made clothing industry was supplying cheap shirts and dungarees to western farmers and southern slaves; by the 1840s it was providing expensive suits for the well-to-do. Fierce competition spurred wage cuts and work speedups in the urban factories. Whereas New England's entrepreneurs had introduced machines, New York City's manufacturers lacked both cheap waterpower and readily available machines. To increase production, New York and Philadelphia factory owners alike hired large numbers of unskilled workers and paid them low wages. A worker would perform one simple hand operation such as stitching cloth or soling shoes. Unlike their colonial counterparts, these workers neither made whole shoes nor saw a customer. Such subdivision of tasks (performed without machines) and specialization of labor characterized much early industrialization. In Massachusetts's boot and shoe industry, workers gradually were gathered into large factories to perform specialized operations in different rooms. But in New York City and Philadelphia, high population density made grouping workers unnecessary; instead, middlemen subcontracted out tasks to widows, immigrants, and others who would fashion parts of shoes or saddles or dresses anywhere that light would enter.

The skilled artisans of New York City and Philadelphia tried to protect their interests by forming trade unions and "workingmen's" political parties. Initially, they sought to restore privileges and working conditions that artisans had once enjoyed, but gradually they joined forces with unskilled workers. When coal heavers in Philadelphia struck for a ten-hour day in 1835, carpenters, cigar makers, leather workers, and other artisans joined in what became the first general strike in the United States. The emergence of organized worker protests underscored the mixed blessings of economic development. Where some people prospered, others found their economic position deteriorating. By 1830 many Americans were questioning whether their nation was truly a land of equality.

## Equality and Inequality

Visitors to the United States sensed changes sweeping the country but could neither describe them nor agree on their direction. One of the most astute of these observers, the French nobleman Alexis de Tocqueville, whose *Democracy in America* (1835, 1840) is a classic, cited the "general equality of condition among the people" as the fundamental shaping force of American society. But Tocqueville also was keenly aware of inequalities in that society, inequalities less visible but no less real than those in France. The United States might not have a permanent servant class, but it surely had its rich and its poor.

Even today historians disagree about the meaning and extent of inequality in antebellum (pre–Civil War) America. Nonetheless, we have a more detailed and complete understanding of that society than did its contemporaries, such as Tocqueville. The following discussion applies mainly to northern society; we examine the South's distinctive social structure in Chapter 12.

### Growing Inequality:
### The Rich and the Poor

The gap between rich and poor continued to widen in the first half of the nineteenth century. Although striking inequalities separated rich and poor farmers, the inequalities were far greater in the cities, where a small fraction of the people owned a huge share of the wealth. In Boston the richest 4 percent of the people owned almost 70 percent of the wealth by 1848, whereas 81 percent of the population owned only 4 percent of the wealth. New York and other major cities mirrored these statistics.

Although commentators celebrated the self-made man and his rise "from rags to riches," few actually fit this pattern. Less than 5 percent of the wealthy had started life poor; almost 90 percent of well-off people had been born rich. Clearly, the old-fashioned way to wealth was to inherit it, to marry more of it, and to invest it wisely. Occasional rags-to-riches stories like that of John Jacob Astor and his fur-trading empire sustained the myth, but it was mainly a myth.

The rich built their splendid residences close to one another. In New York half the city's wealthy families lived on only eight streets, and they belonged to the same clubs. Tocqueville noted these facts and also observed that the rich feigned respect for equality, at least in public. They rode in ordinary carriages, brushed elbows with the less privileged, and avoided the conspicuous display of wealth that marked their private lives.

At the opposite end of the social ladder were the poor. By today's standards most antebellum Americans were poor; they lived at the edge of destitution, depended on their children's labor to meet expenses, had little money for medical care or recreation, and suffered frequent unemployment. In 1850 an estimated three out of eight males over twenty owned little more than their clothing.

Antebellum Americans distinguished between poverty, a common condition, and *pauperism*, which meant both poverty and dependency—the inability to care for oneself. The elderly, the ill, and the widowed often fell into the category of pauperism, although they were not seen as a permanent class. Pauperism caused by illness, old age, or circumstance would not pass from generation to generation.

Moralists' assumption that the United States would be free of a permanent class of paupers was comforting but misleading. Immigrants, especially the Irish who fled famine in their homeland only to settle in wretched slums in New York City, found it difficult to escape poverty. Moreover, as some Americans convinced themselves that success lay within everyone's grasp, they also tended to believe that the poor were responsible for their own poverty. Ironically, even as many Americans blamed the poor for being poor, discrimination mired some groups in enduring poverty. Among the chief victims were northern free blacks.

### Free Blacks in the North

Prejudice against African-Americans was deeply ingrained in white society throughout the nation. Although slavery had largely disappeared in the North by 1820, discriminatory laws remained. The voting rights of African-Americans were severely restricted; for example, New York eliminated property requirements for whites but kept them for blacks. There were attempts to bar free blacks from migrating. And segregation prevailed in northern schools, jails, and hospitals. Most damaging of all to free blacks was the social pressure that forced them into unskilled, low-paying jobs throughout the northern cities. Recalling his youth as a free black in Rhode Island, William J. Brown wrote, "To drive carriages, carry a market basket after the boss, and brush his boots, or saw wood and run errands was as high as a colored man could rise." Although a few free blacks accumulated moderate wealth, free blacks in general were only half as likely as other city dwellers to own real estate.

### The "Middling Classes"

Most antebellum Americans were neither fabulously rich nor grindingly poor but part of the "middling classes." Even though the wealthy owned an increasing proportion of wealth, per capita income grew at 1.5 percent annually between 1840 and 1860, and the standard of living generally rose after 1800.

Americans applied the term *middling classes* to farmers and artisans, who held the ideal of self-employment and were considered steady and dependable. Often, however, farmers and artisans led lives considerably less stable than this ideal. Asa G. Sheldon of Massachusetts described himself as a farmer, offered advice on growing corn and cranberries, and gave speeches glorifying farming. But Sheldon actually practiced it very little; he instead derived his

**Dancing for Eels, Catharine Market, 1820**
*Expressive dancing was part of African-American street festivals in the eighteenth-century cities. Fearing that such street dancing perpetuated white stereotypes of blacks, antislavery whites and black leaders tried to suppress it after 1800, but black dancing survived in dance cellars in New York City's Five Points slum. As this sketch indicates, African-Americans sometimes danced in public for applause, "a bunch of eels" or other fish, and perhaps money. The African-American at the left is "patting juba," which meant keeping time by hand clapping or by beating hands against legs. "Juba" also became the nickname of William Henry Lane. After seeing Lane perform in 1842 in a Five Points cellar, the novelist Charles Dickens labeled him "the greatest dancer known."*

living from transporting grain, harvesting timber, and clearing land for railroads. The Irish immigrants whom he hired did the shoveling and hauling, and Sheldon the "farmer" prospered—but his prosperity owed little to farming.

The increasingly commercial and industrial American economy allowed, and sometimes forced, people to adapt. Not all succeeded. Allan Melville, the father of novelist Herman Melville, was one who failed. An enterprising import merchant with boundless faith in the inevitable triumph of honesty and prudence, Melville did well until the late 1820s, when his business sagged. By 1830 he was "destitute of resources and without a shilling—without immediate assistance I know not what will become of me." Despite loans of $3,500, Melville's downward spiral continued, and he died two years later, broken in spirit.

Artisans shared the perils of life in the middling classes. During the colonial period many had attained the ideal of self-employment, owning their tools, taking orders, making their products, and training their children and apprentices in the craft. By 1850 this self-sufficient artisan class had split into two distinct groups. The few artisans who had access to capital became entrepreneurs who hired journeymen to do the actual work. Without capital, most remained journeymen, working for the artisans-turned-entrepreneurs with little prospect of self-employment.

Like the poor, the middling class was transient. When debt-burdened farmers hoping to get out of debt exhausted land quickly by their intense cultivation of cash crops, they simply moved on. Artisans, increasingly displaced by machines, found that skilled jobs were seasonal, and so they, too, moved from place to place to survive.

The multiplying risks and opportunities that confronted Americans both widened the gap between social classes and increased the psychological burdens on individuals. Commercial and industrial growth placed intense pressure on basic social relationships—for example, between lawyer and client, minister and congregation, and even parents and children.

# The Revolution in Social Relationships

Following the War of 1812 the growth of interregional trade, commercial agriculture, and manufacturing disrupted traditional social relationships and forged new ones. Two broad changes took place. First, Americans began to question traditional forms of authority and to embrace individualism; wealth, education, and social position no longer received automatic deference. Second, Americans created new foundations for authority. For example, women developed the idea that they possessed a "separate sphere" of authority in the home, and individuals formed voluntary associations to influence the direction of society.

## The Attack on the Professions

An intense criticism of lawyers, physicians, and ministers exemplified the assault on and erosion of traditional authority. Between 1800 and 1840 the wave of religious revivals known as the Second Great Awakening (see Chapter 10) sparked fierce attacks on the professions. Revivalists blasted the clergy for creating complex theologies, drinking expensive wines, and fleecing the people. One revivalist accused physicians of inventing fancy Latin and Greek names for diseases to disguise their inability to cure them.

These attacks on the learned professions peaked between 1820 and 1850. Samuel Thomson led a successful movement to eliminate all barriers to entry into the medical profession, including educational requirements. By 1845 every state had repealed laws requiring licenses or education to practice medicine. In religion ministers found little job security as finicky congregations dismissed clergymen whose theology displeased them. In turn, ministers became more ambitious and more inclined to leave poor, small churches for large, wealthy ones.

The increasing commercialization of the economy led to both more professionals and more attacks on them. In 1765 America had one medical school; by 1860 there were sixty-five. The newly minted doctors and lawyers had neither deep roots in the towns where they practiced nor convincing claims to social superiority. "Men dropped down into their places as from clouds," one critic wrote. "Nobody knew who or what they were, except as they claimed." A horse doctor would hang up a sign as "Physician and Surgeon" and "fire at random a box of his pills into your bowels, with a vague chance of killing some disease unknown to him, but with a better prospect of killing the patient."

This questioning of authority was particularly sharp on the frontier. Easterners sneered that every man in the West claimed to be a "judge," "general," "colonel," or "squire." In a society in which *every* person was new, titles were easily adopted and just as readily challenged. Would-be gentlemen substituted an exaggerated sense of personal honor for legal or customary claims of authority. Obsessed with their fragile status, these "gentlemen" could react testily to the slightest insult, and consequently duels were common on the frontier.

## The Challenges to Family Authority

Meanwhile, children quietly questioned parental authority. The era's economic change forced many young people to choose between staying at home to help their parents and venturing out on their own. Writing to her parents just before beginning work at a Lowell textile mill, eighteen-year-old Sally Rice explained:

> I must of course have something of my own before many more years have passed over my head, and where is that something coming from if I go home and earn nothing. You may think me unkind, but how can you blame me if I want to stay here. I have but one life to live and I want to enjoy myself as I can while I live.

This desire for independence fueled westward migration as well. Restless single men led the way. Two young men from Virginia put it succinctly: "All the promise of life now seemed to us to be at the other end of the rainbow—somewhere else—anywhere else but on the farm. . . . All our youthful plans had as their chief object the getting away from the farm."

As young antebellum Americans tried to escape close parental supervision, courtship and marriage patterns also changed. No longer dependent on parents for land, young people wanted to choose their own mates. Romantic love, rather than parental preference, increasingly determined marital decisions. Colonial Puritans had advised young people to choose marriage partners whom they *could* love; but by the early 1800s young men and women viewed romantic love as the indispensable basis for successful marriage.

One clear sign of lessening parental control over courtship and marriage was the number of women marrying out of their birth order. Traditionally, fathers had wanted their daughters to marry in the order of their birth to avoid suspicion that there was something wrong with any of them. Another mark of the times was the growing popularity of long engagements; young women were reluctant to tie the knot, fearing that marriage would snuff out their independence. Equally striking was the increasing number of young women who chose not to marry. Catharine Beecher, for example, the daughter of minister Lyman Beecher, broke off her engagement to a young man during the 1820s, later renewed the engagement, and after her fiancé's death remained single.

Thus young people lived more and more in a world of their own. Moralists reacted with alarm and flooded the country with books of advice to youth, all of which stressed the same message: that the newly independent young people should develop rectitude, self-control, and "character." The self-made adult began with the self-made youth.

## Wives, Husbands

Another class of advice books counseled wives and husbands about their rights and duties. These books were a sign that relations between spouses were also changing. Young men and women accustomed to making their own decisions would understandably approach marriage as a compact among equals. Although inequalities within marriage remained—especially the legal tradition that married women could not own property—the trend was toward a form of equality.

One source of this change was the rise of the doctrine of separate spheres. The traditional view of women as subordinate in all ways yielded to a separate-but-equal doctrine that portrayed men as superior in making money and governing the world and women as superior in exerting moral influence on family members. Most important was the shift of responsibility for child rearing from fathers to mothers. Advice books instructed mothers to discipline children by withdrawing love rather than using corporal punishment. A whipped child might obey but would remain sullen and bitter. The gentler methods advocated in manuals promised to penetrate the child's heart, to make the child want to do the right thing.

The idea of a separate women's sphere blended with the image of family and home as secluded refuges from a disorderly society. Popular culture painted an alluring portrait of the pleasures of home in such sentimental songs as "Home, Sweet Home" and poems such as "A Visit from St. Nicholas." Even the physical appearance of houses changed; one prominent architect published plans for peaceful single-family homes to offset the hurly-burly of daily life. "There should be something to love," he wrote. "There must be nooks about it, where one would love to linger; windows, where one can enjoy the quiet landscape at his leisure; cozy rooms, where all fireside joys are invited to dwell."

But reality diverged far from this ideal. Ownership of a quiet single-family home lay beyond the reach of most Americans, even much of the middle class. Farm homes, far from tranquil, were beehives of activity, and city dwellers often had to sacrifice privacy by taking in boarders to supplement family income.

Nevertheless, these intertwined ideas—separate spheres for men and women and the home as a sanctuary from the harsh world—were virtually the only ones projected in antebellum magazines. Although ideals, they intersected with the real world at points. The decline of cottage industry and the growing number of men (merchants, lawyers, brokers) who worked outside the home gave women more time to lavish on children. Married women found these ideals sources of power: the doctrine of separate spheres subtly implied that women should control not only the discipline but also the number of children.

In 1800 the United States had one of the highest birthrates ever recorded. Statistically, the average woman bore 7.04 children. Children were valuable for the labor they provided and for the relief from the burdens of survival that they could bring to aging parents. The more children, the better, most couples assumed. However, the growth of the market economy raised questions about children's economic value. Unlike a farmer, a merchant or lawyer could not send his children to work at the age of seven or eight. The birthrate gradually dropped, especially in towns and cities, so that statistically, by 1900 the average woman would bear 3.98 children. Birthrates remained higher among African-Americans and immigrants and in the rural West, where land was plentiful.

Abstinence, *coitus interruptus* (the withdrawal of the penis before ejaculation), and abortion were common birth-control methods. Remedies for "female irregularity"—unwanted pregnancy—were widely advertised. The rubber condom and vaginal diaphragm were familiar to many Americans by 1865. Whatever the method, husbands and wives jointly decided to limit family size. Economic and ideological considerations blended together. Husbands could note that the economic value of children was declining; wives, that having fewer children would give them more time to nurture each one and thereby to carry out their womanly duties.

Most supporters of the ideal of separate spheres did not advocate full legal equality for women. Indeed, the idea of separate spheres was an explicit *alternative* to legal equality. But the concept enhanced women's power within marriage by giving them influence in such vital issues as child rearing and the frequency of pregnancies.

## Horizontal Allegiances and the Rise of Voluntary Associations

As some forms of authority weakened, Americans devised new ways by which individuals could extend their influence over others. The antebellum era witnessed the widespread substitution of *horizontal* allegiances for *vertical* allegiances. In vertical allegiances, authority flows from the top down, and people in a subordinate position identify their interests with those of superiors rather than others in the same subordinate roles. The traditional patriarchal family is an example of vertical allegiance, as is the traditional apprentice system. When social relationships assumed a horizontal form, new patterns emerged. Vertical relationships remained but became less important. New relationships linked those who were in a similar position: for example, in the large textile mills, operatives realized they had more in common with one another than with their supervisors. Wives tended to form associations that bound them with other married women, and young men developed associations with other young men.

Voluntary (and horizontal) associations proliferated in the 1820s and 1830s. Tocqueville described Americans as "a nation of joiners." At the most basic level these organizations promoted sociability by providing contact with people who shared similar interests, experiences, or characteristics. Women and free blacks formed their own voluntary associations. Beyond that, voluntary associations allowed members to assert their influence at a time when traditional forms of authority were weakening. To promote the concept of a separate sphere for women, women joined maternal associations to exchange ideas about child rearing; temperance associations to work for abstinence from alcoholic beverages; and moral-reform societies to combat prostitution.

Temperance and moral-reform societies served dual purposes. In addition to trying to suppress well-known vices, they enhanced women's power over men. Temperance advocates assumed that intemperance was a male vice, and moral reformers attributed prostitution to men who, unable to control their passions, exploited vulnerable girls. These organizations represented collective action by middle-class women to increase their influence in society.

## CONCLUSION

Tocqueville described the United States of the 1830s as remarkable not for "the marvellous grandeur of some undertakings" but for the "innumerable multitude of small ones." Indeed, despite grand projects such as the Erie Canal, the era's distinguishing feature was the number of small to medium-sized enterprises that Americans embarked on: commercial farms of modest proportions, railroads of a few hundred miles, manufacturing companies employing five to ten workers. Even so, antebellum Americans thought that the world of their ancestors was breaking apart. As traditional assumptions eroded, however, new ones replaced them. Ties to village leaders and parents weakened, but people of the same age or same ideas formed new bonds. A widening circle of Americans insisted on the right to shape their own economic destinies, but individualism did not mean isolation from others, as the proliferation of voluntary associations testified.

Beyond changing the private lives of Americans, the social transformations of 1815 to 1840 also created a host of new political issues, as we shall see in Chapter 10.

## CHRONOLOGY

| | |
|---|---|
| **1790** | Samuel Slater opens his first Rhode Island mill. |
| **1793** | Eli Whitney invents the cotton gin. |
| **1807** | Robert R. Livingston and Robert Fulton introduce the steamboat *Clermont* on the Hudson River. |
| **1811** | Construction of the National Road begins at Cumberland, Maryland. |
| **1819** | Economic panic, ushering in four-year depression. |
| **1820–1850** | Growth of female moral-reform societies. |
| **1820s** | Expansion of New England textile mills. |
| **1824** | *Gibbons* v. *Ogden*. |
| **1825** | Completion of the Erie Canal. |

| | |
|---|---|
| **1828** | Baltimore and Ohio Railroad chartered. |
| **1830** | Indian Removal Act passed by Congress. |
| **1831** | Alexis de Tocqueville begins visit to the United States to study American penitentiaries. |
| **1832** | *Worcester* v. *Georgia*. |
| **1834** | First strike at the Lowell mills. |
| **1835–1838** | Trail of Tears. |
| **1837** | Economic panic begins a depression that lasts until 1843. |
| **1840** | System of production by interchangeable parts perfected. |

## FOR FURTHER READING

William L. Anderson, ed., *Cherokee Removal Before and After* (1991). An anthology containing the latest research on Cherokee relocation.

Rowland Berthoff, *An Unsettled People: Social Order and Disorder in American History* (1971). A stimulating interpretation of American social history.

Ray A. Billington, *Westward Expansion: A History of the American Frontier* (1949). The standard study of westward movement and settlement.

Carl Degler, *At Odds: Women and the Family in America from the Revolution to the Present* (1980). A fine overview of the economic and social experiences of American women.

Gary Nash, *Forging Freedom: The Formation of Philadelphia's Black Community, 1720–1840* (1988). An imaginative reconstruction of the emergence of a semi-autonomous African-American community.

Harry N. Scheiber, *The Ohio Canal Era: A Case Study of Government and the Economy, 1820–1861* (1969). An analysis that speaks volumes about economic growth in the early republic.

George R. Taylor, *The Transportation Revolution, 1815–1860* (1951). The standard general study of the development of canals, steamboats, highways, and railroads.

Sean Wilentz, *Chants Democratic: New York City and the Rise of the American Working Class, 1788–1850* (1983). A stimulating synthesis of economic, social, and political history.

The 1820s were a period of transition. As the Revolutionary generation passed from the scene—both Thomas Jefferson and John Adams died on July 4, 1826—new generations of Americans grappled with new problems born of westward migration, growing economic individualism, and increasing sectional conflict over slavery. Massive social and economic change shattered old assumptions and created a vigorous new brand of politics.

This transformation led to the birth of a second American party system, with Democrats and Whigs replacing Republicans and Federalists. The changes went far beyond names. The new parties organized grassroots support, molded government in response to the people's will, and welcomed conflict as a way to sustain interest in political issues.

Reform movements paralleled, and sometimes replaced, politics as idealistic men and women worked for temperance, abolition, education reform, and equality for women. Strongly held religious beliefs, often the product of evangelism and nontraditional sects, impelled reformers into

*(Right)* The Liberator *banner*

## Politics, Religion, and Reform in Antebellum America

**The Transformation of American Politics, 1824–1832**

❧

**The Bank Controversy and the Second Party System**

❧

**The Rise of Popular Religion**

❧

**The Age of Reform**

these and other crusades, and they soon discovered that their success rested on their ability to influence politics.

Both the political and the reform agendas of the 1820s and 1830s diverged from those of the nation's founders. They had feared popular participation in politics, left an ambiguous legacy on slavery, and displayed little interest in women's rights. Yet even as Americans shifted their political and social priorities, they continued to venerate the founders. Histories of the United States, biographies of Revolutionary patriots, and torchlight parades that bore portraits of Washington and Jefferson alongside depictions of Andrew Jackson reassured the men and women of the young nation that they were remaining loyal to their heritage.

# The Transformation of American Politics, 1824–1832

In 1824 Andrew Jackson and John Quincy Adams were both members of Jefferson's Republican party; by 1834 Jackson was a Democrat and Adams a Whig. Tensions spawned by industrialization, the rise of the Cotton South, and westward expansion split Jefferson's old party. Generally, supporters of states' rights joined the Democrats, and advocates of national support for economic development became Whigs.

Democrat or Whig, leaders had to adapt to the rising notion that politics should be an expression of the will of the common people rather than an activity that gentlemen conducted on the people's behalf. Americans still looked up to their political leaders, but those leaders could no longer look down on the people.

## Democratic Ferment

Democratizing forces in politics took several forms. One of the most common was the abolition of the requirement that voters own property; no western states had such a requirement, and eastern states gradually liberalized their laws. Moreover, written ballots replaced the custom of voting aloud, which had enabled elites to influence others at the polls. And appointive offices became elective. The selection of members of the electoral college shifted gradually from state legislatures to the voters, and by 1832 only South Carolina followed the old custom.

The fierce tug of war between Republicans and Federalists in the 1790s and early 1800s had taught both parties to court voters and listen to their will. At grand party-run barbecues from Maine to Maryland, potential voters washed down free clams and oysters with free beer and whiskey. Republicans sought to expand suffrage in the North, and Federalists did likewise in the South, each in hopes of transforming itself into a majority party in that section.

The pace of political democratization was uneven, however. The parties were still run from the top down as late as 1820, with candidates nominated by caucus, that is, a meeting of party members in the legislature. Moreover, few party leaders embraced the principle of universal white manhood suffrage. Finally, the democratization of politics did not necessarily draw more voters to the polls. Waning competition between Federalists and Republicans after 1816 deprived voters of clear choices and made national politics boring. Yet no one disputed that to oppose the people or democracy would be a formula for political suicide. The people, one Federalist moaned, "have become too saucy and are really beginning to fancy themselves equal to their betters."

## The Election of 1824

Sectional politics shattered the harmony of the Era of Good Feelings. In 1824 five candidates, all Republicans, battled for the presidency. John Quincy Adams emerged as the New England favorite. John C. Calhoun and William Crawford fought to represent the South. Henry Clay of Kentucky assumed that his leadership in promoting the American System would endear him to the East as well as to his native West. Tennessean Andrew Jackson stunned

## The Election of 1824

| Candidates | Parties | Electoral Vote | Popular Vote | Percentage of Popular Vote |
|---|---|---|---|---|
| JOHN QUINCY ADAMS | Democratic-Republican | 84 | 108,740 | 30.5 |
| Andrew Jackson | Democratic-Republican | 99 | 153,544 | 43.1 |
| William H. Crawford | Democratic-Republican | 41 | 46,618 | 13.1 |
| Henry Clay | Democratic-Republican | 37 | 47,136 | 13.2 |

the four by emerging as a favorite of frontier people, southerners, and some northerners as well.

Most Republicans in Congress refused to support Crawford, the caucus's choice, and a paralyzing stroke soon removed him from the race. Impressed by Jackson's support, Calhoun withdrew to run unopposed for the vice presidency. Jackson won the popular and electoral vote but failed to win the majority electoral vote required by the Constitution. When the election went to the House of Representatives, Clay threw his support, and thus the presidency, to Adams; Adams then promptly appointed Clay secretary of state. Jackson's supporters raged that a "corrupt bargain" had cheated their candidate, "Old Hickory," of the presidency. Although no evidence of any outright deal was uncovered, the widespread belief in a corrupt bargain hung like a cloud over Adam's presidency.

### John Quincy Adams as President

Failing to understand the changing political climate, Adams made several other miscalculations that would cloak his presidency in controversy. For example, he proposed federal support for internal improvements, although Old Republicans had continued to attack them as unconstitutional. Adams then infuriated southerners by proposing to send American delegates to a conference of newly independent Latin American nations. Southerners opposed U.S. participation because it would imply recognition of Haiti, the black republic created by slave revolutionaries. Both the sharp debate over

Missouri and the discovery of Denmark Vesey's conspiracy to ignite a slave rebellion in South Carolina had shaken southern slaveholders. Instead of building new bases of support, Adams clung to the increasingly obsolete view of the president as custodian of the public good, aloof from partisan politics. He alienated his supporters by appointing his opponents to high office and wrote loftily, "I have no wish to fortify myself by the support of any party whatever." Idealistic though his view was, it guaranteed him a single-term presidency.

### The Rise of Andrew Jackson and Martin Van Buren

As Adams's popularity fell, Andrew Jackson's rose. His victory over the British at the Battle of New Orleans made him a national hero, and southerners admired him as a Tennessee slaveholder, a renowned Indian fighter, and an advocate of Indian removal. Too, southerners praised Jackson's demand that they be allowed a free hand in pushing the Indians westward as a noble application of Jeffersonian ideals of states' rights—and a way to satisfy their land hunger. As the only candidate in 1824 not linked to the Monroe administration, Jackson was also in a position to capitalize on discontent after the Panic of 1819, which, in Calhoun's words, left people with "a general mass of disaffection to the Government" and "looking out anywhere for a leader."

By 1826 towns and villages across the country buzzed with political activity. Because supporters of Jackson, Adams, and Clay all still called themselves

Republicans, few realized that a new political system was being born. The man most alert to the new currents was Martin Van Buren, who would be Jackson's vice president and then president.

Van Buren exemplified a new breed of politician. A tavernkeeper's son, he had worked his way up through New York politics and created a powerful statewide machine, the Albany Regency, composed of men like himself from the middling and lower ranks. A genial man who befriended even his political rivals, Van Buren loved the game of politics and possessed an uncanny ability to sense which way the political winds were shifting.

The election of 1824 had convinced Van Buren of the need for two-party competition. Without the discipline imposed by party competition, the Republicans had splintered into sectional factions. The country would be better served, he thought, by reducing the shades of opinion in the country to just two so that parties could clash and a clear winner emerge. Jackson was the logical leader, and presidential nominee, of one new party, becoming known as the Democratic party; its opponents, calling themselves National Republicans, nominated Adams. The second American party system was taking shape.

## The Election of 1828

The 1828 campaign was a vicious, mudslinging affair. The National Republicans attacked Jackson as a murderer, a drunken gambler, and an adulterer. He had in fact killed several men in duels and had several more executed militarily; and in 1791 he had married Rachel Robards, erroneously believing that her divorce from her first husband had become final. Jackson supporters retaliated that Adams was rich and in debt, had tried to gain favor with the Russian tsar by providing him with a beautiful American prostitute, and—perhaps worst of all to westerners—wore silk underwear.

The Adams supporters' charges that Jackson was an illiterate backwoodsman backfired and endeared "Old Hickory" to ordinary people. Jackson's

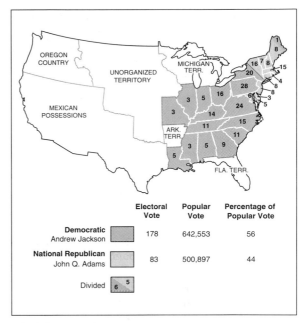

| | Electoral Vote | Popular Vote | Percentage of Popular Vote |
|---|---|---|---|
| **Democratic** Andrew Jackson | 178 | 642,553 | 56 |
| **National Republican** John Q. Adams | 83 | 500,897 | 44 |
| Divided 6 | 5 | | |

**The Election of 1828**

mudslingers, moreover, had the better aim. They proclaimed that Jackson was the common man incarnate—his mind unclouded by learning, his morals simple and true, his will fierce and resolute. Adams, in contrast, was an aristocrat, a scholar whose learning obscured the truth, a man who could write but not fight.

The election swept Jackson into office with twice Adams's electoral votes. The popular vote, much closer, reflected the strong sectional bases of the new parties. Adams doubled Jackson's vote in New England, while Jackson doubled Adams's vote in the South and nearly tripled it in the Southwest.

## Jackson in Office

For all the furor, the campaign had revealed little about Jackson's position on major issues. On such key questions as federal aid for internal improvements and the tariff, Jackson had sent out conflicting signals. He would, as president, use the office to express the will of the majority.

Jackson's first policy on assuming office was to support "rotation in office," the removal of office-holders of the rival party. Jackson neither invented this policy, popularly known as the spoils system, nor abused it, but he moved to new ground in defending it. Rotation in office was fundamentally democratic, he argued. Officeholders' duties were so plain and simple that any intelligent man could perform them. By moving people into and out of office at will, Jackson hoped to prevent the emergence of an elite bureaucracy unresponsive to the will of the people.

Jackson's interpretation of the spoils system ruffled feathers, but the issues of internal improvements and tariffs ignited real controversy. Like most southerners, Jackson believed that federal support for internal improvements was simply a lavish giveaway. He thought that such funding violated the Constitution, which stated that Congress could appropriate money only for national purposes, not for the benefit of particular sections or interests. Accordingly, in 1830 Jackson vetoed a bill to provide federal support for a road in Kentucky between Maysville and Lexington.

The Maysville Road Bill veto and the almost simultaneous Indian Removal Act enhanced Jackson's popularity in the South. The tariff issue, however, would test southern loyalty. In 1828 while Adams was still president, Congress passed a high protective tariff favorable to western agriculture and New England manufacturing. Southerners fumed at the tariff, which raised the price of the manufactured goods that they had to buy and also created the threat of retaliatory tariffs against southern cotton exports. To the surprise of Jackson and his followers, he, rather than Adams, bore the brunt of southern ire.

## Nullification

The 1828 tariff, the "Tariff of Abominations," laid the foundation for a split between Jackson and his vice president, John C. Calhoun. Although he had entered Congress as a "war hawk" and had championed nationalism early in his career, Calhoun had gradually become a states' rights sectionalist. He had supported the tariff of 1816 but would fiercely oppose that of 1828.

Calhoun also burned with ambition to be president. Jackson had stated that he would serve only one term and as vice president Calhoun assumed that he would succeed Jackson. To do so, he needed to maintain the support of the South, which was increasingly taking an anti-tariff stance. Calhoun's own state, South Carolina, had suffered economic decline throughout the 1820s; its citizens blamed protective tariffs for driving up the price of manufactured goods and for threatening cotton prices by lowering American demand for British cotton cloth, which was spun and woven from southern cotton. Whereas New Englanders, among them Senator Daniel Webster of Massachusetts, supported the tariff and protectionism, southerners responded with militant hostility.

Calhoun also accepted the Virginia and Kentucky Resolutions of 1798–1799, which defined the Union as a compact among the states, an association conferring limited powers on the central government. He insisted that the only constitutional tariff was one that raised money for the common national defense, not one that favored a particular section at the expense of others. Calhoun expressed these views anonymously in the widely circulated *South Carolina Exposition and Protest* (1828), which argued not only that the 1828 tariff was unconstitutional but also that states had the right to nullify that tariff within their borders.

More was at stake than the price of manufactured goods. Southerners feared that a government capable of passing tariffs favoring one section over another might also pass laws meddling with slavery. Although this idea seemed far-fetched—Jackson himself was a slaveholder—South Carolina's whites were edgy about the safety of slavery. African-Americans composed a majority of their state's population, the slave Nat Turner's bloody rebellion in Virginia in 1831 raised fears of a similar threat to South Carolina, and William Lloyd Garrison's new newspaper, *The Liberator*, advocated immediate aboli-

(*Near right*)
**Andrew Jackson (1767–1845),** *by Thomas Scully, 1845*

*Jackson, defeated in the presidential election of 1824, won handily four years later. The magnetic Calhoun, Jackson's vice president, broke with Jackson over nullification and the Peggy Eaton affair and resigned the vice presidency in 1832.*

(*Above*) **John C. Calhoun (1782–1850),** *by Charles Bird King, c. 1825*

tion. To many South Carolinians, these were ominous signs warning that a line had to be drawn against tariffs and possible future interference with slavery.

## Jackson Versus Calhoun

Like Calhoun, Jackson was strong-willed and proud. Unlike Calhoun, he already was president and the leader of a national party that included supporters of the tariff. To mollify both pro-tariff and anti-tariff forces, he devised two policies.

First, he distributed surplus federal revenue, largely derived from the tariff duties, to the states, hoping to remove the taint of sectional injustice from the tariff. Second, he tried to ease tariffs down from the sky-high 1828 rates, and Congress passed slight reductions in 1832. But these measures did little to satisfy Calhoun and the South Carolinians.

By the time the somewhat lower tariff was passed, other issues had ruptured relations between the president and vice president. Jackson learned that in 1818, then–Secretary of War Calhoun had urged that Jackson be punished for his unauthorized raid into Spanish Florida. Combined with the snubbing by Calhoun's wife, Floride, of Peggy Eaton, the scandal-tainted spouse of Jackson's ally and secretary of war, John H. Eaton, this revelation convinced Jackson that he had to "destroy [Calhoun] regardless of what injury it might do me or my administration." A Jefferson Day dinner in April 1830 featured a symbolic confrontation between Jackson and Calhoun. Jackson proposed the toast "Our Union: It must be preserved." Calhoun responded, "The Union next to Liberty the most dear. May we always remember that it can only be preserved by distributing equally the benefits and burdens of the Union."

The stage was set for the president and the vice president to clash over nullification. In November 1832 a South Carolina convention, citing Calhoun's states' rights doctrine, nullified the tariffs of

1828 and 1832 and forbade the collection of customs duties within the state. Jackson reacted quickly. He despised nullification as an "abominable doctrine" that would reduce the government to anarchy and denounced the South Carolinians as "unprincipled men who would rather rule in hell than be subordinate in heaven." He sent arms to Unionists in South Carolina and issued a proclamation that lambasted nullification as unconstitutional; the Constitution, he emphasized, had established "a single nation," not a league of states.

In March 1833 the crisis eased as President Jackson signed "the olive branch and the sword," in one historian's words. The Compromise Tariff of 1833, the olive branch or peace offering, provided for a gradual but significant lowering of tariff duties from 1833 to 1842. The Force Bill, the sword, authorized the president to use arms to collect customs duties in South Carolina. Although South Carolina did not abandon the principle of nullification—in fact, it petulantly nullified the Force Bill—it accepted the Compromise Tariff and rescinded its nullification of the tariffs of 1828 and 1832.

This so-called Compromise of 1833 grew out of a mixture of partisanship and statesmanship. Its chief architect was Henry Clay of Kentucky, who had long favored high tariffs. Clay not only feared the outbreak of civil war but also wanted to keep control of the tariff issue away from the Jacksonians, even if that meant a lower tariff. The nullifiers, recognizing that no other states had supported them, preferred giving Clay, not Jackson, credit for defusing the crisis; they therefore supported the Compromise Tariff and rescinded the nullification proclamation. Americans everywhere hailed Henry Clay as the Great Compromiser.

## The Bank Veto

One reason that Jackson signed Clay's Compromise Tariff into law was that he had no strong convictions about an alternative. In fact, he was relatively open-minded on the subject of tariffs. The same could not be said of his attitude toward banks. Owing to disastrous financial speculations early in

his career, Jackson was deeply suspicious of all banks, all paper money, and all monopolies. On each count the Bank of the United States was guilty.

The Bank of the United States had received a twenty-year charter from Congress in 1816. As a creditor of state banks, the Bank of the United States in effect restrained their printing and lending of money by its ability to demand the redemption of state notes in specie (gold or silver coin).

Many other aspects of the Bank of the United States made it controversial. For example, it was widely blamed for the Panic of 1819. Second, it was a privileged institution at a time when privilege was coming under fierce attack. Third, as the official depository for federal revenue, the bank had far greater lending capacity than state banks and thus dominated them. Fourth, although chartered by the federal government, the bank was controlled by its stockholders, who were private citizens—"moneyed capitalists" in Jackson's view. Finally, its location in Philadelphia, rather than Washington, symbolized the bank's independence of supervision by the national government. The bank's president, the aristocratic Nicholas Biddle, saw himself as a public servant duty-bound to keep the bank above politics.

After Jackson questioned "both the constitutionality and the expediency" of the Bank of the United States in his first annual message to Congress, Biddle sought an early rechartering of the bank. He was urged on by Henry Clay, who hoped to ride the probank bandwagon into the White House in 1832. Congress passed, and Jackson promptly vetoed, the recharter bill. The president denounced the bank as a private and privileged monopoly that drained the West of specie, was immune to taxation by states, put inordinate power in the hands of a few men, and made "the rich richer and the potent more powerful."

## The Election of 1832

By 1832 Jackson had made clear his views on major issues. He was simultaneously a strong defender of

| The Election of 1832 | | | | |
| --- | --- | --- | --- | --- |
| Candidates | Parties | Electoral Vote | Popular Vote | Percentage of Popular Vote |
| ANDREW JACKSON | Democratic | 219 | 687,502 | 55.0 |
| Henry Clay | National Republican | 49 | 530,189 | 42.4 |
| William Wirt | Anti-Masonic | 7 } | 33,108 | 2.6 |
| John Floyd | National Republican | 11 } | | |

states' rights *and* a staunch Unionist. Although he cherished the Union, Jackson believed the states far too diverse to accept strong direction from the federal government. The safest course was to allow the states considerable freedom so that they would remain contentedly within the Union and would reject such a dangerous doctrine as nullification.

Throwing aside earlier promises to retire, Jackson ran for the presidency again in 1832, with Martin Van Buren as his running mate. Henry Clay ran on the National Republican ticket, stressing his American System of protective tariffs, national banking, and federal support for internal improvements. Jackson's overwhelming personal popularity swamped Clay, 219 to 49 electoral votes. Secure in office for another four years, Jackson was ready to finish dismantling the Bank of the United States.

## The Bank Controversy and the Second Party System

Coming late in Jackson's first term, the veto of the recharter of the Bank of the United States had little impact on the election of 1832. However, between 1833 and 1840 banking became an issue that ignited popular passion as Jackson's veto of the bank recharter unleashed a tiger that threatened to devour all banks.

Banking created such controversy in part because the United States had no paper currency of its own. Instead, private bankers (widely viewed as sinister figures) issued paper notes, which they promised to redeem in specie. Yet there was a more basic issue: what sort of society would the United States become? Abundant paper money would foster a speculative economy that would enrich some Americans but leave many poor. Would the United States embrace swift economic development at the price of allowing some people to get rich quickly while others languished? Or would the nation undergo more modest growth in traditional molds, anchored by "honest" manual work and frugality?

Before the answer to these questions was clear, the banking issue dramatically transformed politics. It contributed both to the growth of opposition to the Democrats and to the steady expansion of popular interest in politics.

### The War on the Bank of the United States

Jackson could have allowed the Bank of the United States, "the monster," as he termed it, to die a natural death when its charter expired, but he and his followers believed that if the bank escaped with a breath of life, "it will soon recover its wonted strength, its whole power to injure us, and all hope of its destruction must forever be renounced." When Biddle began calling in bank loans and contracting credit to forestall further moves by Jackson, Jacksonians saw their darkest fears confirmed. The bank, Jackson said, "is trying to kill me, but I will kill it." So the president began removing federal deposits from the Bank of the United States and putting them in state banks.

In turn, this policy raised new problems. State banks that were depositories for federal funds could use these moneys as the basis for issuing more notes and extending more loans. Jackson hoped to head off the danger of a credit-fueled speculative economy by limiting the number of state banks used for federal revenue. But he discovered that doing so was impossible; indeed, by the end of 1833 there were twenty-three "pet banks," chosen in part for their loyalty to the Democratic party. Jackson could not stem the rapid economic expansion fueled by paper money and by foreign specie flowing in to purchase cotton. In 1836 the president thus reluctantly signed the Deposit Act, increasing the number of deposit banks and lessening federal control over them.

The Democratic party split between advocates of soft money (paper) and proponents of hard money (specie). The two Democratic camps agreed that the Bank of the United States was evil, but for different reasons. Soft-money Democrats, especially strong in the West, resented the bank's restriction of credit and wanted more paper money. Hard-money Democrats, typically wage-earning urban workers, disliked the speculative economy based on paper money and easy credit, and they deeply feared inflation.

## The Rise of Whig Opposition

During Jackson's second term the National Republicans changed their name to the Whig Party and broadened their base of support in both the North and the South. As Jackson's policies became clearer and sharper, the opposition attracted people alienated by his positions.

For example, Jackson's crushing of nullification led some southerners to the Whigs in order to oppose Jackson. Jackson's war against the Bank of the United States and his opposition to federal aid for internal improvements alienated other southerners and drove them to the Whigs as well. Most of the South remained Democratic, but the Whigs made substantial inroads nonetheless. Northern reformers also joined the Whigs, who were far more willing than the Democrats to effect social change by gov-

ernment intervention. And supporters of Henry Clay's American System joined advocates of public education and temperance in seeking a more activist, interventionist national government.

One remarkable source of Whig strength was Anti-Masonry, a protest movement against the secrecy of Masonic lodges, which had long provided prominent men with fraternal fellowship and exotic rituals. In 1826 William Morgan, a stonemason from Genesee County, New York, was kidnapped after threatening to expose Masonic secrets. Efforts to solve the mystery of Morgan's disappearance foundered because local officials, themselves Masons, obstructed the investigation. Rumors spread that Masonry was a conspiracy of the rich to suppress liberty, a secret order of men who loathed Christianity, and an exclusive retreat for drunkards.

Anti-Masons, who began as a movement of moral protest, organized the Anti-Masonic party, which became a potent political force in part of New England. In many ways Anti-Masons' hatred of vice paralleled that of the Whig reformers, and so their entry into the Whig party was natural. Anti-Masonry brought into the Whig party a broad-based constituency that protested "aristocracy" with the same zeal as Jacksonian Democrats, and the presence of Anti-Masons in the party countered the charge that the Whigs were tools of the rich.

By 1836 the Whigs had become a national party with widespread appeal. Whigs everywhere assailed Andrew Jackson as an imperious dictator, "King Andrew I"; and the name "Whigs" evoked memories of the American patriots who had opposed George III in 1776.

## The Election of 1836

As the election of 1836 approached, the Whigs lacked a national leader. Henry Clay came close, but he carried political scars and a reputation for spending his days at the gaming table and his nights in brothels. In the end the Whigs ran four sectional candidates, hoping to draw enough votes to prevent the Democratic candidate, Martin Van Buren, from gaining a majority of electoral votes. Although the strategy failed—Van Buren captured 170 electoral

| The Election of 1836 | | | | |
| --- | --- | --- | --- | --- |
| Candidates | Parties | Electoral Vote | Popular Vote | Percentage of Popular Vote |
| MARTIN VAN BUREN | Democratic | 170 | 765,483 | 50.9 |
| William H. Harrison | Whig | 73 | | |
| Hugh L. White | Whig | 26 | | |
| Daniel Webster | Whig | 14 | 739,795 | 49.1 |
| W. P. Mangum | Whig | 11 | | |

votes to the Whigs' 124—the Whigs made substantial gains in the South, a clear sign of trouble ahead for the Democrats.

## The Panic of 1837

Hailed as "the greatest man of his age," Jackson left office in 1837 in a sunburst of glory. Yet he bequeathed to his successor a severe depression, the legacy of the bank war and the "pet banks."

In the speculative boom of 1835 and 1836, born of Jackson's policy of placing federal funds in state banks, the total number of banks doubled, the value of bank notes in circulation nearly tripled, and both commodity and land prices soared skyward. But the overheated economy began to cool rapidly in May 1837 as prices tumbled and as bank after bank suspended specie payments. After a short rally, 1839 saw a second crash as banks across the nation again suspended specie payments.

The prolonged depression had multiple roots. Domestically, Jackson's Specie Circular of July 1836, declaring that only specie, not paper money, could be used to purchase public lands, dried up credit. International causes played a large role as well, especially Britain's decision in 1836 to halt the flow of specie from its shores to the United States.

## The Search for Solutions

Van Buren, known as "the sly fox" and "the little magician" for his political craftiness, would need those skills to confront the depression, which was battering ordinary citizens and the Democratic party alike. The president called for the creation of an independent treasury that would hold government revenues and keep them from the grasp of corporations. When Van Buren finally signed the Independent Treasury Bill into law on July 4, 1840, his supporters hailed it as a second Declaration of Independence.

The Independent Treasury reflected the basic Jacksonian suspicion of an alliance between the federal government and banking. However, the Independent Treasury Act failed to address banking on the state level, where newly chartered state banks—more than 900 in number by 1840—lent money to farmers and businessmen, fueling the speculative economy feared by Jacksonians.

Whigs and Democrats differed sharply in their approach to the multiplication of state banks. Whigs, convinced that Jackson's Specie Circular, not banks themselves, had brought on the depression, supported policies allowing any group to start a bank as long as its members met state requirements. Democrats, who tended to blame banks and paper money for the depression, adopted the hard-money position favored by Jackson and his advisers. After 1837 the Democrats were in effect an antibank, hard-money party.

## The Election of 1840

Despite the depression, the Democrats renominated Van Buren. Avoiding the mistake of 1836, the Whigs nominated a single candidate, Ohio's William Henry Harrison, and ran John Tyler of Virginia for vice president. The Whigs chose Harri-

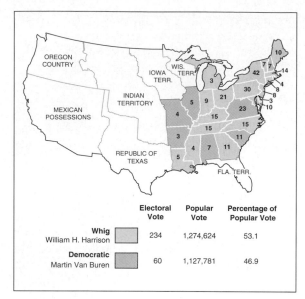

**The Election of 1840**

| | Electoral Vote | Popular Vote | Percentage of Popular Vote |
|---|---|---|---|
| **Whig** William H. Harrison | 234 | 1,274,624 | 53.1 |
| **Democratic** Martin Van Buren | 60 | 1,127,781 | 46.9 |

son, sixty-seven years old, largely because he had few enemies.

Early in the campaign the Democrats made a fatal mistake, ridiculing Harrison as "Old Granny" who desired only to spend his declining years in a log cabin sipping cider. In so doing, they handed the Whigs the most famous campaign symbol in American history. The Whigs saluted Harrison as a rugged frontiersman, the hero of the Battle of Tippecanoe, and a defender of all those people who lived in log cabins. Disdaining a platform, the Whigs ran a "hurrah" campaign using log cabins for headquarters, singing log cabin songs, and ladling out log cabin cider. Instead of a platform, they trumpeted, "Tippecanoe and Tyler, too!" and attacked Van Buren as an aristocrat who lived in "regal splendor."

Harrison was elected in a clear victory. The depression would have made it difficult for any Democrat to win, and Van Buren lacked the halo of military glory that gleamed around Jackson and Harrison. However, many of Van Buren's problems stemmed from his style of campaign. While the Whigs ran a rousing race aimed directly at the "common man," Van Buren quietly wrote letters of

encouragement to key supporters. Ironically, the Whigs beat the master politician at his own game.

### The Second Party System Matures

The strong contrasts between the two parties and the sharp choices they presented jolted the American electorate. Nearly 2.4 million people voted in 1840, up an astonishing 60 percent from 1836. Most of that change was in the number of people who chose to vote; prior to 1840 the proportion of white males who voted had ranged from 55 to 58 percent; in 1840 it rose to 80 percent.

Both the depression and the frenzied log cabin campaign had brought voters to the polls in 1840, but voter turnouts stayed high even after prosperity returned. The second party system reached a high plateau in 1840 and remained there over a decade. The gradual hardening of the line between the two parties piqued popular interest in politics.

By 1840 reform issues were drawing as many to the polls as tariffs and banking. Religion, rather than politics, however, was the source of many of these reforms.

## The Rise of Popular Religion

In *Democracy in America*, Alexis de Tocqueville called religion "the foremost of the political institutions" in the United States. "In France I had almost always seen the spirit of religion and the spirit of freedom pursuing courses dramatically opposed to each other; but in America I found that they were intimately united, and that they reigned in common over the same country."

Tocqueville was referring to the way religious impulses reinforced democracy and liberty. Just as Americans demanded that politics be accessible to average people, they insisted ministers preach doctrines that appealed to ordinary men and women. Successful ministers used plain language to move the heart, not theological complexity to dazzle the intellect. Increasingly, Americans put individuals in charge of their own religious destiny, thrusting aside

Calvinist predestination in favor of the belief that anyone could attain heaven. A series of religious revivals known as the Second Great Awakening contributed to the growing harmony between religion and politics and to the growing conviction that heaven itself was democratic.

## The Second Great Awakening

The Second Great Awakening first flared in Connecticut in the 1790s, and during the following half century it set ablaze one section of the nation after another. As the revivals moved westward, they underwent striking changes, typified by the rise of camp meetings. Here the members of several denominations gathered together in sprawling open-air camps to hear revivalists proclaim that the Second Coming of Jesus was near and that the time for repentance was now. The most famous camp meeting took place at Cane Ridge, Kentucky, in August 1801. A huge crowd gathered on a hillside to listen to thunderous sermons, sing hymns, and experience divine grace.

The Cane Ridge revival was part of the Great Kentucky Revival of 1800–1801. These frontier revivals featured "exercises" in which men and women rolled around like logs, jerked their heads furiously, and grunted like animals. Critics blasted the frontier frenzy for encouraging fleshly lust and complained that "more souls were begot than saved" at the camp meetings. But although these early frontier revivals challenged traditional religious customs—indeed, the most successful preachers were farmers and artisans who had experienced powerful conversions and scorned those whose religion came from books—the revivalists promoted law, order, and morality.

Methodists, the most successful frontier denomination, became the largest American Protestant denomination, soaring from 70,000 members in 1800 to more than 1 million in 1844. The Methodists emphasized that religion was a matter of the heart rather than the head and relied on itinerant circuit riders, young, unmarried men who traveled ceaselessly and preached in houses, open fields, or wherever else listeners would gather. After the Methodist

circuit riders left, their converts held weekly "classes" to provide mutual encouragement and to chastise members for drunkenness, fighting, gossiping, fornication, and even shrewd business practices.

## Eastern Revivals

By the 1820s the Second Great Awakening had begun to shift back to the East. The hottest revival fires blazed in an area of western New York known as the Burned-Over District. No longer a frontier, western New York teemed with descendants of Puritans who hungered for religious experience and with people drawn by the hope of wealth after the completion of the Erie Canal. It was a fertile field of high expectations and bitter discontent. The man who harnessed these anxieties to religion was Charles Grandison Finney, a lawyer-turned-Presbyterian minister. His greatest "harvest" came in the thriving canal city of Rochester in 1830–1831.

Finney's innovations at the Rochester revival justified his reputation as the "father of modern revivalism." First, he pioneered in generating cooperation among Protestants, and all denominations participated in his revivals. In addition, he introduced such novelties as the "anxious seat," a bench where those ready for conversion could be made objects of special prayer, and the "protracted meeting," which ran nightly for a week or more. Finally, although a Presbyterian, Finney rejected the Calvinist doctrine of total depravity, humankind's irresistible inclination to sin. Instead, he proclaimed, sin was a voluntary act, and those who willed themselves to sin could just as readily will themselves not to sin. In theory, men and women could live perfect lives, free of sin. Those converted by Finney or other evangelists believed that they were cleansed of past guilt and were beginning a new life. "I have been born again," a young convert wrote. "I am three days old when I write this letter."

Originally controversial, Finney's ideas came to dominate "evangelical" Protestantism, which focused on the need for an emotional religious conversion. He succeeded because he told people what they wanted to hear: that their destinies were in their own hands. A society that celebrated the "self-made" individual embraced Finney's assertion that even in religion people could make of themselves what they chose. Finney multiplied his success by emphasizing the role of women, who outnumbered male converts nearly two to one. Finney encouraged women to give public testimonials of their conversion, and he often converted men by first winning over their wives and daughters.

## Critics of Revivals: The Unitarians

Although some praised revivals for saving souls, others doubted their lasting effects. The Unitarians were a small but influential group of critics. Although their basic doctrine—that Jesus Christ was less than fully divine—had gained acceptance among religious liberals in the eighteenth century, Unitarianism became a formal denomination only in the early nineteenth century. Hundreds of New England Congregational churches were torn apart by the withdrawal of socially prominent families who had embraced Unitarianism and by legal battles over which group, Congregationalists or Unitarians, could occupy church property. Unitarians won few converts outside New England, but their tendency to attract the wealthy and educated gave them influence beyond their numbers.

Unitarians criticized revivals as uncouth emotional exhibitions and argued that "character building" was more effective than sudden emotional conversion. Yet they and the revivalists agreed in rejecting the Calvinist emphasis on human wickedness. Christianity had only one purpose, a Unitarian leader proclaimed: "the perfection of human nature, the elevation of men into nobler beings."

## The Rise of Mormonism

Far more controversial than the Unitarians were the Mormons and their church, the Church of Jesus Christ of Latter-day Saints, another new denomination of the 1820s. Joseph Smith, its founder, grew up in the heart of the Burned-Over District. Conflict among the various religious denominations that thrived in the region left Smith confused: "Some were contending for the Methodist faith, some for

the Presbyterian, and some for the Baptists," he later wrote. He wondered who was right and who wrong or whether they were "all wrong together."

Smith resolved this conflict, which was not uncommon in the Burned-Over District, in a unique way. He claimed that an angel had led him to a buried book of revelation and to special stones for use in translating it. The Book of Mormon, which Smith translated, tells the story of an ancient Hebrew prophet, Lehi, whose descendants migrated to America and created a prosperous civilization. Jesus had appeared and performed miracles in the New World, but Lehi's descendants had departed from the Lord's ways and quarreled among themselves. God had cursed some of these defectors with dark skin; these were the American Indians, who had long since forgotten their history.

Smith quickly gathered followers. Mormonism's appeal lay partly in its placing America at the center of Christian history and partly in its resolving the conflicting claims within Protestantism by additional revelations beyond those in the Bible. The Mormons moved steadily west, both to escape persecution and to draw closer to the Indians, whom they wished to convert. Smith's claim of a new revelation guaranteed a hostile reception for the Mormons wherever they went because it undermined the authority of the Bible, which, along with the Constitution, contained the ideals on which the American republic rested.

In 1843 Smith added fuel to the fire by proclaiming yet another revelation, this one sanctioning polygyny, the practice of taking multiple wives. Smith's claims that he was a prophet, the "Second Mohammed," also intensified the controversy that boiled around Mormonism. He proclaimed that Mormonism would be to Christianity what Christianity had been to Judaism: a grand, all-encompassing, and higher form of religion. Smith called himself "Prophet of the Kingdom of God." But in 1844 the state of Illinois charged him with treason and jailed him in the town of Carthage. There, in June 1844, a mob murdered Smith and his brother.

Although deprived of a founder, Mormonism grew rapidly in the next three decades; by 1870 it boasted 200,000 believers. Brigham Young, who assumed leadership after Smith's murder, led the Mormons westward into Utah, at the time still under Mexican control. There he established the independent republic of Deseret, and the Mormons prospered. Young's firm control kept the rank and file in line, while polygyny guaranteed that Mormons would remain a people apart from the mainstream of American society. Above all, the Mormons were industrious and deeply committed to the welfare of their people. They transformed the Great Salt Lake Valley into a rich oasis and continued to dominate Utah after it became part of the United States.

Although it pushed against main currents of American society, Mormonism offered the downcast and the outcast an alternative to dominant religious and social practices. In this respect it mirrored the efforts of several religious communal societies, among them the Shakers, whose members likewise set themselves apart from society.

### The Shakers

The founder of the Shakers (who derived their name from a convulsive religious dance that was part of their ceremony) was Mother Ann Lee, the illiterate daughter of an English blacksmith. Lee and her followers had established a series of tightly knit agricultural-artisan communities in America after her arrival in 1774. Shaker artisanship, particularly in furniture, had quickly gained renown for its simple lines, beauty, and strength. Shaker advances in the development of new farm tools and seed varieties would be a boon to the growing market economy. However, the Shakers were fundamentally other worldly and hostile to materialism. Lee had insisted that her followers abstain from sexual intercourse, believed that the end of the world was imminent, and derived many of her doctrines from trances and visions. She had also taught that at the Second Coming, Jesus would take the form of a woman.

Shaker missionaries took advantage of revivalism's appeal. At Cane Ridge and other revivals, Shaker proselytizers attracted converts whom the revivals had loosened from their traditional religious moorings. By the 1830s the Shakers numbered about 6,000.

Although the Shakers and the Mormons lived apart from traditional society, most evangelical Protestants taught that religion and the pursuit of wealth were compatible. Revivalists taught that getting ahead in the world was acceptable as long as people were honest, temperate, and bound by their consciences. By encouraging involvement in society, evangelism provided a powerful stimulus to the multiple social reform movements of the 1820s and 1830s.

## The Age of Reform

Despite rising popular interest in politics between 1824 and 1840, large numbers of people were excluded from political participation. Women and free blacks could not vote, and political parties shunned controversial issues, including slavery and women's rights.

During the 1820s and 1830s unprecedented numbers of men and women joined organizations aimed at improving society. The abolition of slavery, women's rights, temperance, better treatment of criminals and the insane, public education, and even the establishment of perfect, utopian communities were on the various reformers' agenda. Although they occasionally cooperated with political parties, especially the Whigs, reformers gave their loyalty to their causes, not to parties.

Religious revivalism intensified the righteousness of reformers, who believed that they were on God's side of any issue. Abolitionists and temperance reformers tended to come from evangelical backgrounds, but others, school reformers and women's rights advocates particularly, were often hostile or indifferent to revivals. Yet even reformers opposed to revivalism borrowed evangelical preachers' language and psychology by painting drunkenness, ignorance, and inequality as sins calling for immediate repentance and change. Reformers had a dark side. So sure were many reformers of the worthiness of their cause that they became self-righteous, paying more attention, for example, to drunkenness than to conditions that bred drinking.

Reform movements lacked a national scope. New England and those parts of the Midwest settled by New Englanders were hotbeds of reform, while southerners actively suppressed abolition, displayed only mild interest in temperance and educational reform, ignored women's rights, and saw utopian communities as proof of the mental instability of northern reformers.

## The War on Liquor

Agitation for temperance (either total abstinence from alcoholic beverages or moderation in their use) intensified during the second quarter of the nineteenth century. Alcohol abuse was a growing problem: per capita consumption of rum, whiskey, gin, and brandy had risen steadily until it exceeded seven gallons per year by 1830, nearly triple today's rate. The average adult male downed a half pint of liquor a day, and reformers saw alcohol excess as a male indulgence whose bitter consequences (for example, spending money on liquor instead of food) fell on women and children. Not surprisingly, millions of women marched behind the temperance banner.

The movement took off in 1825 when the popular evangelist Lyman Beecher, in six widely acclaimed lectures, thundered against all use of alcohol. Evangelical Protestants established the American Temperance Society the following year, and by 1834 it enjoyed some 5,000 state and local affiliates. The American Temperance Society demanded total abstinence and flooded the country with tracts denouncing the "amazing evil" of strong drink.

The laboring class became a chief target for temperance reformers. Passing a jug around the workplace every few hours had been a time-honored way to relieve on-the-job fatigue, but large factories demanded a more disciplined, sober work force. Manufacturers quickly supported the evangelical temperance reformers. Uninterested in temperance at first, workers flocked to reform after the Panic of 1837, forming the Washington Temperance Societies beginning in 1840. Many workers who joined the Washingtonians were reformed drunkards who had concluded that hard times required temperance and frugality. Because so many of the forces dislocating workers in the late 1830s were beyond their control, they looked to something that they could control: drinking. Take care of temperance, a Washingtonian told his audience, and the Lord would take care of the economy.

As temperance won new supporters, the crusaders shifted their emphasis from the individual drinker to the entire community and demanded that towns and even states ban all traffic in liquor. By the late 1830s prohibition was scoring victories, especially in New England. The steady rise of alcohol consumption halted in the early 1830s and then began to fall; by the 1840s the rate of consumption was less than half that in the 1820s.

## Public-School Reform

Like temperance crusaders, school reformers worked to encourage orderliness and thrift in the common people. Rural "district" schools were a main target. Here students ranging in age from three to twenty crowded into a single room and learned to read and count, but little more.

District schools enjoyed considerable support from rural parents. However, reformers insisted that schools had to equip children for the emerging competitive and industrial economy. In 1837 Horace Mann of Massachusetts, the most articulate and influential of the reformers, became the first secretary of his state's newly created board of education. He presided over sweeping reforms to transform schools from loose organizations into highly structured institutions that occupied most of a child's time and energy. Mann's goals included shifting financial support of schools from parents to the state, compelling attendance, extending the school term, introducing standardized textbooks, and grading schools (that is, classifying students by age and attainment).

School reformers sought to spread uniform cultural values as well as to combat ignorance. Requiring students to arrive at a set time would teach punctuality, and matching children against their peers would stimulate the competitiveness needed in an industrializing society. Children would read the same books and absorb the same moral lessons. The McGuffey readers, which sold 50 million copies between 1836 and 1870, preached industry, honesty, sobriety, and patriotism.

Mann's reforms took root primarily in the North, despite challenges from farmers satisfied with the district school, from Catholics objecting to anti-Catholic and anti-Irish barbs in the textbooks, and from the working poor, who widely saw compulsory education as a menace to families dependent on children's wages. He and other school reformers prevailed in part because their opponents could not cooperate with each other and in part because the reformers attracted influential allies, including urban workers, manufacturers, and women. Many people doubted that a woman could control a one-room school with students of widely variant ages, but managing a classroom of eight-year-olds was different. Reformers predicted that school reform would make teaching a suitable profession for women, and they were right. By 1900, 70 percent of the nation's teachers were women.

School reform also appealed to native-born Americans alarmed by the swelling tide of immigration. The public school became a vehicle for forging a common American culture out of an increasingly diverse society. However, few reformers stressed the integration of black and white children. When black children got any schooling, it was usually in segregated schools; black children in integrated schools encountered such virulent prejudice that African-American leaders in northern cities often preferred segregated schools.

## Abolitionism

Antislavery sentiment had flourished among whites during the Revolutionary era but faded in the early nineteenth century. The American Colonization Society, founded in 1817, was the main antislavery organization of this period. It proposed gradual emancipation, compensation for slave owners when slaves became free, and the shipment to Africa of freed blacks. Although these proposals attracted some support from slave owners in the Upper South, they were unrealizable. The growing cotton economy had made slavery more attractive than ever to most southerners, and few owners would have freed their slaves, even if compensated. The U.S. slave population, fed by natural increase, soared in the early nineteenth century, from 1.2 million in 1810 to more than 2 million by 1830, but only 1,400 blacks migrated to Africa, and most were already free.

Radical antislavery views flourished primarily among African-Americans themselves. Opposing colonization in Africa—for most American blacks were native born—they formed scores of abolition societies. One free black, David Walker of Boston, even called for a rebellion to crush slavery.

In 1821 Benjamin Lundy, a white Quaker, began a newspaper, the *Genius of Universal Emancipation*, that trumpeted repeal of the Constitution's three-fifths clause, the outlawing of the internal slave trade, and the abolition of slavery in U.S. territories. Seven years later Lundy hired a young New Englander, William Lloyd Garrison, as an editorial assistant. The prematurely bald, bespectacled Garrison looked like a genial schoolmaster, but he would become a potent force in the antislavery movement.

In 1831 Garrison launched a newspaper, *The Liberator*, to spread his radical antislavery message. "I am in earnest," he wrote. "I will not equivocate—I will not excuse—I will not retreat a single inch—AND I WILL BE HEARD." His battle cry was "immediate emancipation"; his demand, civil and legal equality for African-Americans. However, even Garrison did not believe that all slaves could be freed overnight. People first had to realize that slavery was sinful and its continued existence intolerable.

Black abolitionists supported Garrison; in its early years three-fourths of *The Liberator*'s subscribers were African-American. Other blacks were emerging as powerful writers and speakers. Frederick Douglass, an escaped slave, could rivet an audience with an opening line: "I appear before the immense

**The Antislavery Alphabet**
*Viewing children as morally pure and hence as natural opponents of slavery, abolitionists produced antislavery toys, games, and, as we see here, alphabet books.*

assembly this evening as a thief and a robber. I stole this head, these limbs, this body from my master, and ran off with them."

Relations between white and black abolitionists were often stormy. Many white abolitionists called for legal, but not civil and social, racial equality; preferred light-skinned to dark-skinned blacks; and hesitated to admit African-Americans to antislavery societies. And widespread white prejudice made the life of any abolitionist precarious. Mobs attacked abolitionists often; one angry crowd, in Alton, Illinois, murdered abolitionist editor Elijah Lovejoy in 1837.

As if external hostility were not enough, abolitionists differed passionately with one another. The largest national abolition group, the American Anti-Slavery Society, founded in 1833, was split by disagreements over whether abolitionists should form their own political party and about what role women should play in antislavery. Abolitionists from the Midwest and the Burned-Over District, most with ties to Charles Grandison Finney, formed the antislavery Liberty party in 1840 and ran a presidential slate. In contrast, Garrison increasingly rejected *all* laws and government. Embracing the doctrine of "nonresistance," he established the New England Non-Resistance Society in 1838. Like slavery, Garrison and his extremist followers argued, all

government depended on force, and because force was the opposite of Christian love, Christians should refuse to vote, to hold office, or to have anything to do with government.

Equally divisive to the abolitionist cause were questions over the role of women in the movement. In 1837 Angelina and Sarah Grimké, the daughters of a South Carolina slaveholder, made an antislavery lecture tour of New England. Women had become deeply involved in antislavery societies by then, but always in female auxiliaries. The Grimké sisters were controversial because they spoke to audiences of both men and women at a time when it was thought indelicate for women to address male audiences. Clergymen chastised the Grimké sisters for lecturing men rather than obeying them.

Such criticism backfired, turning the Grimkés and others to the cause of women's rights. In 1838 Sarah wrote *Letters on the Condition of Women and the Equality of the Sexes*; Angelina penned her equally classic *Letters to Catharine E. Beecher* (a militant opponent of female equality). Many male abolitionists tried to dampen the feminist flames, including the poet John Greenleaf Whittier, who dismissed women's grievances as "paltry" compared to the "great and dreadful wrongs of slavery." Even Theodore Dwight Weld, who married Angelina Grimké, wanted to subordinate women's rights to antislavery. Garrison, welcoming the controversy, promptly espoused women's rights and urged that women be given positions equal to men in the American Anti-Slavery Society. In 1840 the election of Abby Kelley to a previously all-male committee split the American Anti-Slavery Society, with many profeminists splintering off to form their own groups. The split, however, did little to derail the antislavery crusade because local societies—more than 1,500 of them—continued to function more or less independently.

One of the most disruptive abolitionist tactics was to flood Congress with petitions calling for an end to slavery in the District of Columbia. Lacking time to consider the petitions, Congress in effect deprived citizens of their right to have the petitions heard. Then in 1836 southerners secured passage of the "gag rule," which automatically tabled abolitionist petitions and thus prevented congressional discussion of them. In the ensuing battle over the gag rule, congressmen with little sympathy for abolition attacked southerners for suppressing the constitutional right of petition. Ex-president John Quincy Adams, at the time a representative from Massachusetts, led the struggle against the gag rule until it was lifted in 1845.

## Women's Rights

Women occupied a paradoxical position in the 1830s. They could not vote and, if married, had no right to own property or to keep their own wages. At the same time, reform movements gave women unprecedented opportunities for public activity within their own "sphere"; for example, by suppressing liquor, women could claim that they were transforming wretched homes into nurseries of happiness.

The argument that women were natural guardians of family life was double-edged. It justified reform activities on behalf of the family but undercut women's demands for legal equality. So deeply ingrained was sexual inequality that most women came reluctantly to the issue of women's rights as a result of their experience in other reform move-

ments, especially abolitionism. Among the early women's rights advocates who started their reform careers as abolitionists were the Grimké sisters, Lucretia Mott, Lucy Stone, and Abby Kelley.

Like abolitionism, the women's rights cause revolved around the conviction that differences of race and gender were unimportant. "Men and women," wrote Sarah Grimké, "are CREATED EQUAL! They are both moral and accountable beings, and whatever is *right* for a man to do, is *right* for woman." The most articulate and aggressive advocates of women's rights tended to gravitate to William Lloyd Garrison, who stressed the degradation of women under slavery; the entire South was a vast brothel, Garrison wrote, in which slave women were "treated with more indelicacy and cruelty than cattle."

The discrimination within the abolition movement infuriated women and drove them to make women's rights a separate cause. When Lucretia Mott and other American women attended the World Anti-Slavery Convention in London in 1840, they were relegated to a screened-off section. The incident made a deep impression on Mott and on Elizabeth Cady Stanton. In 1848 they organized a women's rights convention at Seneca Falls, New York. The convention issued a Declaration of Sentiments that began, "All men and all women are created equal." The participants passed a series of resolutions, including a call for the right of women to vote, which would become the centerpiece of women's rights activity after the Civil War.

Women's rights had less immediate impact than most other reforms. Temperance and school reform were far more popular, and antislavery created more commotion. Women would not secure the right to vote throughout the nation until 1920, fifty-five years after the Thirteenth Amendment had abolished slavery. One reason for the relatively slow advance of women's rights was that piecemeal gains, such as married women's securing the right to own property in several states before the Civil War, satisfied many women. The cult of domesticity also slowed feminism's advance; by sanctioning women's involvement in other reforms, it provided women

**Lucretia Mott (1793–1880)**

**Dorothea Dix (1808–1887)**

*Mott, a Quaker minister, worked for the antislavery cause as well as for women's rights. Dix, after devoting herself to reforming prison conditions and the treatment of the insane, served her country in the Civil War as superintendent of women nurses.*

with pursuits beyond the family and thus blunted demands for full equality.

## Penitentiaries and Asylums

Beginning in the 1820s, reformers tried to combat poverty, crime, and insanity by establishing regimented institutions, themselves the products of bold new assumptions about the causes of deviancy. As poverty and crime had increased and become more visible in the early nineteenth century, alarmed investigators had concluded that indigence and deviant behavior resulted not from defects in human nature, as colonial Americans had thought, but from drunken fathers and broken homes. The failure of parental discipline, not the will of God or the wickedness of human nature, lay at the root of evil. In light of the growing belief that the moral qualities of the individual could be changed, reformers turned their energies to finding the right combination of moral influences and structured environments to improve human nature.

Reformers created, for example, highly ordered and disciplined penitentiaries as substitutes for failed parental discipline. Sincere reformation, rather than simple incarceration, became the goal. Solitary confinement would purge offenders' violent habits, reformers believed; at new prisons in Auburn and Ossining, New York, prisoners could neither speak nor look at one another during the day and spent their nights in small, windowless cells. Critics of the "Auburn system" preferred the "Pennsylvania system," in which each prisoner was isolated in a single cell and received no news or visits from the outside.

Antebellum America also witnessed a transformation in the treatment of the poor. The infirm poor crowded into almshouses, while the able-bodied poor entered workhouses. Idealistic reformers argued that taking the poor from demoralizing surroundings and putting them into such highly regimented institutions could change them into virtuous, productive citizens. But the results were often dismal. In 1833 a legislative committee found that inmates of the Boston House of Industry were packed seven to a room and included unwed mothers, the sick, and the insane as well as the poor.

Many of the insane were confined in prisons. In 1841 an idealistic Unitarian schoolteacher, Dorothea Dix, discovered insane people kept in an unheated room at the East Cambridge, Massachusetts, jail. After visiting other jails and almshouses, an appalled Dix reported that the insane were confined "in *cages, closets, cellars, stalls, pens! Chained, naked, beaten with rods, and lashed into obedience.*" Supported by Horace Mann and other reformers, she encouraged legislatures to create separate insane asylums, and by 1860, twenty-eight states, four cities, and the federal government had built public mental institutions.

## Utopian Communities

The belief in the perfectibility of human nature and conduct found its most extreme expression in the "utopian" communities that flourished during the reform years. Most of these, founded by intellectuals, were meant to be alternatives to the prevailing competitive economy and models whose success would inspire others.

American interest in utopian communities began in the 1820s. In 1825 British industrialist Robert Owen founded the New Harmony community in Indiana. As a mill owner, Owen had improved his workers' living conditions and educational opportunities; he was convinced that the problems of the early industrial age were social, not political. Vice and misery would vanish if social arrangements were perfected, he thought. The key was the creation of small, planned communities—"Villages of Unity and Mutual Cooperation"—with a perfect balance of occupational, religious, and social groups.

New Harmony was to provide a model for the United States; by 1827, Owen predicted, northern states would embrace its principles. Unfortunately, by 1827 there was little left to embrace, for the community, a magnet for idlers and fanatics, had fallen apart. However, Owen's belief that environment shaped character and that cooperation was superior to competition survived and influenced urban workers in particular throughout the nineteenth century.

Experimental communities with hopeful names such as Fruitlands, Hopedale, and Brook Farm proliferated amid the economic chaos of the late 1830s and 1840s. Brook Farm, near Boston, was the creation of a group of religious philosophers called transcendentalists. Most transcendentalists, including Ralph Waldo Emerson, had started as Unitarians but then tried to revitalize Christianity by proclaiming the infinite spiritual capacities of ordinary men and women. Brook Farm, like other utopias, was both a retreat and a model. Sure that the competitive commercial life of the cities was unnatural, philosophers spent their evenings in lofty musings after a day perspiring in the cabbage patch. Brook Farm attracted several renowned writers, including Emerson and Nathaniel Hawthorne, and its literary magazine, *The Dial*, disseminated transcendentalist ideas about philosophy, art, and literature (see Chapter 11).

The most controversial of the antebellum experiments in communitarian utopianism, the Oneida community in New York State, established in 1848, challenged conventional notions of religion, property, gender roles, marriage, sex, dress, and motherhood. Although contemporaries dismissed its founder, John Humphrey Noyes, as a licentious crackpot, Oneida achieved considerable economic prosperity and attracted new members long after less radical utopian experiments such as Brook Farm had collapsed. By 1875 its membership had swelled to 300. However, by then Noyes had embarked on a project of breeding a perfect race. A committee headed by Noyes decided on the residents' sexual partners, generally mating old men with young women and young men with old women. Children aged four and older were to be raised in a common nursery. Dissatisfaction among younger members of the community turned into dissent, then disunion. Noyes fled to Canada in 1879 to avoid prosecution, and the Oneida community abandoned its communitarianism in 1881.

Few utopias enjoyed success to match their vision. Unlike the religious communities of the Shakers and the Mormans, the utopian communities remained part of the larger society; their members moved back and forth between their communities and antislavery or women's rights conventions. In addition, utopians neither sought nor attained the kind of grip on the allegiance of their members held by a Mother Ann Lee or a Joseph Smith. Widely derided as fit only for cranks, these utopias exemplified in extreme form the idealism and hopefulness that permeated reform in the Jacksonian era.

## CONCLUSION

During the 1820s and 1830s American society burst beyond its traditional physical and intellectual boundaries under the leadership of the generation born after 1775. Free of external threats, Americans wrestled with the implications of a changing society.

Political parties, religious revivals, and reform movements constituted different—but equally novel and inventive—means of response to the same set of problems created by massive social and economic change. Ultimately, both religious leaders and reformers came to see politics as another route to change, and politics became a medium that even those antagonistic to it had to understand.

## CHRONOLOGY

1800–1801  Great Kentucky Revival.

1817–  American Colonization Society founded.

1824  John Quincy Adams elected president by the House of Representatives.

1826  American Temperance Society organized.

1828  Andrew Jackson elected president.
Congress passes the "Tariff of Abominations."
John Calhoun anonymously writes *South Carolina Exposition and Protest.*

1830  Jackson's Maysville Road Bill veto.
Indian Removal Act.

1830–1831  Charles G. Finney's Rochester revival.

1831  William Lloyd Garrison starts *The Liberator.*

1832  Jackson vetoes recharter of the Bank of the United States.
Jackson reelected president.
South Carolina Nullification Proclamation.

1833  Force Bill.
Compromise Tariff.

American Anti-Slavery Society founded.
South Carolina nullifies the Force Bill.

1834  Whig party organized.

1836  Congress imposes the gag rule.
Specie Circular.
Martin Van Buren elected president.

1837  Economic depression sets in.
Elijah Lovejoy murdered by proslavery mob.

1838  Garrison's New England Non-Resistance Society founded.
Publication of Sarah Grimké's *Letters on the Condition of Women and the Equality of the Sexes* and Angelina Grimké's *Letters to Catharine E. Beecher.*

1840  Independent Treasury Act passed.
William Henry Harrison elected president.
First Washington Temperance Society started.

1841  Dorothea Dix begins exposé of prison conditions.
Brook Farm community founded.

1848  Seneca Falls Convention.
Oneida community founded.

# FOR FURTHER READING

Lee Benson, *The Concept of Jacksonian Democracy: New York as a Test Case* (1961). A major revisionist interpretation of the period.

William W. Freehling, *Prelude to Civil War* (1966). A major study of the nullification crisis.

Richard P. McCormick, *The Second American Party System: Party Formation in the Jacksonian Era* (1966). An influential work stressing the role of political leaders in shaping the second party system.

Edward Pessen, *Jacksonian America: Society, Personality, and Politics*, rev. ed. (1979). A comprehensive interpretation of the period, emphasizing the lack of real democracy in American society and politics.

Robert V. Remini, *Henry Clay: Statesman for the Union* (1991). An important new biography of the leading Whig statesman of the period.

Arthur M. Schlesinger Jr., *The Age of Jackson* (1945). A classic study, now dated in some of its interpretations but still highly readable.

Fred Somkin, *Unquiet Eagle: Memory and Desire in the Idea of American Freedom, 1815–1860* (1967). A penetrating study of American political values.

Ronald G. Walters, *American Reformers, 1815–1860* (1978). A balanced study that addresses the negative as well as the positive aspects of nineteenth-century reform.

Chilton Williamson, *American Suffrage: From Property to Democracy, 1760–1860* (1960). The standard study of changing requirements for voting.

# CHAPTER 11

Americans, wrote Alexis de Tocqueville, "care but little for what has been, but they are haunted by visions of what will be." Belief in irreversible progress captivated Americans in the 1840s and 1850s. Each year advances in technology confirmed Thomas Jefferson's prediction that Europe "will have to lean on our shoulders and hobble by our side." Improvements in agriculture, industry, and transportation led to calls for the development of a distinctive American literary and artistic style, and writers and artists responded. For the most part Americans equated material, cultural, and moral progress; inventor Samuel F. B. Morse expected that his telegraph would end war.

But progress had a dark side. It neither prevented nor softened the economic depressions of the late 1830s and 1840s. Cholera epidemics demonstrated that diseases as well as people could travel swiftly by railroad and steamboat. Some leading writers questioned the easy assumption that material progress meant moral progress. And for the first time anxieties arose about the despoliation of the American landscape.

*(Right) Family relaxing in their parlor, c. 1852*

# Life, Leisure, and Culture, 1840–1860

**Technology and Economic Growth**

❧

**The Quality of Life**

❧

**Democratic Pastimes**

❧

**The Quest for Nationality in Literature and Art**

# Technology and Economic Growth

As evidence of progressiveness, Americans increasingly pointed to the march of "technology," the use of scientific principles to transform the practical conveniences of life. "We have invented more useful machines within twenty years," a Bostonian reported, "than have been invented in all Europe."

To optimistic Americans, technology was both democratic and progressive. Machines would advance civilization because they could perform the work of ten people without needing food or clothing, Daniel Webster contended. A Lowell mill girl wrote, "It is emphatically the age of improvement. The arts and sciences have been more fully developed and the great mass of society are feeling its improvement."

The technology that transformed life in antebellum America included the steam engine, the cotton gin, the reaper, the use of interchangeable parts in manufacturing, the sewing machine, and the telegraph. Some of these originated in Europe, but Americans had a flair for investing in others' inventions and perfecting their own. Sadly, these advances did not benefit everyone. The cotton gin, for example, riveted slavery firmly in place by intensifying southern dependence on cotton. By rendering traditional skills obsolete, technology also undercut the position of artisans. Nonetheless, the improved transportation and increased productivity that technology made possible raised the living standards of a sizable body of free Americans between 1840 and 1860.

## Woman at Singer Sewing Machine

*Asked to repair a sewing machine that did not do continuous stitching, Isaac M. Singer invented one that did. Patented in 1851, the Singer machine quickly dominated the market. Although most early sewing machines were used in factories, some had made their way into households by 1860.*

## *Agricultural Advancement*

Although few settlers ventured onto the treeless, semiarid Great Plains before the Civil War, settlement edged west after 1830 from the woodlands of Ohio and Kentucky into parts of Indiana, Michigan, and Illinois where flat grasslands (prairies) alternated with forests. The prairies' matted soil was difficult to break for planting, but in 1837 John Deere invented a steel-tipped plow that halved the labor required to clear prairie for planting. Timber for housing and fencing was available near the prairies, and settlement occurred rapidly.

Wheat quickly became the Midwest's major cash crop. Technology eased the task of harvesting wheat. The traditional hand sickle consumed enormous amounts of time and labor and collecting and binding the cut wheat, even more. Experiments with horse-drawn machines to replace sickles had failed until Cyrus McCormick of Virginia developed the mechanical reaper. In 1834 McCormick patented his machine; in 1847 he opened a factory in

Chicago, and by 1860 he had sold 80,000 reapers. During the Civil War McCormick made immense profits by selling 250,000 reapers. The mechanical reaper, which harvested grain seven times faster than traditional methods with half the labor force, guaranteed that wheat would dominate the midwestern prairies.

Although Americans generally remained wasteful farmers—abundant cheap land made it more "practical" to move west than to try to improve played-out soil—a movement for more efficient cultivation developed before the Civil War, primarily in the East. Because eastern soils could not compete with fertile western lands, eastern farmers had little choice. For example, some farmers in Orange County, New York, fed their cattle only clover and bluegrass; combining better feed with an emphasis on cleanliness in processing dairy products, they could then charge twice as much as others for the superior butter they marketed. Virginia wheat growers fertilized their soil with plaster left over from construction of the James River Canal and raised their average yield 250 percent between 1800 and 1860. In the 1840s cotton planters began importing guano, the droppings of sea birds on islands off Peru, for use as a fertilizer. By applying fertilizers, eastern cotton growers could close the gap created by the superior fertility of soils in the Southwest.

## Technology and Industrial Progress

The early growth of U.S. manufacturing relied primarily on imported technology. That dependence lessened during the 1830s as American industries became more innovative.

Eli Whitney had pioneered in the application of interchangeable parts in the United States in 1798, but the manufacture of guns and other products using interchangeable parts still required a great deal of handwork before the components could be fitted together. By the 1840s, however, American factories had eliminated the need for hand-fitting by improving the quality of machine tools. In 1853 the superintendent of the Springfield, Massachusetts, armory staged a spectacular demonstration of interchangeable parts for a British com-

mission investigating American technology. Rifles that had been produced in ten consecutive years were stripped and their parts easily reassembled at random.

The American system of manufacturing offered multiple advantages. Damaged machines no longer had to be discarded but could be repaired simply by installing new parts. Improved machine tools allowed entrepreneurs to mass-produce new inventions rapidly, and the speed of production attracted investors. By the 1850s Connecticut firms, among them Smith and Wesson, were mass-producing the revolving pistol, which Samuel Colt had invented in 1836. Sophisticated machine tools made it possible to increase production "by confining a worker to one particular limb of a pistol until he had made two thousand." Elias Howe's sewing machine, invented in 1846, entered mass production only two years later.

Americans were eager to use technology to conquer time and space. An impatient people inhabiting a huge area, they seized enthusiastically on Samuel F.B. Morse's invention of the telegraph in 1844. A British engineer noted how quickly Americans adapted the invention: "A system of communication that annihilates distances was felt to be of vital importance, both politically and commercially, in a country so vast, and having a population so widely scattered." The speed with which Americans formed telegraph companies and strung lines stunned that same engineer. By 1852 more than 15,000 miles of lines connected cities as far-flung as Quebec, New Orleans, and St. Louis. And in 1857 a transatlantic cable linked New York and London for four months before snapping. (A new cable had to wait until 1867, after the Civil War.)

## The Railroad Boom

The desire to conquer time and space also drove antebellum Americans to make an extraordinary investment in railroads. Even more than the telegraph, the railroad embodied progress through advances in technology.

In 1790 even European royalty could travel no faster than fourteen miles an hour and that only with frequent changes of horses. By 1850 an ordinary American could travel three times as fast on a train. The swift, comfortable transportation that American railroads provided for the common person dramatized technology's democratic promise. U.S. railroads offered only one class of travel, in contrast to the several classes on European railroads. With the introduction of adjustable upholstered seats that could serve as couches at night, every American in effect traveled first class—except for African-Americans, who often were forced to sit separately.

Americans loved railroads "as a lover loves his mistress," one Frenchman wrote, but there was little to love about the earliest railroads. Sparks from locomotives showered the passengers riding in open cars, which were common. Travelers sometimes had to get out and pull trains to stations. Lacking lights, trains rarely ran at night. Before the introduction of standard time zones in 1883 (see Chapter 18), scheduling was a nightmare; at noon in Boston it was twelve minutes before noon in New York City. Delays were frequent, for trains on single-track lines had to wait on sidings for other trains to pass. Because a train's location was a mystery once it had left the station, these waits could seem endless.

Between 1840 and 1860 the size of the rail network and the power and convenience of trains underwent stunning transformations. Railroad track went from 3,000 to 30,000 miles, flat-roofed coaches replaced open cars, kerosene lamps made night travel possible, and increasingly powerful engines let trains climb even the steepest hills. Fifty thousand miles of telegraph wire enabled dispatchers to communicate with trains en route and thus to reduce delays.

Problems nonetheless lingered. Sleeping accommodations remained crude, and schedules erratic. Because individual railroads used different gauge track, frequent changes of train were necessary: there were eight changes between Charleston and Philadelphia in the 1850s. Yet nothing slowed the advance of railroads or cured America's mania for them. By 1860 the United States had more track than all the rest of the world.

Railroads spearheaded the second phase of the

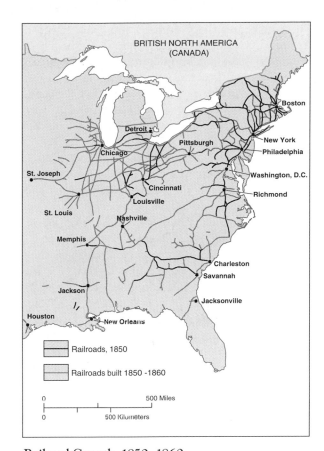

### Railroad Growth, 1850–1860

*Rail ties between the East and the Midwest greatly increased during the railroad "boom" of the 1850s.*

transportation revolution. Canals remained in use, but railroads, both faster and less vulnerable to winter freezes, gradually overtook them, first in passengers and then in freight. By 1860 the value of goods transported by railroads greatly exceeded that carried by canals.

During the 1850s the nation's rail net grew by 22,000 miles, and most of the expansion took place east of the Mississippi River. Cities such as Chicago, Chattanooga, and Atlanta boomed because of the railroads. Most important, the railroads crossed the Appalachian Mountains to link the East and the Midwest. The New York Central and the Erie railroads joined New York City to Buffalo; the Pennsylvania Railroad connected Philadelphia and

Pittsburgh; and the Baltimore and Ohio Railroad linked the Chesapeake Bay to the Ohio-Mississippi system at Wheeling, Virginia (now West Virginia). Trunk lines tied these routes to cities farther west. By 1860 rail routes ran from Buffalo to Cleveland, Toledo, and Chicago; from Pittsburgh to Fort Wayne; and from Wheeling to Cincinnati and St. Louis.

Chicago's growth illustrates the impact of these rail links. In 1849 it was a village of a few hundred people with virtually no rail service. By 1860 it had become a metropolis of 100,000, served by eleven railroads. Farmers in the upper Midwest no longer had to send their grain, livestock, and dairy products down the Mississippi to New Orleans; they could now ship their products directly east. Chicago supplanted New Orleans as the interior's main commercial hub.

The east-west rail lines stimulated the settlement and agricultural development of the Midwest. By 1860 Illinois, Indiana, and Wisconsin had replaced Ohio, Pennsylvania, and New York as the leading wheat-growing states. Enabling farmers to speed their produce to the East, railroads increased the value of farmland and promoted additional settlement. In turn, this population growth stimulated industrial development in cities such as Chicago and Minneapolis, for the new settlers needed lumber for fences and houses and mills to grind wheat into flour. Railroads also spurred the growth of small towns along their midwestern routes. Some lines, such as the Illinois Central, made profits from real-estate speculation. After purchasing land for stations along its route, the Illinois Central laid out towns around the stations and even stipulated street names. By the Civil War, few viewed the Midwest as a frontier or its inhabitants as pioneers.

As the nation's first big business, railroads transformed the conduct of business, particularly in finance. State money had helped to finance many lines, but by the 1840s it began to dry up. Federal aid would not be widely available until the Civil War. Although local and county governments tried to fill the void, the dramatic expansion of the rail net in the 1850s required new sources of financing. Private investors had long purchased railroad stock, but the large trunk lines of the 1850s needed far more capital than small investors could generate. Thus the railroads turned to the capital market in New York City. The railroad boom helped to make Wall Street the nation's greatest capital market, as the securities of all the leading railroads were traded on the floor of the New York Stock Exchange. New York also became the center of modern investment firms. These companies evaluated securities issued by railroads in Toledo or Chattanooga and then found purchasers in New York, Paris, London, and Amsterdam. Controlling the flow of funds to the railroads, investment bankers soon influenced their internal affairs. A Wall Street analyst noted in 1851 that railroad men seeking financing "must remember that money is power, and that the [financier] can dictate to a great extent his own terms."

## Rising Prosperity

Technology also improved life by lowering prices. Clocks that cost $50 to make by hand in 1800 could be produced for 50¢ by 1850. Widespread use of steam power led to a 25 percent rise in the average worker's real income (purchasing power) between 1840 and 1860; unlike water wheels, steam engines could run in all seasons, and so workers did not have to face long winter layoffs. Although cotton textile workers saw little gain in hourly wages, their average annual wages rose from $160 to $201 between 1830 and 1869.

The growth of towns and cities also contributed to the upward trend in average annual wages. In contrast to rural farming areas, with their heavily seasonal labor, urban settings offered year-round opportunities for jobs. Towns and cities also provided women and children—who seldom were paid for farm labor—new opportunities for paid work. Children's wages played an important role in family finances for working-class families. An average New York or Philadelphia working-class family spent $500 to $600 per year on food, rent, clothing, and fuel. However, an average male head of household earned $300 a year. Clearly, the survival of many families depended on the wages of children and wives.

The average urban worker was marginally better off than the average rural worker, primarily because of seasonal fluctuations in agricultural work. Most antebellum Americans continued to see farming as the ideal occupation, but comparatively few could raise the $500 or so in cash necessary to purchase, clear, and stock a farm and then wait three to five years for any reward. The economic advantages of urban life explain in part why so many Americans moved to urban areas in the first half of the nineteenth century. So does the unprecedented range of comforts and conveniences that the city offered.

# The Quality of Life

Subtle but critical changes in the quality of daily life accompanied the large-scale transformations in transportation, production, and income in the two decades before the Civil War. These changes occurred within the home and affected routine activities such as eating, drinking, and washing. Americans became far more comfortable as machine-made furniture, stoves, and fresh food entered the home.

But change occurred unevenly. Technology made it possible for the middle class to enjoy luxuries formerly reserved for the rich, yet it widened the gulf between middle class and poor. As middle-class homes became increasingly lavish, the urban poor crowded into cramped tenements. And some critical elements—medicine, for example—lagged far behind in the technological explosion. Nevertheless, Americans embraced the benefits of progress and ignored its limitations. Few accepted the possibility that progress could neglect such an important aspect of everyday life as health. Lacking medical advances, Americans embraced popular health movements that stressed diet and regimen over doctors.

## Housing

During the early 1800s the unattached and distinctive wood-frame houses dotting colonial urban skylines yielded to quickly constructed, uniform-looking brick row houses. Where some praised the row houses as democratic, others condemned "their extreme uniformity—when you have seen one, you have seen all." The typical row house was narrow and long, fifteen to twenty feet across and thirty to forty feet from front to back. Most had open spaces in the rear for gardens, pigs, privies (outhouses), and cisterns (water-storage vessels). Middle-class row houses, with cast-iron balconies, elegant doors, and curved staircases emphasizing the owner's individuality and taste, were larger and more elaborate than those of the working class.

As land values soared (as much as 750 percent in Manhattan between 1785 and 1815), renting, rather than owning, homes became common. By 1815 more than half of the homes in large cities were rented. Skyrocketing land values also led to the subdivision of row houses for occupancy by several families. The worst of these, known as tenements, were the usual habitats of Irish immigrants and free blacks.

In rural areas the quality of housing depended as much on the date of settlement as on social class. In recently settled areas the standard dwelling was a one-room log cabin with split-log floors that allowed in drafts, roofs that let in snow, crude chimneys made of sticks and clay, and windows covered by oiled paper or cloth. As rural communities matured, log cabins gave way to frame houses of two or more rooms with glass windows and better insulation.

## Home Furniture

Furniture also revealed the widening gap between the prosperous and the poor. Families in the middle and upper classes increasingly decorated their parlors with a style of furniture known as rococo. Such furniture was ornate and featured elaborately carved wooden frames supporting heavily upholstered backs and seats topped with medallions; vines, leaves, and flowers covered both wooden and upholstered surfaces. The fashion of the day required the crowding of seven matched pieces into the parlor. Contemporary style also dictated the hanging of mirrors with intricate gilded moldings depicting birds, flowers, and young women.

Such highly ornamental furniture marked its

possessors as people of substantial wealth. The rise of mass-produced furniture brought rococo style within the reach of the middle class, which could not afford to import furniture from France, as the wealthy did. Most Americans, however, were unable to afford either imported or domestic rococo and had to be content with simpler furniture. Technological advances in furniture making tended to level taste between the middle and upper classes while marking those classes off from everyone else.

## Heating, Cooking, and Diet

The transportation and industrial revolutions also affected heating, cooking, and diet. Iron foundries took advantage of distant markets by specializing in the production of cast-iron stoves, which had displaced open hearths in urban areas by the late 1840s. Country dwellers continued to prefer open wood-fired hearths, partly because clearing farm land left abundant wood. City people, however, increasingly opted for coal-fired stoves. The discovery of high-grade hard coal in eastern Pennsylvania guaranteed a steady supply of the fuel.

Coal burned longer and hotter than wood and reduced the time and expense of acquiring fuel. The drawbacks of using coal, among them its sooty residue and the ever-present danger of carbon monoxide poisoning, paled beside its benefits, which included ease of cooking. With coal, open flames no longer threatened clothing and person, meals could be left unattended, and several dishes could be cooked at once on the stove. In this way stoves contributed to a growing variety in the American diet.

Meanwhile, better transportation brought a greater variety of foodstuffs to urban markets, particularly fresh vegetables. For most people, diet was still subject to seasonal fluctuation; only the rich could afford fruit out of season. Preserving any kind of food was a problem, for few homes had iceboxes—the forerunners of refrigerators—before 1860. Housewives could bury meat in the snow to keep it from spoiling, but salt remained the most

widely used preservative. Americans ate far more pork than beef because salt affected the taste of pork less.

## Water and Sanitation

Rural homes rarely had running water. Instead, water was brought in from wells, springs, or cisterns; once used, it was carried outside and dumped. But antebellum cities had begun constructing public waterworks to deal with threats to well water posed by leakage from outdoor privies. By 1823 Philadelphia had completed a system that brought water from the Schuylkill and Delaware rivers to street hydrants. Charles Dickens marveled that the city "is most bountifully provided with fresh water, which is showered and jerked about, and turned on, and poured off everywhere." By 1860 sixty-eight public water systems were operating in the United States.

Although public waterworks were engineering marvels, their impact was uneven. Most smaller cities had no waterworks before the Civil War, and even in New York less than a tenth of the city's population were customers of the water system. Few urban houses had running water, and so families carried water from street hydrants into their homes. Because hot running water was rare, the water had to be heated on the stove before one could take a bath. Not surprisingly, people rarely bathed.

Infrequent baths meant pungent body odors, but they mingled with a multitude of strong scents. Even fashionable residential streets contained stables backed by mounds of manure. Street cleaning was left to private contractors, who often discharged their duties casually, and so urban Americans relied on hogs, which they let roam freely to scavenge, for cleaning public thoroughfares. Outdoor privies added to the stench. Flush toilets were rare outside cities, and within cities sewer systems lagged behind water systems. Boston had only 5,000 flush toilets in 1860 for a population of 178,000, a far higher ratio of toilets to people than most cities. Americans normally answered calls of nature by trips to outdoor privies and suppressed their odors with shovelsful of dirt.

Stoves and other conveniences did little to liberate women from housework; they merely elevated the standards of housekeeping. Technology would let women fulfill their duty to make every house "a glorious temple." However, middle-class Americans boasted how comfortable their lives were becoming and pointed to the steady improvement in wages, diet, and water supplies as tangible marks of betterment.

## Disease and Health

Despite the slowly rising living standard, Americans remained vulnerable to disease. Epidemic disease swept through antebellum American cities and felled thousands. Yellow fever and cholera killed one-fifth of New Orlean's population in 1832–1833, and cholera alone killed 10 percent of St. Louis's population in 1849.

Ironically, the transportation revolution increased the danger of epidemic diseases. The cholera epidemic of 1832, the first truly national epidemic, followed shipping routes: one branch of the epidemic ran from New York City up the Hudson River, across the Erie Canal to Ohio, and down the Ohio River to the Mississippi and New Orleans; the other branch followed shipping up and down the East Coast from New York.

The inability of physicians to explain epidemic diseases led to general distrust of the medical profession and to the making of public health a low-priority issue (see Chapter 9). No one understood that bacteria caused cholera and yellow fever. Instead, doctors debated the "contagion" theory versus the "miasm" theory of disease. Contagionists, who believed that touch spread disease, called for quarantines of affected areas. Supporters of the miasm theory argued that poisonous gases (miasms) emitted by rotten vegetation or dead animals carried disease through the air. They concluded that swamps had to be drained and streets cleaned. It quickly became apparent that neither theory worked.

Although epidemic disease baffled antebellum physicians, the discovery of anesthesia opened the way for remarkable advances in surgery. Laughing gas (nitrous oxide) had long provided partygoers who inhaled it enjoyable sensations of giddiness and painlessness, but it was difficult to handle. Crawford Long, a Georgia physician who had attended laughing gas frolics in his youth, employed sulfuric ether (an easily transportable liquid with the same properties as nitrous oxide) during surgery. Long did not follow up his discovery, but four years later William T.G. Morton, a dentist, successfully employed sulfuric ether during an operation at Massachusetts General Hospital. Within a few years ether was widely used.

The discovery of anesthesia improved the public image of surgeons, who had long been viewed as brutes hacking away at agonized patients. It also permitted longer and thus more careful operations. However, the failure of most surgeons to recognize the importance of clean hands and sterilized instruments partially offset the value of anesthesia. As early as 1843, Oliver Wendell Holmes Sr., a poet and physician, published a paper on how unclean hands spread puerperal fever among women giving birth, but disinfection was accepted only gradually. Operations remained as dangerous as the conditions they tried to heal. The mortality rate for amputations hovered around 40 percent, and during the Civil War 87 percent of soldiers who suffered abdominal wounds died from them.

## Popular Health Movements

Doubtful of medicine and skeptical of the benefits of public health, antebellum Americans turned to various therapies that promised a longer, healthier life. Hydropathy, the "water cure," offered "an abundance of water of dewy softness and crystal transparency, to cleanse, renovate, and rejuvenate the disease-worn and dilapidated system." Well-to-do women flocked to hydropathic sanitoriums both to relieve pain and to enjoy relaxation and exercise in a congenial gathering place.

Sylvester Graham, a temperance reformer turned health advocate, popularized dietary changes as the way to better health. He urged Americans to eat less; to substitute vegetables, fruits, and whole-grain bread (called Graham bread) for meat; to abstain from spices, coffee, tea, and alcohol; and to avoid sexual "excess" (by which he meant most sex).

Reformers became enthusiastic proponents of Graham's ideas. Abolitionists and others agreed with Graham that Americans' unnatural cravings, whether for red meat or sex, stimulated violence and aggressive impulses. But Graham's doctrines also attracted a broad audience beyond the reform movements. His books sold well, and his public lectures were thronged. His commonsense ideas appealed to Americans wary of orthodox medicine, and he used familiar religious terms to describe disease, which was hell, and health, which amounted to a kind of heaven on earth. Graham provided simple assurances to an audience as ignorant as he was of disease's true causes.

### Phrenology

The belief that each person was master of his or her own destiny underlay not only evangelical religion and health movements but also the most popular of the antebellum scientific fads: phrenology. Created by a Viennese physician, Franz J. Gall, phrenology rested on the idea that the human mind comprised thirty-seven distinct faculties, or "organs," each localized in a different part of the brain. Phrenologists thought that the degree of each organ's development determined skull shape, so that they could accurately analyze an individual's character by examining the bumps and depressions of the skull.

In the United States two brothers, Orson and Lorenzo Fowler, became the chief promoters of phrenology in the 1840s. Orson Fowler was a missionary of sorts for phrenology, opening a publishing house (Fowlers and Wells) that marketed phrenology books everywhere. The Fowlers met criticisms that phrenology was godless by pointing out a huge organ called "Veneration" to prove that people were naturally religious, and they answered charges that phrenology was pessimistic by claiming that exer-

cise could improve every desirable mental organ. Lorenzo Fowler reported that several of his own skull bumps had grown.

Phrenology appealed to Americans as a "practical" science. In a mobile, individualistic society, it promised a quick assessment of others. Merchants sometimes used phrenological charts to hire clerks, and some young women even induced their fiancés to undergo a phrenological analysis before marriage.

Phrenologists had close ties to popular health movements. Fowlers and Wells published the *Water-Cure Journal* and Sylvester Graham's *Lectures on the Science of Human Life*. Orson Fowler filled his popular phrenological books with tips on the evils of coffee, tea, meat, spices, and sex that could have been plucked from Graham's writings. Phrenology shared with the health movement the belief that anyone could understand and obey the "laws" of life.

Unlike hydropathy, phrenology required no money; unlike Grahamism, it required no abstinence. Easily understood and practiced, and filled with the promise of universal betterment, phrenology was ideal for antebellum America. Just as Americans had invented machines to better their lives, they could invent "sciences" that promised human betterment.

## Democratic Pastimes

Between 1830 and 1860 technology transformed recreation into a commodity that could be purchased in the form of cheap newspapers and novels and equally cheap tickets to plays, museums, and lectures. Imaginative entrepreneurs seized technology to make and sell entertainment. Fortunes awaited men who could sense what people wanted and who could use available technology to satisfy them. James Gordon Bennett, one of the founders of the penny press, and P. T. Barnum, the greatest showman of the century, made the public want what they had to sell.

Bennett and Barnum saw themselves as purveyors of democratic entertainment: they sold their wares cheaply to anyone. Barnum's American Museum in New York City catered to varied social classes that paid to see paintings, dwarfs, mammoth bones, and other attractions. By marketing his museum as a family entertainment, Barnum helped to break down barriers between pastimes of husband and wife. Racy news stories in Bennett's *New York Herald* provided a vast audience with common information and topics of conversation.

Technology also changed the way Americans amused themselves. People had long found ways to enjoy themselves, and even the gloomiest Puritans had indulged in games and sports. After 1830, however, individuals increasingly became spectators rather than creators of amusements, relying on entrepreneurs who supplied entertainment.

## Newspapers

In 1830 the typical American newspaper was four pages long, with the front and back pages filled almost completely with advertisements. The interior pages contained editorials, reprints of political speeches, notices of political events, and information about shipping. Even the most prominent papers had a daily circulation of only 1,000 to 2,000; subsidies from political parties or factions supported them. "Journalists," a contemporary wrote, "were usually little more than secretaries dependent upon cliques of politicians, merchants, brokers, and office seekers for their prosperity and bread."

Because they could be profitable without being popular, most early newspapers had limited appeal. Priced at six cents an issue, the average paper was too expensive for a worker who earned less than a dollar a day. Moreover, with few eye-catching news stories or illustrations, papers seemed little more than bulletin boards.

In the 1830s technology began to transform newspapers. Cheaper paper and steam-driven presses drastically lowered production costs, and enterprising journalists, among them James Gordon Bennett, saw the implications: slash prices, boost circulation, and reap vast profits. In 1833 New York's eleven daily newspapers had a combined daily circulation of only 26,500. Two years later the combined circulation of the three largest "penny" newspapers had soared to 44,000. From 1830 to 1840 national newspaper circulation rose from 78,000 to 300,000, and the number of weekly newspapers more than doubled.

The penny press also revolutionized the marketing and format of newspapers. Newsboys hawked the penny papers on busy street corners, and reporters filled the papers with gripping news stories designed to attract readers. As sociologist Michael Schudson observes, "The penny press invented the modern concept of 'news.' " The penny papers also used the telegraph to speed both news and human-interest stories to readers.

Some penny papers were little more than scandal sheets, but others, such as Bennett's *New York Herald* and Horace Greeley's *New York Tribune*, pioneered modern financial and political reporting. The *Herald* featured a daily "money article" that analyzed and interpreted financial events. "The spirit, pith, and philosophy of commercial affairs is what men of business want," Bennett wrote. The relentless snooping by the *Tribune's* Washington reporters outraged politicians. In 1841 *Tribune* correspondents were temporarily barred from the House of Representatives for reporting that an Ohio representative ate his lunch in the House chamber, picked his teeth with a jackknife, and wiped his greasy hands on his pants and coat.

## The Popular Novel

Novels became affordable and enormously popular between 1830 and 1860. In the 1830s technology and transportation began to lower the price of novels, and in the 1840s cheap paperbacks selling for as little as seven cents flooded the national market. Serial versions appeared in newspapers devoted mainly to printing novels.

Sentimental novels dominated the fiction market in the 1840s and 1850s. The tribulations of orphans and deaths of children filled the pages of these tearjerkers. In Susan Warner's *The Wide, Wide World*, the heroine bursts into tears on an average of every other page for two volumes. Another popular writer, Lydia Sigourney, wrote a poem on a canary accidentally starved to death.

Women constituted the main audience for sentimental novels; these works were written by women, about women, and mainly for women. Writing, the most lucrative occupation open to women prior to the Civil War, attracted those desperately in need of cash. Susan Warner, for example, raised in luxury, had been thrown into poverty by her family's ruin in the Panic of 1839. Mrs. E. D. E. N. Southworth turned to writing after a broken marriage left her supporting two children on a teacher's salary of $250 a year.

A major theme in the novels of Warner, Southworth, and their female contemporaries was that women could conquer any obstacle. These novels challenged stereotypes of men as trusty providers and of women as delicate dependents. Instead, men were portrayed as liars, drunken lechers, and vicious misers and women as resourceful and strong-willed. A typical plot featured a female orphan or a spoiled rich girl thrown on hard times or a dutiful daughter plagued by a drunken father. Each learned to master her life. The moral was clear: women could overcome trials and make the world a better place.

## The Theater

During the 1850s popular novelists such as Charles Dickens and Harriet Beecher Stowe were as well known through dramatizations of their work as through sales of their books. Antebellum theaters were large and crowded; cheap seats drew a democratic throng of lawyers and merchants and their wives, artisans and clerks, sailors and noisy boys, and a sizable body of prostitutes. The presence of prostitutes in the audience was only one of many factors that made theaters vaguely disreputable. Theater audiences were notoriously rowdy: they stamped their feet, hooted at villains, and threw potatoes and garbage at the stage when they disliked the characters or the acting.

Actors developed huge followings. In 1849 a long-running feud between leading American actor Edwin Forrest and popular British actor William Macready ended with a riot in New York City that left twenty people dead. The riot demonstrated theater's broad popularity. Forrest's supporters included Irish workers who loathed the British and who appealed to "working men" to rally against the "aristocrat" Macready. Macready, projecting a polished, intellectual image, attracted the better-educated classes. Had not all classes patronized the theater, the riot probably never would have occurred.

The plays themselves were as diverse as the audiences. Melodramas, whose plots resembled those of sentimental novels, were popular; vice was punished, virtue was rewarded, and the heroine married the hero. Yet the single most popular dramatist was William Shakespeare. In 1835 Philadelphia audiences witnessed sixty-five performances of his plays. Shakespeare himself might not have recognized some of these performances, adapted as they were for popular audiences. Theatrical managers highlighted swordfights and assassinations, cut long speeches, and changed tragic endings to happy ones. Producers arranged for short performances or demonstrations between acts. In the middle of *Macbeth*, the audience might see an impersonation of Tecumseh or of Aaron Burr, jugglers and acrobats, a drummer beating twelve drums at once, or a three-year-old who weighed one hundred pounds.

## Minstrel Shows

The minstrel shows that Americans flocked to see in the 1840s and 1850s forged enduring stereotypes that buttressed white Americans' sense of superiority by diminishing blacks. The shows arose in northern cities in the 1840s as blackfaced white men took the stage to present an evening of songs, dances, and humorous sketches.

Although the performances featured elements of African-American culture, especially dance steps,

**Dan Bryant, the Minstrel**
*Bryant was one of many antebellum popularizers of black minstrelsy. One of the earliest known minstrelsy performances occurred in Boston in 1799 when a white man, Gottlieb Graupner, reportedly made up as a black, sang and accompanied himself on the banjo.*

most of the songs were from white culture. Stephen Foster's "Camptown Races" and "Massa's in the Cold, Cold Ground," first performed in minstrel shows, reflected whites' notions of how blacks sang, not authentic black music. The images of blacks projected by minstrelsy catered to the prejudices of the working-class whites who dominated the audiences. Minstrel troupes depicted blacks as stupid, clumsy, and obsessively musical and emphasized their Africanness. At a time of intensifying political conflict over race, minstrel shows planted images and expectations about blacks' behavior through stock characters such as Uncle Ned, the tattered, humble, and docile slave; and Zip Coon, the arrogant urban free black who paraded around in a high hat and long-tailed coat and lived off his girlfriends' money.

## P. T. Barnum

No one understood better than P.T. Barnum how to turn the public's craving for entertainment into a profitable business. He was simultaneously a hustler who cheated his customers before they could cheat him and an idealist who founded a newspaper to attack wrongdoing and who thought of himself as a public benefactor.

After moving to New York City in 1834, Barnum began his career as an entrepreneur of entertainment. His first venture exhibited an African-American woman, Joyce Heth, whom Barnum billed as the 169-year-old former slave nurse of George Washington. In Barnum's mind, the truth or falsehood of the claim was irrelevant. What mattered was that people would pay. It was the beginning of a lifelong game between Barnum and the public.

In 1841 Barnum purchased a run-down museum in New York City, rechristened it the American Museum, and opened a new chapter in the history of popular entertainment. Avoiding the educational slant of other museums, Barnum concentrated on curiosities and faked exhibits; he wanted to interest people, not to educate them. The American Museum included ventriloquists, magicians, albinos, a five-year-old midget named Tom Thumb, and the "Feejee Mermaid," a shrunken oddity "taken alive in the Feejee Islands." By 1850 Barnum's entertainment emporium was the best-known museum in the nation.

A genius at publicity, Barnum recognized that newspapers could invent as well as report news. Thus he frequently wrote letters (under various names) to newspapers hinting that the scientific world was agog over some astonishing curiosity that the public could soon view at the American Museum. Barnum's success rested on more than people's curiosity, however. A temperance advocate, he provided lectures on the evils of alcohol and gave the place a reputation as a center for safe family amusement. In addition, Barnum tapped the public's insatiable appetite for natural wonders. At a time when each year brought new technological marvels, Americans would believe in anything, even the Feejee Mermaid.

## The Quest for Nationality in Literature and Art

Sentimental novels, melodramas, minstrel shows, and the American Museum belonged to the world of popular culture. They did not represent the serious culture in which many Americans sought to reflect the American spirit. During the 1830s Ralph Waldo Emerson emerged as the most influential spokesman for those who sought a national literature and art.

"The American Scholar," an address by Emerson in 1837, constituted an intellectual Declaration of Independence. His message had an electrifying effect. Americans had too long deferred to European precedents, he proclaimed. The democratic spirit of the age had made Americans more self-reliant, and the time had come for them to break free of European standards and to trust themselves. In addition, Emerson's address adopted romanticism, the major intellectual movement of the first half of the nineteenth century, which celebrated the nation and the individual. Rejecting the idea of universal standards, romantics first in Europe and then in the United States insisted that great literature had to reflect both the national character and the author's emotions.

The transcendentalism of Emerson and his colleagues formed a uniquely American romanticism. Transcendentalists argued that knowledge went beyond, or transcended, the intellect. Like sight, it was an instantaneous, direct perception of truth. Intuition and emotion could provide knowledge as accurately as intellect could. Emerson concluded that

learned people had no special advantage in the pursuit of truth. Rather, truth itself was democratic—all could see the truth if only they would trust the promptings of their hearts. Transcendentalist doctrine led to the exhilarating belief that a young, democratic society such as the United States could produce as noble a literature and art as the established societies of Europe simply by drawing on the inexhaustible resources of the common people.

### Literary Geography

"The American Scholar" coincided with the American Renaissance, a flowering of art and literature that had been gaining momentum since the 1820s.

New England's rocky soil had proved fertile ground for literature. Its poets ranged from the urbane Henry Wadsworth Longfellow to the self-taught Quaker John Greenleaf Whittier. Boston was home to George Bancroft, Francis Parkman, William Hickling Prescott, and John Lothrop Motley, the four most distinguished historians of the age. Twenty miles from Boston lay Concord, where Emerson, Nathaniel Hawthorne, the eccentric Henry David Thoreau, and the brilliant philosopher Margaret Fuller lived. Close by was Fruitlands, a utopian community where Louisa May Alcott had spent part of her childhood. West of that lay Amherst, where the shy, reclusive, and brilliant poet Emily Dickinson lived her entire fifty-six years on the same street.

New York, home to Washington Irving, James Fenimore Cooper, Walt Whitman, and Herman Melville, supported a flourishing literary culture. Southerners, including William Gilmore Simms, acquired national reputations. Virginia-born Edgar Allan Poe did most of his writing in New York and Philadelphia.

Many reputations that burned brightly in nineteenth-century America have dimmed, but the genius of seven writers continues to gleam: Cooper, Emerson, Thoreau, Whitman, Hawthorne, Melville, and Poe. Cooper and Emerson were the only writers who basked in public esteem in their day;

neither Hawthorne nor Poe gained the audience that each believed he deserved, and the antebellum public largely ignored Thoreau and Whitman. Melville's light works were popular, but his serious fiction received little acclaim. Creativity, not popularity, linked these seven writers. Each challenged existing literary conventions and created new ones.

## James Fenimore Cooper and the Stirrings of Literary Independence

Until well after 1800 British literature dominated American literary taste. Sir Walter Scott's historical novel *Waverly* (1814) had catapulted the British author to enduring fame and influence in America and created a demand for historical novels. Born in 1789, James Fenimore Cooper, called the American Scott because he wrote historical novels, introduced American characters and American themes to literature. In his frontiersman Natty Bumppo, "Leatherstocking," Cooper created an American archetype. Natty first appears in *The Pioneers* (1823) as an old man, a former hunter, who blames the farmers for wantonly destroying upstate New York's game and turning the silent and majestic forests into deserts of tree stumps. As a spokesman for nature against the march of civilization, Natty became a highly popular figure, and his life unfolded in several other enormously popular novels, such as *The Last of the Mohicans* (1826), *The Pathfinder* (1840), and *The Deerslayer* (1841). The prolific Cooper averaged a novel a year for thirty-four years and said that he found it harder to read his novels than to write them.

The success of James Fenimore Cooper and other early-nineteenth-century writers was the first step in the development of an American literature. Americans still read British novels, but more and more they enjoyed American authors. In 1800 American authors had accounted for a negligible proportion of the output of American publishers, but by 1830, 40 percent of the books published in the United States were written by Americans and by 1850, 75 percent.

## Emerson, Thoreau, and Whitman

Ralph Waldo Emerson's advocacy of a national literature extended beyond "The American Scholar." In his own writing he tried to capture the brisk language of the common people, and he also encouraged younger writers, among them Thoreau and Whitman. Whitman, extravagantly patriotic, contrasted sharply with Emerson and Thoreau, who criticized the materialism and aggressiveness of their compatriots. But all three shared a common trait: their uniquely American work emphasized the spontaneous and vivid expression of personal feeling rather than learned analysis.

Born in 1803, Emerson had served briefly as a Unitarian minister before fashioning a career as a public lecturer. Pungency and vividness characterized his lectures, which Emerson published as essays. The true scholar, he stressed, must be independent: "Let him not quit his belief that a popgun is a popgun, though the ancient and honorable of the earth affirm it to be the crack of doom." A transcendentalist who believed that knowledge reflected the voice of God within every person and that truth was inborn and universal, Emerson relied not on a systematic analysis of the world around him but on vivid and arresting—although unconnected—assertions. Listening to Emerson, someone said, was like trying to see the sun in a fog; one could see light but never the sun.

In addition to dazzling his audiences, Emerson had a magnetic attraction for young intellectuals ill at ease in conventional society. Henry David Thoreau, born in 1817, typified the younger Emersonians. Unlike Emerson, whose adventurousness was largely intellectual, Thoreau was both a thinker and a doer. At one point he went to jail rather than pay poll taxes that would support the Mexican War, a conflict that he saw as part of a southern conspiracy to extend slavery. The experience of jail led Thoreau to write *Civil Disobedience* (1849), in which he defended disobedience of unjust laws.

In spring 1845 Thoreau moved a few miles from Concord into the woods near Walden Pond. He constructed a simple cabin on land owned by Emer-

**Louisa May Alcott, c. 1858**
*Raised in bleak, if genteel, poverty, Louisa May Alcott first gained recognition for her sketches of her experiences as a nurse in a military hospital during the Civil War. The publication of* Little Women, *her largely autobiographical novel of New England family life, brought her fame and enough money to support herself and her sisters.*

son and spent the next two years providing for his wants away from civilization. Thoreau's stated purpose for his retreat to Walden was to write a book about a canoe trip that he and his brother had taken, but he soon discovered a larger purpose and undertook a much more important book. *Walden* (1854), although it abounded with descriptions of nature and wildlife, carried a larger, transcendentalist message. Thoreau proclaimed that his woodland retreat had taught him that only a few weeks' work was needed to satisfy material needs; most of the year could be used to examine life's purpose. The problem with Americans, he wrote, was that they turned themselves into "mere machines" to acquire wealth without asking why.

Thoreau prodded Americans with the uncomfortable truth that material progress and moral progress were not as intimately related as they liked to think.

Emerson sympathized with personalities as dissimilar but distinctively American as Thoreau and Walt Whitman—the former was eccentric, reclusive, and critical, the latter was self-taught, exuberant, outgoing, and in love with everything American except slavery. A journalist and fervent Democrat, Whitman had an intimate, affectionate knowledge of ordinary Americans. His reading of Emerson nurtured his belief that the United States would be the cradle of a new citizen in whom natural virtue would flourish. The threads of Whitman's early career came together in his major work, *Leaves of Grass*, a book of poems first published in 1855.

*Leaves of Grass* shattered existing poetic conventions. Whitman composed in free verse, and his blunt, often lusty words assailed "delicacy." He wrote of "the scent of these armpits finer than prayer" and "winds whose soft-tickling genitals rub against me." Whitman became the subject as well as the writer of his poems, especially in "Song of Myself." He saw himself—crude, plain, self-taught, passionately democratic—as the personification of the American people.

To some contemporary critics, *Leaves of Grass* seemed the work of an escaped lunatic. One derided it as a "heterogeneous mass of bombast, egotism, vulgarity, and nonsense." Emerson and a few others, however, reacted enthusiastically. Emerson had long awaited the appearance of "the poet of America" and knew immediately that in Whitman that poet had arrived.

## Hawthorne, Melville, and Poe

Emerson's call on American writers to create a democratic literature by comprehending "the near, the low, the common" had a negligible impact on the major fiction writers during the 1840s and 1850s: Nathaniel Hawthorne, Herman Melville, and Edgar Allan Poe. Hawthorne, for example, set *The Scarlet Letter* (1850) in New England's Puritan past, *The House of the Seven Gables* (1851) in a mansion haunted by memories of the past, and *The Mar-*

*ble Faun* (1859) in Rome. Poe set several of his short stories in Europe; and Melville's novels *Typee* (1846), *Omoo* (1847), and *Mardi* (1849) took place in the exotic South Seas, and his masterpiece, *Moby-Dick* (1851), aboard a whaler.

In part, these three writers felt that American life lacked the materials for great fiction. Hawthorne bemoaned the difficulty of writing about a country "where there is no shadow, no antiquity, no mystery, no picturesque and gloomy wrong." Psychology, not society, fascinated these writers. Each probed the depths of the human mind rather than the intricacies of social relationships. Their preoccupation with analyzing the characters' mental states grew out of their underlying pessimism about the human condition. All three viewed individuals as bundles of conflicting forces that might never be reconciled.

Pessimism led them to create characters obsessed by pride, guilt, a desire for revenge, or a quest for perfection and then to set their stories along the byways of society, where the authors could freely explore the complexities of human motivation without the jarring intrusions of everyday life. For example, in *The Scarlet Letter* Hawthorne returned to the Puritan era in order to examine the psychological and moral consequences of the adultery committed by Hester Prynne and the minister Arthur Dimmesdale, although he devoted little attention to depicting the Puritan village in which the action takes place. Melville, in *Moby-Dick*, created the frightening Captain Ahab, whose relentless pursuit of a white whale fails to fill the chasm in his soul and brings death to all his crew except the narrator. Poe, too, channeled his pessimism into creative work of the first rank. In his short story "The Fall of the House of Usher" (1839), he interwove the symbol of a crumbling mansion with the mental agony of a crumbling family.

Although these three authors ignored Emerson's call to write about the everyday experiences of their fellow Americans, they fashioned a distinctively American fiction. Their works, preoccupied with analysis of moral dilemmas and psychological states, fulfilled Tocqueville's prediction that writers in democratic nations, while rejecting traditional sources of fiction, would explore the abstract and universal questions of human nature.

## American Landscape Painting

American painters between 1820 and 1860 also sought to develop nationality in their work. Lacking a mythic past of gods and goddesses, they subordinated historical and figure painting to landscape painting. The American landscape, though barren of the "poetry of decay" that Europe's ruined castles and crumbling temples provided, was fresh and relatively unencumbered by the human imprint. These conditions posed a challenge to the painters of the Hudson River school, which flourished from the 1820s to the 1870s. Its best-known representatives—Thomas Cole, Asher Durand, and Frederic Church—painted scenes of the unspoiled region around the Hudson River.

The works of Washington Irving and the opening of the Erie Canal had piqued interest in the Hudson during the 1820s. Then, after 1830 Emerson and Thoreau lauded primitive nature; "in wildness is the preservation of the world," Thoreau wrote. By this time, much of the original American forest already had fallen to pioneer axes, and one writer urgently concluded that "it behooves our artists to rescue from [civilization's] grasp the little that is left before it is too late."

The Hudson River painters did more than preserve a passing wilderness; they also emphasized emotional effect. Cole's rich colors; billowing clouds; massive, gnarled trees; towering peaks; and deep chasms so heightened the dramatic impact of his paintings that poet William Cullen Bryant compared them to "acts of religion." In powerful, evocative canvases, American artists aimed to capture the natural grandeur of their land.

Like Cole, George Catlin tried to preserve a vanishing America through his art. His goal was to paint as many Native Americans as possible in their pure and "savage" state. By 1837 he had created 437 oil paintings and thousands of sketches of faces and customs from nearly fifty tribes. Catlin's romantic view of the Indians as noble savages was a double-edged sword. His admirers delighted in his dignified portrayals of Indians but shared his foreboding that the march of progress had already doomed these noble creatures to oblivion.

Landscape architects tried to create small enclaves of nature to provide spiritual refreshment to harried city dwellers. "Rural" cemetaries with pastoral names such as Harmony Grove, placed near major cities, became tourist attractions, designed as much for the living as for the dead. On a grander scale Frederick Law Olmsted and Calvert Vaux designed New York City's Central Park to look like undisturbed countryside. Drainage pipes carried water to man-made lakes, and trees screened out the surrounding buildings. Central Park became an idealized version of nature, meant to remind visitors of landscapes that they had seen in pictures. Thus nature was made to mirror art.

## The Diffusion of Knowledge

Just as Emerson contended that the democratizing spirit of his age would encourage Americans to discover their cultural identity, many of his contemporaries argued that the educated had a duty to "diffuse," or spread, enlightenment among the common people. Some believed that inexpensive books and magazines would bring fine literature to the masses, but others thought that only organized efforts could instruct and uplift American minds.

Advocates of systematic popular instruction turned to both public schools and lyceums, local organizations that sponsored public lectures on topics as diverse as astronomy, biology, physiology, geology, memory, Iceland, the true mission of women, and the domestic life of the Turks. Audiences usually included professional men, merchants, farmers, artisans, and middle-class women. The lecturers mirrored their audiences' diversity. After 1840 the spread of railroads contributed to the rise of a group of nationally known lecturers, including Ralph Waldo Emerson. Tickets cost as little as 12¢ but the crowds were so large that some lecturers could command the then astounding fee of $250 per talk.

Not only railroads but also the growth of public education and the advent of low-priced newspapers and books helped to bring audiences and lecturers together. Originating in New England, lyceums expanded across the northern states and made inroads into the South. Their spread revealed a popular hunger for knowledge and refinement. By 1840, 3,500 towns had lyceums, yet in that year's presidential election, the Whigs' log cabin campaign blasted Democratic candidate Martin Van Buren for displays of refinement. Americans were clearly of two minds on the subject of learning. Nowhere was this ambivalence sharper than in the West. Westerners prided themselves on their rough ways, but eastern missionaries swarmed across the West to build not only lyceum halls but also academies and colleges. In 1800 there was only one college in what is now the Midwest; by 1850 there were nearly seventy, more than in any other region. Audiences flocked to listen to emissaries of eastern refinement.

The movement to popularize knowledge and art bridged the cultural gap between classes but never closed it. The popularization of culture carried a hidden price, as lyceum lecturers usually softened their ideas to avoid controversy. Even Emerson, whose early pronouncements on religion were controversial, pulled his punches on the lyceum circuit; his vagueness of style made it possible to quote him on both sides of most issues.

## CONCLUSION

Hailed as progressive and democratic, advances in technology transformed the lives of millions of Americans between 1840 and 1860. Mechanical reapers increased the food supply, steam power drove up productivity and income, and coal-burning stoves brought warmer homes and a better diet to millions of people. Even leisure felt the impact of technology, which brought down the cost of printing, stimulated the rise of the penny press and the dime novel, expanded the size of the reading public, and encouraged efforts to popularize knowledge.

The bright possibilities, rather than the dark potential, of technology impressed most antebellum Americans, but technology neither erased class and ethnic differences nor quieted a growing conflict between North and South. As the penny press and the telegraph spread, Americans discovered that speedier communication could not bridge their differences over slavery.

## CHRONOLOGY

1820  Washington Irving, *The Sketch Book*.

1823  Philadelphia completes the first urban water-supply system.

1826  Josiah Holbrook introduces the idea for lyceums. James Fenimore Cooper, *The Last of the Mohicans*.

1832  A cholera epidemic strikes the United States.

1833  The *New York Sun*, the first penny newspaper, is established.

1834  Cyrus McCormick patents the mechanical reaper.

1835  James Gordon Bennett establishes the *New York Herald*.

1837  Ralph Waldo Emerson, "The American Scholar."

1839  Edgar Allan Poe, "The Fall of the House of Usher."

1841  P. T. Barnum opens the American Museum.

1844  Samuel F. B. Morse patents the telegraph. The American Art Union is established.

1846  W. T. G. Morton successfully uses anesthesia.

1849  Second major cholera epidemic.

1850  Nathaniel Hawthorne, *The Scarlet Letter*.

1851  Hawthorne, *The House of the Seven Gables*. Herman Melville, *Moby-Dick*.

1853  Ten small railroads are consolidated into the New York Central Railroad.

1854  Henry David Thoreau, *Walden*.

1855  Walt Whitman, *Leaves of Grass*.

1857  Baltimore–St. Louis rail service completed.

## FOR FURTHER READING

Carl Bode, *The Anatomy of American Popular Culture, 1840–1861* (1959). A useful general survey.

Mary Kupiec Cayton, *Emerson's Emergence: Self and Society in the Transformation of New England* (1989). A sensitive interpretaion of the major figure in the American Renaissance.

William Cronon, *Chicago and the Great West* (1991). Analysis emphasizing environmental factors in the emergence of Chicago as the dominant city in the mid-nineteenth-century West.

Ann Douglas, *The Feminization of American Culture* (1977). An analysis of the role of the middle-class women and liberal ministers in the cultural sphere during the nineteenth century.

Siegfried Giedion, *Mechanization Takes Command* (1948). An interpretive overview of the impact of technology on Europe and America.

Barbara Novak, *Nature and Culture: American Landscape Painting, 1825–1875* (1982). An insightful study of the relationships between landscape painting and contemporary religious and philosophical currents.

Gwendolyn Wright, *Building the Dream: A Social History of Housing in America* (1981). An exploration of the ideologies and policies that have shaped American housing since Puritan times.

# CHAPTER 12

During winter 1831–1832 an intense debate over the future of slavery raged across Virginia. In part, the debate was a continuation of discussions begun during the Revolution; in part, it sprang from the anxieties created by an August 1831 slave insurrection led by Nat Turner. Virginians advanced various plans for the slaves' emancipation, and opponents of slavery, many of them nonslaveholders from western Virginia, briefly held the initiative. Slavery was denounced as "a mildew which has blighted in its course every region it has touched from the creation of the world."

The ultimate victory of proslavery forces in the Virginia legislature marked a point of no return in U.S. history. From this time on southern society increasingly diverged from the rest of the nation; the word *South* referred to a distinct political and economic region. The key to defining the South was the institution of slavery. Although slavery had been spread throughout all thirteen colonies, by the early 1830s it had been banned in every

## The Old South and Slavery, 1800–1860

King Cotton

&

Social Relations in the White South

&

Honor and Violence in the Old South

&

Life Under Slavery

&

The Emergence of
African-American Culture

(*Right*) **Charlotte Helen and Her Faithful Nurse, Lydia,** *1857*

249

northern state and outlawed in the entire British Empire. Opposition to slavery continued to intensify in the United States, Europe, and South America—but not in the South. As Senator James Buchanan of Pennsylvania observed in 1842, "All Christendom is leagued against the South upon the question of domestic slavery."

However, even within the South there existed profound divisions between the slaveholders, who were in the minority, and the nonslaveholders, who made up the majority of the population. Their common race, not slavery, bound them together. Similarly, major differences separated the Upper South (Virginia, North Carolina, Tennessee, and Arkansas) from the Lower South (South Carolina, Georgia, Florida, Alabama, Mississippi, Louisiana, and Texas). Nonetheless, the ties created by slavery powerfully bound the two Souths together.

African-Americans could do little to escape bondage directly. But they defied its most devastating effects indirectly by creating strong families (often extended to include nonblood members) and by undermining the system through sabotage and through the vitality of a distinctive black culture.

Slavery shaped and scarred all social relationships in the Old South: between blacks and whites, among whites, and even among blacks. Without slavery, there would never have been an Old South.

## King Cotton

In 1790 the South was essentially stagnant. Tobacco, its primary cash crop, had lost its economic

**Growth of Cotton Production and the Slave Population, 1790–1860**

*Cotton and slavery rose together in the Old South.*

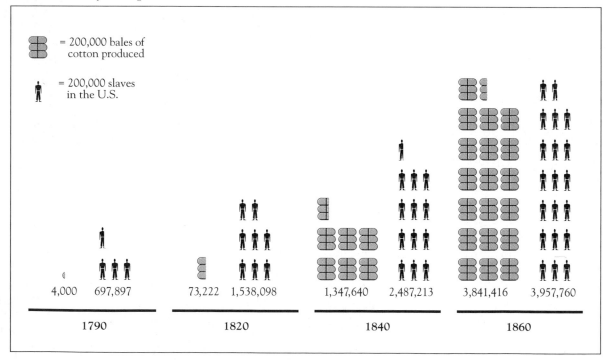

= 200,000 bales of cotton produced

= 200,000 slaves in the U.S.

| 1790 | | 1820 | | 1840 | | 1860 | |
|---|---|---|---|---|---|---|---|
| 4,000 | 697,897 | 73,222 | 1,538,098 | 1,347,640 | 2,487,213 | 3,841,416 | 3,957,760 |

vitality even as it had depleted the once-rich southern soils, and neither rice nor cotton could replace tobacco's economic importance. Three out of four southerners still lived along the Atlantic seaboard, specifically in the Chesapeake and the Carolinas. One of three resided in Virginia alone.

The contrast between that South and the dynamic South of 1850 was stunning. By 1850 southerners had moved south and west—now only one of seven southerners lived in Virginia—and cotton reigned as king, shaping this new South. The growth of the British textile industry had created a huge demand for cotton, while Indian removal had made way for southern expansion into the "Cotton Kingdom," a broad swath of land that stretched from South Carolina, Georgia, and northern Florida in the east through Alabama, Mississippi, central and western Tennessee, and Louisiana, and from there on to Arkansas and Texas.

## The Lure of Cotton

To the British traveler Basil Hall, southerners talked incessantly of cotton. "Every flow of wind from the shore wafted off the smell of that useful plant; at every dock or wharf we encountered it in huge piles or pyramids of bales, and our decks were soon choked with it. All day, . . . the captain, pilot, crew, and passengers were talking of nothing else." A warm climate, wet springs and summers, and relatively dry autumns made the Lower (or Deep) South ideal for cultivating cotton. A cotton farmer needed neither slaves nor cotton gins nor the capital required for sugar cultivation. Indeed, perhaps 50 percent of farmers in the "cotton belt" owned no slaves, and to process their harvest, they could turn to the widely available commercial gins. In short, cotton profited everyone; it promised to make poor men prosperous and rich men kings.

Yet large-scale cotton cultivation and slavery grew together as the southern slave population nearly doubled between 1810 and 1830. Three-fourths of all southern slaves worked in the cotton economy in 1830. Owning slaves enabled a planter

to harvest vast fields of cotton speedily, a crucial advantage because a sudden rainstorm at harvest time could pelt cotton to the ground and soil it.

Cotton offered an added advantage: it was compatible with corn production. Corn could be planted either earlier or later than cotton and harvested before or after. Because the cost of owning a slave remained the same regardless of whether he or she was working, corn production allowed slaveholders to shift slave labor between corn and cotton. By 1860 the acreage devoted to corn in the Old South actually *exceeded* that devoted to cotton. Economically, corn and cotton gave the South the best of two worlds. Intense demand in Britain and New England kept cotton prices high and money flowing into the South. Because of southern self-sufficiency in growing corn and raising hogs that thrived on the corn, money did not drain away to pay for food. In 1860 the twelve wealthiest counties in the United States were all in the South.

## Ties Between the Lower and Upper South

Two giant cash crops, sugar and cotton, dominated agriculture in the Lower South. The Upper South, a region of tobacco, vegetable, hemp, and wheat growers, depended far less on the great cash crops. Nevertheless, a common dependence on slavery unified the Upper and the Lower South and made the Upper South identify more with the Lower South than with the nation's free states.

A range of social, political, and psychological factors promoted this unity. First, many settlers in the Lower South had come from the Upper South. Second, all white southerners benefited from the Constitution's three-fifths clause, which let them count slaves as a basis for congressional representation. Third, abolitionist attacks on slavery stung all southerners and bound them together. Fourth, economic ties linked the two Souths. The profitability of cotton and sugar increased the value of slaves throughout the South. The sale of slaves from the declining plantation states of the Upper South to

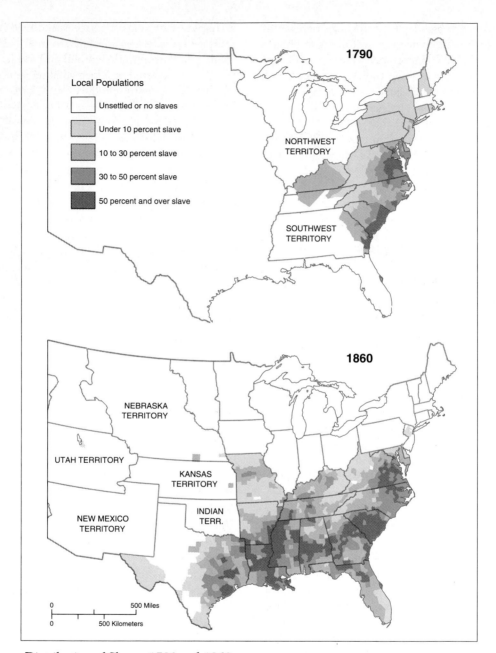

## Distribution of Slaves, 1790 and 1860

*In 1790 the majority of slaves resided along the southeastern seaboard. By 1860, however, slavery had spread throughout the South, and slaves were most heavily concentrated in the Deep South states.*

SOURCE: Reprinted with permission of the McGraw-Hill Companies, from *Ordeal by Fire: The Civil War and Reconstruction*, Second Edition, by James M. McPherson. Copyright © 1992 by the McGraw-Hill Companies.

the booming Lower South was a huge business. Eliminate the slave trade, one Virginian argued, and "Virginia will be a desert."

## The North and South Diverge: Economic Patterns

However, the changes responsible for the dynamic growth of the South widened the distance between it and the North. The South remained predominantly rural as the North became more and more urban.

Lack of industry kept the South rural; by 1850 it had one-third of the U.S. population but accounted for only a tenth of the nation's manufacturing. In 1850 the industrial output of the entire South was less than a third that of Massachusetts alone. Between 1840 and 1860 the southern share of capital invested in U.S. manufacturing actually *declined*, from 20 percent to 16 percent.

Some southerners advocated and created factories in the South, but they were a minority. By 1860 cotton-textile mills were scattered throughout the South, and Richmond boasted the nation's fourth-largest producer of iron products, the Tredegar Iron Works. Despite these successes, industrial output in the South trailed far behind that of the New England and Middle Atlantic states. Southern factories were small; they produced mainly for nearby markets, and they were closely tied to agriculture. While northern factories manufactured cloth and shoes, southern factories turned grain into flour, corn into meal, and trees into lumber.

Slavery posed a major obstacle to southern industrialization, but not because slaves were unfit for factories; the Tredegar Iron Works was among many factories that employed slaves. However, the prospect of industrial slavery troubled slaveholders. Away from the strict discipline and supervision possible on a plantation, slaves sometimes behaved as if they were free, shifting jobs, working overtime, and even negotiating better working conditions. A Virginia planter summed up whites' lamentations about urban, industrial slaves: they "got the habit of roaming about and *taking care of themselves*."

But the chief brake on southern industrialization was money, not labor. To raise the capital needed to build factories, planters would have had to sell their slaves. They seldom did. Cash crops such as cotton and sugar were proved, but the benefits of industrialization were remote and doubtful. Successful industrialization also would disrupt social relations, a southerner contended, by introducing "filthy, overcrowded, licentious factories" and attracting abolitionists. As long as southerners believed that the cash-crop economy remained profitable, they had little reason to plunge into the uncertainties of industrialization.

## The North and South Diverge: Education in a Cotton Economy

In education, as in industry, the South lagged behind the North. Where northerners recognized the benefits of an educated work force for their growing manufacturing economy, agriculturally oriented southerners rejected compulsory education and were reluctant to tax property to support schools. They abhorred the thought of educating slaves, and southern lawmakers made it a crime to teach slaves to read. For most whites, the only available schools were private. White illiteracy thus remained high in the South as it declined in the North.

Southern education trailed northern education for a number of reasons. As the southern states' revenues rose and fell with the fluctuating price of cotton, so did enthusiasm for public education. Low population density also impeded the expansion of southern education. Having a public school within walking distance of each child was virtually impossible. But the primary reason for the South's failure to develop effective public schools was widespread indifference. Agricultural, self-sufficient, and independent, the middling and poor whites of the South remained unconvinced of the need for public education. They had little dependency on the printed word, few complex commercial transactions, and infrequent dealings with urban people. Planters did not need an orderly and disciplined white work force; they already had a black one that they were determined to keep illiterate lest it acquire ideas about freedom.

### Cotton and Southern Progress

Because the South diverged so sharply from the North, outsiders often dismissed it as backward. A northern journalist wrote of white southerners in the 1850s, "They work little, and that little, badly; they earn little, they sell little; they buy little, and have little—very little—of the common comforts and consolations of civilized life."

But the South did not lack progressive features. By 1860 white per capita income in the South exceeded the national average. And although southerners lagged behind northerners in general technology, they did advance in the area that concerned them most: scientific agriculture.

Thus the Old South was not economically backward—it was merely different. Cotton was a wonderful crop, and southerners could hardly be blamed for making it their ruler. As a southern senator wrote in 1858, "You dare not make war upon cotton; no power on earth dares to make war upon it. Cotton is king."

# Social Relations in the White South

Antislavery northerners often charged that slavery warped the South's entire social structure. By creating a permanent black underclass of bond servants, they alleged, slavery robbed lower-class whites of the incentive to work, reduced them to shiftless misery, and rendered the South a premodern throwback in an otherwise progressive era. Southerners retorted that the real center of white inequality was the North, where merchants and financiers paraded in fine silks and never soiled their hands with manual labor.

In reality, the white South mixed aristocratic and democratic, premodern and modern features. Although the South featured considerable class inequality, property ownership was widespread. Rich planters dominated social life and the legislature, but they did not necessarily get their way, and often their political agenda paralleled that of other whites. Like white northerners, white southerners were restless, acquisitive, eager to make money, and skillful at managing complex commercial enterprises. Yet practices such as slaveholding and dueling thrived in the South when they were dying out elsewhere.

### The Social Groups of the White South

There was wide diversity within and between the South's slaveholding and nonslaveholding classes. Although some planters owned hundreds of slaves and lived lavishly, most lived more modestly. In 1860, one-fourth of all white families in the South owned slaves; nearly half of those owned fewer than five slaves, and three-fourths had fewer than ten slaves. Only 12 percent owned twenty or more slaves, and only 1 percent a hundred or more. Nonslaveholders were equally diverse. Most owned farms and drew on the labor of family members, but other whites squatted on land in the pine barrens or piney woods and scratched out a living by raising livestock, hunting, fishing, and planting a few acres of corn, oats, or sweet potatoes.

Planters, small slaveholders, family farmers, and pine-barrens folk composed the South's four main white groups. Many southerners—lawyers, physicians, merchants, and artisans—did not fall into any of these four, but they tended to identify their interests with one or another of the agricultural groups. Urban merchants and lawyers depended on the planters and shared their views on most issues, whereas rural artisans and merchants dealt with, and were thus attuned to, the family farmers, or yeomen.

### Planters and Plantation Mistresses

The plantation, with its porticoed mansion and fields teeming with slaves, stands at the center of the popular image of the Old South. This romanticized view, reinforced by novels and movies such as *Gone with the Wind,* is not entirely false, for the South did contain plantations that travelers found "superb beyond description." Abundant slaves and the division of labor they afforded, and plentiful land, allowed large plantations to generate incomes of $20,000 or more a year, an immense sum in those years.

In the eighteenth century during the initial flush of settlement in the piedmont and trans-Appalachian South, even well-off planters generally had lived in humble log cabins. After 1810, however, elite planters competed with one another to build stately mansions. Yet most planters counted their wealth not in grand mansions and elegant furnishings but in the value of their slaves. A field hand was worth as much as $1,700 in the 1850s, and few planters sold their slaves to buy furniture and silver plate.

But in their constant worry about profit, planters enjoyed neither repose nor security. High fixed costs—housing and feeding slaves, maintaining cotton gins, hiring overseers—led them to search for more and better land, higher efficiency, and greater self-sufficiency. Because cotton prices tended to fluctuate seasonally, planters often assigned their cotton to commercial agents in cities, who held the cotton until the price was right. The agents extended credit so that the planters could pay their bills before the cotton was sold. Indebtedness became part of the plantation economy and intensified the planters' quest for profitability. Psychological strains compounded economic worries. Frequent moves disrupted circles of friends and relatives, particularly as migration to the Southwest (Alabama and Mississippi) carried families into less settled, more desolate areas. Until 1850 this area was still the frontier.

Migration to the Southwest often deeply unsettled plantation women. They suddenly found themselves in frontier conditions with neither friends, neighbors, nor relatives nearby and surrounded by slaves. "I am sad tonight, sickness preys upon my frame," wrote a bride who moved to Mississippi in 1833. "I am alone and more than 150 miles from any near relatives in the wild woods of an Indian nation." Frequent absences by husbands, whether

**Ye Southern Planter, 1838**
*Although they aspired to be leisured gentlemen and live in mansions, most planters resided in modest dwellings and actively managed their estates.*

they were looking for new land, supervising outlying plantations, or conducting business in the city, intensified wives' loneliness.

Planters and their wives found various ways of coping with their isolation. Employing overseers to run the plantation, some lived in cities; in 1850 one-half the planters in the Mississippi Delta lived in New Orleans or Natchez. Most planters acted as their own overseers, however, and dealt with the problems of harsh living conditions by opening their homes to visitors. The responsibility for such hospitality fell heavily on wives, who might have to entertain as many as fifteen people for breakfast and attend to the needs of visitors who stayed for days. Plantation wives also bore the burdens of raising their children, supervising house slaves, making clothes and carpets, looking after smokehouses and dairies, planting gardens, and, often, keeping the plantation accounts. Plantation wives were anything but the delicate idlers of legend.

Among the heaviest sorrows of some plantation mistresses was the presence of mulatto children, constant reminders of their husbands' infidelities. Charlestonian Mary Boykin Chesnut, a famous diarist, observed tartly, "Any lady is ready to tell you who is the father of all the mulatto children in everybody's household but her own. These, she seems to think, drop from clouds." Southern men insisted on sexual purity for white women but allowed themselves a looser standard. The father of abolitionist sisters Sarah and Angelina Grimké fathered three mulatto children after his wife's death. The gentlemanly code usually tolerated such transgressions.

Yet isolation, drudgery, and humiliation did not turn planters' wives against the system. Indeed, when the Civil War came, they supported the Confederacy as enthusiastically as any group. However much they might have hated living as white islands in a sea of slaves, they recognized that their wealth and position depended on slavery.

## The Small Slaveholders

In 1860, 88 percent of all slaveholders owned fewer than twenty slaves, and most possessed fewer than

ten. One out of every five slaveholders worked outside of agriculture, as a lawyer, physician, merchant, or artisan.

Small slaveholders experienced conflicting loyalties and ambitions. In upland regions they absorbed the outlook of the more numerous yeomen (nonslaveowning small farmers); they owned only a few slaves and rarely aspired to become large planters. In contrast, in the plantation-dominated low country and delta regions, small slaveholders often aspired to planter status. There someone with ten slaves could realistically look forward to owning thirty. And ambitious, acquisitive individuals equated success with owning more slaves. The logic of slavery remained the same: the only way to justify the investment in slaves was to set them to work on profitable crops. Such crops demanded more and better land, and both the planters and the small slaveholders of the deltas were restless and footloose.

The social structure of the deltas was fluid. In the early antebellum period large planters had been reluctant to risk transporting their hundreds of valuable slaves in a still turbulent region. It was small slaveholders who led the initial westward push into the cotton belt in the 1810s and 1820s. Gradually, large planters, too, moved westward, buying up the land that the small slave owners had developed and turning the region from Vicksburg to Natchez into large plantations. Small slave owners took the profits from selling their land, bought more slaves, and moved on. They gradually transformed the region from Vicksburg to Tuscaloosa, Alabama, into a belt of medium-sized farms with a dozen or so slaves on each.

## The Yeomen

Nonslaveholding family farmers, or yeomen, composed the largest single group of southern whites. Most owned land, and many hired slaves to help at harvest. In areas of poor soil, such as eastern Tennessee, yeomen were typically subsistence farmers, but most yeomen grew some cash crops. Their landholdings were comparatively small, ranging from 50 to 200 acres. Yeomen generally inhabited uplands far from the rich coastal plains and deltas, such as the piedmont of the East or the hilly upcountry of the Southwest. Young, landless yeomen lived with and worked for relatives.

Above all, the yeomen valued self-sufficiency. Unlike planters, who were driven to acquire more land and to plant more cash crops, the yeomen devoted much of their acreage to subsistence crops such as corn, sweet potatoes, and oats. The planter's ideal was profit with modest self-sufficiency; the yeoman's goal, self-sufficiency with modest profit.

Yeomen living in planter-dominated regions were often dismissed as "poor white trash," but in the upland regions that they dominated, the yeomen were highly respected. Upland slaveholders tended to own only a few slaves; like the yeomen, they were essentially family farmers. With or without the aid of slaves, yeomen fathers and sons cleared the land and cultivated the fields. Wives and daughters planted and tended vegetable gardens, helped at harvest, occasionally cared for livestock, cooked, and made the family's clothes.

Unlike southern planters, yeomen marketed their cash crops locally, trading cotton, wheat, and tobacco for goods and services from nearby artisans and merchants. In some areas yeomen sold their surplus corn to drovers and herdsmen who specialized in raising hogs. Along the French Broad River in eastern Tennessee, for example, 20,000 to 30,000 hogs a year were fattened for market. At peak season a traveler would see 1,000 hogs a mile. The hogs were penned at night in huge stock stands—veritable hog hotels—and fed with corn supplied by the local yeomen.

## The People of the Pine Barrens

Independent whites of the wooded "pine barrens" were one of the most controversial groups in the Old South. About 10 percent of southern whites, they usually squatted on the land; put up crude cabins; cleared some acreage, where they planted corn between tree stumps; and grazed hogs and cattle in the woods. They neither raised cash crops nor en-

gaged in the daily routine of orderly work that characterized family farmers. With their ramshackle houses and handful of stump-strewn acres, they appeared lazy and shiftless.

Abolitionists cited the pine-barrens people as proof that slavery degraded whites, but southerners responded that, while the pine-barrens folk were poor, they could at least feed themselves, unlike the paupers of northern cities. In general, the people of the pine barrens were both self-sufficient and fiercely independent. Pine-barrens men were reluctant to hire themselves out as laborers to do "slave" tasks, and the women refused to become servants.

Neither victimized nor oppressed, these people generally lived in the pine barrens by choice. The grandson of a farmer who had migrated from Emanuel County, Georgia, to the Mississippi pine barrens explained his grandfather's decision: "The turpentine smell, the moan of the winds through the pine trees, and nobody within fifty miles of him, [were] too captivating . . . to be resisted, and he rested there."

## Conflict and Consensus in the White South

Planters tangled with yeomen on several issues. With extensive economic dealings and need for credit, planters inclined toward the Whig party, which generally supported economic development. The independent yeomen, cherishing their self-sufficiency, tended to be Democrats.

Yet few conflicts arose between these groups. An underlying political unity reigned in the South. Geography was in part responsible: planters, small slaveowners, yeomen, and pine-barrens folk tended to cluster in different regions, each independent of the others. In addition, with landownership widespread and factories sparse, few whites worked for other whites, and so friction among whites was minimized.

The white South's political structure was sufficiently democratic to prevent any one group from gaining exclusive control over politics. Planters dominated state legislatures, but they owed their election to the popular vote. And the democratic currents that had swept northern politics between 1815 and 1860 had affected the South as well; newer southern states entered the Union with democratic constitutions that included universal white manhood suffrage—the right of all adult white males to vote.

Although yeomen often voted for planters, the nonslaveholders did not give their elected representatives a blank check to govern as they pleased. During the 1830s and 1840s Whig planters who favored banks faced intense and often successful opposition from Democratic yeomen. These yeomen blamed banks for the Panic of 1837 and pressured southern legislatures to restrict bank operations. The nonslaveholders got their way often enough to nurture their belief that they, not the slaveholders, controlled politics.

## Conflict over Slavery

Nevertheless, considerable *potential* existed for conflict between slaveholders and nonslaveholders. The southern white carpenter who complained in 1849 that "unjust, oppressive, and degrading" competition from slave labor depressed his wages surely had a point. Between 1830 and 1860 the slaveholding class shrank in size in relation to the total white population, but its share of total wealth increased. As a Louisiana editor wrote in 1858, "The present tendency of supply and demand is to concentrate all the slaves in the hands of the few, and thus excite the envy rather than cultivate the sympathy of the people."

Yet although pockets of opposition dotted the South, slavery did not create profound or lasting divisions between slaveholders and nonslaveholders. For example, antagonism to slavery flourished in parts of Virginia up to 1860, but proposals for emancipating the slaves dropped from the state's political agenda after 1832. Kentucky had a history of antislavery activity dating back to the 1790s, but after calls for emancipation suffered a crushing defeat in an 1849 referendum, slavery ceased to be a political issue there.

The rise and fall of pro-emancipation sentiment in the South raises a key question: as most white southerners were non-slaveholders, why did they not attack slavery more consistently? To look ahead, why were so many southerners willing to fight ferociously and to die bravely during the Civil War in defense of an institution in which they apparently had no real stake? There are several reasons. First, some nonslaveholders hoped to become slaveholders. Second, most southerners accepted the racist assumptions on which slavery rested; they dreaded the likelihood that emancipation would encourage "impudent" blacks to entertain ideas of social equality with whites. Slavery appealed to whites as a legal, time-honored, and foolproof way to enforce the social subordination of blacks. Third, no one knew where the slaves, if freed, would go or what they would do. Colonizing freed blacks in Africa was unrealistic, southerners concluded, but they also believed that without colonization, emancipation would lead to a race war. In 1860 Georgia's governor sent a blunt message to his constituents, many of them nonslaveholders: "So soon as the slaves were at liberty thousands of them would leave the cotton and rice fields . . . and make their way to the healthier climate of the mountain region [where] we should have them plundering and stealing, robbing and killing."

## The Proslavery Argument

Between 1830 and 1860 southerners constructed a defense of slavery as a positive good rather than a necessary evil. St. Paul's injunction that servants obey their masters became a biblical justification for some. Others looked to the classical past to argue that slavery was both an ancient and classical institution; the slave society of Athens, they said, had produced Aristotle and Plato, and Roman slaveholders had laid the foundations of Western civilization. A third proslavery argument, advanced particularly by George Fitzhugh of Virginia, contrasted the plight of the northern "wage slaves," callously discarded when they became too ill or too old to work, with the lot of southern slaves, cared for by masters who attended to their health, their clothing, and their discipline.

At the same time, southerners increasingly suppressed any open discussion of slavery within the South. In the 1830s they seized abolitionist literature from southern mails and burned it. Although Kentucky abolitionist Cassius Marcellus Clay protected his press with two cannons, in 1845 a mob dismantled it anyway. By 1860 any southerner found with a copy of Hinton R. Helper's antislavery *The Impending Crises* might well fear for his life.

The rise of the proslavery argument coincided with a shift in the position of southern churches on slavery. During the 1790s and early 1800s some Protestant ministers had assailed slavery as immoral, but by the 1830s most clergymen had convinced themselves that slavery was both compatible with Christianity and necessary for the proper exercise of Christian religion. Slavery, they proclaimed, provided the opportunity to display Christian responsibility toward one's inferiors, and it helped African-Americans to develop Christian virtues such as humility and self-control. Southerners increasingly attacked antislavery evangelicals in the North for disrupting the "superior" social arrangement of the South. In 1837 southerners and conservative northerners had combined forces to drive antislavery New School Presbyterians out of that denomination's main body, in 1844 the Methodist Episcopal Church split into northern and southern wings, and in 1845 Baptists formed a separate Southern Convention. In effect, southern evangelicals seceded from national church organizations long before the South seceded from the Union.

# Honor and Violence in the Old South

Almost everything about the Old South struck northern visitors as extreme. Although inequality flourished in both the North and the South, no group was as deprived as southern slaves. Not only did northerners find the gap between the races in the South extreme, but also individual southerners seemed to run to extremes. One minute they were hospitable and gracious; the next, savagely violent. "The Americans of the South," Tocqueville wrote, "are brave, comparatively ignorant, hospitable, generous, easy to irritate, violent in their resentments, without industry or the spirit of enterprise."

## Violence in the White South

Throughout the colonial and antebellum periods, violence deeply colored the daily lives of white southerners. In the 1760s a minister described backcountry Virginians "biting one anothers Lips and Noses off, and gowging one another—that is, thrusting out anothers Eyes, and kicking one another on the Cods [genitals], to the great damage of many a Poor Woman." Gouging out eyes became a specialty of sorts among poor southern whites. On one occasion a South Carolina judge entered his court to find a plaintiff, a juror, and two witnesses all missing one eye. Stories of eye gougings and ear bitings became part of Old South folklore. Mike Fink, a legendary southern fighter and hunter, boasted that he was so mean in infancy that he refused his mother's milk and howled for whiskey. Yet beneath the folklore lay the reality of violence that gave the Old South a murder rate as much as ten times higher than that of the North.

## The Code of Honor and Dueling

At the root of most violence in the white South lay intensified feelings of personal pride that reflected the inescapable presence of slaves. White southerners saw slaves degraded, insulted, and powerless to resist. In turn, whites reacted violently to even trivial insults to demonstrate that they had nothing in common with slaves.

Among gentlemen this exaggerated pride took the form of a code of honor, with honor defined as an extraordinary sensitivity to one's reputation. Northern moralists celebrated a rival idea, character, the quality that enabled an individual to behave in steady fashion regardless of how others acted toward him or her. In the honor culture of the Old South, however, even the slightest insult, as long as it was perceived as intentional, could become the basis for a duel.

Formalized by French and British officers during the Revolutionary War, dueling gained a secure niche in the Old South as a means by which gentlemen dealt with affronts to their honor. Seemingly trivial incidents—a harmless brushing against the side of someone at a public event, a hostile glance—could trigger a duel. Yet dueling did not necessarily lead to violence. Gentlemen viewed dueling as a refined alternative to the random violence of lower-class life. Instead of leaping at his antagonist's throat, a gentleman remained cool, settled on a weapon with his opponent, and agreed to a meeting place. In the interval, friends of the parties negotiated to clear up the "misunderstanding" that had provoked the challenge. Most confrontations ended peaceably rather than on the field of honor at dawn.

Although dueling was as much a way of settling disputes peacefully as of ending them violently, the ritual could easily end in death or maiming. Dueling bypassed the court system, which would have guaranteed a peaceful result; in disputes involving honor, recourse to the law struck many southerners as cowardly and shameless.

Dueling rested on the assumption that gentlemen could recognize each other and know when to respond to a challenge. Nothing in the code of honor compelled a person to duel with someone who was not a gentleman, for such a person's opinion hardly mattered. An insolent porter who insulted a gentleman might get a whipping but did not merit a duel. Yet it was often difficult to determine who was a gentleman. Indeed, the Old South teemed with would-be gentlemen. A clerk in a country store in Arkansas in 1850 found it remarkable that ordinary farmers who hung around the store talked of their honor, and that the proprietor, a German Jew, carried a dueling pistol.

### The Southern Evangelicals and White Values

With its emphasis on the personal redress of grievances and its inclination toward violence, the ideal of honor conflicted with the values preached by the southern evangelical churches, notably the Baptists, Methodists, and Presbyterians. These denominations stressed humility and self-restraint, virtues that sharply contrasted with the culture of display that buttressed the extravagance and violence of the Old South.

Before 1830 most southern gentlemen looked down on the evangelicals as uncouth fanatics. But the evangelicals shed their backwoods image by founding colleges such as Randolph Macon and Wake Forest and by exhorting women (two-thirds of the average congregation) to make every home "a sanctuary, a resting place, a shadow from the heats, turmoils, and conflicts of life, and an effectual barrier against ambition, envy, jealousy, and selfishness." During the 1830s evangelical values and practices penetrated even the Episcopal church, long preferred by the gentry.

Southern evangelicals rarely attacked honor as such, but they condemned dueling, brawling, intemperance, and gambling. By the 1860s the South counted many gentlemen like the Bible-quoting Presbyterian general Thomas J. "Stonewall" Jackson, fierce in a righteous war but a sworn opponent of strong drink, gambling, and dueling.

## Life Under Slavery

Slavery, the institution at the root of the code of honor and other distinctive features of the Old South, has long inspired controversy among historians. Some have seen slavery as a benevolent institution in which African-Americans lived contentedly under kindly masters; others, as a brutal system that drove slaves into constant rebellion. Neither view is accurate, but both contain a germ of truth. There were kind masters, and some slaves developed genuine affection for their owners. Yet slavery inherently oppressed its African-American victims by forcibly appropriating their life and labor. Even kind masters exploited blacks in order to earn profits. And kindness was a double-edged sword; the benevolent master expected grateful affection from his slaves and interpreted that affection as loyalty to slavery itself. When northern troops descended on the plantations during the Civil War, masters were genuinely surprised and dismayed to find many of their most trusted slaves deserting to Union lines.

The kindness or cruelty of masters was important, but three other factors primarily determined slaves' experience: the kind of agriculture in which they worked, whether they resided in rural or urban areas, and what century they lived in. The experiences of slaves working on cotton plantations in the 1830s differed drastically from those of slaves in 1700, for reasons unrelated to the kindness or brutality of masters.

### The Maturing of the Plantation System

Slavery changed significantly between 1700 and 1830. In 1700 the typical slave was a man in his twenties, recently arrived from Africa or the Caribbean, who worked on an isolated small farm. Drawn from different regions of Africa, few slaves spoke the same language. Because slave ships carried twice as many men as women, and because slaves were widely scattered, blacks had difficulties finding partners and creating a semblance of family life. Severe malnutrition sharply limited the number of children slave women bore. Without continuing importations, the number of slaves in North America would have declined between 1710 and 1730.

In contrast, by 1830 the typical North American slave was as likely to be female as male, had been born in America, spoke English, and worked beside numerous other slaves on a plantation. The rise of plantation agriculture in the eighteenth century was at the heart of the change. Plantation slaves found mates more easily than slaves on scattered farms. The ratio between slave men and women fell into balance, and marriage between slaves on the same or nearby plantations increased. The native-born slave population soared after 1750. The importation of African slaves declined, and in 1808 Congress banned it.

### Work and Discipline of Plantation Slaves

In 1850 the typical slave worked on a large farm or plantation with at least ten other slaves. Almost three-quarters of all slaves belonged to masters with ten or more slaves, and just over one-half lived in units of twenty or more slaves. Thus understanding the life of a typical slave requires examining plantation routines.

An hour before sunrise, a horn or a bell awakened the slaves. After a sparse breakfast, they marched to the fields. A traveler in Mississippi described such a procession: "First came, led by an old driver carrying a whip, forty of the largest and strongest women I ever saw together; they were all in a simple uniform dress of bluish check stuff, the skirts reaching little below the knee; their legs and feet were bare; they carried themselves loftily, each having a hoe over the shoulder, and walking with a free, powerful swing." The plow hands followed, "thirty strong, mostly men, but few of them women. . . . A lean and vigilant white overseer, on a brisk pony, brought up the rear."

Slave men and women worked side by side in the fields. Those female slaves who did not labor in the fields remained busy. A former slave, John Curry, described how his mother milked cows, cared for children whose mothers worked in the fields, cooked for field hands, washed and ironed for her master's household, and looked after her own seven children. Plantations never lacked tasks for slaves of either gender. As former slave Solomon Northup noted, "Ploughing, planting, picking cotton, gathering the corn, and pulling and burning stalks, occupies the whole of the four seasons of the year. Drawing and cutting wood, pressing cotton, fattening and killing hogs, are but incidental labors." In any season the slave's day stretched from dawn to dusk. When darkness made field work impossible, slaves toted cotton bales to the ginhouse, gathered wood for supper fires, and fed the mules. Weary from their labors, they slept in log cabins on wooden planks.

Although virtually all antebellum Americans worked long hours, no others experienced the combination of long hours and harsh discipline that slave field hands endured. Northern factory workers did not live in fear of drivers walking among them with a whip. Repulsive brutality pervaded American

**African-American Women and Men on a Trek Home, South Carolina**
*Much like northern factories, large plantations made it possible to impose discipline and order on their work force. Here African-American women loaded down with cotton join their men on the march home after a day in the fields.*

slavery. For example, pregnant slave women were sometimes forced to lie in depressions in the ground and endure whipping on their backs, a practice that supposedly protected the fetus while abusing the mother. Masters often delegated discipline and punishment to white overseers and black drivers. The barbaric discipline meted out by others twinged the consciences of many masters, but most justified it as their Christian duty to ensure the slaves' proper "submissiveness." Frederick Douglass recalled that his worst master had been converted at a Methodist camp meeting. "If religion had any effect on his character at all," Douglass related, "it made him more cruel and hateful in all his ways."

Despite the system's brutality, some slaves advanced—not to freedom but to semiskilled or skilled indoor work. Some became blacksmiths, carpenters, or gin operators, and others served as cooks, butlers, and dining-room attendants. These house slaves became legendary for their disdain of field hands and poor whites. Slave artisans and house slaves generally enjoyed higher status than the field

hands. But legend often distorted reality, for house slaves were as subject to discipline as field hands.

### Slave Families

Masters thought of slaves as naturally promiscuous and flattered themselves into thinking that they alone held slave marriages together. Masters had powerful incentives to encourage slave marriages: bringing new slaves into the world and discouraging slaves from running away. James Henry Hammond, governor of South Carolina and a large slaveholder, noted in his diary how he "flogged Joe Goodwyn and ordered him to go back to his wife. Ditto Gabriel and Molly and ordered them to come together."

This picture of benevolent masters holding together promiscuous slaves is misleading. Slavery itself posed the keenest challenge to slave families. The law provided neither recognition of nor protection for the slave family. Masters reluctant to break slave marriages by sale could neither bequeath their reluctance to heirs nor avoid economic hardship that might force them to sell slaves. The reality, one historian has calculated, was that on average a slave would see eleven family members sold during his or her lifetime.

Inevitably, the buying and selling of slaves disrupted attempts to create a stable family life. Poignant testimony to the effects of sale on slave families appeared in advertisements for runaway slaves. An 1851 North Carolina advertisement said that a particular fugitive was probably "lurking in the neighborhood of E. D. Walker's, at Moore's Creek, who owns most of his relatives, or Nathan Bonham's who owns his mother; or perhaps, near Fletcher Bell's, at Long Creek, who owns his father." Small wonder that a slave preacher pronounced a couple married "until death or *distance* do you part."

Other factors disrupted slave marriages. The marriage of a slave woman did not protect her against the sexual demands of her master or, indeed, of any white. Slave children of white masters sometimes became targets for the wrath of white mistresses. Sarah Wilson, the daughter of a slave and her white master, remembers that as a child she was "picked on" by her mistress until the master ordered his wife to let Sarah alone because she "got big, big blood in her." Field work kept slave mothers from their children, who were cared for by the elderly or by the mothers of other children.

Despite these enormous obstacles, relationships within slave families were often intimate and, where possible, long lasting. Lacking legal protection, slaves developed their own standards of family morality. A southern white woman observed that slaves "did not consider it wrong for a girl to have a child before she married, but afterwards were extremely severe upon anything like infidelity on her part." Given the opportunity, slaves solemnized their marriages before members of the clergy. White clergymen who accompanied Union armies into Mississippi and Louisiana during the Civil War conducted thousands of marriage rites for slaves who had long viewed themselves as married and desired a formal ceremony and registration.

Broad kinship patterns—close ties between children and grandparents, aunts, and uncles as well as parents—had marked West African cultures, and they were reinforced by the separation of children and parents that routinely occurred under slavery. Frederick Douglass never knew his father and saw his mother rarely, but he vividly remembered his grandmother. In addition, slaves often created "fictive" kin networks, naming friends as their uncles, aunts, brothers, or sisters. In this way they helped to protect themselves against the disruption of family ties and established a broader community of obligation. When plantation slaves greeted each other as "brother," they were not making a statement about actual kinship but about obligations to each other.

## The Longevity, Health, and Diet of Slaves

Of the 10 million to 12 million Africans imported to the New World between the fifteenth and nineteenth centuries, North America received only 550,000 of them (about 5 percent), whereas Brazil received 3.5 million (nearly 33 percent). Yet by 1825, 36 percent of all slaves in the Western Hemisphere lived in the United States, and only 31 percent in Brazil. The reason for this difference is that slaves in the United States reproduced faster and lived longer than those in Brazil and elsewhere in the Western Hemisphere.

Several factors account for U.S. slaves' longer lives and higher rates of reproduction. First, with the gender ratio among slaves equalizing more rapidly in North America, slaves there married earlier and had more children. Second, because raising corn and livestock was compatible with growing cotton, the Old South produced plentiful food. Slaves generally received a peck of cornmeal and three to four pounds of fatty pork a week, which they often supplemented with vegetables grown on small plots and with catfish and game.

Slaves enjoyed greater immunity from malaria and yellow fever than whites but suffered more from cholera, dysentery, and diarrhea. Lacking privies, slaves usually relieved themselves behind bushes, and consequently urine and feces contaminated the sources of their drinking water. Slave remedies for stomach ailments, though commonly ridiculed by whites, often worked. For example, slaves ate white clay to cure dysentery and diarrhea. We now know that white clay contains kaolin, a remedy for these disorders.

Nonetheless, slaves experienced a higher mortality rate than whites. The very young suffered most; infant mortality among slaves was double that among whites, and one in three African-American children died before age ten. Plantations in the disease-ridden lowlands had the worst overall mortality rates, but overworked field hands often miscarried or bore weakened infants even in healthier areas.

### Slaves off Plantations

Greater freedom from supervision and greater opportunities awaited slaves who worked off plantations in towns and cities. Most southern whites succumbed to the lure of cotton and established small farms; the resulting shortage of white labor created a steady demand for slaves outside the plantation economy. Driving wagons, working as stevedores on the docks, manning river barges, and toiling in mining and lumbering gave slaves an opportunity to work somewhere other than the cotton fields. Other African-Americans served as engineers for sawmills or artisans for ironworks. African-American women and children constituted the main labor force for the South's fledgling textile industry.

The draining of potential white laborers from southern cities also provided opportunity for slaves to become skilled artisans. In the eighteenth century Charleston, Savannah, and other cities had a large class of highly skilled slave blacksmiths and carpenters, and the tradition endured into the nineteenth century. Slave or free, blacks found it easier to pursue skilled occupations in southern cities than in northern ones, where immigrant laborers competed with blacks for work.

Despite slavery's stranglehold, urban African-Americans in the South enjoyed opportunities denied their counterparts in the North. Generally, slaves who worked in factories, mining, or lumbering were hired out by their masters rather than owned by their employers. If working conditions for hired-out slaves deteriorated badly, masters would refuse to provide employers with more slaves. Consequently, working conditions for slaves off the plantation generally stayed at a tolerable level. Watching workers load cotton onto a steamboat, Frederick Law Olmsted was amazed to see slaves sent to the top of the bank to roll the bales down to Irishmen who stowed them on the ship. Asking the reason for this arrangement, Olmsted was told, "The niggers are worth too much to be risked here; if the Paddies [Irish] are knocked overboard, or get their backs broke, nobody loses anything."

### Life on the Margin: Free Blacks in the Old South

Free blacks were likelier than southern blacks in general to live in cities. In 1860 one-third of the free blacks in the Upper South and more than half in the Lower South were urban.

Urban specialization allowed free blacks the chance to become carpenters, coopers (barrel makers), barbers, and small traders. Most of the meat, fish, and produce in an antebellum southern market was prepared for sale by free blacks. Urban free blacks formed their own fraternal orders and churches; in New Orleans free blacks also had their own opera and literary journals. In Natchez a free black barber, William Tiler Johnson, invested profits from his shop in real estate, acquired stores that he rented out, and bought a plantation and slaves.

Despite such successes, free blacks were vulnerable in southern society. They continued to increase in absolute numbers (a little more than 250,000 free people of color lived in the South in 1860), but the rate of growth of the free black population slowed radically after 1810. Fewer masters freed their slaves after that time, and following the Nat Turner rebellion in 1831, states legally restricted the liberties of free blacks. Every southern state forbade free blacks to enter, and in 1859 Arkansas ordered all free blacks to leave.

Although a free-black culture flourished in certain cities, that culture did not reflect the conditions under which the majority of blacks lived. Most free blacks dwelled in rural areas, where whites lumped them together with slaves, and a much higher percentage of blacks were free in the Upper South than in the Lower South.

Many free blacks were mulattos, the product of white masters and black women, and looked down on "darky" field hands and laborers. But as discrimination against free people of color intensified during the late antebellum period, many free blacks realized that whatever future they had was as blacks, not whites. Feelings of racial solidarity increased during the 1850s, and after the Civil War, the leaders of the ex-slaves were usually blacks who had been free before the war.

## Slave Resistance

Fear of slave insurrection haunted the Old South. In lowland and delta plantation areas slaves often outnumbered whites. In the cities free blacks could have provided leadership for rebellions. Rumors of slave conspiracies flew within the southern white community, and all whites knew of the massive black revolt that had destroyed French rule in Santo Domingo.

Yet only three organized rebellions occurred in the Old South during the nineteenth century. Taken together, they say more about the futility than the possibility of slave rebellion. In 1800 the Virginia slave Gabriel Prosser's planned rebellion was betrayed by other slaves, and Prosser and his followers were executed. That same year Denmark Vesey, a South Carolina slave, used $1,500 won in a lottery to buy his freedom. Purchasing a carpentry shop in Charleston, Vesey preached at the city's African Methodist Episcopal church and built a sizable African-American following. In 1822 he and his loyalists devised a plan to attack Charleston and seize the city's arms and ammunition; betrayed by other slaves, they were captured and executed.

The Nat Turner rebellion, which occurred in 1831 in Southampton County, Virginia, was the only slave insurrection to lead to white deaths. Gloomy and introspective by nature, the slave Nat Turner taught himself to read and write in childhood. He became an electrifying preacher and gained a reputation for prophecy, including visions of white and black angels warring in the sky. For all his gifts, Turner's life as a field hand was onerous, and the sale of his wife reminded him that whites measured him only by his cash value.

In 1831 Turner's anger over slavery's injustice boiled over. In August he and a handful of slaves set out, armed with axes and clubs. Gathering recruits as they moved from plantation to plantation, Turner and his followers killed all whites whom they encountered, men, women, and children alike. Before the rebellion was suppressed, fifty-five whites and more than a hundred blacks had died.

Turner's rebellion stunned the South. Coupled with the slave uprising of the 1790s on Santo Domingo, it convinced white southerners that a slave insurrection constituted an ever-present threat. Yet the Nat Turner rebellion, like the Prosser and Vesey conspiracies, never had a chance of success. During the Turner rebellion several slaves alerted their masters to the threat, less from loyalty than from a correct assessment of Turner's chances. Despite constant fears of slave rebellion, the Old South experienced far fewer threats than the Caribbean or South America.

Several factors explain this apparent tranquillity. First, although slaves formed a majority in South Carolina and a few other areas, they did not constitute a *large* majority in any state. Second, unlike Caribbean slave owners, most southern masters lived on their plantations; they possessed armed force and were willing to use it. Third, family ties among U.S. slaves made them reluctant to risk death and thereby to orphan their children. Finally, slaves who ran away or plotted rebellion had no allies. Southern Indians routinely captured runaway slaves and claimed rewards for them; some Indians even owned slaves.

Unable to rebel, many slaves tried to escape to freedom in the North. Some light mulattos who passed as whites succeeded. More often, slaves borrowed, stole, or forged passes from plantations or obtained papers describing them as free. Frederick Douglass borrowed a sailor's papers to make his escape from Baltimore to New York City. Some former slaves, including Harriet Tubman and Josiah Henson, returned to the South to assist others to escape. Despite legends of an "Underground Railroad" of abolitionists helping slaves to freedom, fugitive slaves owed little to abolitionists. The "safe houses" of white sympathizers in border states were better known to slave catchers than to runaways. Probably fewer than a thousand slaves actually escaped to the North.

Despite poor prospects for permanent escape, slaves could disappear for prolonged periods into the free-black communities of southern cities. Slaves enjoyed a fair degree of practical freedom to drive wagons to market and to come and go when they were off plantations. Slaves sent to a city might overstay their leave and pass themselves off as free. This kind of practical freedom did not change slavery's underlying oppressiveness, but it did give slaves a sense of having certain rights, and it helped to channel slave resistance into activities that were furtive and relatively harmless rather than open and violent. Theft, for example, was so common that planters kept tools, smokehouses, and closets under lock and key. Overworked field hands might leave tools out to rust, feign illness, or simply refuse to work. Slaves could not be fired for such malingering or negligence. And Frederick Law Olmsted even found masters afraid to punish a slave "lest [he or she] should abscond, or take a sulky fit and not work, or poison some of the family, or set fire to the dwelling." Indeed, not all furtive resistance was harmless. Arson and poisoning, both common forms of vengeance in African culture, flourished in the Old South. So did fear. Masters afflicted by dysentery never knew for sure that they had not been poisoned.

Arson, poisoning, theft, work stoppage, and negligence acted as alternatives to violent rebellion, but their goal was not freedom. Their object was merely to make slavery bearable. Most slaves would have preferred freedom but settled for less. "White folks do as they please," an ex-slave said, "and the darkies do as they can."

# The Emergence of African-American Culture

Enslaved blacks combined elements of African and American culture to create a distinctive culture of their own.

## *The Language and Religion of Slaves*

Before slaves could develop a common culture, they needed a common language. During the colonial period African-born slaves, speaking a variety of languages, had developed a "pidgin"—that is, a language that has no native speakers but in which people with different native languages can communicate. Many African-born slaves spoke English pidgin poorly, but their American-born descendants used it as their primary language.

Like all pidgins, English pidgin was a simplified language. Slaves usually dropped the verb *to be* (which had no equivalent in African tongues) and ignored or confused genders. Instead of saying "Mary is in the cabin," they typically said, "Mary, he in cabin." They substituted *no* for *not,* as in "He no wicked." Some African words, among them *banjo,* moved from pidgin to standard English, and others, such as *goober* (peanut), entered southern white slang. Although many whites ridiculed pidgin, and black house servants struggled to speak standard English, pidgin proved indispensable for communication among slaves.

Religion played an equally important role in forging an African-American culture. Africa contained rich and diverse religious customs and beliefs. Despite the presence of a few Muslims and Christians in the early slave population, most of the slaves brought from Africa followed one of many native African religions. Most of these religions drew little distinction between the spiritual and natural worlds—storms, illnesses, and earthquakes were all assumed to stem from supernatural forces. God, spirits that inhabited woods and waters, and ancestor spirits all constituted these supernatural forces. The religions of West Africa, the region where most American slaves originated, attached special significance to water, which suggested life and hope.

However, African religions did not unify American slaves. African religions differed greatly, and the majority of slaves in the colonial period were young men who had not absorbed this religious heritage. Remnants of African religion remained, however, in part because before the 1790s whites made few attempts to convert slaves to Christianity. When whites' conversion efforts increased, dimly remembered African beliefs such as the reverence for water may have aided Christian missionaries in influencing slaves to accept Christianity and to undergo baptism. Evangelical Christianity, like African religions, drew few distinctions between the sacred and the worldly. Just as Africans believed that droughts and plagues resulted from supernatural forces, revivalists knew in their hearts that every drunkard who fell off his horse and every Sabbath breaker struck by lightning had experienced a deliberate, direct punishment from God.

By the 1790s African-Americans formed about a quarter of the membership of the Methodist and Baptist denominations. The fact that converted slaves played significant roles in the South's three slave rebellions reinforced whites' fears that a Christian slave would be a rebellious slave. These slave uprisings, especially the Nat Turner rebellion, spurred Protestant missionaries to intensify their efforts among slaves. They pointed to the self-taught Turner as proof that slaves could learn about Christianity and claimed that only organized efforts at conversion would ensure that the slaves were taught correct versions of Christianity. After Methodists, Baptists, and Presbyterians split into northern and southern wings, missionaries argued that it was safe to convert slaves, for the southern churches had rid themselves of antislavery elements. Between 1845

and 1860 the number of African-American Baptists doubled.

Christian blacks' experience in the Old South illustrates the contradictions of life under slavery. Urban blacks often had their own churches, but rural blacks and slaves worshipped in the same churches as whites. Although African-Americans sat in segregated sections, they heard the same service as whites. Churches became the most interracial institutions in the Old South, and biracial churches sometimes disciplined whites for abusing black Christian members. But Christianity was not a route to black liberation. Ministers went out of their way to remind slaves that spiritual equality was not the same as civil equality. The conversion of slaves succeeded only to the extent that it did not challenge the basic inequality of southern society.

However, slaves listening to the same sermons as whites often came to different conclusions. For example, slaves drew parallels between their captivity and that of the Jews, the Chosen People. Like the Jews, slaves concluded, they were "de people of de Lord." If they kept the faith, they would reach the Promised Land.

"The Promised Land" could refer to Israel, to heaven, or to freedom. Whites agreed that Israel and heaven were the only permissible meanings, but some African-Americans thought of freedom as well. Many plantations had black preachers, slaves trained by white ministers to spread Christianity among blacks. In the presence of masters or ministers, African-American preachers repeated the familiar biblical command "Obey your master." Often, however, slaves met for services apart from whites, and then the message changed.

Some slaves privately interpreted Christianity as a religion of liberation, but most recognized that their prospects for freedom were slight. Generally, Christianity neither turned blacks into revolutionaries nor made them model slaves. It did provide slaves with a view of slavery different from their masters' outlook. Masters argued that slavery was a benign and divinely ordained institution, but Christianity told slaves that the institution was an afflic-

**The Banjo Lesson,**
*by Henry O. Tanner, c. 1893*
*Tanner, a black artist, captured African-Americans' rich musical traditions and close family bonds in this evocative painting. Africans brought the banza, or banjo, to the Americas.*

tion, a terrible and unjust system that God had allowed in order to test their faith. For having endured slavery, he would reward slaves. For having created it, he would punish masters.

## African-American Music and Dance

African-American culture expressed blacks' feelings. Long after white rituals had grown sober and sedate, the congregation in African-American religious services shouted, "Amen" and let their body movements reflect their feelings. Slaves also expressed their emotions in music and dance. Southern law forbade them to own "drums, horns, or other loud instruments, which may call together or give sign or notice to one another of their wicked designs and intentions." Instead, slaves made rhythmical clapping, called "patting juba," an indispensable accompaniment to dancing. Slaves also played an African instrument, the banjo, and beat tin buckets as substitutes for drums. Slave music was tied to bodily movement; slaves expressed themselves in a dance African in origin, emphasizing shuffling steps and bodily contortions rather than quick footwork and erect backs as in whites' dances.

Whether at work or prayer, slaves liked to sing. Work songs usually consisted of a leader's chant and a choral response. Masters encouraged such songs, believing that singing induced slaves to work harder and that the innocent content of work songs proved that slaves were happy. However, Frederick Douglass, recalling his own past, observed that "slaves sing most when they are most unhappy. The songs of the slave represent the sorrows of his heart; and he is relieved by them, only as an aching heart is relieved by its tears."

African-Americans also sang religious songs, later known as spirituals, which reflected the powerful emphasis that slave religion placed on deliverance from earthly travails. Whites took a dim view of spirituals and tried to make slaves sing "good psalms and hymns" instead of "the extravagant and nonsensical chants, and catches, and hallelujah songs of their own composing." But enslaved blacks clung to their spirituals, drawing hope from them that "we will soon be free, when the Lord will call us home," as one spiritual promised.

## CONCLUSION

The emergence of an African-American culture was one of many features that made the Old South distinctive. With its huge black population, plantation slavery, lack of industries, and scattered white population, the South seemed a world apart to antebellum northerners, who were convinced that slavery had cut the South off from progress and turned it into "sterile land, and bankrupt estates." Southerners, for their part, believed that their agricultural base was far more sta-

ble than northern industry. Southerners portrayed slavery as a time-honored and benevolent response to the natural inequality of the black race and believed that their slaves were content. In reality, however, few slaves accepted slavery. African-Americans resisted slavery covertly, by sabotage or poison, rather than openly, by escape or rebellion. The Christianity that whites used to justify slavery taught slaves the injustice of human bondage.

## CHRONOLOGY

**1790s** Methodists and Baptists start to make major strides in converting slaves to Christianity.

**1793** Eli Whitney invents the cotton gin.

**1800** Gabriel Prosser leads a slave rebellion in Virginia.

**1808** Congress prohibits external slave trade.

**1816–1819** Boom in cotton prices stimulates settlement of the Southwest.

**1822** Denmark Vesey's conspiracy is uncovered in South Carolina.

**1831** William Lloyd Garrison starts *The Liberator*. Nat Turner leads a slave rebellion in Virginia.

**1832** Virginia legislature narrowly defeats a proposal for gradual emancipation.

**1837** Economic panic begins, lowering cotton prices.

**1844–1845** Methodist and Baptist churches split over slavery into northern and southern wings.

**1849** Sugar production in Louisiana reaches its peak.

**1849–1860** Period of high cotton prices.

## FOR FURTHER READING

John B. Boles, *Black Southerners, 1619–1869* (1983). An excellent synthesis of scholarship on slavery.

Wilbur J. Cash, *The Mind of the South* (1941). A brilliant interpretation of southern history.

Bruce Collins, *White Society in the Antebellum South* (1985). A very good, brief synthesis of southern white society and culture.

William J. Cooper, *Liberty and Slavery: Southern Politics to 1860* (1983). A valuable synthesis and interpretation of recent scholarship on the antebellum South in national politics.

Robert W. Fogel, *Without Consent or Contract: The Rise and Fall of American Slavery* (1989). A comprehensive reexamination of the slaves' productivity and welfare.

Robert W. Fogel and Stanley L. Engerman, *Time on the Cross: The Economics of American Negro Slavery* (1974). A controversial book that uses mathematical models to analyze the profitability of slavery. (Fogel won the Nobel Prize in Economics in 1993.)

Lacy K. Ford, *Origins of Southern Radicalism: The South Carolina Upcountry, 1800–1860* (1988). An important recent study that underscores the commitment of poorer whites in the hill regions to their personal independence and to widespread property ownership.

Eugene D. Genovese, *Roll, Jordan, Roll: The World the Slaves Made* (1974). The most influential work on slavery in the Old South written during the last twenty-five years; a penetrating analysis of the paternalistic relationship between masters and slaves.

Peter Kolchin, *Unfree Labor: American Slavery and Russian Serfdom* (1987). A comparative study that sets American slavery within the context of unfree labor in the early nineteenth century.

James Oakes, *The Ruling Race: A History of American Slaveholders* (1982). An important attack on the ideas of Eugene D. Genovese.

James Oakes, *Slavery and Freedom: An Interpretation of the Old South* (1990). A study stressing slavery's development in the context of liberal capitalism.

U. B. Phillips, *American Negro Slavery* (1918) and *Life and Labor in the Old South* (1929). Works marred by racial prejudice but containing a wealth of information about slavery and the plantation system.

Kenneth M. Stampp, *The Peculiar Institution: Slavery in the Antebellum South* (1956). A standard account of the African-American experience under slavery.

# CHAPTER 13

"A mericans regard this continent as their birthright," thundered Sam Houston, the first president of the Republic of Texas, in 1847. Indeed, antebellum Americans widely believed that God had ordained the spread of their civilization, progressive and unique, from ocean to ocean. Indians and Mexicans must make way "for our mighty march," Houston concluded.

This was not idle talk. In less than 1,000 fevered days during President James K. Polk's administration (1845–1849), the United States doubled its land area through annexation, negotiation, and war. Meanwhile, immigrants poured in. The push and pull of expansion and immigration were closely intertwined, and most immigrants gravitated to the expansionist Democratic party.

The benefits of expansion emerged as an article of faith among most antebellum Americans. Opening new lands to settlement, the thinking went, would create more yeoman farmers, and the Jeffersonian ideal of the United States as a nation of

*Immigration, Expansion, and Sectional Conflict, 1840–1848*

**Newcomers and Natives**

℘

**The West and Beyond**

℘

**The Politics of Expansion**

*(Right) California Forty-Niner, c. 1850*

self-sufficient farmers would be recaptured. Westward expansion would reduce sectional strife as well. Such optimism was unfounded. By 1850 expansion would heat sectional antagonisms to the boiling point, split the Democratic party, and set the nation on the path to the Civil War.

# Newcomers and Natives

Between 1815 and 1860, 5 million European immigrants reached the United States. Of these, 4.2 million arrived between 1840 and 1860, and 3 million crowded in just from 1845 to 1854, the largest immigration relative to population in U.S. history. The Irish and the Germans dominated this wave of newcomers; by 1860 three-fourths of foreign-born Americans were Irish or German.

## Expectations and Realities

Although a desire for religious freedom drew some immigrants to U.S. shores, hopes of economic betterment lured the majority. Travelers' accounts and relatives' letters assured Europeans that America was an ideal world, a utopia. Yet typically, emigrants faced hard times. Because ships sailed irregularly, many were forced to spend their small savings in waterfront slums while awaiting departure. Squalid cargo ships carried most of the emigrants, who endured wretched conditions in quarters as crowded as those of slave ships.

But for many, the greatest shock came after landing. In the depression years of the 1840s, immigrants quickly discovered that farming in America was a perilous prospect, radically different from what they had known in Europe. Unlike the compact farming communities of Europe, American agricultural areas featured scattered farms, and Americans' individualism led them to speculate in land and to move frequently.

Clear patterns emerged amid the shocks and dislocations of immigration. For example, most Irish immigrants lacked the capital to purchase land and consequently crowded into urban areas of New England, New York, New Jersey, and Pennsylvania, where they could find jobs. German immigrants often arrived at southern ports, but slavery, climate, and lack of economic opportunity gradually drove them north to settle in Illinois, Ohio, Wisconsin, and Missouri.

Cities, rather than farms, attracted most antebellum immigrants; by 1860 German and Irish newcomers constituted half or more of the population of St. Louis, New York, Chicago, Cincinnati, Milwaukee, Detroit, and San Francisco. These fast-growing cities needed people with strong backs willing to work for low wages. Irish construction gangs built the houses, streets, and aqueducts that were changing the face of urban America and dug the canals and railroads that linked these cities. In addition to jobs, cities provided immigrants with the community life lacking in farming areas.

## The Germans

In 1860 there was no German nation-state, only a collection of principalities and kingdoms. Immigrants from this area thought of themselves as Bavarians, Westphalians, or Saxons, not Germans. They included Catholics, Protestants, Jews, and freethinkers who denounced all religions.

German immigrants spanned a wide spectrum of class and occupation. Most were farmers, but professionals, artisans, and tradespeople made up a sizable minority. For example, Levi Strauss, a Jewish tailor from Bavaria, reached the United States in 1847. When gold was discovered in California the next year, Strauss gathered rolls of cloth and sailed for San Francisco. There he fashioned tough work overalls from canvas. Demand soared, and Strauss opened a factory to produce his cheap overalls, later known as blue jeans or Levi's.

A common language transcended the differences among German immigrants and bound them together. They clustered in the same neighborhoods, formed their own militia and fire companies, and established German-language parochial schools and newspapers. The diversity of the German-speaking population further fostered solidarity. Because Germans supplied their own lawyers, doctors, teachers, and merchants from their midst, they had no need to go outside their neighborhoods. Native-born Americans simultaneously admired German industriousness and resented German self-sufficiency, which they interpreted as clannishness. In a vicious cycle, the Germans responded by becoming even more clannish. In effect, they isolated themselves from gaining the political influence that Irish immigrants acquired.

## The Irish

There were three waves of Irish immigration. Between 1815 and the mid-1820s, most Irish immigrants were Protestants, small landowners and tradespeople drawn by enthusiastic veterans of the War of 1812 who reported that America was a paradise where "all a man needed was a gun and sufficient ammunition to be able to live like a prince." From the mid-1820s to the mid-1840s, Irish immigration became both more Catholic and poorer, primarily comprising tenant farmers evicted by Protestant landlords as "superfluous." Rich or poor, Protestant or Catholic, nearly a million Irish crossed the Atlantic to the United States between 1815 and 1845.

Then, between 1845 and the early 1850s the character of Irish immigration changed dramatically. In Ireland blight destroyed harvest after harvest of potatoes, virtually the only food of the peasantry, and triggered one of the most gruesome famines in history. The Great Famine killed a million people. Those who survived, a landlord wrote, were "famished and ghastly skeletons." To escape suffering and death, 1.8 million Irish migrated to the United States in the decade after 1845.

Overwhelmingly poor and Catholic, these newest Irish immigrants entered the work force at the bottom. Paddy with his pickax and Bridget the maid were simultaneously stereotypes and realities. While Irish men dug streets and canals and railroads, Irish women worked as maids and textile workers. Poverty drove women to work at early ages, and the outdoor, all-season labor performed by their husbands turned many of them into working widows. Because the Irish usually married late, almost half the Irish immigrants were single adult women, many of whom never married. Most of these Irish-Americans lived a harsh existence. One immigrant described the life of the average Irish-born laborer as "despicable, humiliating, [and] slavish"; there was "no love for him—no protection of life—[he] can be shot down, run through, kicked, cuffed, spat upon—and no redress." Nevertheless, a few Irish struggled up the social ladder, becoming foremen in factories or small storeowners.

It sometimes seemed that no matter what the Irish did, they clashed with other Americans. The poorer Irish who dug canals, took in laundry, or worked as domestics competed with equally poor free blacks. The result was Irish animosity toward blacks and Irish hatred of abolitionists. At the same time, the Irish who secured skilled or semiskilled jobs clashed with native-born white workers.

## Anti-Catholicism, Nativism, and Labor Protest

In the 1840s swelling Catholic immigration led to a Protestant counterattack in the form of nativist (anti-immigrant) societies. Many nativist societies began as secret or semisecret fraternal orders but developed political offshoots; for example, the Order of the Star-Spangled Banner evolved into the "Know-Nothing" party, a major political force in the 1850s. During the 1840s, however, nativist societies played their most influential part in flare-ups over local issues. In 1844 after a nativist political party won a handful of offices in Philadelphia, fiery Protestant orators denounced "popery," and Protestant mobs put Catholic neighborhoods to the torch. By the time militia quelled these "Bible Riots," sixteen people lay dead and thirty buildings had been reduced to charred ruins.

An explosive mixture of fears and discontents fueled nativism. Protestants generally saw their doctrines such as the responsibility of each individual to interpret scripture as far more democratic than Catholicism, which made doctrine the province of the pope and the hierarchy. Native-born artisans and journeymen, already hard pressed by the subdivision of tasks and the aftermath of the Panic of 1837, feared that desperately poor Catholic immigrants represented threats to their jobs. Nativism fed on such fears and anxieties.

Demands for land reform joined nativism as a proposed solution to workers' economic woes. Americans had long believed that abundant land guaranteed security against a permanent class of "wage slaves." In 1844 George Henry Evans, an English-born radical, organized the National Reform Association and exhorted workers to "Vote Yourself a Farm." Such neo-Jeffersonian ideas gained Evans support among artisans and middle-class intellectuals. Land reformers argued that workers in an industrial economy abandoned all possibility of economic independence; their only hope lay in claiming land and becoming farmers. However, in an age when a horse cost the average worker three months' pay, and most factory workers dreaded "the horrors of wilderness life," the idea of solving industrial problems by turning "wage slaves" into self-sufficient farmers seemed a pipe dream.

Labor unions appealed to workers left cold by the promises of the land reformers. For example, desperately poor Irish immigrants, refugees from an agricultural society, believed that they could gain more through unions and strikes than through farming. Even women workers organized unions in these years; the leader of a seamstresses' union proclaimed, "Too long have we been bound down by tyrant employers."

Probably the most important development for workers in the 1840s was a state court decision. In *Commonwealth* v. *Hunt* (1842), the Massachusetts Supreme Court ruled that labor unions were not illegal monopolies that restrained trade. However, because less than 1 percent of the work force at that time belonged to unions, their impact was sharply limited. Thus Massachusetts employers easily brushed aside the *Commonwealth* decision, firing union agitators and replacing them with cheap immigrant labor. "Hundreds of honest laborers," a labor paper reported in 1848, "have been dismissed from employment in the manufactories of New England because they have been suspected of knowing their rights and daring to assert them." This repression effectively blunted agitation for a ten-hour

workday in an era when the twelve- or fourteen-hour day was typical.

Ethnic and religious tensions also split the antebellum working class during the 1830s and 1840s. Friction between native-born and immigrant workers inevitably became intertwined with the political divisions of the second party system.

## Labor Protest and Immigrant Politics

Few immigrants had voted before reaching America, and even fewer had fled political persecution. Political upheavals had erupted in Austria and some German states in the turbulent year 1848, but among the 1 million German immigrants to the United States, only 10,000 were political refugees, or "Forty-Eighters." Once settled in the United States, however, many immigrants became politically active. They discovered that urban political organizations could help them to find housing and jobs—in return for votes. Both the Irish and the Germans identified overwhelmingly with the Democratic party. By 1820 the Irish controlled Tammany Hall, the New York City Democratic organization; Germans became staunch Democrats in Milwaukee, St. Louis, and other cities.

Immigrants' fears about jobs partly explained their widespread Democratic support. Former president Andrew Jackson had given the Democratic party an antiprivilege, anti-aristocratic coloration, making the Democrats seem more sympathetic than the Whigs to the common people. In addition, antislavery was linked to the Whig party, and the Irish loathed abolitionism because they feared that freed slaves would become their economic competitors. Moreover, the Whigs' moral and religious values seemed to threaten those of the Irish and Germans. Hearty-drinking Irish and German immigrants shunned temperance-crusading Whigs, many of whom were also rabid anti-Catholics. Even public-school reform, championed by the Whigs, was perceived as a menace to the Catholicism of Irish children and as a threat to the integrity of German language and culture.

The Bible Riots illustrate both the interplay of

**Defenders of the True Faith**
*This cartoon portrays the mob that attacked a Roman Catholic convent in Charlestown, Massachusetts, in 1834, as composed of bigoted ruffians who flatter themselves that their deed will live as a heroic act in the national memory.*

nativism, religion, and politics and the way in which local issues shaped the immigrants' political loyalties. Both Democrats and Whigs became adept at attracting voters initially drawn to politics by local issues such as liquor regulations and school laws. Nativists usually voted for Whig candidates rather than those of overtly nativist parties, while immigrants followed the Democratic party from local battles into national politics. There the Democrats taught immigrants to revere George Washington, Thomas Jefferson, and Andrew Jackson; to view "moneyed capitalists" as parasites who would tremble when the people spoke; and to think of themselves as Americans. During the 1830s the Democrats had persuaded immigrants that such national issues as the Bank of the United States and the tariff were vital to them. Similarly, in the 1840s the Democrats would try to convince immigrants that national territorial expansion would advance their interests.

## The West and Beyond

As late as 1840 the American West meant the area between the Appalachian Mountains and the Mississippi River or just beyond. West of that lay the inhospitable Great Plains. A semiarid treeless plateau, the Plains sustained huge buffalo herds and the nomadic Indians who lived off the buffalo. Because the Great Plains presented would-be farmers with formidable obstacles, public interest shifted toward the Far West, the fertile region beyond the Rockies.

### The Far West

By the Transcontinental (or Adams-Onís) Treaty of 1819, the United States had relinquished to Spain its claims to Texas west of the Sabine River and in return had received Spanish claims to the Oregon Country north of California. Two years later the

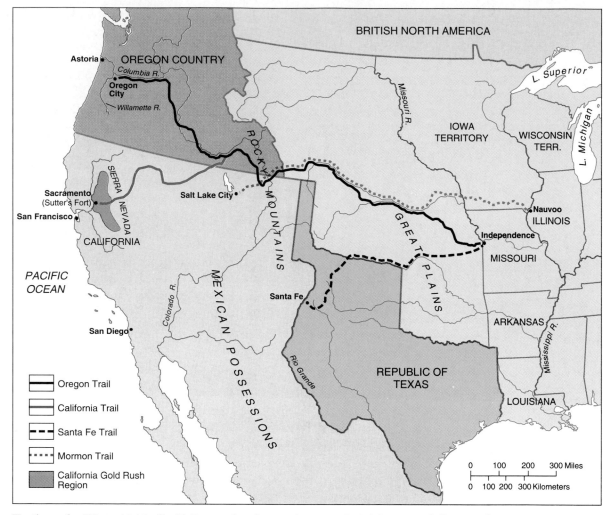

**Trails to the West, 1840**  *By 1840 several trails carried pioneers from Missouri and Illinois to the West.*

Mexican Revolution had brought Mexico independence from Spain and possession of all North American territory claimed by Spain—Texas, California, and the southwest quadrant of the continent. In 1824 and 1825 Russia yielded its claims to Oregon south of Alaska, and in 1827 the United States and Great Britain revived an earlier agreement for the joint occupation of the Oregon Territory.

Despite these agreements and treaties, the vast Far West remained a remote and shadowy frontier during the 1820s. The American line of settlement reached only to Missouri, a 2,000-mile trek (allowing for mountains) from the West Coast.

### Far Western Trade

After sailing around South America and up the Pacific coast, early merchants had established American and British outposts on the West Coast. Between the late 1790s and the 1820s, for example, Boston merchants had built a thriving trade, exchanging goods from the eastern United States for western sea-otter fur, cattle, hides, and tallow (rendered from cattle fat and used for making candles and soap). The British Hudson's Bay Company developed a similar trade in Oregon and northern California. The California trade generated little friction with Mexico. Californians were as eager to buy as the traders were to sell. Traders who settled in California, such as the Swiss-born John Sutter, learned to speak Spanish and became assimilated into Mexican culture.

Also during the 1820s, trading links developed between St. Louis and Santa Fe. Each spring, midwesterners loaded wagon trains with tools, clothing, and household sundries and rumbled westward to Santa Fe, where they traded their goods for mules and silver. Mexico welcomed the trade. By the 1830s more than half the goods trucked west along the Santa Fe Trail trickled into the mineral-rich Mexican provinces of Chihuahua and Sonora and were exchanged for Mexican silver pesos, which became the principal medium of exchange in Missouri.

Some Americans ventured north from Santa Fe to trap beaver in what is today western Colorado and eastern Utah. Americans from St. Louis soon found themselves competing with both the Santa Fe traders and the agents of the Hudson's Bay Company for lucrative beaver pelts. In 1825 William Ashley of St. Louis initiated an annual rendezvous along the Green River in Mexican territory, where midwestern traders could exchange beaver pelts for supplies and thereby save themselves the long trip back to St. Louis. Gradually, the St. Louis traders wrested the beaver trade from their Santa Fe competitors.

For the most part, American traders and trappers operating on the northern Mexican frontier in the 1820s and 1830s provided a service to Mexico's provinces. The Mexican people of New Mexico and California depended on American trade for manufactured goods, and the Mexican government in both provinces needed revenues from customs duties. The New Mexican government often had to wait until the caravan of American traders arrived from St. Louis before it could pay its officials and soldiers.

Yet despite the mutually beneficial relations between Mexicans and Americans, the potential for conflict was always present. Spanish-speaking, Roman Catholic, and accustomed to a hierarchical society, the Mexicans formed a striking contrast to the Protestant, individualistic Americans. Furthermore, American traders returned to the United States with glowing reports about the fertility and climate of Mexico's northern provinces. Consequently, by the 1820s American settlers were moving into eastern Texas. At the same time, the ties binding Mexico's government to its northern provinces were fraying.

## Mexican Government in the Far West

Spain, and later Mexico, recognized that the key to controlling their frontier provinces lay in promoting settlement there by Spanish-speaking people—Spaniards, Mexicans, and Indians who had embraced Catholicism and agriculture. Thus by the early nineteenth century, Spanish missions, which had long been the chief instrument of Spanish expansion, stretched up the California coast as far as San Francisco and into the interior of New Mexico and Texas.

The Spanish missions combined political, economic, and religious goals. Paid by the government, the Franciscan priests who staffed the missions tried to convert Native Americans and to settle them on mission lands. By 1823 more than 20,000 Indians lived on the lands of the twenty-one California missions, most of them protected by a fort, or presidio, like that at San Francisco.

In the late 1820s the mission system began to decline, the victim of Mexican independence and the new government's decision to secularize the missions by distributing their lands to ambitious government officials and private ranchers. Some of the mission Indians became forced laborers, but most returned to their nomadic ways and joined with Indians who had resisted the missions. During the 1820s and 1830s these "barbaric Indians"—notably the Comanches, Apaches, Navajos, and Utes—terrorized the Mexican frontier, carrying off women and children as well as livestock. Mexican policy was partly responsible for the upsurge in terrorism. With the secularization of the missions, Hispanic ranchers had made some Native Americans virtual slaves on ranches bloated by the addition of mission lands. Frontier dwellers, moreover, sometimes raided Native American tribes for domestic servants. "To get Indian girls to work for you," a descendant of Hispanic settlers recalled, "all you had to do was organize a company against the Navajos or Utes or Apaches and kill all the men you could and bring captive the children." Thus the "barbaric Indians" had many scores to settle.

Overofficered and corrupt, the Mexican army had little taste for frontier fighting and less for protecting frontier settlers. Consequently, few people ventured into the undeveloped, lawless territories, and most of the Mexican empire remained underpopulated. In 1836 New Mexico contained 30,000 settlers of Hispanic culture; California, about 3,200; and Texas, 4,000. Separated by vast distances from an uncaring government in Mexico City, and dependent on American traders for the necessities of civilization, the frontier Mexicans constituted a frail barrier against the advance of Anglo-American settlement.

## American Settlements in Texas

Unlike the provinces of New Mexico and California, the Mexican state known as Coahuila-Texas had neither mountains nor deserts to protect its boundaries. By 1823, 3,000 Americans had drifted into eastern Texas, some in search of cotton lands, others in flight from creditors after the Panic of 1819. In 1824 the Mexican government began to encourage American colonization of Texas as a way to bring in manufactured goods and to gain protection against the Indians. The government bestowed generous land grants on agents known as *empresarios* to recruit peaceful American settlers for Texas. Stephen F. Austin, the most successful of the *empresarios*, had brought in 300 families by 1825. By 1830, 7,000 Americans lived in Texas, more than double the Mexican population there.

This large number of Americans proved a mixed blessing. Unlike the assimilated traders of California, the American settlers in Texas were generally farmers living in their own communities, far from the Mexican settlements to the west. Although naturalized Mexican citizens and nominal Catholics, the American settlers distrusted the Mexicans and complained constantly about the creaking, erratic Mexican judicial system. Mexico had not bargained for the size and speed of American immigration. The first news of the Americans, wrote a Mexican general in 1828, "comes from discovering them on land already under cultivation."

As early as 1826 an American *empresario*, Haden Edwards, led a revolt against Mexican rule, but Mexican forces, aided by Austin, crushed the uprising. However, Mexican policies in the early 1830s quickly eroded the American settlers' allegiance to the Mexican government. In 1830 the government closed Texas to further immigration from the United States and forbade the introduction of more slaves to Texas, a troubling matter because many American settlers were slaveholders. But Mexico could not enforce its decrees, and between 1830 and 1834 the number of Americans in Texas doubled. Austin secured repeal of the prohibition against American migration in 1834; within a year an estimated 1,000 Americans a month were entering Texas. In 1836 Texas counted some 30,000 white Americans, 5,000 black slaves, and 4,000 Mexicans.

At the same time, the Mexican government grew more and more erratic. "The political character of this country," Austin wrote, "seems to partake of its geological features—all is volcanic." From the beginning, the government had featured a precarious balance between liberals who favored decentralized government and conservatives who wanted a highly centralized state with power in the hands of the military and church officials in Mexico City. When Antonio López de Santa Anna became president of Mexico in 1834, he restricted the power of the individual states, including Coahuila-Texas. His actions ignited a series of rebellions in the Mexican states, the most important of which became the Texas Revolution.

## The Texas Revolution

At first the insurgent Anglo-Texans sought the restoration of the liberal Constitution of 1824 and greater autonomy for Texas, not independence. But Santa Anna's brutal treatment of the rebels alarmed the initially moderate Austin and others. When Santa Anna invaded Texas in fall 1835, Austin cast his lot with the radicals who wanted outright independence.

Santa Anna's armies met with initial success. In February 1836, 4,000 of his men laid siege to San Antonio, where 200 rebels had retreated into an abandoned mission, the Alamo. On March 6—four days after Texas had declared its independence, although they did not know about it—the defenders of the Alamo were overwhelmed by Mexican troops. Under Santa Anna's orders, the Mexican army killed all the Alamo's defenders, including the wounded. A few weeks later Mexican troops massacred 350 Texas prisoners at Goliad.

Meanwhile, the Texans had formed an army with Sam Houston at its head. A giant man of extensive political and military experience, Houston retreated east to pick up recruits, many of them Americans who crossed the Sabine River border to fight Santa Anna. On April 21, 1836, Houston's army turned and surprised the complacent Mexican forces under Santa Anna, which had encamped on a prairie just to the east of what is now the city of Houston. Shouting, "Remember the Alamo!" and "Remember Goliad!" Houston's army of 1,200 tore through the Mexican lines, killing nearly half of Santa Anna's men in fifteen minutes and capturing the general himself. This engagement, the Battle of San Jacinto, gave Texas its independence from Mexico, although the Mexican government never ratified the treaty that Santa Anna signed. However, Texas became an independent republic, not the American state that most had envisioned.

## American Settlements in California, New Mexico, and Oregon

Before 1840 California and New Mexico, both less

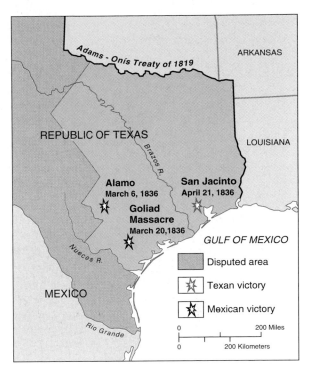

**Major Battles in the Texas Revolution, 1835–1836**
*Sam Houston's victory at San Jacinto was the decisive action of the war and avenged the massacres at the Alamo and Goliad.*

accessible than Texas, exerted only a mild attraction for American settlers. That year a mere 100 Americans lived in New Mexico and perhaps 400 in California. According to a contemporary, these Americans "are scattered throughout the whole Mexican population, and most of them have Spanish wives. . . . They live in every respect like the Spanish."

Yet the beginnings of change were evident. During the 1840s Americans streamed into the Sacramento Valley, lured by favorable reports of the region and welcomed by the Hispanic population as a way to encourage economic development. To these land-hungry settlers, geographically and culturally separated from the Mexican population, no sacrifice was too great if it led to California.

To the north, Oregon's abundant farmland

**Sam Houston (1793–1863)**
*This photo shows Houston as a prosperous, successful elder statesman. But in his youth, Houston had a reputation for wildness. In 1829 he resigned Tennessee's governorship and lived dissolutely for three years among the Cherokee Indians.*

beckoned settlers from the Mississippi Valley. By 1840 some 500 Americans had settled there, in what was described as a "pioneer's paradise" where "the pigs are running around under the great acorn trees, round and fat and already cooked, with knives and forks sticking in them so that you can cut off a slice whenever you are hungry." To some, Oregon was more attractive than California, especially because the joint British-American occupation seemed to herald eventual U.S. annexation.

## The Overland Trail

Whether bound for California or Oregon, Ameri-

cans faced a four-month ordeal crossing terrain little known in reality but vividly depicted in fiction as an Indian killing ground. Cautious pioneers stocked up on enough guns to equip an army in jump-off towns such as Independence and St. Joseph, Missouri. In fact, they were more likely to shoot one another than to be shot by the usually cooperative Indians and much more likely to be scalped by Independence or St. Joseph merchants selling their goods at inflated prices.

Along the Overland Trail the emigrants faced hardships and hazards: ornery mules that kicked, bit, and balked; oxen that collapsed from thirst; and overloaded wagons that broke down. Trails were difficult to follow and too often marked by the debris of broken wagons and the bleached bones of oxen. Guidebooks were more like guessbooks. The Donner party, which left Illinois in 1846, lost so much time following one such guidebook that it became snowbound in the High Sierra during a bitter winter. To survive, members of the party guaranteed themselves a place in future textbooks by turning to cannibalism.

Emigrants met the challenges of the overland trail by close cooperation with one another, traveling in huge wagon trains rather than alone. Men yoked and unyoked the oxen, drove the wagons and stock, and hunted. Women packed, cooked, and assisted in childbirths. Men also stood guard against Indian raids, although these were rare.

Between 1840 and 1848, an estimated 11,500 pioneers followed an overland trail to Oregon, and some 2,700 reached California. Such small numbers made a difference, for the British did not settle Oregon at all and the Mexican population of California was small and scattered. By 1845 California was clinging to Mexico by the thinnest of threads. The territory's Hispanic population, the *californios*, felt little allegiance to Mexico, which they contemptuously called "the other shore." Some of them wanted independence from Mexico, while others contemplated British or French rule. By the mid-1840s these *californios*, with their tenuous allegiances, faced a growing number of American settlers with definite political sympathies.

# The Politics of Expansion

Westward expansion raised the question of whether the United States should annex Texas. In the 1840s the Texas issue sparked political passions and became entangled with other unsettling issues about the West. Between 1846 and 1848 a war with Mexico and a dramatic confrontation with Britain settled these questions on terms favorable to the United States.

At the start of the 1840s western issues received little attention in a nation concerned with issues relating to economic recovery—tariffs, banking, and internal improvements. Only after politicians failed to address the economic problems coherently did opportunistic leaders thrust expansion-related issues to the top of the political agenda.

## The Whig Ascendancy

The election of 1840 brought the Whig candidate William Henry Harrison to the presidency and installed Whig majorities in both houses of Congress. The Whigs proposed to replace Van Buren's Independent Treasury (see Chapter 10) with some sort of national fiscal agency such as the Bank of the United States. The Whig party also favored a revised tariff that would increase government revenues but remain low enough to permit the importation of foreign goods. According to the Whig plan, the states would then receive tariff-generated revenues for internal improvements.

The Whig program might well have breezed into law. But Harrison died after only a month in office, and his successor, John Tyler, a Virginia aristocrat put on the ticket for his southern appeal, proved a disaster for the Whigs. A former Democrat, Tyler continued to favored the Democratic philosophy of states' rights. As president, he used the veto to shred his new party's program. In August 1841 a Whig measure to create a new national bank fell to Tyler's veto, as did a subsequent modification.

Tyler also played havoc with Whig tariff policy by vetoing one bill to lower tariffs to 20 percent in accord with the Compromise Tariff and rejecting another to distribute revenue from a higher tariff to the states. Whig leaders were understandably furious; some Whigs talked of impeaching Tyler. In August 1842 the president, needing money to run the government, signed a new bill that maintained some tariffs above 20 percent but abandoned distribution to the states.

Tyler's erratic course confounded and disrupted his party. By maintaining some tariffs above 20 percent, the tariff of 1842 satisfied northern manufacturers, but by abandoning distribution, it infuriated southerners and westerners. The issue cut across party lines. In the congressional elections of 1842, the Whigs paid a heavy price for failing to enact their program; they lost control of the House to the Democrats. Now the nation had one party controlling the Senate, another controlling the House, and a president who appeared to belong to neither.

## Tyler and Texas Annexation

Although disowned by his party, Tyler ardently desired a second term as president. Domestic issues offered him little hope of building a popular following, but foreign policy was another matter. In 1842 Tyler's secretary of state, Daniel Webster, concluded the Webster-Ashburton Treaty with Great Britain, settling a long-festering dispute over the Maine-Canadian border. Tyler reasoned that if he could follow the treaty, which was highly popular in the North, with the annexation of Texas, he could build a national following.

The issue of slavery clouded every discussion of Texas. Antislavery northerners saw proposals to annex Texas as part of a southern conspiracy to extend American territory into Mexico, Cuba, and Central America. Thus an unlimited number of new slave states could be created, but British Canada would eliminate the possibility of free states expanding to the north. And some southerners talked openly of carving Texas into four or five slave states.

Nevertheless, in summer 1843 Tyler launched a campaign for Texas annexation. He justified his crusade by reporting that he had learned of an attempt to make Texas a British, rather than an

American, ally. John C. Calhoun, who became secretary of state in 1844, embroidered these reports with his own theories of British plans to use abolition as a way to destroy rice, sugar, and cotton production in the United States.

In spring 1844 Tyler and Calhoun submitted to the Senate a treaty annexing Texas. Accompanying the treaty was a letter from Calhoun to the British minister in Washington defending slavery as beneficial to African-Americans, the only way to protect them from "vice and pauperism." Abolitionists now had evidence that the annexation of Texas was linked to a conspiracy to extend slavery. Consequently, both Whig and Democratic leaders came out in opposition to the annexation of Texas, and the treaty went down to crushing defeat in the Senate. But however ostensibly decisive, the Senate vote simply dumped the annexation question into the upcoming presidential election.

## The Election of 1844

Tyler's ineptitude turned the presidential campaign into a free-for-all. Unable to gather support as an independent, he dropped out of the race. Henry Clay had a secure grip on the Whig nomination, but Martin Van Buren's apparently clear path to the head of the Democratic ticket vanished as the issue of annexation split his party. A deadlocked Democratic party finally turned to James K. Polk of Tennessee, the first "dark-horse" nominee in American history.

Little known outside the South, the slaveholding Polk enjoyed broad southern support as the "bosom friend of [Andrew] Jackson, and a pure whole-hogged Democrat, the known enemy of banks and distribution." Polk supported the immediate "reannexation" of Texas—like Jackson, he believed that Texas had been part of the Louisiana Purchase until ceded to Spain in the Transcontinental (Adams-Onís) Treaty of 1819. Indeed, Polk followed Old Hickory's lead so often that he became known as Young Hickory.

Jeering "Who is James K. Polk?" the Whigs derided the nomination. However, Polk, a wily campaigner, convinced many northerners that annexation of Texas would benefit them. In an imaginative scenario, Polk and his supporters argued that if Britain succeeded in abolitionizing Texas, slavery would not be able to move westward, racial tensions in existing slave states would intensify, and the chances of a race war would increase. However farfetched, this argument played effectively on northern racial phobias and helped Polk to detach annexation from Calhoun's narrow, prosouthern defense.

In contrast to the Democrats, whose position was clear, Clay and the Whigs wobbled. After several shifts Clay finally came out against annexation, but not until September. His wavering alienated his southern supporters and prompted some of his northern supporters to bolt the Whigs for the antislavery Liberty party, formed in 1840. The Whigs also infuriated Catholic immigrant voters by nominating Theodore Frelinghuysen for the vice presidency. A supporter of temperance and an assortment of other causes, Frelinghuysen confirmed fears that the Whigs were the orthodox Protestant

### The Election of 1844

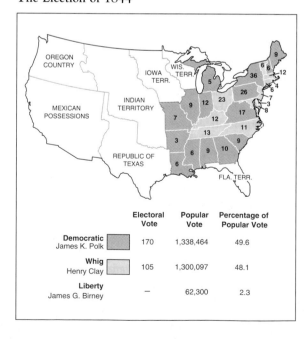

| | Electoral Vote | Popular Vote | Percentage of Popular Vote |
|---|---|---|---|
| **Democratic** James K. Polk | 170 | 1,338,464 | 49.6 |
| **Whig** Henry Clay | 105 | 1,300,097 | 48.1 |
| **Liberty** James G. Birney | — | 62,300 | 2.3 |

party. Catholic immigrants turned out in large numbers to vote for the Democrats.

On the eve of the election in New York City, so many Irish marched to the courthouse to be qualified for voting that the windows had to be opened to allow people to enter and leave. "Ireland has reconquered the country which England lost," moaned an embittered Whig. Polk won the electoral vote 170–105, but his margin in the popular vote was only 38,000 out of 2.6 million votes cast. A shift of 6,000 votes in New York, where the immigrant vote and Whig defections to the Liberty party had hurt Clay, would have given Clay the state and the presidency.

## Manifest Destiny

The election of 1844 demonstrated the strength of national support for the annexation of Texas. The surging popular sentiment for expansion reflected a growing conviction that America's natural destiny was to expand into Texas and all the way to the Pacific Ocean.

Expansionists emphasized extending the "area of freedom" and talked of "repelling the contaminating proximity of monarchies upon the soil that we have consecrated to the rights of man." For young Americans such as Walt Whitman, such restless expansionism knew few limits. "The more we reflect upon annexation as involving a part of Mexico, the more do doubts and obstacles resolve themselves away," Whitman wrote. "Then there is California, on the way to which lovely tract lies Santa Fe; how long a time will elapse before they shine as two new stars in our mighty firmament?" Americans needed only a phrase to capture this ebullient spirit. In 1845 John L. O'Sullivan, a New York Democratic journalist, supplied that phrase when he wrote of "our manifest destiny to overspread and to possess the whole of the continent which Providence has given us for the development of the great experiment of liberty and federated self-government entrusted to us."

Advocates of Manifest Destiny used lofty language and invoked God and nature to justify expansion. Because most champions of Manifest Destiny were Democrats who favored annexing Texas, northern Whigs dismissed Manifest Destiny as a smoke screen to conceal an evil intent to extend slavery. In fact, many expansionists supported neither slavery nor annexation. Most had their eyes not on Texas but on Oregon and California. Blaming the post-1837 depression on the failure of Americans to find markets for their agricultural surplus, they saw California and Oregon as solutions. A Missouri Democrat observed that "the ports of Asia are as convenient to Oregon as the ports of Europe are to the eastern slope of our confederacy, with an infinitely better ocean for navigation." An Alabama Democrat praised California's "safe and capacious harbors," which "invite to their bosoms the rich commerce of the East."

More than trade was at stake. To many, expansion presented an opportunity to preserve the agricultural character of the American people and thus to safeguard democracy. Fundamentally Jeffersonian, expansionists equated industrialization and urbanization with social stratification and class strife. To avoid the "bloated wealth" and "terrible misery" that afflicted Britain, the United States *had to* expand.

Democrats saw expansion as a logical complement to their support of low tariffs and their opposition to centralized banking. High tariffs and banks tended to "favor and foster the factory system," but expansion would provide farmers with land and with access to foreign markets. Americans would continue to be farmers, and the foundations of the Republic would remain secure.

This message, trumpeted by the penny press, made sense to the working poor, many of them Irish immigrants. Expansion would open economic opportunity for the common people and thwart British plans to free American slaves, whom the poor viewed as potential competition for already scarce jobs.

Expansionism drew on the ideas of Thomas Jefferson, John Quincy Adams, and other leaders of the early Republic who had proclaimed the American people's right to displace any people, uncivilized or European, from their westward path. Early expansionists had feared that overexpansion might create an ungovernable empire, but their successors had no such qualms. Although they pointed with alarm to the negative effects of industrialization, the expansionists also relied on the technology of industrialization. The railroad and the telegraph, they said, had annihilated the problem of distance and made expansion safe.

## Polk and Oregon

The growing spirit of Manifest Destiny intensified the Oregon issue. To soften northern criticism of the pending annexation of Texas, the Democrats had included in their 1844 platform the assertion that American title "to the whole of the Territory of Oregon is clear and unquestionable." Taken literally, this statement, which Polk repeated in his inaugural address, pressed an American claim to the entire Oregon Territory between California and 54°40', a claim never before advanced.

Polk's objectives in Oregon were far subtler than his language. He knew that it would take a war with Britain for the United States to claim the entire Oregon Territory, and he wanted to avoid war. He hoped the belligerent language would persuade the British to accept what they had previously rejected, a division of Oregon at the forty-ninth parallel. This settlement would give the United States the superb deep-water harbor of Puget Sound and the southern tip of Vancouver Island.

Polk's position succeeded in rousing furious interest in the nation's acquiring the entire territory. Mass meetings adopted such resolutions as "The Whole or None!" Each year brought new American settlers into Oregon. John Quincy Adams, though no supporter of the annexation of Texas or the 54°40' boundary for Oregon, believed that American settlements gave the United States a stronger claim than discovery and exploration had given the British. The United States, not Britain, he contended, was destined "to make the wilderness blossom as the rose, to establish laws, to increase, multiply, and subdue the earth," all "at the first behest of God Almighty."

In April 1846 Polk forced the issue by notifying Britain that the United States was terminating the joint British-American occupation of Oregon. In effect, this message was that the British could either go to war over the American claims to 54°40' or negotiate. They chose to negotiate. Although raging against "that ill-regulated, overbearing, and aggressive spirit of American democracy," Britain faced too many other problems to wage war over "a few miles of pine swamp." The ensuing treaty divided Oregon at the forty-ninth parallel, although Britain retained all of Vancouver Island and navigation rights on the Columbia River. On June 15, 1846, the Senate ratified the treaty, stipulating that Britain's navigation rights on the Columbia were temporary.

## The Origins of the Mexican War

While Polk challenged Britain over Oregon, the United States and Mexico moved toward war. The conflict had both immediate and remote causes. One long-standing grievance lay in the failure of the Mexican government to pay $2 million in debts

**Oregon Boundary Dispute**
*Although demanding that Britain cede the entire Oregon Territory south of 54°40', the United States settled for a compromise at the forty-ninth parallel.*

**Patriotism and the Mexican War**
*U.S. soldiers commonly wore tall hats known as shako caps during the Mexican War. The caps were adorned with decorative plates showing the eagle spreading its wings, the symbol of Manifest Destiny. Inexpensive and mass-produced lithographs such as the one on the left, depicting the Battle of Sacramento, aroused patriotic support for the war.*

owed to U.S. citizens. Bitter memories of the Alamo and of the Goliad massacre, moreover, reinforced American loathing of Mexico. Above all, the issue of Texas poisoned relations. Mexico still hoped to regain Texas or to keep it independent of the United States. Should Texas join the United States, Mexico feared, Americans might seize other provinces and even Mexico itself and treat Mexicans as they treated slaves.

Polk's election increased the strength of the pro-annexationists, as his campaign had persuaded many northerners that Texas's annexation would bring national benefits. In February 1845 both houses of Congress responded to popular sentiment by passing a resolution annexing Texas. However, Texans balked, in part because some feared that union with the United States would provoke a Mexican invasion and war on Texas soil.

Polk moved rapidly. To sweeten the pot for Texans, he supported their claim that the Rio Grande constituted Texas's southern border, despite Mexico's contention that the Nueces River, 100 miles farther north, bounded Texas. Because the Rio Grande meandered west and north nearly 2,000 miles, it encompassed a huge territory, including

part of modern New Mexico. The Texas that Polk proposed to annex thus was far larger than the Texas that had gained independence from Mexico. On July 4, 1845, reassured by Polk's support, Texas voted to accept annexation. To counter Mexican belligerency, Polk ordered American troops under General Zachary Taylor to the edge of the disputed territory. Taylor deployed his army at Corpus Christi, south of the Nueces River, in territory still claimed by Mexico.

California and its fine harbors influenced Polk's actions, for he had entered the White House with the firm intention of extending American control over that province, too. If Mexico went to war with the United States over Texas, Polk's supporters claimed, "the road to California will be open to us." Reports from American agents convinced Polk that the way lay open for California to join the United States as Texas would—by revolution and then annexation.

Continued turmoil in Mexican politics further complicated this complex situation. In early 1845 a new Mexican government agreed to negotiate with the United States, and Polk decided to give negotiations a chance. In November 1845 he dispatched John Slidell to Mexico City with instructions to gain Mexican recognition of the annexation of Texas with the Rio Grande border. In exchange, the U.S. government would assume the debt owed by Mexico to American citizens. Polk also authorized Slidell to offer up to $25 million for California and New Mexico. However, by the time Slidell reached Mexico City, the government there had become too weak to make concessions to the United States, and its head, General José Herrara, refused to receive Slidell. Polk then ordered Taylor to move southward to the Rio Grande, hoping to provoke a Mexican attack and to unite the American people behind war.

The Mexican government, however, dawdled over taking the bait. Polk was about to send a war message to Congress when word finally arrived that Mexican forces had crossed the Rio Grande and attacked the U.S. army. *"American blood has been shed on American soil!"* Polk's followers jubilantly proclaimed. On May 11, 1846, Polk informed Congress that war "exists by the act of Mexico herself" and called for $10 million to fight the war.

Polk's disingenuous assertion that the United States was already at war provoked furious opposition in Congress. For one thing, the Mexican attack on Taylor's troops had taken place on land never before claimed by the United States. Equally grievous, in announcing that war already existed, Polk seemed to undercut congressional power to declare war. He was using a mere border incident as a pretext to plunge the nation into a general war to acquire more slave territory. Whig papers warned readers that Polk was "precipitating you into a fathomless abyss of crime and calamity." But Polk had backed the Whigs into a corner. They could not afford to appear unpatriotic—they remembered vividly what opposition to the War of 1812 had cost the Federalists—so they swallowed their outrage and supported war.

Polk's single-minded pursuit of his goals had prevailed. A humorless, austere man who banned dancing and liquor at White House receptions, Polk inspired little personal warmth. But he had clear objectives and pursued them unflinchingly. He triumphed over all opposition, in part because of his

opponents' fragmentation, in part because of expansion's popular appeal, and in part because of his foreign antagonists' weakness. Reluctant to fight over Oregon, Britain had negotiated. Too weak to negotiate, Mexico chose to fight over territory that it had already lost (Texas) and where its hold was feeble (California and New Mexico).

## The Mexican War

Most European observers expected Mexico to win the war. Its army was four times the size of the American forces, and it was fighting on home ground. The United States, having botched its one previous attempt to invade a neighbor, Canada in 1812, now had to sustain offensive operations in an area remote from American settlements. American expansionists, however, hardly expected the Mexicans to fight at all. Racism and arrogance convinced many Americans that the Mexican people, degraded by their mixed Spanish and Indian population, were "as sure to melt away at the approach of [American] energy and enterprise as snow before a southern sun," as one newspaper publisher insisted.

In fact, the Mexicans fought bravely and stubbornly, although unsuccessfully. In May 1846 Taylor, "Old Rough and Ready," routed the Mexican army in Texas and pursued it across the Rio Grande, eventually to capture the major city of Monterrey in September. War enthusiasm surged in the United States, and recruiting posters blared, "Here's to old Zach! Glorious Times! Roast Beef, Ice Cream, and Three Months' Advance!" After taking Monterrey, Taylor, starved for supplies, halted and granted Mexico an eight-week armistice. Eager to undercut Taylor's popularity—the Whigs were already touting him as a presidential candidate—Polk stripped him of half his forces and reassigned them to General Winfield Scott. He was to mount an amphibious attack on Vera Cruz and proceed on to Mexico City, following the path of Cortés and his *conquistadores*. Events outstripped Polk's scheme, however, when Taylor defeated a far larger Mexican army at the Battle of Buena Vista, on February 22–23, 1847.

Farther north, American forces took advantage of the shakiness of Mexican rule to strip away New

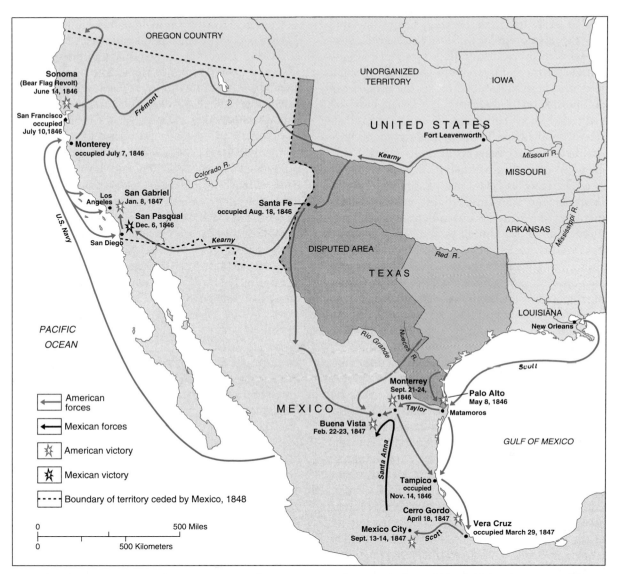

**Major Battles of the Mexican War**

*The Mexican War's decisive campaign began with General Winfield Scott's capture of Vera Cruz and ended with his conquest of Mexico City.*

Mexico and California. In spring 1846 Colonel Stephen Kearny led an army from Fort Leavenworth, Kansas, toward Santa Fe. Having overcome immense natural obstacles to reach New Mexico, Kearny took the territory by a combination of bluff, bluster, and, perhaps, bribery. The Mexican governor, who had said that "it is better to be thought brave than to be so," fled at Kearny's approach. Once he had suppressed a brief rebellion by Mexicans and Indians, Kearny controlled New Mexico securely enough that he could dispatch part of his army south into Mexico to support Taylor at Buena Vista.

California also fell easily into American hands.

In 1845 Polk had ordered the Pacific Squadron under Commodore John D. Sloat to occupy California's ports in event of war. The president had also dispatched a courier overland with secret orders for one of the most colorful actors in the conquest of California, John C. Frémont. A Georgia-born adventurer, Frémont had taken advantage of his marriage to the daughter of a powerful senator to have accounts of his explorations in the Northwest published as official government documents, then basked in glory as "the Great Pathfinder." Polk's courier caught up with Frémont in Oregon. Instructed to proceed to California and "watch over the interests of the United States," Frémont interpreted his orders liberally. In June 1846 he rounded up some American insurgents, captured the town of Sonoma, and proclaimed the independent "Bear Flag Republic." The combined efforts of Frémont, Sloat, and Kearny (who had continued on to California after his successful New Mexico campaign) established U.S. control over California.

The war's final and most important campaign brought Winfield Scott to glory in the conquest of Mexico City itself. In March 1847 Scott carried out a successful amphibious landing near Vera Cruz, pounded the city into submission, and moved inland to attack Mexico City. The U.S. army encountered a Mexican force under Santa Anna at the seemingly impregnable Cerro Gordo pass, but a young captain, Robert E. Lee, helped to find a trail that outflanked the Mexicans and led to a small peak overlooking the pass. The Americans planted howitzers there, stormed the pass, and routed the Mexican army. On September 13, 1847, Mexico City fell to Scott, and he joined Zachary Taylor in the pantheon of new American heroes.

Although the Mexican army had outnumbered the U.S. forces in virtually every battle, it could not match the superior artillery or the superior logistics and organization of the "barbarians of the North." American soldiers died like flies from yellow fever, and they carried into battle the agonies of venereal disease, which they picked up (and left) in every Mexican town they captured, but they benefited enormously from the unprecedented quality of their weapons, supplies, and organization.

By the Treaty of Guadalupe-Hidalgo (February 2, 1848), Mexico ceded Texas with the Rio Grande boundary, New Mexico, and California to the United States; from the Mexican cession would come the states of New Mexico, California, Nevada, and Utah, most of Arizona, and parts of Colorado and Wyoming. In turn, the United States assumed the claims of U.S. citizens against the Mexican government and paid Mexico $15 million. Although some rabid expansionists denounced the treaty because it failed to include all of Mexico, Polk, like most Americans, was satisfied. Empty territory was fine, but few Americans wanted to annex the mixed Spanish and Indian population of Mexico itself and incorporate into the United States "ignorant and indolent half-civilized Indians," in one writer's words. On March 10, 1848, the Senate ratified the treaty by a vote of 38–10.

## The Mexican War in the Popular Mind

Occurring amid the rise of the penny press and the popular novel, the Mexican War became the most fully reported war that the United States had yet fought and the first conflict in which war correspondents were employed. The extensive coverage given to battlefield victories fueled soaring nationalism and helped to submerge political divisions. "We are now all Whigs and all Democrats," an Indiana newspaper exulted.

Romance as well as patriotism gripped the popular mind. Writers portrayed the war as evidence that the noble streak in the American character could prevail over the grasping materialism of U.S. society. A generation raised on the historical novels of Sir Walter Scott believed that the age of chivalry had returned. Popular novels such as *The Texas Ranger; or, the Maid of Matamoros* mingled patriotism and romance in tales of how American soldiers routed Mexican men, only to fall in love with Mexican women.

Zachary Taylor became the main beneficiary of public infatuation with the war. "Old Rough and Ready" seemed to combine, in equal parts, military genius, a democratic bearing, and a conspicuously ordinary manner. In contrast to the more punctilious Winfield Scott ("Old Fuss and Feathers"), Taylor went into battle wearing a straw hat and plain brown coat. To a people searching for heroes, even his short, stocky stature seemed vaguely Napoleonic. The war made Taylor a hero, and the conflicts spinning out of that war would now boost his political career.

## Intensifying Sectional Divisions

Despite wartime patriotic enthusiasm, sectional conflict sharpened between 1846 and 1848. Questions related to territorial expansion intensified this conflict, but so, too, did President Polk's uncompromising and literal-minded Jacksonianism.

Polk had restored the Independent Treasury, to the Whigs' dismay, and had eroded Democratic unity by pursuing Jacksonian policies on tariffs and internal improvements. Despite Polk's campaign promise to combine a revenue tariff with mild protection, his administration's Tariff of 1846 slashed duties to the minimum necessary for revenue. Having alienated his northern supporters, Polk then disappointed western Democrats, thirsting for federal aid to internal improvements, by vetoing the Rivers and Harbors Bill of 1846.

Important as these issues were, territorial expansion generated the Polk administration's major battles. To Polk, it mattered little whether new territories were slave or free. Expansion would meet its purposes by dispersing the population, weakening dangerous tendencies toward centralized government, and ensuring the agricultural and democratic character of the United States. Focusing attention on slavery in the territories struck him as "not only unwise but wicked." To Polk, the Missouri Compromise, prohibiting slavery north of 36°30', embodied a simple, permanent solution to the question of territorial slavery.

But many northerners were coming to see slavery in the territories as a profoundly disruptive issue that neither could nor should be solved simply by extending the 36°30' line. Abolitionist Whigs, who opposed any expansion of slavery on moral grounds, posed a lesser threat to Polk than northern Democrats who feared that extending slavery into New Mexico and California would deter free laborers from settling those territories. Those Democrats argued that competition with slavery degraded free labor, that the westward extension of slavery would create a barrier to the westward migration of free labor, and that such a barrier would intensify social problems already evident in the East: excessive concentration of population, labor protest, class strife, and social stratification.

## The Wilmot Proviso

A young Democratic congressman from Pennsylvania, David Wilmot, galvanized these disaffected northern Democrats. In August 1846 he introduced an amendment to an appropriations bill. This amendment, which became known as the Wilmot Proviso, stipulated that slavery be prohibited in any territory acquired by the negotiations. Wilmot represented the Democrats who had supported annexing Texas on the assumption that it would be the last slave state. Like other northern Democrats, he believed that Polk had made an implicit bargain: Texas for slaveholders, California and New Mexico for free labor. But Polk and southern Democrats opposed any barrier to the expansion of slavery south of the Missouri Compromise line; they believed that the westward expansion of slavery would reduce the concentration of slaves in older southern regions and thus lessen the chances of a slave revolt.

The proviso raised unsettling constitutional questions. Calhoun and other southerners contended that because slaves were property, the Constitution protected slaveholders' right to carry their slaves wherever they chose. This position led to the conclusion that the Missouri Compromise was unconstitutional. On the other side, many northerners cited the Northwest Ordinance of 1787, the Missouri Compromise, and the Constitution itself, which gave Congress the power to "make all needful rules and regulations respecting the territory or other property belonging to the United States," as justification for congressional legislation over slavery in the territories.

## The Election of 1848

The Whigs watched in dismay as prosperity returned under Polk's program of an independent treasury and low tariffs. Never before had Henry Clay's American System of national banking and high tariffs seemed so irrelevant. But the Wilmot Proviso gave the Whigs a political windfall; originating in the Democratic party, it allowed the Whigs to portray themselves as the South's only dependable friends.

These considerations inclined the majority of Whigs toward Zachary Taylor. As a Louisiana slaveholder, he had obvious appeal to the South. As a political newcomer, he had no loyalty to a discredited American System. And as a war hero, he had broad national appeal. Nominating Taylor as presidential candidate in 1848, the Whigs presented him as an ideal man "without regard to creeds or principles" and ran him without any platform.

The Democrats faced a greater challenge because David Wilmot was one of their own. They could not ignore the issue of slavery in the territories, but if they embraced the positions of either Wilmot or Calhoun, the party would split along sectional lines. When Polk declined to run for reelection, the Democrats nominated Lewis Cass of Michigan, who solved their dilemma by announcing the doctrine of "squatter sovereignty," or popular sovereignty as it was later called. Cass argued that Congress should let the question of slavery in the territories be decided by the people who settled there. Squatter sovereignty appealed to many because of its arresting simplicity and vagueness; it loftily ignored such questions as whether Congress actually possessed power to prohibit territorial slavery and (if squatter sovereignty were to become law) what timetables for territorial action should be followed. In fact, few Democrats wanted definitive answers. As long as the doctrine remained vague, northern and southern Democrats alike could interpret it to their respective benefit.

In the campaign both parties tried to avoid the issue of slavery in the territories, but neither succeeded. A pro-Wilmot faction of the Democratic party linked up with the abolitionist Liberty party and antislavery "Conscience" Whigs to form the Free-Soil party. Declaring their dedication to "Free Trade, Free Labor, Free Speech, and Free Men," the Free-Soilers nominated Martin Van Buren on a platform opposing any extension of slavery.

Zachary Taylor benefited from the opposition's alienation of key northern states over the tariff issue, from Democratic disunity over the Wilmot Proviso, and from his war-hero stature. He captured a majority of electoral votes in both North and South. Although it failed to carry any state, the Free-Soil party ran well enough in the North to demonstrate the grassroots popularity of opposition to the extension of slavery. By showing that opposition to the spread of slavery had far more appeal than outright abolitionism, the Free-Soilers sent both Whigs and Democrats a message that they would be unable to ignore in future elections.

## The California Gold Rush

When Wilmot had introduced his proviso, the issue of slavery in the West was more abstract than immediate, for Mexico had not yet ceded any territory. The picture quickly changed when an American carpenter discovered gold while building a sawmill in the foothills of California's Sierra Nevada only

| The Election of 1848 | | | | |
| --- | --- | --- | --- | --- |
| Candidates | Parties | Electoral Vote | Popular Vote | Percentage of Popular Vote |
| ZACHARY TAYLOR | Whig | 163 | 1,360,967 | 47.4 |
| Lewis Cass | Democratic | 127 | 1,222,342 | 42.5 |
| Martin Van Buren | Free-Soil | | 291,263 | 10.1 |

**San Francisco Saloon,**
*by Frank Marryat*

*Mexicans, Chinese, Yankees, and southerners drink together in an ornate San Francisco saloon in the booming gold-rush days.*

nine days before the Treaty of Guadalupe-Hidalgo was signed. A frantic gold rush erupted. A San Francisco paper complained that "the whole country from San Francisco to Los Angeles, and from the shore to the base of the Sierra Nevada, resounds with the sordid cry to gold, GOLD, GOLD! while the field is left half-planted, the house half-built, and everything neglected but the manufacture of shovels and pickaxes." By December 1848 pamphlets with such titles as *The Emigrant's Guide to the Gold Mines* had hit the streets of New York City, and the gold rush was on. Overland emigrants to California rose from 400 in 1848 to 44,000 in 1850.

The gold rush made the issue of slavery in the West an immediate, practical concern. The newcomers to California included Mexicans, free blacks, and slaves brought by southern planters. White prospectors loathed the idea of competing with these groups and wanted to drive them from the gold fields. Violence mounted, and demands grew for a strong civilian government to replace the ineffective military government left over from the war. The gold rush guaranteed that the question of slavery in the Mexican cession would be the first item on the agenda for Polk's successor and the nation.

## CONCLUSION

By calling their destiny manifest, Americans of the 1840s implied that they had no choice but to annex Texas, to seize California and New Mexico, and to take the lion's share of Oregon. The idea of inevitable expansion had deep roots in American experiences and values. Fed by immigration, the population had grown dramatically, increasing nearly 500 percent between 1800 and 1850. Overwhelming numbers of U.S. settlers did as much to seal the fate of Texas as did Sam Houston's victory in the Battle of San Jacinto. Expansion also rested on ideas that seemed self-evident to antebellum Americans: that a nation of farmers would never experience sustained misery, that most Americans would rather work on farms than in factories, and that expansion would provide more land for farming, reduce the dangerous concentration of people in cities, and restore opportunity for all.

But expansion did little to heal deepening divisions between immigrants and native-born Americans or between northerners and southerners. Instead, it split the Democratic party, widened the gap between northern and southern Whigs, and spurred the emergence of the Free-Soil party. As the 1840s ended, Americans, victorious over Mexico and enriched by the discovery of gold in California, would begin to discover the high price of expansion.

## CHRONOLOGY

1818    The United States and Britain agree on joint occupation of Oregon for a ten-year period.

1819    Transcontinental (Adams-Onís) Treaty.

1821    Mexico gains independence from Spain.

1822    Stephen F. Austin founds the first American community in Texas.

1824–    Russia abandons its claims to Oregon south
1825      of 50°40'.

1826    Haden Edwards leads an abortive rebellion against Mexican rule in Texas.

1827    The United States and Britain renew their agreement on joint occupation of Oregon for an indefinite period.

1830    Mexico closes Texas to further American immigration.

1834    Antonio López de Santa Anna comes to power in Mexico.
Austin secures repeal of the ban on American immigration into Texas.

1835    Santa Anna invades Texas.

1836    Texas declares its independence from Mexico.
Fall of the Alamo.
Goliad massacre.
Battle of San Jacinto.

1840    William Henry Harrison elected president.

1841    Harrison dies; John Tyler becomes president.
Tyler vetoes Whig National Banking Bill.

1842    Webster-Ashburton Treaty.

1843    Tyler launches campaign for Texas annexation.

1844    Philadelphia Bible Riots.
Senate rejects treaty annexing Texas.
James K. Polk elected president.

1845    Texas accepts annexation by the United States.
Mexico rejects Slidell mission.

1846    Congress ends the joint occupation of Oregon.
Zachary Taylor defeats the Mexicans in two battles north of the Rio Grande.
The United States declares war on Mexico.
John C. Frémont proclaims the Bear Flag Republic in California.
Congress votes to accept a settlement of the Oregon boundary issue with Britain.
Colonel Stephen Kearny occupies Santa Fe.
Wilmot Proviso introduced.
Taylor takes Monterrey.

1847    Taylor defeats Santa Anna at the Battle of Buena Vista.
Vera Cruz falls to Winfield Scott.
Mexico City falls to Scott.
Lewis Cass's principle of "squatter sovereignty."

1848    Gold discovered in California.
Treaty of Guadalupe-Hidalgo signed.
Taylor elected president.

## FOR FURTHER READING

Ray A. Billington, *The Far Western Frontier, 1830–1860* (1956). A comprehensive narrative of the settlement of the Far West.

William R. Brock, *Parties and Political Conscience: American Dilemmas, 1840–1850* (1979). An excellent interpretive study of the politics of the 1840s.

William H. Goetzmann, *When the Eagle Screamed: The Romantic Horizon in American Diplomacy, 1800–1860* (1966). A lively overview of antebellum expansionism.

Maldwyn A. Jones, *American Immigration* (1960). An excellent brief introduction to immigration.

Patricia Nelson Limerick, *Legacy of Conquest* (1987). A provocative interpretation of western history.

Charles G. Sellers, *James K. Polk: Continentalist, 1843–1846* (1966). An outstanding political biography.

Henry Nash Smith, *Virgin Land: The American West as Symbol and Myth* (1950). A classic study of westward expansion in the American mind.

From December 1859 to February 1860 Congress deadlocked over the selection of the Speaker of the House of Representatives. Tempers flared as northerners and southerners collided ideologically. A South Carolinian observed that "the only persons who do not have a revolver and a knife are those who have two revolvers." The election of an inoffensive New Jersey congressman to the speakership broke the deadlock, but the tension in Congress reflected the divisions between North and South that would lead to civil war.

Confrontations with the North over slavery in the territories fed a deepening desperation in the South and spawned thoughts of secession—withdrawal from the Union. During the 1850s a growing number of northerners embraced the doctrine of free soil, the belief that Congress had to prohibit slavery in all the territories. Prominent free-soilers such as William Seward of New York and Abraham Lincoln of Illinois, who sought to limit but not to abolish slavery, made the

# From Compromise to Secession, 1850–1861

The Compromise of 1850

⚮

The Collapse of the
Second Party System

⚮

The Crisis of the Union

*(Right)* **John Brown** *by John Steuart Curry, 1939*

conflict over slavery a national issue. Seward spoke of an "irrepressible conflict" between slavery and freedom, and Lincoln said, "I believe this government cannot endure permanently half *slave* and half *free*."

To free-soil advocates, the ideal society was composed of free people working to achieve economic self-sufficiency as landowning farmers, self-employed artisans, and small shopkeepers. Southerners also valued economic independence, but they insisted that without slaves to do menial jobs, whites could never attain self-sufficiency. By 1850 most southerners had persuaded themselves that slavery treated blacks humanely while enabling whites to live comfortably.

These differing images of the good society made conflict over slavery in the territories virtually unavoidable. Free-soil attacks on territorial slavery infuriated southerners, who believed they should be able to take slaves—their property—anywhere they wanted. They interpreted free-soilers' hostility as a thinly disguised attempt to erode slavery's foundations. When abolitionist John Brown recklessly attempted to launch a slave insurrection in 1859, many southerners concluded that secession offered their only protection. "Not only our property," a southern editor proclaimed, "but our honor, our lives and our all are involved."

# The Compromise of 1850

Ralph Waldo Emerson's grim prediction that a U.S. victory in the Mexican War would be like swallowing arsenic proved disturbingly accurate. When the war ended in 1848, the United States contained an equal number (fifteen each) of free and slave states, but the vast territory gained by the war threatened to upset this balance. Any solution to the question of slavery in the Mexican cession—a free-soil policy, extension of the Missouri Compromise line, or popular sovereignty—ensured controversy. The prospect of free soil angered southerners, while extension of the Missouri Compromise line antagonized free-soil northerners as well as southern

extremists who proclaimed that Congress could not bar slavery's expansion. Popular sovereignty offered the greatest hope for compromise by taking the question of slavery out of national politics and handing it to each territory, but this notion pleased neither free-soil nor proslavery extremists.

As the rhetoric escalated, events plunged the nation into crisis. Utah and then California, both acquired from Mexico, sought admission to the Union as free states. Texas, admitted to the Union as a slave state in 1845, aggravated matters by claiming the eastern half of New Mexico, thus potentially opening the door to slavery's extension into other newly acquired territory.

By 1850 other issues had become intertwined with territorial questions. Northerners had grown increasingly unhappy with slavery in the District of Columbia, within the shadow of the Capitol; southerners complained about lax enforcement of the Fugitive Slave Act of 1793. Any broad compromise would have to take both matters into account.

## Zachary Taylor at the Helm

President Zachary Taylor believed that the South must not kindle the issue of slavery in the territories because neither New Mexico nor California was suited for slavery. In 1849 he asserted that "the people of the North need have no apprehension of the further extension of slavery."

Taylor's position differed significantly with the thinking behind the still controversial Wilmot Proviso, which proposed that Congress bar slavery in the territories ceded by Mexico. Taylor's plan, in contrast, left the decision to the states. He prompted California to apply for admission as a free state, bypassing the territorial stage, and hinted that he expected New Mexico (where the Mexican government had abolished slavery) to do the same. This strategy appeared to offer a quick, practical solution to the problem of extending slavery. The North would gain two new free states, and the South would gain acceptance of the right of the individual state to bar or to permit slavery.

But southerners rejected Taylor's plan. Not

only would it yield the Wilmot Proviso's goal—the banning of slavery from the lands acquired from Mexico—but it rested on the shaky assumption that slavery could never take root in California or New Mexico. Southerners also protested the addition of two new free states. "If we are to be reduced to a mere handful . . . wo, wo, I say to this Union," John C. Calhoun warned. Disillusioned with Taylor, a slaveholder from whom they had expected better, nine southern states agreed to send delegates to a convention to meet in Nashville in June 1850.

### Henry Clay Proposes a Compromise

Had Taylor held a stronger position in the Whig party, he might have blunted mounting southern opposition. But many leading Whigs had never accepted this political novice, and in early 1850 Kentucky senator Henry Clay challenged Taylor's leadership by forging a compromise bill to resolve the whole range of contentious issues. Clay proposed (1) the admission of California as a free state; (2) the division of the remainder of the Mexican cession into two territories, New Mexico and Utah, without federal restrictions on slavery; (3) the settlement of the Texas–New Mexico boundary dispute on terms favorable to New Mexico; (4) as a pot-sweetener for Texas, an agreement that the federal government would assume the state's large public debt; (5) continuation of slavery in the District of Columbia but abolition of the slave trade; and (6) a more effective fugitive slave law.

Clay rolled all these proposals into a single "omnibus" bill. The debates over the compromise bill during late winter and early spring 1850 marked the last major appearance on the public stage of Clay, Calhoun, and Webster, the trio who had stood at the center of American political life since the War of 1812. Clay, the conciliator as ever, warned the South against the evils of secession and assured the North that nature would check the spread of slavery. Gaunt and gloomy, the dying Calhoun listened as another senator read Calhoun's address for him, a repetition of his warnings that only if the North treated the South as an equal could the

**Henry Clay (1777–1852)**
*Eloquent but at the same time earthy, Clay was first elected to the Senate during Jefferson's administration. Subsequently, Clay himself made five unsuccessful bids for the presidency. A European visitor was struck by his penchant for chewing tobacco, drinking whiskey, putting his legs on the table, and spitting "like a regular Kentucky hog-driver."*

Union survive. Webster spoke vividly in favor of compromise, "not as a Massachusetts man, nor as a Northern man, but as an American," and chided the North for trying to "reenact the will of God" by excluding slavery from the Mexican cession. Strident voices countered these attempts at conciliation. The antislavery Whig William Seward of New York enraged southerners by talking of a "higher law than the Constitution"—namely, the will of God against the extension of slavery. Clay's compromise faltered as Clay broke with President Taylor, who attacked him as a glory hunter.

Even as the Union faced its worst crisis since 1789, events in summer 1850 eased the way toward

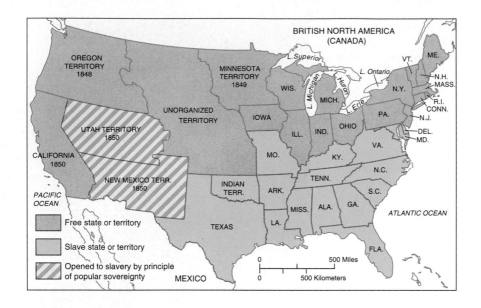

**The Compromise of 1850**

*The Compromise of 1850 admitted California as a free state. Utah and New Mexico were left open to slavery or freedom according to the principle of popular sovereignty.*

resolution. When the Nashville convention met in June, only nine of the fifteen slave states, primarily in the Lower South, sent delegates. Despite the reckless pronouncements of the "fire-eaters" (extreme advocates of "southern rights"), moderates dominated. Then Zachary Taylor celebrated too extravagantly on July 4 and died five days later of a stomach ailment. His successor, Millard Fillmore of New York, supported Clay's compromise. Finally, Senator Stephen A. Douglas of Illinois took over stewardship of the bill from the exhausted Clay and ingeniously secured its passage by chopping the omnibus bill into a series of individual measures. By summer's end Congress had passed each component of Clay's plan and the Compromise of 1850 had become reality.

### Assessing the Compromise

Although President Fillmore hailed the compromise as a final settlement of sectional issues, it failed to bridge the underlying differences between North and South. Few members of Congress had supported each separate proposal: southerners had voted against the admission of California and northerners against the Fugitive Slave Act. Only shifting alliances between moderates and northerners or southerners on specific issues had achieved passage of the compromise.

Each section could claim victories from the compromise. Northern victories were clear: admission of California and abolition of the slave trade in the District of Columbia. However, southern victories, such as the stricter fugitive slave law, were clouded by the legislators' failure to resolve the issue of congressional authority over slavery in territories outside the Mexican cession.

Southerners therefore reacted ambivalently to the Compromise of 1850. In state elections during fall 1850 and 1851, procompromise candidates generally thrashed the law's opponents. At the same time, Unionists in Georgia wrote the celebrated Georgia platform, which threatened secession if Congress prohibited slavery in the Mexican cession or repealed the Fugitive Slave Act. And the South's one clear victory, the passage of a new, more stringent fugitive slave law, quickly proved a mixed blessing.

## Enforcement of the Fugitive Slave Act

Northern moderates accepted the Fugitive Slave Act of 1850 as the price of saving the Union, but the law outraged antislavery northerners. It denied alleged fugitives the right of trial by jury, forbade them to testify at their own trial, permitted their return to slavery merely on the testimony of a claimant, and enabled court-appointed commissioners to collect ten dollars if they ruled for the slaveholder but only five if they ruled for the fugitive. As one commentator noted, the law threatened to turn the North into "one vast hunting ground." It targeted *all* runaways, putting at risk even fugitives who had lived as free blacks for thirty years or more. Above all, the law brought home to northerners the uncomfortable truth of their own complicity in slavery's continuation. By legalizing the activities of slave catchers on northern soil, the law reminded northerners that slavery was a national problem, not merely a southern institution. Antislavery northerners assailed the law in such terms as the "vilest monument of infamy of the nineteenth century."

Efforts to catch and return runaways inflamed emotions in both North and South. In 1854 a Boston mob aroused by antislavery speeches killed a courthouse guard in an abortive effort to rescue fugitive slave Anthony Burns. Determined to enforce the law, President Franklin Pierce sent federal troops to escort Burns to the harbor, where a ship carried him back to slavery. As five platoons of troops marched Burns to the ship, 50,000 people lined the streets. One Bostonian hung from his window a black coffin bearing the words "THE FUNERAL OF LIBERTY." The Burns incident shattered the complacency of conservative supporters of the Compromise of 1850. "We went to bed one night old fashioned conservative Compromise Union Whigs," textile manufacturer Amos A. Lawrence wrote, "and waked up stark mad Abolitionists." A Boston committee later purchased Burns's freedom, but other fugitives had worse fates. Margaret Garner, about to be captured and sent back to Kentucky as a slave, tried to kill her children rather than witness their return to slavery.

**Harriet Beecher Stowe (1811–1896)**
*Stowe did extensive research before writing* Uncle Tom's Cabin. *By making the demonic Simon Legree a northerner and by portraying southerners as well meaning, she effectively indicted slavery as an institution.*

Northerners devised ways to interfere with the enforcement of the Fugitive Slave Act. "Vigilance" committees spirited endangered blacks to Canada, lawyers dragged out hearings to raise slave catchers' expenses, and "personal liberty laws" hindered state officials' enforcement of the law. These obstructionist tactics convinced southerners that opposition to slavery boiled just beneath the surface of northern opinion. The southern "victory" represented by the passage of the Fugitive Slave Act seemed increasingly illusory.

## Uncle Tom's Cabin

Harriet Beecher Stowe's novel *Uncle Tom's Cabin* (1852) drummed up wide northern support for fugitive slaves. Stowe, the daughter of famed evangeli-

| The Election of 1852 | | | | |
|---|---|---|---|---|
| Candidates | Parties | Electoral Vote | Popular Vote | Percentage of Popular Vote |
| FRANKLIN PIERCE | Democratic | 254 | 1,601,117 | 50.9 |
| Winfield Scott | Whig | 42 | 1,385,453 | 44.1 |
| John P. Hale | Free-Soil | | 155,825 | 5.0 |

cal Lyman Beecher, greeted the Fugitive Slave Act with horror. In one of the novel's most memorable scenes, she depicted the slave Eliza, clutching her infant son, bounding across ice floes on the Ohio River to freedom. Slavery itself was Stowe's main target. Much of her novel's power derives from its view that good intentions mean little in the face of so evil an institution. The good intentions of a kindly slave owner die with him, and Uncle Tom is sold to the vicious Yankee Simon Legree, who whips Tom to death. Stowe also played effectively to the emotions of her audience by demonstrating how slavery ripped slave families apart.

Three hundred thousand copies of *Uncle Tom's Cabin* were sold in 1852, and 1.2 million by summer 1853. Stage dramatizations reached perhaps fifty times as many people as the novel did. As a play, *Uncle Tom's Cabin* enthralled working-class audiences normally indifferent or hostile to abolitionism. Yet the impact of *Uncle Tom's Cabin* cannot be precisely measured. Although it hardly lived up to the prediction of one abolitionist leader that it would convert 2 million people to abolitionism, it did push many waverers toward an aggressive anti-slavery stance. As historian David Potter concluded, the northern attitude toward slavery "was never quite the same after *Uncle Tom's Cabin*."

## The Election of 1852

The Fugitive Slave Act fragmented the Whig party. Northern Whigs took the lead in defying the law, and southern Whigs had a difficult time explaining away the power of vocal free-soil Whigs.

In 1852 the Whigs' nomination of Mexican War hero General Winfield Scott as their presidential candidate widened the sectional split in the party. Although a Virginian, Scott owed his nomination to the northern free-soil Whigs. His single, feeble statement endorsing the Compromise of 1850 undercut southern Whigs trying to portray the Democrats as the party of disunion and themselves as the party of both slavery and the Union.

The Democrats had their own problems. Substantial numbers of free-soilers who had left the party in 1848 gravitated to the Whig party in 1852. The Democrats nominated Franklin Pierce of New Hampshire, a dark-horse candidate whose chief attraction was that no faction of the party violently opposed him. The "ultra men of the South," a friend of his noted, "say they can cheerfully go for him, and none, none say they cannot." Northern and southern Democrats alike rallied behind the Compromise of 1850 and behind the ideal of popular sovereignty, and Pierce won a smashing victory. In the most one-sided election since 1820, he carried twenty-seven of the thirty-one states and collected 254 of 296 electoral votes. Following the Whigs' devastating defeats throughout the South in both presidential and local elections, one stalwart lamented "the decisive breaking-up of our party."

## The Collapse of the Second Party System

Franklin Pierce was the last presidential candidate of the nineteenth century to carry the popular and electoral vote in both North and South. Not until Franklin D. Roosevelt swept into office in 1932

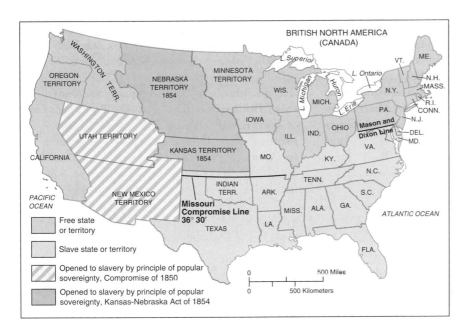

**The Kansas-Nebraska Act, 1854**

*Kansas and Nebraska lay within the Louisiana Purchase, north of 36°30', and hence were closed to slavery until Stephen A. Douglas introduced his bills in 1854.*

would another president do so. Pierce also became the last president to hold office under the second party system—Whigs against Democrats. Within four years of Pierce's election, the Whig party would disintegrate, to be replaced by two newcomers, the American (Know-Nothing) party and the Republican party.

Unlike the Whigs, the Republican party was a purely sectional, northern party, drawing its support from both former Whigs and discontented Democrats. The Democrats survived as a national party, but with a base so shrunken in the North that the newborn Republican party captured two-thirds of the free states in the election of 1856.

For decades the second party system had kept the conflict over slavery in check by providing Americans other issues to argue about—banking, internal improvements, tariffs, and temperance. By the 1850s the debate over slavery extension overshadowed such issues and exposed raw divisions in each party. Whigs, with their larger, more aggressive free-soil wing, were much more vulnerable to disruption than the Democrats. Thus when Stephen A. Douglas put forth a proposal in 1854 to organize the vast Nebraska territory with no restrictions on

slavery, he ignited a fire-storm that consumed the Whig party.

## The Kansas-Nebraska Act

Signed in late May 1854, the Kansas-Nebraska Act shattered the already weakened second party system and triggered renewed sectional strife. The bill's roots lay in the seemingly uncontroversial desire of farmers to organize the large territory west of Iowa and Missouri. Railroad enthusiasts who dreamed of a rail line linking the Midwest to the Pacific also wanted the territory organized.

In January 1854 Democratic senator Stephen A. Douglas of Illinois proposed a bill to organize Nebraska as a territory. Douglas believed that a railroad to the Pacific would bring national benefits, including a continuous line of settlement, and thought that a railroad-based western expansion would unite the splintering Democratic factions.

Two sources of potential conflict loomed. First, some southerners advocated a southern-based Pacific route rather than a midwestern one. Second, Nebraska lay north of the Missouri Compromise line in the Louisiana Purchase, a region closed to slavery. Under Douglas's bill, the South would lose the Pacific rail route *and* face the possibility of more free territory in the Union. To placate southerners and win their votes, Douglas made two concessions. First, he proclaimed the Missouri Compromise now void, superseded by the Compromise of 1850 and its doctrine of popular sovereignty. Second, Douglas agreed to divide the territory into northern and southern parts, Nebraska and Kansas. Implicit in this, at least to southerners, was the idea that Nebraska would be free soil but Kansas would be open to slavery.

These modifications to Douglas's original bill set off a storm of protest. Despite Douglas's belief that national expansion was the critical issue, most attention focused on the extension of slavery. Anti-slavery northerners assailed the bill as "an atrocious plot" to violate the Missouri Compromise and to turn Kansas into a "dreary region of despotism, inhabited by masters and slaves." Their anger provoked an equal response among southerners and added the issue of regional pride to the already volatile mix of expansion and slavery.

Despite the uproar, Douglas guided the bill easily through the Senate. Matters were far more tumultuous in the House, where the bill passed by a narrow margin. Ominously, not a single northern Whig in the House voted for the bill, and northern Democrats split evenly.

## The Surge of Free Soil

Amid the clamor over his bill, Douglas ruefully observed that he could now travel to Chicago by the light of his own burning effigies. Neither a fool nor a political novice, he was the victim of a political bombshell, free soil, that exploded under his feet.

Support for free soil united many who agreed on little else. Many free-soilers were racists who opposed allowing any African-Americans, slave or free, into the West. Others repudiated slavery on moral grounds and rejected blatantly racist legislation. However, as one abolitionist noted, the free-soil convictions of many westerners rested on a "perfect, if not supreme" hatred of African-Americans.

Although split over the morality of slavery, most free-soilers agreed that slavery impeded whites' progress. Most accepted Abraham Lincoln's portrayal of the North as a society of upwardly mobile farmers, artisans, and small-business operators. Any enterprising individual could escape wage labor and attain self-employment. "The man who labored for another last year," Lincoln insisted, "this year labors for himself, and next year he will hire others to labor for him." Because a slave worked for nothing, free-soilers claimed, no free laborer could compete with a slave. In any territory that allowed slavery, free labor would therefore vanish. Wherever slavery appeared, a free-soiler argued, "labor loses its dignity; industry sickens; education finds no schools; religion finds no churches, and the whole land of slavery is impoverished." Free-soilers also rejected the idea that slavery had natural limits. "Slavery is as certain to invade New Mexico and Utah, as the sun is to rise," insisted a free-soiler. If slavery secured a toehold in Kansas, free-soilers warned, Minnesota would fall to slavery as well.

The Kansas-Nebraska Act, in free-soilers' opinion, was "a part of a continuous movement of slaveholders to advance slavery over the entire North." Free-soilers saw southern planters, southern politicians, and their northern dupes, such as Stephen A. Douglas, entangled in a gigantic conspiracy to extend slavery. To free-soilers, a *pattern* of events—the Fugitive Slave Act, the repeal of the Missouri Compromise, and the division of Nebraska—demonstrated that a diabolical "Slave Power" was spreading its tentacles like an octopus.

## The Ebbing of Manifest Destiny

The uproar over the Kansas-Nebraska Act embarrassed the Pierce administration. It also doomed Manifest Destiny, the one issue that had held the Democrats together in the 1840s.

Franklin Pierce had come to office championing Manifest Destiny, but increasing sectional rivalries sidetracked his efforts. In 1853 his emissary James Gadsden negotiated the purchase of a strip of land south of the Gila River (now southern Arizona and part of southern New Mexico), an acquisition favored by advocates of a southern railroad route to the Pacific. Fierce opposition to the Gadsden Purchase revealed mounting free-soilers' suspicions of expansion, and the Senate approved the treaty only after slashing 9,000 square miles from the purchase. The sectional rivalries beginning to engulf the Nebraska bill clearly threatened any proposal to gain new territory.

Cuba provided even more vivid proof of the change in public attitudes toward expansion. In 1854 a former Mississippi governor, John A. Quitman, planned a filibuster (an unofficial military expedition) to seize Cuba from Spain. Pierce wanted to acquire Cuba and may first have encouraged Quitman's plans, but the president backed down in the face of northern opposition. Northerners saw the filibuster as another manifestation of the Slave Power's conspiracy to grab more territory for the South's "peculiar institution."

Events, however, slipped out of Pierce's control. In October 1854 the American ambassadors to Great Britain, France, and Spain, two of them southerners, met in Belgium and issued the unofficial Ostend Manifesto, calling on the United States to acquire Cuba by any means, including force. Beset by the storm over the Kansas-Nebraska Act and northern fury over Quitman's proposed filibuster, Pierce repudiated the manifesto.

Despite the Pierce administration's disavowal of the Ostend Manifesto, the idea of expansion into the Caribbean continued to attract southerners, including the Tennessee-born adventurer William Walker. Between 1853 and 1860, the year a firing squad in Honduras executed him, Walker led a succession of filibustering expeditions into Mexico and Nicaragua. Taking advantage of civil chaos in Nicaragua, he made himself the chief political force there, reinstituted slavery, and talked of making Nicaragua a U.S. colony. Southern expansionists, moreover, kept the acquisition of Mexico and Cuba at the top of their agenda and received some support from northern Democrats. As late as 1859 James Buchanan, Pierce's successor, asked Congress to appropriate funds to purchase Cuba.

Although some southerners were against expansion—among them the Louisiana sugar planters who opposed acquiring Cuba because Cuban sugar would compete with their product—southern expansionists stirred up enough commotion to worry antislavery northerners that the South aspired to establish a Caribbean slave empire. Like a card in a poker game, the threat of expansion southward was all the more menacing for not being played. As long as the debate on the extension of slavery focused on territories in the continental United States, slavery's prospects for expansion were limited. However, adding Caribbean territory to the equation changed all calculations.

## The Whigs Disintegrate

While straining Democratic unity, the Kansas-Nebraska Act wrecked the Whig party. Although Democrats lost ground in the 1854 congressional elections, the Whigs failed to benefit. No matter how furious the free-soil Democrats were at Douglas for introducing the act, they could not forget that southern Whigs had supported him. Northern Whigs split into two camps: antislavery "Conscience" Whigs, led by Senator William Seward of New York, and conservatives, led by former president Millard Fillmore. The conservatives believed that the Whig party had to adhere to the Compromise of 1850 to maintain itself as a national party.

This deep division within the Whig party repelled anti-slavery Democrats and prompted anti-slavery Whigs to look for an alternative party. By 1856 the new Republican party would become home for these anti-slavery refugees; however, in 1854 and 1855 the American, or Know-Nothing, party emerged as the principal alternative to the faltering established parties.

## The Rise and Fall of the Know-Nothings

The Know-Nothings evolved out of a nativist organization, the Order of the Star-Spangled Banner. (The party's popular name derived from its members' standard response to inquiries about its activities: "I know nothing.") One of many nativist societies that had mushroomed in response to the immigration boom of the 1840s, the Order of the Star-Spangled Banner had pressured existing parties to nominate and appoint only native-born Protestants. It had also urged lengthening the naturalization period before immigrants could vote.

Winfield Scott's compaign for the presidency in 1852 had alienated many nativists, who had previously voted Whig. Trying to revitalize his badly split party, Scott had courted the traditionally Democratic Catholic vote. Most Catholics had voted for Franklin Pierce, but many nativists bailed out of the Whig party. The Kansas-Nebraska Act cemented nativist allegiance to the Know-Nothings, opposed both to the extension of slavery and to Catholicism. An obsessive fear of conspiracies unified the Know-Nothings. They simultaneously denounced a papal conspiracy against the American republic and a Slave Power conspiracy reaching its tentacles throughout the United States.

The Know-Nothings enjoyed a meteoric rise and an equally rapid fall. For example, in 1854 they captured the governorship, almost the entire state legislature, and all the congressional seats of Massachusetts. Such Know-Nothing successes wrecked Whig hopes of capitalizing on hostility to the Kansas-Nebraska Act.

By 1856 the Know-Nothings had become a falling star soon to plummet below the horizon. They proved as vulnerable to sectional conflicts over slavery as the Whigs. In 1855 southern Know-Nothings, mainly proslavery former Whigs, combined with northern conservatives to make acceptance of the Kansas-Nebraska Act part of the Know-Nothing platform, blurring the attraction of Know-Nothingism to northern voters more antislavery than anti-Catholic. One such former Whig, Illinois congressman Abraham Lincoln, asked pointedly, "How can anyone who abhors the oppression of negroes be in favor of degrading classes of white people?" Most Know-Nothings eventually concluded that, as one observer put it, "neither the Pope nor the foreigners ever can govern the country or endanger its liberties, but the slavebreeders and slavetraders *do* govern it, and threaten to put an end to all government but theirs." Chief beneficiary of the Know-Nothing dilemma was the emerging Republican party, which had no southern wing to blunt its antislavery message.

## The Origins of the Republican Party

Born in the chaotic aftermath of the Kansas-Nebraska Act, the Republican party would become the main opposition to the Democratic party by 1856 and would win each presidential election from 1860 until 1884. In 1855, however, few might have predicted such a bright future. Although united in opposition to the Kansas-Nebraska Act, the fledgling party was host to conservatives who wanted to restore the Missouri Compromise, radicals who had been part of the Liberty party abolitionists, and a sizable middle of free-soilers.

Building organizations at the state level was essential, for state issues often shaped voters' allegiances. The Know-Nothings, for example, linked support for temperance, strong at the state level, with anti-Catholicism and antislavery. Frequently antislavery voters were also protemperance and anti-Catholic, believing that addiction to alcohol and submission to the pope were both forms of enslavement to be eradicated. Competing with the Know-Nothings for these intensely moralistic voters at the state level, Republicans faced a dilemma: if they attacked the Know-Nothings for stressing anti-Catholicism over antislavery, they might well alienate the voters, but if they compromised with the Know-Nothings, they might well lose their own identity as a party.

Alternately attacking and conciliating, the Republicans succeeded in some state elections in 1855 but lost ground as popular ire against the Kansas-Nebraska Act cooled. By the start of 1856 they were organized in only half the northern states and lacked any national organization. The Republicans desperately needed something to make voters more concerned about the Slave Power than about rum or Catholicism. Salvation for the nascent party came in the form of violence in Kansas, which quickly became known as Bleeding Kansas. This violence united the party around its free-soil center, intensified antislavery feelings, and boosted Republican fortunes.

## Bleeding Kansas

In the wake of the Kansas-Nebraska Act, Boston abolitionists had organized a company to send antislavery settlers into Kansas, but most of the territory's early settlers came from Missouri or other parts of the Midwest. Few of these opposed slavery on moral grounds. Some supported slavery; others wanted to keep all African-Americans out of Kansas. "I kem to Kansas to live in a free state," exclaimed one clergyman, "and I don't want niggers a-trampin' over my grave."

Despite most settlers' racist leanings and hatred of abolitionists, Kansas became a battleground between proslavery and antislavery forces. In March 1855 thousands of proslavery Missouri "border ruffians" crossed into Kansas to vote illegally in the first elections for the territorial legislature. Drawing revolvers, they quickly silenced judges who challenged their right to vote in Kansas. Ironically, proslavery forces probably would have won an honest election. But the proslavery legislature established in 1855 in Lecompton, Kansas, operated under a cloud of fraud. "There is not a proslavery man of my acquaintance in Kansas," wrote the antislavery wife of a farmer, "who does not acknowledge that the Bogus Legislature was the result of a gigantic and well-planned fraud, that the elections were carried by an invading mob from Missouri." The Lecompton legislature shredded what little good reputation it had by passing a series of outrageous laws, punishing the harboring of fugitive slaves by ten years' imprisonment, and making the circulation of abolitionist literature a capital offense.

The legislature's actions set off a chain reaction. In summer 1855 free-staters, including many aroused to oppose the Lecompton legislature, organized a rival government at Topeka. In May 1856 the Lecompton government dispatched a posse to Lawrence, where some free-staters were organizing a militia. The Lecompton posse, bearing banners emblazoned "SOUTHERN RIGHTS" and "LET YANKEES TREMBLE AND ABOLITIONISTS FALL," tore through Lawrence, burning buildings and destroying two printing presses. There were no deaths, but Republicans immediately dubbed the incident "THE SACK OF LAWRENCE."

The next move belonged to John Brown, a Connecticut-born abolitionist with an overpowering sense of divinely ordained mission. The "sack" of Lawrence convinced Brown that God now beckoned him "to break the jaws of the wicked." In late May Brown led seven men, including his four sons and his son-in-law, toward Pottawatomie Creek near Lawrence. They shot to death one man associated with the Lecompton government and hacked four others to pieces with broadswords. Brown's "Pottawatomie Massacre" terrified southerners and transformed "Bleeding Kansas" into a battleground between North and South. Supporters of slavery armed themselves for, as one South Carolinian wrote, "no Proslavery man knows when he is safe in this Ter[ritory]."

Popular sovereignty had failed in Kansas. Instead of resolving the issue of the extension of slavery, popular sovereignty had institutionalized the division over slavery by creating two rival governments. The Pierce administration compounded its problems, and Kansas's, by denouncing the antislavery Topeka government and recognizing the proslavery Lecompton government, thus forcing northern Democrats into the awkward appearance of supporting the "Bogus Legislature" at Lecompton. Nor did popular sovereignty keep the slavery issue out of politics. On the day before the proslavery attack on Lawrence, Republican senator Charles Sumner of Massachusetts delivered a wrathful speech, "The Crime Against Kansas," in which he verbally lashed the Senate for its complicity in slavery. Sumner singled out Senator Andrew Butler of South Carolina for making "the harlot, slavery" his mistress. The speech stunned the Senate. Two days later a relative of Butler, Democratic representative Preston Brooks of South Carolina, strode into the

| The Election of 1856 | | | | |
| --- | --- | --- | --- | --- |
| Candidates | Parties | Electoral Vote | Popular Vote | Percentage of Popular Vote |
| JAMES BUCHANAN | Democratic | 174 | 1,832,955 | 45.3 |
| John C. Frémont | Republican | 114 | 1,339,932 | 33.1 |
| Millard Fillmore | American | 8 | 871,731 | 21.6 |

Senate chamber and beat Sumner with a cane. The hollow cane broke after five or six blows, but Sumner, who required stitches, took three years to recuperate. Brooks immediately became a hero in the South.

Now "Bleeding Kansas" and "Bleeding Sumner" united the North. The "sack" of Lawrence, President Pierce's recognition of the proslavery Lecompton government, and Brooks's actions seemed to clinch the Republican argument that an aggressive slaveocracy was in power and holding white northerners in contempt. By denouncing the Slave Power rather than slavery, the Republicans sidestepped the divisive question of slavery's morality. Instead, they focused on portraying planters as arrogant aristocrats, the natural enemies of the laboring people of the North.

## The Election of 1856

The presidential race of 1856 revealed the scope of the political realignment of the preceding few years. The Republicans, in their first presidential contest, nominated John C. Frémont, the "pathfinder" of California "Bear State" fame. Northern Know-Nothings also endorsed Frémont, while southern Know-Nothings nominated Millard Fillmore, the last Whig president. The Democrats dumped the battered Pierce for James Buchanan of Pennsylvania, who had had the luck to be out of the country (as minister to Great Britain) during the Kansas-Nebraska furor. A signer of the Ostend Manifesto, Buchanan was popular in the South.

The campaign became two separate races: Frémont versus Buchanan in the free states and Fillmore versus Buchanan in the slave states. Buchanan in effect was the only national candidate. Although Frémont attracted wide support in the North and Fillmore equal support in the South, Buchanan carried enough votes in both North and South to win the presidency.

The election of 1856 made three facts clear. First, the American party was finished as a major national force. Having worked for the Republican Frémont, most northern Know-Nothings joined that party. Fillmore's dismal showing in the South convinced southern Know-Nothings to abandon their party and seek a new political affiliation. Second, although in existence for barely a year, lacking any base in the South, and running a political novice, the Republican party did very well. A purely sectional party had nearly captured the presidency. Third, as long as the Democrats could unite behind a single national candidate, they would be hard to defeat. To achieve unity, however, the Democrats would have to find more James Buchanans—"doughface" moderates acceptable to southerners and northerners alike.

# The Crisis of the Union

No one ever accused James Buchanan of impulsiveness or fanaticism. Although a moderate who wished to avoid controversy, Buchanan would preside over one of the most controversy-ridden administrations in American history. A Supreme Court decision concerning Dred Scott, a Missouri slave who had resided in free territory for several years; the creation of the proslavery Lecompton constitution in Kansas; a raid by John Brown on Harpers Ferry, Virginia; and secession itself would wrack Buchanan's administration. The forces driving the nation apart were spinning out of control by 1856, and Buchanan could not stop them. By his inauguration, southerners saw creeping abolitionism in the guise of free soil and northerners detected an ever more insatiable Slave Power. Once these potent images took hold in the minds of the American people, politicians could do little to erase them.

## The Dred Scott Case

Pledged to congressional "noninterference" with slavery in the territories, Buchanan looked to the courts for resolution of the vexatious issue of slavery's extension. A case that appeared to promise a solution had been winding its way through the courts for years; on March 6, 1857, two days after Buchanan's inauguration, the Supreme Court handed down its decision in *Dred Scott* v. *Sandford.*

During the 1830s his master had taken Dred Scott, a slave, from the slave state of Missouri into Illinois and the Wisconsin Territory, both closed to slavery. After his master's death, Scott sued for his freedom on the grounds of his residence in free territory. Scott's case reached the Supreme Court in 1856.

The Court faced two key questions. Did Scott's residence in free territory during the 1830s make him free? Did Scott, again enslaved in Missouri, have the right to sue in the federal courts? The Supreme Court could have neatly sidestepped controversy by ruling that Scott had no right to sue, but it chose not to.

Instead, Chief Justice Roger B. Taney, a seventy-nine-year-old Marylander, handed down a sweeping decision that touched off another firestorm. First, Taney wrote, Scott, a slave, could not sue for his freedom. Further, no black, whether a slave or a free descendant of slaves, could become a U.S. citizen. Continuing his incendiary opinion, Taney ruled that even had Scott been entitled to sue, his residence in free territory did not make him free because the Missouri Compromise, whose provisions prohibited slavery in the Wisconsin Territory, was itself unconstitutional. The compromise, declared Taney, violated the Fifth Amendment's protection of property (including slaves).

The *Dred Scott* decision, instead of settling the issue of expansion of slavery, touched off another blast of controversy. The antislavery press flayed it as "willful perversion" filled with "gross historical falsehoods." Republicans saw the decision as further evidence that the fiendish Slave Power gripped the nation. The Slave Power, a northern paper bellowed, "has marched over and annihilated the boundaries of the states. We are now one great homogeneous slaveholding community."

Like Stephen A. Douglas after the Kansas-Nebraska Act, James Buchanan now appeared as another northern dupe of an evil slaveocracy. Republicans restrained themselves from open defiance of the decision only by insisting that it did not bind the nation; Taney's comments on the constitutionality of the Missouri Compromise, they contended, were opinions unnecessary to settling the case and therefore technically not binding.

The savage reaction to the decision provided more proof that no "judicious" or nonpartisan solution to slavery was possible. Any doubter needed only to read the fast-breaking news from Kansas.

## The Lecompton Constitution

While the Supreme Court wrestled with the abstract issues raised by the expansion of slavery, President Buchanan sought a concrete solution to the problem of Kansas, where the free-state government at Topeka and the officially recognized proslavery government at Lecompton regarded each other with profound distrust. Buchanan's plan for Kansas looked simple: an elected territorial convention would draw up a constitution that would either prohibit or permit slavery; Buchanan would submit the constitution to Congress; Congress would then admit Kansas as a state.

Unfortunately, the plan exploded in Buchanan's face. Popular sovereignty, the essence of the plan, demanded fair play, a commodity scarce in

**Stephen A. Douglas**
*Douglas's politics was founded on his unflinching convic-
tion that most Americans favored national expansion and
would support popular sovereignty as the fastest and least
controversial way to achieve it. Douglas's self-assurance
blinded him to rising northern sentiment for free soil.*

**Abraham Lincoln**
*Clean-shaven at the time of his famous debates
with Douglas, Lincoln would soon grow a beard to
give himself a more distinguished appearance.*

Kansas. The territory's history of fraudulent elections left both sides reluctant to commit their fortunes to the polls. In June 1857 an election for a constitutional convention took place, but free-staters, by now a majority in Kansas, boycotted the election on grounds that the proslavery forces would rig it. A constitutional convention dominated by proslavery delegates then met and drew up the Lecompton constitution, which protected the rights of slaveholders already residing in Kansas and provided for a referendum to decide whether to allow more slaves into the territory.

Buchanan faced a dilemma. A supporter of popular sovereignty, he had favored letting Kansas voters decide the slavery issue. But now he confronted a constitution drawn up by a convention chosen by less than 10 percent of the eligible voters, a referendum that would not allow voters to remove slaves already in Kansas, and the prospect that the proslavery side would conduct the referendum no more honestly than it had other elections. However, there were compelling reasons to accept the Lecompton constitution. The South, which had provided Buchanan's winning margin in the 1856 election, supported it. To Buchanan, the wrangling over slavery in Kansas was a case of extremists' turning minor issues into major ones, especially because only about 200 slaves resided in Kansas and because prospects for slavery in the remaining territories were slight. The admission of Kansas to the Union as free or slave seemed the quickest way to end the commotion, and so in December 1857 Buchanan endorsed the Lecompton constitution.

Stephen A. Douglas and other northern Democrats broke with Buchanan. To them, the Lecompton constitution, in allowing voters to decide only whether more slaves could enter Kansas, violated the spirit of popular sovereignty. "I care not whether [slavery] is voted down or voted up," Douglas proclaimed, but refusal to allow any vote on slavery amounted to "a system of trickery and jugglery to defeat the fair expression of the will of the people."

Meanwhile, the turbulent swirl of events continued in Kansas. The newly elected territorial legislature called for a referendum on the Lecompton constitution and thus for a referendum on slavery itself. Two elections followed. In December 1857 the referendum called by the constitutional convention took place. Free-staters boycotted it, and the Lecompton constitution passed overwhelmingly. Two weeks later the election called by the territorial legislature took place. This time proslavery forces boycotted, and the constitution went down to crushing defeat. Buchanan tried to ignore this second election, but when he attempted to bring Kansas into the Union under the Lecompton constitution, Congress blocked him and forced yet another referendum. In this third election Kansans could accept or reject the entire constitution, with the proviso that rejection would delay statehood. Despite the proviso, Kansans overwhelmingly voted down the Lecompton constitution.

Buchanan simultaneously had failed to tranquilize Kansas and alienated northerners in his own party, who now more than ever believed that the southern Slave Power pulled all the important strings in the Democratic party. Douglas emerged as the hero of the hour for northern Democrats but saw his cherished formula of popular sovereignty become a prescription for strife rather than harmony.

## The Lincoln-Douglas Debates

Despite the acclaim that he received for his stand against the Lecompton constitution, Douglas faced a stiff challenge in the 1858 Illinois senatorial election. Of his Republican opponent, Abraham Lincoln, Douglas remarked: "I shall have my hands full. He is the strong man of his party—full of wit, facts, and dates—and the best stump speaker with his droll ways and dry jokes, in the West." Indeed, the campaign pitted the Republican party's rising star against the Senate's leading Democrat. Thanks to the railroad and the telegraph, it received unprecedented national attention.

Physically and ideologically, the two candidates presented a striking contrast. Tall and gangling, Lincoln possessed energy, ambition, and a passion for self-education that had carried him from the

Kentucky log cabin where he was born into law and politics in his adopted Illinois. First elected as a Whig, he joined the Republican party in 1856. The New England–born Douglas stood a foot shorter than Lincoln, but to the small farmers of southern origin who populated the Illinois flatlands, he was the "little giant," the personification of the Democratic party in the West.

Despite Douglas's position against the Lecompton constitution, Lincoln saw him as author of the Kansas-Nebraska bill and a man who cared not whether slavery was voted up or down as long as the vote was honest. Opening his campaign with his famous "House Divided" speech ("this government cannot endure permanently half *slave* and half *free*"), Lincoln stressed the gulf between his free-soil position and Douglas's popular sovereignty. Douglas dismissed the house-divided doctrine as an invitation to secession. What mattered to him was not slavery but the continued expansion of white settlement. Both men wanted to keep slavery out of the path of white settlement, but Douglas believed that popular sovereignty was the surest way to do so without disrupting the Union.

The high point of the campaign came in a series of seven debates held from August to October 1858. Douglas used the debates to portray Lincoln as a virtual abolitionist and advocate of racial equality. Lincoln replied that Congress had no constitutional authority to abolish slavery in the South. He also asserted that "I am not, nor ever have been in favor of bringing about the social and political equality of the white and black man."

In the debate at Freeport, Illinois, Lincoln tried to make Douglas squirm by asking how popular sovereignty could be reconciled with the *Dred Scott* decision. Douglas responded that, although the Supreme Court had ruled that Congress could not exclude slavery from the territories, the voters in a territory could do so by refusing to enact laws that gave legal protection to slave property. This "Freeport doctrine" salvaged popular sovereignty but did nothing for Douglas's reputation among southerners, who preferred the guarantees of *Dred Scott* to the uncertainties of popular sovereignty. Trying to move beyond debates on free soil and

popular sovereignty, Lincoln shifted in the closing debates to attacks on slavery as "a moral, social, and political evil."

Neither man scored a clear victory in the debates, and the senatorial election, which Douglas won, settled no major issues. Nonetheless, the candidates' contest was crucial. It solidified the sectional split in the Democratic party and made Lincoln famous in the North—and infamous in the South.

## John Brown's Raid

Although Lincoln explicitly rejected abolitionism, he called free soil a step toward the "ultimate extinction" of slavery. Many southerners ignored the differences between free soil and abolitionism, seeing them as inseparable components of an unholy alliance against slavery. To many in the South, the entire North seemed locked in the grip of demented leaders bent on civil war.

Nothing reinforced this image more than John Brown's raid on the federal arsenal at Harpers Ferry, Virginia. Brown, the religious zealot responsible for the Pottawatomie massacre, seized the arsenal on October 16, 1859, hoping to ignite a slave rebellion throughout the South. Federal troops overpowered the raiders, and Brown, apprehended and convicted of treason, was hanged on December 2, 1859.

Had Brown been a lone fanatic, southerners might have dismissed the raid, but captured correspondence revealed that he enjoyed ties to prominent abolitionists. They had provided both moral and financial support for Brown's plan to "purge this land with blood." When the North responded to Brown's execution with memorial services and tolling bells, southerners saw proof positive of widespread northern support for abolition and even for race war. Although Republicans, including Lincoln and Senator William Seward of New York, denounced Brown's raid, southerners suspected that they regretted the conspiracy's failure more than the attempt itself.

Brown's abortive raid also rekindled southern fears of a slave insurrection. Rumors flew around the South, and vigilantes turned out to battle conspiracies that existed only in their own minds. Volunteers, for example, mobilized to defend northeastern Texas against thousands of abolitionists supposedly on their way to pillage Dallas and its environs. The hysteria generated by such rumors played into the hands of the extremists known as fire-eaters, who encouraged the witch hunts in order to gain political support.

Although fears of a slave insurrection proved groundless, they strengthened southern anxieties about abolitionism. More and more southerners concluded that the Republican party itself directed abolitionism and deserved blame for John Brown's plot as well. After all, had not influential Republicans assailed slavery, unconstitutionally tried to ban it, and spoken of an "irrepressible conflict" between slavery and freedom? The Tennessee legislature reflected southern views when it passed resolutions declaring that the Harpers Ferry raid was "the natural fruit of this treasonable 'irrepressible conflict' doctrine put forth by the great head of the Black Republican party and echoed by his subordinates."

## The South Contemplates Secession

Convinced that the menace to southern rights lay not just with eccentrics such as abolitionist editor William Lloyd Garrison but also with the Republican party that had swept two-thirds of the northern states in the election of 1856, some southerners saw secession from the United States as their only recourse. "The South must dissever itself," a South Carolinian insisted, "from the rotten Northern element." Most southerners, however, reached this conclusion gradually and reluctantly. In 1850, insulated from the main tide of immigration, southerners thought themselves the most American of Americans. The events of the 1850s led growing numbers of southerners to conclude that the North had deserted the principles of the Union and had virtually declared war on the South by using such headline-grabbing phrases as "irrepressible conflict" and "a higher law." To southerners, the North, not slavery, was the problem. For some, venturing into the North became entering "enemy territory" and "a totally different country."

As sectional ties frayed, John Brown's raid electrified southern opinion. A Richmond editor observed that thousands of southerners "who, a month ago, scoffed at the idea of a dissolution of the Union as a madman's dream . . . now hold the opinion that its days are numbered, its glory perished."

Secession made no sense as a tactic to win concrete goals, but logic had yielded to emotion in much of the South. Fury at what southerners considered the irresponsible, unconstitutional course taken by Republicans in attacking slavery drove the talk of secession, and so did the belief that the North treated the South as inferior, even as a slave. "Talk of Negro slavery," wrote one angry southerner, "is not half so humiliating and disgraceful as the slavery of the South to the North." White southerners, certain that slavery made it possible for them to enjoy unprecedented freedom and equality, took great pride in their homeland. They bitterly resented Republican portrayals of the South as a region of arrogant planters and degraded common whites.

As long as the pliant James Buchanan occupied the White House, southerners only talked of secession. However, once Buchanan declined to seek reelection, they anxiously awaited the next presidential election.

## The Election of 1860

Republicans had done well in the elections of 1856 as a single-issue, free-soil party, but they had to broaden their base in order to win in 1860. Republican leaders needed an economic program to complement their advocacy of free soil. A severe economic slump following the Panic of 1857 provided them an opening. The depression shattered a decade of prosperity and thrust economic concerns to the fore. In response, the Republicans developed an economic program based on support for a protective tariff, federal aid for internal improvements, and grants to settlers of free 160-acre homesteads carved from public lands.

To broaden their appeal, the Republicans chose Abraham Lincoln as their presidential candidate

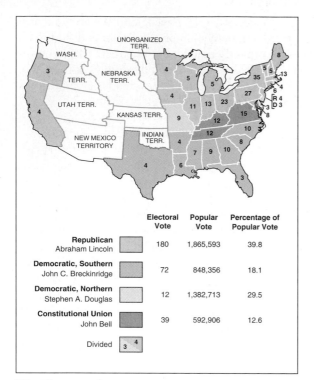

| | | Electoral Vote | Popular Vote | Percentage of Popular Vote |
|---|---|---|---|---|
| **Republican** Abraham Lincoln | | 180 | 1,865,593 | 39.8 |
| **Democratic, Southern** John C. Breckinridge | | 72 | 848,356 | 18.1 |
| **Democratic, Northern** Stephen A. Douglas | | 12 | 1,382,713 | 29.5 |
| **Constitutional Union** John Bell | | 39 | 592,906 | 12.6 |
| Divided | | | | |

**The Election of 1860**

The Democratic party's internal turmoil boiled over at its Charleston convention in spring 1860. Failing to win a platform guaranteeing the federal protection of slavery in the territories, delegates from the Lower South stormed out. The convention adjourned to Baltimore, where a new fight erupted over whether to seat the pro-Douglas delegates hastily chosen to replace the absent delegates from the Lower South. When the convention voted to seat these new delegates, representatives from Virginia and the Upper South walked out. What remained of the original Democratic convention nominated Douglas, but the seceders marched off to yet another hall in Baltimore and nominated Buchanan's vice president, John C. Breckinridge of Kentucky, on a platform calling for the congressional protection of slavery in the territories. The spectacle of two different Democratic candidates for the presidency signaled the complete disruption of the party.

The South still contained a sizable number of moderates, often former Whigs. In 1860 these southern moderates joined former northern Whigs in the new Constitutional Union party. They nominated John Bell of Tennessee, a slaveholder who had opposed the Kansas-Nebraska Act and the Lecompton constitution. Calling for the Union's preservation, the new party took no stand on slavery's extension.

The four candidates presented a relatively clear choice. At one end of the spectrum, Lincoln conceded that the South had the constitutional right to preserve slavery, but he demanded that Congress prohibit its extension. At the other end, Breckinridge insisted that Congress had to protect slavery anywhere it existed. In the middle were Bell and Douglas, the latter still trying to salvage popular sovereignty. In the end Lincoln won 180 electoral votes; his three opponents, only 123. However, Lincoln's popular votes, 39 percent of the total, came almost completely from the North. Douglas, the only candidate to run in both sections, ran second in the popular vote but carried only Missouri. Bell won most of the Upper South, and Breckinridge took Maryland and the Lower South.

over the better-known William H. Seward. Lincoln offered a stronger possibility of carrying key states such as Pennsylvania and his home state of Illinois and projected a more moderate image than Seward, whose penchant for phrases like "irrepressible conflict" and "higher law" made him appear radical. In contrast, Lincoln repeatedly had said that Congress had no constitutional right to interfere with slavery in the South and had rejected the "higher law" doctrine.

The Democrats, still clinging to national party status, had to bridge their own sectional divisions. The *Dred Scott* decision and the conflict over the Lecompton constitution had weakened northern Democrats and strengthened southern Democrats. While Douglas still desperately defended popular sovereignty, southern Democrats stretched *Dred Scott* to conclude that Congress now had to protect slavery in the territories.

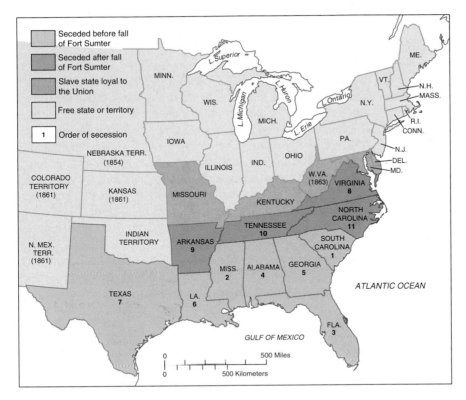

**Secession**
*Four key states—Virginia, Arkansas, Tennessee, and North Carolina—did not secede until after the fall of Fort Sumter. The border slave states of Maryland, Delaware, Kentucky, and Missouri stayed in the Union.*

## The Movement for Secession

Southerners faced a dilemma. The president-elect was so unpopular in the South that his name had not even appeared on the ballot in many southern states. Lincoln's victory struck many southerners as a calculated insult. The North, a South Carolina planter said, "has got so far toward being abolitionized as to elect a man avowedly hostile to our institutions." Few southerners believed that Lincoln would fulfill his promise to protect slavery in the South, and most feared that he would act as a tool for more John Browns.

Some southerners had threatened secession at the prospect of Lincoln's election, and now the moment of decision had arrived. On December 20, 1860, a South Carolina convention voted unanimously for secession; in short order Alabama, Mississippi, Florida, Georgia, Louisiana, and Texas followed. On February 4, 1861, delegates from these seven states met in Montgomery, Alabama, and established the Confederate States of America. But uncertainty colored the secession movement. Many southerners, even in the Deep South, had resisted the fire-eaters' call to leave the Union. Jefferson Davis, inaugurated in February 1861 as president of the Confederacy, was a reluctant secessionist who had remained in the Senate two weeks after his own state of Mississippi had seceded.

At first the Upper South rejected secession completely. More economically dependent on the North, it had proportionately fewer slaves and more nonslaveholders, whose loyalty in case of secession was dubious. Finally, if secession precipitated a war, the Upper South was the likely battleground. Consequently, the secession movement that South Carolina had begun so boldly in December 1860 seemed to be falling apart by March 1861.

## The Search for Compromise

The lack of southern unity confirmed the view of most Republicans that the secessionists were more bluster than substance. Seward described secession as the work of "a relatively few hotheads," and Lincoln believed that the loyal majority of southerners would soon wrest control from the fire-eating minority.

This perception stiffened Republican resolve to resist compromise. Moderate John J. Crittenden of Kentucky suggested compensation for owners of runaway slaves, repeal of northern personal-liberty laws, a constitutional amendment to prohibit the federal government from interfering with slavery in southern states, and another amendment to restore the Missouri Compromise line. But in the face of adamant Republican opposition, the Crittenden plan collapsed.

Lincoln's faith in a "loyal majority" of southerners exaggerated both their numbers and their dedication to the Union. Many southern opponents of the fire-eating secessionists sat on the fence, waiting for major concessions from the North; their allegiance to the Union thus was conditional. But compromise would have meant the abandonment of free soil, a basic principle on which the Republican party had been founded, and Lincoln, who misread southern opinion, resisted.

Beyond the issue of compromise, the precipitous secession of the Lower South had changed the question that Lincoln faced. The issue no longer revolved around slavery's extension but around secession. The Lower South had left the Union in the face of losing a fair election. For Lincoln to cave in to such pressure would violate majority rule, the sacred principle on which the nation had been founded.

## The Coming of War

By the time Lincoln took office in March 1861, only a spark was needed to set off a war. Lincoln pledged in his inaugural address to "hold, occupy, and possess" federal property in the states that had seceded, a statement that committed him to the defense of Fort Pickens in Florida and Fort Sumter in the harbor of Charleston, South Carolina. Accordingly, the president informed South Carolina's governor of his intention to supply Fort Sumter with provisions but neither reinforcements nor ammunition. Shortly before dawn on April 12, 1861, Confederate shore batteries bombarded the fort, which surrendered the next day.

Proclaiming an insurrection in the Lower South, Lincoln called for 75,000 militia to suppress the rebellion. The outbreak of hostilities ended fence-sitting in the Upper South. "I am a Union man," one southerner wrote, "but when they [the Lincoln administration] send men south it will change my notions. I can do nothing against my own people." In quick succession Virginia, North Carolina, Arkansas, and Tennessee joined the Confederacy. Acknowledging that "I am one of those dull creatures that cannot see the good of secession," Robert E. Lee resigned from the U.S. Army rather than lead troops against his native Virginia.

The North, too, was ready for a fight, less to abolish slavery than to punish secession. Stephen Douglas, exhausted by his efforts to find a peaceable solution to the issue of slavery extension, assaulted "the new system of resistance by the sword and bayonet to the results of the ballot-box" and affirmed, "I deprecate war, but if it must come I am with my country, under all circumstances, and in every contingency."

## CONCLUSION

During the 1850s disagreements over the extension of slavery drove the North and the South far apart. When popular sovereignty failed, support for free soil grew in the North, while at the same time southerners decided that the *Dred Scott* decision mandated the congressional protection of slavery in the territories and elsewhere.

The decade had begun with the Compromise of 1850, which papered over, rather than solved, divisive issues. Decades of industrial expansion had left northerners convinced of the value of free labor, and decades of agricultural prosperity had left southerners equally convinced of the economic and moral value of slavery.

Nonetheless, secession festered ten years before erupting. Southerners would not take the drastic step of seceding until they believed that the North aimed not merely to bar the expansion of slavery but also to corrode the moral and political foundations of southern society. The Kansas-Nebraska furor, the emergence of the purely sectional Republican party, northern opposition to the *Dred Scott* decision, and John Brown's raid on Harpers Ferry finally persuaded southerners that the North intended to reduce them to subjection and "slavery." Secession seemed a natural recourse.

These conflicts were deeply embedded in the nation's political heritage, with the North and the South holding vastly different views of what that heritage was. For northerners, liberty meant an individual's freedom to pursue self-interest without competition from slaves. For white southerners, liberty meant freedom to use their legal property, including slaves, as they saw fit. Each side proclaimed that *it* subscribed to the rule of law, which it accused the other of deserting. Ultimately, war broke out between siblings who, although they claimed the same inheritance, had become virtual strangers.

## CHRONOLOGY

1846  Wilmot Proviso.

1848  Treaty of Guadalupe-Hidalgo ends Mexican War.
      Free-Soil party formed.
      Zachary Taylor elected president.

1849  California seeks admission to the Union as a free state.

1850  Nashville convention assembles to discuss the South's grievances.
      Compromise of 1850.

1852  Harriet Beecher Stowe, *Uncle Tom's Cabin*.
      Franklin Pierce elected president.

1854  Ostend Manifesto.
      Kansas-Nebraska Act.

1854–  Know-Nothing and Republican parties emerge.
1855

1855  Proslavery forces steal the election for a territorial legislature in Kansas.
      Proslavery Kansans establish a government in Lecompton.
      Free-soil government established in Topeka, Kansas.

1856  The "sack" of Lawrence, Kansas.
      John Brown's Pottawatomie massacre.
      James Buchanan elected president.

1857  *Dred Scott* decision.
      President Buchanan endorses the Lecompton constitution in Kansas.
      Panic of 1857.

1858  Congress refuses to admit Kansas to the Union under the Lecompton constitution.
      Lincoln and Douglas debate.

1859  John Brown's raid on Harpers Ferry.

1860  Abraham Lincoln elected president.
      South Carolina secedes from the Union.

1861  The remaining Lower South states secede.
      Confederate States of America established.
      Crittenden compromise plan collapses.
      Lincoln takes office.
      Firing on Fort Sumter; Civil War begins.
      Upper South secedes.

## FOR FURTHER READING

Tyler Anbinder, *Nativism and Slavery: The Northern Know Nothings and the Politics of the 1850s* (1992). A study of the Know-Nothings' striking success in the North in the mid-1850s.

Eric Foner, *Free Soil, Free Labor, Free Men: The Ideology of the Republican Party Before the Civil War* (1970). An outstanding analysis of the thought, values, and components of the Republican party.

William W. Freehling, *The Road to Disunion: Secessionists at Bay, 1776–1854* (1990). A major study that traces the roots of secession.

William E. Gienapp, *The Origins of the Republican Party, 1852–1856* (1988). A major recent study of the party's formative period.

Michael F. Holt, *The Political Crisis of the 1850s* (1978). A lively reinterpretation of the politics of the 1850s.

Allan Nevins, *The Ordeal of the Union* (vols. 1–2, 1947). A very detailed, highly regarded account of the coming of the Civil War.

David Potter, *The Impending Crisis, 1848–1861* (1976). The best one-volume overview of the events leading to the Civil War.

# CHAPTER

With Fort Sumter's fall in April 1861, northerners and southerners rushed to arms. "They sing and whoop, they laugh; they holler to de people on de ground and sing out 'Good-by,'" remarked a slave watching rebel troops depart. "All going down to die." Longing for the excitement of battle, the first troops enlisted with hopes of adventure and glory. Neither the volunteers nor the politicians expected a long or bloody war.

These expectations of military glory and quick fame proved the first of many miscalculations. Actual battlefield experiences scarcely conformed to the early volunteers' rosy visions. War brought not glory but fetid army camps and the stench of death. "We don't mind the sight of dead men no more than if they were dead hogs," a Union soldier claimed.

One out of every five soldiers who fought in the Civil War died in it. The 620,000 American soldiers killed between 1861 and 1865 nearly equaled the number of U.S. soldiers killed in all other American wars combined. As it became clear

---

*(Right) Armless or legless veterans were a common sight in American cities, towns, and rural districts well into our present century.*

## Reforging the Union: Civil War, 1861–1865

Mobilizing for War

❧

In Battle, 1861–1862

❧

Emancipation Transforms the War

❧

War and Society, North and South

❧

The Union Victorious, 1864–1865

that a few battles would not decide the war, leaders on both sides contemplated, and often adopted, previously unthinkable strategies. The Confederacy, despite its states' rights basis, had to draft men into its army and virtually extort supplies from civilians. By the end of the war, the Confederacy was even prepared to arm slaves in a desperate effort to save a society founded on slavery. The North, which began the war with the objective of overcoming secession, explicitly disclaiming any intention of interfering with slavery, found that in order to win, it had to destroy slavery.

## Mobilizing for War

Neither North nor South was prepared for war. In April 1861 most of the Union's small army, a scant 16,000 men, was scattered across the West. One-third of its officers had resigned to join the Confederacy. The nation had not had a strong president since James K. Polk in the 1840s, and many viewed the new president, Abraham Lincoln, as a yokel. It seemed doubtful that such a government could marshal its people for war. The Confederacy was even less prepared: it had no tax structure, no navy, only two tiny gunpowder factories, and poorly equipped, unconnected railroad lines.

During the first two years of war, both sides would have to overcome these deficiencies, raise and supply large armies, and finance the war. In each region mobilization would expand the powers of the central government to a degree that few had anticipated.

### Recruitment and Conscription

The Civil War armies were the largest organizations ever created in America; by the end of the war, more than 2 million men had served in the Union army and 800,000 in the Confederate army. In the first flush of enthusiasm for war, volunteers rushed to the colors. "War and volunteers are the only topics of conversation or thought," an Oberlin College student wrote to his brother in April 1861. "I cannot study. I cannot sleep. I cannot work."

At first the raising of armies was a local, rather than a national or state, effort. Regiments usually consisted of volunteers from the same locale. Southern cavalrymen provided their own horses, and uniforms were left to local option. In both armies the troops themselves elected officers up to the rank of colonel. This informal, democratic way of raising and organizing soldiers reflected the nation's political traditions but could not withstand the stresses of the Civil War. As early as July 1861 the Union began examinations for officers. With casualties mounting, moreover, military demand exceeded the supply of volunteers. The Confederacy felt the pinch first and in April 1862 enacted the first conscription law in American history, requiring all able-bodied white men aged eighteen to thirty-five to serve in the military. (By war's end the limits would be seventeen and fifty.) The Confederacy's Conscription Act aroused little enthusiasm. A later amendment exempting owners or overseers of twenty or more slaves evoked complaints about "a rich man's war but a poor man's fight."

Despite opposition, the Confederate draft became increasingly difficult to evade, and this fact stimulated volunteering. Only one soldier in five was a draftee, but four out of every five eligible white southerners served in the Confederate army. An 1864 law requiring all soldiers to serve for the duration of the war ensured that a high proportion of Confederate soldiers would be battle-hardened veterans.

Once the army was raised, the Confederacy had to supply it. At first the South imported arms and ammunition from Europe or relied on weapons taken from federal arsenals and captured on the battlefield. Gradually, the Confederacy assigned contracts to privately owned factories such as the Tredegar Iron Works in Richmond, provided loans to establish new plants, and created government-owned industries such as the giant Augusta Powder Works in Georgia. The South lost few, if any, battles for want of munitions.

Supplying troops with clothing and food proved more difficult. When the South invaded Maryland in 1862, thousands of Confederate soldiers remained behind because they could not march barefoot on Maryland's gravel-surfaced roads. Late in the war, Robert E. Lee's Army of Northern Virginia ran out of food but never out of ammunition. Supply problems had several sources: railroads that fell into disrepair or were captured, an economy that grew more cotton and tobacco than food, and Union capture of the livestock and grain-raising districts of central Tennessee and Virginia. Close to desperation, the Confederate Congress in 1863 passed the Impressment Act, authorizing army officers to take food from reluctant farmers at prescribed rates. One provision, bitterly resented, empowered agents to impress slaves into labor for the army. Slave owners were willing to give up their relatives to military service, a Georgia congressman noted, "but let one of their negroes be taken and what a howl you will hear."

The industrial North more easily supplied its troops with arms, clothes, and food, but keeping a full army was another matter. When the initial tide of enthusiasm for enlistment ebbed, Congress turned to conscription with the Enrollment Act of March 1863. Every able-bodied white male citizen aged twenty to forty-five faced the draft.

The Enrollment Act provided some exemptions and offered two ways of escaping the draft: substitution, or paying another man to serve; and commutation, or paying a $300 fee to the government. As enrollment districts competed for volunteers by offering cash bounties, "bounty jumpers" repeatedly enrolled and then deserted after collecting their payment. Democrats denounced conscription as a violation of individual liberties and states' rights, and ordinary citizens resented the substitution and commutation privileges and leveled their own "poor man's fight" charges. Nevertheless, as in the Confederacy, the law stimulated volunteering: only 8 percent of all Union soldiers were draftees or substitutes.

## Financing the War

The recruitment and supply of huge armies lay far beyond the capacity of American public finance at the start of the war. During the 1840s and 1850s federal spending had averaged only 2 percent of the gross national product.* With such meager expenditures, the federal government met its revenue needs from tariff duties and income from the sale of public lands. During the war, however, as annual federal expenditures rose to 15 percent of the gross national product, the need for new sources of revenue became urgent. When neither additional taxes nor war bond sales produced enough revenue, the Union and the Confederacy began to print paper money. Early in 1862 President Lincoln signed into law the Legal Tender Act, authorizing the issue of $150 million in paper "greenbacks." Although the North's financial officials distrusted paper money, they resorted to it because, as the Union's treasury secretary bluntly put it, *"The Treasury is nearly empty."* Unlike gold and silver, which had established market values, the value of paper money depended on the public's confidence in the government that issued it. To bolster that confidence, Union officials made the greenbacks legal tender (that is, acceptable in payment of most public and private debts).

In contrast, the Confederacy never made paper money legal tender, and so suspicions arose that the southern government had little faith in its own money. The fact that the Confederacy raised little of its wartime revenue from taxes compounded the problem. Northern invasions and poor internal transportation made collecting taxes difficult, and ultimately the South raised less than 5 percent of its wartime revenue from taxes (compared to 21 percent in the North).

Confidence in the Confederacy's paper money quickly evaporated, and the value of paper money in relation to gold plunged. The Confederate response—printing more paper money—merely accelerated inflation. Prices in the North rose 80 percent during the war, but those in the South soared more than 9,000 percent.

---

*Gross national product (GNP): the sum, measured in dollars, of all goods and services produced in a given year. By contrast, in the 1980s the federal budget averaged about 25 percent of GNP.

By raising taxes, floating bonds, and printing paper money, both North and South broke with the hard-money, minimal-government traditions of American public finance. In the North, Republicans took advantage of the departure of southern Democrats to push through Congress a measure that they and their Whig predecessors had long advocated: a national banking system. Passed in February 1863, the National Bank Act allowed banks to obtain federal charters and to issue national bank notes (backed by the federal government). The North's ability to revolutionize its system of public finances reflected both its greater experience with complex financial transactions and its stronger political cohesion.

## Political Leadership in Wartime

The Civil War pitted rival political systems as well as armies and economies against each other. The South entered the war with several apparent political advantages. Lincoln's call for militiamen to suppress the rebellion had transformed southern waverers into secessionists. "Never was a people more united or more determined," wrote a New Orleans resident. "There is but one mind, one heart, one action." Since the founding of the United States, the South had produced a disproportionate share of the nation's strong presidents: Washington, Jefferson, Madison, Monroe, Jackson, and Polk. Jefferson Davis, the president of the Confederacy, possessed experience, honesty, courage, and what one commentator called "a jaw sawed in *steel*."

In contrast, the Union's list of political liabilities appeared lengthy. Loyal but contentious northern Democrats wanted no conscription, no National Bank, and no abolition of slavery. Even within the Republican party, Lincoln, with little national experience, had trouble commanding respect. A small but vocal group of Republicans known as the Radicals—including Secretary of the Treasury Salmon P. Chase, Senator Charles Sumner of Massachusetts, and Representative Thaddeus Stevens of Pennsylvania—vigorously criticized Lincoln. First they focused on his failure to make the slaves' emancipation a war goal, and later they would lash

**Abraham Lincoln**
*When Lincoln became president in March 1861, he faced more severe problems than any predecessor. Washington photographer Matthew Brady captured this image of the solemn president-elect on February 23, 1861, a few weeks after the formation of the Confederacy and shortly before Lincoln's inauguration.*

him for being too eager to readmit the conquered rebel states into the Union.

Lincoln's style of leadership both encouraged and disarmed opposition within the Republican party. Keeping his counsel to himself until ready to act, he met criticism with homespun anecdotes that threw his opponents off guard. Caught between Radicals and conservatives, Lincoln used his cautious reserve to maintain open communications with both wings of the party and to fragment his opposition. He also co-opted some members of the opposition, including Chase, by bringing them into his cabinet.

In contrast, Jefferson Davis had a knack for making enemies. A West Pointer, he would rather have led the army than the government, and he used his sharp tongue to win arguments rather than friends. Davis's cabinet suffered frequent resignations; for example, the Confederacy had five secretaries of war in four years. Relations between Davis and his vice president, Alexander Stephens of Georgia, were disastrous. Stephens left Richmond, the Confederate capital, in 1862 and spent most of the war in Georgia sniping at Davis as "weak and vacillating, timid, petulant, peevish, obstinate."

The clash between Davis and Stephens involved not just personalities but also the ideological divisions that lay at the heart of the Confederacy. The Confederate Constitution explicitly guaranteed the sovereignty of the Confederate states and prohibited the government from enacting protective tariffs or supporting internal improvements. For Stephens and other influential Confederate leaders, the Confederacy existed to protect slavery and to enshrine states' rights. For Davis, the overriding objective of the Confederacy was to secure the independence of the South from the North, if necessary at the expense of states' rights.

This difference between Davis and Stephens somewhat resembled the discord between Lincoln and the northern Democrats. Lincoln believed that winning the war demanded increasing the central government's power; like Stephens, northern Democrats resisted centralization. But Lincoln could control his opponents more effectively than Davis controlled his. By temperament Lincoln was more suited to reconciliation than Davis was, and the different nature of party politics in the two sections favored him as well.

In the South the Democrats and the remaining Whigs agreed to suspend party politics for the war's duration. Although intended to encourage unity, this decision led to discord. As southern politics disintegrated along personal and factional lines, Davis found himself without organized political support. In contrast, in the Union northern Democrats' opposition to Lincoln tended to unify the Republicans. After Democrats won control of five states in the election of 1862, Republicans swallowed a bitter lesson: no matter how much they disdained Lincoln, they had to rally behind him or risk being driven from office. Ultimately, the Union developed more political cohesion than the Confederacy not because it had fewer divisions but because it managed those divisions more effectively.

## Securing the Union's Borders

Even before large-scale fighting began, Lincoln moved to safeguard Washington, which was bordered by two slave states (Virginia and Maryland) and filled with Confederate sympathizers. A week after Fort Sumter's fall, a Baltimore mob attacked a Massachusetts regiment bound for Washington, but enough troops slipped through to protect the capital. Lincoln then dispatched federal troops to Maryland and suspended the writ of habeas corpus;* federal troops could now arrest Marylanders without formally charging them with specific offenses. Both Maryland and Delaware, another border slave state, voted down secession. Next Lincoln authorized the arming of Union sympathizers in Kentucky, a slave state with a Unionist legislature, a secessionist governor, and a thin chance of staying neutral. Lincoln also stationed troops just across the Ohio River from Kentucky, in Illinois, and when a Confederate army invaded Kentucky early in 1862, those troops drove it out. Officially, at least, Kentucky became the third slave state to declare for the Union. Four years of murderous fighting ravaged the fourth, Missouri, as Union and Confederate armies and bands of guerrillas clashed. Despite savage fighting and the divided loyalties of its people, Missouri never left the Union.

By holding the border slave states in the

---

*Habeas corpus: a court order requiring that the detainer of a prisoner bring the person in custody to court and show cause for his or her detention.

Union, Lincoln kept open his lines to the free states and gained access to the river systems in Kentucky and Missouri that led into the heart of the Confederacy. Lincoln's firmness, particularly in the case of Maryland, scotched charges that he was weak-willed.

# In Battle, 1861–1862

The Civil War was the first war in which both sides relied extensively on railroads, the telegraph, mass-produced weapons, joint army-navy tactics, iron-plated warships, rifled guns and artillery, and trench warfare. Thus there is some justification for its description as the first modern war.

## Armies, Weapons, and Strategies

Compared to the Confederacy's 9 million people, who included 3 million slaves, the Union had 22 million people in 1861. The North also enjoyed 3.5 times as many white men of military age, 90 percent of all U.S. industrial capacity, and two-thirds of its railroad track. But the North faced a daunting challenge: to force the South back into the Union. The South, in contrast, fought only for independence. To subdue the Confederacy, the North would have to sustain offensive operations over an area comparable in size to the part of Russia that Napoleon had invaded in 1812 with disastrous results.

Measured against this challenge, the North's advantages in population and technology shrank. The North had more men but needed them to defend long supply lines and to occupy captured areas. Consequently, it could commit a smaller proportion of its overall force to combat. The South, relying on slaves for labor, could assign a higher proportion of its white male population to combat. And although the Union had superior railroads, it had to move its troops and supplies huge distances, whereas the Confederacy could shift its troops relatively short distances within its defense area without railroads. The South's poor roads hampered the supply-heavy northern forces as well. Finally, southerners had

an edge in morale, for Confederate troops usually fought on home ground.

The Civil War witnessed experiments with a variety of new weapons, including the submarine, the repeating rifle, and the multibarreled Gatling gun, the predecessor of the machine gun. Whereas smoothbore muskets had an effective range of 80 yards, the Springfield or Enfield rifles widely in use by 1863 were accurate at 400 yards. The rifle's development posed a challenge to long-accepted military tactics, which stressed the mass infantry charge. Armed with muskets, defenders could fire only a round or two before being overwhelmed. Armed with rifles, however, defenders could fire several rounds before closing with the enemy.

As the fighting wore on, both sides recognized the value of trenches, which offered defenders protection against withering rifle fire. In addition, the rifle forced generals to depend less on cavalry. Traditionally, cavalry had been among the most prestigious components of an army, in part because cavalry charges were often devastatingly effective and in part because the cavalry helped to maintain class distinctions within the army. More accurate rifles reduced the cavalry's effectiveness, for the bullet that missed a rider could hit his horse. Thus the cavalry increasingly was relegated to reconnaissance and raids.

Much like previous wars, the Civil War was fought basically in a succession of battles during which exposed infantry traded volleys, charged, and countercharged. The side that withdrew first from the battlefield was considered the loser, even though it frequently sustained lighter casualties than the "victor." The defeated army usually moved back a few miles to lick its wounds; the winners stayed in place to lick theirs. Although politicians raged at generals for not pursuing a beaten foe, they seldom understood the difficulties that a mangled victor faced in gathering horses, mules, supply trains, and exhausted soldiers for an attack. Not surprisingly, generals on both sides concluded that the best defense was a good offense.

What passed for long-range Union strategy in 1861 was the Anaconda plan, which called for the

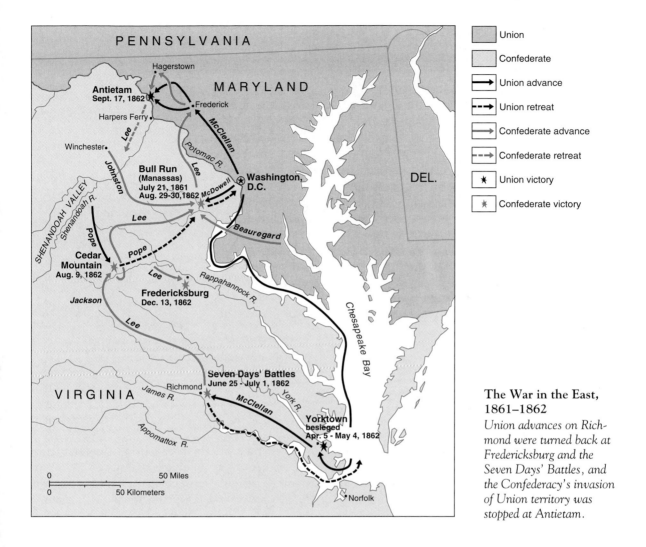

**The War in the East, 1861–1862**
*Union advances on Richmond were turned back at Fredericksburg and the Seven Days' Battles, and the Confederacy's invasion of Union territory was stopped at Antietam.*

Union to blockade the southern coast and to thrust, like a huge snake, down the Mississippi River. In theory, sealing off and severing the Confederacy would make the South recognize the futility of secession and end the war as bloodlessly as possible. However, the lack of adequate ships and men to seize the Mississippi in 1861 prevented the implementation of this ambitious plan.

Early in the war the need to secure the border slave states, especially Kentucky and Missouri, dictated Union strategy in the West, sending northern armies plunging southward from Kentucky into Tennessee. The Appalachian Mountains tended to separate this western theater from the eastern theater. East of the mountains, the Confederates' decision to locate their capital in Richmond, Virginia, shaped Union strategy. "Forward to Richmond!" became the Union's first war cry.

## Stalemate in the East

Before Union troops could reach Richmond, one hundred miles southwest of Washington, they

**Dead Soldiers at Antietam**
*These dead rebel gunners lie next to the wreckage of their battery at Antietam. The building, a Dunker church, was the site of furious fighting.*

would have to dislodge a Confederate army brazenly encamped at Manassas Junction, Virginia, only twenty-five miles from the Union capital. Lincoln ordered General Irvin McDowell to attack the rebel force. In the resulting First Battle of Bull Run (or First Manassas\*), amateur armies clashed in bloody chaos under a blistering sun in July 1861 as well-dressed, picnicking Washington dignitaries watched the carnage. The Confederates routed the larger Union army.

After Bull Run, Lincoln appointed General George B. McClellan to replace McDowell as commander of the Union's Army of the Potomac. McClellan, a master of administration and training, transformed a ragtag mob into a disciplined fighting force. His soldiers adored him, but Lincoln became

disenchanted. To the president, the key to victory lay in launching simultaneous attacks on several fronts so that the North could exploit its advantages in manpower and communications. McClellan, a proslavery Democrat, hoped for a series of relatively bloodless victories that would result in the readmission of southern states into the Union with slavery still intact.

In spring 1862 McClellan got an opportunity to demonstrate the value of his strategy. After Bull Run, the Confederates had pulled back behind the Rappahannock River to block a Union march toward Richmond. McClellan decided to go around the southerners by transporting his troops down the Chesapeake Bay to the tip of the peninsula formed by the York and James rivers and then to attack Richmond from the rear.

At first McClellan's Peninsula Campaign unfolded smoothly. But after luring the Confederacy to the brink of defeat, he hesitated, refusing to

---

\*Because the North often named battles after local landmarks, usually bodies of water, and the South after the nearest town, some Civil War battles are known by two names.

launch the final attack without the reinforcements he expected. Confederate forces under General Thomas "Stonewall" Jackson had turned back the reinforcements. As McClellan delayed, General Robert E. Lee assumed command of the Confederacy's Army of Northern Virginia. An opponent of secession, a man so courteous that he seemed almost too gentle, Lee nevertheless was McClellan's opposite, bold and willing to accept casualties.

Lee immediately took the offensive, attacking the much larger Union forces in the Seven Days' Battles (June–July 1862). Raging through forests east of Richmond, the battles cost the Confederacy nearly twice as many men as the Union, but McClellan, not Lee, blinked. Unnerved by mounting casualties, he sent a series of panicky reports to Washington. Lincoln, who cared little for McClellan's peninsula strategy, ordered him to call off the campaign and return to Washington.

With McClellan out of the picture, Lee and his lieutenant, Stonewall Jackson, pushed north, routing a Union army at the Second Battle of Bull Run (Second Manassas) in August 1862. Lee followed up this victory with a typically bold stroke: he took his army across the Potomac and northward into Maryland, hoping that the fall harvest could provide him with desperately needed supplies. McClellan met Lee at the Battle of Antietam (Sharpsburg) on September 17, 1862. North and South together suffered 24,000 casualties in this bloodiest day of the entire war. Tactically, the battle was a draw, but strategically it constituted a major Union victory because it forced Lee to withdraw south of the Potomac. Most important, Antietam provided Lincoln the occasion to issue the Emancipation Proclamation, freeing all slaves under rebel control.

Lincoln complained that McClellan had "the slows" and faulted him for not pursuing Lee after Antietam. McClellan's replacement, General Ambrose Burnside, thought himself unfit for high command. He was right. In December 1862 he led 122,000 federal troops against 78,500 Confederates at the Battle of Fredericksburg (Virginia). Burnside captured the town but then sacrificed his army in futile charges up the heights west of the town. The carnage shook even Lee. "It is well that war is so terrible—we should grow fond of it," he told an aide during the battle. Richmond remained, in the words of a southern song, "a hard road to travel." The war in the East had become a stalemate.

## The War in the West

The Union fared better in the West. Unlike the geographically limited eastern theater, the war in the West shifted over a vast terrain that provided access to rivers leading directly into the South. The West also spawned new leadership in the person of an obscure Union general, Ulysses S. Grant. A West Point graduate with a reputation for heavy drinking, and a failed farmer and businessman, Grant soon proved one of the Union's best leaders.

In 1861–1862 Grant had stabilized control of Missouri and Kentucky and then moved south to attack Corinth, Mississippi, a major rail junction. In early April 1862 Confederate forces staged a surprise attack on Grant's army, encamped at Shiloh Church in southern Tennessee. Driven back on the first day, Union forces counterattacked on the second day and drove the Confederate army from the field. Of 77,000 men who fought at Shiloh, 23,000 were killed or wounded. Perhaps the most important casualty was General Albert Sydney Johnston, whose death deprived the Confederacy of its best commander west of the Appalachians. Defeated at Shiloh, the Confederates evacuated Corinth.

For the Corinth-Shiloh Campaign, the Confederacy had stripped New Orleans of its defenses, leaving its largest city guarded by only 3,000 militia. A combined land-sea force under Union general Benjamin Butler and Admiral David G. Farragut took advantage of the weakened defenses and captured New Orleans in late April. Farragut continued up the Mississippi as far as Natchez. When a Union flotilla moved down the river in June and took Memphis, the North controlled the great river except for a 200-mile stretch between Port Hudson, Louisiana, and Vicksburg, Mississippi.

In 1862 Union and Confederate forces also clashed in the Transmississippi West, a vast region that stretched from the Midwest to the Pacific Coast. On the banks of the Rio Grande, Union vol-

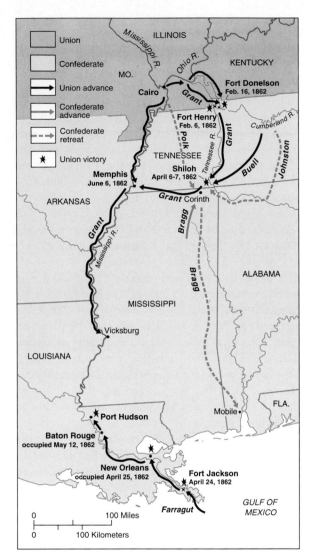

**The War in the West, 1861–1862**
*By the end of 1862 the North held New Orleans and the entire Mississippi River except for the stretch between Vicksburg and Port Hudson.*

unteers and Mexican-American companies drove a Confederate army from Texas out of New Mexico. A thousand miles to the east, opposing armies battled for control of the crucial Missouri River. In Pea Ridge, Arkansas, in March 1862, northern troops scattered a Confederate force of 16,000.

These Union victories changed the Trans-Mississippi war. As the rebel threat faded, western volunteers who had mobilized to crush Confederates turned to fighting Indians. Conflict between Union forces and Native Americans erupted in Minnesota, Arizona, Nevada, Colorado, and New Mexico. After 1865 federal troops moved west to complete the rout of the Indians that had begun during the Civil War.

## Ironclads and Cruisers: The Naval War

By plunging the navy into the Confederacy like a dagger, the Union exploited one of its clearest advantages. The North began the war with more than forty active warships—the South had none—and by 1865 northern industrial advantages had given the United States the largest navy in the world. Steamships could penetrate the South's river systems from any direction. Yet the Union navy faced an extraordinary challenge in its efforts to blockade the South's 3,500 miles of coastline. Sleek Confederate blockade runners darted in and out of southern harbors with little chance of capture early in the war. Their chances of success gradually diminished, however, as the North tightened the blockade and began to capture key southern ports. In 1861 almost 90 percent of blockade runners made it through; by 1865 the rate had sunk to 50 percent.

Despite meager resources, the South made impressive efforts to offset the North's naval advantages. Early in the war the Confederates raised a scuttled Union frigate, the *Merrimac;* sheathed its sides in iron; rechristened it the *Virginia;* and deployed it to attack wooden Union ships at Hampton Roads, Virginia. The *Virginia*'s success ended on March 9, 1862, when it tangled with the hastily built Union ironclad *Monitor* in the first battle ever fought between ironclads. The battle ended in a draw, but the South eventually lost the naval war because it could not build enough ships to overcome the northern lead. Even successful commerce raiders, such as the British-built *Alabama* and the *Florida,* although they wreaked havoc on the Union's merchant marine, did comparatively little to tip the balance in the South's favor because the North did not depend on imports for war materials.

## The Diplomatic War

While armies and navies clashed in 1861–1862, conflict developed on a third front, diplomacy. At the war's start southerners had confidently opened a campaign to gain swift diplomatic recognition for the Confederacy. They were sure of the support of Britain and France's upper classes and even more certain that Britain, dependent on the South for four-fifths of its cotton, would have to break the Union blockade.

In 1861 Confederate diplomats James Mason and John Slidell sailed for Europe to lobby for recognition of an independent South, but their ship, the *Trent,* fell into Union hands. When the pair ended up as prisoners in Boston, British tempers exploded. Considering one war at a time quite enough, President Lincoln ordered Mason and Slidell released. But settling the *Trent* affair did not eliminate friction between the United States and Britain. Union diplomats protested the construction of Confederate commerce raiders such as the *Alabama* and the *Florida* in British shipyards and threatened war if two British-built ironclads were turned over to the Confederacy. Britain gave in and purchased the vessels for its own navy.

The South fell far short of its diplomatic objectives. Neither Britain nor France ever recognized the Confederacy as a nation. Southerners had badly overestimated the leverage of "cotton diplomacy" and the power of King Cotton, exaggerating the impact of their threats to withhold raw cotton supplies. Britain had an enormous cotton surplus on hand when the war began and developed other sources of cotton during the war, especially in India and Egypt. Although the South's share of England's cotton imports plummeted from 77 percent to 10 percent during the war, Britain's textile industry never faltered.

Lincoln's issuance of the Emancipation Proclamation, freeing the slaves, effectively preempted any British or French move toward recognition of the Confederacy. By transforming the war into a struggle about slavery, Lincoln won wide support among liberals and the working class in Britain. The proclamation, wrote Henry Adams (diplomat Charles Francis Adams's son) from London, "has done more for us here than all of our former victories and all our diplomacy."

# Emancipation Transforms the War

"I hear old John Brown knocking on the lid of his coffin and shouting 'Let me out! Let me out!'" abolitionist Henry Stanton wrote to his wife after the fall of Fort Sumter. "The Doom of Slavery is at hand." In 1861 this prediction seemed wildly premature. In the inaugural address Lincoln had stated bluntly, "I have no purpose, directly or indirectly, to interfere with the institution of slavery in the states where it exists." Yet within two years both necessity and ideology made emancipation a primary northern goal.

The rise of emancipation as a war goal reflected the changing character of the conflict itself. As the fighting raged on, demands for the prosecution of a "total war" intensified in the North, and many people who were unconcerned about the morality of slavery accepted abolition as a military necessity.

## From Confiscation to Emancipation

The Union's policy on emancipation developed in several stages. As soon as northern troops invaded the South, questions arose about captured rebel property, including slaves. Generally, slaves who fled behind Union lines were considered "contraband"—enemy property liable to seizure—and were put to work for the Union army. In August 1861 Congress passed the first Confiscation Act, which authorized the seizure of all property, including slaves, used in military aid of the rebellion. This law did not free slaves, nor did it apply to those who had not worked for the Confederate army.

Several factors determined the Union's cautious approach. For one thing, Lincoln maintained that the South could not legally secede and thus argued that the Constitution's protection of property still applied. Second, Lincoln did not want to alienate slaveholders in the border states and proslavery Democrats. In December 1861 he assured Congress that the war would not become a "remorseless revolutionary struggle." At the same time, however, the Radical Republicans pressured Lincoln to make the Civil War a second American Revolution, one that would abolish slavery. Thaddeus Stevens urged that the Union "free every slave—slay every traitor—burn every Rebel mansion, if these things be necessary to preserve this temple of freedom." Radicals agreed with African-American abolitionist Frederick Douglass that "to fight against slaveholders without fighting against slavery, is but a half-hearted business."

Emancipation also took on military significance with each Union setback, as northerners began to recognize that slavery permitted the South to commit a higher percentage of its white men to battle. In July 1862 Congress therefore passed the second Confiscation Act, which authorized the seizure of property belonging to all rebels, stipulated that slaves who entered Union lines "shall be forever free," and authorized the use of blacks as soldiers.

Nevertheless, Lincoln continued to stall. "My paramount object in this struggle *is* to save the Union, and is *not* either to save or destroy slavery," Lincoln averred. "If I could save the Union without freeing *any* slave, I would do it, and if I could save it by freeing *all* the slaves, I would do it; and if I could save it by freeing some and leaving others alone, I would also do that." But Lincoln, who had always loathed slavery, gradually came around to the view that the war had to lead to abolition. Reluctant to push the issue while Union armies reeled in defeat, he drafted a proclamation of emancipation and waited for the right moment to announce it. After the Union victory at Antietam, Lincoln issued the

Preliminary Emancipation Proclamation (September 1862), which declared all slaves under rebel control free as of January 1, 1863. The final Emancipation Proclamation, issued on January 1, 1863, declared "forever free" all slaves in areas in rebellion.

The proclamation had limited practical impact. It applied only to areas in which it could not be enforced, those still in rebellion, and did not touch slavery in the border states. But the Emancipation Proclamation was a brilliant political stroke. By making it a military measure, Lincoln pacified northern conservatives, and by issuing the proclamation himself, he stole the initiative from the Radical Republicans. Through the proclamation, moreover, Lincoln mobilized support for the Union among European liberals, pushed the border states toward emancipation (both Missouri and Maryland abolished slavery before the war's end), and increased slaves' incentives to escape as Union troops neared. Fulfilling the worst of Confederate fears, the proclamation also enabled African-Americans to join the Union army.

The Emancipation Proclamation did not end slavery everywhere or free "*all* the slaves," but it changed the war. From 1863 on the war for the Union was also a war against slavery.

## Crossing Union Lines

The attacks and counterattacks of the opposing armies turned many slaves into pawns of the war, free when Union troops overran their area, slaves again if the Confederates regained control. One North Carolina slave celebrated his liberation twelve different times. By 1865 about 500,000 former slaves were in Union hands.

Although in the first year of the war masters could retrieve slaves from Union armies, after 1862 slaves who crossed Union lines were considered free. The continual influx of freed slaves created a huge refugee problem for army commanders. Many freed slaves served in army camps as cooks, teamsters, and laborers. Some worked for pay on abandoned plantations or were leased out to planters who swore allegiance to the Union. Whether in camps or on plantations, freedmen questioned the value of liberation. Deductions for clothing and food ate up most of their earnings, and labor contracts bound them for long periods of time. Moreover, the freedmen encountered fierce prejudice among Yankee soldiers, who widely feared that emancipation would propel blacks northward after the war. The best solution to the widespread "question of what to do with the darkies," wrote one northern soldier, "would be to shoot them."

But this was not the whole story. Contrabands who aided the Union as spies and scouts helped to break down bigotry. "The sooner we get rid of our foolish prejudice the better for us," a Massachusetts soldier wrote home. In March 1865 Congress established the Freedmen's Bureau to provide relief, education, and work for the former slaves. The same law also provided that forty acres of abandoned or confiscated land could be leased to each freedman or southern Unionist, with an option to buy after

three years. This was the first and only time that Congress provided for the redistribution of confiscated Confederate property.

## African-American Soldiers in the Union Army

During the first year of the war the Union had rejected African-American soldiers. Only after the Emancipation Proclamation did the large-scale enlistment of blacks begin. Prominent blacks, including Frederick Douglass, worked as recruiting agents in northern cities. Douglass clearly saw the link between military service and citizenship. "Once let the black man get upon his person the brass letters, U.S.; let him get an eagle on his button, and a musket on his shoulder and bullets in his pocket, and there is no power on earth which can deny that he has earned the right to citizenship." By the war's end 186,000 African-Americans had served in the

**African-American Artillerymen**

*African-American troops were organized after the Emancipation Proclamation. The soldiers in the photograph belonged to the Second U.S. Colored Light Artillery, which took part in the Battle of Nashville in 1864.*

Union army, one-tenth of all Union soldiers. One-half came from the Confederate states.

White Union soldiers commonly objected to the new recruits on racial grounds. Others, including Colonel Thomas Wentworth Higginson, a liberal minister and former John Brown supporter who led a black regiment, welcomed the black soldiers. "There is a fierce energy about them [in battle] beyond anything of which I have ever read, except it be the French Zouaves [troops in North Africa]," he observed. Even Union soldiers who held African-Americans in contempt came to approve of "anything that will kill a rebel." Black recruitment offered opportunities for whites to secure commissions, for blacks served in separate regiments under white officers. For most of the war, black soldiers earned far less pay than whites. "We have come out Like men and Expected to be Treated as men but we have bin Treated more Like Dogs then men," an African-American soldier complained. Not until June 1864 did Congress belatedly equalize the pay of black and white soldiers.

African-American soldiers also suffered a far higher mortality rate than whites. Seldom committed to combat, they were far more likely to die of disease in bacteria-ridden garrisons. The Confederacy refused to treat captured black Union soldiers as prisoners of war; instead they were sent back to the states from which they had come to be reenslaved or executed. In an especially gruesome incident, when Confederate troops captured Fort Pillow, Tennessee, in 1864, they massacred 262 blacks.

Although fraught with inequities and hardships, military service symbolized citizenship for African-Americans. A black private explained, "If we hadn't become sojers, all might have gone back as it was before. But now things can never go back because we have showed our energy and our courage . . . and our natural manhood." And the Union's use of African-American soldiers, especially former slaves, struck a military as well as psychological blow at the Confederacy. "They will make good soldiers," General Grant wrote in 1863, "and taking them from the enemy weakens him in the same proportion they strengthen us."

## Slavery in Wartime

Anxious white southerners on the home front felt as if they were perched on a volcano. To maintain control over their 3 million slaves, they tightened slave patrols, spread scare stories among slaves, and sometimes even moved entire plantations to relative safety in Texas. "The whites would tell the colored people not to go to the Yankees, for they would harness them to carts . . . in place of horses," remembered one African-American fugitive.

Some slaves remained faithful to their owners, hiding treasured belongings from marauding Union soldiers. Others were torn between loyalty and desire for freedom; one body servant, for example, accompanied his master to war, rescued him when he was wounded, and then escaped on his master's horse. Given the chance to flee to Union lines, most slaves did. Freedom was irresistible. But the majority of southern slaves stayed on their plantations under the nominal control of their masters. Despite the fears of southern whites, no general slave uprising occurred, and the Confederate war effort continued to utilize slave labor. Thousands of slaves worked in war plants, toiled as teamsters and cooks in army camps, and served as nurses in field hospitals. However, wartime conditions reduced overall slave productivity. The women and boys who remained on plantations complained of hard-to-control slaves who refused to work, worked inefficiently, or even destroyed property.

Whether slaves fled to freedom or merely stopped working, they effectively undermined the plantation system. Slavery disintegrated even as the Confederacy fought to preserve it. By 1864 a desperate Confederate Congress considered impressing slaves into the army in exchange for their freedom at the war's end. Although Robert E. Lee himself favored making slaves into soldiers, others were adamantly opposed. "If slaves will make good soldiers," a Georgia general argued, "our whole theory of slavery is wrong." In March 1865 the Confederate Congress passed a bill to arm 300,000 slave soldiers.

Although the plan to arm the slaves never took effect, the debate over it damaged southern morale

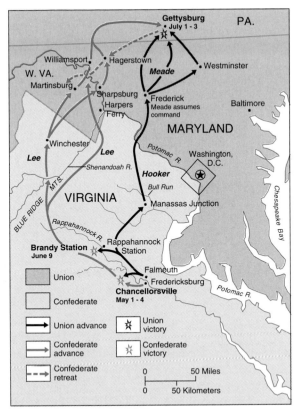

**The War in the East, 1863**
*Victorious at Chancellorsville in May 1863, Lee again invaded Union territory but was decisively stopped at Gettysburg.*

**Robert E. Lee (1807–1870)**
*Lee had a distinguished military career before assuming command of the Army of Northern Virginia in 1862. He had served in the Mexican War under Winfield Scott and as lieutenant colonel of the cavalry performed frontier duty in Texas beginning in 1855. In 1859 he had led the troops that put down John Brown's raid on Harpers Ferry.*

by revealing deep internal divisions over war goals. Even before these conflicts had become obvious, the South's military position had deteriorated.

## The Turning Point of 1863

In summer and fall 1863 Union fortunes improved dramatically in every theater of the war. However, the spring had gone badly as General Joseph "Fighting Joe" Hooker, a windbag fond of issuing pompous proclamations to his troops, suffered a crushing defeat at Chancellorsville, Virginia, in May 1863. Although Chancellorsville cost the South dearly—

Stonewall Jackson was accidentally killed by his own troops—it humiliated the North, whose forces had outnumbered the Confederate troops two to one. "What will the country say?" Lincoln moaned. Reports from the West brought no better news: Grant was still unable to take Vicksburg, and the rebels clung to a vital 200-mile stretch of the Mississippi.

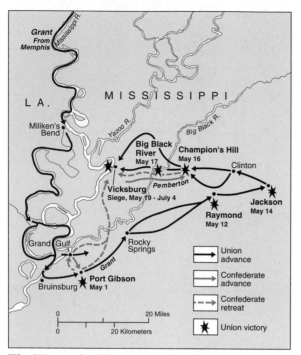

**The War in the West, 1863: Vicksburg**
*Grant first moved his army west of Vicksburg to a point on the Mississippi south of the town. Then he marched northeast, taking Jackson, and finally west to Vicksburg.*

Union fortunes rose when Lee determined to invade the North. The decision provoked dissension within the Confederate government, but Lee needed supplies that war-racked Virginia could no longer provide. He also hoped that Lincoln would move troops from Vicksburg back into the eastern theater, and he believed that a major Confederate victory on northern soil could tip the balance to propeace northern Democrats and gain European recognition for the Confederacy. Lee led his 75,000 men into Maryland and then pressed forward into southern Pennsylvania. Lincoln, rejecting Hooker's plan to attack a virtually unprotected Richmond, replaced him with General George G. Meade.

Early in July 1863 Lee's offensive ground to a halt at a Pennsylvania road junction, Gettysburg. Confederates foraging for shoes in the town stumbled into Union cavalry, and both sides called for re-inforcements. Thus began the war's greatest battle. The Union fielded 90,000 troops against Lee's 75,000, and the struggle raged for the first three days of July. On the afternoon of the third day, Lee ordered a direct frontal assault on the Union lines, and 15,000 men under General George E. Pickett charged across the open field, flags bright in the brilliant sunshine. Union rifles poured volley after volley into the onrushing Confederates, whose line wavered and then broke. More than one-half of Pickett's force lay dead, dying, or captured. When Lee withdrew to Virginia the next day, July 4, he had lost seventeen generals and more than one-third of his army. Total Union and Confederate casualties numbered 50,000. Although Meade failed to pursue the retreating rebels, the Union men rejoiced that they had parried Lee's stab northward.

Almost simultaneously, the North won a strategically vital battle in the West, at Vicksburg. After arduous maneuvering, Grant had besieged Vicksburg, the key to the Mississippi. After six weeks, during which southern soldiers and civilians alike survived by eating mules and even rats, the Confederate commander surrendered his 30,000-man garrison to Grant on July 4, the day that Lee began his withdrawal from Pennsylvania. Port Hudson, the last Confederate stronghold on the Mississippi, soon surrendered. "The Father of Waters flows unvexed to the sea," Lincoln proclaimed.

A second crucial Union victory in the West soon followed as armies stormed back and forth across Tennessee. By November 1863 the Union forces had finally captured and held Chattanooga, and the way lay open for a Union strike into Georgia.

Coming on the heels of reverses that had driven northern morale to its lowest point of the war, Union successes in the second half of 1863 stiffened the North's will to continue fighting and plunged some Confederate leaders into despair. After the fall of Vicksburg, chief of ordnance Josiah Gorgas lamented, "Yesterday we rode the pinnacle of success—today absolute ruin seems our portion. The Confederacy totters to its destruction."

Totter it might, but the South was far from falling. Lee and his Army of Northern Virginia still defended Virginia and Richmond. Although the loss of Vicksburg had cut the Confederacy in half, southern states west of the Mississippi could still provide soldiers. And the heart of the Confederacy—the Carolinas, Georgia, Florida, Mississippi, and Virginia—remained in southern hands. Few contemporaries thought that the fate of the Confederacy had been sealed.

# War and Society, North and South

The Civil War, engulfing two economies and societies, extended far beyond the battlefields. By 1863 the contrasts between North and South were stark: superior resources enabled the Union to meet wartime demands that the imperiled Confederacy could not. But both sides confronted similar problems: labor shortages, inflation, and disunity and dissent. The war disrupted and dislocated families in the Union and Confederacy alike but especially in the South. Women on both sides took on new roles at home, in the workplace, and in relief efforts.

### The War's Economic Impact: The North

The war had a wildly uneven effect on the Union's economy. Deprived of southern markets, the shoe industry in Massachusetts declined; deprived of raw cotton, the textile industry went into a tailspin. But northern industries directly related to the war effort, such as the manufacture of arms and uniforms, benefited from huge government contracts. Railroads flourished. Now an overwhelming majority in Congress, and with no need to balance southern interests against those of the North, the Republican party carried through a vigorous probusiness legislative agenda. Congress hiked the tariff in 1862 and again in 1864 to protect domestic industries. In 1862 it passed the Pacific Railroad Act to build a transcontinental railroad. The government chartered the Union Pacific and Central Pacific corporations and gave each large land grants and generous loans, a total of 60 million acres of land and $20 million. The issuance of greenbacks and the creation of a national banking system brought a measure of uniformity to the nation's financial system.

The Republicans designed these measures to help all social classes and partially succeeded. The Homestead Act (passed in May 1862), embodying the party's ideal of "free soil, free labor, free men," granted 160 acres of public land to settlers after five years of residence on the land. By 1865, 20,000 homesteaders had occupied new land in the West under this act. To bring higher education within the reach of the common people, the Morrill Land Grant Act of July 1862 gave states proceeds from public land to establish universities emphasizing "such branches of learning as are related to agriculture and mechanic arts [engineering]."

Despite the idealistic goals underlying such laws, the war benefited the wealthy more than the average citizen. Corrupt contractors grew rich by selling the government substandard merchandise such as the notorious "shoddy," clothing made from compressed rags, which quickly disintegrated. Speculators made millions in the gold market, profiting more from Union defeats than from Union victories. Dealers with access to scarce commodities reaped astonishing profits. Manpower shortages in agricultural areas stimulated demand for Cyrus McCormick's mechanical reaper. McCormick redoubled his profits by investing in pig iron and watching as wartime demand drove the price of iron from twenty-three to forty dollars a ton.

Ordinary workers suffered. Protective tariffs, wartime excise taxes, and inflation bloated the price of finished goods, while wages lagged 20 percent or more behind cost increases. As boys and women poured into government offices and factories to replace men serving in the army, they drew lower pay, and the threat that employers could hire more youths and females undercut the bargaining power of men remaining in the labor force.

### The War's Economic Impact: The South

The war shattered the South's economy. In fact, if both regions are considered together, the war retarded *American* economic growth. For example, the U.S. commodity output, which had increased 51 percent and 62 percent in the 1840s and 1850s, respectively, rose only 22 percent during the 1860s. Even this modest gain depended wholly on the North, for during that same decade commodity output in the South *declined* 39 percent.

Multiple factors offset the South's substantial wartime industrial growth. For example, the war destroyed the South's railroads. Cotton production plunged from 4 million bales in 1861 to 300,000 in 1865. Southern food production also declined because of Union occupation and a shortage of manpower. Food scarcities occurred late in the war. "The people are subsisting on the ungathered crops and nine families out of ten are left without meat," lamented one Mississippian.

Part of the blame for the South's food shortage rested with the planters. Despite government pleas to grow more food, many planters continued to raise cotton. To feed its hungry armies, the Confederacy impressed food from civilians. Farms and plantations run by the wives of active soldiers provided the easiest targets for food-impressment agents, and the women sent desperate pleas to their husbands to return home. By late 1864, half the Confederacy's soldiers were absent from their units.

In one respect the persistence of cotton growing aided the South as cotton became the basis for the Confederacy's flourishing trade with the enemy. In July 1861 the U.S. Congress virtually legalized this trade by allowing northern commerce with southerners loyal to the Union. In practice, it proved impossible to tell loyalists from rebels, and northern traders happily swapped bacon, salt, blankets, and other necessities with whomever would sell them southern cotton. By 1864 traffic through the lines was providing the South with enough food daily to feed Lee's Army of Northern Virginia. To one disenchanted northern congressman, it seemed that the Union's policy was "to feed an army and fight it at the same time."

Trading with the enemy alleviated the South's food shortages but intensified its morale problems. The prospect of traffic with the Yankees gave planters an incentive to keep growing cotton, and it fattened merchants and middlemen. "Oh! the extortioners," complained a War Office clerk in Richmond. "Our patriotism is mainly in the army and among the ladies of the South. The avarice and cupidity of men at home could only be exceeded by ravenous wolves."

## Dealing with Dissent

Both wartime governments faced mounting dissent and disloyalty. Within the Confederacy, dissent assumed two basic forms. First, a vocal group of states' rights supporters persistently attacked Jefferson Davis's government as a despotism. Second, loyalty to the Union flourished among the nonslaveholding small farmers who lived in the Appalachian region. To these people, the Confederate rebellion was a slave owners' conspiracy. An Alabama farmer complained of the planters, "All they want is to get you pupt up and to fight for their infurnal negroes and after you do there fighting you may kiss there hine parts for o they care." On the whole, the South responded mildly to such popular disaffection. In 1862 the Confederate Congress gave President Davis the power to suspend the writ of habeas corpus, but he used it sparingly.

Lincoln faced similar challenges in the North, where the Democratic minority opposed both emancipation and the wartime growth of centralized power. One faction, the "Peace Democrats" (called Copperheads by their opponents, to suggest a resemblance to a species of easily concealed poisonous snakes), demanded a truce and a peace conference. They charged that the administration's war policy would "exterminate the South," make reconciliation impossible, and spark "terrible social change and revolution" nationwide.

Strongest in the border states, the Midwest, and northeastern cities, the Democrats mobilized farmers of southern background and the urban working class, especially recent immigrants, who feared losing their jobs to free blacks. In 1863 this volatile mix of political, ethnic, racial, and class antagonisms exploded into antidraft protests in several cities. By far the most violent eruption occurred in July 1863 in New York City, where mobs of Irish working-class men and women roamed the streets for four days until federal troops suppressed them. The Irish loathed the idea of being drafted to fight a war on behalf of slaves who, once freed, might compete with them for jobs. They also bitterly resented the provision of the draft law that allowed the rich to purchase substitutes. The mobs' targets reflected their grievances: the rioters lynched at least a dozen blacks, injured hundreds more, and burned draft offices and the homes of wealthy Republicans.

President Lincoln's speedy dispatch of federal troops to quash these riots typified his forceful response to dissent. Lincoln imposed martial law with far less hesitancy than Davis; he suspended the writ of habeas corpus nationwide in 1863 and authorized the arrest of rebels, draft resisters, and anyone engaged in "any disloyal practice." The contrasting responses of Davis and Lincoln to dissent underscored the differences between the two regions' wartime political systems. Lincoln and the Republicans used dissent to rally patriotic fever against the Democrats, but Davis lacked the institutionalization of dissent provided by party conflict and thus had to tread lightly lest he be branded a despot.

Yet Lincoln did not unleash a reign of terror against dissent. In general, the North preserved freedom of the press, speech, and assembly. In 1864 the Union became the first warring nation in history to hold a contested national election. Moreover, most of the 15,000 civilians arrested in the North were quickly released. A few cases aroused concern. In 1864 a military commission sentenced an Indiana man to be hanged for an alleged plot to free Confederate prisoners. Two years later in *Ex parte* Milligan (1866), the Supreme Court overturned the conviction, ruling that military courts could not try civilians when civil courts were open. The arrest of outspoken dissident politicians raised protests as well. Clement L. Vallandigham, an Ohio Peace Democrat, challenged the administration, denounced the suspension of habeas corpus, and proposed an armistice. In 1863 a military commission

sentenced him to jail for the duration of the war; when Ohio Democrats nominated him for governor, Lincoln changed the sentence to banishment. Escorted to enemy lines in Tennessee, Vallandigham was left in the hands of bewildered Confederates and escaped to Canada. The Supreme Court refused to review his case.

## The Medical War

The Union and the Confederacy alike witnessed remarkable wartime patriotism that propelled civilians, especially women, to work tirelessly to alleviate soldiers' suffering. The United States Sanitary Commission, organized to assist the Union's medical bureau, depended on women volunteers. Described by one woman as a "great artery that bears the people's love to the army," the commission raised funds, bought and distributed supplies, and ran special kitchens to supplement army rations. One widow, Mary Ann "Mother" Bickerdyke, served sick and wounded Union soldiers as both nurse and surrogate mother.

Women also reached out to aid the battlefront through the nursing corps. Some 3,200 women served the Union and the Confederacy as nurses. Dorothea Dix, famed for her campaigns on behalf of the insane, became head of the Union's nursing corps. Clara Barton, an obscure clerk in the Patent Office, found ingenious ways of channeling medicine to the sick and wounded. Catching wind of Union movements before the Battle of Antietam, she showed up at the battlefield on the eve of the clash with a wagonload of supplies. When army surgeons ran out of bandages and started to dress wounds with corn husks, she raced forward with lint and bandages. In 1881 she would found the American Red Cross. The Confederacy also had extraordinary nurses, among them Belle Boyd, who served as both nurse and spy and once dashed through a field, waving her bonnet, to give Stonewall Jackson information. Nurses witnessed horrible sights. One reported, "About the amputating table lay large piles of human flesh—legs, arms, feet, and hands."

Pioneered by British reformer Florence Nightingale in the 1850s, nursing was a new vocation for women. In the eyes of critics, it marked a brazen departure from women's proper sphere. Male doctors were unsure about how to react to female nurses and sanitary workers. Some saw a potential for mischief in women's presence in male hospital wards. But other physicians viewed nursing and sanitary work as useful. The miasm theory of disease (see Chapter 11) won wide respect among physicians and stimulated valuable sanitary measures. In partial consequence, the ratio of disease to battle deaths was much lower in the Civil War than in the Mexican War. Nonetheless, for every soldier killed during the Civil War, two died of disease. The germ theory of disease was unknown, and arm and leg wounds often led to gangrene or tetanus. Typhoid, malaria, diarrhea, and dysentery were rampant in army camps.

Prison camps posed a special problem. The two sides had far more prisoners than they could handle, and prisoners on both sides suffered gravely. The worst conditions plagued the southern camps. Squalor and insufficient rations turned the Confederate prison camp at Andersonville, Georgia, into a virtual death camp; 3,000 prisoners a month (out of a total of 32,000) were dying there by August 1864. After the war an outraged northern public demanded, and got, the execution of Andersonville's commandant. Although the commandant was partly to blame, the deterioration of the southern economy was primarily responsible for such wretched conditions. Union prison camps were only marginally better.

### The War and Women's Rights

Nurses and Sanitary Commission workers were not the only women to serve society in wartime. In North and South alike, women took over jobs vacated by men. In rural areas, where manpower shortages were most acute, women often plowed, planted, and harvested.

Northern women's rights advocates hoped that the war would yield equality for women as well as for slaves. A grateful North, they contended, should reward women for their wartime service and recognize the link between black rights and women's rights. In 1863 feminists Elizabeth Cady Stanton and Susan B. Anthony organized the National Woman's Loyal League. Its members principally gathered signatures on petitions calling for a constitutional amendment to abolish slavery, but Stanton and Anthony used the organization to promote woman suffrage as well. Despite high expectations, the war did not bring women significantly closer to economic or political equality. Nor did it much change the prevailing definition of women's sphere. Men continued to dominate the medical profession, and for the rest of the century the census classified nurses as domestic help.

This failure to win the vote for women by capitalizing on the rising sentiment for abolition keenly disappointed women's rights advocates. The North had compelling reasons to abolish slavery, but northern politicians saw little practical value in woman suffrage. The *New York Herald*, which supported the Loyal League's attack on slavery, dismissed its call for woman suffrage as "nonsense and tomfoolery." Stanton wrote bitterly, "So long as woman labors to second man's endeavors and exalt his sex above her own, her virtues pass unquestioned; but when she dares to demand rights and privileges for herself, her motives, manners, dress, personal appearance, and character are subjects for ridicule and detraction."

# The Union Victorious, 1864–1865

Successes at Gettysburg and Vicksburg in 1863 notwithstanding, the Union stood no closer to taking Richmond at the start of 1864 than in 1861, and most of the Lower South remained under Confederate control. The North's persistent inability to destroy the main Confederate armies eroded the Union's will to attack. War weariness strengthened

| The Election of 1864 | | | | |
| --- | --- | --- | --- | --- |
| Candidates | Parties | Electoral Vote | Popular Vote | Percentage of Popular Vote |
| ABRAHAM LINCOLN | Republican | 212 | 2,206,938 | 55.0 |
| George B. McClellan | Democratic | 21 | 1,803,787 | 45.0 |

the Democrats and jeopardized Lincoln's reelection in 1864.

The year 1864 was crucial for the North. A Union army under General William Tecumseh Sherman captured Atlanta in September, boosting northern morale and helping to reelect Lincoln. Sherman then marched unimpeded across Georgia and into South Carolina and devastated the states. In Virginia Grant backed Lee into trenches around Petersburg and Richmond and forced the evacuation of both cities—and ultimately the Confederacy's collapse.

## The Eastern Theater in 1864

Early in 1864 Lincoln made Grant the commander of all Union armies and promoted him to lieutenant general. At first glance, the stony-faced, cigar-puffing Grant seemed an unlikely candidate for so exalted a rank, held previously only by George Washington. But Grant's successes in the West had made him the Union's most popular general. He moved his headquarters to the Army of the Potomac in the East and mapped a strategy for final victory.

Grant shared Lincoln's belief that the Union had to coordinate its attacks on all fronts to exploit its numerical advantage. He planned a sustained offensive against Lee in the East while ordering Sherman to attack the rebel army in Georgia. Sherman's mission was "to break it [the Confederate army] up, and to get into the interior of the enemy's country . . . inflicting all the damage you can."

In early May 1864 Grant led 118,000 men against Lee's 64,000 in a forested area near Fredericksburg, Virginia, called the Wilderness. The Union army fought the Army of Northern Virginia in a series of bloody engagements in May and June. These battles ranked among the war's fiercest; at Cold Harbor, Grant lost 7,000 men in one hour. Instead of recoiling from such an immense "butcher's bill," Grant pressed on, forcing Lee to pull back to trenches guarding Petersburg and Richmond.

Once entrenched, Lee could not threaten the Union rear with rapid moves as he had done for three years. Lee sent General Jubal A. Early on raids down the Shenandoah Valley, which served the Confederacy as a granary and as an indirect way to menace Washington. Grant countered by ordering General Philip Sheridan to march down the valley from the north and lay it waste. By September 1864 Sheridan controlled the devastated valley.

## Sherman in Georgia

While Grant and Lee grappled in the Wilderness, Sherman led 98,000 men into Georgia. Opposing him with 53,000 men (later reinforced to 65,000), General Joseph Johnston slowly retreated toward Atlanta, conserving his strength for a defense of the city. Dismayed by this defensive strategy, President Davis replaced Johnston with the adventurous John B. Hood. He gave Davis what he wanted, a series of attacks on Sherman, but Sherman pressed relentlessly forward against Hood's increasingly depleted army. Unable to defend Atlanta, Hood evacuated the city, which Sherman took on September 2, 1864.

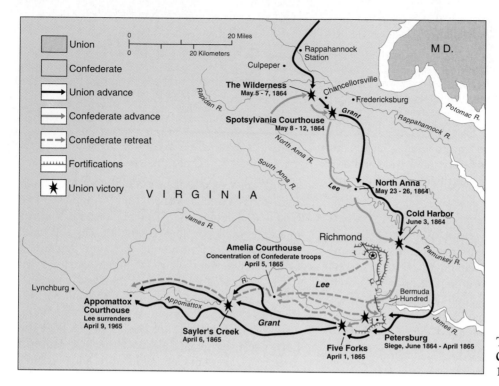

The Final Virginia
Campaign,
1864–1865

## The Election of 1864

Atlanta's fall came at a timely moment for Lincoln, in the thick of a tough campaign for reelection. Radical Republicans opposed his renomination, largely because of his desire to restore occupied parts of the Confederacy to the Union, and rallied around Secretary of the Treasury Salmon P. Chase. The Democrats, meanwhile, had never forgiven Lincoln for making emancipation a war goal, and now the Copperheads demanded an immediate armistice followed by negotiations.

Lincoln, however, benefited from his own resourcefulness and his foes' problems. Chase's challenge failed, and by the time of the Republican convention, Lincoln's managers controlled the nomination. To isolate the Peace Democrats, the Republicans formed a temporary organization, the National Union party, and chose a southern Unionist, Democratic senator Andrew Johnson of Tennessee, for the vice presidency. The Democrats nominated George B. McClellan, former commander of the Army of the Potomac, who advocated military victory and tried to distance himself from the Democratic platform, which called for peace without victory.

Lincoln doubted that he would be reelected, but the fall of Atlanta provided an enormous boost. With 55 percent of the popular vote and 212 out of 233 electoral votes, he swept to victory.

## Sherman's March Through Georgia

Meanwhile, Sherman gave the South a lesson in total war. Refusing to chase Hood back into Tennessee, he decided to abandon his own supply lines, to march his army across Georgia to Savannah, and to live off the countryside. He would break the South's will to fight, terrify its people, and "make war so terrible . . . that generations would pass before they could appeal to it again."

Sherman began by burning much of Atlanta and forcing the evacuation of its civilian population. This harsh measure freed him of the need to feed and garrison the city. Then he led the bulk of his army, 62,000 men, out of Atlanta toward Savannah. Four columns of infantry, augmented by cavalry squads and followed by thousands of jubilant slaves, moved on a front sixty miles wide and at a pace of ten miles a day, destroying everything that could aid the Confederacy—arsenals, railroads, munitions plants, cotton gins, crops, and livestock. This ruin far exceeded Sherman's orders. Although told not to destroy civilian property, foragers ransacked and demolished homes. Indeed, havoc seemed a vital part of Sherman's strategy. By the time he occupied Savannah, he estimated that his army had destroyed $100 million worth of property. After taking Savannah in December 1864, Sherman's army wheeled north toward South Carolina and advanced unimpeded to Columbia, where fires set by looters, slaves, soldiers of both sides, and liberated Union prisoners razed the city. Sherman headed for North Carolina. By spring 1865 his army had left behind 400 miles of ruin. Other Union armies controlled the entire Confederacy, except Texas and Florida, and destroyed its wealth. "War is cruelty and you cannot refine it," Sherman wrote. "Those who brought war into our country deserve all the curses and maledictions a people can pour out."

## Toward Appomattox

While Sherman headed north, Grant renewed his assault on the entrenched Army of Northern Virginia. His main objective was Petersburg, a railroad hub south of Richmond. The fall of Atlanta and the devastation wrought by Sherman's army took a heavy toll on Confederate morale. Desertions reached epidemic proportions. Late in March 1865 Grant, reinforced by Sheridan, swung his army around the western flank of the Petersburg defenders. Lee could not stop him. On April 2 a courier brought the grim news to Jefferson Davis, attending church in Richmond: "General Lee telegraphs that he can hold his position no longer."

Davis left his pew, gathered his government, and fled. On the morning of April 3 Union troops entered Richmond, pulled down the Confederate flag, and raised the Stars and Stripes over the capital. Explosions set by retreating Confederates left the city "a sea of flames." Union troops liberated the jail, which held slaves awaiting sale, and its rejoicing inmates poured into the streets. On April 4 Lincoln toured the city and, for a few minutes, sat at Davis's desk with a dreamy expression on his face.

Lee led a last-ditch effort to escape westward to Lynchburg and its rail connections. But Grant and Sheridan choked off the route, and on April 9 Lee bowed to the inevitable. He asked for terms of surrender and met Grant in a private home in the village of Appomattox Courthouse, east of Lynchburg. As stunned troops gathered outside, Lee appeared in full dress uniform, complete with sword. Grant entered in his customary disarray, smoking a cigar. The final surrender came four days later as Lee's troops laid down their arms between federal ranks. "On our part," wrote a Union officer, "not a sound of trumpet . . . nor roll of drum; not a cheer . . . but an awed stillness rather." Grant paroled Lee's 26,000 men and sent them home with the horses and mules "to work their little farms." Within a month the remnants of Confederate resistance collapsed.

Grant headed back to Washington. On April 14 he turned down a theater date with the Lincolns; his wife found Mrs. Lincoln overbearing. That night at Ford's Theater an unemployed pro-Confederate actor, John Wilkes Booth, entered Lincoln's box and shot him in the head. Assassination attempts on the secretary of state and vice president failed, and Booth escaped. Within two weeks Union troops hunted him down and shot him to death (or he shot himself). Four accused accomplices were hanged, and four more were imprisoned. On April 15 Lincoln died and Andrew Johnson became president. Six days later Lincoln's funeral train left Washington on its mournful journey to Springfield, Illinois. Crowds of thousands gathered at stations to weep as the black-draped train passed.

## CONCLUSION

The Civil War took a larger human toll than any other war in American history. More than 600,000 persons died during the tragic four years of war. Most families in the nation suffered losses. Vivid reminders remained well into the twentieth century. For many years armless and legless veterans gathered at regimental reunions, and thousands of communities built monuments to the dead.

The war's costs were high, but only the southern economy was destroyed. By war's end the North had most of the nation's wealth and industrial capacity. Spurring economic modernization, the war provided opportunities for industrial development and capital investment. No longer the largest slave-owning power in the world, the United States would become a major industrial nation.

The war had political ramifications as well. States never regained their antebellum range of powers. The national banking system gradually supplanted state banks, and greenbacks provided a national currency. The war also promoted large-scale organization in both the business world and public life.

Finally, the Civil War fulfilled abolitionists' prophecies as well as Union goals, producing the very sort of radical upheaval within southern society that Lincoln had tried to avoid. Beaten Confederates wondered whether blacks and Yankees would permanently take over the South. "Hello, massa," an African-American Union soldier called out when he spotted his former owner among Confederate prisoners whom he was guarding. "Bottom rail top dis time." The nation now shifted its attention to the reconstruction of the conquered South and the fate of 3.5 million newly freed slaves.

## CHRONOLOGY

**1861**  President Abraham Lincoln calls for volunteers to suppress the rebellion (April).
Virginia, Arkansas, Tennessee, and North Carolina join the Confederacy (April–May).
Lincoln imposes a naval blockade on the South (April).
First Battle of Bull Run (July).
First Confiscation Act (August).

**1862**  Legal Tender Act (February).
George B. McClellan's Peninsula Campaign (March–July).
Battle of Shiloh (April).
Confederate Congress passes the Conscription Act (April).
David G. Farragut captures New Orleans (April).
Homestead Act (May).
Seven Days' Battles (June–July).
Pacific Railroad Act (July).

Morrill Land Grant Act (July).
Second Confiscation Act (July).
Second Battle of Bull Run (August).
Battle of Antietam (September).
Preliminary Emancipation Proclamation (September).
Battle of Fredericksburg (December).

**1863**  Emancipation Proclamation issued (January).
Lincoln suspends writ of habeas corpus nationwide (January).
National Bank Act (February).
Congress passes the Enrollment Act (March).
Battle of Chancellorsville (May).
Battle of Gettysburg (July).
Surrender of Vicksburg (July).
New York City draft riots (July).
Battle of Chickamauga (September).

**1864** Ulysses S. Grant given command of all Union armies (March).
Wilderness campaign (May–June).
Surrender of Atlanta (September).
Lincoln reelected (November).
William T. Sherman's march to the sea (November–December).

**1865** Sherman moves through South Carolina (January–March).
Grant takes Richmond (April).
Robert E. Lee surrenders at Appomattox (April).
Lincoln dies (April).
Joseph Johnston surrenders to Sherman (April).

## FOR FURTHER READING

Iver Bernstein, *The New York Draft Riots: The Significance for American Society and Politics in the Age of the Civil War* (1990). An exploration of the social, economic, and political facets of the riots, and their ramifications.

Albert Castel, *Decision in the West: The Atlanta Campaign of 1864* (1992). A critical examination of William T. Sherman's legendary brilliance of command.

Catherine Clinton and Nina Silber, eds., *Divided Houses: Gender and the Civil War* (1992). Essays focusing on changes in women's roles and activities.

David H. Donald, *Lincoln* (1995). An impressive new biography of one of America's greatest presidents.

Alvin M. Josephy Jr., *The Civil War in the American West* (1993). A penetrating look at a relatively unexamined arena of the war.

Leon Litwack, *Been in the Storm So Long: The Aftermath of Slavery* (1979). A prize-winning examination of slaves' responses to the process of emancipation, continuing into the Reconstruction era.

James M. McPherson, *Battle Cry of Freedom: The Civil War Era* (1988). An award-winning study of the war years, skillfully integrating political, military, and social history.

Philip Shaw Paludan, *The Presidency of Abraham Lincoln* (1994). An assessment of Lincoln as statesman, party leader, commander in chief, and emancipator.

Charles Royster, *The Destructive War: William Tecumseh Sherman, Stonewall Jackson, and the Americans* (1991). An insightful exploration of the meaning of violence and nationality in the Civil War era.

Emory M. Thomas, *The Confederate Nation, 1861–1865* (1979). An engaging narrative history, emphasizing the rise and fall of southern nationalism.

# CHAPTER 16

When the Civil War ended, parts of the South resembled a wasteland. The landscape "looked for many miles like a broad black streak of ruin and desolation," wrote a Union general. Homes, crops, and railroads had been destroyed; farming and business had come to a standstill. Refugees, demobilized soldiers, and former slaves flooded the roads. The prevailing mood was as grim as the landscape. "The South lies prostrate—their foot is on us—there is no help," a Virginia woman lamented. That 200,000 Union troops occupied the former Confederacy contributed to the sense of despair.

After most wars victors care little for the mood of the vanquished, but the Civil War was different. The Union had sought not merely victory but the return of national unity. The federal government faced unprecedented questions. How could the Union be restored and the South reintegrated? Who would control the process—Congress or the president? Should Confederate leaders be tried for treason? Most important, what would happen to the 3.5 million former slaves?

## The Crises of Reconstruction, 1865–1877

**Reconstruction Politics**

✤

**Reconstruction Governments**

✤

**The Impact of Emancipation**

✤

**New Concerns in the North**

✤

**Reconstruction Abandoned**

*(Right) Richmond in ruins, 1865*

The freedmen's future was *the* crucial postwar issue, for emancipation had set in motion the most profound upheaval in the nation's history. Slavery had been both a labor system and a means of racial control; it had determined the South's social, economic, and political structure. The end of the Civil War, in short, posed two huge challenges that had to be addressed simultaneously: readmitting the Confederate states to the Union and defining the status of free blacks in society.

From 1865 to 1877 the drama of Reconstruction—the restoration of the former Confederate states to the Union—unfolded in several theaters. In Washington conflict between president and Congress led to stringent measures. In the South Republicans temporarily took power, and far-reaching social and economic changes transformed the former Confederacy. Freed slaves wrestled with new identities and new problems. Meanwhile, the North hurtled headlong into an era of industrial expansion, labor unrest, and financial crises. By the mid-1870s, however, northern Republicans had abandoned Reconstruction and southern Democrats had regained control of their states. Reconstruction collapsed in 1877, and the nature and causes of its failure have engaged historians ever since.

## Reconstruction Politics

The end of the Civil War offered multiple possibilities for chaos and vengeance. The federal government could have imprisoned Confederate leaders; former rebel troops could have become guerrillas; freed slaves could have waged a racial war against their former masters. None of this happened. Instead, intense *political* conflict dominated the immediate postwar period. The political upheaval, sometimes attended by violence, produced new constitutional amendments, an impeachment crisis, and some of the most ambitious domestic legislation ever enacted by Congress, the Reconstruction Acts of 1867–1868. It culminated in something that few

expected, the enfranchisement of African-American men.

In 1865 only a handful of Radical Republicans advocated African-American suffrage. Any plan to restore the Union, Representative Thaddeus Stevens of Pennsylvania proclaimed, would have to "revolutionize Southern institutions, habits, and manners . . . or all our blood and treasure have been spent in vain." In the complex political battles of Reconstruction, the Radicals won broad support for their program, including African-American male enfranchisement. Just as the Civil War had led to emancipation, so Reconstruction led to African-American suffrage.

### Lincoln's Plan

Conflict over Reconstruction began even before the war ended. In December 1863 President Lincoln issued the Proclamation of Amnesty and Reconstruction, which allowed southern states to form new governments if at least 10 percent of those who had voted in the 1860 elections swore an oath of allegiance to the Union and accepted emancipation. This plan excluded most Confederate officials and military officers, who would have had to apply for presidential pardons, as well as African-Americans, who had not voted in 1860. Lincoln hoped both to undermine the Confederacy and to build a southern Republican party.

Radical Republicans in Congress wanted a slower readmission process that would exclude even more ex-Confederates from political life. The Wade-Davis bill, passed by Congress in July 1864, provided that a military government would rule each former Confederate state and that at least one-half of the eligible voters would have to swear allegiance before they could choose a convention to repeal secession and abolish slavery. In addition, to qualify as a voter or a delegate, a southerner would have to take the "ironclad" oath, swearing that he had never voluntarily supported the Confederacy. The Wade-Davis bill would have delayed readmission of southern states almost indefinitely.

Lincoln pocket-vetoed* the Wade-Davis bill, and an impasse followed. Arkansas, Louisiana, Tennessee, and parts of Virginia moved toward readmission under variants of Lincoln's plan, but Congress refused to seat their delegates. Lincoln hinted that he might be moving toward a more rigorous policy than his original one, a program that would include African-American suffrage. But his death foreclosed the possibility that he and Congress might draw closer to agreement, and Radicals now looked with hope to the new president, Andrew Johnson.

## Presidential Reconstruction Under Johnson

At first glance, Andrew Johnson seemed a likely ally for the Radicals. The only southern senator to remain in Congress when his state seceded, Johnson had taken a strong anti-Confederate stance and had served as military governor of Tennessee for two years. Self-educated, an ardent Jacksonian, a foe of the planter class, a supporter of emancipation—Johnson carried impeccable credentials. However, as a lifelong Democrat he had his own political agenda, sharply different from that of the Radicals.

In May 1865, with Congress out of session, Johnson shocked Republicans by announcing his own program to bring the southern states still without Reconstruction governments—Alabama, Florida, Georgia, Mississippi, North Carolina, South Carolina, and Texas—back into the Union. Virtually all southerners who took an oath of allegiance would receive pardon and amnesty, and all their property except slaves would be restored to them. Confederate civil and military officers would still be disqualified, as would well-to-do former Confederates (anyone owning taxable property worth $20,000 or more). By purging the plantation aristocracy, Johnson claimed, he would aid "humble men, the peasantry and yeomen of the South, who have been decoyed . . . into rebellion." Oath takers could elect delegates to state conventions, which would call regular elections, proclaim secession illegal, repudiate debts incurred under the Confederacy, and ratify the Thirteenth Amendment, which abolished slavery.

This presidential Reconstruction took effect in summer 1865, with unforeseen results. Johnson handed out pardons liberally (some 13,000) and dropped his plans for the punishment of treason. By the end of 1865 all seven states had created new civil governments that in effect restored the *status quo ante bellum*. Confederate officers and large planters resumed state offices, and former Confederate congressmen and generals won election to Congress. Because many of these new representatives were former Whigs who had not supported secession, southerners believed that they genuinely had elected "Union" men. Some states refused to repudiate their Confederate debts or to ratify the Thirteenth Amendment.

Most infuriating to the Radicals, every state passed a "black code" intended to ensure a landless, dependent black labor force—to "secure the services of the negroes, teach them their place," in the words of one Alabamian. These codes, which replaced earlier slave codes, guaranteed the freedmen some basic rights—marriage, ownership of property, the right to testify in court against other blacks—but also harshly restricted freedmen's behavior. Some states established segregation, and most prohibited racial intermarriage, jury service by blacks, and court testimony by blacks against whites. Most harmful, black codes included economic restrictions to prevent blacks from leaving the plantation, usually by establishing a system of labor contracts and then stipulating that anyone who had not signed a labor contract was a vagrant and thus subject to arrest.

These codes left freedmen no longer slaves but not really liberated. Although many of their provisions never actually took effect—for example, the Union army and the Freedmen's Bureau suspended the enforcement of the racially discriminatory laws—

---

*Pocket-vetoed: failed to sign the bill within ten days of Congress's adjournment.

**King Andrew**

*This Thomas Nast cartoon, published just before the 1866 congressional elections, conveyed Republican antipathy to Andrew Johnson. The president is depicted as an autocratic tyrant. Radical Republican Thaddeus Stevens, upper right, has his head on the block and is about to lose it. The Republic sits in chains.*

the black codes reflected white southern attitudes and showed what "home rule" would have been like without federal intervention.

When former abolitionists and Radical Republicans decried the black codes, Johnson defended them and his restoration program. Former Confederates should not become "a degraded and debased people," he said. To many northerners, both the black codes and the election of former Confed-

erates to high office reeked of southern defiance. "What can be hatched from such an egg but another rebellion?" asked a Boston newspaper. When the Thirty-ninth Congress convened in December 1865, it refused to seat the southern delegates and prepared to dismantle the black codes and to lock ex-Confederates out of power.

## Congress Versus Johnson

Southern blacks' status became the major issue in Congress. With Congress split into four blocs—Democrats, and radical, moderate, and conservative Republicans—a politically adroit president could have protected his program. Ineptly, Johnson alienated the moderates and pushed them into the Radicals' arms by vetoing some key moderate measures.

In late 1865 Congress voted to extend the life of the Freedmen's Bureau for three more years. Staffed mainly by army officers, the bureau provided relief, rations, and medical care; built schools for former slaves; put them to work on abandoned or confiscated lands; and tried to protect their rights as laborers. To strengthen the bureau, Congress had voted to allow it to run special military courts that would settle labor disputes and invalidate labor contracts forced on African-Americans under the black codes. In February 1866 Johnson vetoed the bill; the Constitution, he declared, neither sanctioned military trials of civilians in peacetime nor supported a system to care for "indigent persons." Then in March 1866 Congress passed the Civil Rights Act of 1866, which made African-Americans U.S. citizens with the same civil rights as other citizens and authorized federal intervention to ensure African-Americans' rights in court. Johnson vetoed this measure also, arguing that it would "operate in favor of the colored and against the white race." In April Congress overrode his veto, and in July it enacted the Supplementary Freedmen's Bureau Act over another presidential veto.

These vetoes puzzled many Republicans, for the new laws did not undercut the basic structure of presidential Reconstruction. Although the vetoes gained support for Johnson among northern Democrats, they cost him dearly among moderate Republicans, who began to ally with the Radicals. Was Johnson a political incompetent, or was he merely trying, unsuccessfully, to forge a centrist coalition? Whatever the case, he drove moderate and Radical Republicans together toward their next step: the passage of a constitutional amendment to protect the new Civil Rights Act.

## The Fourteenth Amendment

In April 1866 Congress adopted the Fourteenth Amendment, its most ambitious attempt to deal with the problems of Reconstruction and the freed slaves. In the first clause, the amendment proclaimed that all persons born or naturalized in the United States were citizens and that no state could abridge their rights without due process of law or deny them equal protection under the law. Second, the amendment guaranteed that if a state denied suffrage to any male citizen, its representation in Congress would be proportionally reduced. Third, the amendment disqualified from state and national offices *all* prewar officeholders who had supported the Confederacy. Finally, it repudiated the Confederate debt and maintained the validity of the federal debt. In effect, the Fourteenth Amendment nullified the *Dred Scott* decision, threatened southern states that deprived African-American men of the right to vote, and invalidated most of the pardons that President Johnson had ladled out. Beyond demonstrating widespread receptivity to the Radicals' demands, including African-American male suffrage, the Fourteenth Amendment represented the first national effort to limit the states' control of civil and political rights.

Passage of the amendment created a fire-storm. Abolitionists said that it did not go far enough to protect African-American voting rights, southerners blasted it as vengeful, and President Johnson denounced it. The president's unwillingness to compromise solidified the new alliance between moderate and Radical Republicans and transformed the congressional elections of 1866 into a referendum on the Fourteenth Amendment.

Over the summer Johnson set off on a whistle-stop train tour campaigning against the amendment. Humorless and defensive, the president made fresh enemies, however, and doomed his hope of creating a new political party, the National Union party, opposed to the amendment. Meanwhile, the moderate and Radical Republicans defended the amendment, condemned President Johnson, and branded the Democratic party "a common sewer . . . into which is emptied every element of treason, North and South."

Republicans carried the congressional elections of 1866 in a landslide, winning nearly two-thirds of the House and three-fourths of the Senate. They had secured a mandate for the Fourteenth Amendment and their own Reconstruction program.

## Congressional Reconstruction

The congressional debate over reconstructing the South began in December 1866 and lasted three months. Radical leaders, anxious to stifle a resurgence of Confederate power, called for African-American suffrage, federal support for public schools, confiscation of Confederate estates, and extended military occupation of the South. Moderate Republicans accepted part of this plan. The lawmakers debated every ramification of various legislative proposals, and in February 1867, after complex political maneuvers, Congress passed the Reconstruction Act of 1867. Johnson vetoed it, and on March 2 Congress passed the law over his veto. Three more Reconstruction acts, passed in 1867 and 1868 over presidential vetoes, refined and enforced the first act.

The Reconstruction Act of 1867 invalidated the state governments formed under the Lincoln and Johnson plans; only Tennessee, which had already ratified the Fourteenth Amendment and had been readmitted to the Union, escaped further Reconstruction. The new law divided the other ten former Confederate states into five military districts. It provided that voters—all black men, plus whites not disqualified by the Fourteenth Amendment—

NEBRASKA TERRITORY

IOWA

ILLINOIS    INDIANA    OHIO    PA.

MD.    DEL.

COLORADO TERRITORY

WEST VIRGINIA (new state 1863)    VIRGINIA

**Military District No. 1**

KANSAS    MISSOURI

KENTUCKY

NORTH CAROLINA

TENNESSEE    **Military District No. 2**

INDIAN TERRITORY    ARKANSAS    SOUTH CAROLINA

NEW MEXICO TERRITORY    **Military District No. 4**

ALABAMA    GEORGIA

MISSISSIPPI    **Military District No.3**

**Military District No. 5**

LOUISIANA

TEXAS

MEXICO    FLORIDA

0    300 Miles

0    300 Kilometers

Reconstruction government set up under Lincoln

Reconstruction government set up under Johnson

Boundaries of the five military districts

### The Reconstruction of the South

*The Reconstruction Act of 1867 divided the former Confederate states, except Tennessee, into five military districts and set forth the steps by which new state governments could be created.*

could elect delegates who would write a new state constitution granting African-American suffrage. After congressional approval of the state constitution, and after the state legislature's ratification of the Fourteenth Amendment, Congress would readmit the state into the Union. The enfranchisement of African-Americans and disfranchisement of so many ex-Confederates made the Reconstruction Act of 1867 far more radical than Johnson's program. Even then, however, it provided only temporary military rule, made no provisions to prosecute Confederate leaders for treason, and neither confiscated nor redistributed property.

Radical Republican leader Thaddeus Stevens had proposed confiscation of large Confederate estates to "humble the proud traitors" and to provide land for the former slaves. He hoped to create a new class of self-sufficient African-American yeomen farmers. Because political independence rested on economic independence, he contended, land grants would be far more valuable to African-Americans than the vote. But moderate Republicans and others backed away from Stevens's proposal. Tampering with property rights in the South might well jeopardize them in the North, they argued, and could endanger the entire Reconstruction program. Thus Congress rejected the most radical parts of the Radical Republican program.

Congressional Reconstruction took effect in spring 1867, but Johnson impeded its implementation by replacing pro-Radical military officers with conservative ones since Reconstruction could not be enforced without military power. Furious and more suspicious than ever of the president, congressional moderates and Radicals again joined forces to block Johnson from further hampering Reconstruction.

## The Impeachment Crisis

In March 1867, responding to Johnson's obstructionist tactics, Republicans in Congress passed two laws to restrict presidential power. The Tenure of Office Act prohibited the president from removing civil officers without Senate consent. Its purpose was to protect Secretary of War Edwin Stanton, a Radical ally needed to enforce the Reconstruction acts. The other law banned the president from issuing military orders except through the commanding general, Ulysses S. Grant, who could not be removed without the Senate's consent. Not satisfied with clipping the president's wings, Radicals also began to look for grounds for impeachment and conviction to remove all possible obstacles to Reconstruction. Intense investigations by the House Judiciary Committee and private detectives turned up no impeachable offenses, but Johnson himself soon provided the charges that his opponents needed.

In August 1867 Johnson suspended Stanton and in February 1868 tried to remove him. The president's defiance of the Tenure of Office Act drove moderate Republicans back into alliance with the Radicals. The House approved eleven charges of impeachment, nine of them based on violation of the Tenure of Office Act and the other two accusing Johnson of being "unmindful of the high duties of the office," of seeking to disgrace Congress, and of not enforcing the Reconstruction acts.

Johnson's trial by the Senate, which began in March 1868, riveted public attention for eleven weeks. Seven congressmen, including leading Radicals, served as prosecutors, or "managers." Johnson's lawyers maintained that he was merely seeking a court test of a law that he believed unconstitutional, the Tenure of Office Act, by violating it. They also contended that the law did not protect Stanton because Lincoln, not Johnson, had appointed him. And they asserted that Johnson was guilty of no crime indictable in a regular court.

The congressional "managers" countered that impeachment was a political process, not a criminal trial, and that Johnson's "abuse of discretionary power" constituted an impeachable offense. Some Senate Republicans wavered, fearful that the removal of a president would destroy the balance of power within the federal government. They also were reluctant to see Benjamin Wade, a Radical Republican who was president pro tempore of the Senate, become president, as the Constitution then provided.

Intense pressure weighed on the wavering Republican senators. Ultimately, seven Republicans risked political suicide by voting with the Democrats against removal, and the Senate failed by one vote to convict Johnson. In so doing, the legislators set two critical precedents: in the future, no president would be impeached on political grounds, nor would he be impeached because two-thirds of Congress disagreed with him. In the short term, nonetheless, the anti-Johnson forces achieved their goals, for Andrew Johnson had no future as president. Republicans in Congress could now pursue their last major Reconstruction objective: guaranteeing African-American male suffrage.

## The Fifteenth Amendment

African-American suffrage was the linchpin of congressional Reconstruction. Only with the support of African-American voters could Republicans secure control of the southern states. The Reconstruction Act of 1867 had forced southern states to enfranchise black men in order to reenter the Union, but most northern states still refused to grant suffrage to African-Americans. The Fifteenth Amendment, drawn up by Republicans and approved by Congress in 1869, aimed both to protect black suffrage in the South and to extend it to the northern and border states, on the assumption that newly enfranchised African-Americans would gratefully vote Republican. The amendment prohibited the denial of suf-

## The Reconstruction Amendments

| Amendment and Date of Congressional Passage | Provisions | Ratification |
|---|---|---|
| Thirteenth (January 1865) | Prohibited slavery in the United States. | December 1865 |
| Fourteenth (June 1866) | Defined citizenship to include all persons born or naturalized in the United States. | July 1868, after Congress made ratification a prerequisite for readmission of ex-Confederate states to the Union. |
| | Provided proportional loss of congressional representation for any state that denied suffrage to any of its male citizens. | |
| | Disqualified prewar officeholders who supported the Confederacy from state or national office. | |
| | Repudiated the Confederate debt. | |
| Fifteenth (February 1869) | Prohibited the denial of suffrage because of race, color, or previous condition of servitude. | March 1870; ratification required of Virginia, Texas, Mississippi, and Georgia for readmission to the Union. |

frage by the states to anyone on account of race, color, or previous condition of servitude.

Democrats opposed the amendment on the grounds that it violated states' rights, but they did not control enough states to prevent its ratification. However, to some southerners, the amendment's omissions made it acceptable; as a Richmond newspaper pointed out, it had "loopholes through which a coach and four horses can be driven." Indeed, the new amendment did not guarantee African-American officeholding, nor did it prohibit restrictions on suffrage such as property requirements and literacy tests, both of which might be used to deny African-Americans the vote.

The debate over black suffrage drew new participants into the fray. Women's rights advocates had tried to promote both black suffrage and woman suffrage, but Radical Republicans rejected any linkage between the two, preferring to concentrate on black suffrage. Supporters of women's rights were themselves divided. Frederick Douglass argued that

black suffrage had to receive priority. "If the elective franchise is not extended to the Negro, he is dead," explained Douglass. "Woman has a thousand ways by which she can attach herself to the ruling power of the land that we have not." Women's rights leaders Elizabeth Cady Stanton and Susan B. Anthony disagreed. If the Fifteenth Amendment did not include women, they emphasized, it would establish an "aristocracy of sex" and increase the disabilities under which women already labored. The argument fractured the old abolition–women's rights coalition and would lead to the development of an independent women's rights movement.

By the time the Fifteenth Amendment was ratified in 1870, Congress could look back on five years of momentous achievement. Three constitutional amendments had broadened the scope of democracy by abolishing slavery, affirming the rights of citizens, and prohibiting the denial of suffrage on the basis of race. Congress had readmitted the former Confederate states into the Union. At the same time, momentum had slowed at the federal level. In 1869 the center of action shifted to the South, where tumultuous change was under way.

# Reconstruction Governments

During the years of presidential Reconstruction, 1865–1867, the southern states faced formidable tasks: creating new governments, reviving war-torn economies, and dealing with the impact of emancipation. Racial tensions flared as freedmen organized political meetings to protest ill treatment and demand equal rights, and deadly race riots erupted in major southern cities. In May 1866 white crowds attacked African-American veterans in Memphis and rampaged through African-American neighborhoods, killing forty-six people. Two months later in New Orleans, whites assaulted black delegates on their way to a political meeting and left forty people dead.

Congressional Reconstruction, supervised by federal troops, began in spring 1867 with the dismantling of existing governments and the formation of new state governments dominated by Republicans. By 1868 most former Confederate states had rejoined the Union, and within two years the process was complete.

But Republican rule did not long endure in the South. Opposition from southern Democrats, the landowning elite, vigilantes, and most white voters proved insurmountable. Nevertheless, these Reconstruction governments were unique because African-American men, including former slaves, participated in them. Slavery had ended in other societies, too, but only in the United States had freedmen gained democratic political rights.

## A New Electorate

The Reconstruction laws of 1867–1868 transformed the southern electorate by temporarily disfranchising 15 percent of potential white voters and by enfranchising more than 700,000 freed slaves. Black voters outnumbered whites by 100,000 overall and held voting majorities in five states.

This new electorate provided a base for the Republican party, which had never existed in the South. To scornful Democrats, the Republicans comprised three types of scoundrels: northern "carpetbaggers" who had come south for wealth and power; southern scalawags, poor and ignorant, looking to profit from Republican rule; and hordes of uneducated freedmen, easily manipulated. In fact, the hastily assembled Republican party, crossing racial and class lines, constituted a loose coalition of diverse factions with often contradictory goals.

To northerners who moved south after the war, the former Confederacy was an undeveloped region, ripe with possibilities. The carpetbaggers included many former Union soldiers who hoped to buy land, open factories, build railroads, or simply enjoy the warmer climate. Wielding disproportionate political power—they held almost one in three state offices—carpetbaggers recruited African-American support through a patriotic society called the Union League, which urged African-Americans to vote and escorted them to the polls.

A handful of scalawags (white southerners who supported the Republicans) were old Whigs, but most were small farmers from the mountain regions of North Carolina, Georgia, Alabama, and Arkansas. Former Unionists who had owned no slaves and who felt no loyalty to the old plantation elite, they wanted to improve their economic position and cared little one way or the other about black suffrage. Scalawags held the most political offices during Reconstruction but proved the least stable element of the Republican coalition. Many drifted back into the Democratic fold.

Freedmen, the backbone of southern Republicanism, provided eight out of ten Republican votes. They sought land, education, civil rights, and political equality and remained loyal Republicans. "We know our friends," an elderly freedman said. Although Reconstruction governments depended on African-American votes, freedmen held at most one in five political offices and constituted a legislative majority only in South Carolina, whose population was more than 60 percent black. No African-Americans won the office of governor, and only two served in the U.S. Senate. A mere 6 percent of southern members of the House were African-American, and almost 50 percent came from South Carolina.

A significant status gap divided high-level African-American officials from African-American voters. Most freedmen cared mainly about their economic future, especially about acquiring land, whereas African-American officeholders concerned themselves far more with attaining equal rights. Still, both groups shared high expectations and prized enfranchisement. "We are not prepared for this suffrage," admitted a former slave. "But we can learn. Give a man tools and let him commence to use them and in time he will learn a trade. So it is with voting. . . . In time we shall learn to do our duty."

## Republican Rule

Large numbers of African-Americans participated in government for the first time in the state constitutional conventions of 1867–1868. The South Carolina convention had an African-American majority, and in Louisiana one-half the delegates were freedmen. In general, these conventions instituted democratic changes such as universal manhood suffrage and public-school systems but failed to provide either integrated schools or land reform. Wherever proposed, plans for the confiscation and redistribution of land failed.

Once civil power shifted to the new state governments, Republican administrations began ambitious public-works programs. They built roads and bridges, promoted railroad development, and funded institutions to care for orphans, the insane, and the disabled. Republican regimes also expanded state government and formed state militia in which African-Americans often were heavily represented. Finally, they created public-school systems, almost nonexistent in the antebellum South.

These reforms cost millions, and state debts and taxes skyrocketed. During the 1860s taxes rose 400 percent. Although northern tax rates still exceeded southern tax rates, southerners, particularly landowners, resented the new levies. In their view, Reconstruction strained the pocketbooks of the propertied in order to finance the vast expenditures of Republican legislatures, the "no property herd."

Opponents of Reconstruction viewed Republican rule as wasteful and corrupt, the "most stupendous system of organized robbery in history." Indeed, corruption did permeate some state governments, as in Louisiana and South Carolina. The main profiteers were government officials who accepted bribes and railroad promoters who doled them out. But neither group was exclusively Republican. In fact, corruption increasingly characterized government *nationally* in these years and was both more flagrant and more lucrative in the North. But such a comparison did little to quiet the critics of Republican rule.

## Counterattacks

For ex-Confederates, African-American enfranchisement and the "horror of Negro domination" created nightmares. As soon as congressional Reconstruction began, it fell under attack. Democratic newspapers assailed delegates to the North Carolina constitutional convention as an "Ethiopian minstrelsy . . . baboons, monkeys, mules . . . and other jackasses." They demeaned Louisiana's constitution as "the work of ignorant Negroes cooperating with a gang of white adventurers."

But Democrats delayed any political mobilization until the readmission of the southern states was completed. Then they swung into action, often calling themselves Conservatives to attract former Whigs. At first, they pursued African-American votes, but when that initiative failed, they switched tactics. In every southern state the Democrats contested elections, backed dissident Republican factions, elected some Democratic legislators, and lured scalawags away from the Republican Party.

Vigilante efforts to reduce black votes bolstered Democratic campaigns to win white ones. Antagonism toward free blacks, long present in southern

**The Ku Klux Klan**

*The menacing symbol and hooded disguise characterized the Ku Klux Klan's campaign of intimidation during Reconstruction. Hooded Klansmen, like this Tennessee nightrider, wore colored robes with astrological symbols such as the moon and stars. The Klan strove to end Republican rule, restore white supremacy, and obliterate, in a southern editor's words, "the preposterous and wicked dogma of negro equality."*

life, grew increasingly violent. As early as 1865 Freedmen's Bureau agents itemized a variety of outrages against blacks, including shooting, murder, rape, arson, and "severe and inhuman beating." White vigilante groups sprang up in all parts of the former Confederacy, but one organization became dominant. In spring 1866 six young Confederate war veterans in Tennessee formed a social club, the Ku Klux Klan, distinguished by elaborate rituals, hooded costumes, and secret passwords. New Klan dens spread rapidly. By the election of 1868, when African-American suffrage had become a reality, the Klan had become a terrorist movement directed against potential African-American voters.

The Klan sought to suppress black voting, to reestablish white supremacy, and to topple the Reconstruction governments. It targeted Union League officers, Freedmen's Bureau officials, white Republicans, black militia units, economically successful blacks, and African-American voters. Some Democrats denounced Klan members as "cut-throats and riff-raff," but some prominent Confederate leaders, including General Nathan Bedford Forrest, were active Klansmen. Vigilantism united southern whites of different social classes and drew on the energy of many Confederate veterans.

Republican legislatures tried to outlaw vigilantism, but when state militia could not enforce the laws, state officials turned to the federal government for help. In response, between May 1870 and February 1871 Congress passed three Enforcement Acts, each progressively more stringent. The First Enforcement Act protected African-American voters. The Second Enforcement Act provided for federal supervision of southern elections, and the Third Enforcement Act (also known as the Ku Klux Klan Act) authorized the use of federal troops and the suspension of habeas corpus. Although thousands were arrested under the Enforcement Acts, most terrorists escaped conviction.

By 1872 the federal government had effectively suppressed the Klan, but vigilantism had served its purpose. A large military presence in the South could have protected black rights, but instead troop levels fell steadily. Congress allowed the Freedmen's Bureau to die in 1869, and the Enforcement Acts became dead letters. White southerners, a Georgia politician explained in 1871, could not discard "a feeling of bitterness, a feeling that the Negro is a sort of instinctual enemy of ours." The battle over Reconstruction was in essence a battle over the implications of emancipation, and it had begun as soon as the war had ended.

**The Freedmen's School**
*Supported by the Freedmen's Bureau, northern freedmen's aid societies, and African-American denominations, freedmen's schools reached about 12 percent of school-age African-American children in the South by 1870. Here, a northern teacher poses with her students at a school in rural North Carolina.*

# The Impact of Emancipation

"The master he says we are all free," a South Carolina slave declared in 1865. "But it don't mean we is white. And it don't mean we is equal." Yet despite the daunting handicaps they faced—illiteracy, lack of property, lack of skills—most former slaves found the exhilaration of freedom overwhelming. Emancipation had given them the right to their own labor and a sense of autonomy, and during Reconstruction they asserted their independence by casting off white control and shedding the vestiges of slavery.

## Confronting Freedom

For the ex-slaves, mobility was often liberty's first fruit. Some left the slave quarters; others fled the plantation completely. "I have never in my life met

with such ingratitude," a South Carolina mistress exclaimed when a former slave ran off.

Emancipation stirred waves of migration within the former Confederacy. Some slaves headed to the Deep South, where desperate planters would pay higher wages for labor, but more moved to towns and cities. Urban African-American populations doubled and tripled after emancipation. The desire to find lost family members drove some migrations. "They had a passion, not so much for wandering as for getting together," explained a Freedmen's Bureau official. Parents sought children who had been sold; husbands and wives who had been separated reunited; and families reclaimed children who were being raised in masters' homes. The Freedmen's Bureau helped former slaves to get information about missing relatives and to travel to find them, and bureau agents also tried to resolve entanglements over the multiple alliances of spouses who had been separated under slavery.

Not all efforts at reunion succeeded. Some fugitive slaves had died during the war or were untraceable. Other ex-slaves had formed new partnerships and could not revive old ones. But the success stories were poignant. "I's hunted an' hunted till I track you up here," one freedman told the wife whom he found twenty years after their separation by sale.

Once reunited, freed blacks quickly legalized unions formed under slavery, sometimes in mass ceremonies of up to seventy couples. Legal marriage had a tangible impact on family life. In 1870 eight out of ten African-American families in the cotton-producing South were two-parent families, about the same proportion as white families. Men asserted themselves as household heads, and their wives and children often withdrew from the work force. Thus severe labor shortages followed immediately after the war because women had made up half of all field workers. However, by Reconstruction's end, many African-American women had rejoined the work force out of economic necessity, either in the fields or as cooks, laundresses, and domestic servants.

## African-American Institutions

The freed blacks' desire for independence also led to the growth of African-American churches. The African Methodist Episcopal Church, founded by Philadelphia blacks in the 1790s, gained thousands of new southern members. Negro Baptist churches, their roots often in plantation "praise meetings" organized by slaves, sprouted everywhere.

The influence of African-American churches extended far beyond religion. They provided relief, raised funds for schools, and supported Republican policies. African-American ministers assumed leading political roles. Even after southern Democrats excluded most freedmen from political life at Reconstruction's end, ministers remained the main pillars of authority within African-American communities.

Schools, too, played a crucial role for freedmen as the ex-slaves sought literacy for themselves and above all for their children. At emancipation, African-Americans organized their own schools, which the Freedmen's Bureau soon supervised. Northern philanthropic organizations paid the wages of instructors, half of whom were women. In 1869 the bureau reported more than 4,000 African-American schools in the former Confederacy. Within three more years each southern state had a public-school system, at least in principle, generally with separate schools for blacks and whites. The Freedmen's Bureau and others also helped to establish Howard, Atlanta, and Fisk Universities in 1866–1867 and Hampton Institute in 1868. Nonetheless, African-American education remained limited. Few rural blacks could reach the schools, and those who tried were sometimes the targets of vigilante attacks. Thus by the end of Reconstruction, more than 80 percent of the African-American population remained illiterate, although literacy was rising among children.

Not only school segregation but also other forms of racial separation were taken for granted. Whether by law or by custom, segregation continued on streetcars and trains as well as in churches, theaters, and restaurants. In 1875 Congress passed the Civil Rights Act, banning segregation except in schools, but in the 1883 *Civil Rights Cases,* the Supreme Court threw the law out. The Fourteenth Amendment did not prohibit discrimination by individuals, the Court ruled, only that perpetrated by the state.

White southerners adamantly rejected the prospect of racial integration, which they insisted would lead to racial amalgamation. "If we have social equality, we shall have intermarriage," contended one white southerner, "and if we have intermarriage, we shall degenerate." Urban blacks occasionally protested segregation, but most freed blacks were less interested in "social equality" than in African-American liberty and community. Moreover, the new black elite—teachers, ministers, and politicians—served African-American constituencies and thus had a vested interest in separate black institutions. Too, rural blacks had little desire to mix with whites; rather, they sought freedom from white control. Above all, they wanted to secure personal independence by acquiring land.

## Land, Labor, and Sharecropping

"The sole ambition of the freedman," a New Englander wrote from South Carolina in 1865, "appears to be to become the owner of a little piece of land, there to erect a humble home, and to dwell in peace and security, at his own free will and pleasure." Indeed, to free blacks everywhere, "forty acres and a mule" promised emancipation from plantation labor, white domination, and cotton, the "slave crop." Landownership signified economic independence. "We want to be placed on land until we are able to buy it and make it our own," an African-American minister told General Sherman in Georgia during the war.

But the freedmen's visions of landownership failed to materialize, for large-scale land reform never occurred. Proposals to confiscate or to redistribute Confederate property failed. A few slaves did obtain land, either through the pooling of resources or through the Southern Homestead Act. In 1866 Congress passed this law, setting aside 44 million acres of land in five southern states for freedmen; but the land was poor, and few slaves had resources to survive until their first harvest. About 4,000 blacks claimed homesteads, though few could establish farms. By the end of Reconstruction, only a fraction of former slaves owned working farms. Without large-scale land reform, barriers to African-American landownership remained overwhelming.

Three obstacles impeded African-American landownership. Freedmen lacked capital to buy land or tools. Furthermore, white southerners generally opposed selling land to blacks. Most important, planters sought to preserve a cheap labor force and forged laws to ensure that black labor would remain available on the plantations.

The black codes written during presidential Reconstruction were designed to preserve a captive labor force. Under labor contracts in effect in 1865–1866, freedmen received wages, housing, food, and clothing in exchange for field work. But cash was scarce, and wages often became a small share of the crop, typically one-eighth or less, to be divided among the entire work force. Freedmen's Bureau agents encouraged African-Americans to sign the contracts, seeing wage labor as a step toward economic independence. "You must begin at the bottom of the ladder and climb up," bureau head O. O. Howard told the freedmen.

Problems arose immediately. Freedmen disliked the new wage system, especially the use of gang labor, which resembled the work pattern under slavery. Moreover, postwar planters had to compete for labor even as many scorned African-American workers as lazy or inefficient. One landowner estimated that workers accomplished only "two-fifths of what they did under the old system." As productivity fell, so did land values. Plummeting cotton prices and poor harvests in 1866 and 1867 combined with these other factors to create an impasse: landowners lacked labor, and freedmen lacked land.

Southerners began experimenting with new labor schemes, including the division of plantations into small tenancies. Sharecropping was the most widespread arrangement. Under this system, landowners subdivided large plantations into farms of thirty to fifty acres and rented them to freedmen under annual leases for a share of the crop, usually one-half. Freedmen liked this decentralized system, which let them use the labor of family members and represented a step toward independence. A half share of the crop far exceeded the fraction that they had received under the black codes. Planters benefited, too, for the leases gave them leverage over their tenants and tenants shared the risk of poor harvests with them. Most important, planters retained control of their land. The most productive land thus remained in the hands of a small group of owners, and in effect sharecropping helped to preserve the planter elite.

Although the wage system continued on sugar and rice plantations, by 1870 the plantation tradition had yielded to sharecropping in the cotton South. A severe depression in 1873 drove many blacks and independent white farmers into sharecropping. By 1880 sharecroppers, white and black, farmed 80 percent of the land in cotton-producing states. In fact, white sharecroppers outnumbered black,

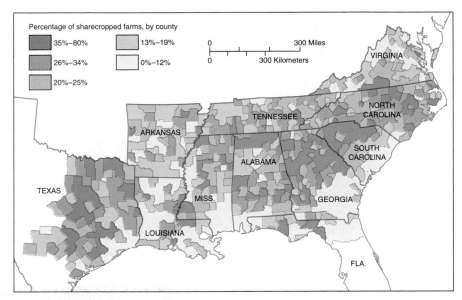

**Southern Sharecropping, 1880**

*The depressed economy of the late 1870s caused poverty and debt, increased tenancy among white farmers, and forced many renters, black and white, into sharecropping. By 1880 the sharecropping system pervaded most southern counties, with highest concentrations in the cotton belt from South Carolina to eastern Texas.*

SOURCE: U.S. Census Office, Tenth Census, 1880, *Report of the Production of Agriculture* (Washington, D.C.: Government Printing Office, 1883), Table 5.

although a higher proportion of southern blacks, almost 75 percent, were involved in the system. Changes in marketing and finance, meanwhile, made the sharecroppers' lot increasingly precarious.

### Toward a Crop-Lien Economy

Before the Civil War planters had depended on factors, or middlemen, who sold them supplies, extended credit, and marketed their crops through urban merchants. Because the high value of slave property had backed these long-distance credit arrangements, this system collapsed with the end of slavery. The postwar South, with its hundreds of thousands of tenant farmers and sharecroppers, needed a local credit system.

Into this gap stepped rural merchants, who advanced supplies to tenants and sharecroppers on credit and sold their crops to wholesalers. Because renters had no property to serve as collateral, merchants secured their loans with a lien, or claim, on each farmer's next crop. Exorbitant interest rates, 50 percent or more, quickly forced many tenants and sharecroppers into a cycle of indebtedness. The sharecropper might well owe part of his crop to the landowner and another part (the rest of his crop, or more) to the merchant. Illiterate tenants who could not keep track of their financial arrangements were at the mercy of sometimes unscrupulous merchants. "A man that didn't know how to count would always lose," an Arkansas freedman explained. Once a tenant's real or alleged debts exceeded the value of his crop, he was tied to the land, to cotton, and to sharecropping.

By the end of Reconstruction, sharecropping and crop liens had bound the South to easily marketable cash crops such as cotton and prevented crop diversification. Soil depletion, land erosion, and outmoded equipment stranded capital-short planters in a cycle of poverty. Postwar changes in southern agriculture left the region with bleak economic prospects.

Trapped in perpetual debt, tenant farmers became the chief victims of the new agricultural order. Cotton remained the only survival route open to poor farmers, regardless of race, but low income from cotton locked them into sharecropping and crop liens. African-American tenants, for whom neither landownership nor economic independence ever materialized, saw their political rights dwindle as rapidly as their hopes for economic freedom. When Reconstruction ended, neither state governments nor the national government offered them protection, for northern politicians were preoccupied with their own problems.

# New Concerns in the North

The nomination of Ulysses S. Grant for president in 1868 launched a chaotic era in national politics. His eight years in office featured political scandals, a party revolt, a massive depression, and a steady retreat from Reconstruction. By the mid-1870s northern voters cared more about economics, unemployment, labor unrest, and currency problems than the "southern question." Eager to end sectional conflict, Republicans turned their backs on the freedmen.

## Grantism

Republicans had good reason to nominate General Grant. A war hero, he was endorsed by veterans, admired throughout the North, and unscathed by the bitter feuds of Reconstruction politics. To oppose Grant, the Democrats nominated Horatio Seymour, arch-critic of the Lincoln administration and an opponent of Reconstruction and greenbacks. Grant ran on his personal popularity more than on issues. Although he carried all but eight states, the popular vote was close; newly enfranchised freedmen provided Grant's margin in the South. When he was inaugurated, Grant pledged to execute all the laws, whether he agreed with them or not, to support sound money, and to follow a humane policy toward the Indians.

Grant's presidential leadership proved as weak as his war leadership had been strong. He had little political skill; his cabinet appointments were at best mediocre, and a string of scandals plagued his administration. In 1869 financier Jay Gould and his partner Jim Fisk attempted to corner the gold market with the help of Grant's brother-in-law. When gold prices tumbled, investors were ruined, and Grant's reputation was tarnished. Near the end of Grant's first term, his vice president, Schuyler Colfax, got caught up in the Crédit Mobilier scandal, an elaborate scheme to skim off the profits of the Union Pacific Railroad. Then in 1875 Grant's personal secretary, Orville Babcock, was found guilty of accepting bribes from the "whiskey ring," distillers who preferred bribery to payment of federal taxes. And in 1876 voters learned that Grant's secretary of war, William E. Belknap, had taken bribes to sell lucrative Indian trading posts in Oklahoma.

| The Election of 1868 | | | | |
| --- | --- | --- | --- | --- |
| Candidates | Parties | Electoral Vote | Popular Vote | Percentage of Popular Vote |
| ULYSSES S. GRANT | Republican | 214 | 3,013,421 | 52.7 |
| Horatio Seymour | Democratic | 80 | 2,706,829 | 47.3 |

| The Election of 1872 | | | | |
| --- | --- | --- | --- | --- |
| Candidates | Parties | Electoral Vote | Popular Vote | Percentage of Popular Vote |
| ULYSSES S. GRANT | Republican | 286 | 3,596,745 | 55.6 |
| Horace Greeley* | Democratic | | 2,843,446 | 43.9 |

*On Greeley's death shortly after the election, the electors supporting him divided their votes among minor candidates.

Although Grant was not personally involved in the scandals, he did little to restrain such activities, and "Grantism" came to stand for fraud, bribery, and corruption in office. Such evils, however, spread far beyond Washington. The New York City press in 1872 revealed that Democrat boss William M. Tweed led a ring that had looted the city treasury and collected some $200 million in kickbacks and bribes. When Mark Twain and coauthor Charles Dudley Warner published their scathing satire *The Gilded Age* (1873), readers recognized the novel's speculators, self-promoters, and maniacal opportunists as familiar types in public life.

Grant did enjoy some foreign policy successes. His administration engineered the settlement of the *Alabama* claims with England: an international tribunal ordered Britain to pay $15.5 million to the United States in compensation for damage inflicted by Confederate-owned but British-built raiders. But the administration went astray when it tried to add nonadjacent territory to the Union. In 1867 the Johnson administration had purchased Alaska from Russia at the bargain price of $7.2 million. The purchase had rekindled expansionists' hope, and in 1870 Grant decided to annex the Caribbean island nation of Santo Domingo (the modern Dominican Republic). The president believed that annexation would promote Caribbean trade and provide a haven for persecuted southern blacks. Despite speculators' hopes for windfall profits, the Senate rejected the annexation treaty and further diminished Grant's reputation.

As the election of 1872 approached, dissident

Republicans feared that "Grantism" would ruin the party. Former Radicals and other Republicans left out of Grant's "Great Barbecue" formed their own party, the Liberal Republicans.

## The Liberals' Revolt

The Liberal Republican revolt split the Republican party and undermined Reconstruction. Liberals demanded civil service reform to bring the "best men" into government. In the South they demanded an end to "bayonet rule" and argued that African-Americans, now enfranchised, could fend for themselves. Corruption in government posed a greater threat than Confederate resurgence, the Liberals claimed, and they demanded that the "best men" in the South, ex-Confederates barred from holding office, be returned to government.

*New York Tribune* editor Horace Greeley, inconsistently supporting both a stringent Reconstruction policy and leniency toward the ex-Confederates, received the Liberal Republican nomination, and the Democrats endorsed Greeley as well. Republican reformers found themselves allied with the party that they had recently castigated as a "sewer" of treasonable sentiments.

Despite Greeley's arduous campaigning (he literally worked himself to death on the campaign trail and died a few weeks after the election), Grant carried 56 percent of the popular vote and won the electoral vote handily. But his victory had come at a high price: to nullify the Liberals' issues, "regular" Republicans passed an amnesty act allowing all but a few hundred ex-Confederates to resume office. And during Grant's second term Republicans' desire to discard the "southern question" grew as a depression gripped the nation.

## The Panic of 1873

The postwar years brought accelerated industrialization, rapid economic expansion, and frantic speculation as investors rushed to take advantage of seemingly unlimited opportunities. Railroads led the speculative boom. The transcontinental line reached completion in 1869 (see Chapter 17), and by 1873 almost 400 railroads crisscrossed the Northeast. But in addition to transforming the northern economy, the railroad boom led entrepreneurs to overspeculate, with drastic results.

In 1869 Philadelphia banker Jay Cooke took over a new transcontinental line, the Northern Pacific. For four years Northern Pacific securities sold briskly, but in 1873 construction costs outran bond sales. In September Cooke, his bank vaults stuffed with unsalable bonds, defaulted on his obligations. His bank, the largest in the nation, shut down. Then the stock market collapsed and smaller banks and other firms followed; and the Panic of 1873 plunged the nation into a devastating five-year depression. Thousands of businesses went bankrupt. By 1878 unemployment had risen to more than 3 million. Labor protests mounted, and industrial violence spread (see Chapter 18). The depression of the 1870s demonstrated ruthlessly that conflicts born of industrialization had replaced sectional divisions.

The depression also fed a dispute over currency that had begun in 1865. During the Civil War Americans had used greenbacks, a paper currency not backed by a specific weight in gold. "Sound-money" supporters demanded the withdrawal of greenbacks from circulation as a means of stabilizing the currency. Their opponents, "easy-money" advocates such as farmers and manufacturers dependent on easy credit, wanted to expand the currency by issuing additional greenbacks. The deepening depression created even more demand for easy money, and the issue split both major parties.

Controversy over the type of currency was compounded by the question of how to repay the federal debt. In wartime the Union government had borrowed astronomical sums through the sale of war bonds. Bond holders wanted repayment in "coin," gold or silver, even though many of them had paid for the bonds in greenbacks. The Public Credit Act of 1869 promised payment in coin.

Senator John Sherman, the author of the Public Credit Act, put together a series of compromises to satisfy both "sound-money" and "easy-money" advocates. Sherman's measures, exchanging Civil War bonds for new ones payable over a longer period of time and defining "coin" as gold only, preserved the public credit, the currency, and Republican unity. His Specie Resumption Act of 1875 promised to put the nation back on the gold standard by 1879.

But Sherman's measures, however ingenious, did not placate the Democrats, who gained control of the House in 1875. Many Democrats, and a few Republicans, were "free-silver" advocates who wanted the silver dollar restored in order to expand the currency and end the depression. The Bland-Allison Act of 1878 partially restored silver coinage by requiring the government to buy and coin several million dollars' worth of silver each month. In 1876 other expansionists formed the Greenback party to keep the paper money in circulation for the sake of debtors, but they enjoyed little success. As the depression receded, the clamor for "easy money" subsided, only to return in the 1890s (see Chapter 21). Although never settled, the controversial "money question" diverted attention away from Reconstruction and thus contributed to its demise.

## Reconstruction and the Constitution

During the 1870s the Supreme Court also played a role in weakening northern support for Reconstruction as new constitutional questions surfaced.

Would the Court support laws to protect freedmen's rights? The decision in *Ex Parte* Milligan (1866) had suggested not. In *Milligan*, the Court had ruled that a military commission could not try civilians in areas where civilian courts were functioning, thus dooming the special military courts that had been established to enforce the Supplementary Freedmen's Bureau Act. Would the Court sabotage the congressional Reconstruction plan? In 1869 in *Texas* v. *White,* the Court had let Reconstruction stand, ruling that Congress had the power to ensure each state a republican form of government and to recognize the legitimate government in any state.

However, during the 1870s the Supreme Court backed away from Reconstruction. The process began with the *Slaughterhouse* decision of 1873. In this case the Court ruled that the Fourteenth Amendment protected the rights of *national* citizenship, such as the right to interstate travel, but that it did not protect the civil rights that individuals derived from *state* citizenship. The federal government, in short, did not have to safeguard such rights against violation by the states. The *Slaughterhouse* decision effectively gutted the Fourteenth Amendment, which was intended to secure freedmen's rights against state encroachment.

The Supreme Court retreated even further from Reconstruction in two cases involving the Enforcement Act of 1870. In *U.S.* v. *Reese* (1876), the Court threw out the indictment of Kentucky officials who had barred African-Americans from voting. The Fifteenth Amendment, the Court said, did not "confer the right of suffrage upon anyone"; it merely prohibited the hindrance of voting on the basis of race, color, or previous condition of servitude. Crucial sections of the Enforcement Act, the Court ruled, were invalid. Another decision that same year, *U.S.* v. *Cruikshank,* again weakened the Fourteenth Amendment. In the *Cruikshank* case, the Court ruled that the amendment barred *states,* but not *individuals,* from encroaching on individual rights. The decision threw out the indictments against white Louisianians charged with murdering more than thirty black militiamen who had surrendered after a battle with armed whites.

Continuing this retreat from Reconstruction, the Supreme Court in 1883 invalidated both the Civil Rights Act of 1875 and the Ku Klux Klan Act of 1871; later it would uphold segregation laws (see Chapter 21). Taken cumulatively, these decisions dismantled Republican Reconstruction and confirmed rising northern sentiment that Reconstruction's egalitarian goals were unenforceable.

### Republicans in Retreat

The Republicans gradually disengaged from Reconstruction, beginning with the election of Grant as president in 1868. Grant, like most Americans, hesitated to approve the use of federal authority in state or local affairs.

In the 1870s Republican idealism waned. Instead, commercial and industrial interests dominated both the Liberal and "regular" wings of the party, and few had any taste left for further sectional strife. When Democratic victories in the House of Representatives in 1874 showed that Reconstruction had become a political liability, the Republicans prepared to abandon it.

By 1875, moreover, the Radical Republicans had virtually disappeared. The Radical leaders Chase, Stevens, and Sumner had died, and others had grown tired of "waving the bloody shirt," or defaming Democratic opponents by reviving wartime animosity. Party leaders reported that voters were "sick of carpet-bag government" and tired of the "southern question" and the "Negro question." It seemed pointless to prop up southern Republican regimes that even President Grant found corrupt. Finally, Republicans generally agreed with southern Democrats that African-Americans were inferior. To insist on black equality, many party members believed, would be a thankless, divisive, and politically suicidal course that would quash any hope of reunion between North and South. The Republican retreat set the stage for Reconstruction's end in 1877.

## Reconstruction Abandoned

"We are in a very hot political contest just now," a Mississippi planter wrote his daughter in 1875, "with a good prospect of turning out the carpetbag thieves by whom we have been robbed for the past six to ten years." Indeed, an angry white majority had led a Democratic resurgence throughout the South in the 1870s, and by the end of 1872 four ex-Confederate states had already returned the Democrats to power. By 1876 Republican rule survived in only three southern states. Democratic victories in state elections that year and political bargaining in Washington in 1877 ended what little remained of Reconstruction.

## "Redeeming" the South

After 1872 the Republican collapse in the South accelerated. Congressional amnesty enabled virtually all ex-Confederate officials to regain office, divided Republicans lost their grip on the southern electorate, and attrition diminished Republican ranks. Carpetbaggers returned North or joined the Democrats, and scalawags deserted the Republicans in large numbers. Tired of northern interference and seeing the possibility of "home rule," scalawags decided that staying Republican meant going down with a sinking ship. Unable to win new white votes

or retain the old ones, the fragile Republican coalition crumbled.

Meanwhile, the Democrats mobilized formerly apathetic white voters. Although still faction-ridden—businessmen who dreamed of an industrialized "New South" had little in common with the old planter elite, the so-called Bourbons—the Democrats shared one goal: kicking the Republicans out. The Democrats' tactics varied. In several Deep South states Democrats resorted to violence. In Vicksburg in 1874 rampaging whites slaughtered about 300 blacks and terrorized thousands of potential voters. Vigilante groups in several southern states disrupted Republican meetings and threatened blacks who had registered to vote. "The Republicans are paralyzed through fear and will not act," the carpetbag governor of Mississippi wrote his wife. "Why should I fight a hopeless battle . . . when no possible good to the Negro or anybody else would result?"

Terrorism did not completely squelch black voting, but it did deprive Republicans of enough African-American votes to win state elections.

| The Duration of Republican Rule in the Ex-Confederate States | | | |
| --- | --- | --- | --- |
| *Former Confederate States* | *Readmission to the Union Under Congressional Reconstruction* | *Democrats (Conservatives) Gain Control* | *Duration of Republican Rule* |
| Alabama | June 25, 1868 | November 14, 1874 | 6½ years |
| Arkansas | June 22, 1868 | November 10, 1874 | 6½ years |
| Florida | June 25, 1868 | January 2, 1877 | 8½ years |
| Georgia | July 15, 1870 | November 1, 1871 | 1 year |
| Louisiana | June 25, 1868 | January 2, 1877 | 8½ years |
| Mississippi | February 23, 1870 | November 3, 1875 | 5½ years |
| North Carolina | June 25, 1868 | November 3, 1870 | 2 years |
| South Carolina | June 25, 1868 | November 12, 1876 | 8 years |
| Tennessee | July 24, 1866* | October 4, 1869 | 3 years |
| Texas | March 30, 1870 | January 14, 1873 | 3 years |
| Virginia | January 26, 1870 | October 5, 1869[†] | 0 years |

*Admitted before start of Congressional Reconstruction.
[†]Democrats gained control before readmission.

SOURCE: Reprinted by permission from John Hope Franklin, *Reconstruction After the Civil War* (Chicago: University of Chicago Press, 1962), 231.

Throughout the South economic pressures reinforced intimidation; labor contracts included clauses barring attendance at political meetings, and planters threatened to evict sharecroppers who stepped out of line.

*Redemption,* the word that Democrats used to describe their return to power, introduced sweeping changes. States rewrote constitutions, cut expenses, lowered taxes, eliminated social programs, limited the rights of tenants and sharecroppers, and shaped laws to ensure a stable African-American labor force. Legislatures restored vagrancy laws, strengthened crop-lien statutes, and remade criminal law. New criminal codes directed at African-Americans imposed severe penalties for what formerly were misdemeanors: stealing livestock or wrongly taking part of a crop became grand larceny, punishable by five years at hard labor. By Reconstruction's end, a large African-American convict work force had been leased out to private contractors.

Freedmen whose hopes had been raised by Republicans saw their prospects destroyed by the redeemers. The new laws, Tennessee blacks stated at an 1875 convention, imposed "a condition of servitude scarcely less degrading than that endured before the late civil war." In the late 1870s an increasingly oppressive political climate gave rise to an "exodus" movement among African-Americans. Nearly 15,000 African-American "exodusters" from the Deep South moved to Kansas and set up homesteads. But scarce resources left most of the freed slaves stranded. Not until the twentieth century would the mass migration of southern blacks to the Midwest and North gain momentum.

## The Election of 1876

By autumn 1876, with redemption almost complete, both parties were moving to discard the animosity left by the war and Reconstruction. The Republicans nominated Rutherford B. Hayes, the governor of Ohio, for president. Popular with all factions and untainted by the Grant scandals, Hayes, a "moderate," favored "home rule" in the South and civil and political rights for all—clearly contradictory goals.

The Democrats nominated Governor Samuel J. Tilden of New York, a political reformer known for his assaults on the Tweed Ring that had plundered New York City's treasury. Both candidates were fiscal conservatives, favored sound money, endorsed civil service reform, and decried corruption.

Tilden won the popular vote by a small margin, but the Republicans challenged pro-Tilden electoral votes from South Carolina, Florida, and Louisiana. Giving those nineteen electoral votes to Hayes would make him the winner. The Democrats, for their part, requiring a single electoral vote to put Tilden in the White House, challenged one electoral vote from Oregon. But Southern Republicans managed to throw out enough Democratic ballots in the contested states to proclaim Hayes the winner.

The nation now faced an unprecedented dilemma. Each party claimed victory, and each accused the other of fraud. In fact, both sets of

**The Disputed Election of 1876**

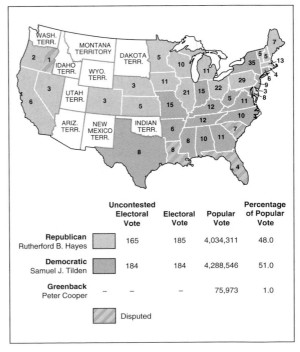

| | Uncontested Electoral Vote | Electoral Vote | Popular Vote | Percentage of Popular Vote |
|---|---|---|---|---|
| **Republican** Rutherford B. Hayes | 165 | 185 | 4,034,311 | 48.0 |
| **Democratic** Samuel J. Tilden | 184 | 184 | 4,288,546 | 51.0 |
| **Greenback** Peter Cooper | – | – | 75,973 | 1.0 |
| Disputed | | | | |

southern votes were fraudulent: Republicans had discarded legitimate Democratic ballots, and Democrats had illegally prevented freedmen from voting. In January 1877 Congress created a special electoral commission to resolve the conflict. The commission originally consisted of seven Republicans, seven Democrats, and one independent, but when the independent resigned, a Republican replaced him. The commission gave the Republican Hayes the election by an 8–7 vote.

Congress now had to certify the new electoral vote. But the Democrats controlled the House, and some planned to forestall approval of the electoral vote. For many southern Democrats, regaining control of their states was far more important than electing a Republican president—*if* the new Republican administration would leave the South alone. Republican leaders, for their part, were willing to bargain, for Hayes wanted not just victory but also southern approval. Informal negotiations followed, with both parties exchanging promises. Ohio Republicans and southern Democrats agreed that if

Hayes won the election, he would remove federal troops from all southern states. Other negotiations led to the understanding that southerners would receive federal patronage, federal aid to railroads, and federal support for internal improvements. In turn, southerners promised to accept Hayes as president and to treat the freedmen fairly.

Congress thus ratified Hayes's election. Once in office, Hayes fulfilled many of the agreements made by his colleagues. Republican rule toppled in Louisiana, South Carolina, and Florida. But some of the bargains struck in the so-called Compromise of 1877 fell apart, particularly Democratic promises to treat the freedmen fairly and Hayes's pledges to ensure the freed slaves' rights. "When you turned us loose, you turned us loose to the sky, to the storm, to the whirlwind, and worst of all . . . to the wrath of our infuriated masters," Frederick Douglass had charged at the 1876 Republican convention. "The question now is, do you mean to make good to us the promises in your Constitution?" By 1877 the answer was clear: "No."

## CONCLUSION

The end of Reconstruction benefited both major political parties. The "southern question" no longer burdened the Republicans. The Democrats, who had regained power in the ex-Confederate states, would remain entrenched there for almost a century. The postwar South was tied to sharecropping and economic backwardness as surely as it once had been tied to slavery; but "home rule" was firmly in place.

Reconstruction's end also signaled the triumph of nationalism and reconciliation. Battlefields became national parks. Jefferson Davis, who had served two years in prison but had never gone to trial, urged young men to "lay aside all rancor, all bitter sectional feeling." Americans increasingly dismissed Reconstruction as a fiasco, a tragic interlude of "radical rule" and "black reconstruction" fashioned by carpetbaggers, scalawags, and Radical Republicans.

Historians, too, still consider Reconstruction a failure, although for different reasons from those of Americans who lived through the era. Today scholars view Reconstruction as an unsuccessful democratic experiment that did not go far enough.

They cite two main failings. First, Congress did not promote land reform and thus left African-Americans propertyless, without the economic power to defend their rights. More important, the federal government did not back congressional Reconstruction militarily. Reconstruction's failure lay with the federal government's inability to fulfill its own goals and to create a biracial democracy in the South. Consequently, the nation's adjustment to emancipation would continue into the twentieth century.

The Reconstruction era left significant legacies, including the Fourteenth and Fifteenth Amendments, monuments to Congress's democratic zeal in the 1860s. Above all, Reconstruction gave freedmen the opportunity to reconstitute their families, to form schools and churches, and to participate in government for the first time in U.S. history. However, in the 1880s the United States would consign Reconstruction to history and the freed slaves to their fate as Americans focused on their economic futures—on railroads, factories, and mills and on the exploitation of bountiful natural resources.

## CHRONOLOGY

**1863**  President Abraham Lincoln issues Proclamation of Amnesty and Reconstruction.

**1864**  Wade-Davis bill passed by Congress and pocket-vetoed by Lincoln.

**1865**  Freedmen's Bureau established.
Civil War ends.
Lincoln assassinated; Andrew Johnson becomes president.
Johnson issues Proclamation of Amnesty and Reconstruction.
Ex-Confederate states hold constitutional conventions (May–December).
Thirteenth Amendment added to the Constitution.
Presidential Reconstruction completed.

**1866**  Congress enacts the Civil Rights Act of 1866 and the Supplementary Freedmen's Bureau Act over Johnson's vetoes.
Ku Klux Klan founded in Tennessee.
Congress proposes the Fourteenth Amendment.
Race riots in southern cities.
Thirty-ninth Congress begins debates over Reconstruction policy.

**1867**  Reconstruction Act of 1867.
William Seward negotiates the purchase of Alaska.
Constitutional conventions meet in the ex-Confederate states.
Howard University founded.

**1868**  President Johnson is impeached, tried, and acquitted.
Fourteenth Amendment added to the Constitution.
Ulysses S. Grant elected president.

**1869**  Transcontinental railroad completed.

**1870**  Fifteenth Amendment added to the Constitution.
Enforcement Act of 1870.

**1871**  Second Enforcement Act.
Ku Klux Klan Act.

**1872**  Liberal Republican Party formed.
*Alabama* claims settled.
Grant reelected president.

**1873**  Panic of 1873 begins (September–October), setting off a five-year depression.

**1875**  Civil Rights Act of 1875.
Specie Resumption Act.

**1876**  Disputed presidential election: Rutherford B. Hayes versus Samuel J. Tilden.

**1877**  Electoral commission decides election in favor of Hayes.
The last Republican-controlled governments overthrown in Florida, Louisiana, and South Carolina.

**1879**  "Exodus" movement spreads through several southern states.

## FOR FURTHER READING

Eric Foner, *Reconstruction: America's Unfinished Revolution, 1863–1877* (1988). A thorough exploration of Reconstruction that draws on recent scholarship and stresses the centrality of the African-American experience.

John Hope Franklin, *Reconstruction After the Civil War* (1961). An overview that dismantles the traditional view of Reconstruction as a disastrous experiment in radical rule.

William Gillette, *Retreat from Reconstruction, 1869–1879* (1979). A survey of the era's national politics, indicting Republican policy makers for vacillation and lack of commitment to racial equality.

Leon Litwack, *Been in the Storm So Long: The Aftermath of Slavery* (1979). A comprehensive study of the African-American response to emancipation in 1865–1866.

Roger L. Ransom and Richard Sutch, *One Kind of Freedom: The Economic Consequences of Emancipation* (1977). Economic assessment of the impact of free black labor on the South and explanation of the rise of sharecropping and the crop-lien system.

Kenneth M. Stampp, *The Era of Reconstruction, 1865–1877* (1965). A classic revisionist interpretation of Reconstruction, focusing on the establishment and fall of Republican governments.

Joel Williamson, *The Negro in South Carolina During Reconstruction, 1861–1877* (1965). A pioneer study of African-American life and institutions after emancipation.

# Appendix

# Declaration of Independence

*IN CONGRESS, JULY 4, 1776*

*The Unanimous Declaration of the Thirteen United States of America*

When, in the course of human events, it becomes necessary for one people to dissolve the political bands which have connected them with another, and to assume, among the powers of the earth, the separate and equal station to which the laws of nature and of nature's God entitle them, a decent respect to the opinions of mankind requires that they should declare the causes which impel them to the separation.

We hold these truths to be self-evident: That all men are created equal; that they are endowed by their Creator with certain unalienable rights; that among these are life, liberty, and the pursuit of happiness; that, to secure these rights, governments are instituted among men, deriving their just powers from the consent of the governed; that whenever any form of government becomes destructive of these ends, it is the right of the people to alter or to abolish it, and to institute new government, laying its foundation on such principles, and organizing its powers in such form, as to them shall seem most likely to effect their safety and happiness. Prudence, indeed, will dictate that governments long established should not be changed for light and transient causes; and accordingly all experience hath shown that mankind are more disposed to suffer, while

evils are sufferable, than to right themselves by abolishing the forms to which they are accustomed. But when a long train of abuses and usurpations, pursuing invariably the same object, evinces a design to reduce them under absolute despotism, it is their right, it is their duty, to throw off such government, and to provide new guards for their future security. Such has been the patient sufferance of these colonies; and such is now the necessity which constrains them to alter their former systems of government. The history of the present King of Great Britain is a history of repeated injuries and usurpations, all having in direct object the establishment of an absolute tyranny over these states. To prove this, let facts be submitted to a candid world.

He has refused his assent to laws, the most wholesome and necessary for the public good.

He has forbidden his governors to pass laws of immediate and pressing importance, unless suspended in their operation till his assent should be obtained; and, when so suspended, he has utterly neglected to attend to them.

He has refused to pass other laws for the accommodation of large districts of people, unless those people would relinquish the right of representation in the legislature, a right inestimable to them, and formidable to tyrants only.

He has called together legislative bodies at places unusual, uncomfortable, and distant from the depository of their public records, for the sole purpose of fatiguing them into compliance with his measures.

He has dissolved representative houses repeatedly, for opposing, with manly firmness, his invasions on the rights of the people.

He has refused for a long time, after such dissolutions, to cause others to be elected; whereby the legislative powers, incapable of annihilation, have returned to the people at large for their exercise; the state remaining, in the mean time, exposed to all the dangers of invasions from without and convulsions within.

He has endeavored to prevent the population of these states; for that purpose obstructing the laws of naturalization of foreigners; refusing to pass others to encourage their migration hither, and raising the conditions of new appropriation of lands.

He has obstructed the administration of justice, by refusing his assent to laws for establishing judiciary powers.

He has made judges dependent on his will alone, for the tenure of their offices, and the amount and payment of their salaries.

He has erected a multitude of new offices, and sent hither swarms of officers to harass our people and eat out their substance.

He has kept among us, in times of peace, standing armies, without the consent of our legislatures.

He has affected to render the military independent of, and superior to, the civil power.

He has combined with others to subject us to a jurisdiction foreign to our constitution, and unacknowledged by our laws, giving his assent to their acts of pretended legislation:

For quartering large bodies of armed troops among us;

For protecting them, by a mock trial, from punishment for any murders which they should commit on the inhabitants of these states;

For cutting off our trade with all parts of the world;

For imposing taxes on us without our consent;

For depriving us, in many cases, of the benefits of trial by jury;

For transporting us beyond seas, to be tried for pretended offenses;

For abolishing the free system of English laws in a neighboring province, establishing therein an arbitrary government, and enlarging its boundaries, so as to render it at once an example and fit instrument for introducing the same absolute rule into these colonies;

For taking away our charters, abolishing our most valuable laws, and altering fundamentally the forms of our governments;

For suspending our own legislatures, and declaring themselves invested with power to legislate for us in all cases whatsoever.

He has abdicated government here, by declaring us out of his protection and waging war against us.

He has plundered our seas, ravaged our coasts, burned our towns, and destroyed the lives of our people.

He is at this time transporting large armies of foreign mercenaries to complete the works of death, desolation, and tyranny already begun with circumstances of cruelty and perfidy scarcely paralleled in the most barbarous ages, and totally unworthy of the head of a civilized nation.

He has constrained our fellow-citizens, taken captive on the high seas, to bear arms against their country, to become the executioners of their friends and brethren, or to fall themselves by their hands.

He has excited domestic insurrection among us, and has endeavored to bring on the inhabitants of our frontiers the merciless Indian savages, whose known rule of warfare is an undistinguished destruction of all ages, sexes, and conditions.

In every stage of these oppressions we have petitioned for redress in the most humble terms; our repeated petitions have been answered only by repeated injury. A prince, whose character is thus marked by every act which may define a tyrant, is unfit to be the ruler of a free people.

Nor have we been wanting in our attentions to our British brethren. We have warned them, from time to time, of attempts by their legislature to extend an unwarrantable jurisdiction over us. We have reminded them of the circumstances of our emigration and settlement here. We have appealed to their native justice and magnanimity; and we have conjured them by the ties of our common kindred, to disavow these usurpations, which would inevitably interrupt our connections and correspondence. They, too, have been deaf to the voice of justice and of consanguinity. We must, therefore, acquiesce in the necessity which denounces our separation, and hold them, as we hold the rest of mankind, enemies in war, in peace friends.

We, therefore, the representatives of the United States of America, in General Congress assembled, appealing to the Supreme Judge of the world for the rectitude of our intentions, do, in the name and by the authority of the good people of these colonies, solemnly publish and declare, that these United Colonies are, and of right ought to be, FREE AND INDEPENDENT STATES; that they are absolved from all allegiance to the British crown, and that all political connection between them and the state of Great Britain is, and ought to be, totally dissolved; and that, as free and independent states, they have full power to levy war, conclude peace, contract alliances, establish commerce, and do all other acts and things which independent states may of right do. And for the support of this declaration, with a firm reliance on the protection of Divine Providence, we mutually pledge to each other our lives, our fortunes, and our sacred honor.

JOHN HANCOCK [*President*]
[*and fifty-five others*]

# Constitution of the United States of America

## PREAMBLE

We the people of the United States, in order to form a more perfect union, establish justice, insure domestic tranquility, provide for the common defense, promote the general welfare, and secure the blessings of liberty to ourselves and our posterity, do ordain and establish this CONSTITUTION for the United States of America.

## ARTICLE I

**Section 1.** All legislative powers herein granted shall be vested in a Congress of the United States, which shall consist of a Senate and a House of Representatives.

**Section 2.** The House of Representatives shall be composed of members chosen every second year by the people of the several States, and the electors in each State shall have the qualifications requisite for electors of the most numerous branch of the State Legislature.

No person shall be a Representative who shall not have attained to the age of twenty-five years, and been seven years a citizen of the United States, and who shall not, when elected, be an inhabitant of that State in which he shall be chosen.

Representatives and direct taxes shall be apportioned among the several States which may be included within this Union, according to their respective numbers, *which shall be determined by adding to the whole number of free persons, including those bound to service for a term of years and excluding Indians not taxed, three-fifths of all other persons.* The actual enumeration shall be made within three years after the first meeting of the Congress of the United States, and within every subsequent term of ten years, in such manner as they shall by law direct. The number of Representatives shall not exceed one for every thirty thousand, but each State shall have at least one Representative; *and until such enumeration shall be made, the State of New Hampshire shall be entitled to choose three, Massachusetts eight, Rhode Island and Providence Plantations one, Connecticut five, New York six, New Jersey four, Pennsylvania eight, Delaware one, Maryland six, Virginia ten, North Carolina five, South Carolina five, and Georgia three.*

When vacancies happen in the representation from any State, the Executive authority thereof shall issue writs of election to fill such vacancies.

The House of Representatives shall choose their Speaker and other officers; and shall have the sole power of impeachment.

**Section 3.** The Senate of the United States shall be composed of two Senators from each State, *chosen by the legislature thereof,* for six years; and each Senator shall have one vote.

*Immediately after they shall be assembled in consequence of the first election, they shall be divided as equally as may be into three classes. The seats of the Senators of the first class shall be vacated at the expiration of the second year, of the second class at the expiration of the fourth year, and of the third class at the expiration of the sixth year, so that one-third may be chosen every second year; and if vacancies happen by resignation or otherwise, during the recess of the legislature of any State, the Executive thereof may make*

---

NOTE: Passages no longer in effect are printed in italic type.

*temporary appointments until the next meeting of the legislature, which shall then fill such vacancies.*

No person shall be a Senator who shall not have attained to the age of thirty years, and been nine years a citizen of the United States, and who shall not, when elected, be an inhabitant of that State for which he shall be chosen.

The Vice President of the United States shall be President of the Senate, but shall have no vote, unless they be equally divided.

The Senate shall choose their other officers, and also a President *pro tempore,* in the absence of the Vice President, or when he shall exercise the office of the President of the United States.

The Senate shall have the sole power to try all impeachments. When sitting for that purpose, they shall be on oath or affirmation. When the President of the United States is tried, the Chief Justice shall preside: and no person shall be convicted without the concurrence of two-thirds of the members present.

Judgment in cases of impeachment shall not extend further than to removal from the office, and disqualification to hold and enjoy any office of honor, trust or profit under the United States; but the party convicted shall nevertheless be liable and subject to indictment, trial, judgment and punishment, according to law.

**Section 4.** The times, places and manner of holding elections for Senators and Representatives shall be prescribed in each State by the legislature thereof; but the Congress may at any time by law make or alter such regulations, except as to the places of choosing Senators.

The Congress shall assemble at least once in every year, and such meeting *shall be on the first Monday in December, unless they shall by law appoint a different day.*

**Section 5.** Each house shall be the judge of the elections, returns and qualifications of its own members, and a majority of each shall constitute a quorum to do business; but a smaller number may

adjourn from day to day, and may be authorized to compel the attendance of absent members, in such manner, and under such penalties, as each house may provide.

Each house may determine the rules of its proceedings, punish its members for disorderly behavior, and with the concurrence of two-thirds, expel a member.

Each house shall keep a journal of its proceedings, and from time to time publish the same, excepting such parts as may in their judgment require secrecy; and the yeas and nays of the members of either house on any question shall, at the desire of one-fifth of those present, be entered on the journal.

Neither house, during the session of Congress, shall, without the consent of the other, adjourn for more than three days, nor to any other place than that in which the two houses shall be sitting.

**Section 6.** The Senators and Representatives shall receive a compensation for their services, to be ascertained by law and paid out of the treasury of the United States. They shall in all cases except treason, felony and breach of the peace, be privileged from arrest during their attendance at the session of their respective houses, and in going to and returning from the same; and for any speech or debate in either house, they shall not be questioned in any other place.

No Senator or Representative shall, during the time for which he was elected, be appointed to any civil office under the authority of the United States, which shall have been created, or the emoluments whereof shall have been increased, during such time; and no person holding any office under the United States shall be a member of either house during his continuance in office.

**Section 7.** All bills for raising revenue shall originate in the House of Representatives; but the Senate may propose or concur with amendments as on other bills.

Every bill which shall have passed the House of Representatives and the Senate, shall, before it become a law, be presented to the President of the United States; if he approve he shall sign it, but if not he shall return it with objections to that house in which it originated, who shall enter the objections at large on their journal, and proceed to reconsider it. If after such reconsideration two-thirds of that house shall agree to pass the bill, it shall be sent, together with the objections, to the other house, by which it shall likewise be reconsidered, and, if approved by two-thirds of that house, it shall become a law. But in all such cases the votes of both houses shall be determined by yeas and nays, and the names of the persons voting for and against the bill shall be entered on the journal of each house respectively. If any bill shall not be returned by the President within ten days (Sundays excepted) after it shall have been presented to him, the same shall be a law, in like manner as if he had signed it, unless the Congress by their adjournment prevent its return, in which case it shall not be a law.

Every order, resolution, or vote to which the concurrence of the Senate and House of Representatives may be necessary (except on a question of adjournment) shall be presented to the President of the United States; and before the same shall take effect, shall be approved by him, or being disapproved by him, shall be repassed by two-thirds of the Senate and House of Representatives, according to the rules and limitations prescribed in the case of a bill.

**Section 8.**  The Congress shall have power

To lay and collect taxes, duties, imposts, and excises, to pay the debts and provide for the common defense and general welfare of the United States; but all duties, imposts and excises shall be uniform throughout the United States;

To borrow money on the credit of the United States;

To regulate commerce with foreign nations, and among the several States, and with the Indian tribes;

To establish an uniform rule of naturalization, and uniform laws on the subject of bankruptcies throughout the United States;

To coin money, regulate the value thereof, and of foreign coin, and fix the standard of weights and measures;

To provide for the punishment of counterfeiting the securities and current coin of the United States;

To establish post offices and post roads;

To promote the progress of science and useful arts by securing for limited times to authors and inventors the exclusive right to their respective writings and discoveries;

To constitute tribunals inferior to the Supreme Court;

To define and punish piracies and felonies committed on the high seas and offenses against the law of nations;

To declare war, grant letters of marque and reprisal, and make rules concerning captures on land and water;

To raise and support armies, but no appropriation of money to that use shall be for a longer term than two years;

To provide and maintain a navy;

To make rules for the government and regulation of the land and naval forces;

To provide for calling forth the militia to execute the laws of the Union, suppress insurrections, and repel invasions;

To provide for organizing, arming, and disciplining the militia, and for governing such part of them as may be employed in the service of the United States, reserving to the States respectively the appointment of the officers, and the authority of training the militia according to the discipline prescribed by Congress;

To exercise exclusive legislation in all cases whatsoever, over such district (not exceeding ten miles square) as may, by cession of particular States, and the acceptance of Congress, become the seat of government of the United States, and to exercise like authority over all places purchased by the consent of the legislature of the State, in which the same shall be, for erection of forts, magazines, arsenals, dock-yards, and other needful buildings;—and

To make all laws which shall be necessary and proper for carrying into execution the foregoing powers, and all other powers vested by this Constitution in the government of the United States, or in any department or officer thereof.

**Section 9.** *The migration or importation of such persons as any of the States now existing shall think proper to admit shall not be prohibited by the Congress prior to the year 1808; but a tax or duty may be imposed on such importation, not exceeding $10 for each person.*

The privilege of the writ of habeas corpus shall not be suspended, unless when in cases of rebellion or invasion the public safety may require it.

No bill of attainder or ex post facto law shall be passed.

No capitation, or other direct, tax shall be laid, unless in proportion to the census or enumeration herein before directed to be taken.

No tax or duty shall be laid on articles exported from any State.

No preference shall be given by any regulation of commerce or revenue to the ports of one State over those of another; nor shall vessels bound to, or from, one State, be obliged to enter, clear, or pay duties in another.

No money shall be drawn from the treasury, but in consequence of appropriations made by law; and a regular statement and account of the receipts and expenditures of all public money shall be published from time to time.

No title of nobility shall be granted by the United States: and no person holding any office of profit or trust under them, shall, without the consent of the Congress, accept of any present, emolument, office, or title, of any kind whatever, from any king, prince, or foreign state.

**Section 10.** No State shall enter into any treaty, alliance, or confederation; grant letters of marque and reprisal; coin money; emit bills of credit; make anything but gold and silver coin a tender in payment of debts; pass any bill of attainder, ex post facto law, or law impairing the obligation of contracts, or grant any title of nobility.

No State shall, without the consent of Congress, lay any imposts or duties on imports or exports, except what may be absolutely necessary for executing its inspection laws: and the net produce of all duties and imposts, laid by any State on imports or exports, shall be for the use of the treasury of the United States; and all such laws shall be subject to the revision and control of the Congress.

No State shall, without the consent of Congress, lay any duty of tonnage, keep troops or ships of war in time of peace, enter into any agreement or compact with another State, or with a foreign power, or engage in war, unless actually invaded, or in such imminent danger as will not admit of delay.

## ARTICLE II

**Section 1.** The executive power shall be vested in a President of the United States of America. He shall hold his office during the term of four years, and, together with the Vice President, chosen for the same term, be elected as follows:

Each state shall appoint, in such manner as the legislature thereof may direct, a number of electors, equal to the whole number of Senators and Representatives to which the State may be entitled in the Congress; but no Senator or Representative, or person holding an office of trust or profit under the United States, shall be appointed an elector.

*The electors shall meet in their respective States, and vote by ballot for two persons, of whom one at least shall not be an inhabitant of the same State with themselves. And they shall make a list of all the persons voted for, and of the number of votes for each; which list they shall sign and certify, and transmit sealed to the seat of government of the United States, directed to the President of the Senate. The President of the Senate shall, in the presence of the Senate and the House of Representatives, open all the certificates, and the votes shall then be counted. The person having the greatest number of votes shall be the President, if such number be a majority of the whole number of electors appointed; and if there be more than one who have such majority, and have an equal number of votes, then the House of Representatives shall immediately choose by ballot one of them for President; and if no person have a majority, then from the five highest on the list said house shall in like manner choose the President. But in choosing the President the votes shall be taken by States, the representation from each State having one vote; a quorum for this purpose shall consist of a member or members from two-thirds of the States, and a majority of all the States shall be necessary to a choice. In every case, after the choice of the President, the person having the greatest number of votes of the electors shall be the Vice President. But if there should remain two or more who have equal votes, the Senate shall choose from them by ballot the Vice President.*

The Congress may determine the time of choosing the electors and the day on which they shall give their votes; which day shall be the same throughout the United States.

No person except a natural-born citizen, *or a citizen of the United States at the time of the adoption of this Constitution,* shall be eligible to the office of President; neither shall any person be eligible to that office who shall not have attained to the age of thirty-five years, and been fourteen years a resident within the United States.

In case of the removal of the President from office or of his death, resignation, or inability to discharge the powers and duties of the said office, the same shall devolve on the Vice President, and the Congress may by law provide for the case of removal, death, resignation, or inability, both of the President and Vice President, declaring what officer shall then act as President, and such officer shall act accordingly, until the disability be removed, or a President shall be elected.

The President shall, at stated times, receive for his services a compensation, which shall neither be increased nor diminished during the period for which he shall have been elected, and he shall not receive within that period any other emolument from the United States, or any of them.

Before he enter on the execution of his office, he shall take the following oath or affirmation:—"I do solemnly swear (or affirm) that I will faithfully execute the office of the President of the United States, and will to the best of my ability preserve, protect and defend the Constitution of the United States."

**Section 2.**    The President shall be commander in chief of the army and navy of the United States, and of the militia of the several States, when called into the actual service of the United States; he may require the opinion, in writing, of the principal officer in each of the executive departments, upon any subject relating to the duties of their respective offices, and he shall have power to grant reprieves and pardons for offenses against the United States, except in cases of impeachment.

He shall have power, by and with the advice and consent of the Senate, to make treaties, provided two-thirds of the Senators present concur; and he shall nominate, and by and with the advice and consent of the Senate, shall appoint ambassadors, other public ministers and consuls, judges of the Supreme Court, and all other officers of the United States, whose appointments are not herein otherwise provided for, and which shall be established by law: but Congress may by law vest the appointment of such inferior officers, as they think proper, in the President alone, in the courts of law, or in the heads of departments.

The President shall have power to fill up all vacancies that may happen during the recess of the Senate, by granting commissions which shall expire at the end of their next session.

**Section 3.**    He shall from time to time give to the Congress information of the state of the Union, and recommend to their consideration such measures as he shall judge necessary and expedient; he may, on extraordinary occasions, convene both houses, or either of them, and in case of disagreement between them, with respect to the time of adjournment, he may adjourn them to such time as he shall think proper; he shall receive ambassadors and other public ministers; he shall take care that the laws be faithfully executed, and shall commission all the officers of the United States.

**Section 4.** The President, Vice President and all civil officers of the United States shall be removed from office on impeachment for, and on conviction of, treason, bribery, or other high crimes and misdemeanors.

## ARTICLE III

**Section 1.** The judicial power of the United States shall be vested in one Supreme Court, and in such inferior courts as the Congress may from time to time ordain and establish. The judges, both of the Supreme and inferior courts, shall hold their offices during good behavior, and shall, at stated times, receive for their services a compensation which shall not be diminished during their continuance in office.

**Section 2.** The judicial power shall extend to all cases, in law and equity, arising under this Constitution, the laws of the United States, and treaties made, or which shall be made, under their authority;—to all cases affecting ambassadors, other public ministers and consuls;—to all cases of admiralty and maritime jurisdiction;—to controversies to which the United States shall be a party;—to controversies between two or more States;—*between a State and citizens of another State;*—between citizens of different States;—between citizens of the same State claiming lands under grants of different States, and between a State, or the citizens thereof, and foreign states, citizens or subjects.

In all cases affecting ambassadors, other public ministers and consuls, and those in which a State shall be party, the Supreme Court shall have original jurisdiction. In all the other cases before mentioned, the Supreme Court shall have appellate jurisdiction, both as to law and fact, with such exceptions, and under such regulations, as the Congress shall make.

The trial of all crimes, except in cases of impeachment, shall be by jury; and such trial shall be held in the State where said crimes shall have been committed; but when not committed within any State, the trial shall be at such place or places as the Congress may by law have directed.

**Section 3.** Treason against the United States shall consist only in levying war against them, or in adhering to their enemies, giving them aid and comfort. No person shall be convicted of treason unless on the testimony of two witnesses to the same overt act, or on confession in open court.

The Congress shall have power to declare the punishment of treason, but no attainder of treason shall work corruption of blood, or forfeiture except during the life of the person attainted.

## ARTICLE IV

**Section 1.** Full faith and credit shall be given in each State to the public acts, records, and judicial proceedings of every other State. And the Congress may by general laws prescribe the manner in which such acts, records, and proceedings shall be proved, and the effect thereof.

**Section 2.** The citizens of each State shall be entitled to all privileges and immunities of citizens in the several States.

A person charged in any State with treason, felony, or other crime, who shall flee from justice, and be found in another State, shall on demand of the executive authority of the State from which he fled, be delivered up, to be removed to the State having jurisdiction of the crime.

*No person held to service or labor in one State, under the laws thereof, escaping into another, shall, in consequence of any law or regulation therein, be discharged from such service or labor, but shall be delivered up on claim of the party to whom such service or labor may be due.*

**Section 3.**   New States may be admitted by the Congress into this Union; but no new State shall be formed or erected within the jurisdiction of any other State; nor any State be formed by the junction of two or more States, or parts of States, without the consent of the legislatures of the States concerned as well as of the Congress.

The Congress shall have power to dispose of and make all needful rules and regulations respecting the territory or other property belonging to the United States; and nothing in this Constitution shall be so construed as to prejudice any claims of the United States, or of any particular State.

**Section 4.**   The United States shall guarantee to every State in this Union a republican form of government, and shall protect each of them against invasion; and on application of the legislature, or of the executive (when the legislature cannot be convened), against domestic violence.

## ARTICLE V

The Congress, whenever two-thirds of both houses shall deem it necessary, shall propose amendments to this Constitution, or, on the application of the legislatures of two-thirds of the several States, shall call a convention for proposing amendments, which, in either case, shall be valid to all intents and purposes, as part of this Constitution, when ratified by the legislatures of three-fourths of the several States, or by conventions in three-fourths thereof, as the one or the other mode of ratification may be proposed by the Congress; provided *that no amendments which may be made prior to the year one thousand eight hundred and eight shall in any manner affect the first and fourth clauses in the ninth section of the first article;* and that no State, without its consent, shall be deprived of its equal suffrage in the Senate.

## ARTICLE VI

All debts contracted and engagements entered into, before the adoption of this Constitution, shall be as valid against the United States under this Constitution, as under the Confederation.

This Constitution, and the laws of the United States which shall be made in pursuance thereof; and all treaties made, or which shall be made, under the authority of the United States, shall be the supreme law of the land; and the judges in every State shall be bound thereby, anything in the Constitution or laws of any State to the contrary notwithstanding.

The Senators and Representatives before mentioned, and the members of the several State legislatures, and all executive and judicial officers, both of the United States and of the several States, shall be bound by oath or affirmation to support this Constitution; but no religious test shall ever be required as a qualification to any office or public trust under the United States.

## ARTICLE VII

The ratification of the conventions of nine States shall be sufficient for the establishment of this Constitution between the States so ratifying the same.

Done in Convention by the unanimous consent of the States present, the seventeenth day of September in the year of our Lord one thousand seven hundred and eighty-seven and of the Independence of the United States of America the twelfth. In witness whereof we have hereunto subscribed our names.

[Signed by]
G° WASHINGTON
*Presidt and Deputy from Virginia*
[*and thirty-eight others*]

# Amendments to the Constitution

## ARTICLE I*

Congress shall make no law respecting an establishment of religion, or prohibiting the free exercise thereof; or abridging the freedom of speech, or of the press; or the right of the people peaceably to assemble, and to petition the government for a redress of grievances.

## ARTICLE II

A well-regulated militia being necessary to the security of a free State, the right of the people to keep and bear arms shall not be infringed.

## ARTICLE III

No soldier shall, in time of peace, be quartered in any house without the consent of the owner, nor in time of war, but in a manner to be prescribed by law.

## ARTICLE IV

The right of the people to be secure in their persons, houses, papers, and effects, against unreasonable searches and seizures, shall not be violated, and no warrants shall issue but upon probable cause, supported by oath or affirmation, and particularly describing the place to be searched, and the persons or things to be seized.

## ARTICLE V

No person shall be held to answer for a capital, or otherwise infamous crime, unless on a presentment or indictment of a grand jury, except in cases arising in the land or naval forces, or in the militia, when in actual service in time of war or public danger; nor shall any person be subject for the same offense to be twice put in jeopardy of life or limb; nor shall be compelled in any criminal case to be a witness against himself, nor be deprived of life, liberty, or property, without due process of law; nor shall private property be taken for public use without just compensation.

## ARTICLE VI

In all criminal prosecutions, the accused shall enjoy the right to a speedy and public trial, by an impartial jury of the State and district wherein the crime shall have been committed, which district shall have been previously ascertained by law, and to be informed of the nature and cause of the accusation; to be confronted with the witnesses against him; to have compulsory process for obtaining witnesses in his favor, and to have the assistance of counsel for his defense.

## ARTICLE VII

In suits at common law, where the value in controversy shall exceed twenty dollars, the right of trial by jury shall be preserved, and no fact tried by a jury shall be otherwise reexamined in any court of the United States, than according to the rules of the common law.

## ARTICLE VIII

Excessive bail shall not be required, nor excessive fines imposed, nor cruel and unusual punishments inflicted.

## ARTICLE IX

The enumeration in the Constitution, of certain rights, shall not be construed to deny or disparage others retained by the people.

*The first ten Amendments (Bill of Rights) were adopted in 1791.

## ARTICLE X

The powers not delegated to the United States by the Constitution, not prohibited by it to the States, are reserved to the States respectively, or to the people.

## ARTICLE XI    [Adopted 1798]

The judicial power of the United States shall not be construed to extend to any suit in law or equity, commenced or prosecuted against one of the United States by citizens of another State, or by citizens or subjects of any foreign state.

## ARTICLE XII    [Adopted 1804]

The electors shall meet in their respective States, and vote by ballot for President and Vice President, one of whom, at least, shall not be an inhabitant of the same State with themselves; they shall name in their ballots the person voted for as President, and in distinct ballots the person voted for as Vice President, and they shall make distinct lists of all persons voted for as President, and of all persons voted for as Vice President, and of the number of votes for each, which lists they shall sign and certify, and transmit sealed to the seat of government of the United States, directed to the President of the Senate;—the President of the Senate shall, in the presence of the Senate and House of Representatives, open all the certificates and the votes shall then be counted;—the person having the greatest number of votes for President shall be the President, if such number be a majority of the whole number of electors appointed; and if no person have such majority, then from the persons having the highest numbers not exceeding three on the list of those voted for as President, the House of Representatives shall choose immediately, by ballot, the President. But in choosing the President, the votes shall be taken by States, the representation from each State having one vote; a quorum for this purpose shall consist of a member or members from two-thirds of the States, and a majority of all the States shall be necessary to a choice.

And if the House of Representatives shall not choose a President whenever the right of choice shall devolve upon them, before *the fourth day of March* next following, then the Vice President shall act as President, as in the case of the death or other constitutional disability of the President.

The person having the greatest number of votes as Vice President shall be the Vice President, if such a number be a majority of the whole number of electors appointed; and if no person have a majority, then from the two highest numbers on the list the Senate shall choose the Vice President; a quorum for the purpose shall consist of two-thirds of the whole number of Senators, and a majority of the whole number shall be necessary to a choice. But no person constitutionally ineligible to the office of President shall be eligible to that of Vice President of the United States.

## ARTICLE XIII    [Adopted 1865]

**Section 1.** Neither slavery nor involuntary servitude, except as a punishment for crime whereof the party shall have been duly convicted, shall exist within the United States, or any place subject to their jurisdiction.

**Section 2.** Congress shall have power to enforce this article by appropriate legislation.

## ARTICLE XIV    [Adopted 1868]

**Section 1.** All persons born or naturalized in the United States, and subject to the jurisdiction thereof, are citizens of the United States and of the State wherein they reside. No State shall make or enforce any law which shall abridge the privileges or immunities of citizens of the United States; nor shall any State deprive any person of life, liberty, or property, without due process of law; nor deny to any person within its jurisdiction the equal protection of the laws.

**Section 2.** Representatives shall be apportioned among the several States according to their respective numbers, counting the whole number of persons in each State, excluding Indians not taxed. But when the right to vote at any election for the choice of Electors for President and Vice President of the United States, Representatives in Congress, the executive and judicial officers of a State, or the members of the legislature thereof, is denied to any of the male inhabitants of such State, being twenty-one years of age and citizens of the United States, or in any way abridged, except for participation in rebellion, or other crime, the basis of representation therein shall be reduced in the proportion which the number of such male citizens shall bear to the whole number of male citizens twenty-one years of age in such State.

**Section 3.** No person shall be a Senator or Representative in Congress or Elector of President and Vice President, or hold any office, civil or military, under the United States, or under any State, who, having previously taken an oath, as a member of Congress, or as an officer of the United States, or as a member of any State legislature, or as an executive or judicial officer of any State, to support the Constitution of the United States, shall have engaged in insurrection or rebellion against the same, or given aid and comfort to the enemies thereof. Congress may, by a vote of two-thirds of each house, remove such disability.

**Section 4.** The validity of the public debt of the United States, authorized by law, including debts incurred for payment of pensions and bounties for services in suppressing insurrection or rebellion, shall not be questioned. But neither the United States nor any State shall assume or pay any debt or obligation incurred in aid of insurrection or rebellion against the United States, or any claim for the loss or emancipation of any slave; but all such debts, obligations, and claims shall be held illegal and void.

**Section 5.** The Congress shall have the power to enforce, by appropriate legislation, the provisions of this article.

## ARTICLE XV     [*Adopted 1870*]

**Section 1.** The right of citizens of the United States to vote shall not be denied or abridged by the United States or by any State on account of race, color, or previous condition of servitude.

**Section 2.** The Congress shall have power to enforce this article by appropriate legislation.

## ARTICLE XVI     [*Adopted 1913*]

The Congress shall have power to lay and collect taxes on incomes, from whatever source derived, without apportionment among the several States, and without regard to any census or enumeration.

## ARTICLE XVII     [*Adopted 1913*]

**Section 1.** The Senate of the United States shall be composed of two Senators from each State, elected by the people thereof, for six years; and each Senator shall have one vote. The electors in each State shall have the qualifications requisite for electors of [voters for] the most numerous branch of the State legislatures.

**Section 2.** When vacancies happen in the representation of any State in the Senate, the executive authority of such State shall issue writs of election to fill such vacancies: Provided, that the Legislature of any State may empower the executive thereof to make temporary appointments until the people fill the vacancies by election as the Legislature may direct.

**Section 3.** This amendment shall not be so construed as to affect the election or term of any Senator chosen before it becomes valid as part of the Constitution.

## ARTICLE XVIII     [*Adopted 1919; repealed 1933*]

**Section 1.** *After one year from the ratification of this article the manufacture, sale, or transportation of intoxicating liquors within, the importation thereof into,* *or the exportation thereof from the United States and all territory subject to the jurisdiction thereof, for beverage purposes, is hereby prohibited.*

**Section 2.**   *The Congress and the several States shall have concurrent power to enforce this article by appropriate legislation.*

**Section 3.**   *This article shall be inoperative unless it shall have been ratified as an amendment to the Constitution by the legislatures of the several States, as provided by the Constitution, within seven years from the date of the submission thereof to the States by the Congress.*

## ARTICLE XIX   [Adopted 1920]

**Section 1.**   The right of citizens of the United States to vote shall not be denied or abridged by the United States or by any State on account of sex.

**Section 2.**   The Congress shall have the power to enforce this article by appropriate legislation.

## ARTICLE XX   [Adopted 1933]

**Section 1.**   The terms of the President and Vice President shall end at noon on the 20th day of January, and the terms of Senators and Representatives at noon on the 3d day of January, of the years in which such terms would have ended if this article had not been ratified; and the terms of their successors shall then begin.

**Section 2.**   The Congress shall assemble at least once in every year, and such meeting shall begin at noon on the 3d day of January, unless they shall by law appoint a different day.

**Section 3.**   If, at the time fixed for the beginning of the term of the President, the President-elect shall have died, the Vice President-elect shall become President. If a President shall not have been chosen before the time fixed for the beginning of his term, or if the President-elect shall have failed

to qualify, then the Vice President-elect shall act as President until a President shall have qualified; and the Congress may by law provide for the case wherein neither a President-elect nor a Vice President-elect shall have qualified, declaring who shall then act as President, or the manner in which one who is to act shall be selected, and such persons shall act accordingly until a President or Vice President shall have qualified.

**Section 4.**   The Congress may by law provide for the case of the death of any of the persons from whom the House of Representatives may choose a President whenever the right of choice shall have devolved upon them, and for the case of the death of any of the persons from whom the Senate may choose a Vice President whenever the right of choice shall have devolved upon them.

**Section 5.**   Sections 1 and 2 shall take effect on the 15th day of October following the ratification of this article.

**Section 6.**   This article shall be inoperative unless it shall have been ratified as an amendment to the Constitution by the Legislatures of three-fourths of the several States within seven years from the date of its submission.

## ARTICLE XXI   [Adopted 1933]

**Section 1.**   The eighteenth article of amendment to the Constitution of the United States is hereby repealed.

**Section 2.**   The transportation or importation into any State, Territory, or Possession of the United States for delivery or use therein of intoxicating liquors, in violation of the laws thereof, is hereby prohibited.

**Section 3.**   This article shall be inoperative unless it shall have been ratified as an amendment to the Constitution by conventions in the several States, as provided in the Constitution, within seven years from the date of submission thereof to the States by the Congress.

## ARTICLE XXII   [*Adopted 1951*]

**Section 1.**   No person shall be elected to the office of President more than twice, and no person who has held the office of President, or acted as President, for more than two years of a term to which some other person was elected President shall be elected to the office of President more than once. But this article shall not apply to any person holding the office of President when this article was proposed by the Congress, and shall not prevent any person who may be holding the office of President, or acting as President, during the term within which this article becomes operative from holding the office of President or acting as President during the remainder of such term.

**Section 2.**   This article shall be inoperative unless it shall have been ratified as an amendment to the Constitution by the legislatures of three-fourths of the several States within seven years from the date of its submission to the States by the Congress.

## ARTICLE XXIII   [*Adopted 1961*]

**Section 1.**   The District constituting the seat of Government of the United States shall appoint in such manner as the Congress may direct:

A number of electors of President and Vice President equal to the whole number of Senators and Representatives in Congress to which the District would be entitled if it were a State, but in no event more than the least populous State; they shall be in addition to those appointed by the States, but they shall be considered for the purposes of the election of President and Vice President, to be electors appointed by a State; and they shall meet in the District and perform such duties as provided by the twelfth article of amendment.

**Section 2.**   The Congress shall have the power to enforce this article by appropriate legislation.

## ARTICLE XXIV   [*Adopted 1964*]

**Section 1.**   The right of citizens of the United States to vote in any primary or other election for President or Vice President, for electors for President or Vice President, or for Senator or Representative in Congress, shall not be denied or abridged by the United States or any State by reason of failure to pay any poll tax or other tax.

**Section 2.**   The Congress shall have the power to enforce this article by appropriate legislation.

## ARTICLE XXV   [*Adopted 1967*]

**Section 1.**   In case of the removal of the President from office or of his death or resignation, the Vice President shall become President.

**Section 2.**   Whenever there is a vacancy in the office of the Vice President, the President shall nominate a Vice President who shall take office upon confirmation by a majority vote of both Houses of Congress.

**Section 3.**   Whenever the President transmits to the President pro tempore of the Senate and the Speaker of the House of Representatives his written declaration that he is unable to discharge the powers and duties of his office, and until he transmits to them a written declaration to the contrary, such powers and duties shall be discharged by the Vice President as Acting President.

**Section 4.**   Whenever the Vice President and a majority of either the principal officers of the executive departments or of such other body as Congress may by law provide, transmit to the President pro tempore of the Senate and the Speaker of the House of Representatives their written declaration that the President is unable to discharge the powers and duties of his office, the Vice President shall immediately assume the powers and duties of the office as Acting President.

Thereafter, when the President transmits to the President pro tempore of the Senate and the

Speaker of the House of Representatives his written declaration that no inability exists, he shall resume the powers and duties of his office unless the Vice President and a majority of either the principal officers of the executive department[s] or of such other body as Congress may by law provide, transmit within four days to the President pro tempore of the Senate and the Speaker of the House of Representatives their written declaration that the President is unable to discharge the powers and duties of his office. Thereupon Congress shall decide the issue, assembling within forty-eight hours for that purpose if not in session. If the Congress, within twenty-one days after receipt of the latter written declaration, or, if Congress is not in session, within twenty-one days after Congress is required to assemble, determines by two-thirds vote of both Houses that the President is unable to discharge the powers and duties of his office, the Vice President shall continue to discharge the same as Acting President; otherwise, the President shall resume the powers and duties of his office.

## ARTICLE XXVI   [Adopted 1971]

**Section 1.**   The right of citizens of the United States, who are eighteen years of age or older, to vote shall not be denied or abridged by the United States or by any State on account of age.

**Section 2.**   The Congress shall have power to enforce this article by appropriate legislation.

## ARTICLE XXVII*   [Adopted 1992]

No law, varying the compensation for services of the Senators and Representatives, shall take effect, until an election of Representatives shall have intervened.

---

*Originally proposed in 1789 by James Madison, this amendment failed to win ratification along with the other parts of what became the Bill of Rights. However, the proposed amendment contained no deadline for ratification, and over the years other state legislatures voted to add it to the Constitution; many such ratifications occurred during the 1980s and early 1990s as public frustration with Congress's performance mounted. In May 1992 the Archivist of the United States certified that, with the Michigan legislature's ratification, the article had been approved by three-fourths of the states and thus automatically became part of the Constitution. But congressional leaders and constitutional specialists questioned whether an amendment that took 202 years to win ratification was valid, and the issue had not been resolved by the time this book went to press.

## Presidential Elections, 1789–1996

| Year | States in the Union | Candidates | Parties | Electoral Vote | Popular Vote | Percentage of Popular Vote |
|------|------|------|------|------|------|------|
| 1789 | 11 | GEORGE WASHINGTON | No party designations | 69 | | |
| | | John Adams | | 34 | | |
| | | Minor candidates | | 35 | | |
| 1792 | 15 | GEORGE WASHINGTON | No party designations | 132 | | |
| | | John Adams | | 77 | | |
| | | George Clinton | | 50 | | |
| | | Minor candidates | | 5 | | |
| 1796 | 16 | JOHN ADAMS | Federalist | 71 | | |
| | | Thomas Jefferson | Democratic-Republican | 68 | | |
| | | Thomas Pinckney | Federalist | 59 | | |
| | | Aaron Burr | Democratic-Republican | 30 | | |
| | | Minor candidates | | 48 | | |
| 1800 | 16 | THOMAS JEFFERSON | Democratic-Republican | 73 | | |
| | | Aaron Burr | Democratic-Republican | 73 | | |
| | | John Adams | Federalist | 65 | | |
| | | Charles C. Pinckney | Federalist | 64 | | |
| | | John Jay | Federalist | 1 | | |
| 1804 | 17 | THOMAS JEFFERSON | Democratic-Republican | 162 | | |
| | | Charles C. Pinckney | Federalist | 14 | | |
| 1808 | 17 | JAMES MADISON | Democratic-Republican | 122 | | |
| | | Charles C. Pinckney | Federalist | 47 | | |
| | | George Clinton | Democratic-Republican | 6 | | |
| 1812 | 18 | JAMES MADISON | Democratic-Republican | 128 | | |
| | | DeWitt Clinton | Federalist | 89 | | |
| 1816 | 19 | JAMES MONROE | Democratic-Republican | 183 | | |
| | | Rufus King | Federalist | 34 | | |
| 1820 | 24 | JAMES MONROE | Democratic-Republican | 231 | | |
| | | John Quincy Adams | Independent Republican | 1 | | |
| 1824 | 24 | JOHN QUINCY ADAMS | Democratic-Republican | 84 | 108,740 | 30.5 |
| | | Andrew Jackson | Democratic-Republican | 99 | 153,544 | 43.1 |
| | | William H. Crawford | Democratic-Republican | 41 | 46,618 | 13.1 |
| | | Henry Clay | Democratic-Republican | 37 | 47,136 | 13.2 |
| 1828 | 24 | ANDREW JACKSON | Democratic | 178 | 642,553 | 56.0 |
| | | John Quincy Adams | National Republican | 83 | 500,897 | 44.0 |
| 1832 | 24 | ANDREW JACKSON | Democratic | 219 | 687,502 | 55.0 |
| | | Henry Clay | National Republican | 49 | 530,189 | 42.4 |
| | | William Wirt | Anti-Masonic | 7 } | 33,108 | 2.6 |
| | | John Floyd | National Republican | 11 } | | |

Because candidates receiving less than 1 percent of the popular vote are omitted, the percentage of popular vote may not total 100 percent.

Before the Twelfth Amendment was passed in 1804, the electoral college voted for two presidential candidates; the runner-up became vice president.

| Year | States in the Union | Candidates | Parties | Electoral Vote | Popular Vote | Percentage of Popular Vote |
|---|---|---|---|---|---|---|
| 1836 | 26 | MARTIN VAN BUREN | Democratic | 170 | 765,483 | 50.9 |
| | | William H. Harrison | Whig | 73 | | |
| | | Hugh L. White | Whig | 26 | | |
| | | Daniel Webster | Whig | 14 | 739,795 | 49.1 |
| | | W. P. Mangum | Whig | 11 | | |
| 1840 | 26 | WILLIAM H. HARRISON | Whig | 234 | 1,274,624 | 53.1 |
| | | Martin Van Buren | Democratic | 60 | 1,127,781 | 46.9 |
| 1844 | 26 | JAMES K. POLK | Democratic | 170 | 1,338,464 | 49.6 |
| | | Henry Clay | Whig | 105 | 1,300,097 | 48.1 |
| | | James G. Birney | Liberty | | 62,300 | 2.3 |
| 1848 | 30 | ZACHARY TAYLOR | Whig | 163 | 1,360,967 | 47.4 |
| | | Lewis Cass | Democratic | 127 | 1,222,342 | 42.5 |
| | | Martin Van Buren | Free Soil | | 291,263 | 10.1 |
| 1852 | 31 | FRANKLIN PIERCE | Democratic | 254 | 1,601,117 | 50.9 |
| | | Winfield Scott | Whig | 42 | 1,385,453 | 44.1 |
| | | John P. Hale | Free Soil | | 155,825 | 5.0 |
| 1856 | 31 | JAMES BUCHANAN | Democratic | 174 | 1,832,955 | 45.3 |
| | | John C. Frémont | Republican | 114 | 1,339,932 | 33.1 |
| | | Millard Fillmore | American | 8 | 871,731 | 21.6 |
| 1860 | 33 | ABRAHAM LINCOLN | Republican | 180 | 1,865,593 | 39.8 |
| | | Stephen A. Douglas | Democratic | 12 | 1,382,713 | 29.5 |
| | | John C. Breckinridge | Democratic | 72 | 848,356 | 18.1 |
| | | John Bell | Constitutional Union | 39 | 592,906 | 12.6 |
| 1864 | 36 | ABRAHAM LINCOLN | Republican | 212 | 2,206,938 | 55.0 |
| | | George B. McClellan | Democratic | 21 | 1,803,787 | 45.0 |
| 1868 | 37 | ULYSSES S. GRANT | Republican | 214 | 3,013,421 | 52.7 |
| | | Horatio Seymour | Democratic | 80 | 2,706,829 | 47.3 |
| 1872 | 37 | ULYSSES S. GRANT | Republican | 286 | 3,596,745 | 55.6 |
| | | Horace Greeley | Democratic | * | 2,843,446 | 43.9 |
| 1876 | 38 | RUTHERFORD B. HAYES | Republican | 185 | 4,034,311 | 48.0 |
| | | Samuel J. Tilden | Democratic | 184 | 4,288,546 | 51.0 |
| | | Peter Cooper | Greenback | | 75,973 | 1.0 |
| 1880 | 38 | JAMES A. GARFIELD | Republican | 214 | 4,453,295 | 48.5 |
| | | Winfield S. Hancock | Democratic | 155 | 4,414,082 | 48.1 |
| | | James B. Weaver | Greenback-Labor | | 308,578 | 3.4 |
| 1884 | 38 | GROVER CLEVELAND | Democratic | 219 | 4,879,507 | 48.5 |
| | | James G. Blaine | Republican | 182 | 4,850,293 | 48.2 |
| | | Benjamin F. Butler | Greenback-Labor | | 175,370 | 1.8 |
| | | John P. St. John | Prohibition | | 150,369 | 1.5 |

*When Greeley died shortly after the election, his supporters divided their votes among the minor candidates. Because candidates receiving less than 1 percent of the popular vote are omitted, the percentage of popular vote may not total 100 percent.

| Year | States in the Union | Candidates | Parties | Electoral Vote | Popular Vote | Percentage of Popular Vote |
|------|------|------------|---------|-------|-------|-------|
| 1888 | 38 | BENJAMIN HARRISON | Republican | 233 | 5,477,129 | 47.9 |
|      |    | Grover Cleveland | Democratic | 168 | 5,537,857 | 48.6 |
|      |    | Clinton B. Fisk | Prohibition |     | 249,506 | 2.2 |
|      |    | Anson J. Streeter | Union Labor |     | 146,935 | 1.3 |
| 1892 | 44 | GROVER CLEVELAND | Democratic | 277 | 5,555,426 | 46.1 |
|      |    | Benjamin Harrison | Republican | 145 | 5,182,690 | 43.0 |
|      |    | James B. Weaver | People's | 22 | 1,029,846 | 8.5 |
|      |    | John Bidwell | Prohibition |     | 264,133 | 2.2 |
| 1896 | 45 | WILLIAM McKINLEY | Republican | 271 | 7,102,246 | 51.1 |
|      |    | William J. Bryan | Democratic | 176 | 6,492,559 | 47.7 |
| 1900 | 45 | WILLIAM McKINLEY | Republican | 292 | 7,218,491 | 51.7 |
|      |    | William J. Bryan | Democratic; Populist | 155 | 6,356,734 | 45.5 |
|      |    | John C. Wooley | Prohibition |     | 208,914 | 1.5 |
| 1904 | 45 | THEODORE ROOSEVELT | Republican | 336 | 7,628,461 | 57.4 |
|      |    | Alton B. Parker | Democratic | 140 | 5,084,223 | 37.6 |
|      |    | Eugene V. Debs | Socialist |     | 402,283 | 3.0 |
|      |    | Silas C. Swallow | Prohibition |     | 258,536 | 1.9 |
| 1908 | 46 | WILLIAM H. TAFT | Republican | 321 | 7,675,320 | 51.6 |
|      |    | William J. Bryan | Democratic | 162 | 6,412,294 | 43.1 |
|      |    | Eugene V. Debs | Socialist |     | 420,793 | 2.8 |
|      |    | Eugene W. Chafin | Prohibition |     | 253,840 | 1.7 |
| 1912 | 48 | WOODROW WILSON | Democratic | 435 | 6,296,547 | 41.9 |
|      |    | Theodore Roosevelt | Progressive | 88 | 4,118,571 | 27.4 |
|      |    | William H. Taft | Republican | 8 | 3,486,720 | 23.2 |
|      |    | Eugene V. Debs | Socialist |     | 900,672 | 6.0 |
|      |    | Eugene W. Chafin | Prohibition |     | 206,275 | 1.4 |
| 1916 | 48 | WOODROW WILSON | Democratic | 277 | 9,127,695 | 49.4 |
|      |    | Charles E. Hughes | Republican | 254 | 8,533,507 | 46.2 |
|      |    | A. L. Benson | Socialist |     | 585,113 | 3.2 |
|      |    | J. Frank Hanly | Prohibition |     | 220,506 | 1.2 |
| 1920 | 48 | WARREN G. HARDING | Republican | 404 | 16,143,407 | 60.4 |
|      |    | James N. Cox | Democratic | 127 | 9,130,328 | 34.2 |
|      |    | Eugene V. Debs | Socialist |     | 919,799 | 3.4 |
|      |    | P. P. Christensen | Farmer-Labor |     | 265,411 | 1.0 |
| 1924 | 48 | CALVIN COOLIDGE | Republican | 382 | 15,718,211 | 54.0 |
|      |    | John W. Davis | Democratic | 136 | 8,385,283 | 28.8 |
|      |    | Robert M. La Follette | Progressive | 13 | 4,831,289 | 16.6 |
| 1928 | 48 | HERBERT C. HOOVER | Republican | 444 | 21,391,993 | 58.2 |
|      |    | Alfred E. Smith | Democratic | 87 | 15,016,169 | 40.9 |

Because candidates receiving less than 1 percent of the popular vote are omitted, the percentage of popular vote may not total 100 percent.

| Year | States in the Union | Candidates | Parties | Electoral Vote | Popular Vote | Percentage of Popular Vote |
|---|---|---|---|---|---|---|
| 1932 | 48 | FRANKLIN D. ROOSEVELT | Democratic | 472 | 22,809,638 | 57.4 |
| | | Herbert C. Hoover | Republican | 59 | 15,758,901 | 39.7 |
| | | Norman Thomas | Socialist | | 881,951 | 2.2 |
| 1936 | 48 | FRANKLIN D. ROOSEVELT | Democratic | 523 | 27,752,869 | 60.8 |
| | | Alfred M. Landon | Republican | 8 | 16,674,665 | 36.5 |
| | | William Lemke | Union | | 882,479 | 1.9 |
| 1940 | 48 | FRANKLIN D. ROOSEVELT | Democratic | 449 | 27,307,819 | 54.8 |
| | | Wendell L. Willkie | Republican | 82 | 22,321,018 | 44.8 |
| 1944 | 48 | FRANKLIN D. ROOSEVELT | Democratic | 432 | 25,606,585 | 53.5 |
| | | Thomas E. Dewey | Republican | 99 | 22,014,745 | 46.0 |
| 1948 | 48 | HARRY S TRUMAN | Democratic | 303 | 24,105,812 | 49.5 |
| | | Thomas E. Dewey | Republican | 189 | 21,970,065 | 45.1 |
| | | Strom Thurmond | States' Rights | 39 | 1,169,063 | 2.4 |
| | | Henry A. Wallace | Progressive | | 1,157,172 | 2.4 |
| 1952 | 48 | DWIGHT D. EISENHOWER | Republican | 442 | 33,936,234 | 55.1 |
| | | Adlai E. Stevenson | Democratic | 89 | 27,314,992 | 44.4 |
| 1956 | 48 | DWIGHT D. EISENHOWER | Republican | 457 | 35,590,472 | 57.6 |
| | | Adlai E. Stevenson | Democratic | 73 | 26,022,752 | 42.1 |
| 1960 | 50 | JOHN F. KENNEDY | Democratic | 303 | 34,227,096 | 49.7 |
| | | Richard M. Nixon | Republican | 219 | 34,108,546 | 49.5 |
| | | Harry F. Byrd | Independent | 15 | 502,363 | .7 |
| 1964 | 50 | LYNDON B. JOHNSON | Democratic | 486 | 43,126,506 | 61.1 |
| | | Barry M. Goldwater | Republican | 52 | 27,176,799 | 38.5 |
| 1968 | 50 | RICHARD M. NIXON | Republican | 301 | 31,770,237 | 43.4 |
| | | Hubert H. Humphrey | Democratic | 191 | 31,270,533 | 42.7 |
| | | George C. Wallace | American Independent | 46 | 9,906,141 | 13.5 |
| 1972 | 50 | RICHARD M. NIXON | Republican | 520 | 47,169,911 | 60.7 |
| | | George S. McGovern | Democratic | 17 | 29,170,383 | 37.5 |
| 1976 | 50 | JIMMY CARTER | Democratic | 297 | 40,827,394 | 49.9 |
| | | Gerald R. Ford | Republican | 240 | 39,145,977 | 47.9 |
| 1980 | 50 | RONALD W. REAGAN | Republican | 489 | 43,899,248 | 50.8 |
| | | Jimmy Carter | Democratic | 49 | 35,481,435 | 41.0 |
| | | John B. Anderson | Independent | | 5,719,437 | 6.6 |
| | | Ed Clark | Libertarian | | 920,859 | 1.0 |
| 1984 | 50 | RONALD W. REAGAN | Republican | 525 | 54,451,521 | 58.8 |
| | | Walter F. Mondale | Democratic | 13 | 37,565,334 | 40.5 |
| 1988 | 50 | GEORGE H. W. BUSH | Republican | 426 | 47,946,422 | 54.0 |
| | | Michael S. Dukakis | Democratic | 112 | 41,016,429 | 46.0 |
| 1992 | 50 | WILLIAM J. CLINTON | Democratic | 370 | 43,728,275 | 43.2 |
| | | George H. W. Bush | Republican | 168 | 38,167,416 | 37.7 |
| | | H. Ross Perot | Independent | | 19,237,247 | 19.0 |
| 1996 | 50 | WILLIAM J. CLINTON | Democratic | 379 | 47,401,185 | 49.2 |
| | | Robert Dole | Republican | 159 | 39,197,469 | 40.7 |
| | | H. Ross Perot | Reform | | 8,085,294 | 8.4 |

Because candidates receiving less than 1 percent of the popular vote are omitted, the percentage of popular vote may not total 100 percent.

## Supreme Court Justices

| Name | Terms of Service | Appointed By |
|------|------------------|--------------|
| JOHN JAY | 1789–1795 | Washington |
| James Wilson | 1789–1798 | Washington |
| John Rutledge | 1790–1791 | Washington |
| William Cushing | 1790–1810 | Washington |
| John Blair | 1790–1796 | Washington |
| James Iredell | 1790–1799 | Washington |
| Thomas Johnson | 1792–1793 | Washington |
| William Paterson | 1793–1806 | Washington |
| JOHN RUTLEDGE* | 1795 | Washington |
| Samuel Chase | 1796–1811 | Washington |
| OLIVER ELLSWORTH | 1796–1800 | Washington |
| Bushrod Washington | 1799–1829 | J. Adams |
| Alfred Moore | 1800–1804 | J. Adams |
| JOHN MARSHALL | 1801–1835 | J. Adams |
| William Johnson | 1804–1834 | Jefferson |
| Brockholst Livingston | 1807–1823 | Jefferson |
| Thomas Todd | 1807–1826 | Jefferson |
| Gabriel Duvall | 1811–1835 | Madison |
| Joseph Story | 1812–1845 | Madison |
| Smith Thompson | 1823–1843 | Monroe |
| Robert Trimble | 1826–1828 | J. Q. Adams |
| John McLean | 1830–1861 | Jackson |
| Henry Baldwin | 1830–1844 | Jackson |
| James M. Wayne | 1835–1867 | Jackson |
| ROGER B. TANEY | 1836–1864 | Jackson |
| Philip P. Barbour | 1836–1841 | Jackson |
| John Cartron | 1837–1865 | Van Buren |
| John McKinley | 1838–1852 | Van Buren |
| Peter V. Daniel | 1842–1860 | Van Buren |
| Samuel Nelson | 1845–1872 | Tyler |
| Levi Woodbury | 1845–1851 | Polk |
| Robert C. Grier | 1846–1870 | Polk |
| Benjamin R. Curtis | 1851–1857 | Fillmore |
| John A. Campbell | 1853–1861 | Pierce |
| Nathan Clifford | 1858–1881 | Buchanan |
| Noah H. Swayne | 1862–1881 | Lincoln |
| Samuel F. Miller | 1862–1890 | Lincoln |
| David Davis | 1862–1877 | Lincoln |
| Stephen J. Field | 1863–1897 | Lincoln |
| SALMON P. CHASE | 1864–1873 | Lincoln |

NOTE: The names of chief justices are printed in capital letters.

*Although Rutledge acted as chief justice, the Senate refused to confirm his appointment.

| Name | Terms of Service | Appointed By |
|---|---|---|
| William Strong | 1870–1880 | Grant |
| Joseph P. Bradley | 1870–1892 | Grant |
| Ward Hunt | 1873–1882 | Grant |
| MORRISON R. WAITE | 1874–1888 | Grant |
| John M. Harlan | 1877–1911 | Hayes |
| William B. Woods | 1881–1887 | Hayes |
| Stanley Matthews | 1881–1889 | Garfield |
| Horace Gray | 1882–1902 | Arthur |
| Samuel Blatchford | 1882–1893 | Arthur |
| Lucious Q. C. Lamar | 1888–1893 | Cleveland |
| MELVILLE W. FULLER | 1888–1910 | Cleveland |
| David J. Brewer | 1890–1910 | B. Harrison |
| Henry B. Brown | 1891–1906 | B. Harrison |
| George Shiras, Jr. | 1892–1903 | B. Harrison |
| Howell E. Jackson | 1893–1895 | B. Harrison |
| Edward D. White | 1894–1910 | Cleveland |
| Rufus W. Peckham | 1896–1909 | Cleveland |
| Joseph McKenna | 1898–1925 | McKinley |
| Oliver W. Holmes | 1902–1932 | T. Roosevelt |
| William R. Day | 1903–1922 | T. Roosevelt |
| William H. Moody | 1906–1910 | T. Roosevelt |
| Horace H. Lurton | 1910–1914 | Taft |
| Charles E. Hughes | 1910–1916 | Taft |
| EDWARD D. WHITE | 1910–1921 | Taft |
| Willis Van Devanter | 1911–1937 | Taft |
| Joseph R. Lamar | 1911–1916 | Taft |
| Mahlon Pitney | 1912–1922 | Taft |
| James C. McReynolds | 1914–1941 | Wilson |
| Louis D. Brandeis | 1916–1939 | Wilson |
| John H. Clarke | 1916–1922 | Wilson |
| WILLIAM H. TAFT | 1921–1930 | Harding |
| George Sutherland | 1922–1938 | Harding |
| Pierce Butler | 1923–1939 | Harding |
| Edward T. Sanford | 1923–1930 | Harding |
| Harlan F. Stone | 1925–1941 | Coolidge |
| CHARLES E. HUGHES | 1930–1941 | Hoover |
| Owen J. Roberts | 1930–1945 | Hoover |
| Benjamin N. Cardozo | 1932–1938 | Hoover |
| Hugo L. Black | 1937–1971 | F. Roosevelt |
| Stanley F. Reed | 1938–1957 | F. Roosevelt |
| Felix Frankfurter | 1939–1962 | F. Roosevelt |
| William O. Douglas | 1939–1975 | F. Roosevelt |
| Frank Murphy | 1940–1949 | F. Roosevelt |
| HARLAN F. STONE | 1941–1946 | F. Roosevelt |

| Name | Terms of Service | Appointed By |
| --- | --- | --- |
| James F. Byrnes | 1941–1942 | F. Roosevelt |
| Robert H. Jackson | 1941–1954 | F. Roosevelt |
| Wiley B. Rutledge | 1943–1949 | F. Roosevelt |
| Harold H. Burton | 1945–1958 | Truman |
| FREDERICK M. VINSON | 1946–1953 | Truman |
| Tom C. Clark | 1949–1967 | Truman |
| Sherman Minton | 1949–1956 | Truman |
| EARL WARREN | 1953–1969 | Eisenhower |
| John Marshall Harlan | 1955–1971 | Eisenhower |
| William J. Brennan, Jr. | 1956–1990 | Eisenhower |
| Charles E. Whittaker | 1957–1962 | Eisenhower |
| Potter Stewart | 1958–1981 | Eisenhower |
| Byron R. White | 1962–1993 | Kennedy |
| Arthur J. Goldberg | 1962–1965 | Kennedy |
| Abe Fortas | 1965–1970 | L. Johnson |
| Thurgood Marshall | 1967–1991 | L. Johnson |
| WARREN E. BURGER | 1969–1986 | Nixon |
| Harry A. Blackmun | 1970–1994 | Nixon |
| Lewis F. Powell, Jr. | 1971–1987 | Nixon |
| William H. Rehnquist | 1971–1986 | Nixon |
| John Paul Stevens | 1975– | Ford |
| Sandra Day O'Connor | 1981– | Reagan |
| WILLIAM H. REHNQUIST | 1986– | Reagan |
| Antonin Scalia | 1986– | Reagan |
| Anthony Kennedy | 1988– | Reagan |
| David Souter | 1990– | Bush |
| Clarence Thomas | 1991– | Bush |
| Ruth Bader Ginsburg | 1993– | Clinton |
| Stephen Breyer | 1994– | Clinton |

## Growth of U.S. Population and Area

| Census | Population of United States | Increase over the Preceding Census | | Land Area (Sq. Mi.) | Pop. Per. Sq. Mi. | Percentage of Pop. in Urban and Rural Territory | |
|---|---|---|---|---|---|---|---|
| | | Number | Percentage | | | Urban | Rural |
| 1790 | 3,929,214 | | | 867,980 | 4.5 | 5.1 | 94.9 |
| 1800 | 5,308,483 | 1,379,269 | 35.1 | 867,980 | 6.1 | 6.1 | 93.9 |
| 1810 | 7,239,881 | 1,931,398 | 36.4 | 1,685,865 | 4.3 | 7.2 | 92.8 |
| 1820 | 9,638,453 | 2,398,572 | 33.1 | 1,753,588 | 5.5 | 7.2 | 92.8 |
| 1830 | 12,866,020 | 3,227,567 | 33.5 | 1,753,588 | 7.3 | 8.8 | 91.2 |
| 1840 | 17,069,453 | 4,203,433 | 32.7 | 1,753,588 | 9.7 | 10.8 | 89.2 |
| 1850 | 23,191,876 | 6,122,423 | 35.9 | 2,944,337 | 7.9 | 15.3 | 84.7 |
| 1860 | 31,433,321 | 8,251,445 | 35.6 | 2,973,965 | 10.6 | 19.8 | 80.2 |
| 1870 | 39,818,449 | 8,375,128 | 26.6 | 2,973,965 | 13.4 | 24.9 | 75.1 |
| 1880 | 50,155,783 | 10,337,334 | 26.0 | 2,973,965 | 16.9 | 28.2 | 71.8 |
| 1890 | 62,947,714 | 12,791,931 | 25.5 | 2,973,965 | 21.2 | 35.1 | 64.9 |
| 1900 | 75,994,575 | 13,046,861 | 20.7 | 2,974,159 | 25.6 | 39.7 | 60.3 |
| 1910 | 91,972,266 | 15,997,691 | 21.0 | 2,973,890 | 30.9 | 45.7 | 54.3 |
| 1920 | 105,710,620 | 13,738,354 | 14.9 | 2,973,776 | 35.5 | 51.2 | 48.8 |
| 1930 | 122,775,046 | 17,064,426 | 16.1 | 2,977,128 | 41.2 | 56.2 | 43.8 |
| 1940 | 131,669,275 | 8,894,229 | 7.2 | 2,977,128 | 44.2 | 56.5 | 43.5 |
| 1950 | 150,697,361 | 19,028,086 | 14.5 | 2,974,726* | 50.7 | 64.0 | 36.0 |
| 1960† | 179,323,175 | 28,625,814 | 19.0 | 3,540,911 | 50.6 | 69.9 | 30.1 |
| 1970 | 203,235,298 | 23,912,123 | 13.3 | 3,536,855 | 57.5 | 73.5 | 26.5 |
| 1980 | 226,504,825 | 23,269,527 | 11.4 | 3,536,855 | 64.0 | 73.7 | 26.3 |
| 1990 | 249,975,000 | 22,164,068 | 9.8 | 3,536,855 | 70.3 | N.A. | N.A. |

*As measured in 1940; shrinkage offset by increase in water area.
†First year for which figures include Alaska and Hawaii.

SOURCES: Census Bureau, *Historical Statistics of the United States*, updated by relevant *Statistical Abstract of the United States*.

## Admission of States into the Union

| State | Date of Admission | State | Date of Admission |
|---|---|---|---|
| 1. Delaware | December 7, 1787 | 26. Michigan | January 26, 1837 |
| 2. Pennsylvania | December 12, 1787 | 27. Florida | March 3, 1845 |
| 3. New Jersey | December 18, 1787 | 28. Texas | December 29, 1845 |
| 4. Georgia | January 2, 1788 | 29. Iowa | December 28, 1846 |
| 5. Connecticut | January 9, 1788 | 30. Wisconsin | May 29, 1848 |
| 6. Massachusetts | February 6, 1788 | 31. California | September 9, 1850 |
| 7. Maryland | April 28, 1788 | 32. Minnesota | May 11, 1858 |
| 8. South Carolina | May 23, 1788 | 33. Oregon | February 14, 1859 |
| 9. New Hampshire | June 21, 1788 | 34. Kansas | January 29, 1861 |
| 10. Virginia | June 25, 1788 | 35. West Virginia | June 20, 1863 |
| 11. New York | July 26, 1788 | 36. Nevada | October 31, 1864 |
| 12. North Carolina | November 21, 1789 | 37. Nebraska | March 1, 1867 |
| 13. Rhode Island | May 29, 1790 | 38. Colorado | August 1, 1876 |
| 14. Vermont | March 4, 1791 | 39. North Dakota | November 2, 1889 |
| 15. Kentucky | June 1, 1792 | 40. South Dakota | November 2, 1889 |
| 16. Tennessee | June 1, 1796 | 41. Montana | November 8, 1889 |
| 17. Ohio | March 1, 1803 | 42. Washington | November 11, 1889 |
| 18. Louisiana | April 30, 1812 | 43. Idaho | July 3, 1890 |
| 19. Indiana | December 11, 1816 | 44. Wyoming | July 10, 1890 |
| 20. Mississippi | December 10, 1817 | 45. Utah | January 4, 1896 |
| 21. Illinois | December 3, 1818 | 46. Oklahoma | November 16, 1907 |
| 22. Alabama | December 14, 1819 | 47. New Mexico | January 6, 1912 |
| 23. Maine | March 15, 1820 | 48. Arizona | February 14, 1912 |
| 24. Missouri | August 10, 1821 | 49. Alaska | January 3, 1959 |
| 25. Arkansas | June 15, 1836 | 50. Hawaii | August 21, 1959 |

## Profile of the U.S. Population

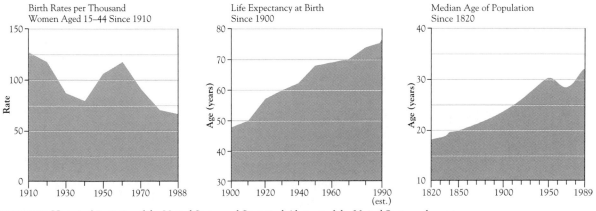

SOURCES: *Historical Statistics of the United States* and *Statistical Abstract of the United States*, relevant years.

# Political and Physical Map of the United States

Puget Sound
WASH.
Olympia ★
Mt. Rainier ▲
Salem ★
CASCADE MTS.
COLUMBIA
Columbia R.
PLATEAU
OREGON
IDAHO
Boise ★
Snake R.
ROCKY
Helena ★
MONTANA
WYOMING
HIGH
Red River of the North
N. DAKOTA
Bismarck ★
Pierre ★
S. DAKOTA
GREAT
NEBRASKA
COASTAL RANGES
SIERRA NEVADA
Central Valley
Sacramento ★
Carson City ★
GREAT BASIN
Great Salt Lake
Salt Lake City ★
Cheyenne ★
FRONT RANGE
PLAINS
Platte R.
Linco
NEVADA
UTAH
Mt. Whitney ▲
Denver ★
COLO.
Arkansas R.
KANSAS
To
CALIFORNIA
Colorado R.
Grand Canyon
Mesa Verde ▲
MOUNTAINS
Santa Fe ★
Red R.
OKLA.
Oklahoma City ★
PACIFIC OCEAN
ARIZONA
Phoenix ★
Gila R.
NEW MEXICO
Rio Grande
TEXAS
Extent of Continental Shelf
Austin ★

Arctic Circle
Bering Strait
ARCTIC OCEAN
BROOKS RANGE
Yukon R.
Mt. McKinley (Denali) ▲
Ancient Alaska-Siberia land bridge
ALASKA RANGE
Juneau ★
ALASKA
N. PACIFIC OCEAN

M E X I C O

Niihau
Kauai
Oahu
Honolulu ★
Molokai
Lanai
Maui
Mauna Kea ▲
Hawaii
PACIFIC OCEAN
HAWAII

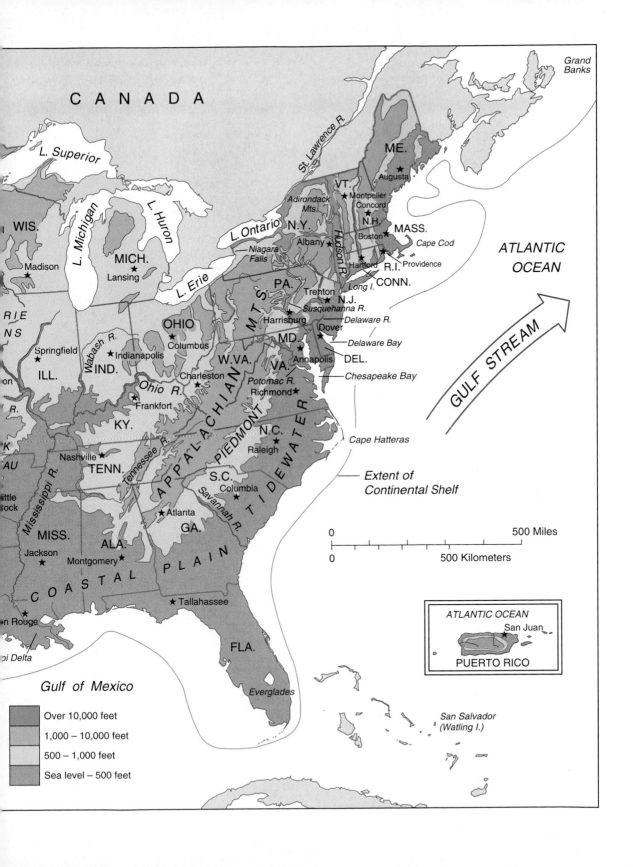

CANADA

L. Superior

L. Michigan

L. Huron

L. Ontario

L. Erie

St. Lawrence R.

Grand Banks

ME.
★ Augusta

VT.
★ Montpelier
Concord ★
N.H.

Adirondack Mts.

N.Y.
Albany ★

Niagara Falls

Hudson R.

Boston ★
MASS.

Cape Cod

Hartford ★
R.I.
★ Providence

CONN.
Long I.

ATLANTIC OCEAN

WIS.
Madison ★

MICH.
Lansing ★

PA.

Trenton ★
N.J.
Susquehanna R.
Harrisburg ★
Delaware R.

Dover ★
Delaware Bay

GULF STREAM

OHIO
Columbus ★

MD.

Annapolis ★
DEL.

Chesapeake Bay

Wabash R.

Springfield ★

Indianapolis ★

W.VA.

VA.
Richmond ★

ILL.

IND.

Charleston ★
Potomac R.

Ohio R.

Frankfort ★

N.C.

Cape Hatteras

KY.

Raleigh ★

PIEDMONT

APPALACHIAN MTS.

Extent of Continental Shelf

Nashville ★

TENN.

Tennessee R.

S.C.
Columbia ★

Savannah R.

0          500 Miles
0      500 Kilometers

TIDEWATER

Atlanta ★

GA.

MISS.

ALA.

Jackson ★

Montgomery ★

Mississippi R.

COASTAL

PLAIN

Tallahassee ★

n Rouge ★

oi Delta

Gulf of Mexico

FLA.

Everglades

San Salvador
(Watling I.)

ATLANTIC OCEAN
San Juan ★
PUERTO RICO

Over 10,000 feet
1,000 – 10,000 feet
500 – 1,000 feet
Sea level – 500 feet

# Photograph Credits

**Chapter 1**  p. 1: Ohio Historical Society; p. 8: Field Museum of Natural History, Chicago/Art Resource, New York; p. 9: Courtesy of Cahokia Mounds Historic Site, painting by Lloyd K. Townsend.

**Chapter 2**  p. 15: John Carter Brown Library; p. 18: Entwistle Gallery, London/Werner Forman Archive/Art Resource, New York; p. 25: Pierpont Morgan Library, New York. MS 3900, Folio 100; p. 28: Arizona State Museum, University of Arizona. Helen Teiwes, photographer; p. 32: By permission of The British Library.

**Chapter 3**  p. 39: Library Company of Philadelphia; p. 41: Courtesy, American Antiquarian Society; p. 53: The British Museum, London; p. 56: Arents Tobacco Collection, New York Public Library. Miriam and Ira D. Wallach Division of Art, Prints & Photographs. Astor, Lenox, and Tilden Foundation; p. 61 (both): Historical Society of Pennsylvania; p. 64: Photograph by John K. Hillers. Courtesy, Museum of New Mexico, Neg. No. 16096.

**Chapter 4**  p. 67: Newport Historical Society; p. 73: Peabody Essex Museum, Salem, Massachusetts; p. 75: Courtesy, Wethersfield Historical Society; p. 86: Yale University. Bequest of Eugene Phelps Edwards, 1938.

**Chapter 5**  p. 90: Courtesy, Winterthur Museum. Bequest of Henry Francis du Pont; p. 98: Courtesy, American Antiquarian Society; p. 104: Deposited by the City of Boston. Courtesy, Museum of Fine Arts, Boston; p. 108: Library of Congress.

**Chapter 6**  p. 117: New York Historical Society; p. 121: Metropolitan Museum of Art. Bequest of Charles Allen Munn, 1924; p. 136 (detail): Boston Athenaeum; p. 138: Colonial Williamsburg Foundation.

**Chapter 7**  p. 144: New York State Historical Association, Cooperstown; p. 150: Yale University Art Gallery; p. 155: Smithsonian Institution. Photo #BAE1169-L-3.

**Chapter 8**  p. 168: White House Historical Association; p. 170 (left): Monticello/Thomas Jefferson Memorial Foundation, Inc.; p. 170 (right): Collection of Mr. and Mrs. Jack W. Warner, Tuscaloosa, Alabama; p. 179: Granger Collection.

**Chapter 9**  p. 190: Walters Art Gallery, Baltimore; p. 192: Metropolitan Museum of Art, Rogers Fund, 1942. #42.95.12; p. 193: William L. Clements Library/ University of Michigan, Ann Arbor; p. 199: University of Massachusetts, Lowell, Center for Lowell History, Lyndon Library; p. 202: Witt Library/Courtauld Institute of Art.

**Chapter 10**  p. 208: Massachusetts Historical Society; p. 213 (left): Andrew W. Mellon Collection © 1996 Board of Trustees, National Gallery of Art; p. 213 (right): Redwood Library and Athenaeum, Newport, Rhode Island; p. 224: Boston Athenaeum; p. 226 (left): Chicago Historical Society; p. 226 (right): Library of Congress.

**Chapter 11**  p. 230: Courtesy George Eastman House; p. 231: AP/Wide World Photos; p. 241: Corbis-Bettmann; p. 244: Photograph courtesy of the Louisa May Alcott Memorial Association.

**Chapter 12**  p. 249: Gibbes Museum of Art/Carolina Art Association; p. 255: Collection of Dr. Richard G. Saloom; p. 262: New York Historical Society; p. 268: Hampton University Museum, Hampton, Virginia.

**Chapter 13**  p. 271: Amon Carter Museum, Fort Worth, Texas; p. 275: Boston Athenaeum; p. 280: Courtesy George Eastman House; p. 285: Chicago Historical Society; p. 291: Courtesy, Bancroft Library.

**Chapter 14**  p. 293: Metropolitan Museum of Art, Arthur Hoppock Hearn Fund #50.94.1; p. 295: Library of Congress; p. 297: Metropolitan Museum of Art, Gift of I.N. Phelps Stokes, Edward S. Hawes, Alice Mary Hawes, Marion Augusta Hawes, 1937 #37.14.40; p. 306 (left): National Portrait Gallery, Washington, DC/Art Resource, NY; p. 306 (right): Corbis-Bettmann.

**Chapter 15**  p. 315: Cook Collection, Valentine Museum, Richmond, Virginia; p. 318: Corbis-Bettmann; p. 322: Library of Congress; p. 327: Chicago Historical Society; p. 329: National Archives.

**Chapter 16**  p. 341: Library of Congress; p. 344: Harper's Weekly, 1866; p. 351: Tennessee State Museum Collection. Copy photograph by June Dorman; p. 352: The William Gladstone Collection.

# Index